LEGAL SYSTEMS OF THE PACIFIC

LEGAL SYSTEMS OF THE PACIFIC

Introducing Sixteen Gems

Edited by
Jennifer Corrin
Tony Angelo

INTERSENTIA
Cambridge – Antwerp – Chicago

Intersentia Ltd
8 Wellington Mews
Wellington Street | Cambridge
CB1 1HW | United Kingdom
Tel: +44 1223 736 170
Email: mail@intersentia.co.uk
www.intersentia.com | www.intersentia.co.uk

Distribution for the UK and
Rest of the World (incl. Eastern Europe)
NBN International
1 Deltic Avenue, Rooksley
Milton Keynes MK13 8LD
United Kingdom
Tel: +44 1752 202 301 | Fax: +44 1752 202 331
Email: orders@nbninternational.com

Distribution for Europe
Lefebvre Sarrut Belgium NV
Hoogstraat 139/6
1000 Brussels
Belgium
Tel: +32 (0)800 39 067
Email: mail@intersentia.be

Distribution for the USA and Canada
Independent Publishers Group
Order Department
814 North Franklin Street
Chicago, IL 60610
USA
Tel: +1 800 888 4741 (toll free) | Fax: +1 312 337 5985
Email: orders@ipgbook.com

Artwork on cover: Best-Backgrounds / Shutterstock

ISBN 978-1-83970-153-5
D/2021/7849/113
NUR 820

British Library Cataloguing in Publication Data. A catalogue record for this book is available from the British Library.

This book is dedicated with fond memories and gratitude
and as a token of an abiding legacy

to the memory of Donald Paterson (1934–2021),
Professor Emeritus of the University of the South Pacific and
founder of the University of the South Pacific law school

an ever-present mentor and friend.

FOREWORD

Malo e lelei, Ni sa bula vinaka, Kia orana, Taloha ni, Faka'alofa lahi atu, Kam na mauri, Talofa, Gud de tru, Halo olgeta, Ia orana, Aloha mai e, Kia ora, Talofa lava, and warm Pacific greetings.

The island nations of the Pacific were amongst the last places on earth to be inhabited by the human species. The islands of Papua New Guinea were perhaps the first settled and Aotearoa-New Zealand the last. The early settlers of the Pacific islands established systems of governance to regulate their communities. The first 'laws' of the Pacific were oral by nature and debated and memorised through *stori* and *talanoa*. The indigenous legal systems of the Pacific islands were refined over millennia, developing into sophisticated codes designed to regulate customary ways of life, *kastom*, traditional practices, relationships between people and communities, behaviour, the environment and other aspects of community life. Traditional legal systems were unique to each island community across the Pacific.

European explorers, traders and missionaries entered the Blue Pacific universe, shattering the peace of these fragile communities. Imperial systems of governance and European legal systems were established. British, French, German and American laws were imposed on the people of the Pacific as the European powers established colonial governance.

As they struggled for political independence in the 20th century, emerging Pacific island nations developed new legal and constitutional frameworks. In some nations imported legal systems were adopted (or imposed) wholesale. Some other nations, for example Papua New Guinea and Samoa, developed unique legal systems that aimed to marry the indigenous with the imported. The result is a Pacific-wide range of legal systems that continue to evolve.

Pacific legal systems have been described in the *Encyclopedia of Comparative Law*, in various publications by the late Professor Ron Crocombe, in the *South Pacific Islands Legal Systems* volume by Michael A Ntumy, and in the books of the late Professor Guy Powles. These publications are no longer current or are out of print.

In their Introduction to this volume, Emeritus Professors Jennifer Corrin and Tony Angelo state: '... that there is a need for an up-to-date and accessible reference book for legal systems of the South Pacific'.

Legal Systems of the Pacific: Introducing Sixteen Gems aims to address that need. The legal systems of 16 Pacific island nations are described and discussed in detail including historical backgrounds, the source of the laws and indigenous elements. Cross-country comparisons are also made, including the discussion of cases of custom and customary law. Importantly, reflecting the growth of the legal profession in the Pacific, most of the chapters are written by local authors who are lawyers and authorities on their nation's legal systems.

This book provides a handy overview of Pacific legal systems and directs students, scholars and practitioners to where they can find more detail on the law of each of the 16 countries.

For much of our history, the people of the Pacific regulated our Blue Pacific universe through our customary legal systems. That all changed with the imposition of imported legal systems during the colonial period. The post-colonial period has seen the development of new legal systems for Pacific nations that are led by Pacific people familiar with Western law and knowledgeable of indigenous custom.

The new Pacific legal systems have their complexities, are still evolving and are subject to debate and challenge in the legal community and the political sphere, as recent events in Samoa demonstrate.

Since its independence, 'Samoa has sought to build a legal system that supports the modern ideal of democracy without significantly compromising its cultural heritage and uniqueness'.[1] There is an inbuilt tension between Samoan customary law, which 'developed as a means to defend and protect the group (family, village) and 'uphold the authority of *matai*', and a legal system that 'is based on principles of individual rights'. In Samoa, the judges of the Supreme and Magistrate's Courts deal with criminal offences and civil matters, and the *Fa'amasino Samoa* of the Land and Titles Court deal with matters relating to disputes over customary lands and titles. Former Chief Justice Patu Sapolu uses the term 'legal pluralism', to refer to a country with two legal systems.[2] Recent constitutional amendments that institutionalise legal pluralism have led to deep divisions in Samoa's legal and political communities.

In my view, public debate is a healthy sign of the development and evolution of new Pacific legal systems. It is my hope that this book will provide up-to-date and accessible information to inform these debates.

I acknowledge the many contributors to this volume and the leadership of Emeritus Professors Jennifer Corrin and Tony Angelo. *Fa'afetai tele lava.*

---

1 See Patu Falefatu Sapolu et al. 'Law and Custom' in Ellie Meleisea, Leasiolagi Malama Meleisea and Penelope Schoeffel (eds) *Samoa's Journey 1962–2012, Aspects of History* (Victoria University Press, 2012) 18.

2 'Comments to Special Parliamentary Committee' *Samoa Observer* (12 May 2020).

I commend *Legal Systems of the Pacific: Introducing Sixteen Gems* to students, scholars, law practitioners and to all who are interested in the evolving legal systems of the island nations of the Pacific.

Ia manuia.

Associate Professor Luamanuvao Dame Winnie Laban
Assistant Vice Chancellor (Pasifika)
Victoria University of Wellington

ACKNOWLEDGEMENTS

The authors and editors extend their thanks to The University of Queensland and to the Victoria University of Wellington for the support provided for the production of this book. They would also like to thank Dame Winnie Laban for generously agreeing to write the foreword.

The vital support provided by Sir David Carruthers, Lily Fu, Billie Haddleton, Weichu Huang, Madeline Lilly-Howe and Jamie Molea (both for assistance in addition to their authorship), Ian Macintosh, Dr Yves-Louis Sage, and Kari Young is here gratefully acknowledged.

We would also like to thank Intersentia for continuing to support South Pacific scholars and its wonderful staff for assistance in getting this book from manuscript to publication.

CONTENTS

LIST OF CASES

COOK ISLANDS

FIJI

FRENCH POLYNESIA

KIRIBATI

NAURU

NIUE

PAPUA NEW GUINEA

PITCAIRN

SAMOA

SOLOMON ISLANDS

TOKELAU

TONGA

TUVALU

VANUATU

WALLIS AND FUTUNA

AUSTRALIA

UNITED KINGDOM

LIST OF LEGISLATION

COOK ISLANDS

FIJI

FRENCH POLYNESIA

KIRIBATI

NAURU

NEW CALEDONIA

NIUE

PAPUA NEW GUINEA

PITCAIRN

SAMOA

SOLOMON ISLANDS

TOKELAU

TONGA

TUVALU

VANUATU

WALLIS AND FUTUNA

AUSTRALIA

COMMONWEALTH

QUEENSLAND

FRANCE

NEW ZEALAND

UNITED KINGDOM

LIST OF CONTRIBUTORS

Tony Angelo is Professor Emeritus at Victoria University of Wellington. He has a long-standing interest in the law of small states and has published extensively on the laws of Mauritius, Seychelles and the small countries of the Pacific.

Jennifer Corrin is Professor Emerita at The University of Queensland. She is an academic, researching on law reform and development in plural legal regimes and legal issues affecting small states. She is the author of *Contract Law in the South Pacific* (now in its second edition) and co-author of *Introduction to South Pacific Law* (now in its fourth edition) and *Courts and Civil Procedure in the South Pacific.*

Gregory Dale is completing a doctorate at Monash University law school. He is an Associate Lecturer in the TC Beirne School of Law at The University of Queensland and is admitted to practice in the Supreme Courts of New South Wales and Queensland. He worked as the Associate to the Chief Justice of Western Australia for two years and later worked as a Senior Legislation Officer, Assistant Parliamentary Counsel within the Queensland Government and as a Legal Officer on the Queensland Child Protection Commission of Inquiry.

Carine David is a Professor of Public Law, at the University of French West Indies. She worked for 20 years in New Caledonia (1998–2018), as PhD student and then Senior Lecturer at the University of New Caledonia. Her research activities mainly focus on French Overseas Territories and small islands territories' political regimes, environmental law and right to happiness. She is currently Editorial Director of the *Happiness Law Review.*

Victor David has a PhD in Law and Social Sciences (University of Paris/EHESS). He is a Research Fellow at the French National Research Institute for Sustainable Development (IRD). His research and expertise focus on environmental law, rights of nature, law and political strategies for CC adaptation. He is the scientific coordinator of the participatory development of the Environmental Code of the Loyalty Islands province in New Caledonia and initiated a feasibility study for the recognition of the Pacific Ocean as a legal entity.

Joel Fangalasuu has a LLB (USP) and is currently an LLM candidate at the Australian National University in Canberra, Australia. He has a particular interest in the interaction between law and custom and their role in development within the South Pacific.

Kahealani Sinahemana Hekau is a lawyer and entrepreneur. Since graduating law school from Emalus Campus, Vanuatu in 2002, she has worked for the Government of Niue serving as legal counsel in public law in the areas of good governance, culture and climate change. Since 2010 she, along with her late sister Toepenina Krystal Ann Hekau, established the Hekau Attorneys At Law. Niue's first private law firm serving the community and private citizens with a keen interest in Niuean land, property and energy. For the last 20 years, Sina has been dedicated to the delivery of quality legal services to the people of Niue.

Reimen Hii is an Australian barrister and mediator. He has a broad practice throughout the Asia-Pacific region which includes commercial litigation, international law, public and administrative law, family law, property law and human rights. He previously held a position as a registrar of the Supreme Court of Tonga and has worked as a solicitor in private practice, a judge's associate and at a UN-backed war crimes tribunal. His publications include the *Tonga Magistrates' Bench Book* (2nd ed 2014).

Lise Hope-Suveinakama BA/LLB (Waikato) is the Director of Olatia Consulting Ltd of Auckland, New Zealand. She is a registered Legal Practitioner of Tokelau and a Barrister and Solicitor of the High Court of New Zealand. From 2008 to September 2020 she worked as the Senior Legal Adviser for the Government of Tokelau and as the Judicial Coordinator for the Judiciary of Tokelau.

Christopher Karaiye holds a Bachelor of Laws with Honours, Bachelor of Business and Management with Honours (economics major), and Bachelor of Economics degrees from the University of Papua New Guinea. He has practiced law for over 10 years and worked as an economist for a year at the Papua New Guinea Department of Treasury and as an academic for eight years at the University of Papua New Guinea and Divine Word University, PNG. He practices law as a private practitioner in Papua New Guinea, appearing in the District Court, National Court and Supreme Court of Papua New Guinea.

Hervé Raimana Lallemant-Moe has a PhD in Law. He is an associate member of the research unit Governance and Insular Development at the University of French Polynesia (UPF) and an associate member of the International Law Center at the University of Lyon III. He is a temporary lecturer at the UPF and a member of the French Polynesian Competition Authority as the Chief Counsellor of the president and the board. His research focuses mainly on environmental law and also the legal status of French oversea territories and small island states in the Pacific. He graduated from the UPF, the University of the South Pacific and the University of Western Brittany.

Madeline Lilly-Howe is a fifth-year law student at The University of Queensland. She is currently studying a Bachelor of Arts/Bachelor of Laws (Honours), majoring in history and political science. She has worked as a research assistant in the TC Beirne School of Law and has completed pro bono research for the Environmental Defenders Office (Qld). Since 2017, she has worked on the Queensland Judgments Project with the ICLRQ.

Mike Mitchell graduated with an LLB (VUW). Since then he has practised law in London, Uganda, New Zealand and the Cook Islands. He was Solicitor-General of the Cook Islands in 1979–1986 and returned to this role in 2007 before being appointed Secretary for Foreign Affairs in 2008. In 2010 he then became the Cook Islands High Commissioner to New Zealand. He resigned from this position in 2011 and is currently a practitioner in the Cook Islands.

Jamie Molea has a LLB (USP), LLM (VUW) and is currently a Policy Advisor at the Ministry of Justice in New Zealand where he works in the criminal justice space. He has a particular interest in human rights, international law and legal pluralism in Solomon Islands.

Morsen Mosses is a Lecturer in Law and Acting Discipline Coordinator for Law at the School of Law and Social Sciences, the University of the South Pacific. He teaches and conducts research in public international law, human rights law and legal pluralism. He is particularly interested in right to self-determination, territorial disputes, right to equality and the intersection of law and custom/culture. He is currently the General Editor of the *Journal of South Pacific Law*.

Unaisi Narawa graduated from the School of Law, University of the South Pacific (USP) in 2008. She has a Bachelor's Degree and a Master's Degree in Law, as well as a post graduate certificate in tertiary teaching. Her research interests include family law, environmental law, deep sea mining, customary law, legal pluralism and blackbirding and its displacement of Melanesians in Fiji, Australia and other Pacific Island States. In 2020, Unaisi began her PhD studies at The University of Queensland.

Yves-Louis Sage is Maître de Conférences Hdr (Honorary) in Private Law. He is also the Editor-in-Chief of the *Comparative Law Journal of the Pacific – Journal de Droit Comparé du Pacifique*. His research focuses on various aspects of comparative law in the Pacific, including land law, to which he has devoted several books, articles and chronicles. He has taught at the University of French Polynesia, the Faculty of Law at Victoria University of Wellington and the Dispute Resolution Centre at Massey University.

Beatrice Tabangcora was raised in Samoa. Beatrice is an alumna of the University of the South Pacific (USP) and the Victoria University of Wellington (VUW). She is an Assistant Lecturer in Law at the University of the South Pacific in Port-Vila, Vanuatu. Her research interests include tort law, human rights and legal pluralism in the South Pacific.

INTRODUCTION

Tony ANGELO and Jennifer CORRIN

This book arose from the perception that there is a need for an up-to-date and accessible reference book for legal systems of the South Pacific. In the past there have been several descriptions of Pacific systems: in the *Encyclopaedia of Comparative Law* (vol 1), in specific areas in the various publications of Professor Ron Crocombe, in the more developed legal statements in the two Pacific courts and justice books by Professor Guy Powles,[1] and, primarily, in the seminal work *South Pacific Legal Systems* edited by Mike Ntumy.[2] None of those texts is now current and many are out of print.

The goal for this volume, the next in the field, was that it should be prepared for each country by an author of that country who is a lawyer and who is an emerging authority. A concerted effort was made to that end and the goal of having a local author was achieved in respect to 10 of the 16 legal systems included in the book. The chapters on Kiribati and Tuvalu were to be written by local authors but this did not eventuate, so Kiribati was written by one of the editors and Tuvalu was put together by the editorial team, including some of those mentioned in the acknowledgements. It is for a future team to achieve the ideal.

Primarily the countries surveyed are of the South Pacific and of British or French colonial background.

Whilst the material in this work is mainly descriptive, the task for the authors should not be underestimated. Access to up-to-date South Pacific legal sources is often a convoluted task, even where authors are based in country. Not all materials are available online. Where consolidations of legislation exist, they are rarely up to date. Not all countries have published law reports and existing series are often outdated.

This book provides a compendium of data to guide students, scholars and practitioners into and around the legal systems discussed. It presents an

1 *Pacific Courts and Justice* (Institute of Pacific Studies, University of the South Pacific, 1977). Guy Powles and Mere Pulea (eds) *Pacific Courts and Legal Systems* (Institute of Pacific Studies, University of the South Pacific, 1988).

2 *South Pacific Islands Systems* (University of Hawaii Press, 1993).

informative description of each system, its sources of law and the available legal materials. There is also comparative interest in the material: in the continued influence of the historical background in the post-colonial laws, in inter-country comparisons.

Pacific countries are commonly divided into three subregions, that is, Melanesia, Micronesia and Polynesia. The 16 'gems' fall across all three subregions. The boundaries of the subregions are contested, particularly in the case of Papua New Guinea and Fiji, whose peoples do not all belong in the same group.[3] However, the categories have endured as a rough and fluid indication of cultural and biological affinities. Countries within this work that are generally regarded as falling within Melanesia are Fiji, New Caledonia, Papua New Guinea, Solomon Islands, Vanuatu and Wallis and Futuna. Those regarded as being within Micronesia are Nauru and Kiribati. The Cook Islands, French Polynesia, Niue, Pitcairn, Samoa, Tokelau, Tonga and Tuvalu are usually placed within Polynesia. Interestingly, the divergences and convergences emerging from the chapters in this book do not present a pattern that follows these subregional delineations. Rather, they suggest a link to historical pathways, particularly those embedded during the colonial era.

The book deals with various cultural groups of law; for instance, those with a United Kingdom colonial background have at their origin the Orders in Council for the Western Pacific High Commission and the common law of England (typically at a given date) as the default or residual source of law. In some areas, such as procedure, the continuing influence is clearly visible. For example, as discussed in the relevant chapters, in Kiribati and Tuvalu, the High Court (Civil Procedure) Rules 1964 (Western Pacific) continue to govern civil proceedings. For those that had or have a French colonial background, the major codes of France continue, often with considerable local supplementation. The chapter on Vanuatu is particularly interesting here, as it highlights the repercussions of the country's history as a condominium, which, as discussed further below, brought it within the British 'Western Pacific Islands', but also subjected it to the French Codes as applied in New Caledonia.

There is a clear distinction between the common law and equity of England and the common law in the sense of a *droit commun*. 'Common law' in the French systems means basically the law of the Civil Code – the droit commun. In many cases in the Pacific, 'common law and equity' refers specifically to the body of law developed by the royal courts in England. There is also now in the Pacific a body of common law which is the law developed by the local courts, often independently of the common law of England. In some cases, this is based

---

3 See eg Ann Chowning *An Introduction to the Peoples and Cultures of Melanesia* (Cummings Publishing Company, 1977); Serge Tcherkezoff 'A Long and Unfortunate Voyage Toward the Invention of the Melanesia-Polynesia Distinction 1595–1832' (2003) 38(2) Journal of Pacific History 175–196.

on the common law in other parts of the Commonwealth, such as Australia, New Zealand and Canada. In others, it forms part of a unique local jurisprudence. However, it is also clear from the chapters that, although there are common models influencing legislation in some areas of law, there is no evidence of what might be referred to as South Pacific jurisprudence. An endeavour has been made in the chapters to reflect these different manifestations of law.

In particular instances, the colonial policies and the individuals who draft legislation come through clearly and give a specific flavour to the legislation of each country. The consequence is that understanding the background to the systems greatly assists an understanding of the systems as they now exist and operate. As emerges from the following chapters, the extent to which South Pacific countries have abandoned colonial laws differs dramatically from place to place. As discussed in the relevant chapters, this covers a spectrum from a complete repeal of British legislation in Tonga[4] to a continued reliance on a raft of inherited British legislation in Kiribati.[5]

The impact of colonial administration on present-day legal systems is well illustrated by the chapters dealing with countries which were part of the British Western Pacific that existed between 1877 and 1976.[6] At one time or another, the British Western Pacific included the islands which now constitute Fiji, Kiribati, Nauru, Niue, Pitcairn, Solomon Islands, Tokelau, Tonga, Tuvalu and Vanuatu. The Chief Justice of Fiji was appointed as the Judicial Commissioner of the Western Pacific,[7] and later the Chief Justice presided over what became known as the High Court of the Western Pacific;[8] it formed a common apex for appeals from countries within British Western Pacific, subject to a further right of appeal in some cases to the Judicial Committee of the Privy Council. As can be seen from the following chapters, in addition to this common source of jurisprudence, many of these countries were subjected to the general introduction of English statutes and English common law and equity. These laws were carried forward at independence and, in many cases, remain in force as a feature of the commonalities presented in the relevant chapters.

The colonial influence is also evident in the discussion of constitutions and constitutional law. Again, membership of the British Western Pacific resulted in similarities between independence constitutions, particularly in those of Fiji, Kiribati, Solomon Islands and Tuvalu, although, as will be seen, Fiji and Tuvalu have since enacted new constitutions.[9] Some commonalities also appeared in

4 Civil Law (Amendment) Act 2003, s 3.
5 For example, the Sale of Goods Act 1893 (UK) and the Adoption Act 1958 (UK) continue to apply.
6 Western Pacific Order in Council 1877 made under the Pacific Islanders Protection Act 1875, the British Settlements Act 1887, and the Foreign Jurisdiction Act 1890.
7 Western Pacific Order in Council 1877, art 12.
8 Western Pacific (Courts) Order 1961.
9 Constitution of the Republic of Fiji (2013); Constitution of Tuvalu Cap 1.02.

the constitutions of the Cook Islands and Niue,[10] until the Cook Islands made substantial amendments.[11] All these constitutions were drafted and enacted by the departing colonial power or controlling country. The Nauru Constitution was drafted by Australia but made by a locally constituted body. These documents form a stark contrast with the Constitution of Papua New Guinea, revealed in the relevant chapter to be 'home-grown or autochthonous' and 'in many ways ... unique in its outlook'. Perhaps ironically, given that it is still non-self-governing, the Constitution of Tokelau is also 'home-grown' and unique.

The chapters' discussion of arrangements for accommodating, and in many cases corralling, custom and customary laws also provides an interesting field of comparison. This is not just a matter of contrasting countries where customary laws are given general recognition as part of State law, such as Samoa and Solomon Islands, with those where it is not, such as French Polynesia and Tonga. Much richer seams for exploration lie in the differing depths and manner of separation and recognition. For instance, the chapter on Tokelau reveals that in practice custom is the primary source of law. As will be seen in other chapters, including those on Nauru and Solomon Islands, in some countries customary laws are recognised and ranked above common law and equity. The Papua New Guinea chapter shows a unique approach to customary law, treating it as a source of underlying law which is subject only to the Constitution and legislation. In other countries, such as Fiji, recognition is limited to land.

The goal of the book was to provide a handy overview of the 16 chosen legal systems for the purpose of quick and easy reference, and to provide information about where to find data on specific aspects of each of those countries. The authors approached this task with enthusiasm and in English. Generally, the chapters are structured in a similar way, commencing with some brief background, including local history relevant to the current legal system. The chapters then set out the sources of law and explore each of them as relevant in the particular legal system. The chapters also deal with constitutional law: the constitution, the legislature, the judiciary, and constitutional offices and entities, the law profession, court procedure, and dispute resolution. The chapters then address a series of specific subject areas, including the law of persons, the law of obligations, property law and cultural protection, key points of commercial law, environmental law, including responses to climate change, natural resources law, criminal law, international law, including human rights, and the law relating to civil society organisations such as churches and trade unions. Despite the common writing brief, the character of each system is evident in the writing of the authors and their responses to the writing brief. This reflects the fact that authors were invited to include a more personalised and targeted comment about

[10] Constitution of the Cook Islands 1964; Constitution of Niue 1974.
[11] Constitution Amendment Acts 1968–69 to 2009.

the particularities of their system. Undoubtedly this manifests not only their areas of interest within their system, but also the culture of the system, whether it be English common law, French law or of some other origin. Just as the place of training of a judge is evidenced in a judge's judgments, so the training and experiences of the authors is evident in the chapters. These differences make for an interesting comparative study in its own right.

THE COOK ISLANDS

Madeline LILLY-HOWE and Mike MITCHELL

1. CONTEXT

The Cook Islands is a self-governing state in free association with New Zealand. It is located in the South Pacific Ocean and consists of 15 islands,[1] which are separated into a northern and southern group.[2] The islands cover a total land area of 240 square kilometres; the exclusive economic zone of the Cook Islands is 1,900,000 square kilometres.[3] The capital is Avarua, located on the main and most populous island, Rarotonga. The population of the Cook Islands at 2018 was 17,500.[4] Approximately 78 per cent of the population identify as fully or partially Cook Islands Maori.[5] Many Cook Islanders have migrated to and live permanently in New Zealand.[6] In the 2018 New Zealand census, there were approximately 80,500 Cook Islanders in New Zealand.[7] The Te Reo Maori Act 2003 declares English and Maori as the two official languages of the Cook Islands.[8] Various dialects of Cook Islands Maori, of which the most dominant is Rarotongan, are widely spoken.

---

1 See the Constitution of the Cook Islands, art 1(1) for a territorial description of the Cook Islands.
2 Norman Douglas and Ngaire Douglas (eds) *Pacific Islands Yearbook* (17th ed, Fiji Times, 1994).
3 Christina Newport 'Polynesia in Review: Issues and Events, 1 July 2017 to 30 June 2018: Cook Islands' (2019) 31 The Contemporary Pacific 188 at 188.
4 Cook Islands Statistics Office *Census of Population and Dwellings 2016* (Report, 2018) 15.
5 Cook Islands Statistics Office *Census of Population and Dwellings 2016* (Report, 2018) 19.
6 Cook Islands Statistics Office *Census of Population and Dwellings 2016* (Report, 2018) 15.
7 Stats New Zealand <https://www.stats.govt.nz/tools/2018-census-ethnic-group-summaries/cook-islands-maori>.
8 Te Reo Maori Act 2003, ss 4–5.

The Cook Islands has a long history. Polynesian settlement has been evidenced to date back to at least 600 AD. In the pre-colonial era, custom and orders given by individual chiefs regulated the communities of the Cook Islands. There was no central government for the whole territory. In 1888, a British protectorate was declared over the southern islands.[9]

The Cook Islands' colonial period commenced in 1901.[10] Following the Rarotongan Ariki petition, New Zealand came to control the Cook Islands. The Cook Islands, which then included Niue, were annexed to the British colony of New Zealand. During the colonial period, the New Zealand Parliament enacted legislation to provide for a Cook Islands government structure. The Cook Islands Act 1915 (NZ) was the significant legislation of the time.[11] It set out the relationship between the law of the Cook Islands and New Zealand.

Self-government was developed progressively.[12] Island Councils enacted Ordinances with the New Zealand Resident Commissioner's assent, from 1901 to 1946.[13] From 1947 to 1965, a Resident Commission enacted Ordinances, with the assent of the Legislative Council, later the Legislative Assembly.[14]

The Cook Islands ceased to be a colony on 4 August 1965, following the enactment by the Parliament of New Zealand of an entrenched written constitution for the Cook Islands.[15] This process involved consultation with leaders in the Cook Islands.[16] At international law, the Cook Islands is a state of a different character from that of an independent state, because of the free association arrangement with New Zealand. In 1965, the association with New Zealand chosen by the Cook Islands was internationally a novel, formal legal structure.[17] A key feature of the arrangement is that Cook Islanders are New Zealand citizens.[18]

---

9 See Richard Gilson *The Cook Islands 1820–1950* (Victoria University Press in association with the Institute of Pacific Studies of the University of the South Pacific, 1980) 60.

10 Cook and Other Islands Government Act 1901 (NZ).

11 Commenced on 1 April 1916. It repealed the 1901 Act. For background to that Act see Alex Frame *Salmond Southern Jurist* (VUP, 1995) 184–189.

12 Cook Islands Amendment Act 1946 (NZ); Cook Islands Amendment Act 1957 (NZ).

13 Jennifer Corrin and Don Paterson (eds) *Introduction to South Pacific Law* (4th ed, Intersentia, 2017).

14 Cook Islands Amendment Act 1946 (NZ), s 2.

15 Cook Islands Constitution Act 1964 (NZ); Cook Islands Constitution Amendment Act 1965 (NZ).

16 Don Paterson 'New Impulses in the Interaction of Law and Religion: A South Pacific Perspective' (2003) 2 Brigham Young University Law Review 593 at 605–606.

17 Greg Fry *Framing the Islands: Power and Diplomatic Agency in Pacific Regionalism* (ANU Press, 2019) 123; Jon Fraenkel 'Post-Colonial Political Institutions in the South Pacific Islands: A Survey' in David Hegarty and Darrell Tryon (eds) *Politics, Development and Security in Oceania* (ANU Press, 2013) 39.

18 Cook Islands Constitution Act 1964 (NZ), s 6; Citizenship Act 1977 (NZ).

2. SOURCES OF LAW

The sources of law in the Cook Islands include the Constitution, ordinary legislation, the common law and custom.[19] The Constitution has, as at 31 December 2019, been amended by the Cook Islands Parliament on 30 occasions.

2.1. THE CONSTITUTION

The Constitution is the supreme law of the Cook Islands. The Constitution outlines provisions relating to the government, executive, legislature, judiciary, fundamental human rights and freedoms, public revenues and the public service of the Cook Islands. The Constitution is complemented by the Letters Patent constituting the Office of the Governor-General of New Zealand[20] and by the Kirk Henry letters of 1973.[21]

2.2. LEGISLATION

Statute is a key source of law. Article 77 of the Constitution provides that the existing law was to continue in force in the Cook Islands until it was specifically repealed by the legislature.[22] Such laws were to continue provided there was consistency with the newly enacted Constitution.[23] Consequently, applicable forms of legislation include:

- Acts of the Cook Islands;
- Ordinances that were in force at 4 August 1965;[24]
- New Zealand Acts of Parliament specifically extended to the Cook Islands by the Cook Islands Act 1915 (NZ), or adopted by the New Zealand Laws Acts of 1966–70, 1973 and 1979 of the Cook Islands, or by direct enactment;[25]
- Acts of the Parliament of the United Kingdom that were in force in New Zealand on 1 April 1916 and consistent with the Cook Islands Act 1915;[26]
- Regulations made by the Queen's Representative in Executive Council.

---

19 A substantial survey of all legislation of the Cook Islands was completed in 1981 by Alex Frame. That material as at 1994 is available in *Laws of the Cook Islands 1994* Vol 1 at 25–108.

20 SR 1983/225 (NZ).

21 App HR 1973 A10.

22 Constitution of the Cook Islands, art 77.

23 Constitution of the Cook Islands, art 77.

24 See above n 19.

25 By the request and consent procedure under art 46 of the Constitution as in force until 5 June 1981; Constitution Amendment (No 9) Act 1980–81.

26 In accordance with s 615 of the Cook Islands Act 1915. Don Paterson 'Cook Islands: Sources of Law' *PacLII* (1999) <http://www.paclii.org/ck/sources.html>.

2.3. COMMON LAW

A further source of law is the common law. The English law in existence on 14 January 1840 was received and forms part of the law of the Cook Islands, provided it was consistent with the Cook Islands Act 1915; this includes established common law and equitable principles.[27]

2.4. CUSTOM

Prior to 1995, customary law was not constitutionally recognised as a formal source of law in the Cook Islands. Its role was limited to particular areas of law including land law, succession and customary adoption disputes.[28] Individual Acts could also make reference to custom.[29]

In 1995, the Constitution was amended to insert art 66A which concerned customary law.[30] This constitutional recognition of the role of customary law coincided with growing recognition that customary law is an important and legitimate source of law in the Pacific.[31] Article 66A provides:[32]

> 66A. Custom –
>
> (1) In addition to its powers to make laws pursuant to Article 39, Parliament may make laws recognising or giving effect to custom and usage.
>
> (2) In exercising its powers pursuant to this Article, Parliament shall have particular regard to the customs, traditions, usages, and values of the indigenous people of the Cook Islands.
>
> (3) Until such time as an Act otherwise provides, custom and usage shall have effect as part of the law of the Cook Islands, provided that this subclause shall not apply in respect of any custom, tradition, usage or value that is, and to the extent that it is, inconsistent with a provision of this Constitution or of any other enactment.
>
> (4) For the purposes of this Constitution, the opinion of the Aronga Mana of the island or vaka to which a custom, tradition or value relates, as to matters relating

---

27 Cook Islands Act 1915, ss 615–616. Don Paterson 'Cook Islands: Sources of Law' *PacLII* (1999) <http://www.paclii.org/ck/sources.html>.

28 New Zealand Law Commission, *Converging Currents: Custom and Human Rights in the Pacific* (Study Paper 17, September 2006) 3.5; see Cook Islands Act 1915, parts 12–15.

29 For example House of Arikis Act 1966, s 2 (definition of '*ariki*').

30 Constitution Amendment (No 17) Act 1994–95, s 7.

31 Alex Frame *The Sources of Cook Islands Law* (Cook Islands Law Society Education Programme 2018, session 2, Wednesday 7 March 2018) 4; *Hunt v de Miguel* [2016] CKCA 2; CA 2.14 (19 February 2016) at [56].

32 Constitution of the Cook Islands, art 66A.

> to and concerning custom, tradition, usage or the existence, extent or application of custom, shall be final and conclusive and shall not be questioned in any court of law.

Subclauses (1) and (2) add little to Parliament's pre-existing power to legislate at it sees fit. Subclause (3) provides that custom and usage can be generally applied in the Cook Islands provided they are not inconsistent with the Constitution or any other enactment. Under subclause (4), it is for the Aronga Mana to conclusively determine what constitutes custom. It is however, for the High Court of the Cook Islands to determine if the custom is inconsistent with the Constitution or any other enactment of the Parliament of the Cook Islands under sub-clause (3).[33] The Court applies the custom in any given dispute.[34] Elements of paragraph (4) remain unclear: who constitutes Aronga Mana in relation to a particular custom is not clear; it is uncertain who determines Aronga Mana's composition; it is also not determined how Aronga Mana is to express its opinion regarding a particular custom.[35] Article 66A does not impose a duty on the Crown to consult with Aronga Mana in every administrative law decision and if the Crown is not aware of a custom, it does not bind it.[36]

3. CONSTITUTIONAL LAW

3.1. PARLIAMENT

The legislature is the Parliament of the Cook Islands. The Constitution confers primary legislative power on the Parliament.[37] There are 25 members of the unicameral Parliament; each member represents a constituency.[38] The members are elected by secret ballot under a system of universal suffrage. The electoral system's particulars are outlined in the Electoral Act 1966. The Speaker of Parliament is elected by Parliament, in a manner decided on by Parliament.[39] Under art 44 of the Constitution, a Bill passed by Parliament and assented to by the Queen's Representative becomes law as an Act of Parliament.[40]

---

33 Alex Frame *The Sources of Cook Islands Law* (Cook Islands Law Society Education Programme 2018, session 2, Wednesday 7 March 2018) 5–6; *Framhein v Attorney-General* [2017] CKHC 37 at [138]; *Hunt v de Miguel* [2016] CKCA 2; CA 2.14 at [63]–[64]; *Browne v Munokoa* [2017] CKCA 1; CA 1.2017.

34 *Hunt v de Miguel* at [52].

35 *Hunt v de Miguel* at [73]; *Browne v Munokoa* at [38].

36 *Framhein v Attorney-General* at [143]–[147].

37 Constitution of the Cook Islands, art 27.

38 Constitution Amendment Act (No 9) 1980–81, Part 5.

39 Constitution of the Cook Islands, art 31.

40 Constitution of the Cook Islands, art 44.

3.2. HOUSE OF ARIKIS

The House of Arikis was established by the Cook Islands Constitution Amendment Act 1965 (NZ).[41] The House of Arikis considers matters related to the people's welfare that are submitted by Parliament.[42] It performs its advisory function by making recommendations and expressing its opinion to Parliament.[43] The House is made up of 15 members appointed by the Queen's Representative. The *ariki* are hereditary chiefs and represent the 15 islands.[44] There is to be at least one meeting annually.[45] Under s 7(1)(aa) of the House of Arikis Act, a member of the House may face disqualification upon the making of a declaration that fails to recognise the head of state, specifically the Queen in right of New Zealand.

3.3. EXECUTIVE

Article 2 of the Constitution declares that Her Majesty the Queen in right of New Zealand is the head of state of the Cook Islands and vests executive authority in the head of state.[46] The Constitution confers limited, express powers on the Queen, as head of state.[47] The executive branch of government is based on the Westminster model.[48] Articles 3–7 outline the position of the Queen's Representative. The Queen's Representative is appointed by the Sovereign for a three-year term and is required to act on the advice of Cabinet, the Prime Minister, or the appropriate minister.[49]

The Prime Minister is formally appointed by the Queen's Representative. The Prime Minister must be a Member of Parliament and command the confidence of the Parliament. The Prime Minister leads a Cabinet composed of the Prime Minister and no more than six other Ministers.[50] Ministers are responsible to the legislature.[51]

---

41 Cook Islands Constitution Amendment Act 1965 (NZ), s 8.

42 Constitution of the Cook Islands, arts 8–11B.

43 Constitution of the Cook Islands, arts 8–11B.

44 Norman Douglas and Ngaire Douglas (eds) *Pacific Islands Yearbook* (17th ed, Fiji Times, 1994).

45 House of Arikis Act 1966, Schedule.

46 Constitution of the Cook Islands, art 2. As at 2020, the head of state was Queen Elizabeth II of the Realm of New Zealand. See Letters Patent.

47 Jennifer Corrin and Don Paterson (eds) *Introduction to South Pacific Law* (4th ed, Intersentia, 2017) 88.

48 Jennifer Corrin and Don Paterson (eds) *Introduction to South Pacific Law* (4th ed, Intersentia, 2017) 94.

49 Constitution of the Cook Islands, arts 3 and 5.

50 Constitution of the Cook Islands, art 13.

51 Constitution of the Cook Islands, art 14.

There is an Executive Council, which consists of the Queen's Representative and members of Cabinet.[52]

3.4. JUDICIARY

Part IV of the Constitution covers the judiciary. The courts in the Cook Islands include[53] the High Court, Court of Appeal and Judicial Committee of the Privy Council.[54]

Article 47 of the Constitution establishes the High Court. The Constitution confers all necessary jurisdiction on the High Court to administer the law in force in the Cook Islands, subject to the Constitution and the law.[55] The High Court has the right to interpret and enforce the Constitution. The High Court is divided into civil, criminal and land divisions.[56]

Each High Court judge is appointed by the Queen's Representative and may exercise all the powers of the High Court.[57] There must be at least one judge of the Cook Islands.[58] In circumstances where the High Court consists of only one judge, that judge may be the Chief Justice.[59] If more than one judge is appointed to the High Court, one of them shall be the Chief Justice.[60] There are constitutional limitations on the terms of judges who do not reside in the Cook Islands.[61] Under art 53(2) of the Constitution, non-citizen judges may serve a maximum three-year term in office, but may be reappointed. Judges may be removed or suspended only on limited, express grounds.[62] Justices of the peace are appointed by the Queen's Representative.[63] The High Court 'may be constituted as an inferior court' specifically when justices of the peace preside over the matters.[64]

Article 56 establishes the Court of Appeal. This is a superior court of record with jurisdiction to hear and determine appeals from the High Court.[65] Article 57(1) provides that any three judges of the Court of Appeal may exercise

52 Constitution of the Cook Islands, art 22.
53 There are other tribunals, for example the Small Claims Tribunal.
54 See Privy Council (Judicial Committee) Act 1984. See also *Browne v Munokoa* [2018] UKPC 18.
55 Constitution of the Cook Islands, art 47(2).
56 Constitution of the Cook Islands, art 47(3).
57 Constitution of the Cook Islands, arts 47(4)–(6) and 49–52.
58 Constitution of the Cook Islands, art 49(1).
59 Constitution of the Cook Islands, art 49(2).
60 Constitution of the Cook Islands, art 49(2).
61 Constitution of the Cook Islands, art 53(2).
62 Constitution of the Cook Islands, art 54.
63 Constitution of the Cook Islands, art 62(1).
64 Jennifer Corrin and Don Paterson (eds) *Introduction to South Pacific Law* (4th ed, Intersentia, 2017) 339.
65 Constitution of the Cook Islands, art 60.

all of the powers of the Court. Judgments of the Court of Appeal must reflect the opinion of the majority on the Bench.[66] Further appeal may be made in limited circumstances to the Privy Council.[67]

The Law Practitioners Act 1993–94 regulates the practice of law in the Cook Islands. The basic provision is s 3, which deals with admission to practice. Every practitioner is by s 30 of the Act a member of the Cook Islands Law Society. As at 2020 there were more than 20 listed law practitioners.

3.5. ADDITIONAL CONSTITUTIONAL STRUCTURES

Part VI of the Constitution governs the public service of the Cook Islands. The Public Service Commissioner, who is appointed by the Queen's Representative for a term determined by Cabinet, is responsible for the public service.[68] The Queen's Representative may remove the Public Service Commissioner for disability, bankruptcy, neglect of duty, breach of the terms of appoint, or misconduct.[69] Article 76 establishes the Public Service Board of Appeal.

Part IVA of the Constitution contains fundamental human rights and freedoms.[70] This Part was added by an amendment to the Constitution in 1981.[71] It follows the Canadian Charter of Rights and Freedoms model, which outlines human rights in general terms.[72]

The Constitution's amendment procedure is contained in art 41. Most amendments require a special majority of two-thirds of Parliament.[73] Specifically, two-thirds of the total membership of the Parliament, including vacancies, must vote in favour of the amendment on two separate occasions,[74] with a minimum of a 90-day interval between the votes.[75] Some amendments additionally require approval by two-thirds of electors.[76] This further requirement applies to amendments to ss 2–6 of the Cook Islands Constitution Act 1964 and to arts 2 and 41 of the Constitution.[77]

---

66 Constitution of the Cook Islands, art 57(2).
67 Constitution of the Cook Islands, art 59(2).
68 Constitution of the Cook Islands, arts 73 and 74(1).
69 Constitution of the Cook Islands, art 74(3).
70 Constitution of the Cook Islands, art 64. Article 64(1) deals with rights; art 64(2) with duties.
71 Constitution Amendment Act (No 9) 1980–81.
72 Canada Act 1982 (UK) c 11, Sch B, Part I.
73 Constitution of the Cook Islands, art 41.
74 Constitution of the Cook Islands, art 41(1)(a).
75 Constitution of the Cook Islands, art 41(1)(b).
76 Constitution of the Cook Islands, art 41(2).
77 Constitution of the Cook Islands, arts 2 and 41; Cook Islands Constitution Act 1964 (NZ), ss 2–6. These are the main provisions relating to the free association arrangement with New Zealand. On amendment processes see *Henry v Attorney-General* [1983] CKCA 1.

3.6. PROTECTION FOR INDIVIDUALS

The office of the Ombudsman provides an accountability mechanism for individuals in the Cook Islands in relation to administrative decisions made by the executive. The Ombudsman Act 1984 establishes the position of the Ombudsman. The Ombudsman is an officer of and is responsible to Parliament.[78] The Queen's Representative acting on the advice of the Prime Minister appoints the Ombudsman.[79]

Section 11 outlines the functions of the Ombudsman. It states that it is a function of the Ombudsman to investigate any decision, recommendation or act by a department or specified organisation, provided the decision, recommendation or act relates to a matter of administration and affects any person or body of persons in their personal capacity. The function has wide coverage encompassing all relevant decisions and recommendations made, and all acts done or omitted to be done, by officers, employees and members of departments and specified organisations in their capacity as officer, employee or member. The Ombudsman may initiate and conduct an investigation on a complaint made to him or her, or of his or her own motion.[80]

The Ombudsman may refuse to investigate a complaint if it appears that there is an adequate remedy or right of appeal under the law or existing administrative practice that it would have been reasonable for the complainant to resort to, excluding the right to petition Parliament.[81] The Ombudsman may also refuse to investigate a complaint within the Ombudsman's jurisdiction further, on the basis that additional investigation is unnecessary, by having regard to all the circumstances of the case.[82] Furthermore, the Ombudsman may refuse to commence or continue an investigation in relation to a complaint on various express grounds such as triviality of the complaint's subject matter.[83] Where an Ombudsman refuses to investigate, the Ombudsman is required to inform and state the reasons for the decision to the complainant.[84]

The reach of the Ombudsman's investigative powers has expanded over the past decade. Under the Official Information Act 2008, it is a function of the Ombudsman to investigate and review particular decisions made by ministries or ministers of the Crown or organisations.[85] This investigation must follow from a complaint made to the Ombudsman in writing.[86] The Disability Act 2008

78 Ombudsman Act 1984, s 3(1).
79 Ombudsman Act 1984, ss 3(2) and 7.
80 Ombudsman Act 1984, s 11(3).
81 Ombudsman Act 1984, s 14(1)(a).
82 Ombudsman Act 1984, s 14(1)(b).
83 Ombudsman Act 1984, s 14(2).
84 Ombudsman Act 1984, s 14(3).
85 Official Information Act 2008, ss 30(1)–(2).
86 Official Information Act 2008, s 30(3).

further extended the Ombudsman's power. Section 16 empowers the Ombudsman to investigate a complaint made by a person with a disability or their agent in relation to unlawful discrimination.[87] A person with a disability or their agent may make a compliant to the Ombudsman where they believe there has been unlawful discrimination in respect of a person or persons with a disability.[88] The Ombudsman may elect to pursue an investigation of such complaint under this Act or under the Ombudsman Act.[89]

The Ombudsman can also investigate complaints in relation to the conduct of police officers, under the Police Act 2012. Section 91 permits the Ombudsman to investigate a complaint which had previously been made by the complainant to the Police Commissioner, but for which an investigation failed to occur. Also, a complaint may be investigated if there was, in the complainant's opinion, an unsatisfactory outcome in the original investigation. The Act imposes duties of notification on the Ombudsman and Police Commissioner respectively.[90] The Ombudsman must notify the Commissioner of every complaint received as soon as practicable, and in any case within five working days after receipt.[91]

Further, s 92 imposes a duty on the Police Commissioner to notify the Ombudsman of certain incidents involving death or serious bodily harm. Specifically, where a member of the police acting in the execution of duty causes death or serious bodily harm to any person, the Commissioner must notify the Ombudsman in writing with particulars about the incident, as soon as practicable, and in any case within five working days of the incident.[92] The Ombudsman may investigate any such incident following notification, provided the Ombudsman is satisfied that there are reasonable grounds to carry out an investigation in the public interest.[93]

4. THE LAW OF PERSONS

4.1. MARRIAGE

The Marriage Act 1973 governs marriage in the Cook Islands. The minimum age to marry without parental consent is 16.[94] Persons younger than 16 may marry with parental consent or judicial approval from the High Court.[95] The minimum

87 Disability Act 2008, ss 16(1) and 20.
88 Disability Act 2008, s 16(1).
89 Disability Act 2008, ss 16(2)–(3); Ombudsman Act 1984, s 11(1).
90 Police Act 2012, ss 92–93.
91 Police Act 2012, s 93.
92 Police Act 2012, s 92.
93 Police Act 2012, ss 91(2) and 92.
94 Marriage Act 1973, s 17.
95 Marriage Act 1973, s 18.

age has been criticised by international human rights bodies, which advise that the legal age for marriage should be 18 years.[96] The Act states that a marriage that involves a prohibited relationship is void.[97]

All marriages must be registered.[98] Part IV of the Act lists the formal requirements for marriage. For example, one party is required to give notice to a registrar and the registrar is subsequently to issue a marriage licence.[99] The solemnisation of marriage must occur before a registrar or an officiating minister, and in the presence of two or more witnesses.[100] Part VII contains various offences relating to marriage.

The Marriage Act 1973 was amended by the Marriage Amendment Act 2007 to expressly prohibit same-sex marriage. Under s 15A, marriage between persons of the same sex is prohibited. The Act employs a restrictive definition of gender; pursuant to s 15A(2), a person's sex at birth is that person's sex for legal purposes. This deeming provision is applicable regardless of any surgical or medical treatment.

4.2. DIVORCE

Divorce is governed by Part 2 of the Family Protection and Support Act 2017. The 2017 Act replaced the then existing law relating to divorce and separation. A stated principal purpose of the Act in s 3 is to provide for the orderly and equitable settlement of the affairs of spouses and de facto partners when a marriage or de facto relationship breaks down. This law reform eliminated the fault-based divorce system.[101]

The divorce procedure is outlined in ss 9–12 of the Act. Under s 9, an application for divorce may be made jointly or by either party to the marriage, provided at least one of the parties has resided in the Cook Islands for more than two years. The court must make a divorce order if the parties have been separated for a minimum of 12 months.[102] Alternatively, the court may make a divorce order on a number of other bases. The court may exercise its discretionary power to make a divorce order if the parties have not been separated for 12 months, the

96 Article 1 of the Convention on the Rights of the Child; Committee on the Rights of the Child 'Consideration of Reports Submitted by States Parties under Article 44 of the Convention', CRC/C/COK/CO/1, 22 February 2012, at 5.

97 Marriage Act 1973, s 15; Second Schedule.

98 Marriage Act 1973, Part VI.

99 Marriage Act 1973, ss 23, 24, 28.

100 Marriage Act 1973, ss 30–32.

101 Committee on the Elimination of Discrimination against Women 'Convention on the Elimination of All Forms of Discrimination against Women', CEDAW/C/COK/CO/2-3, 25 July 2018, at 1.

102 Family Protection and Support Act 2017, s 10(1).

application for divorce is made jointly and neither party lives with a child of the marriage on a permanent basis.[103]

A period of separation begins when a joint application is made, notice of one party's application is served or the parties cease living together.[104] Once a period of separation has commenced, the court may make additional or alternative orders on a party's application.[105]

Part 3 deals with domestic and child support. The court may make a support order relating to the provision of domestic support by one former partner to the other, childbearing expenses and child support for a child or children.[106] Following separation, a partner may apply to the court for a support order requiring payment of domestic support.[107] The court's power is to be exercised on the basis of express factors including age, health and earning capacity of each partner.[108] The court's power to order payment of childbearing expenses by the child's father is contained in s 19. The court may order payment of child support upon application.[109] Child support may extend to an adult child if there is necessity relating to the education or disability, mental or physical, of the child.[110]

Part 4, which concerns parenting arrangements, makes it clear that the child's best interests are paramount.[111] Section 40 confers power on the court to make a parenting order, which must include details of caregivers, times of care and any restricted or prohibited persons. A parenting order prevails in cases of inconsistency with a person's parental responsibility.[112] The interaction of orders and foreign jurisdictions is dealt with in ss 130–133, including offences relating to the removal of a child from the Cook Islands.

4.3. ADOPTION

Under the Cook Islands Act 1915, jurisdiction is conferred on the High Court to make adoption orders where an application is made by the adopting parent or adopting parents jointly.[113] The Act regulates statutory adoptions. Customary adoptions are regulated by customary law.

103 Family Protection and Support Act 2017, s 10(2).
104 Family Protection and Support Act 2017, s 11(1).
105 Family Protection and Support Act 2017, s 12.
106 Family Protection and Support Act 2017, s 14.
107 Family Protection and Support Act 2017, s 16.
108 Family Protection and Support Act 2017, ss 17–18.
109 Family Protection and Support Act 2017, ss 20–22.
110 Family Protection and Support Act 2017, s 23.
111 Family Protection and Support Act 2017, s 33.
112 Family Protection and Support Act 2017, s 43.
113 Cook Islands Act 1915 (NZ), s 573A.

The Cook Islands' Family Protection and Support Act 2017 addresses children and adoptive parents' status. The Act imposes a duty on the Secretary to establish, facilitate, and supervise the use of *uipaanga kopu tangata* in the making of an agreed *kaveinga a te kopu tangata* regarding the care and protection of children.[114] The meaning of *uipaanga kopu tangata*, namely a meeting about a child, is contained in s 80. Section 81 defines a *kaveinga a te kopu tangata* as a written and signed agreement, between the Ministry of Internal Affairs and the relevant *uipaanga kopu tangata* participants, which specifies the relevant arrangements for the care and protection of a child. The Family Protection and Support Act 'explicitly integrates and builds on customary and community practices through the use of *uipaanga kopu tangata* (family meetings) in care planning'.[115]

There has consistently been a lack of clarity surrounding the land rights and entitlements of adopted children, particularly in the context of customary adoptions. Legislative intervention has not occurred. This is despite recommendations and judicial comments voicing the need for intervention. *Hunt v de Miguel* provides an illustration of such judicial concern.[116] A notable example of the uncertainty concerning customary adoptions is the Privy Council decision of *Browne v Munokoa*.[117] International human rights bodies have criticised the lack of legislative attention to informal adoptions, as well as the discriminatory and non-uniform provisions regarding adoption based on residency.[118]

4.4. OTHER

The Registry Office is responsible for recording births and deaths within the Cook Islands. Births and deaths occurring outside the country's borders are not recorded by the Registry Office. The applicable time for the registration of a birth is 14 days from the date of birth.[119] Non-compliance with specified time periods may result in a financial penalty.[120]

Succession matters are covered by the Administration Act 1969, the Wills Act 1837 (UK) and Part XIV of the Cook Islands Act 1915.

---

114 Family Protection and Support Act 2017, s 49(3)(b).

115 United Nations Children's Fund *Situation Analysis of Children in the Cook Islands* (UNICEF, 2017) 81.

116 *Hunt v de Miguel* [2016] CKCA 2, CA 2.14.

117 *Browne v Munokoa* [2018] UKPC 18.

118 Committee on the Rights of the Child 'Consideration of Reports Submitted by States Parties under Article 44 of the Convention', CRC/C/COK/CO/1, 22 February 2012, at 9.

119 Department of Justice 'Death' (10 April 2014) <http://www.justice.gov.ck/index.php/bdm/3-death>; Department of Justice 'Birth' (10 April 2014) <http://www.justice.gov.ck/index.php/bdm/2-birth>.

120 Department of Justice 'Birth' (10 April 2014) <http://www.justice.gov.ck/index.php/bdm/2-birth>.

5. LAW OF OBLIGATIONS

5.1. TORTS

The common law applies to the area of tort law. Many of the torts that apply in the Cook Islands stem from the principles of English common law.[121] For example, in relation to the tort of negligence, key cases in common law jurisdictions, such as *Donoghue v Stevenson*, are persuasive.[122]

The case law of the Cook Islands is significant in the area of torts. To illustrate, in 2013 the High Court considered the torts of false imprisonment and liability for misfeasance in public office in *Samatua v Attorney-General* (*Samatua*).[123] This case concerned the detention and treatment of Mr Samatua at a lockup at Penrhyn and on a ship by police officers. Among other claims, Mr Samatua alleged false imprisonment and misfeasance in public office. In order to establish the tort of false imprisonment, Grice J considered it necessary for a plaintiff to prove that they were imprisoned by the act of the defendant, whether intentionally or negligently.[124] In relation to the tort of misfeasance in public office, Grice J identified two forms, which have different requirements. Targeted malice by a public officer is the first form. This requires conduct specifically intended to injure.[125] The second form of the tort requires the public officer to have acted in bad faith or maliciously.[126] In considering the bad faith requirement, Grice J commented: 'The element of bad faith is the absence of an honest belief in the lawfulness of the conduct which gives rise to the risk of probable loss'.[127] Grice J held that neither tort was established and that the detention of Mr Samatua and the force used against him were reasonable. The bad faith and malice requirements failed because there was no factual basis for inferring bad faith, malice or improper motive.

While codification has not occurred, there are a number of statutes that regulate aspects of tort law and related processes and procedures in the Cook Islands. One such statute is the Crown Proceedings Act 1950, which is an inherited New Zealand Act. Section 6(1)(a) provides that the Crown is subject to

---

121 Sections 615–616 of the Cook Islands Act 1915. Don Paterson 'Cook Islands: Sources of Law' *PacLII* (1999) <http://www.paclii.org/ck/sources.html>.

122 *Donoghue v Stevenson* [1932] UKHL 100; *Marine Resources (Cook Islands) Ltd v Solicitor-General* [1986] CKCA 2; *Anns v London Borough of Merton* [1977] 2 A ER 492 at 498 (Lord Wilberforce); *Hedley Byrne & Co Ltd v Heller & Partners Ltd* [1964] AC 465; *Home Office v Dorset Yacht Co Ltd* [1970] UKHL 2.

123 *Samatua v Attorney-General* [2015] CKHC 14.

124 *Samatua v Attorney-General* [2015] CKHC 14 at [293] (Grice J).

125 *Samatua v Attorney-General* [2015] CKHC 14 at [307] (Grice J); *Three Rivers District Council v Bank of England (No 3)* [2001] 2 All ER 513 at [46] (Lord Steyn).

126 *Samatua v Attorney-General* [2015] CKHC 14 at [308]–[309] (Grice J); *Three Rivers District Council v Bank of England* [2000] 3 All ER 1 at [42] (Lord Hutton).

127 *Samatua v Attorney-General* [2015] CKHC 14 at [308] (Grice J).

all the liabilities in tort it would be subject to if it were a private person of full age and capacity, in respect of torts committed by its servants or agents. The Crown's liability relates to actions done by servants and agents in the course of their employment. In *Rolls v Attorney-General*, the High Court held the Attorney-General liable for the negligence of the prison authorities, which included the total prison administration and prison officers concerned, under this Act.[128] The breach of duty of care owed by the prison authorities in that case related to the repeated escape of a prisoner.[129] The liability of the Crown in tort does not extend to the exercise of judicial functions.[130] Specifically, no proceedings lie against the Crown in respect of anything done or omitted to be done by any person while discharging any responsibilities of a judicial nature, or any responsibilities in connection with the execution of judicial process.[131]

In *Samatua*, Grice J considered that the Penrhyn Justices of the Peace had been 'acting throughout the proceedings as judicial officers'.[132] This was because in presiding over the court hearings, the Justices necessarily 'made findings, determinations and sentenced Mr Samatua', and signed 'the record of proceedings', which are characteristic tasks of judicial officers.[133] Consequently, Grice J held that the Crown could not be liable for the alleged tortious conduct of the Justices of the Peace.[134]

Furthermore, statute may regulate the law surrounding a particular tort. In relation to defamation, the Defamation Act 1993 abolished the libel and slander distinction. Under the Act, proof of special damage is not required.[135]

Generally, for cases involving torts, dispute resolution mainly occurs through conciliation, arbitration and customary dispute settlement mechanisms.

5.2. CONTRACT

Contract law in the Cook Islands is regulated largely by the common law. There are also a number of Acts of relevance – several from the colonial period, including the Bills of Exchange Act 1908, Carriage of Goods Act 1998 and Sale of Goods Act 1908. More recent consumer protection laws are the Consumer

128 *Rolls v Attorney-General of the Cook Islands* [1991] CKHC 3; Crown Proceedings Act 1950, s 6(1)(a).

129 *Rolls v Attorney-General of the Cook Islands* [1991] CKHC 3.

130 Crown Proceedings Act 1950, s 6(5).

131 Crown Proceedings Act 1950, s 6(5).

132 *Samatua v Attorney General* [2015] CKHC 14 at [332] (Grice J).

133 *Samatua v Attorney General* [2015] CKHC 14 at [332] (Grice J).

134 Crown Proceedings Act 1950, s 6(5); *Samatua v Attorney-General* [2015] CKHC 14 at [333s] (Grice J).

135 Other torts-related statutes are the Cook Islands Workers Compensation Ordinance 1964, and the Deaths by Accident Compensation Act 1952.

Guarantees Act 2008 and the Fair Trading Act 2008. Under statute, the High Court may modify oppressive contracts. Specifically, s 645 of the Cook Islands Act 1915 allows the High Court to modify or refuse to enforce 'a contract made by a Cook Islands Maori if the court is of the opinion that it is oppressive, unreasonable, or improvident'.[136]

The Illegal Contracts Act 1987 governs contracts that are the subject of judicial declarations of illegality. Under s 5, illegal contracts have no effect, and no persons become entitled to property under an illegal contract. The statute's coverage is wide.[137] The definition of illegal contract in s 3 includes any contract considered illegal at law or in equity. The contract's formation or performance can render it illegal.[138] The Act also covers contracts with severable illegal provisions.[139] A court may grant relief 'by way of restitution, compensation, variation of the contract, validation of the contract in whole or part or for any particular purpose, or otherwise howsoever as the Court in its discretion thinks just'.[140] A relief order, which may be made to, for example, any party to an illegal contract, may be 'subject to such terms and conditions as the Court thinks fit'.[141]

6. LAND, PERSONAL PROPERTY AND CULTURAL PROTECTION

6.1. LAND

The sources of land law are the common law, legislation and customary law. Historically, the sole source was custom. Most land is customary land. Section 422 of the Cook Islands Act 1915 provides that all titles to and interests in customary law are to be determined by custom. Customary land is 'land which, being vested in the Crown, is held by Natives or the descendants of Natives under the Native customs and usages of the Cook Islands'.[142] The Constitution establishes a land division of the High Court to determine claims relating to land.[143] Formally, all land is vested in the Crown.[144] But there are constitutional limits on the entitlement of the Crown. Under art 40 of the Constitution, no property can be compulsorily taken without compensation.

136 Cook Islands Act 1915, s 645; Jennifer Corrin and Don Paterson (eds) *Introduction to South Pacific Law* (4th ed, Intersentia, 2017) 246.
137 Illegal Contracts Act 1987, ss 3 and 8.
138 Illegal Contracts Act 1987, s 3.
139 Illegal Contracts Act 1987, s 3.
140 Illegal Contracts Act 1987, s 6(1).
141 Illegal Contracts Act 1987, ss 6(1)(a) and (1)(b).
142 Cook Islands Act 1915, s 2.
143 Constitution of the Cook Islands, art 47(3)(c).
144 Cook Islands Act 1915, s 354.

6.2. PERSONAL PROPERTY

The use and ownership of personal property is governed by the common law, as well as by the Chattels Transfer Act 1924 and the Property Law Act 1952 (NZ). These Acts were inherited from the law of New Zealand. The Personal Property Securities Act 2017 introduced a Personal Property Securities Registry (PPSR). Security interests over moveable property can be registered on this Registry.

6.3. INTANGIBLE PROPERTY

Copyright law provides the predominant protection mechanism for intangible property in the Cook Islands. The Copyright Act 2013 is the central piece of legislation. This Act clarified and amended the law relating to copyright and other forms of protection for intellectual creations.[145] Notably, the Cook Islands became a member of the Berne Convention for the Protection of Literary and Artistic Works in 2017, after acceding on 3 May 2017.[146]

The Copyright Act defines copyright as a property right that exists in original works and confers exclusive rights on the owner of the copyright in the works.[147] The owner of copyright enjoys various exclusive rights in respect of the work, including rights to copy, publish, perform, display, distribute, modify and communicate the original work.[148] The copyright owner may also authorise another person to exercise these rights.[149] The duration of the copyright is the life of the author plus 50 years, in most circumstances.[150] There are various exceptions to copyright infringement, including where the copying of work occurs only temporarily or for the purposes of research, private study, education, law or reporting current events to the public.[151]

In addition to economic rights, the Act confers moral rights on the author.[152] These are non-transferable during the author's lifetime, but may be passed by testamentary disposition or operation of law upon the author's death.[153] The moral rights an author has in relation to a work include a right to receive

---

145 Miranda Forsyth and Kalissa Alexeyeff 'Regulating Cultural Performances in Oceania: The Complicated Relationship between Law, Creativity and Cultural Property' (2016) 142–143 Journal de la Société des Oceanistes 117 at 124.

146 World Intellectual Property Organization 'Berne Notification No. 277' (3 May 2017) <https://www.wipo.int/treaties/en/notifications/berne/treaty_berne_277.html>.

147 Copyright Act 2013, s 7(1).

148 Copyright Act 2013, s 8(1).

149 Copyright Act 2013, s 8(1)(l).

150 Copyright Act 2013, s 13(1).

151 Copyright Act 2013, ss 14–25.

152 Copyright Act 2013, s 26(1).

153 Copyright Act 2013, s 26(2).

prominent attribution by name or pseudonym in particular circumstances, to object to any modification or derogatory treatment that would be prejudicial to their honour or reputation, and to object to any other action in relation to their work.[154] Under s 27, authors may waive their moral rights.

Part 4 relates to enforcement. There are civil and criminal protections for rights conferred on owners of copyright. In civil proceedings for an infringement or breach of rights, the person who enjoys rights under the Act is entitled to damages, and may be granted additional discretional remedies by the court.[155] The Act creates a number of offences.[156] For example, it is an offence to intentionally infringe or breach a protected right for a profit-making purpose or to provide the means for making infringing copies.[157] Generally, the penalty for committing an offence listed in this Part is a substantial fine.[158] Further orders may also be made at the discretion of the court, provided civil proceedings have not also been taken.[159]

The Copyright Act is supplemented on matters of intellectual property by the Designs Act 1953, the Patents Act 1953 and the Trade Marks Act 1953.

6.4. CULTURAL PROTECTION

Cultural protection occurs in a number of ways in the Cook Islands. Specific statutes apply to protect various aspects of the culture of the Cook Islands. The Cultural and Historic Places Act 1994–95 aims to preserve the historic heritage of the Cook Islands. The Act establishes the Cultural and Historic Places Trust.[160] Section 26 empowers the Trust to issue a declaration that a building and associated land is to be protected. Any works that are contrary to a protection notice are prohibited.[161]

In addition, the Traditional Knowledge Act 2013 provides for the protection of knowledge. The Act gives legal recognition to rights in the traditional knowledge of the traditional communities of the Cook Islands. It also contributes to the protection of the rights of the traditional communities for the benefit of the people of the Cook Islands. The Act establishes a system of registration for recognised forms of traditional knowledge and confers certain rights and protections on rights-holders. The definition of traditional knowledge includes

---

154 Copyright Act 2013, s 26(5).
155 Copyright Act 2013, ss 39–40.
156 Copyright Act 2013, ss 41–45.
157 Copyright Act 2013, ss 41–42.
158 Copyright Act 2013, ss 41–45.
159 Copyright Act 2013, s 46.
160 Cultural and Historic Places Act 1994–95, ss 4 and 6.
161 Cultural and Historic Places Act 1994–95, s 28.

tangible and intangible knowledge transmitted from generation to generation that originates from a traditional community or was inspired for traditional purposes.[162] The Act outlines the various types of dealings with registered traditional knowledge that require written authorisation, and those which are not subject to restrictions.[163] It further specifies the circumstances in which acts in relation to registered sacred knowledge or sacred-secret knowledge are prohibited.[164]

Importantly, s 7 of the Act sets out the various rights of rights-holders of registered traditional knowledge. Rights enjoyed exclusively by registered rights-holders are listed in s 7(1). These include the right to use such knowledge, to receive commercial returns, to authorise use by other persons, to be acknowledged upon publication or public issuing of the knowledge, and to exercise the rights and remedies under the Act. The rights are personal, inalienable and continue in perpetuity.[165]

Section 12(1) creates a number of offences relating to sacred knowledge and sacred-secret knowledge. A person commits an offence if they, for example, receive commercial returns from or attempt to authorise another person's use of the knowledge. An offender can receive a fine of NZ$50,000, or NZ$500,000 in the case of a body corporate.[166] In addition, the court may make an order for delivery up or disposal of any offending material.[167] A relevant defence is contained in s 46.[168] Civil relief is also available to rights-holders following breaches of certain provisions.[169] The Act confers a wide discretion on the court to grant relief including the grant of an injunction on any terms the Court considers appropriate, damages or an account of profits, an order for delivery up, an order for disposal and any additional ancillary order the court considers desirable.[170]

Registration is a key aspect of the Traditional Knowledge Act. Under s 14, any rights-holder may apply to the Secretary of Cultural Development in order to register traditional knowledge. The Secretary is required to establish and maintain a register of traditional knowledge for the purposes of providing a record and enabling members of the public to have access to and share such knowledge.[171] The Act incorporates the Are Korero into the registration process

---

162 Traditional Knowledge Act 2013, s 4.
163 Traditional Knowledge Act 2013, ss 8–9.
164 Traditional Knowledge Act 2013, ss 10–12.
165 Traditional Knowledge Act 2013, s 13(1).
166 Traditional Knowledge Act 2013, s 45.
167 Traditional Knowledge Act 2013, s 47.
168 Traditional Knowledge Act 2013, s 46.
169 Traditional Knowledge Act 2013, ss 7(3), 8(2), 10(2) and 42.
170 Traditional Knowledge Act 2013, s 42.
171 Traditional Knowledge Act 2013, ss 56 and 58.

in a 'meaningful' way.[172] Furthermore, the Act requires the Minister to appoint a Traditional Knowledge Advisory Committee.[173]

Although the Traditional Knowledge Act is quite far-reaching, misappropriations of traditional knowledge which occur outside of the Cook Islands are not covered by the Act,[174] despite this having been a key motivation for the legislation.[175] Furthermore, the Act's model of registration and adoption of 'Western mechanisms' has been criticised on the basis that the legal 'creation of boundaries of private ownership creates tension with principles of public access', which is a value central to the traditions of the Cook Islands.[176]

The Environment Act 2003 also provides cultural protection. According to the statutory definition, the environment is 'the ecosystems and the equality of those ecosystems as well as the physical, biological, cultural, spiritual, social and historic processes and resources in those ecosystems'.[177] This includes the 'natural, physical, cultural, demographic, and social qualities and characteristics of an area that contribute to people's appreciation of its pleasantness, aesthetic coherence, and cultural and recreational attributes'.[178]

Specific mechanisms that provide for cultural protection are management plans and protection areas. Under the Act, a stated purpose for which management plans can be prepared is the conservation and management of historical, archaeological and cultural sites.[179] Furthermore, an Island Environment Authority may propose to designate an area with importance as a protected area.[180] Where it does, the

---

172 Traditional Knowledge Act 2013, Part 3; Miranda Forsyth 'Making Room for Magic in Intellectual Property Policy' in Steward Firth and Vijay Naidu (eds) *Understanding Oceania: Celebrating the University of the South Pacific and its Collaboration with The Australian National University* (ANU Press, 2019) 115.

173 Traditional Knowledge Act 2013, ss 62–64.

174 Miranda Forsyth and Kalissa Alexeyeff 'Regulating Cultural Performances in Oceania: The Complicated Relationship between Law, Creativity and Cultural Property' (2016) 142-143 Journal de la Société des Oceanistes 117 at 125; Miranda Forsyth 'Legal Pluralism: The Regulation of Traditional Medicine in the Cook Islands' in Peter Drahos (ed) *Regulatory Theory* (ANU Press, 2017) 233 at 241.

175 Miranda Forsyth and Kalissa Alexeyeff 'Regulating Cultural Performances in Oceania: The Complicated Relationship between Law, Creativity and Cultural Property' (2016) 142-143 Journal de la Société des Oceanistes 117 at 122; Miranda Forsyth 'Legal Pluralism: The Regulation of Traditional Medicine in the Cook Islands' in Peter Drahos (ed) *Regulatory Theory* (ANU Press, 2017) 233 at 241.

176 Miranda Forsyth and Kalissa Alexeyeff 'Regulating Cultural Performances in Oceania: The Complicated Relationship between Law, Creativity and Cultural Property' (2016) 142-143 Journal de la Société des Oceanistes 117 at 127; Miranda Forsyth 'Legal Pluralism: The Regulation of Traditional Medicine in the Cook Islands' in Peter Drahos (ed) *Regulatory Theory* (ANU Press, 2017) 233 at 243–244; William Gallagher 'Intellectual Property' *UC Berkeley: Center for the Study of Law and Society Jurisprudence and Social Policy Program* (2008) <https://escholarship.org/uc/item/008853bp> xxiii.

177 Environment Act 2003, s 2.

178 Environment Act 2003, s 2.

179 Environment Act 2003, s 37(1)(h).

180 Environment Act 2003, s 41(1).

Authority may cause a notification to be issued.[181] Such notifications must specify the area, the management plan's name, viewing location and 'particulars of the ecological, cultural, archaeological, historical or scenic importance and the resources, animals, plants and their habitats'.[182]

7. COMMERCIAL LAW

7.1. CORPORATION AND RELATED LAW

There have been significant recent reforms in the field of company law. The legislature aimed to improve business law by introducing the Companies Act 2017 and the Personal Property Securities Act 2017, in conjunction with the making of notable amendments to the Incorporated Societies Act 1994. This comprehensive legislative reform package was intended to promote efficiency in the corporate and business sector of the Cook Islands.

Other Acts of relevance are the Partnership Act 1908 (NZ) and the Foundations Act 2012.

7.1.1. Cook Islands Companies Act 2017

The Companies Act 2017 repealed the Companies Act 1970–71.[183] The 2017 Act is based on the Companies Act 1993 of New Zealand with changes incorporated to meet the conditions of the Cook Islands.[184]

A significant aspect of the reform was the introduction of an electronic registry, namely the Cook Islands Companies and Incorporated Societies Registry. This requires all companies to be registered and allows for the searching of a company's details. The time limit for reregistration was 10 December 2020.[185] Non-compliance with reregistration requirements results in the company's removal from the active roll.[186] These requirements extended to overseas companies.[187]

An additional reform made by the Act was the elimination of the distinction between public and private companies.[188] The Act provides a simplified

---

181 Environment Act 2003, s 41(1).

182 Environment Act 2003, s 41(2).

183 The Companies Act 1970–71 had modified the New Zealand Companies Act 1955 to reflect the needs and context of the Cook Islands.

184 Department of Justice *Company Act Detailed Section by Section Analysis* (2019) <https://registry.justice.gov.ck/documentation/ck/Company_Act_Detailed_Section%20by%20Section_Analysis_Dec10_2019.pdf>.

185 Companies Act 2017, s 407.

186 Companies Act 2017, ss 407–408.

187 Companies Act 2017, s 409.

188 Companies Act 2017, s 6(d).

process for corporate formation. It is mandatory for all companies to submit a company constitution.[189] This reform eliminates the previous procedure, which involved submitting various documents such as a memorandum and articles of association, registration of registered office, particulars of directors and secretaries, and a compliance declaration.[190] A company's constitution outlines relevant governance rules. Companies may elect to draft a constitution or to adopt a standard constitution contained in the Act.[191] There are three different default constitutions that may apply to a company depending on the company's number of shareholders.[192] The number of shareholders of a company is not limited by the Act.[193] Part 6 strengthens the position of shareholders.

Rules concerning company shares are contained in ss 18–55 of the Act. Primarily, a company must have issued a minimum of one share to a shareholder.[194] According to s 18, shares are personal property. Accordingly, shares can act as collateral for loans under the Personal Property Securities Act 2017.

The Companies Act has residency requirements for company directors. Specifically, at least one of the directors of a company is required to live in the Cook Islands or in New Zealand.[195] This residency provision does not extend to shareholders.[196] Section 76 requires every director to sign a consent form to undertake the position; the document is to be retained for potential inspection, but does not have to be lodged with the Registrar.[197]

Enforcement provisions are contained in ss 109–127. The receivership of companies is governed by ss 296–336. The removal of a company from the active roll on the register concludes the process of closing a business.[198] A business that is removed from the register ceases to exist.[199] Any remaining assets of the company are vested in the Crown.[200]

7.1.2. Incorporated Societies Act 1994

The statutory amendments to the Incorporated Societies Act 1994 modernised the law relating to incorporated societies. Comparable to the Companies Act 2017, the Incorporated Societies Amendment Act 2019 introduced a

189 Companies Act 2017, ss 6(b) and 15.
190 Companies Act 2017, s 6(b).
191 Companies Act 2017, s 15.
192 Companies Act 2017, s 15.
193 Companies Act 2017, s 6(d).
194 Companies Act 2017, s 20.
195 Companies Act 2017, s 6(e).
196 Companies Act 2017, s 6(e).
197 Companies Act 2017, s 76.
198 Companies Act 2017, Part 16.
199 Companies Act 2017, Part 16.
200 Companies Act 2017, s 344.

searchable register of incorporated societies. The Act allows registration materials to be filed on the electronic register; this promotes accuracy, efficiency and ease in the sector.

7.1.3. Personal Property Securities Act 2017

A further aspect of the reform was the enactment of the Personal Property Securities Act 2017. This modified the law relating to security interests and personal property in the Cook Islands. The Act established the Personal Property Securities Registry (PPSR). Creditors can 'register their interest over movable property used as collateral to secure a payment obligation' on this online register.[201] The Act repeals the previously applicable Chattels Transfer Act 1924 and the Hire Purchase Act 1986. The Act applies only to personal property.

7.2. INTERNATIONAL COMMERCIAL ACTIVITIES

The International Companies Act 1981–82 deals with the incorporation and administration of international companies. International partnerships are covered by the International Partnerships Act 1984.

7.3. SHIPPING

The carriage of goods by sea is regulated by the Maritime Transport Act 2008. This statute provides for maritime safety, the implementation of international obligations, responsibility of industry workers and marine environment protection.[202] Part 2 outlines relevant duties, with s 8 detailing the general duties expected of participants in the maritime system. Part 3 contains the maritime rules and Part 4 establishes the Secretary's powers. Part 5 sets out numerous offences including offences relating to safety and maritime documents. Part 6 provides for the liability of vessel owners. A duty of assistance is imposed by s 84 of the Act. Part 10 deals with the carriage of goods by sea.

The International Shipping Act 1999 also has application. One of the purposes of the Act was to safeguard and maintain competition in the Cook Islands' international shipping services. The Ship Registration Act 2007 regulates the important ship registration industry.

201 Department of Justice 'Registry' (2020) <https://registry.justice.gov.ck/public/howto.aspx?cn=AccessTheRegistry&ctk=PPSRHowTo>.

202 Maritime Transport Act 2008, s 6.

7.4. BANKING

The law relating to banking is provided by the Bank of the Cook Islands Act 2003 and the Banking Act 2011. The Bank of the Cook Islands Act 2003 established the Bank of the Cook Islands Holdings Corporation. The Act further provided for the incorporation and establishment of the Bank of the Cook Islands Limited. The Banking Act 2011 covers the licensing, regulation and supervision of banking businesses, and circumstances involving the insolvency of a licensee. Under s 23(1), a licensee is required to immediately notify the Financial Supervisory Commission in writing of their insolvency. The mandatory notification requirement also applies to situations where licensees consider insolvency to be likely.[203] The Act also empowers the Commission to take enforcement action.[204] When a licensee is, or is likely to become, insolvent, the Commission may take action against the licensee.[205]

7.5. OFFSHORE FINANCING

Offshore or asset protection trusts are common in the Cook Islands. The International Trusts Act 1984 is a key piece of legislation. In the last 10 years, the legislature introduced the Foundations Act 2012 and the Captive Insurance Act 2013 in relation to offshore financing. The Foundation Act offers a civil law alternative to the common law trust.[206] Foundations have an independent legal personality due to their incorporation. The mechanisms enshrined in the Act in relation to foundations reflect the benefits against creditors contained in s 13B of the International Trusts Act 1984. Furthermore, the Captive Insurance Act 2013 improves the appeal for captive insurance businesses to be established in the Cook Islands. Under the Act, the strict requirements under the Cook Islands Insurance Act 2008 do not cover captive insurance businesses. The Cook Islands has improved its desirability as a location for offshore financing through such statutory devices.

7.6. OTHER

The principal fiscal legislation is in the Income Tax Act 1997 and the Value Added Tax Act 1997.

---

203 Banking Act 2011, s 23(1)(b).
204 Banking Act 2011, s 20(1).
205 Banking Act 2011, s 20(1)(a).
206 Tony Angelo 'Pacific Islands Review' (2014) 3 NZL Rev 489 at 505–509.

8. ENVIRONMENTAL LAW

8.1. ENVIRONMENTAL PROTECTION

The environment receives no direct constitutional protection. Protection is provided predominately by Acts. The Marae Moana Act 2017 is an important piece of legislation in the field of environmental law and protection. It established the Marae Moana, which is a marine protected area in the Cook Islands,[207] and the Marae Moana Council.[208] The Act primarily aims to protect and conserve the ecological, biodiversity, and heritage values of the Cook Islands marine environment.[209] The Marae Moana is claimed to be 'the world's largest marine protected area'.[210]

The Environment Act 2003 provides for the protection, conservation and management of the environment of the Cook Islands in a sustainable manner. According to a legislative review, this Act 'aims to be a comprehensive instrument that provides for all environmental aspects within the country, from the distribution of powers and functions both at a central and a local level to the prescription of specific environmental requirements and management procedures', as well as outlining 'a strategy for the domestic implementation of the international environmental obligations assumed by the Cook Islands under international law'.[211]

Part 1 of the 2003 Act establishes the National Environment Service.[212] The Part further outlines the structures and procedures of the Service, including the location of the head office,[213] location of separate divisions[214] and annual reporting requirements to the relevant minister and Parliament.[215] Under Part 2 of the Act, the Island Environment Authorities are established[216] and their functions outlined.[217] Part 3 concerns the National Environment Council and Part 4 provides for environmental officers.

Part 5 of the Act outlines the law related to environmental impact assessments. Pursuant to s 36, all persons must submit an application inclusive

---

207 Marae Moana Act 2017, s 8.

208 Marae Moana Act 2017, s 9.

209 Marae Moana Act 2017, s 3(1).

210 *Polynesia in Review: Issues and Events*, 1 July 2017 to 30 June 2018, 188; Adrian Burton 'Dispatches: Cook Islands Establish Marine Protected Area' (2017) 15(7) Frontiers in Ecology and the Environment 353.

211 Secretariat of the Pacific Regional Environment Programme and EDO NSW *Cook Islands: Review of Natural Resource and Environment Related Legislation* (Report, January 2018) 8–9.

212 Environment Act 2003, s 5.

213 Environment Act 2003, s 5(3).

214 Environment Act 2003, s 5(3).

215 Environment Act 2003, s 6.

216 Environment Act 2003, s 11.

217 Environment Act 2003, s 12.

of an environmental impact assessment to the Service for a project permit for activities which cause or are likely to cause significant environmental impacts.[218] Environmental impact assessments are to include details about environmental impacts,[219] proposed mitigation and monitoring techniques,[220] and alternatives.[221] The permitting authority, namely the Service, assesses the application and may issue a permit specifying terms and conditions, request submission of modifications, or refuse to issue a permit.[222] Relevant activities are only to be undertaken in accordance with a s 36 permit.[223] The Court of Appeal case of *Framhein v Attorney-General* concerned environmental impact assessments. In that case, an assessment had not been conducted.[224]

Part 6 provides for management plans and protected areas. Under s 37(1), at the request of the Island Environment Authority, the Service is empowered to prepare a draft management plan for listed purposes. Liability to a fine of up to NZ$5,000 follows the contravention of a management plan without lawful justification.[225] Section 41 concerns protected areas; particularly vulnerable areas are identified in Part 8; and Part 9 establishes the Environment Protection Fund. The Queen's Representative is empowered to make regulations in relation to pollution and waste.[226]

The Maritime Transport Act 2008 also aims, among its other purposes, to protect the marine environment.[227]

8.2. RESPONSES TO CLIMATE CHANGE

Climate change poses a significant threat to the Cook Islands. The intense risks faced by the Cook Islands are disproportionate to the Cook Islands' current contributions to levels of global emissions.[228] Across the Cook Islands, records indicate increases in annual temperatures, rainfall (at Penrhyn), sea levels and ocean acidification.[229] In a report prepared by the Cook Islands government for

218 Environment Act 2003, s 36.
219 Environment Act 2003, s 36(3)(a).
220 Environment Act 2003, s 36(3)(b).
221 Environment Act 2003, s 36(3)(c).
222 Environment Act 2003, s 36(7).
223 Environment Act 2003, s 36(1).
224 *Framhein v Attorney-General* [2018] CKCA 5.
225 Secretariat of the Pacific Regional Environment Programme and EDO NSW *Cook Islands: Review of Natural Resource and Environment Related Legislation* (Report, January 2018) 12.
226 Environment Act 2003, s 70.
227 Maritime Transport Act 2008, s 6(d) and Part 12.
228 National Environment Service *Climate Change* (2015) <https://environment.gov.ck/island-futures-division/climate-change>.
229 Cook Islands Meteorological Service and Pacific Climate Change Science Program *Current and Future Climate of the Cook Islands* (Report, 2013).

the United Nations in 2011, the anticipated, potential consequences of climate change on the Cook Islands were described as 'severe' and 24 vulnerable areas were identified.[230]

The Cook Islands has committed to international action aimed at combatting climate change, despite not being a member of the United Nations. Specifically, the Cook Islands has signed the Framework Convention on Climate Change and Kyoto Protocol, as well as the Paris Climate Accord in 2016.[231] The Cook Islands has undertaken a range of projects to respond and adapt to climate-related challenges, including the Strengthening the Resilience of the Cook Islands to Climate Change project from 2012 to 2018 and resilience-building plans assisted by a grant of NZ$3,000,000 provided by the Adaption Fund.[232]

9. NATURAL RESOURCES

9.1. MINERALS

Various pieces of legislation regulate the use and management of natural resources in the Cook Islands. For example, the Seabed Minerals Act 2019 governs the management of seabed minerals.[233] The Act aims to establish an effective and responsible regulatory scheme for the management of seabed minerals. The purposes refer to upholding international principles, providing a stable regulatory framework and promoting transparent decision-making.[234] Importantly, the statute also aims to 'maximise the benefits of seabed mineral activities for present and future generations of Cook Islanders'.[235] Under s 5, the Crown is vested with all rights to the seabed and mineral resources to be managed. The Cook Islands Seabed Minerals Authority provides a register of titles. In addition, a Cook Islands Seabed Minerals Advisory Committee is established.[236] Part 4 of the statute regulates the issuing of permits and licences for

---

230 Government of the Cook Islands *Cook Islands Second National Communication under the United Nations Framework Convention on Climate Change* (Government of Cook Islands, 2011), 89; Kirsten Hastrup and Martin Skrydstrup (eds) *The Social Life of Climate Change Models: Anticipating Nature* (Routledge, 2012) 58–59.

231 Stephen Eliot Smith 'Uncharted Waters: Has the Cook Islands become Eligible for Membership in the United Nations' (2010) 8(2) New Zealand Journal of Public and International Law 169.

232 United Nations Development Programme 'Strengthening the Resilience of the Cook Islands to Climate Change' *Climate Change Adaption* (2020) <https://www.adaptation-undp.org/projects/af-strengthening-resilience-cook-islands-climate-change>; UN Environment 'With International Support, the Cook Islands Braces for Climate Change' *UN Environment Programme* (story, 7 May 2018) <https://www.unenvironment.org/news-and-stories/story/international-support-cook-islands-braces-climate-change>.

233 Seabed Minerals Act 2019, s 7.

234 Seabed Minerals Act 2019, s 3(1)(a)–(c).

235 Seabed Minerals Act 2019, s 3(1)(d).

236 Seabed Minerals Act 2019, s 35.

seabed mineral activities and Part 5 outlines various duties and responsibilities. Part 6 deals with financial arrangements, including a royalty system,[237] and Part 7 concerns enforcement powers. Part 8 covers seabed mining in international seabed areas.

9.2. FISHERIES

In regard to fisheries, the Fisheries Protection Act 1976 aims to protect the fishing resources of the Cook Islands by restricting foreign fishing vessels from fishing in the territorial waters of the Cook Islands. The Marine Resources Act 2005 covers the conservation of marine resources. Under the Act, the Minister may enter into access agreements and fisheries management agreements,[238] and the Secretary is to establish and administer a system for the administration of fishing rights.[239] The Cook Islands Pearl Authority Act 1993 governs the pearl industry.

10. CRIMINAL LAW

The source of criminal law in the Cook Islands is legislation. Article 64 of the Constitution forms the basis for the criminal justice system. Article 47 of the Constitution establishes a criminal division of the High Court. A jury may be present for certain criminal cases.[240]

Legislation is the primary source of criminal law in the Cook Islands. The Crimes Act 1969 is at the core of the criminal law of the Cook Islands.[241] Pursuant to s 4, the application of the Act is to all acts done or omitted in the Cook Islands and offenders who may be tried in the Cook Islands.[242] The Act lists the various criminal offences and penalties in the Cook Islands, for example a maximum penalty of life imprisonment for the offences of murder or manslaughter,[243] one year for common assault[244] and 10 years for robbery and burglary.[245] The Act does not recognise a distinction between felonies and misdemeanours. The Crimes Amendment Act 2007 abolished the death penalty.

237 Seabed Minerals Act 2019, Part 6; Seabed Minerals (Royalties) Regulations 2013.
238 Marine Resources Act 2005, s 9(1).
239 Section 12(1).
240 Judicature Act 1980–81, ss 13–17.
241 Other important Acts are the Criminal Justice Act 1967 and the Criminal Procedure Act 1980–81.
242 Crimes Act 1969, s 4.
243 Sections 192 and 197.
244 Section 216.
245 Sections 256 and 263.

A notable aspect of the legislation is that sexual offences are framed in gendered language.[246] For example, rape can be committed against females exclusively.[247] Additionally, sentencing and punishment are subject to gender differentiation. To illustrate, the severity of the penalty for the offence of sodomy depends on the gender of the victim. If an act of sodomy is committed on a male under the age of 15 years and the offender is over 21 years, there is a maximum penalty of 14 years.[248] The maximum penalty is reduced to seven years where the act is committed on a male victim outside of those conditions.[249] In contrast, a maximum penalty of 14 years applies when there is a female victim, irrespective of age considerations.[250]

Offences include abortion[251] and prostitution.[252] The Committee on the Elimination of Discrimination against Women in relation to the Cook Islands expressed its concern at the existence of these particular criminal offences.[253] The Committee recommended that the legislature of the Cook Islands should legalise abortion, in certain circumstances at least, and should decriminalise prostitution.[254] This international advice expressed the view that such reforms would ensure compliance with the Convention on the Elimination of Discrimination against Women, which the Cook Islands ratified in 2006.

Additional criminal offences are established in other statutes. Offences are established in the Transport Act 1966, Narcotics and Misuse of Drugs Act 2004 and the Cook Islands Arms Ordinance 1954. Various offences relating to marriage are also contained in Part VII of the Marriage Act 1973.

In regard to the common law, s 8 of the Crimes Act 1969 states that no person can be proceeded against for any criminal offence at common law. The Act however makes clear that common law excuses and justifications remain relevant and applicable.[255]

In terms of criminal capacity, persons in the Cook Islands aged 16 and 17 years old are treated as adults and do not have child procedural protections.[256] Specifically, the Prevention of Juvenile Crime Act 1968 defines a child as a person

---

246 Crimes Act 1969, ss 140–155.

247 Crimes Act 1969, s 141(1)(a).

248 Crimes Act 1969, s 155(1)(b).

249 Crimes Act 1969, s 155(1)(c).

250 Crimes Act 1969, s 155(1)(a).

251 Crimes Act 1969, ss 202–207.

252 Crimes Act 1969, ss 161–163.

253 Committee on the Elimination of Discrimination against Women 'Convention on the Elimination of All Forms of Discrimination against Women', CEDAW/C/COK/CO/2-3, 25 July 2018, at 6 and 10.

254 Committee on the Elimination of Discrimination against Women 'Convention on the Elimination of All Forms of Discrimination against Women', CEDAW/C/COK/CO/2-3, 25 July 2018, at 6 and 10.

255 Crimes Act 1969, s 23.

256 Prevention of Juvenile Crime Act 1968, ss 2, 12–13 and 21–37.

under the age of 16 years.[257] Section 21 provides that all judicial proceedings of offences committed by children are to be heard and determined in the Children's Court.[258] In addition to the limiting age requirement, all proceedings involving charges of murder or manslaughter are conducted in line with criminal justice procedures applying to adults.[259] Children under 10 cannot be criminally responsible, and children aged between 10 and 14 can be convicted only if they had knowledge of the wrongfulness or unlawfulness of the act or omission.[260] Furthermore, according to a situation analysis conducted by the United Nations, '[c]hild sexual offences are framed in outdated language and do not provide equal protection to boys and girls in the Cook Islands'.[261]

11. INTERNATIONAL LAW AND TREATIES

The Cook Islands is a self-governing state in free association with New Zealand. The Cook Islands is not a member state of the United Nations.[262]

Although the Cook Islands is not an independent state, the Cook Islands has entered into various bilateral, regional and international treaties and organisations. A notable early illustration is the Cook Islands' involvement in and signing of the South Pacific Nuclear Free Zone Treaty, the Treaty of Rarotonga, in 1985. The Cook Islands 'interacts with the international community as a sovereign and independent state'.[263] Due to constitutional amendments and the application of constitutional conventions, it is clear that 'the Cook Islands should be treated as having the attributes of an independent and sovereign State at international law'.[264]

The Cook Islands has signed in excess of 100 multilateral conventions.[265] Support has been given to diverse conventions such as the United Nations Convention on the Law of the Sea, the Framework Convention on Climate Change and Kyoto Protocol, the Pacific Island Countries Trade Agreement, the Convention on the Elimination of Discrimination against Women, the Chemical Weapons Convention, the Convention on the Rights of the Child, the Geneva

---

257 Prevention of Juvenile Crime Act 1968, s 2.

258 Prevention of Juvenile Crime Act 1968, s 21(1).

259 Prevention of Juvenile Crime Act 1968, s 21(2).

260 Crimes Act 1969, ss 24–25.

261 United Nations Children's Fund *Situation Analysis of Children in the Cook Islands* (UNICEF, 2017) 81.

262 The Cook Islands are represented by New Zealand at the United Nations.

263 Joint Centenary Declaration of the Principles of the Relationship between New Zealand and the Cook Islands (Rarotonga, 11 June 2001), cl 4(1).

264 Stephen Eliot Smith 'Uncharted Waters: Has the Cook Islands become Eligible for Membership in the United Nations' (2010) 8(2) New Zealand Journal of Public and International Law 169.

265 Stephen Eliot Smith 'Uncharted Waters: Has the Cook Islands become Eligible for Membership in the United Nations' (2010) 8(2) New Zealand Journal of Public and International Law 169.

Conventions, the Convention on the Rights of Persons with Disabilities, the Rome Statute of the International Criminal Court, and the Terrorism Financing Convention.[266]

The Cook Islands has not ratified the International Covenants on Civil and Political Rights or on Economic, Social and Cultural Rights, the Convention on the Elimination of All Forms of Racial Discrimination, or the Convention against Torture and Other Cruel Inhuman or Degrading Treatment or Punishment.

12. CIVIL SOCIETY ORGANISATIONS

12.1. CHURCHES

The Cook Islands Christian Church is a dominant feature of civil society in the Cook Islands. The London Missionary Society originally founded the Cook Islands Christian Church. In 1821, English missionaries arrived in the Cook Islands and the Missionary Society commenced evangelisation in Aitutaki. By 1852, the Church operated on all of the islands.[267]

The Cook Islands Christian Church Incorporation Act 1968–69 incorporated the Cook Islands Christian Church. Approximately half of the population belongs to the Cook Islands Christian Church. Seventeen per cent identify as Roman Catholic and 13 per cent belong to other Protestant Churches.

12.2. OTHER ORGANISATIONS

The Cook Islands Civil Society Organisations Inc (CICSO) consists of 25 members, such as women's, youth and church organisations. There is also the Cook Islands Workers Association (CIWA). Sporting organisations and cultural celebrations are further key features of civil society. Under the Incorporated Societies Act 1994, any society consisting of at least 15 persons associated for lawful purpose, but not for pecuniary gain, may become incorporated as a society upon application to the Registrar.[268]

---

266 Stephen Eliot Smith 'Uncharted Waters: Has the Cook Islands become Eligible for Membership in the United Nations' (2010) 8(2) New Zealand Journal of Public and International Law 169; Rangiau Fariu, Valentino Wichman, Michelle Funk, Zoe Mulliez and Natalie Drew *WHO Profile on Mental Health in Development (WHO proMIND): Cook Islands* (World Health Organization, 2014).

267 Gary Bouma, Rodney Ling and Douglas Pratt *Religious Diversity in Southeast Asia and the Pacific* (Springer, 2010).

268 Incorporated Societies Act 1994, s 3.

13. PARTICULARITIES OF THE SYSTEM

Tourism is a major industry in the Cook Islands. Annually, approximately two-thirds of the GDP of the Cook Islands comes from tourism. In 2017, in excess of 150,000 people visited the Cook Islands[269] and over 168,000 people in 2018. Sixty-one per cent of the 2018 tourist numbers were from New Zealand and 13 per cent were from Australia. There is concern about the impact of climate change on the tourism industry.[270] Sea level increases accelerated by climate change pose a threat to the physical survival of the various islands of the Cook Islands.[271]

Offshore financing is also a central industry of the country. Other important contributors to the Cook Islands' economy are agricultural exports of fruit, particularly tropical and citrus varieties, and marine exports such as pearl and pearl shell. Due to significant reliance on imports, the Cook Islands suffers an unfavourable trade balance. As a result, the Cook Islands receives foreign aid and is dependent on these financial contributions to sustain its economy. The country that supplies the Cook Islands with the majority of its aid is New Zealand.

BIBLIOGRAPHY

Adzoxornu, Isaacus and the Editorial Committee 'The Cook Islands' in Michael A Ntumy (ed) *South Pacific Islands Legal Systems* (University of Hawaii Press, 1993).

Angelo, Tony and Elisabeth Perham 'Report of the Foreign Affairs, Defence and Trade Committee on New Zealand's Relationships with South Pacific Countries' (2010) 8 New Zealand Yearbook of International Law 193.

Corrin, Jennifer and Don Paterson (eds) *Introduction to South Pacific Law* (4th ed, Intersentia, 2017).

Department of Justice *Company Act: Detailed Section by Section Analysis* (2019) <https://registry.justice.gov.ck/documentation/ck/Company_Act_Detailed_Section%20by%20Section_Analysis_Dec10_2019.pdf>.

Frame, Alex 'Cook Islands Appeals in the Privy Council' [2013] New Zealand Law Review 132.

269 Radio New Zealand 'Cook Islands Visitors Up But Concern Over Sustainability' (6 December 2017) <https://www.radionz.co.nz/international/pacific-news/345519/cook-islands-visitors-up-but-concern-over-sustainability>.

270 Kirsten Hastrup and Martin Skrydstrup (eds) *The Social Life of Climate Change Models: Anticipating Nature* (Routledge, 2012).

271 Cook Islands Meteorological Service and Pacific Climate Change Science Program *Current and Future Climate of the Cook Islands* (Report, 2013).

Gilson, Richard *The Cook Islands 1820–1950* (Victoria University Press in association with the Institute of Pacific Studies of the University of the South Pacific, 1980).

Pacific Islands Legal Information Institute *Cook Islands Primary Materials* <http://www.paclii.org/countries/ck.html>.

Quentin-Baxter, Alison 'Pacific States and Territories: The Cook Islands' in *The Laws of New Zealand* (Butterworths, 2001).

Roper, Christopher *The Cook Islands Justices Bench Book* (2nd ed, High Court of the Cook Islands, 2012).

Secretariat of the Pacific Regional Environment Programme and EDO NSW *Cook Islands: Review of Natural Resource and Environment Related Legislation* (Report, January 2018).

FIJI

Unaisi NARAWA

1. CONTEXT

Fiji is an archipelago of more than 300 islands covering about 400,000 square kilometres.[1] The two major islands are Viti Levu and Vanua Levu. In recent centuries, Polynesian, especially Tongan, culture and politics influenced the eastern part of the group and the southeast of Viti Levu, where Suva, the capital, is located.[2]

Fiji became a British colony in 1874 following the signing of the Deed of Cession between the British Crown and Fijian Chiefs.[3] In reliance on the justice and generosity of Queen Victoria, the Fijian Chiefs agreed to cede the possession of and full sovereignty and dominion over the Fiji Islands to Queen Victoria.[4]

Although not immediately apparent, British colonial policies[5] that focused on the indigenous people may have been at the root of the subsequent ethnic conflict in the country. The British maintained the economic segregation of the races in Fiji by ensuring that the majority of Fijians were engaged in subsistence agriculture, combined with some production of food for urban and plantation consumption.[6] Another British policy was the preservation of those Fijian lands not already 'legally' alienated to white settlers. The Native Lands Ordinance[7] was enacted in 1880. Section 3(iii) of the Native Lands Ordinance declared 'all native land shall be inalienable from the native owners to any person not a native Fijian except through the Crown and the said lands shall be alienable to the Crown' only under specific conditions.[8] The prohibition of any further land alienation, although sound in principle, imposed a uniformity and inflexibility that bore little resemblance to pre-colonial Fijian practices.[9] The need to keep the indigenous Fijians apart from other ethnic groups in Fiji may have sowed discord and later served as a catalyst for the political upheavals experienced

---

1 Aubrey L Parke, Mathew Spriggs and Deryk Scarr *Degei's Descendants: Spirits, Place and People in Pre-Cession Fiji* (ANU Press, 2014) 2.

2 Stephen Sherlock *Constitutional and Political Change in Fiji* (Research Paper 7, 1997–98) <https://www.aph.gov.au/About_Parliament/Parliamentary_Departments/Parliamentary_Library/pubs/rp/RP9798/98RP07#MAJOR>.

3 At the head of this was Ratu Seru Epenisa Cakobau, a paramount chief from Bau.

4 Joeli Baledrokadroka 'The Fijian Understanding of the Deed of Cession Treaty of 1874' (LLM Dissertation, University of Auckland, 2003).

5 This is sometimes referred to as Arthur Gordon's Native Policy. See further Kenneth Lowell Gillion *A History of Indian Migration and Settlement in Fiji* (PhD Dissertation, Australia National University, March 1958) <https://openresearch-repository.anu.edu.au/bitstream/1885/16380/2/b12443918-Gillion.pdf>.

6 Sherlock, above n 2.

7 Now iTaukei Lands Act 1905.

8 Native Lands Ordinance 1880.

9 Stephanie Lawson 'The Military Versus Democracy in Fiji: Problems for Contemporary Political Development' in Ronald James May and Virberto Selochan (eds) *The Military and Democracy in Asia and the Pacific* (ANU E-Press, 2004) <http://press-files.anu.edu.au/downloads/press/p33231/mobile/index.html>.

since 1987. In 1970 Fiji gained its independence and became a sovereign democratic state.[10] Following the military-led coup d'état in 1987, the country was declared a republic.[11]

The population is approximately 884,887, the majority of whom are indigenous Fijians and Fijians of Indian descent, with different ethnic groups including Chinese, European, Rotuman and other Pacific Islanders making up the minority.[12]

2. SOURCES OF LAW

2.1. CONSTITUTION

Since independence in 1970, Fiji has had four constitutions. These are the independence Constitution,[13] which lasted until a coup 19 years later when it was replaced by the 1990 Constitution. The 1997 Constitution came into force with the aim of strengthening the multiracial foundations of Fiji;[14] the legislature retained a strong communal element with 25 open seats, the rest elected by communities – 23 by the *iTaukei*, 19 by the Indo-Fijians, one by Rotumans and three general seats.[15]

The 1997 Constitution was challenged in both the 2000 and the 2006 coups.[16] The Constitution survived the 2000 coup as a result of the decision by the Court of Appeal in *Republic of the Fiji Islands v Prasad.*[17] In 2006, Voreqe Bainimarama dissolved Parliament, dismissed Prime Minister Laisenia Qarase and seized power.[18] In *Qarase v Bainimarama*[19] the Court of Appeal declared that in the circumstances it would be lawful for the President of Fiji, as a matter of necessity, to appoint a caretaker Prime Minister to advise that Parliament be dissolved and writs issued for an election.[20] Instead of adhering to the decision, President Josefa Iloilovatu abrogated the Constitution and appointed Voreqe Bainimarama as Prime Minister until the holding of elections in 2014.[21]

---

10 Constitution of Fiji 1970, art 1.
11 Declaration – Republic of Fiji Decree 1987 No 8.
12 Fiji Bureau of Statistics, *Census information* (5 January 2018) <https://www.statsfiji.gov.fj/>.
13 Constitution 1970.
14 Yash Ghai and Jill Cottrell 'A Tale of Three Constitutions: Ethnicity and Politics in Fiji' (October 2007) 5(4) IJCL 639 at 640.
15 Article 51 Constitution Amendment Act 1997 (Fiji).
16 Ghai and Cottrell, above n 14.
17 [2001] 2 FLR 59.
18 Anne Twomey 'The Fijian Coup Cases – The Constitution, Reserve Powers and the Doctrine of Necessity' (Research Paper, University of Sydney, 2009) <http://ssrn.com/abstract=1399803> 1.
19 *Qarase v Bainimarama* [2009] FJCA 9.
20 Twomey, above n 18.
21 Twomey, above n 18.

In 2013, the Constitution of the Republic of Fiji[22] (the Constitution) was brought into force and stated to be the supreme law.[23] The Constitution contains a Bill of Rights and sets up the basic structures of government and other State services. The Constitution replaced the former bicameral Parliament with a unicameral Parliament made up of 50 members elected for a period of four years.

The Constitution makes no distinction based on ethnicity, and all citizens[24] are known as Fijians.[25] Chapter 10 continues in force the clause in Chapter XIV of the 1990 Constitution[26] which provides absolute immunity for any actions taken by Fiji military forces during the 1987 coup. Chapter 10 extends immunity to actions taken during the 2006 coup.[27] The immunity extends to protection from any criminal prosecution and to civil or other liability in any court, tribunal or commission, which resulted from any direct or indirect participation, appointment or involvement in the government from 5 December 2006 to the date of the first sitting of the first Parliament elected after the commencement of the Constitution. Such immunity does not extend to bribery, corruption, sexual assault, prostitution, abortion, theft, fraud, or destruction of property-related offences under the Crimes Act 2009, and certain other crimes.[28]

Constitutional amendments are to be executed in accordance with Chapter 11. Chapter 11 also explicitly prohibits any repeal of the immunity provisions in Chapter 10 and prevents amendments that infringe or diminish the effect of the transitional provisions in Part D of Chapter 12.[29] Section 51 of the Constitution gives Parliament the authority over treaties and conventions, stating that an international treaty or convention binds the State only after it has been approved by Parliament.

The Constitution changed the system of voting, which was previously based along ethnic lines. Section 53(1) provides that the election of Members of Parliament is by a multi-member open list system of proportional representation, under which each voter has one vote, with each vote being of equal value, in a single national electoral roll comprising all the registered voters.

---

22 Constitution 2013.

23 Constitution, Preamble and s 2.

24 As previously provided in s 51 of the Constitution (Amendment) Act 1997 for the electoral roll and the division of such into ethnicities.

25 Constitution 2013, s 5.

26 Constitution 2013, s 155.

27 This includes the office of the President, Prime Minister and Cabinet ministers, the Republic of Fiji military forces, the Fiji police force, Fiji corrections service, judiciary, public service and any other public office.

28 Crimes Act 2009, ss 133–146, 148–236, 288–351, 356–361, 364 –374 and 377–386.

29 Immunity clause.

2.2. LEGISLATION

During Fiji's colonial period, legislation was enacted by the Governor of Fiji through Ordinances.[30] Also, statutes of general application in force in England on 2 January 1875 (the 'cut-off date') were introduced into Fiji during the colonial period.[31] These laws were kept in force at independence to avoid a vacuum pending the creation of 'local' laws by the new legislature and development of a body of case law by local courts,[32] but only to the extent that they were not inconsistent with legislation enacted by the Parliament of Fiji or inappropriate to local circumstances.[33] Subsequent constitutions have carried forward these laws.[34]

Since the first coup d'état in 1987 and the subsequent political upheaval in 2000 and 2006, there have been periods where the country has been without a Parliament. During those times, laws were made by an interim government through Decrees and Promulgations.[35] The last consolidation of Fiji's laws in 2016 renamed these 'Acts', to correspond with laws enacted by the Parliament.[36]

2.3. COMMON LAW

The common law has effect as part of Fiji's laws, provided it is not inconsistent with the Constitution or legislation. Chapter 2 of the Constitution provides that in the determination of any matters according to common law, courts must respect constitutional rights and freedoms, and must interpret the Chapter contextually, having regard to the content and consequences of the law, including its impact on individuals.[37] Common law is developed by the courts through the doctrine of precedent, including decisions interpreting existing legislation and the Constitution.[38]

The common law of England is applicable only to the extent that it is not inconsistent with any law of Fiji.[39] In practice, Fijian courts have not been

---

30 Jennifer Corrin and Don Paterson *Introduction to South Pacific Law* (4th ed, Intersentia, 2017) at 21.

31 Supreme Court Act Cap 13, s 22.

32 Fiji Independence Order 1970 (UK), s 2(1). See further, Jennifer Corrin 'Discarding the Relics of the Past: Patriation of Laws in the South Pacific' (2008) 39 VUWLR <http://www.austlii.edu.au/nz/journals/VUWLawRw/2008/36.pdf>.

33 Supreme Court Act Cap 13, ss 22 and 24.

34 Constitution of Fiji 1990, s 8(1); Constitution Amendment Act 1997, s 195(2)(d); Constitution, s 173(1).

35 During the 1987, 2000 and 2006 military coups d'état.

36 A complete collection of Fiji's laws consolidated quarterly is available at <https://www.laws.gov.fj/Home/laws>.

37 Constitution 2013, s 7(4) and (5).

38 Pacific Judicial Education Programme *Fiji Magistrates Bench Book* (April 2004) [16].

39 Supreme Court Act Cap 13, s 22.

limited to English common law and have routinely found persuasive value in the decisions of courts of other Commonwealth countries, notably Australia and New Zealand.[40] The Fijian courts have, at times, established their own precedents, particularly when it comes to issues relevant to the Fijian context specifically.[41]

2.4. CUSTOMARY LAW

The recognition of customary law in Fiji has gone through many changes. Section 100 of the 1990 Constitution required Parliament to make provision for the application of laws, including customary law. However, no laws were created to put the provision into effect. Section 100 also provided that decisions of the *iTaukei* Lands Commission regarding customary ownership and use rights to Fijian land, or matters relating to Fijian custom, usage and tradition, were not reviewable in any court of law.

Section 186 of the Constitution (Amendment) Act 1997 had provided for the recognition of traditional Fijian processes. This section required Parliament to make provision for customary law and dispute resolution while having regard to the customs, traditions, usages, values and aspirations of the Fijian and Rotuman people. This mandate was never fulfilled. The 2013 Constitution does not include any provision recognising customary law in general, but it does include sections dealing with customary land ownership and fishing rights.[42] The sections protect customary owners, their land and also their interest in that land. These are explained in detail later in this chapter.

3. CONSTITUTIONAL LAW

3.1. PARLIAMENT

The legislative authority in Fiji lies with the Parliament.[43] Chapter 3 of the Constitution sets out the composition and legislative authority of a unicameral

---

40 See eg *Nair v Public Trustee of Fiji and the Attorney-General of Fiji*, unreported, High Court, Fiji, Lyons J, 8 March 1996, 24.

41 See *Narawa v NLTB* (Fiji Court of Appeal, 31 May 2002) and *Narawa v NLTB* [2004] FJSC 7 (21 May 2004), which finally dispatches from Fijian law the CANZUS perception of *iTaukei* title in Fijian law as a sui generis interest which is not a common law tenure protected in rem. See further, Kenneth Chambers 'Native Title and the Torrens System: A Comparative Law Analysis of Tenure Conversion in the Fiji Islands' (PhD Dissertation, University of the South Pacific, 2015).

42 Constitution 2013, ss 28, 29 and 30.

43 Constitution 2013, s 46.

Parliament elected for a period of four years. Members of Parliament are elected according to a one person, one vote system. All laws passed by Parliament require the assent of the President as the head of state.[44] The lack of a presidential assent does not render the law invalid. Rather, the law will be taken to have been assented to within seven days of being presented to the President for his assent.[45] Members of Parliament are covered by privilege, but subject to the Constitution and the Standing Orders of Parliament.[46]

3.2. EXECUTIVE

The executive consists of the Cabinet and the President of the Republic. The President, as the head of state, is commander-in-chief of Fiji's military forces. The President may act only on the advice of the Cabinet, a minister or of some other body or authority prescribed by the Constitution for a particular purpose as the body or authority on whose advice the President acts in that case.[47] The President holds office for three years, and is eligible for re-appointment for one further term of three years, but is not eligible for re-appointment after that.[48] Major General Jioji Konrote is the first non-*iTaukei* to hold the office of President.

The Cabinet consists of the Prime Minister, as head of the government, along with the government ministers. The Attorney-General is also part of the Cabinet as its chief legal advisor and must be a legal practitioner of standing.[49] The Constitution allows for a person who is not a Member of Parliament to be appointed by the Prime Minister to be the Attorney-General.[50] If an appointee is not a Member of Parliament, the person may sit in Parliament but is not entitled to vote.[51]

3.3. JUDICIARY

The judiciary is the third branch of the State. The courts are the Supreme Court, the Court of Appeal, the High Court, the Magistrates Court, and other courts or tribunals created by law.[52] The judiciary is independent of the other

44 Constitution 2013, s 48.
45 Constitution 2013, s 48(2) and (3).
46 Standing Orders, s 133.
47 Constitution 2013, ss 81 and 82.
48 Constitution 2013, s 85.
49 See Constitution 2013, s 96(2).
50 Constitution 2013, s 96(3).
51 The 1997 Constitution gave powers to the President to appoint the Attorney-General, but the appointment had to be made from within the Members of Parliament (the Senate and the House of Representatives).
52 Constitution 2013, ss 98–102.

branches of government and responsible for interpreting and applying the laws made by Parliament, creating and interpreting case law (common law) and solving disputes of fact and law between individuals and between the State and individuals.[53]

The judiciary is subject only to the Constitution and although its budget is sourced from the funds of the State, it has control of its own finances.[54] The Supreme Court is the final appellate court and has original jurisdiction to hear and determine constitutional questions referred under s 91(5).[55] Section 91(5) allows Cabinet to seek an opinion from the Supreme Court on any matter concerning the interpretation or application of the Constitution.

The Chief Justice, as head of the judiciary, is President of the Supreme Court. The Chief Justice is appointed by the President on the advice of the Prime Minister following consultation by the Prime Minister with the Attorney-General. Other judges and justices of appeal are appointed by the President on the recommendation of the Judicial Services Commission following consultation with the Attorney-General.[56]

Each court is regulated by its own Act: the Supreme Court Act 1998, the High Court Act 1875 and the Magistrates Court Act 1944. Each of these Acts further provides the power to make rules of procedure.[57] Criminal procedure is governed by the Criminal Procedure Act 2009. The Act makes comprehensive provision in relation to the powers and procedures to be applied in relation to the apprehension of offenders and the conduct of criminal trials. Civil procedure is governed by several laws.

There are specialist tribunals established to hear specific types of cases. An example is the Small Claims Tribunal, which was first promulgated by the President pursuant to the Small Claims Tribunal Act 1991, but not formally established until 1996. Its role is to 'provide prompt and inexpensive relief to claimants' and 'to attempt to bring the parties to a dispute to an agreed settlement'[58] in certain specified types of disputes involving monetary claims up to a specified maximum sum.[59] In accordance with s 16 of the Act, the Tribunal has jurisdiction to hear claims of up to FJ$5,000. However, there is one exception where, in certain circumstances, a Magistrates Court or a High Court

---

53 Constitution 2013, s 97.
54 Constitution 2013, s 97(6).
55 Constitution 2013, s 98.
56 Constitution 2013, s 106(1) and (2).
57 Supreme Court Rules 2016, High Court Rules 1988, High Court (Constitutional Redress) Rules 2015, High Court (Admiralty) Rules 1893, High Court (Notarial Acts Abroad) Rules 1951, Magistrates Courts Rules 1945, and Magistrates Courts (Justices of the Peace) Rules 1950.
58 Small Claims Tribunal Act 1991, s 15.
59 Ganesh Chand *The Small Claims Tribunal: An Effectiveness Study, A Consumer Council of Fiji Report 2009* (Consumer Council of Fiji, 2009) <http://www.consumersfiji.org/upload/Reports/SCT%20BOOKLET_Final.pdf> 9.

may transfer proceedings filed with them to the Small Claims Tribunal.[60] If any of these courts do so without the consent of the parties, the requirement that a claimant abandon any claim exceeding the limit is dispensed with.[61]

The Employment Relations Tribunal[62] has the general function of assisting employers, their representatives and workers, and representative trade unions in achieving and maintaining effective employment relations, in particular by adjudicating and determining any grievance or dispute between parties to employment contracts.[63] The Tribunal's jurisdiction extends to employees who are not citizens of Fiji.[64]

Other tribunals include the Agricultural Tribunal, established by s 16 of the Agricultural and Landlord Tenant Act 1966 as and when it is needed; the Land Transport Appeals Tribunal, which is set up to hear and determine appeals against the Land Transport Authority dealing with licensing and other matters provided for in the Land Transport Act;[65] and the Appeals Tribunal,[66] which hears and determines appeals from decisions of the *iTaukei* Lands Commission[67] and the *iTaukei* Fisheries Commission.[68]

3.4. OTHER INSTITUTIONS

The Constitution continued in existence with the Independent Legal Services Commission,[69] the Fiji Independent Commission Against Corruption,[70] the Office of the Solicitor-General,[71] the Office of the Director of Public Prosecutions,[72] the Legal Aid Commission,[73] and the Commission on the Prerogative of Mercy.[74]

The Constitution also established some new legal institutions. The Public Service Disciplinary Tribunal is established under s 120 of the Constitution and is the body that presides over disciplinary cases coming from the Public Service Commission. Section 121 of the Constitution establishes the Accountability and Transparency Commission. A Code of Conduct Bill has been tabled

60 Small Claims Tribunal Act 1991, s 23.
61 Small Claims Tribunal Act 1991, s 23(4).
62 Established under the Employment Relations Act 2007, s 202.
63 Employment Relations Act 2007, s 210.
64 See *Sanchez v Sheraton Fiji Resorts* [2019] FJET 3.
65 Land Transport Act 1998, s 40.
66 Established under s 7 of the *iTaukei* Lands Act 1905.
67 See s 7 of the *iTaukei* Lands Act 1905.
68 See s 17 of the Fisheries Act 1941.
69 Legal Practitioners Act 2009.
70 Fiji Independent Commission Against Corruption Promulgation 2007.
71 State Services Decree 2009.
72 State Services Decree 2009.
73 Legal Aid Act 1996.
74 State Services Decree 2009.

in Parliament; it sets out the authority, functions and responsibilities of the Commission but is yet to advance past its first reading in Parliament.

4. THE LEGAL PROFESSION

The legal profession in Fiji is governed by the Legal Practitioners Act 2009, which sets out the requirements for a person to be eligible for admission as a legal practitioner in the country. These include the completion of a course of study approved by the Board of Legal Education,[75] being in receipt of a certificate issued by the Board certifying the educational qualifications and unless exempted by the Chief Justice, and being resident in Fiji for at least three months prior to applying for admission to practice.[76] Persons may be admitted temporarily if they are appearing for a specific cause or matter.[77]

Practising certificates are issued by the Registrar of the High Court for a year and expire on the last day of February each year.[78] The Act makes provision for continuing legal education, and any person applying for a practising certificate must have participated in a programme approved by the Board and such involvement must be no less than 10 hours.[79]

The Fiji Law Society that was established under the Legal Practitioners Act 1997 is continued under the 2009 Act.[80] Membership of the Society consists of legal practitioners holding practising certificates under the Act who apply for membership, persons elected as honorary members of the Society and other persons that the Council of the Society admits to its membership.[81]

Free legal services are available to Fiji residents through the Legal Aid Commission established under the Legal Aid Act 1996 and given Constitutional recognition in s 118 of the 2013 Constitution. The Commission provides free legal aid services to those members of the public who cannot afford the services of a legal practitioner.[82] The Commission had previously only provided services for criminal matters, but this was extended to family law matters with the Commission employing a means and merits test. To improve citizens' access to justice, the Commission maintains a list of private legal practitioners (not employed by the Commission) who may appear on behalf of legally assisted persons.[83]

---

75 Legal Practitioners Act 2009, s 3.
76 Legal Practitioners Act 2009, s 35.
77 Legal Practitioners Act 2009, s 39.
78 Legal Practitioners Act 2009, s 48.
79 Legal Practitioners Act 2009, s 7.
80 Legal Practitioners Act 2009, s 12.
81 Legal Practitioners Act 2009, s 14.
82 Constitution 2013, s 118.
83 Legal Aid Act 1996, s 11.

5. LAW OF PERSONS

The Family Law Act was passed in 2003 and came into effect in 2005. One of the most significant features of the new law was the removal of a fault-based system of divorce. The replacement of the 14 grounds for divorce with a simple requirement of a one-year separation period made it procedurally simpler and less discriminatory, especially for women and children, who often got caught up in the process.[84]

The Act provides for counselling and reconciliation in situations where the court feels that, although dissolution of marriage proceedings have been instituted, there is a possibility of reconciliation between the parties. In such circumstances, if the judge or magistrate thinks it is desirable, he or she may nominate counselling.[85] The best interests of the child is an important factor in the law, which attempts to maintain this through procedures such as child counselling. This type of counselling is really for the parents to discuss issues pertaining to residence and contact between the parents and their child.[86] This approach is based on the idea that parents, rather than courts and lawyers, are the best persons to make decisions about their children.[87]

Marriages are dealt with under the Marriages Act 1968. An amendment made in 2009 outlawed the marriage of any person under the age of 18.[88] This was a significant change that aligned the law with Fiji's obligations under the Convention on the Rights of the Child. De facto relationships have also been given recognition through various laws. An amendment was made in 2012 to update the definitions in s 154 of the Family Law Act 2003 to include de facto relationships in property settlements.[89] Furthermore, de facto relationships are recognised by Fijian law under the Fiji National Provident Fund Regulations 2014, made under the Fiji National Provident Fund Act 2011, and for the purposes of property distribution upon intestacy under the Succession, Probate and Administration Act 1970 as amended by the Succession, Probate and Administration (Amendment) Act 2018.

The Adoption Act 2020 received presidential assent on 4 September 2020. As per s 1(2), the Act comes into force on a date to be appointed by the Minister in the *Gazette*.[90] The Act provides for local and intercountry adoption and other

---

84 Unaisi Narawa-Daurewa 'The Family Law Act of Fiji, 2003: A Brief Review of Some Provisions in the Act; Their Impact on the Family (With Emphasis on Women's Access to Justice)' (LLM Dissertation, University of the South Pacific, 2010).

85 Family Law Act 2003, s 9(2)(c).

86 Narawa-Daurewa, above n 84.

87 P Imrana Jalal, 'Children and the Family Law' (2003) <http://www.rrrt.org/page.asp?active_page_id=144> in Narawa-Daurewa, above n 84.

88 Marriage (Amendment) Act 2010, s 12.

89 Family Law (Amendment) Act 2012.

90 At the time of writing, there has been no date appointed for the commencement of the Act.

related purposes. The 2020 Act repeals the Adoption of Infants Act 1944 but saves any subsidiary laws and forms made under the repealed Act.[91]

The Act domesticates the Hague Convention on Protection of Children and Co-operation in Respect of Intercountry Adoption, which will allow intercountry adoption with countries that have ratified the Convention.[92]

Online safety and the safety of children have become major concerns, and in 2018 the Online Safety Act 2018 was enacted to establish the Online Safety Commission for the promotion of online safety, deterrence of harmful electronic communication and related purposes. Pursuant to s 17(d), school principals or head teachers may bring proceedings on behalf of a child, provided the child consents. This is a measure intended to allow for protection of a child's rights where parents or guardians are unable or unwilling to do so.

6. WILLS AND SUCCESSION LAW

A person who is over the age of 18 has the legal capacity to make a will in accordance with s 4 of the Wills Act 1972. The Act follows the usual common law requirements for the execution of a valid will, which includes the capacity to make such will as provided in s 4.[93] In addition, the will must be signed in the presence of two witnesses, who must sign the will in the presence of the testator and each other.[94] The court has powers under s 6A to declare a document to be a valid will even though it has not been executed in accordance with s 6, but in this case the burden is on the party seeking the declaration to prove that the document was intended to be a will.

A will is automatically revoked by the subsequent marriage of the testator unless it is expressly stated that the will is made in contemplation of marriage.[95] The Fiji National Provident Fund Act 2011 also made amendments to cater for circumstances where there was no will. This is complemented by the Succession, Probate and Administration (Amendment) Act 2018, which introduces recognition of de facto relationships for the purpose of property distribution upon intestacy.[96]

The Succession, Probate and Administration Act 1970 governs circumstances in which a person dies intestate. Application for probate to execute a will or for letters of administration to administer the property of a deceased intestate

91 Adoption Act 2020, s 60(1) and (2).

92 Anuleshni Neelta 'Adoption in Fiji' in Jennifer Corrin and Sue Farran (eds) *The Plural Practice of Adoption in Pacific Island States* (Springer, 2019) 15.

93 Wills Act 1972, s 6.

94 Wills Act 1972, s 6.

95 Wills Act 1972, s 13.

96 Succession, Probate and Administration (Amendment) Act 2018, s 6.

must be made to the High Court.[97] If a person dies testate or intestate and adequate provision is not made for their spouse, child or dependant, then in accordance with the Inheritance (Family Provision) Act 2004 that spouse, child or dependant may apply to the court for further maintenance to be paid out from the deceased's estate.[98] A child includes stepchildren, adopted children and a child *en ventre sa mère*.[99] The British and Colonial Probates Act 1893 continues in force and provides for the recognition by Fiji courts of any probate or letters of administration granted by a British court or 'in any part of Her Majesty's dominion'.[100]

7. LAW OF OBLIGATIONS

7.1. TORTS

The Occupiers Liability Act 1968 remains in force in its original form. The Act sets out a statutory standard governing tort liabilities of owners and occupiers of premises, requiring such care as is reasonable in the circumstances.[101] Also in force is the Compensation to Relatives Act 1920, with relatively minor amendments only.[102] The Act permits wrongful death actions to be instituted by the spouse, parent or child of a person killed.[103] In such circumstances, the court has a discretion to allocate any damages awarded among those relatives.[104]

The Accident Compensation Act 2017 establishes the Accident Compensation Commission Fiji and provides for compensation in respect of persons who suffer personal injury or death as a result of an accident in Fiji. An accident is defined in the Schedule to the Act (as amended by regulation in 2018) as an accident caused by a motor vehicle, an accident arising out of and in the course of employment (including incidents causing prescribed diseases) and an accident occurring on school premises. The Act sets up a no-fault compensation scheme in which a lump-sum payment is made for any personal injury or death as a result of an accident in Fiji, without the need to establish fault or negligence for the accident.[105] The acceptance of an offer of compensation from the Commission is a bar to civil proceedings in the High Court.[106]

---

97 Succession, Probate and Administration Act 1970, s 7.
98 Inheritance (Family Provision) Act 2004, s 3.
99 Inheritance (Family Provision) Act 2004, s 2.
100 Don Paterson and Stephen A Zorn 'Fiji' in Michael A Ntumy (ed) *South Pacific Islands Legal Systems* (University of Hawaii Press, 1993) 26.
101 Occupiers Liability Act 1968, s 4(1).
102 Amendments were made in 1935, 1956, 1967 and 1971.
103 Compensation to Relatives Act 1920, s 4.
104 Compensation to Relatives Act 1920, s 6.
105 Accident Compensation Act 2017, s 19.
106 Accident Compensation Act 2017, s 24.

Furthermore, payment of compensation is also a bar to proceedings to recover damages or claim any contribution from the person who had suffered the injury or death for which the compensation was paid.[107]

The Law Reform (Contributory Negligence and Tortfeasors) Act amends the law relating to contributory negligence. It eliminates the common law defence of contributory negligence and replaces it with a comparative negligence standard. Relevantly, the court is authorised to reduce a plaintiff's damages to such extent as the court thinks just and equitable having regard to the claimant's share in responsibility.[108]

The State Proceedings Act 1951 waived the defence of sovereign immunity in torts committed by government employees and agents, duties owed to government employees, and breach of common law duties to the owner or occupier of property.[109] An amendment in 2012 created an immunity provision for defamatory statements made by the Prime Minister, any minister or the State, in their personal or official capacity.[110] However, this was repealed by the State Proceedings (Amendment) Act 2014.

The Defamation Act 1971 remains in force. Apart from consequential amendments made in 2016 for the purpose of law revision, the Act has not been amended since its enactment. The Act provides that 'fair and accurate' newspaper reports and broadcasts of court and similar proceedings, public meetings, and information released by the government and certain charitable and commercial organisations are privileged.[111] The now repealed State Proceedings (Amendment) Act 2012 had provided an exception for media organisations publishing statements made by persons named in that Act.

7.2. CONTRACT LAW

The legal principles regulating the making and the effect of contracts in Fiji have generally followed other Pacific island states that are guided by principles of common law and equity.[112] There have been some laws enacted by the Parliament to make provision for particular aspects of contracts.[113] The Sale of Goods Act 1979 deals with contracts of sale of goods and provides a definition of these.[114]

---

107 Accident Compensation Act 2017, s 29A as inserted by the Workmen's Compensation (Repeal) Act 2008, s 3.

108 Law Reform (Contributory Negligence and Tortfeasors) Act 1946, s 3.

109 State Proceedings Act 1951, s 3.

110 State Proceedings (Amendment) Act 2012.

111 Defamation Act 1971, ss 13 and 14.

112 Jennifer Corrin *Contract Law in the South Pacific* (2nd ed, Intersentia, 2020) 1.

113 As discussed in Paterson and Zorn, above n 100, these include the Property Law Act (Cap 130) and the Indemnity, Guarantee and Bailment Act (Cap 232) (repealed).

114 Sale of Goods Act 1979, s 3(1).

The Electronic Transactions Act 2008 recognises the validity of and promotes the development of electronic communications in commercial and non-commercial dealings with government entities, and it also removes the uncertainty that often surrounds the use of electronic methods in legal documents.[115] The Act also facilitates and gives effect to the domestic implementation of the United Nations Convention on the Use of Electronic Communications in International Contracts. An amendment in 2017 created general provisions governing electronic communications in international contracts.[116]

8. PROPERTY LAW

8.1. LAND LAW

Before colonisation, all land in Fiji was held according to custom. Today, land in Fiji is divided into: freehold, State, and *iTaukei* (customary).[117] 89.75 per cent of the land is customary land, approximately six per cent is freehold and approximately four per cent is State land.[118]

Until the creation of the *iTaukei* Lands Commission in 1880, indigenous 'ownership' of land was unclassified. The *iTaukei* Lands Commission introduced the *Vola Ni Kawa Bula*[119] and created a system that assigned exclusive possession of contiguous blocks of land to social groupings or 'landowning units'.[120] It was at this point that the *mataqali* or landowning unit was essentially formalised outside of the indigenous Fijian community.

'Ownership' of customary land in Fiji does not have the same meaning as under common law. The perspective of fee simple absolute in possession or freehold ownership is not the essence of indigenous land ownership, which is philosophically vested in communalism.[121] In theory, indigenous landowners are at liberty to use a portion of their landowning unit's land. However, there are protocols and practices that must be observed. There is little difficulty for

115 Electronic Transactions Act 2008, s 2.

116 Electronic Transactions Act 2008, Part 3A, ss 16A–16C.

117 Krishn Shah 'Facilitating Property Developments in the Fiji Islands: The Legal Mechanisms, A Review of ALTA and NLTA: Reforms' (Paper presented at the Pacific Rim Real Estate Society Conference, Thailand, January 2004).

118 *iTaukei* Land Trust Board 'Land Ownership in Fiji' (17 April 2020) *iTaukei* Land Trust Board website <https://www.tltb.com.fj/getattachment/Media/Brochures/Land-Ownership-in-Fiji-Booklet-(1).pdf.aspx?lang=en-US>.

119 This is an official record or Register of indigenous Fijian landowning units.

120 Mathew Dodd 'Reform of Leasing Regimes for Customary Land in Fiji' (LLB (Hons) Dissertation, University of Otago, 2012).

121 Spike Boydell and Krishn Shah 'An Inquiry into the Nature of Land Ownership in Fiji' (Paper presented at the International Association for the Study of Common Property Meeting, Brisbane, Australia, September 2003).

landowners living in the village or on the land, and who participate in the unit's social obligations. In contrast, those who are 'absentee landowners'[122] often have to prove their entitlement before being given permission to use the land.[123]

The *iTaukei* Lands Act 1905 recognises that all indigenous land is to be held by the *iTaukei* according to their customs as evidenced by their usage and tradition.[124] The Act provides that in the event of any dispute arising regarding the tenure of land amongst the *iTaukei*, all courts of law must determine the matter according to such regulations or *iTaukei* custom and usage. Despite ownership being vested in the indigenous landowners, indigenous land cannot be permanently alienated in Fiji except to the State, but subject to conditions prescribed in ss 27 and 28 of the Constitution.

The *iTaukei* Land Trust Act 1940 vests all *iTaukei* land in the *iTaukei* Land Trust Board (iTLTB). Pursuant to s 8 of the Act, the iTLTB is lawfully authorised to grant leases of portions of *iTaukei* land which are not included in the *iTaukei* reserves.[125] Landowners must also be in agreement when the Board plans to lease any land. This means that, on the one hand, the plans of the landowners are dependent on the acceptance by the iTLTB and the statutory planning authorities. On the other hand, the iTLTB's own plans are dependent on the acceptance by the landowners.[126]

Section 20 of the *iTaukei* Lands Act 1905 allows a minister to cancel the rights of a custom owner after a certain period of absence, but this first requires a request from members of the landowning unit.[127] In practice, such a request is unlikely to be made, due to existing social relations within the landowning unit.[128] The ownership of Rotuman and Banaban lands remains with the customary owners and the land may not be permanently alienated.[129]

Freehold titles, leases of State land and indigenous land, and mining leases must be registered in accordance with the Land Transfer Act 1971.[130] The Act adopts the Torrens title approach as used in Australia, providing that the certificate of registration will generally be conclusive as to all interests and charges on the land.[131] The sale of land is regulated by the Land Sales Act 1974. This regulates speculative and other dealings in land, including any taxation of

---

122 *iTaukei* Lands Act 1905, s 20.

123 Timoci Waqaisavou 'Tourism in Fiji: Native Landowner Attitude and Involvement' (Paper presented at the Pacific Rim Real Estate Society Conference, Adelaide, Australia, January 2001).

124 *iTaukei* Lands Act 1905, s 3.

125 *iTaukei* Land Trust Act 1940, s 4. See also the regulations made under the Act.

126 Waqaisavou, above n 123.

127 *iTaukei* Lands Act 1905, s 20.

128 Donald Paterson 'Some Thoughts About Customary Law' (2009) 13(1) JSPL <http://www.paclii.org/journals/fJSPL/vol05/7.shtml#fnB26>.

129 Constitution 2013, s 28.

130 Section 5 of the Land Transfer Act 1971 provides a list of all lands subject to the Act and therefore subject to the registration requirements.

131 Paterson and Zorn, above n 100, at 56.

profits derived from it. Amendments to the Act in 2014[132] and 2016[133] require non-residents who purchase vacant land in Fiji to construct a house on it within two years of the purchase.[134] Buildings constructed on such lands must be valued at FJ$250,000 or more,[135] and if owners fail to comply with the requirements in s 7A(6) regarding construction within two years, they face a fine of 10 per cent of the value of the land for every six months until the construction is completed.[136]

State or freehold land for residential purpose that is situated within the boundary of any town or city cannot be sold, transferred or leased to a non-resident.[137] Those who already own property within the boundaries are therefore restricted from selling it to a foreigner.

8.2. INTELLECTUAL PROPERTY LAW

Intellectual property in Fiji is governed by the Copyright Act 1999, the Trade-Marks Act 1933, the Merchandise Marks Act 1933 and the Patents Act 1879. The Copyright Act protects the economic interests of the authors of intellectual property and creative efforts by giving them the right to exploit their works and to control any unauthorised use.[138] Exceptions are made for copying of work that is not deliberate and for the purposes of broadcast or cable programmes.[139]

The Patents Act 1879 provides for patents to be granted to the inventors of any new manufacture or process of manufacture and any new methods of application or improvements of known processes.[140] Section 3A of the Act provides an exception where it is not an infringement of patents in pharmaceuticals for any person to make, construct use or sell a patented product or substance solely for uses reasonably related to the development and submission of information required under any law of Fiji or of another country.[141] There is provision also for patents granted in the United Kingdom to be registered in Fiji if done within three years of the issue of the patent.[142]

A similar provision regarding the registration of patents from the United Kingdom in Fiji under the Patents Act 1879 exists in the Trade-Marks Act 1933. The 1933 Act provides for applications for registered trade marks to be made

132 Land Sales (Amendment) Act 2014.
133 Land Sales (Budget Amendment) 2016.
134 Land Sales (Budget Amendment) 2016, s 7A(6)(b).
135 Land Sales (Budget Amendment) 2016, s 7A(9).
136 Land Sales (Budget Amendment) 2016, s 7A(7).
137 Land Sales (Budget Amendment) 2016, s 7A(1).
138 Copyright Act 1999.
139 Copyright Act 1999, s 40.
140 Patents Act 1879, s 4.
141 Patents Act 1879, s 3A.
142 Patents Act 1879, s 23.

to the Solicitor-General[143] who then advertises the application[144] and if no one opposes the application then it is registered for 14 years[145] and renewable upon the expiration of those 14 years. Furthermore, there is the Merchandise Marks Act 1933, which makes it an offence for a person to forge a trade mark; falsely apply to goods a trade mark or a similar mark calculated to deceive; make, have possession of, or dispose of any die or machine for the purpose of forging a trade mark; mark any false description of the quantity, weight, country of origin, mode of manufacture, composition, or ingredients of goods; or falsely state that the goods are the subject of an existing patent, privilege or copyright.[146]

9. COMMERCIAL LAW

The Companies Act 2015 regulates private and public companies carrying on business in Fiji.[147] Division 2 of the Act sets out the requirements for the registration of a company and Division 3 deals with company names. Names are available to a company unless identical to the name of another company.[148] A name may also be reserved as a company or business name, if it is not acceptable or in the opinion of the Registrar the name is undesirable.[149] The Companies (Budget Amendment) Act 2019 required all companies previously registered to be reregistered.[150] The Companies Act 2015 also deals with issues of insolvency.[151] Section 513 provides circumstances in which companies may be wound up by the courts, insolvency being one factor. Section 514 defines solvency as being a state where a company or foreign company is able to pay all its debts as and when they are due. Of course, the opposite of this would be insolvency, which is an inability to pay debt.[152]

The Partnership Act 1910 remains in force in its original form. The Act provides that a partnership exists if persons are carrying on a business in common with a view to profit, unless they are registered as a company or incorporated in some other way.[153] Cooperatives are governed by the Cooperatives Act 1996, which provides for the registration and regulation of cooperatives.

---

143 Trade-Marks Act 1933, s 11.
144 Trade-Marks Act 1933, s 12.
145 Trade-Marks Act 1933, s 27.
146 Merchandise Marks Act 1933, s 3(1) as discussed in Paterson and Zorn, above n 100.
147 Companies Act 2015, s 15. The Companies Act repealed the Companies Act 1983, the Capital Markets Act 2009, the Unit Trusts Act 1978 and the Registration of Business Names Act 1923.
148 Companies Act 2015, s 25.
149 Companies Act 2015, s 25.
150 Companies (Budget Amendment) Act 2019, s 11.
151 Companies Act 2015, ss 513–515.
152 Section 515 of the Companies Act 2015 defines inability to pay debt.
153 Partnership Act 1910, s 2.

Fiji has a Bankruptcy Act that lists acts of bankruptcy as including, but not limited to, filing a declaration in court of an inability to pay a debt, leaving the country or one's place of residence in order to avoid creditors or fraudulently transferring property to another person.[154]

No company is permitted to carry on any banking business[155] without a licence.[156] The licensing authority that receives and determines all applications for a banking licence is the Reserve Bank of Fiji. The Act explicitly states that non-resident controlled financial institutions must endeavour to place Fijian citizens in management positions and present to the Reserve Bank a programme of training in order to place Fijian citizens in management positions in the institution's Fiji operations.[157] There are also insolvency provisions under the Banking Act 1995, giving the Reserve Bank certain powers to deal with the insolvency application.[158]

In 2017, Parliament enacted the Personal Property Securities Act 2017, which covers lenders, borrowers, people who lease any movable property and any person who supplies goods on credit. The Act was the Fijian government's initiative to reform laws to facilitate the financing of movable or personal property in order to provide access to credit for micro, small and medium-sized enterprises and individuals.[159] The Act regulates the lending of money secured by personal property, mandates the registration of all interests in personal property and also makes consequential amendments to 18 other laws.[160] It also establishes a searchable registration system, which is very convenient and efficient.[161]

International arbitration is covered under the International Arbitration Act 2017, which is based on the law model adopted by the United Nations Commission on International Trade Law on International Commercial Arbitration.[162] Parties seeking arbitration must have an arbitration agreement clause in their contract or in a separate document[163] and initiate arbitration by activating that clause in the contract.

---

154 Bankruptcy Act 1944, s 3.

155 As defined under s 2 of the Banking Act 1995.

156 Banking Act 1995, ss 3 and 8.

157 Banking Act 1995, s 20.

158 Banking Act 1995, s 30.

159 Standing Committee on Justice, Law and Human Rights 'Report on the Personal Property Securities Bill 2017' (Parliamentary Paper No 110 of 2017).

160 Personal Property Securities Act 2017. Section 114 refers to the Schedule of the Act, which contains a list of all the laws amended by this Act.

161 Personal Property Securities Act 2017, s 69.

162 International Arbitration Act 2017, long title.

163 International Arbitration Act 2017, s 11(1).

10. REVENUE LAW

An income tax and a social responsibility tax is imposed on all residents and non-residents of Fiji under the Income Tax Act 2015, which came into force on 1 January 2016. The 2015 Act repealed the Income Tax Act (Cap 201), the Capital Gains Decree 2011 and the Fringe Benefits Tax Decree 2012 and made consequential amendments to the Tax Administration Act 2009. The 'pay-as-you-earn' (PAYE) tax system in the Act means that tax is calculated on the gross income earned reduced by the amount of deductions allowed[164] per annum.[165] Income tax is chargeable only on those earning over FJ$30,000 per annum.[166] In August 2017, an environment and climate adaptation levy was included as a tax on prescribed income,[167] which forms a part of the social responsibility tax under the Income Tax Act 2015.

In addition to income tax, there is a capital gains tax[168] payable on the sale of a capital asset[169] and calculated on the consideration given deducted by the actual cost of the asset at the time of the sale. Exceptions on assets not subject to the capital gains tax are set out in s 67 of the Act. The Act also includes a fringe benefits tax that was first levied in 2012 and consolidated under the Income Tax Act 2015. Fringe benefits as defined under the Act are those benefits provided to an employee by an employer and include, but are not limited to, water, meals or accommodation.[170]

Under the Value Added Tax Act 1991, a tax of nine per cent is levied on goods and services sold in Fiji. This is an indirect tax that consumers pay only when they spend. Persons who carry on taxable activities must be registered in accordance with the Act.[171] Taxable activities are defined in s 4 of the Act. The supply of remote services[172] is not subject to VAT. The Value Added Tax Act 1991 has refund clauses that apply to those constructing premises for diplomatic missions, tourists purchasing specific types of goods and for film production companies.[173]

164 Allowable deductions are provided for in s 21 of the Act.
165 Income Tax Act 2015, s 13.
166 Income Tax (Rates of Tax and Levies) Regulations 2016 (Fiji), reg 3 (Schedule).
167 Part 4 of the Environment and Climate Adaptation Levy Act 2015.
168 First introduced in 2011 pursuant to the Capital Gains Decree but now consolidated in the Income Tax Act 2015, s 65.
169 As defined in s 2 of the Income Tax Act 2015 (Fiji), it includes real property, a ship, boat, yacht, membership interest in a company, security or financial asset, intangible asset, airplane, helicopter, etc., but does not include an asset that is trading stock, a depreciable asset or a business intangible.
170 Income Tax Act 2015, s 72.
171 Value Added Tax Act 1991, s 22.
172 For example, in online shopping where there is no physical contact at all between the buyer and the seller.
173 Value Added Tax Act 1991, ss 70A, 70B and 70C.

11. ENVIRONMENTAL AND NATURAL RESOURCES LAW

Environmental law in Fiji takes the form of legislation specifically covering the environment, as well as provisions within general laws that make reference to the protection or conservation of the environment or to various environmental offences. Certain pieces of legislation are confined to the marine environment or alternatively the land. The purpose of the Environment Management Act 2005 is to apply the principles of sustainable use and development of natural resources, and to identify matters of national importance for Fiji, as set out in s 3 of the Act.[174] Environment impact assessments (EIAs) are required under the Act.[175]

The Act requires that any activity or undertaking that the approving authority determines will cause a significant environmental or resource management impact is subject to an EIA.[176] These activities include, but are not limited to, mining, commercial logging and any other proposal that may harm or destroy designated or proposed protected areas.[177] Section 50 of the Act allows persons who have suffered loss as a result of any pollution incident to institute a civil claim for damages. This may include a claim for economic loss, loss of earnings, loss to or of any natural environment or resource, and any costs incurred in any inspection, audit or investigation to determine the pollution incident.[178]

The Environment and Climate Adaptation Levy Act 2015 imposes an environment and climate adaptation levy (ECAL) on prescribed services, items and income. This tax is payable by the person who receives the goods and services.[179] An amendment was made to the Act in 2017 imposing a levy of 10 cents on single-use plastic bags.[180] Subsequent amendments were passed in 2018[181] and 2019. The 2019 amendment, which took effect on 1 January 2020, banned all single-use plastic bags that are less than 50 microns thick and increased the ECAL to 50 cents on the remaining thicker bags.[182]

Efforts to respond to the impending threat of climate change have resulted in other laws. An example of this is the Climate Action Trust Fund Act 2017. This Act was originally the COP23 Presidency Trust Fund Act 2017, but was renamed and repurposed as a trust fund for climate action generally in 2019.[183] Also significant is the Climate Relocation of Communities Trust Fund Act 2019

174 Environment Management Act 2005, s 3(2)(a) and (b).
175 Environment Management Act 2005, Part 4.
176 Environment Management Act 2005, s 27(4).
177 Environment Management Act 2005, Sch 2.
178 Environment Management Act 2005, s 50(1).
179 Environmental Levy Act 2015, s 3(2).
180 Environmental Levy (Budget Amendment) Act 2017.
181 Environment and Climate Adaptation Levy (Budget Amendment) Act 2018.
182 Environment Management (Budget Amendment) Act 2019, s 45A(1)(a)(i).
183 Done through the COP 23 Presidency Trust Fund (Amendment) Act 2019.

which established a trust fund to finance the relocation of communities adversely affected by climate change. The Trustee Act 1966 does not apply to the Climate Relocation of Communities Trust Fund established under the Act.[184] The Ozone Depleting Substances Act 1998 was enacted to regulate the importation, exportation, sale, storage and use of ozone-depleting substances.[185] This Act was also important to give effect to Fiji's obligations under the Vienna Convention for the Protection of the Ozone Layer and the Montreal Protocol on Substances that Deplete the Ozone Layer.[186]

There is no dedicated policy or legislation specifically dealing with protected areas in Fiji and the different laws have resulted in a mix of conservation areas having different values and levels of legal status and protection.[187] The Forest Act 1992 establishes the position of the Conservator of Forests, who is responsible for administering the Act.[188] The Act gives the Minister the power to declare forest or nature reserves, but these powers are subject to any customary rights of the indigenous landowners.[189] The protection of these forests and other natural resources is provided for under other legislation. The Environment Management Act 2005 sets out the laws relating to protection of natural resources. The Fiji Forest Policy 2007 sets the foundation for sustainable forest management for Fiji and recognises that the most important means of conserving the vast majority of Fiji's endemic flora and fauna is through the establishment of a comprehensive system of reserves and conservation areas at the national and local level. The Rural Land Use Policy 2005 provides an umbrella framework for forest policy with regard to land use planning. Finally, there is the Fiji National Biodiversity Strategy and Action Plan 2007–2011, which was developed as part of Fiji's obligations under the Convention on Biodiversity.[190]

Fiji's international commitment under the Convention on International Trade in Endangered Species (CITES) is fulfilled by the Endangered and Protected Species Act 2002. The Act establishes a CITES Management Authority and CITES Council and requires permits for the importing and exporting of flora and fauna listed in the Act.[191] The Offshore Fisheries Management Regulations 2014 made under the Offshore Fisheries Management Act 2012 further incorporate

---

184 Climate Relocation of Communities Trust Fund Act 2019, s 3(3).

185 Ozone Depleting Substances Act 1998, long title.

186 Ozone Depleting Substances Act 1998.

187 Wildlife Conservation Society 'Kilaka Forest Conservation Area Management Plan' (24 November 2016) <https://fiji.wcs.org/Portals/82/management_tools/smallKilaka%20Management%20Plan%20booklet%2023%205%2017%20amended8.pdf?ver=2017-07-05-171037-910> 7.

188 Forest Act 1992, s 3.

189 Forest Act 1992, ss 6 and 7.

190 Wildlife Conservation Society, above n 187.

191 Secretariat of the Pacific Regional Environment Programme (SPREP) 'Fiji: Review of Natural Resource and Environment Related Legislation' (January 2018) <https://www.sprep.org/attachments/Publications/EMG/sprep-legislative-review-fiji.pdf>.

protection for species listed in CITES.[192] Subsidiary laws are also created under the Endangered and Protected Species Act 2002.[193]

Marine and coastal fisheries were previously only covered under laws inherited from the colonial era,[194] but these laws have since been modernised. The Offshore Fisheries Management Act 2012, for example, contains a number of mechanisms for the conservation, management and development of fisheries, including the concept of designated fisheries, fisheries management plans and fisheries treaties, as well as regulation by licences.[195] Like land rights, traditional fishing area rights are defined and owned by *vanua* or *tikina* (social units that include a number of villages in a district), which regulate their use and exploitation.[196] Accordingly, with regard to fishing licences, commercial fishers operating within customary fishing areas in Fiji are granted licences only if the head of the customary unit owning the fishing area has given approval.[197]

Although all minerals in or under any land or water are owned by the State, the owners of any particular land (whether customary or freehold), or of any particular registered customary fishing rights are entitled to receive a fair share of royalties or other money paid to the State in respect of the grant by the State of the rights to extract minerals from that land or the seabed in the area of those fishing rights.[198] This particular provision is embedded in the Bill of Rights, which signals the efforts made to include customary landowners in shares of their indigenous lands. The Fair Share of Mineral Royalties Act 2018 gives effect to this constitutional provision. The Act also establishes a process for the fair distribution of royalties from the extraction of minerals.

A topical field in Fiji is deep seabed mining and to cater to this Fiji enacted the International Seabed Mineral Management Act 2013, which governs engagement in seabed mineral activities in the area beyond national jurisdiction. The Act establishes the Fiji International Seabed Authority and a system of sponsorship that allows the sponsored parties to engage in seabed mineral activities and for the sponsoring state[199] to receive payment for that sponsorship.[200] However, at the writing of this chapter, this Act has not commenced.

192 Offshore Fisheries Management Regulations 2014, reg 5 and Sch 2B.

193 Endangered and Protected Species Regulations 2003.

194 Rivers and Streams Act 1882, Fisheries Act 1941, Water Supply Act 1955 and Continental Shelf Act 1970.

195 Secretariat of the Pacific Regional Environment Programme (SPREP), above n 191.

196 Joeli Veitayaki 'Chapter 9: Fisheries Resource-Use Culture in Fiji and its Implications' in Antony Hooper (ed) *Culture and Sustainable Development in the Pacific* (Asia Pacific Press, 2005) 116.

197 Veitayaki, above n 196, at 122.

198 Constitution 2013, s 30(1).

199 International Seabed Mineral Management Act 2013, s 2. A sponsoring state is a state party to the UN Convention on the Law of the Sea who sponsors a person to carry out exploration in the area in accordance with art 153(2)(b) of the UNCLOS.

200 At the time of the writing of this chapter, Fiji has not sponsored any party to carry out any exploration or mining activities.

12. CRIMINAL LAW

The Crimes Act 2009 makes comprehensive provision in relation to the elements of criminal responsibility and prescribes a range of criminal offences. Common law offences which were previously preserved in the Penal Code 1944 ceased to apply on the commencement of the Act.[201]

The Act advanced the rights of victims of sexual offences in various ways, such as by removing the gender tag that had often been attached to such offences. For example, the definition of rape in the repealed Penal Code referred only to the unlawful carnal knowledge of a woman or girl,[202] whereas the Crimes Act refers to a person, which would include both male and female victims.[203]

The Act creates exceptions for persons performing abortions. Under the repealed Penal Code, it was an offence to perform an abortion,[204] but under the Crimes Act an abortion may be performed by a medical practitioner if done in good faith with reasonable care and skill where the pregnancy is a result of incest or rape.[205]

With the advent of technology, the Act creates computer offences where persons may be prosecuted whether or not the conduct constituting the alleged offence occurs in Fiji and whether or not a result of the conduct constituting the alleged offence occurs in Fiji.[206] The death penalty, which covered treason and genocide offences in the Penal Code, was not retained by the 2009 Act.

The Domestic Violence Act 2009 was created to extend greater protection to victims of domestic violence and to promote rehabilitation for perpetrators. The 2009 Act defines domestic violence in s 4. The Act is taken to apply to domestic violence committed in Fiji and overseas, and the Attorney-General may request the appropriate court or authority in a foreign country to make arrangements for the enforcement in that country of a domestic violence restraining order made under the Fiji Act.[207]

The Illicit Drugs Control Act 2004 regulates and controls the cultivation, manufacture, importation, exportation, sale, supply, possession and use of illicit drugs and controlled chemicals. The Juveniles Act 1973 provides a separate system for dealing with offenders under the age of 18.[208] Section 16 of the Act creates a Juveniles Court, which is a Magistrates Court that sits for that specific purpose.[209] According to the Act, the words 'conviction' and 'sentence' are not to

---

[201] Crimes Act 2009, s 2.

[202] Penal Code (repealed), s 149.

[203] Crimes Act 2009, s 207.

[204] Penal Code (repealed), ss 172, 173 and 174.

[205] Crimes Act 2009, s 234.

[206] Crimes Act 2009, s 338.

[207] Domestic Violence Act 2009, s 61.

[208] Previously 17.

[209] Paterson and Zorn, above n 100.

be used in relation to juveniles,[210] and photographs and fingerprints may only be taken on an order by the magistrate.[211] The Minor Offences Act 1971 deals with minor offences such as begging, indecency, loitering and being drunk and disorderly.[212] Under this Act, it is an offence for a person to receive payment to tell fortunes or to pretend to have any knowledge in any occult signs to discover or find things that may have been lost.[213]

13. INTERNATIONAL LAW AND HUMAN RIGHTS

As a dualist state, all international treaties and conventions must be domesticated before they can be applied in Fiji. Pursuant to s 51 of the Constitution 2013, '[a]n international treaty or convention binds the State only after it has been approved by Parliament.' This is further articulated in the Standing Orders of the Parliament of Fiji under Standing Order 130, which states that all international treaties must be approved by Parliament and provides the process to be followed for the purpose of s 51. The Attorney-General must give notice of a motion for the Standing Committee on Foreign Affairs and Defence to review the treaty.[214] This must be accompanied by a copy of the treaty and a written analysis, inclusive of a summary of the treaty, the requirements for its implementation within a signatory state and a statement of the impact of the treaty on Fiji.[215] This will then be reviewed by the Standing Committee. Once the Committee submits its report (or on the expiry of 30 days) and the motion to have the treaty approved is passed by a majority of the Members, the Speaker will then issue a notice to notify the public of the approval of that treaty.[216]

Chapter 2 of the Constitution contains the Bill of Rights. This provides for the rights of all persons in Fiji, including for the protection of land and customary ownership of land.[217] Section 43 limits certain rights during a state of emergency. Pursuant to s 45, the Human Rights Commission, established under the Human Rights Commission Act 2009, continues in existence as the Human Rights and Anti-Discrimination Commission. The Commission, amongst other functions, promotes and protects the rights encapsulated in the Constitution, as well as monitoring the State's compliance with international treaties and conventions. In addition to its obligations under international environmental

210 Juveniles Act 1973, s 20.
211 Juveniles Act 1973, s 25.
212 Minor Offences Act 1971, s 3–20.
213 Minor Offences Act 1971, s 20.
214 Standing Orders of the Parliament of Fiji, SO 130(2).
215 Standing Orders of the Parliament of Fiji, SO 130(2).
216 See an example <http://www.parliament.gov.fj/wp-content/uploads/2019/05/Approval-of-International-TreatiesMay-2019.pdf>.
217 Constitution 2013, ss 28, 29 and 30.

laws discussed earlier in this chapter, Fiji has ratified a number of treaties and conventions, including all nine of the core human rights treaties,[218] as well as being a signatory to several Optional Protocols.[219]

Fiji has been a part of international peacekeeping efforts, which first began in 1978. The first soldiers were deployed to Lebanon, and Fiji has since taken part in more peacekeeping operations – maybe more than any other nation in the world.[220]

14. CIVIL SOCIETY ORGANISATIONS

Fiji has a vibrant civil society mainly made up of ethnic and human rights groups, women's affairs groups, and environmental non-governmental organisations (NGOs).[221] Two prominent women's NGOs are the Fiji Women's Crisis Centre and the Fiji Women's Rights Movement; both campaign and advocate to protect vulnerable women and for the achievement of greater gender equality. These organisations often work with religious groups and organisations to provide assistance, for example the Fiji Women's League and the Young Women's Christian Organisation.[222] There are also those groups organised around specific causes such as disabilities or professional affiliation.[223]

Civil society in Fiji plays a significant role in the achievement of a democratic society. The engagement of young people and civil society in human rights dialogues and discussions is a key contributing factor to the long-term sustainability of democracy. This is because they could be engaged as 'advocates of change' in promoting human rights-related issues in their communities.[224]

---

218 Convention against Torture and Other Cruel Inhuman or Degrading Treatment or Punishment, International Covenant on Civil and Political Rights, Convention on the Elimination of all Forms of Discrimination against Women, Convention for the Protection of all Persons from Enforced Disappearance, Convention on the Elimination of all Forms of Racial Discrimination, International Covenant on Economic, Social and Cultural Rights, Convention on the Protection of the Rights of All Migrant Workers and Members of their Families, Convention on the Rights of the Child, and Convention on the Rights of Persons with Disabilities.

219 A full list is available on the Parliament of Fiji website <http://www.parliament.gov.fj/treaties/>.

220 Andrew Roberts *A History of the English-speaking Peoples Since 1900* (Widenfeld and Nicolson, 2006) 644 as cited in Joeli Baledrokadroka 'The Unintended Consequences of Fiji's International Peacekeeping' (2012) 8(4) Security Challenges 105.

221 Commonwealth of Nations Network *Civil Society Areas: Fiji* <http://www.commonwealthofnations.org/sectors-fiji/civil_society/>.

222 For a 2012 list of non-governmental organisations see <http://www.experiencesuva.com/wp-content/uploads/2012/05/LIST-OF-NGO1.pdf>.

223 For example, the Fiji Law Society and Fiji Society for the Blind.

224 United Nations Development Programme 'Dialogue in Fiji strengthen youth and civil society engagement to support good governance and democracy-enabling conditions' (15 September 2017) <https://www.pacific.undp.org/content/pacific/en/home/presscenter/

Civil societies act as a check and balance on the government, and in order to effectively carry out this function, they must be completely separate. However, some NGOs are aligned so closely with the government that they are effectively 'subcontracted' to carry out work it would otherwise do, as in the case of the *Soqosoqo Vakamarama iTaukei* in Fiji.[225] The *Soqosoqo Vakamarama iTaukei* is a Methodist organisation for indigenous Fijian women, founded in 1924 and known initially as *Qele ni Ruve*,[226] which was sometimes seen to be advancing only indigenous Fijian nationalism in post-coup Fiji, as its members endorsed the platform of indigenous Fijian nationalist parties.[227]

Civil societies are involved in many areas, including environmental conservation, human rights, women's empowerment, food security, and healthcare and climate resilience. They have also worked to try to ensure that the State meets its obligations in respect of international conventions that have been signed, or commitments the State has agreed to through UN conferences.[228] An example is how the Fiji Women's Rights Movement played a key role in shadow-reporting on Fiji's performance in relation to its obligations to the Convention on the Elimination of Racial Discrimination and the Convention on the Elimination of All Forms of Discrimination against Women.[229]

15. CONCLUDING REMARKS

Fiji's laws are derived from the Constitution, legislation, subsidiary laws, common law and customary law. Modernisation of these laws is essential, especially as a large percentage of laws were inherited during the colonial period. In the Pacific region, Fiji has taken the lead in reforming many of its laws and replaced them with legislation that is more applicable to the changing circumstances of the country.

---

articles/2017/09/15/dialogues-in-fiji-strengthen-youth-and-civil-society-engagement-to-support-good-governance-and-democracy-enabling-conditions.html>.

225 Australia National University 'NGO constraints and challenges: Chapter 2. Treading Water in Rapids? Non-Governmental Organisations and Resistance to Neo-Liberalism in Pacific Island States' <http://press-files.anu.edu.au/downloads/press/p55871/mobile/ch02s05.html>.

226 Jacqueline Leckie 'The complexities of women's agency in Fiji' in Brenda Yeoh, Peggy Teo and Shirlena Huang (eds) *Gender Politics in the Asia-Pacific Region* (Routledge, 2002) 156, as cited in Nicole George *Situating Women: Gender Politics and Circumstance in Fiji* (ANU E-Press, 2012) 41 <https://press-files.anu.edu.au/downloads/press/p154311/pdf/book.pdf>.

227 Jacqueline Leckie 'Women's Agency in Fiji' in (1999) 3(2) Fijian Studies: A Journal of Contemporary History and Nicole George 'Advocacy or Activism: Gender Politics in Fiji' (Doctoral Dissertation, Department of International Relations, ANU, 2004) 84–85, as cited in Margaret Mishra 'A History of Women's Activism (1900–2010)' (2012) 24(2) Journal of Women's History 115 at 122 <https://muse.jhu.edu/article/478324/pdf>.

228 Australia National University, above n 225.

229 Australia National University, above n 225.

Land, and its connection to indigenous peoples in Fiji, has remained a contentious issue, especially when it comes to finding a balance between State laws and customary laws. Land disputes involving customary land in Fiji have several main dimensions: land administration, land tenure and ownership and land boundaries.[230] These must be taken into account whenever decisions are made regarding, amongst other things, the indigenous people, the economic use of the land and any conservation efforts of the State or non-governmental organisations. Changes in the ownership of minerals on indigenous land is an indication that more regard is now being given to the traditional landowners. Environmental management is being carried out under more traditional methods and with the consent of the indigenous people.

Law is not static and must change with the circumstances. There are positive and negative features in the Westminster and presidential systems, and different combinations will succeed or fail according to local circumstances. Looking to the future, there is a need for Pacific states to evolve and 'own' their legal and political systems.[231]

BIBLIOGRAPHY

Colvin, Eric 'Criminal Procedure in the South Pacific' (2009) 13(1) JSPL, available at <http://www.paclii.org/journals/fJSPL/vol08no1/1.shtml>.

Corrin, Jennifer *Contract Law in the South Pacific* (2nd ed, Intersentia, 2020).

Corrin, Jennifer 'Discarding the Relics of the Past: Patriation of Laws in the South Pacific' (2008) 39 Victoria University of Wellington Law Review, available at <http://www.austlii.edu.au/nz/journals/VUWLawRw/2008/36.pdf>.

Corrin, Jennifer 'The Status of Customary Law in Fiji Islands After the Constitutional Amendment Act 1997' (2000) 4 Journal of South Pacific Law, available at <https://www.usp.ac.fj/index.php?id=13193>.

Corrin, Jennifer and Don Paterson *Introduction to South Pacific Law* (4th ed, Intersentia, 2017).

Farran, Sue and Donald Paterson *South Pacific Property Law* (Routledge, 2013).

Fonmanu, Keresi R, Lisa Ting and Ian P Williamson *Dispute Resolution For Customary Lands: Some Lessons From Fiji* (University of Melbourne, 2003), available at <https://minerva-access.unimelb.edu.au/bitstream/handle/11343/33965/66324_00001243_01_DisputeResolutionFiji.pdf?sequence=1&isAllowed=y>.

230 Keresi R Fonmanu, Lisa Ting and Ian P Williamson 'Dispute Resolution For Customary Lands: Some Lessons From Fiji' (University of Melbourne, 2003) <https://minerva-access.unimelb.edu.au/bitstream/handle/11343/33965/66324_00001243_01_DisputeResolutionFiji.pdf?sequence=1&isAllowed=y>.

231 John Henderson 'Governance and Constitutional Issues: Reflections on Current Problems and Future Options' in Michael Powles (ed) *Pacific Futures* (Pirion, 2006) 10 at 18.

Ghai, Yash and Jill Cottrell 'A Tale of Three Constitutions: Ethnicity and Politics in Fiji' (October 2007) 5(4) IJCL, 639.

Lawson, Stephanie 'The Military Versus Democracy in Fiji: Problems for Contemporary Political Development' in R J May and Virberto Selochan (eds) *The Military and Democracy in Asia and the Pacific* (UIN, 2004), available at <http://press-files.anu.edu.au/downloads/press/p33231/mobile/index.html>.

Mishra, Margaret 'A History of Women's Activism (1900–2010)' (2012) 24(2) Journal of Women's History 115, available at <https://muse.jhu.edu/article/478324/pdf>.

Neelta, Anuleshni 'Adoption in Fiji' in Jennifer Corrin and Sue Farran (eds) *The Plural Practice of Adoption in Pacific Island States* (Springer, 2019).

Newton Cain, Tess 'Convergence or Clash? The Recognition of Customary Law and Practice in Sentencing Decisions of the Courts of the Pacific Island Region' (2001) 2 Melbourne Journal of International Law, available at <https://law.unimelb.edu.au/__data/assets/pdf_file/0013/1679998/Cain.pdf>.

Pacific Islands Legal Information Institute *Fiji Primary Materials*, available at <http://www.paclii.org/countries/fj.html>.

Parke, Aubrey L, Mathew Spriggs and Deryk Scarr *Degei's Descendants: Spirits, Place and People in Pre-Cession Fiji* (ANU Press, 2014).

Parliament of Fiji, Standing Orders, available at <http://www.paclii.org/fj/other/fijiparliamentstandingorders.html>.

Paterson, Don 'Some Thoughts About Customary Law' (2009) 13(1) Journal of South Pacific Law, available at <http://www.paclii.org/journals/fJSPL/vol05/7.shtml>.

Paterson, Don and Stephen A Zorn 'Fiji' in Michael A Ntumy (ed) *South Pacific Islands Legal Systems* (University of Hawaii Press, 1993).

Ravuvu, Asesela *The Facade of Democracy: Fijian Struggles for Political Control, 1830–1987* (Reader Publishing House, 1991).

Secretariat of the Pacific Regional Environment Programme (SPREP) 'Fiji: Review of Natural Resource and Environment Related Legislation' (January 2018), available at <https://www.sprep.org/attachments/Publications/EMG/sprep-legislative-review-fiji.pdf>.

United Nations Development Programme 'Dialogue in Fiji strengthen youth and civil society engagement to support good governance and democracy-enabling conditions' (15 September, 2017), available at <https://www.pacific.undp.org/content/pacific/en/home/presscenter/articles/2017/09/15/dialogues-in-fiji-strengthen-youth-and-civil-society-engagement-to-support-good-governance-and-democracy-enabling-conditions.html>.

Veitayaki, Joeli 'Chapter 9: Fisheries Resource-Use Culture in Fiji and its Implications' in Antony Hooper (ed) *Culture and Sustainable Development in the Pacific* (Asia Pacific Press, April 2005).

FRENCH POLYNESIA – POLYNÉSIE FRANÇAISE

Hervé Raimana LALLEMANT-MOE

1. CONTEXT

French Polynesia is an overseas *collectivité* of the French Republic comprising 118 islands and atolls in the Pacific Ocean. Of these islands and atolls, 67 are inhabited. The islands are divided into five groups: the Society Islands archipelago, the Tuamotu Archipelago, the Gambier Islands, the Marquesas Islands and the Austral Islands. The total land area is 4,167 square kilometres and its exclusive economic zone is 4,537,730 square kilometres.

The estimated population of French Polynesia in 2020 is 280,908. Tahiti, located in the Society Islands, is the most populous island, with close to 69 per cent of the total population according to the 2017 census. 78 per cent of the population is Polynesian, 12 per cent are Chinese, and the remaining 10 per cent is made up of local and metropolitan French. French and Tahitian are the official languages of French Polynesia but other Polynesian languages are also spoken.

The main religion is Christianity. 54 per cent of the population are Protestant, 30 per cent are Roman Catholic and a minority are Latter-Day Saints and Jehovah's Witnesses.

Tourism plays a large part in French Polynesia's economy, accounting for about 13 per cent of its GDP. Traditional exports such as vanilla have declined, but the development of the fishing industry has partially compensated for this. Pearl exports make up about two-thirds of export earnings. The country's major export destinations are Japan, Hong Kong, the United States and France; imports mostly come from France, the United States, China and New Zealand.

Polynesian society, and in particular that of the Society Islands, was structured around strong power held by the *hui ari'i*. The arrival of London Missionary Society missionaries in 1797 marked an important stage in the development of the island of Tahiti, which at the time was witnessing conflicts between the Pomare and Teva clans. After 1815 and several fights, Pomare II established himself as absolute monarch of a kingdom of the Society Islands archipelago, taking the British Crown as his model.

Although it seems that a code of ethical and moral principles of a largely customary nature, the *code tetuna'e*, existed before the arrival of the Europeans, the first written law codifications date from 1819 for Pomare II, from 1820 for Tamatoa in Raiatea, and from 1822 for Teri'itara in Huahine. This codification work was closely linked to the growing influence of the missionaries on the local ruling classes. Other documents were developed later along the lines of the *Book of Laws of Tahiti and Moorea* of 1842. There were institutions and, providing a counterbalance to the royal power, an assembly of legislators composed of persons elected in each district. It could be said that at this time a part of Polynesia was clearly a unified state in the international law sense because of the high level of autonomy it enjoyed: outright sovereignty.

A treaty was made on 9 September 1842 between the French Admiral Dupetit-Thouars and Queen Pomare IV. It established a protectorate in respect of the Kingdom of Tahiti; it was made without the approval of the King of France (Louis-Philippe I) in order to avoid British domination of the islands. The Queen was guaranteed her sovereignty over the local people but the agreement was clearly imposed by the French officials. The Queen denounced the treaty and that resulted in the annexation of the kingdom by France. The Queen was reinstated on 6 February 1847, the French King having in the meantime renounced the annexation. Despite this, the powers of the Tahitian kingdom were progressively reduced to the benefit of France.

France exercised its exclusive right to maintain public order through the Council of Government. The Queen shared the exercise of her power for internal matters with a French government official (the Royal Commissioner).

The Legislative Assembly that existed before the protectorate was continued for the purpose of enacting legislation. It was composed of deputies elected in the districts for a term of three years. It stopped functioning in 1866 when the powers of France were strengthened. There was also a General Council with power over fiscal matters; it was composed mainly of Europeans.

On 29 June 1880, King Pomare V abdicated and ceded the Kingdom of Tahiti to France, receiving significant financial compensation in this process. The Tahitian State disappeared and Tahiti became a colony of the French Establishments of Oceania (EFO). This was the beginning of the annexation and unification of all of the Polynesian archipelagos; that unification was finally achieved in the early 1900s. All power was then concentrated in the hands of a Governor appointed by the President of the Republic. The Governor was assisted by a Privy Council (its role was consultative from 1885). It was not until 1930 that a local assembly was established. There was also a Colonial Council of members elected by universal suffrage, but it had only a consultative role; it had 12 members, of whom only six were Polynesians.

This Colonial Council was wound up in 1884 and replaced by a General Council (18 members elected by universal suffrage), which had a number of powers (including budget) but was under the control of the Governor. The General Council was disestablished in 1903 and replaced by an administrative council of a consultative nature whose members were public officials. In 1932 a consultative assembly, which had economic and financial powers, was created.

Things did not develop further until the establishment of the Fourth Republic on 27 October 1946. At that time, the category of TOM (overseas territory) was established, as was the principle of legislative specialty (French rules could apply overseas only if there was express extension of them to the overseas territory). The Governor remained the uncontested head of the local executive, with powers identical to those of 1885. There was however a representative assembly (31 August 1945 and 25 October 1946), with authority mainly of a budgetary nature. Its members were elected for five years by a vote of two rounds. The Assembly had 25 members from 1952.

After a period of stagnation, the Defferre Law of 23 June 1956 and the decree of 22 July 1957 allowed Polynesia to enjoy significant autonomy and extensive power. The islands became known as French Polynesia. There was still a Governor, but there was also a Council of Government led by a Vice-President and a Territorial Assembly with strong powers.

The prospect of the installation of the Nuclear Experimentation Centre for the Pacific and concern that there was movement from autonomy towards independence led to a sharp reduction in the autonomy of French Polynesia. The Council of Government and the Territorial Assembly very quickly lost importance and the Governor again became all-powerful. The Council of Government was reduced to five counsellors with very limited authority.

It was also at this same time (11 November 1958) that Pouvana'a a Oopa (the Vice-President of the Council) was arrested.[1]

It was only with the statute of 12 July 1977 (entitled 'Autonomy of Management') that a form of autonomy was regained by the territory. This date marks the point where the current autonomy of French Polynesia and movement towards a greater decentralisation in the island group began. The office of High Commissioner (the chief officer of the executive) and of the Council of Government rapidly gained importance (the Vice-President of the Council becoming its leader). Moreover, this was the era in which French Polynesia gained general power, with the French State retaining competence only in respect of a limited number of matters. This was also the period when the Economic and Social Committee was established.

Autonomy was greatly strengthened by the French Polynesian statute of 6 September 1984 (entitled 'Internal Autonomy'). The most important change was that the head of the executive was from then on elected as a member of the Assembly and by the Assembly members. This official was named the President of the Government. From then on, the French High Commissioner was simply the delegate of the central government. The Council of Government was replaced by a body made up of 12 ministers as a maximum.[2] In the beginning, the government appointed by the President had to be approved by the Assembly, but that requirement disappeared in 1990. The President of the Government was assisted by a General Secretariat for the first time and in 1990, the local Assembly obtained financial autonomy. The President of the Territorial Assembly also gained importance as the controller of the budget and the person responsible for sittings of the Assembly. The Economic, Social and Cultural Council (CESC) began its activity under this name in 1990 and obtained the power to self-manage. It is necessarily concerned with economic, social and cultural matters. The general authority of French Polynesia has been much strengthened. Certain powers are shared between the State and the territorial authority. There was also the establishment of the French Administrative Tribunal in Tahiti which was considered better (because it is locally based and not based in France) even if the Tribunal falls under the French State jurisdiction. Furthermore, French Polynesia was given the power to choose its national symbols and things that relate to its territorial persona (eg flag, anthem).

The Organic Law of 12 April 1996 (entitled 'Autonomy') provided for some slight developments in the local status and transferred new powers to the government of French Polynesia. Overall, the changes made were not

1 He was later deported to Europe. It should be noted that on 25 October 2018, the Court of Review of Penal Sanctions, sitting in public in the criminal chamber of the Court of Cassation in Paris, reinstated Pouvana'a a Oopa, and held that the procedures followed in 1959 were totally irregular.

2 Following the amendment to the statute on 12 July 1990.

revolutionary. Revision of the Constitution had been expected to give French Polynesia a status similar to that of New Caledonia, but the reform initiative failed in 2000 because the French National Congress did not support the President of the Republic, Jacques Chirac.

Finally, the category of overseas territories (TOMs) was abolished and the category of overseas *collectivités* was established in its place.[3] On the basis of the new art 74 in the Constitution, Organic Law No 2004-192 of 27 February 2004 relating to the autonomous status of French Polynesia was adopted and French Polynesia became an overseas *collectivité* with autonomy within the French State.[4] There are now four institutions: the President of French Polynesia, the Government of French Polynesia, the Assembly of French Polynesia (APF), and the Economic, Social, Environmental and Cultural Council (CESEC).

Furthermore, the General Assembly of the United Nations[5] reinscribed French Polynesia as a territory for decolonisation: at international law, France became an 'administering power' and French Polynesia a 'non-self-governing territory' which has to be 'decolonised'. This recognition had effect only at the international law level.

2. SOURCES OF LAW

The sources of law in French Polynesia are (in order of importance):

(1) the French Constitution (the Constitution of 4 October 1958 – Fifth Republic), the Declaration of the Rights of Man and of the Citizen of 26 August 1789, the Preamble to the Constitution of 27 October 1946 (Fourth Republic), the Environmental Charter of 2004 (Constitutional Law of 1 March 2005), constitutional principles;
(2) international treaties ratified by France;
(3) Organic Law No 2004-192 of 27 February 2004 relating to the autonomous status of French Polynesia (2004 LOPF);
(4) French laws (but only regarding the State's jurisdiction and even then, they must with some minor exceptions be clearly extended to French Polynesia because of the legislative specialty process);
(5) French decrees (same as 4°);
(6) laws of the country (*lois du pays*): adopted by the Assembly of French Polynesia on topics that are within the jurisdiction of French Polynesia – related to legislative power but considered to be 'decrees' in nature;

---

3 Constitutional Law No 2003-276 of 28 March 2003.
4 This is the governing document as at July 2020.
5 Via Resolution No 67/265 of 17 May 2013.

(7) resolutions (*délibérations*): adopted by the Assembly of French Polynesia on topics within the jurisdiction of French Polynesia – not related to legislative power;
(8) government decrees (*arrêtés pris en Conseil des ministres*): adopted by the government of French Polynesia or individual ministers. This executive power is applied for the implementation of Laws of the Country or resolutions but the local government also possess an autonomous capacity to adopt rules.

The sources of law in French Polynesia are closely linked to those of the French State, given that French Polynesia is a decentralised *collectivité* (territorial authority)[6] and not a sovereign state. Apart from constitutional rules (and international treaties), which apply automatically, other laws are governed by a system specific to French Polynesia.

As at 2019, the overseas *collectivités* are Saint-Pierre-et-Miquelon, the islands of Wallis and Futuna, French Polynesia, Saint-Barthelemy and Saint Martin. They have a status that is fixed by an organic law which takes account of the specific needs of each of them within the Republic.[7] Their legal status distances them from the basic law but the nature of the difference in status within the group differentiates them from one another. French Polynesia, in addition to being an overseas *collectivité*, is also a country and overseas territory (OCTs) of the European Union. The OCTs are not part of the European Union.

Although they are not under European law (eg the Directives and the Regulations in particular), the OCTs benefit from the status of association which was granted to them by the Lisbon Treaty of 13 December 2007.[8] This status has as its main objective contribution to the economic and social development of the OCTs.

Since 1977, the powers of French Polynesia are not reduced to a definitive list. As of 1977, French Polynesia has general authority and the State retains only its prerogative powers. It follows that when a matter which does not fall within the authority of the State arises, the power lies with French Polynesia.[9] As far as the power of the French State is concerned, French Polynesia is governed by the principle of legislative specialty, which means that the laws and regulations of the State are not applicable in French Polynesia unless they have been expressly extended to do so.

---

6 This classification is the result of the constitutional amendment of 28 March 2003 and is governed by art 74 of the Constitution.
7 Article 74-1 of the Constitution.
8 This system is based mainly on art 198 and following of the Treaty on the Functioning of the European Union and a decision (2013/755/EU) on overseas association of the Council of the European Union of 25 November 2013, which came into force on 1 January 2014.
9 Articles 13 and 14 of the Organic Law of 2004.

3. CONSTITUTIONAL LAW

The sources of constitutional law applicable in French Polynesia are those of the French State. They are superior to all Polynesian norms. This body of constitutional norms includes the following:

(1) the Constitution of 4 October 1958 (Fifth Republic);
(2) the Declaration of the Rights of Man and of the Citizen of 26 August 1789;
(3) the Preamble to the Constitution of 27 October 1946 (Fourth Republic);
(4) the Environmental Charter of 2004 (Constitutional Law of 1 March 2005);
(5) additionally, a judge in constitutional matters has access to other rules. These complement and reinforce the degree of control of constitutionality. Among them are the 'objectives of constitutional value' and 'principles and rules of constitutional value'.

The control of constitutionality is carried out by the Constitutional Council of France (which checks conformity of statutes with the Constitution) and by other courts, notably those with administrative authority, which check conformity of regulations with the main body of constitutional law. The rule-making activities of the institutions of French Polynesia can thus be controlled by the Administrative Tribunal of French Polynesia and by the Council of State (Conseil d'État).

4. LAW PROFESSIONS

Since 1984, French Polynesia has the jurisdiction to regulate the legal and judicial professions, such as that of notaries. Barristers (*avocats*) are the exception and their regulation falls under the jurisdiction of the French State (art 14 2° of the 2004 LOPF). Nevertheless, the State remains competent in matters of judicial organisation.

In 2004, the Administrative Court of French Polynesia (Tribunal Administratif de la Polynésie française) ruled that the provisions of Decision No 99-54 APF of 22 April 1999 were illegal in that they affected judicial organisation. The decision entrusted part of the disciplinary procedure for notaries to the General Assembly of Magistrates of the Court of Appeal de Papeete (Cour d'Appel de Papeete). This ruling was confirmed by the Council of State.[10] It results from the combination of arts 13 and 14 of the 2004 LOPF that only the French State can entrust to the judiciary the task of supervising and sanctioning notaries.

[10] Conseil d'Etat, No 385.488, interior section, 19 July 2011.

5. LAW OF PERSONS

The following provisions of Book I of the Civil Code relating to nationality, status and capacity of individuals, in particular documents of civil status, absence, marriage, divorce and parenthood, are, in accordance with art 7(4) of the 2004 LOPF, automatically applicable in French Polynesia:

(1) Title I bis, 'French nationality';
(2) Title II, 'Acts of civil status';
(3) Title III, 'Domicile';
(4) Title IV, 'Absentees';
(5) Title V, 'Marriage';
(6) Title VI, 'Divorce';
(7) Title VII, 'Filiation';
(8) Title VIII, 'Adoptive parentage';
(9) Title X, 'Minority and descent';
(10) Title XI, 'Majority and adults protected by law';
(11) Title XII, 'Management of the property of minors and adults under guardianships'.

The following provisions of the Civil Code which relate to parental authority, matrimonial property regimes and inheritance and gifts, or which fall within the scope of the guarantee of public freedoms, fall within the competence of the State by application of art 14(1) of the 2004 LOPF. They are applicable in French Polynesia only if they have been expressly extended:

(1) in Book I, Title IX, 'Parental authority';
(2) in Book III:
    (a) Title I, 'Succession';
    (b) Title V, 'The marriage contract and matrimonial regimes'.

Because of art 7 of the 2004 LOPF, the current Civil Code provisions apply in French Polynesia. Nevertheless, specific rules may be adopted by the French Parliament for French Polynesia (eg succession to land: Law No 2019-786 of 26 July 2019 relating to French Polynesia).

The law of persons is governed in French law by the Civil Code. The Civil Code in French Polynesia is not completely under the authority of the State,[11] except in respect of 'nationality, civil rights, status and capacity of individuals, in particular, documents of civil status, absence, marriage, divorce,

[11] In accordance with art 14 of Organic Law No 2004-194 of 27 February 2004 relating to the autonomous status of French Polynesia.

parenthood (*filiation*), parental authority, matrimonial property regimes, succession and gifts'.[12] Furthermore, pursuant to art 7 of the Organic Law, 'legislative and regulatory provisions relating to nationality, to the status and capacity of individuals' are applicable ipso jure in French Polynesia, without prejudice to the provisions which adapt them to a particular organisation; these provisions replaced those of Law No 70-589 of 9 July 1970 relating to civil status and common law in the overseas territories. Consequently, the law of persons that applies in French Polynesia is the same as that which applies in France and in particular that of the Civil Code.

Pursuant to arts 7 and 14 of the 2004 LOPF, the nationality, status and capacity of individuals are issues that fall within the exclusive jurisdiction of the French State. Because this is a competence included in art 7, the legislative specialty process does not apply and the French rules are mostly automatically extended to French Polynesia (it must be noted that there are some topics relating to these powers that impact on the French Polynesian jurisdiction). With some minor exceptions (like the PACS mechanism – a 'wedding-lite' with no divorce mechanism necessary to end it – which is legal in French Polynesia but cannot be contracted there), all the French rules of the Civil Code regarding nationality, marriage, divorce, matrimonial regimes and succession are the same in French Polynesia as in France.

French nationality is a legal attribute whose holders are governed by the Civil Code when it comes to their civil rights, and by the Constitution of the French Republic and particularly its Preamble (Declaration of 1789 of the Rights of the Citizen) when it comes to their civic or political rights. The concept of French nationality is linked to that of French citizenship. In French Polynesia, a person is both a French and a European Union citizen. There is no French Polynesian citizenship.

Articles 143 and following of the Civil Code govern civil marriage, which is the consecration by the law of a couple's union. Marriage is a solemn legal act by which two individuals are united and the effects of which are determined by law. Marriage is also an institution and not a simple contract because the spouses cannot arrange its effects as they choose.

Article 229 of the Civil Code recognises four types of divorce: divorce by mutual consent; divorce by acceptance of the principle of marriage breakdown; divorce for definitive deterioration of the marital bond; and divorce for fault. There is also legal separation where the spouses remain married but are separated.

The marriage contract signed by the future spouses before the celebration of the union allows them to define precisely what their property relations will be during the marriage, the fate of the property, the advantages conferred on the spouses, and their professional constraints.

---

12 Article 13 of the 2004 LOPF.

Without a marriage contract, the spouses are subject to the legal regime of the community of acquests (*régime de la communauté réduite aux acquets*) – everything acquired during the marriage is common, even if only one of the spouses pays for it.

If the spouses choose the regime of the separation of property pure and simple, nothing is pooled. This matrimonial regime makes it possible to differentiate what each spouse has on the day of the marriage, but also what he or she then acquires in terms of property, investments and inheritance. All property owned before or after the marriage remains the property of the individual spouse, as do their wages or income from property.

Alternatively, the spouses may choose the scheme of participation in acquisitions. This regime mixes separation and community, with property separated during marriage and becoming communal at the end of the union. Upon dissolution, the notary measures the enrichment of each spouse during the marriage and what will be shared equally between them.

Opening of successions and referral to heirs are regulated by art 720 and following of the French Civil Code. Sharing of the succession consists in attributing to each heir property with a value equal to that of their rights in joint possession.

6. OBLIGATIONS

As a result of the 2004 LOPF, French Polynesia has civil law authority in respect of obligations: sale, deposit, impounding of property, lease, usufruct, property, company law, contracts, loans, and guarantees are in the sole power of French Polynesia. Broadly they follow the French national law of contracts.

The law of delict and law of contract are under the jurisdiction of French Polynesia.[13] The provisions of the Civil Code, as in force in French Polynesia in 2004 (which are now within the competence of the institutions of French Polynesia pursuant to the last autonomous status), remain applicable without prejudice to their modification by these institutions under the conditions set out in art 11 of the Organic Law.

7. LAWS RELATING TO LAND AND CULTURAL PROTECTION

Since 1993 French Polynesia has had the authority to deal with matters of civil procedure and since 2004 with property (ownership and its acquisition and loss)

[13] Constitutional Council, No 2014-7 LOM, 19 November 2014, Dispositions de droit civil en Polynésie française.

and matters of administrative procedure. French Polynesia can therefore regulate all matters relating to the administrative aspects of expropriation.

Article 17 of the Declaration of the Rights of Man and of the Citizen provides that: 'Since property is an inviolable and sacred right, no one shall be deprived thereof except where public necessity, legally determined, shall clearly demand it, and then only on condition that the owner shall have been previously and equitably indemnified'. French Polynesia must, within the framework of the exercise of its regulatory power, guarantee the constitutional protection of the right to property and ensure that there is no unjustified expropriation of property, and that there is fair and prior compensation with equality of rights between the expropriator and the deprived. In respect of other provisions (transfer of title, establishment and payment of compensation, taking of possession), French Polynesia can change the law, provided that the rules do not impact on the judicial organisation (the position and powers of the judge of expropriation). Indeed, the French State retains competence in matters relating to public freedom, judicial organisation and the procedure in respect of administrative disputes. The State alone is therefore competent to appoint a judge (one specialising in matters of land valuation) and to establish the qualifications for the role (the rules for expropriation, visit to the locus in quo and valuation of the compensation).

Legal protection of Polynesian cultural heritage, and in particular of its historical monuments, has been in place since 1952, with different rules, such as those provided by: Law No 865 apa of 23 June 1952 relating to the classification for their protection of monuments and significant sites in the French establishments of Oceania; Law No 1156 aa of 3 September 1952 relating to the classification for their protection of monuments in the Austral Islands; Resolution No 61-44 of 8 April 1961 relating to the general regulation for the management of the territory in relation to urbanism, habitat, housing, subdivisions, the preservation of monuments and sites, the hygiene and cleanliness of public paths and constructions, dangerous, unhealthy and poorly designed buildings and publicly accessible places; and Law No 97 aa of 10 January 1962, which established the categories of things with a historic, legendary, scientific or folk interest the export of which is subject to administrative control. These laws have been re-established in a code of local heritage by a statute of the country (*Loi du pays* No 2015-10 of 19 November 2015 relating to a code of patrimony of French Polynesia); Book 6 of this relates to historic monuments, sites and protected spaces.

As of 2004, French Polynesia is competent in property law (which includes the right to property and therefore the conditions of acquisition or deprivation of property) as well as in matters of non-contentious administrative procedure. French Polynesia may modify the provisions relating to the transfer of property, the fixing and payment of compensation and the taking of possession, provided that the modifications do not relate to the judiciary (the office and powers of the judge). The State is competent in matters of public freedoms, the judicial branch and contentious administrative procedure.

8. COMMERCIAL LAW

The adoption of the 2004 LOPF transferred all commercial law authority to French Polynesia. French Polynesia also has authority in relation to consumer protection and competition law where the contracts are between traders and consumers. The Council of State has stated that the State has no authority to extend class action procedures to French Polynesia or New Caledonia because competition and consumer protection are within the sole competence of those countries.[14]

Since French Polynesia has authority in respect of contract law and consumer protection, it may therefore set the rules of limitation relating to consumer actions and those relating to traders. The Council of State has determined similarly in respect of matters of social welfare.[15]

The law relating to transport is limited by the 2004 LOPF. The State has authority in relation to sea and air transport only in respect of the following matters: air services between French Polynesia and other parts of the Republic,[16] policing and security of sea and civil aviation traffic,[17] and the mechanism of subsidised travel between French Polynesia and metropolitan France, which arises from the policies of financial aid to citizens which the French State retains total competence to establish. French Polynesia has authority, by virtue of its general competence, to regulate passenger transport throughout French Polynesia, to organise transport services for people other than communal services, and to regulate and organise the transport of goods and specialised types of transport, such as for school children and hospital patients. The local government bodies of French Polynesia are competent to establish the principles for the organisation of intercommunal transport.[18] The purpose of transport services of communal interest is 'the servicing of different points within the community and if necessary by intercommunity cooperation, the servicing of different points of the territory of adjacent communities notably where an urban area extends into the territories of several communities'.[19]

The French State has power in relation to 'coins, credit, exchange, and currency'.[20] According to the Council of State, the State has the power to regulate

14 Council of State, Opinion No 387492, 25 April 2013.

15 Council of State, 13 June 2013, Nos 361767, 361768, 3613912, 369193, 361990, 361991, 362028, *Mrs Clark and others*.

16 Article 14(8) of the Organic Law 2004.

17 Article 14(8) and (9) of the Organic Law 2004.

18 For example regular services, which have an identified point of departure and a terminus and a series of established stopping places, days of operation, and for which timetables are published in advance. Article 43 of the Organic Law 2004.

19 Council of State, Opinion No 373.494, 26 September 2006.

20 Article 14(7) of the Organic Law 2004.

and set rates for bank loans to preserve and maintain the stability of the financial system and the protection of savings.[21]

This is also the case in matters of excessive borrowing where the State has set the national figure for repayments.[22] So in a sense, as a matter of consumer protection, the State has authority concerning the rules relating to information for consumers, the making of contracts or indebtedness when these have an impact on credit. On the contrary, provisions relating to the formalities of contracts of guarantee which are linked to a debt the origin of which is not a credit (eg leases) are entirely within the control of French Polynesia.

The French Commercial Code (resulting from Ordinance No 2000-912 of 18 September 2000) includes provisions applicable in French Polynesia as well as their adaptations. Under the Organic Law in force before 2000 (Organic Law No 96-312 of 12 April 1996), the State was competent to enact in French Polynesia rules on 'civil and commercial obligations'. The Council of State had inferred from this division of powers that, in the field of commercial law, French Polynesia could enact the standards pertaining to the field.[23] The 2004 LOPF transferred the entirety of the field of commercial law to the competence of French Polynesia.

9. COMPETITION LAW

Jurisdiction in respect of competition law is also totally transferred to French Polynesia. A 'code de la concurrence' was adopted in 2015 by French Polynesia's Act No. 2015-2 of 23 February 2015. The same Act created the Polynesian Competition Authority (APC). The APC was created in accordance with art 30-1 of the 2004 LOPF. Within the Republic, it is the first independent administrative authority which was not established by the French State, but by French Polynesia itself. This particular status makes it a real innovation within the Polynesian administrative landscape. It carries out several missions: providing opinions about local laws regarding competition, merger control, creation/extension of retail space control, or anti-competitive practices sanctioning.

10. CURRENCY

French Polynesia uses the Pacific franc (XPF or CFP, Change Franc du Pacifique). There is a fixed exchange rate of 119.332 XPF to 1 euro. The official parity of the

---

21 Council of State, Opinion No 384.124, 10 June 2010, on the sharing of power between the State and New Caledonia in relation to bank rates.

22 Council of State, Opinion, 28 November 2000, on the sharing of power between the State and French Polynesia relating to the difficulties concerning the indebtedness of individuals.

23 Council of State, Opinion No 364.157, 14 March 2000.

Pacific franc was first fixed by the decree of 31 December 1998, and then by the Monetary and Financial Code.

11. THE FISCAL REGIME

Taxation comes under the exclusive jurisdiction of French Polynesia. There are many rules on customs and taxation and on imports and sales.

French Polynesia has created many artificial barriers to the entry of goods. These include tariff protections (customs duties, import taxes), non-tariff protections (quotas, import bans), and the control of foreign investments, all of which constitute barriers to accessing the Polynesian market. Thus, although in theory oriented towards the protection of local production, several of these local regulations increase the price of imported products and reduce the competitive viability of the domestic markets. With respect to tariff barriers alone, on average miscellaneous import taxes and duties represent the same share of the sale price to the consumer as shipping costs by sea (around eight per cent of the price) and less than VAT[24] (which is 13 per cent). One of the best-known examples is the *taxe de développement local* (local development tax, TDL), which can be as high as 82 per cent for some products (eg imported beer).

12. ENVIRONMENTAL LAW

There is a Code of the Environment for French Polynesia, but rules relating to the environment are not new. A typical example of a longstanding environmental rule is that of *rahui*, which could traditionally be of a religious, political or natural resources-conservation nature.

The autonomy given in the statute of 12 July 1977 brought the environment back within the scope of the powers of French Polynesia, and it was in the 2004 LOPF that the law on the environment became a matter for the local law (*loi du pays*). However, because it is an overseas *collectivité* with autonomy,[25] French Polynesia – although competent in matters of environmental law – is still governed by the broad body of constitutional laws of the Republic and particularly by the Charter for the Environment of 2004, as well as by international treaties.

The French Polynesian rules relating to the environment are spread among many separate provisions or codes. Since 2003, the main source of law for the environment has been the Environment Code, as noted above.[26] The latest

24 Value-added tax, or VAT (taxe sur la valeur ajoutée, TVA), in France is a general, broadly based consumption tax assessed on the value added to goods and services.

25 Article 74 of the Constitution.

26 Established by Order No 1843-CM of 15 December 2003.

changes have been achieved by *Lois du pays* No 2017-25 of 5 October 2017 and by Order No 466-CM of 22 March 2018, which relates to the part of the Environment Code headed *Arrêtés*.

The 2003 Code had three books and a supplement. Book 1 covered the basic provisions relating to the protection of the natural environment; Book 2 covered the prevention of pollution, environmental risk and harm; Book 3 covered consultative bodies and 'various texts (sic)'. This structure was a completely artificial one in terms of the content of the three books, which were a patchwork of often-unrelated provisions. It changed in 2017 with now four Books within the code (principles, protection of the natural environment, natural resources management, and pollution management).

There is a dedicated Ministry for the environment in French Polynesia. The Minister controls an administrative body called the Department for the Environment of French Polynesia, which replaced the Agency for the Environment.[27] The Department for the Environment of French Polynesia was created by Decision No 2003-35 APF of 27 February 2003; the rules relating to Department's organisation and operation are set out in Order No 428-CM of 22 February 2005. Its purposes are listed in art 1 of the decision. The Department must:

(1) ensure the oversight and protection of the physical surroundings;
(2) ensure the conservation and valuing of protected natural spaces;
(3) ensure the classification, oversight and preservation of flora and fauna in all their diversity;
(4) implement a policy for prevention, reduction or removal of pollution and damage related to economic and human activities;
(5) contribute its technical ability and attention to the long-term goals of development in the establishment of public policies for management, equipment and urbanisation;
(6) undertake the research and studies necessary for the best possible understanding of the environment and its sustainable development;
(7) develop and put in practice programmes for public facilities at a territorial level for the protection of the environment;
(8) contribute to the development of education about the environment, training and information for users about environmental matters;
(9) ensure the promotion of environmental management within the private sector; and
(10) develop and implement regulations relating to the environment.

27 The Agency for the Environment had been created by Decision No 85-1040 AT of 30 May 1985 under Law No 84-820 of 6 September 1984.

The French Polynesian Environment Code considers the prevention of climate change as an objective only in art LP3100-3, which relates to the balanced and sustainable management of water resources, which must take into account the necessary adaptations for climate change. This idea is also present in art LP3200-1 concerning air quality, which makes clear in its last paragraph that the struggle against the increasing effect of greenhouse gases and the prevention of risks linked to climate change are matters of general interest. Independently of these internal French Polynesian provisions, the *collectivité* is party to all the international conventions relating to climate change to which France is a party.

13. NATURAL RESOURCES

The laws relating to natural resources in French Polynesia are mainly found in the Organic Law of 2004, the Environment Code, the Development Code and the Mining Code. These different areas are all within the competence of French Polynesia.

Article 47 of the Statute of French Polynesia is clear that the *collectivité* manages all its resources. This article provides:

> French Polynesia regulates and exercises conservation rights and management rights, the right to explore and the right to exploit natural biological and non-biological resources, in particular rare earths, in internal waters, in particular harbours and lagoons of the sea bed and the subsoil of the sea bed and of the marine areas adjacent to the territorial sea and the exclusive economic zone respecting international obligations.

However, there is a general exception relating to 'matters of a primarily strategic nature', which arises from the power of the State under art 14-4 of the Organic Law. The lack of detail in the definition of this notion by the rules in force should be noted.[28]

French Polynesia has competence in matters relating to mining law.[29] However, matters which are supplementary to mining law, such as penal provisions, penal procedural law, security and public order, and matters relating to strategic materials, remain the domain of the French State.[30] However, the

28 Decision of the President of the Republic and of the Overseas Community of 14 April 1959, which provided an initial list of matters classed as strategic dash capital – JORF, 18 April 1959, 4292. Also to be noted is the absence of any significant case law – this could lead to a situation where any type of resource could be regarded as relating to 'matters of a primarily strategic nature' and thus the matter would fall within the authority of the French State.

29 Law No 77-772 of 12 July 1977.

30 Article 74 of the Constitution and arts 14 and 27 of the Organic Law No 2004-192 of 27 February 2004.

Mining Code of France – which was reformed by Ordinance No 2011-91 of 20 January 2011 and is in force at the national level – is not entirely applicable to French Polynesia; in fact, French Polynesia has its own Mining Code.[31] This means that French Polynesia has competence in mining matters relating to:

(1) the legal regime for mines (Book 1);
(2) the legal regime relating to underground resources (Book 2);
(3) the legal regime relating to quarries (Book 3); and
(4) excavations and geophysical dumps (Book 4).

Various regulations relating to fishing and the environment, development and the blue economy have been put in place by French Polynesia.

As far as fishing is concerned, the waters of French Polynesia, as an OCT, are not part of the EU community fishing zone and thus not subject to European legislation. France, which is an active party in about 10 regional fishing organisations on behalf of the overseas *collectivités*, participates in those organisations as a French territorial delegation, independently of the EU, to represent the interests of metropolitan France. French Polynesia has authority in fishing matters, but the French State retains competence in relation to maritime surveillance for fishing purposes.[32]

Two main texts apply to fishing: Decision No 88-183 AT, as amended on 8 December 1988, and Decision No 88-184 AT, as amended on 8 December 1998. These two decisions relate to the protection of certain marine and freshwater species as part of the Polynesian patrimony. These decisions as amended establish the rules relating to fishing at sea and notably set out the prohibitions on machines, methods and equipment that are applicable 'at all times and all places within the French Polynesian territory', i.e. the internal waters, the territorial sea and the exclusive economic zone. Article 17bis of Decision No 88-183 AT of 8 December 1988 envisages the possibility of regulations to supplement the general rules with decisions taken by the Council of Ministers:

> With the aim of ensuring the protection of the resources of the sea, of the rivers and aquaculture and, generally all activity of economic, educational or research interest, the Council of Ministers can, on the motion of the Minister responsible for the sea and in respect of parts of the public domain which are specifically identified, establish restrictions or permanent or temporary prohibitions relating to the use of certain fishing methods and equipment.

---

31 Decision No 85-10 51 AT of 25 June 1985. This is the result, on the one hand, of art 14 of the Organic Law No 2004 192 of 27 February 2004 and, on the other hand, of an opinion of the Council of State (Public Works Section, REC, Opinion No 382.125, 25 November 2008). The Polynesian Mining Code is expected to be reviewed in full in 2020.

32 Article 49 of the Organic Law 2004.

The purpose of these regulated fishing zones (ZPR) is very broad since the goal is to 'ensure the protection of the marine resources' (not only sea fisheries but 'every activity of economic educational or research interest'). There is therefore more involved than simply the management of fisheries. However, only fishing activities can be regulated.

In respect of rules for the development of resources there is a General Plan for the Development of Maritime Areas (PGEM). The PGEM seems to closely resemble town planning rules. These rules have the purpose of ensuring the harmonious sharing of buildings in the area, or at least grouping buildings and other forms of land use in a way that will avoid the most serious problems, such as pollution, the waste of natural spaces and so on; the PGEM decides 'the conditions for the use, development, protection, and the maximising of the value of lagoons or of littoral areas'.[33] These rules take a similar form to town and country planning documents. These documents for planning are characterised as 'documents drawn up on the initiative of the local authority and which have as their purpose the establishing of rules relating to the use and occupation of land which bind public or private persons'.[34] The rules that can be established are graded and distinctions can be made relating to different zones which have different uses attributed to them. The PGEM 'determines the general role for each different zone and particularly those set aside for aquaculture, port developments and touristic and recreational activity. PGEM identifies the uses to which different parts of the lagoon or the maritime area can be put'.[35] This spatial allocation takes its formal shape in maps which are attached to the administrative regulations. This matter is covered principally in arts D.133-2 and D.133-4 of the Management Code, the PGEM itself being made up of maps and a report. Although the PGEM is an urban planning document, the Plan 'identifies the ways to protect the marine environment' and 'can prescribe particular restrictions relating to the maritime river and land areas if those are necessary for the protection of the seashore and particularly for the maintenance of biological balance'.[36] It therefore seems that the protection of species and places in the marine environment and on the seashore is also a basic objective of the PGEM. This mechanism therefore makes it possible to deal with and plan for uses of marine areas[37] within a single document.

In relation to the law on the environment, the possibilities for the protection of the marine environment and its biodiversity have been improved with the

---

33 Article D 133-1 of the Polynesian Development Code.

34 Council of State, Opinion, 17 January 1997, the Association for the Protection of the Environment Site of Galluis.

35 Article D.133-3 of the Land Use Code.

36 Article D.133-3(3) and (4) of the Land Use Code.

37 Fishing, diving, boating, jet skiing, anchorages, extractions, pearl farming, bungalows over the water, archaeological exploration, feeding of stingrays and sharks, the protection and observation of whales, the protection of the natural environment, etc.

latest reforms in French Polynesia. The government in effect had the goal of creating the most extensive 'marine managed area' (AMG) in the world. It will cover all of the exclusive economic zone of French Polynesia. This goal was achieved following the publication of a new edition of the Environment Code with a decision taken by the Council of Ministers on 3 April 2018. This creation of an immense AMG in French Polynesia is linked with the possibility of legal recognition of *rahui*. Art LP 2122-1 of the Code defines *rahui* as follows:

> *Rahui* is an area of land or of the sea over which non-written rules dictated by a management imperative are applied in a traditional manner. These rules which restrict or prohibit the exploitation of one or more of the natural resources or the cultivated resources for a specified period and in a specified area, allow the resources identified to re-establish themselves and to be self-sufficient when the *rahui* is lifted.
>
> These unwritten rules which are applied in a traditional manner cannot contradict legislation that is in force in French Polynesia and, in particular, not the provisions of this code.[38]

The notion of *rahui* is also used to specify the seasons and the size limits in relation to the taking of creatures from the sea, but this kind of control is closer to the Polynesian notion of *tapu* than to *rahui*, which relates specifically to a geographical area. The definition given in the aforementioned article is however not the same as the traditional concept of *rahui*, which has a range of application that is more limited in nature, particularly in that it is limited to 'unwritten rules'. Polynesian communities did not wait for the integration of this notion into the Environment Code of French Polynesia and created *rahui* following the models used in the islands of Rapaiti or Maiao. Nevertheless, the inclusion of this traditional notion into the Polynesian legal corpus is a rare demonstration of the integration of a mechanism originating in a popular initiative being converted or taken over by the central government authorities.

14. CRIMINAL LAW

Under the Organic Law of 27 February 2004, all criminal matters fall within the competence of the State, in accordance with arts 73 and 74 of the Constitution. This allows the authorities of French Polynesia to establish, within certain limits, penalties for lesser offences. The provisions are brought together in the Penal Code and the Penal Procedure Code, both of which are French national law.

The criminal law in its entirety is subject to the principle of legislative specialty, and therefore the general provisions of the Penal Code and the penal provisions

---

38 Article LP2122-1 of the Environment Code.

in special legislation[39] are governed by the specialty regime. Thus, depending on whether the legislator has taken the steps necessary to provide expressly for the application of norms in French Polynesia, the general criminal law in force in French Polynesia could be significantly different from the provisions applicable elsewhere in the State – at least for the period of time that it takes the legislator to remedy the situation.

15. INTERNATIONAL LAW

The international obligations of France can have an impact on the authority of French Polynesia and generally on the overseas *collectivités* governed by art 74 of the French Constitution, despite the constitutional rules which require an Organic Law to determine their powers and, since the constitutional revision of 28 March 2003, to establish the 'conditions under which Acts and Regulations are applicable'. The Constitutional Council determined that the constitutional revision of 25 June 1992 led to the need for an Organic Law to establish the authority of French Polynesia:

> neither the purpose nor the effect of amending article 53 of the Constitution in relation to the international obligations of France which, whatever their field of application territorially as determined by provisions or rules of the international organisation under which they were established, is subordinated to approval given by an ordinary law.[40]

Furthermore, 'the field of territorial application of a treaty is determined by its provisions or by the rules of the international organisation under whose authority it was concluded; determining its field of application is therefore not a matter for the law which ratifies it'; in the absence of an express provision or indications to the contrary, such a treaty is applicable in French Polynesia. Some treaties provide a 'territorial clause' that the French government can, by a declaration at the time of depositing the instrument of ratification, extend the effects of the treaty to the non-metropolitan territories for whose international relations France is responsible; this is particularly the case in relation to the European Convention on Human Rights.

Although French Polynesia does not have any authority in matters of 'foreign affairs', or international relations more generally, it is permitted to participate in the exercise of that power by France. Thus, French Polynesia is a member in its own right of the Pacific Islands Forum, of the Secretariat of the Pacific

39 This does not always apply in French Polynesia given the power-sharing between France and French Polynesia.

40 Constitutional Council, No 92-312, 2 September 1992.

Community and of the Polynesian Leaders Group (PLG).[41] The PLG adopted the Taputapuatea Declaration on 16 July 2015 and the Declaration on the Ocean Te Moana O Hiva (People of the Ocean) on 28 June 2016. These two Declarations confirm the importance of the ocean for the cultural identity and social cohesion of all Polynesians and consequently the need to protect it and its rich biodiversity. French Polynesia is also a member of the Ocean Pathway Initiative, which was promoted officially by Fiji at COP23 in Bonn. The purpose of this Initiative is to have the existing links between the ocean and climate change recognised in the process of the United Nations Framework Convention on Climate Change (UNFCCC). French Polynesia participates in international negotiations on biodiversity beyond national jurisdictions under the authority of the United Nations.[42]

16. CIVIL SOCIETY ORGANISATIONS

The right to associate is a fundamental freedom and a matter for the French State. The Constitutional Council has recognised that the freedom of association is a fundamental principle recognised by the laws of France and forms part of the body of basic constitutional provisions.[43] The Constitutional Council stated expressly that the principle of freedom of association is at the basis of the general legal provisions of 1 July 1901 relating to the contract of association. French Polynesia therefore has no control over these matters.

Following the promulgation of the law of 9 December 1905 relating to the separation of Church and State, France is a secular state in the sense that it does not recognise, pay for or subsidise any religion. The law of separation of Church and State of 1905 does not however apply in French Polynesia, even though the principle of secularism is one that has constitutional value. That constitutional value applies throughout French territory, the overseas parts included. Moreover, this matter is within the competence of the French State as matter of fundamental freedom. In effect, what is guaranteed is the freedom of conscience and the freedom to manifest religious belief. To this end, French law allows each religion to be self-regulating to the extent that this self-regulation does not run counter to the rules of the Republic. Religious freedom presupposes the freedom

---

41 The PLG was created on 19 November 2011 by a Memorandum of Understanding made at Apia, Samoa as an organisation for inter-governmental cooperation in the Polynesian region.

42 Resolution No 72/249 of 24 December 2017. A preparatory committee was created by United Nations resolution 69/292 of 19 June 2015 to prepare an international document that would legally constrain states and lead to the conservation and sustainable use of the marine resources within state jurisdictions. In 2017 the General Assembly of the United Nations resolved at an inter-governmental conference to examine the recommendation of the working party.

43 Constitutional Council, Decision of 16 July 1971.

of each person to express their religion, to practise it and to renounce it with due respect for public order. This means that in the State, French Polynesia and its public services, neutrality is guaranteed vis-à-vis all religions and all beliefs. In other words, the public authority can never discriminate between those using public services on the basis of those users' beliefs.

BIBLIOGRAPHY

Conte, Eric et al (eds) *Une histoire de Tahiti. Des origines à nos jours* (A Story of Tahiti. From the origins to our days) (Aux vents des îles, 2019).

Moyrand, Alain *Droit administratif de la Polynésie française* (Administrative law of French Polynesia) (L'Harmattan, 2018) Vols 1 and 2.

Moyrand, Alain and A H Angelo 'Administrative Regimes of French Overseas Territories: New Caledonia and French Polynesia' (2010) Comparative Law Journal of the Pacific, Hors Serie Vol X: *Gouvernance et autonomie dans les Societes du Pacifique Sud: Etudes Comparees/Governance and Self-Reliance in Pacific Island Societies: Comparative Studies*, 193.

Moyrand, Alain and Herve Raimana Lallemant-Moe *Introduction à l'étude des institutions politiques et administratives de la Polynésie française* (Introduction to the political and administrative institutions of French Polynesia) (2nd ed, Creaprint, 2020).

Ntumy, Michael A 'French Polynesia' in Michael A Ntumy (ed) *South Pacific Islands Legal Systems* (University of Hawaii Press, 1993).

Regnault, Jean-Marc *Tahiti tu connais ?* (You know of Tahiti?) (Api Tahiti, 2021).

KIRIBATI

Jennifer CORRIN

1. BACKGROUND

Prior to colonisation, Kiribati, then known as the Gilbert Islands, was regulated by custom and the orders of individual chiefs. The Gilbert Islands, together with the Ellice Islands, became a British Protectorate in 1893.[1] Constituent laws were issued by the British Crown in Letters Patent, Orders in Council, and Royal Instructions.[2] In 1915, the Gilbert and Ellice Islands became a colony, which also included the Union Islands (present-day Tokelau).[3] The normal British practice of appointing a Governor was not followed; instead the colony was governed by the High Commissioner of the Western Pacific, who was stationed in Fiji until 1950 and then in Solomon Islands. In the 1960s, in the lead-up to independence, a Resident Commissioner was authorised to make Ordinances for the colony, with the advice and consent of an advisory council, and later a governing council. In 1975, the Ellice Islands became the separate colony of Tuvalu,[4] and Gilbert Islands got its own Constitution.[5] An elected House of

---

1 Pacific Order in Council 1893 (UK).

2 These were issued both under the legal authority granted by the common law to the British Crown to make constituent laws for overseas territories not settled by British citizens, and also under the legal authority provided by the Pacific Islanders' Protection Acts 1872 and 1875, and the Foreign Jurisdiction Act 1890 (UK).

3 Gilbert and Ellice Islands Order 1915 (UK).

4 Tuvalu Order 1975 (UK).

5 Gilbert Islands Order 1975 (UK), as amended by Gilbert Islands (Amendment) Order 1976; Gilbert Islands (Amendment) Order 1977; and Gilbert Islands (Amendment) (No 2) Order 1977.

Assembly was established to advise the Resident Commissioner. The Gilbertese retained sole possession of the Revenue Equalization Reserve Fund, established in 1956 in anticipation of the expected exhaustion of phosphate minerals.[6] Kiribati achieved independence in 1979.[7]

2. SOURCES OF LAW

2.1. STATE LAWS

During the colonial era, 'the substance of the law for the time being in force in England' was applied to Gilbert and Ellice Islands.[8] This was later amended to 'the statutes of general application in force in England on the 1st day of January 1961' and 'the substance of the English common law and doctrines of equity'.[9] The courts are expressly stated not to be bound by any decision of an overseas court handed down after 1989.[10] The English laws were all stated to be in force only so far as they were not inappropriate to the circumstances of the Gilbert Islands. In addition, a number of specific, named statutes of the British Parliament were applied to the country. Locally, regulations were made by the High Commissioner of the Western Pacific and Ordinances by the Resident Commissioner.

At independence, these laws were retained in force.[11] There is a cut-off date of 1 January 1961 for English statutes[12] and probably for common law and equity as well.[13] The Laws of Kiribati Act 1989 contains a process for patriating United Kingdom Acts that require little adaptation. Patriation is to be carried out through adaption by the Attorney-General and presentation to the Maneaba ni Maungatabu.[14] Examples of patriated laws are the Arbitration Act,[15] the Aircraft Security Act 1990, and legislation patriated by the Criminal Law and Procedure (Patriation) Act 1991. More recently, some United Kingdom Acts

---

6 The RERF is now deemed to have been established under the Public Finance (Control and Audit) Ordinance Cap 79, s 12. See further, Asian Development Bank *Revenue Equalization Reserve Fund: Overview* <https://www.adb.org/sites/default/files/linked-documents/47314-001-sd-03.pdf>.

7 Kiribati Independence Order 1979 (UK).

8 Pacific Order in Council 1893 (UK), s 20.

9 Western Pacific (Courts) Order 1961 (UK), s 15.

10 Laws of Kiribati Act 1989, s 13(2).

11 Kiribati Independence Order 1979, s 5.

12 Laws of Kiribati Act 1989, s 7(1).

13 Laws of Kiribati Act 1989, s 13(2). See further Jennifer Corrin and Don Paterson *Introduction to South Pacific Law* (4th ed, Intersentia, 2017) 40–42.

14 Laws of Kiribati Act 1989, ss 8–12.

15 Applied Law No 1 of 1990.

have been repealed and replaced by locally drafted Acts, rather than patriated. Examples are the Evidence Act 2003, the Limitation Act 2004 and the Statutory Declarations Act 2015.

2.2. CUSTOMARY LAW

Customary law is defined as meaning 'the customs and usages, existing from time to time, of the natives of Kiribati'.[16] The written law makes express provision for customary law to be taken into account by all courts when considering specified matters. In criminal proceedings those matters are:

- the existence of a state of mind;
- the reasonableness of a person's action or inaction;
- whether or not a conviction should be entered;
- the penalty that should be imposed; and
- any other matter where an injustice may be done if customary law is not taken into account.[17]

In civil proceedings, the courts must take account of customary laws in considering the following matters:

- ownership or possession of land, lagoons, reefs, the seabed and water;
- administration, devolution or partition of customary land;
- defamation;
- legitimacy, legitimisation or adoption of children;
- custody and guardianship of children;
- rights arising from marriage or termination of marriage;
- rights of support from family members;
- duties of community members to contribute to community projects;
- any transaction that was intended by the parties, or which justice requires, to be regulated by custom;
- the reasonableness of a person's action or inaction;
- the existence of a state of mind; and
- any other matter where an injustice may be done if customary law is not taken into account.[18]

---

16 Laws of Kiribati Act 1989, s 5(1).
17 Laws of Kiribati Act 1989, Sch 1, para 3.
18 Laws of Kiribati Act 1989, Sch 1, para 4.

Customary law does not apply if it is inconsistent with the Constitution or legislation,[19] or where its application 'would result … in injustice or would not be in the public interest'.[20] On the other hand, customary laws prevail over common law and equity,[21] and, as discussed below, particularly in relation to decisions regarding children.[22]

Where customary laws conflict, the court may adopt the rules of customary law or of the common law, with such modifications 'as the justice of the case requires'.[23]

3. CONSTITUTIONAL LAW

3.1. THE CONSTITUTION

The Constitution of Kiribati was drafted by the UK Foreign and Commonwealth Office and was enacted as a Schedule to an Order of the British Privy Council.[24] It came into effect on 12 July 1979. The Constitution commences with a prefatory provision setting out the basic values underpinning the Constitution, in the following terms:

> We the people of Kiribati, acknowledging God as the Almighty Father in whom we put our trust, and with faith in the enduring value of our tradition and heritage, do now grant ourselves this Constitution establishing a sovereign democratic State. In implementing this Constitution, we declare that–
>
> 1. the will of the people shall ultimately be paramount in the conduct of the government of Kiribati;
> 2. the principles of equality and justice shall be upheld;
> 3. the natural resources of Kiribati are vested in the people and their Government;
> 4. we shall continue to cherish and uphold the customs and traditions of Kiribati.

The enacting parts of the Constitution commence with a declaration of Kiribati as a sovereign democratic state[25] and the establishment of the Constitution as

19 Laws of Kiribati Act 1989, s 5(2). See eg *Koru v Tabiteuea Meang Island Council* [2020] KIHC 30.
20 Laws of Kiribati Act 1989, Sch 1, para 2.
21 Laws of Kiribati Act 1989, s 6(3)(b); Laws of Tuvalu Act 1987, s 6(3)(b).
22 Laws of Kiribati Act 1989, Sch 1, para 5.
23 Laws of Kiribati Act 1989, Sch 1, para 6.
24 Kiribati Independence Order 1979 (UK).
25 Constitution of Kiribati 1979, s 1.

the supreme law of Kiribati.[26] This is followed by a Bill of Rights, modelled on the Universal Declaration of Human Rights 1948, and the European Convention for the Protection of Human Rights and Fundamental Freedoms 1950. The following rights and freedoms are guaranteed, subject to specified exceptions:[27]

- life, liberty and protection from slavery and forced labour;
- freedom from torture and inhuman and degrading treatment;
- protection from deprivation of property;
- freedom from search and entry;
- protection of the law in relation to alleged criminal offences and certain other matters;
- protection of freedom of conscience, expression, assembly and association, and movement; and
- protection from discrimination and inequality of treatment on the grounds of race, place of origin, political opinions, colour or creed.[28]

The Constitution also establishes the executive, legislative and judicial branches of government, the public service, and public finance controls. It provides for amendment, suspension and repeal of the Constitution. Transitional provisions provide for the continued existence of laws and public officers and institutions, with certain specific exceptions.

3.2. THE HEAD OF STATE AND THE EXECUTIVE

The head of state, called Te Beretitenti, is also the head of government.[29] Te Beretitenti is elected directly by the electorate from a panel of three or four persons drawn from and selected by the legislature via a preferential ballot.[30] Te Beretitenti may be removed from office by a vote of no confidence in the legislature.[31]

Whilst there are some similarities with the Westminster model of executive government, ministers are appointed and dismissible by Te Beretitenti, rather than by a prime minister.[32] Te Beretitenti also convenes and presides

---

26 Constitution of Kiribati 1979, s 2.

27 Constitution of Kiribati 1979, Chap II.

28 Constitution of Kiribati 1979, s 15. Interestingly gender is not mentioned in this section, but it is included in the introductory section of Chapter II: s 3. For a discussion of this section see Jennifer Corrin and Don Paterson *Introduction to South Pacific Law* (4th ed, Intersentia, 2017) 90–91.

29 Constitution of Kiribati 1979, s 30(2).

30 Constitution of Kiribati 1979, ss 32–33; Election of Beretitenti Act Cap 29A, ss 4–6.

31 Constitution of Kiribati 1979, s 33.

32 Constitution of Kiribati 1979, ss 30–36 and 39–41.

over meetings of Cabinet to determine government policy.[33] The executive may be removed by a motion of no confidence passed by a majority of all Members of Parliament.[34]

3.3. THE LEGISLATURE

Kiribati's legislature is relatively large, with 46 members. It is an elected unicameral house called the Maneaba ni Maungatabu. It is empowered to enact legislation with the assent of the head of state. The Constitution provides for separate electoral rolls and constituencies based on ethnicity. The assent of Te Beretitenti is required in order for a Bill which has been approved by the legislature to become law.[35] However, Te Beretitenti must assent or refer the Bill to the courts to determine its constitutionality.[36]

Legislation to amend the Constitution requires a special majority of two-thirds of voters.[37]

3.4. THE JUDICIARY

The Constitution of Kiribati establishes the High Court and Court of Appeal and provides for the appointment and tenure of judges,[38] giving the judiciary the protection of the supreme law. However, it allows judges of the High Court and Court of Appeal to be appointed for a limited term.[39] This reflects the fact that the Chief Justice is recruited from overseas on a contractual appointment, and the Court of Appeal is made up of judges from overseas, who visit for a sitting about once a year.

Appointment of the Chief Justice is by Te Beretitenti, acting in accordance with the advice of Cabinet after consultation with the Public Service Commission.[40] Additional judges are appointed in the same way, but also with the advice of the Chief Justice.[41] The judges of the Court of Appeal are the Chief Justice and other High Court judges, together with judges appointed by Te Beretitenti,[42] acting in

---

33 Constitution of Kiribati 1979, ss 39–48.
34 Known as the Maneaba ni Maungatabu: Constitution of Kiribati 1979, s 78(1); see *Takataake v Attorney-General* [2003] KICA 4.
35 Constitution of Kiribati 1979, s 66(2).
36 Constitution of Kiribati 1979, s 66(3)–(6).
37 Constitution of Kiribati 1979, s 69(3).
38 Constitution of Kiribati 1979, Part VI.
39 Constitution of Kiribati 1979, ss 83(1) and 91(2).
40 Constitution of Kiribati 1979, s 81(1).
41 Constitution of Kiribati 1979, s 81(2).
42 Constitution of Kiribati 1979, s 30(1).

accordance with the advice of the Chief Justice sitting with the Public Service Commission.[43]

Judges may be removed before the expiry of their term only on the recommendation of an independent tribunal of inquiry, and only on grounds of incapacity, inability to perform the functions of office, or misbehaviour.[44]

3.5. THE LEGAL PROFESSION

The head of the legal profession is the Attorney-General, who is a constitutional officer appointed by Te Beretitenti and is a legal advisor to the government.[45]

The Constitution establishes a Rules Committee, which is responsible for regulating the admission of legal practitioners.[46] In 1992, the Committee made the Lawyers' Admission (Amendment) Rules (No 2), which provide that candidates for admission must obtain a certificate of qualification from the Attorney-General[47] and then be admitted to practice by the Chief Justice.[48] Discipline of the profession is dealt with by the Kiribati Law Society.[49]

The Office of the People's Lawyer provides free legal advice and assistance to people in Kiribati who are unable to pay a private lawyer. In 2018, the Public Legal Services Act gave the Office legal status as an independent government body reporting to the Minister for Justice.

3.6. THE COURTS

The court structure in Kiribati consists of an inferior court (the Magistrates' Court), established by statute,[50] and a superior court (the High Court) and the Court of Appeal, established by the Constitution.[51] In South Tarawa, a Youth Justice Court and Family Court were established in 2019.[52] There is a possible additional appeal to the Privy Council in England on a limited range of matters.[53]

---

43 Constitution of Kiribati 1979, s 91(1).
44 Constitution of Kiribati 1979, ss 83 and 93.
45 Constitution of Kiribati 1979, s 42.
46 Constitution of Kiribati 1979, s 97.
47 Lawyers' Admission (Amendment) Rules (No 2), r 3.
48 Lawyers' Admission (Amendment) Rules (No 2), r 4.
49 Kiribati Law Society Act 2006. See also Professional Conduct & Practice (Kiribati Lawyers) Rules 2011.
50 Magistrates' Courts Ordinance Cap 52.
51 Constitution of Kiribati 1979, ss 81 and 90.
52 Chief Magistrate *Draft Concept Paper for Independent Inquiry Magistracy Division, Judiciary Kiribati* (6 December 2020).
53 Constitution of Kiribati 1979, s 123.

3.6.1. *Constitution*

The Court of Appeal is constituted by the Chief Justice and other judges of the High Court.[54] It must sit with no fewer than three judges.[55] The High Court is constituted by the Chief Justice and other judges.[56] Magistrates' Courts dealing with civil or criminal matters are composed of three magistrates sitting together, one of whom is the presiding magistrate,[57] except in South Tarawa and Christmas Island, where a single magistrate may preside.[58] In land cases five magistrates must sit.[59] There are currently three legally qualified magistrates and over 120 lay magistrates. In June 2019, arrangements were introduced to separate the administration of the Magistrates' Courts from the High Court.[60]

3.6.2. *Jurisdiction*

The Privy Council has jurisdiction to hear appeals from any High Court decision which involves the interpretation of the Constitution where application to the High Court was made on the basis of contravention of the rights of any Banaban or of the Rabi Council under Chapters III or IX of the Constitution.[61]

The Court of Appeal has jurisdiction to hear appeals as of right from any decision of the High Court exercising original civil jurisdiction.[62] It also has jurisdiction to hear appeals from the High Court with leave in certain other civil cases.[63] In criminal cases, appeals from convictions by the Supreme Court are as of right on a question of law, or otherwise with leave of the Court of Appeal.[64] Where the High Court is exercising appellate jurisdiction, the Court of Appeal has jurisdiction to hear appeals on a question of law or a question of mixed fact and law.[65]

The High Court has unlimited original jurisdiction.[66] It is specifically empowered to determine questions as to the interpretation of the Constitution,[67]

---

54 Constitution of Kiribati 1979, s 80(2).
55 Court of Appeal Act Cap 16B, s 5(1).
56 Constitution of Kiribati 1979, s 80(2).
57 Constitution of Kiribati 1979, s 7(1).
58 Acting Chief Registrar *Annual Report on the Judiciary of Kiribati* (2012 to 2014) 36.
59 Constitution of Kiribati 1979, s 7(4).
60 Chief Magistrate *Draft Concept Paper for Independent Inquiry Magistracy Division, Judiciary Kiribati* (6 December 2020) 1–2.
61 Constitution of Kiribati 1979 1979, s 123.
62 Court of Appeal Act Cap 16B, s 10(1)(a).
63 Court of Appeal Act Cap 16B, s 10(2).
64 Court of Appeal Act Cap 16B, s 19.
65 Court of Appeal Act Cap 16B, ss 10(1)(b) and 21 (as amended by the Court of Appeal (Amendment) Act 2010, s 7. See further *Mataio v Republic* [2019] KICA 10).
66 Criminal Procedure Code Cap 17, s 4.
67 Constitution of Kiribati 1979, s 88(6).

and alleged breaches of the Constitution.[68] It also has exclusive jurisdiction to determine questions as to the membership of Parliament.[69]

Appeals lie to the High Court as of right from decisions of a Magistrates' Court exercising its jurisdiction in divorce,[70] in claims exceeding $20,[71] in land cases,[72] and in criminal cases.[73] The High Court is also empowered to determine disputes as to the validity of election of any member of the Maneaba ni Maungatabu and as to vacation of seats.[74] Cases may also be reviewed by the High Court,[75] referred to by way of case stated and the High Court may 'confirm, reverse or vary' the Magistrates' Court's decision.[76]

Magistrates' Courts may exercise jurisdiction within the district within which they are situated.[77] They may determine petitions for divorce and adoption where the parties are I-Kiribati, and actions in contract or tort where the amount in issue is under $8,000,[78] and disputes concerning customary land and associated matters.[79] The jurisdiction may be extended by the Chief Justice[80] or statute to empower it to deal with specific matters.[81] They may also deal with criminal offences where the maximum punishment is a fine of $500 and five years' imprisonment and certain other specified offences.[82]

3.6.3. Procedure

Criminal procedure is governed by the Criminal Procedure Code.[83] Civil procedure is governed by the High Court (Civil Procedure) Rules 1964.[84]

Specific provision is made for the determination of questions as to the existence and applicability of customary laws. They are to be determined as matters of law, and courts may consult reported cases, treatises, works of reference or official reports and statements made by local government councils, and may

---

68 Constitution of Kiribati 1979, s 88.

69 Constitution of Kiribati 1979, s 60(1) and (4).

70 Magistrates' Courts Ordinance Cap 52, s 66(1)(a).

71 Magistrates' Courts Ordinance Cap 52, s 66(1)(b). The currency referred to in this chapter is the Kiribati dollar, which is pegged at a 1:1 ratio to the Australian dollar.

72 Magistrates' Courts Ordinance Cap 52, s 75(1).

73 Magistrates' Courts Ordinance Cap 52, Part IX.

74 Constitution of Kiribati 1979, s 60.

75 Magistrates' Courts Ordinance Cap 52, s 81(1). See eg *R v Naaua* [1979] Kiribati LR 24.

76 Magistrates' Courts Ordinance Cap 52, s 280.

77 Magistrates' Courts Ordinance Cap 52, s 4.

78 Magistrates' Courts Ordinance Cap 52, s 23 and Sch 1, as amended.

79 Magistrates' Courts Ordinance Cap 52, s 23 and Sch 3.

80 Magistrates' Courts Ordinance Cap 52, s 23(2).

81 See eg Extension of All Magistrates' Courts Jurisdiction Order 1979.

82 Magistrates' Courts Ordinance Cap 52, s 23 and Sch 2.

83 Cap 17.

84 High Court (Civil Procedure) Rules 1964 (UK), O 61.

admit and consider such evidence, including hearsay evidence and expressions of opinion, and otherwise inform themselves as they think fit, without being bound by strict legal procedure or the technical rules of evidence.[85] However, the civil procedure rules require custom to be expressly pleaded, in the same way as matters of fact.[86]

3.7. JUDICIAL REVIEW

Leave of the High Court is required before a substantive application for judicial review is filed.[87] Applications for judicial review are made to the High Court and require leave may be granted ex parte. The application for leave must be accompanied by a supporting statement setting out the relief that is sought and the grounds for that relief, which must be verified by affidavit.

4. THE LAW OF PERSONS

4.1. MARRIAGE

There are two statutory regimes of marriage. Marriage between indigenous parties is governed by local legislation.[88] Marriage between expatriates is governed by colonial Orders in Council.[89] Customary marriage is also recognised, although this is not expressly provided for in legislation.[90]

There are several prerequisites to the formation of a valid marriage, including the following:

- parties to a marriage are required to have reached 18 years;[91] both parents must consent to the marriage of a person under 21;[92]

---

85 Laws of Kiribati Act 1989, Sch 1, para 1.

86 High Court (Civil Procedure) Rules 1964 (WP), O 21 r 6. See eg *Nakau v Attorney-General* [2013] KIHC 41.

87 High Court (Civil Procedure) Rules 1964 (UK), O 61.

88 Marriage Ordinance Cap 54 (Kiribati). The Ordinance does not explicitly exclude expatriates from its ambit, and in practice they seem to have a choice between the local Act and the colonial orders.

89 Pacific Order 1893 (UK), Part XV and Pacific Islands Civil Marriages Order 1907 (UK).

90 But see Salaries and Allowances of Members of Maneaba Ni Maungatabu and Salaries Tribunal (Amendment) Act 2002, which defines 'spouse' to mean a partner in marriage formed under the Marriage Ordinance or recognised by custom: s 2.

91 Marriage Ordinance Cap 54, s 5, as amended by Marriage (Amendment) Act 2002 (Kiribati), s 2.

92 Marriage Ordinance Cap 54, s 7, as amended by Marriage (Amendment) Act 2002 (Kiribati), s 3.

- parties within close blood relationships or close marriage relationships set out in the Marriage Acts may not marry;[93] and
- formalities, which include:
  - 21 days' notice;[94]
  - issue of a certificate of marriage or a licence;[95]
  - two witnesses to the ceremony, which must take place at a specified place and between specified times.[96]

Marriages may only be performed by registered ministers of religion or lay preachers,[97] or a registrar.[98]

4.2. TERMINATION OF MARRIAGE

Marriages may be terminated by a declaration of nullity of the marriage, or a decree of dissolution (divorce). Grounds for divorce are still fault-based for expatriates,[99] but there is a mixture of fault and no-fault grounds for I-Kiribati.[100] The main fault based grounds are adultery, cruelty and desertion.[101] The minimum period of desertion required to found a ground of divorce is three years.[102] Three additional grounds are the respondent's wilful refusal to or incapability of consummating the marriage;[103] being of unsound mind for five years continuously prior to the presentation of the petition;[104] and, for divorcing expatriates, a conviction for rape, sodomy or bestiality on the part of the respondent husband.[105] I-Kiribati parties may also petition for divorce on the basis of incompatibility.[106]

Collusion, condonation, connivance or conduct inducing or contributing to the wrong complained of are discretionary bars to a grant of divorce for expatriates.[107] In the case of condonation and connivance, the bar is absolute,

93 Marriage Ordinance Cap 54, s 4 and Sch 1, as amended by Marriage (Amendment) Act 2002 (Kiribati), s 5.
94 Marriage Ordinance Cap 54, Part III.
95 Marriage Ordinance Cap 54, ss 9 and 11.
96 Marriage Ordinance Cap 54 (Kiribati), ss 14 and 15.
97 Marriage Ordinance Cap 54, ss 3 and 14.
98 Marriage Ordinance Cap 54, s 3.
99 Matrimonial Causes Act 1950 (UK), s 4.
100 Native Divorce Ordinance Cap 60, s 4.
101 Native Divorce Ordinance Cap 60, s 4.
102 Native Divorce Ordinance Cap 60, s 4(b); Matrimonial Causes Act 1950 (UK), s 1(b).
103 Native Divorce Ordinance Cap 60, s 4(d).
104 Native Divorce Ordinance Cap 60, s 4(e); Matrimonial Causes Act 1950 (UK), s 1(d).
105 Matrimonial Causes Act 1950 (UK), s 1.
106 Native Divorce Ordinance Cap 60, s 4(j).
107 Matrimonial Causes Act 1950 (UK), s 4.

rather than discretionary.[108] The legislation governing divorce between I-Kiribati does not refer to any bars.[109] Expatriates may also obtain a decree of judicial separation, which authorises them to live apart.[110]

Customary marriages must be terminated in accordance with custom. There are no fixed 'grounds' for divorce. Rather, this will depend on the customs of the group in which the parties live and may be a matter to be negotiated between relatives and traditional leaders, although the wishes and behaviour of the parties are likely to be taken into account.

4.3. FINANCIAL PROVISION

There is no authority to make a maintenance order under the Native Divorce Ordinance,[111] but there is provision under the Maintenance (Miscellaneous Provisions) Ordinance.[112] The Ordinance empowers a court to make an order for maintenance of any person if satisfied that there is a legal or customary obligation to do so.[113]

There is no legislation empowering the courts to adjust property rights on divorce. The Married Woman's Property Act 1882 (UK), which may apply in Kiribati as an Act of general application, does not give the court power to change defined rights. Notwithstanding, the High Court has been prepared to make such orders.[114]

4.4. CHILDREN

The Laws of Kiribati Act 1989 provides that customary laws are to prevail over the principles of common law in relation to the legitimacy, legitimation and adoption of children, and in relation to the custody or guardianship of children.[115] This is of particular significance in view of the reluctance of other Pacific island courts to apply customs or customary law in decisions relating to the custody and guardianship of children, preferring instead to regard the best interests of the child as the predominant consideration.[116]

---

108 Matrimonial Causes Act 1950 (UK), s 4.
109 Native Divorce Ordinance Cap 60.
110 Matrimonial Causes Act 1950 (UK), s 14.
111 Cap 60.
112 Cap 53, s 3.
113 Maintenance (Miscellaneous Provisions) Ordinance Cap 53, s 3(1).
114 *Boitou v Ieremia* [2005] KIHC 52.
115 Laws of Kiribati Act 1989, Sch 1, para 5.
116 See eg *Sasango v Beliga* [1987] SILR 91.

4.5. CUSTODY

The Custody of Children Ordinance[117] empowers the court to make such custody order as it thinks fit on an application by any person.[118] The guiding principle is that the court must act in the best interests of the child,[119] but this is subject to the application of customary law.[120]

4.6. ADOPTION

State adoptions are governed by the Adoption Act 1958 (UK).[121] Under this Act, the court must be satisfied that the order is for the welfare of the child. However, as with custody orders, customary law may be applied in any proceedings relating to statutory adoption if the court thinks that an injustice would otherwise be done, and will override any common law principles.[122]

Adoption under customary law is also recognised in Kiribati.[123] Customary adoptions must be approved and registered by the Magistrates' Court in order to be recognised by the State.[124]

5. LAW OF OBLIGATIONS

5.1. TORTS

The law of torts is derived from the common law of England.[125] The courts of Kiribati have not created their own jurisprudence in this area. An exception is *Teitinnang v Ariong*,[126] where a claim for breach of the right to freedom of movement was dismissed on the basis that the right was not enforceable amongst individuals. However, the court was prepared to grant an injunction on the basis that the restriction imposed by the village elders on the plaintiff banning him and his family from the village amounted to unlawful interference with his legal rights.

117 Cap 21.
118 Cap 21, s 3.
119 Custody of Children Ordinance Cap 21, s 3(1) and (3).
120 Laws of Kiribati Act 1989, Sch 1, para 5.
121 *Clark v Mote* [2003] KIHC 37 refers to the Adoption of Children Act 1926 (UK).
122 Laws of Kiribati Act 1989, Sch 1, paras 4 and 5.
123 Native Lands Ordinance Cap 61, s 2. See also eg *Kakianako v Maua* [2007] KIHC 96. *Tuiko v Waueri* [1997] KIHC 62.
124 Magistrates' Court Ordinance Cap 52, ss 61 and 64(1)(d).
125 Laws of Kiribati Act 1989, s 6(1).
126 [1987] LRC (Const) 517.

There is some legislation of relevance in the field of torts. The Occupiers' Liability Act 1957 (UK) imposes a duty to take reasonable care to ensure that premises are reasonably safe for the purposes for which invitees or licensees are permitted to enter. The Defamation Act 1952 (UK) is also theoretically in force, but the courts appear to rely on the common law.[127] Another example is the Dogs Act 1906 (UK), which renders the owner of a dog liable for any injury done by the dog to farm animals or poultry, regardless of whether the dog is known to be dangerous.[128]

Claims against the government in tort are regulated by the Government Liability Act 2010.[129] A statutory compensation scheme has been introduced for employees injured at work. The scheme is modelled on the Workmen's Compensation Act 1897 (UK).[130]

5.2. CONTRACT

The law of contract is derived from the common law and equity.[131] The courts in Kiribati mainly apply the English common law, but have followed the Australian law as developed in *Waltons Stores (Interstate) Ltd v Maher*,[132] which allows estoppel to operate as a right, rather than only as a defence.[133]

The Consumer Protection Act 2001, as amended in 2009,[134] implies certain terms into consumer contracts.[135] Claims against the government in contract are regulated by the Government Liability Act 2010.

There are also some relevant United Kingdom Acts in force.[136] These include the Sale of Goods Acts 1893 (UK), and the Law of Property Acts 1925 (UK), as amended by the Law Reform (Enforcement of Contracts) Act 1954 (UK). The Law Reform (Frustrated Contracts) Act 1943 (UK) would appear to apply, but the courts have gone their own way with its interpretation, allowing increased expense to justify a finding of frustration.[137]

---

127 See eg *Orme v Schutz* [1979] Kiribati LR 102; *Doucet v Marshall* [1979] Kiribati LR 115.

128 Dogs Act 1906 (UK), s 1.

129 See eg *Angiraoi v Attorney-General* [2018] KIHC 42.

130 Workmen's Compensation Act Cap 94 (Fiji); Workmen's Compensation Ordinance Cap 102 (Kiribati); Workers' Compensation Ordinance 1956–67 (Nauru); Workmen's Compensation Act Cap 78 (Solomon Islands); Workmen's Compensation Ordinance Cap 83 (Tuvalu).

131 Laws of Kiribati Act 1989, s 6(1).

132 (1984) 164 CLR 387. See also *Commonwealth of Australia v Verwayen* (1990) 170 CLR 394.

133 *Nubono v Attorney-General* [2006] KIHC 16.

134 Consumer Protection (Amendment) Act 2009.

135 See eg *Bongia v Manager TTT Enterprises* [2015] KIHC 37.

136 Constitution of Kiribati 1979, s 5, read with Western Pacific (Courts) Order 1961 (UK), s 15.

137 *Kiribati Supplies Company Ltd v Raiha* [2010] KIHC 46.

The courts take an objective approach in determining whether a contract has been entered into.[138] However, the objective test is applied in the context of local circumstances. For example, in *Compass Rose v Taomati Iuta*,[139] in considering whether there had been a meeting of the minds, the court took into account the fact that shaking hands was not a Kiribati custom and had no significance.

5.3. RESTITUTION

Restitution is part of the law introduced into Kiribati within the field of unjust enrichment, which has been received in Kiribati as one of the principles of equity.[140]

6. PROPERTY LAW

6.1. LAND LAW

During the colonial period most customary land was subject to compulsory systematic registration. About 45 per cent of the land is still under customary tenure; about 50 per cent is public and some five per cent is freehold.[141] Customary land is often held by a group of families or extended families, called a *kaainga*. However, individual ownership is not uncommon.[142] Traditionally, customary land could be acquired as a means of compensation; in return for sexual favours; as recompense for providing care; to acknowledge an adopted child; or through exchange between landowners on different islands. Alienation of customary land to indigenous persons now requires court approval.[143] Transfer to foreigners is prohibited.[144]

Legislation provides for land disputes to be determined in accordance with customary law.[145] However, there is evidence that, historically, courts

138 See eg *Kiribati Shipping Services Ltd v Waysang Kum Kee* [2009] KICA 15, [18].

139 Unreported, High Court, Kiribati, 14 May 1982.

140 See eg *Tabuanaba v Teitoi* [2007] KIHC 81; *Takiro v Tiimi* [2004] KICA 5.

141 AusAID *Making Land Work* (AusAID, vol 1) 4.

142 Whilst an individual may be registered as owner of land, in reality, residual rights still remain with the community: Pole Atanraoi 'Customary land and development in an Atoll Nation – the case of Kiribati' in Ron Crocombe (ed) *Customary Land Tenure and Sustainable Development: Complementarity or Conflict* (SPC, 1995) 64–65.

143 Magistrates' Courts Act Cap 52, s 64(1)(a).

144 Native Lands Ordinance Cap 61, s 5.

145 Magistrates' Court Act Cap 52, s 58(1) provides that Magistrates' Courts 'shall hear and adjudicate in accordance with the provisions of the Lands Code applicable or, where the Code is not applicable, the local customary law, all cases concerning land, land boundaries and transfer of title to native land registered in the registers of native lands and any disputes concerning the possession and utilisation of native land'.

and administrative bodies have not always understood or applied the relevant customary laws when determining interests in customary land.[146]

6.2. INTANGIBLE PROPERTY

Kiribati provides some protection for copyright under the Copyright Ordinance,[147] but also relies on the Copyright Act 1956 (UK). Only patents and trade marks registered in the United Kingdom can be registered in Kiribati.[148]

7. COMMERCIAL LAW

All business entities must register their business name under the Business Names Act 2021, which contributes to a recent modernisation of business laws.

7.1. COMPANY LAW

Companies must be registered under the Companies Act 2021, designed to modernise the law relating to companies in Kiribati. As part of these reforms, Parliament also passed the Company Insolvency Act 2021.

7.2. PARTNERSHIP

Kiribati does not have its own partnership legislation, apart from the requirement that partnerships must be registered.[149] The Partnership Act 1890 (UK) would appear to apply as a statute of general application.

7.3. SECURITIES

Land may be mortgaged in Kiribati.[150]

---

146 Pole Atanraoi 'Customary tenure and sustainability in an Atoll Nation – the case of Kiribati' in Ron Crocombe (ed) *Customary Land Tenure and Sustainable Development: Complementarity or Conflict* (SPC, 1995) 60–65.

147 Cap 16.

148 Registration of UK Patent Act Cap 80; Registration of United Kingdom Trademarks Act Cap 87.

149 Registration of Business Names Act 1988. See eg *Republic v Tekiree* [2004] KIHC 175.

150 Property Law Act 1925 (UK), s 1.

Charges over moveable property are governed by the Bills of Sale Ordinance.[151] This provides that Bills transferring ownership are void as against the trustee in bankruptcy or an execution creditor if not made in the proper form and registered under the Act. Bills creating a security with a right of redemption when the money secured is repaid are void if they do not comply with these requirements.

The Bills of Exchange Act 1882 (UK) provides that a bill of exchange or a promissory note and the acceptance of a bill of exchange must be made in writing.[152] Borrowing by companies is regulated by the Companies Ordinance.[153]

7.4. INSOLVENCY

Kiribati does not have its own bankruptcy Act, but the Bankruptcy Act 1914 (UK) would appear to apply.[154] Insolvent companies may be wound up under the Company Insolvency Act 2021, designed to modernise the law.

7.5. CARRIAGE BY SEA

The Carriage of Goods by Sea Act[155] gives effect to the Hague–Visby Rules[156] and implies an obligation to exercise due diligence to make a ship seaworthy in contracts for the carriage of goods by sea.[157] In the event of an accident, the onus of proving that this obligation was complied with is on the carrier.

The Marine Insurance Act 1906 (UK) would appear to apply in Kiribati. This requires contracts of marine insurance to be made in writing in the form of a policy.[158]

---

151 Cap 4.

152 Bills of Exchange Act 1882 (UK), ss 3(1) and 17(2).

153 Companies Ordinance Cap 10A, ss 48–52.

154 The application of the Act appears to have been accepted, obiter, in *Defiance Mills Ltd v Attorney-General* [1997] KICA 26.

155 Cap 7.

156 International Convention for Unification of Certain Rules of Law Relating to Bills of Lading (Hague–Visby Rules, as amended), opened for signature 25 August 1924, TS17 (1931), cmd 380.

157 Sea Carriage of Goods Act Cap 231 (Fiji), Sch, art III, r 1.

158 Marine Insurance Act 1906 (UK), s 22.

8. ENVIRONMENTAL LAW

Environmental law is governed by the Environment Act 1999, which focuses on controlling pollution and the impacts of development. The Act was amended by the Environment (Amendment) Act 2006, which implements the provisions of the Convention for the Protection of the World Cultural and National Heritage, the Convention on the Prevention of Marine Pollution by Dumping of Wastes and Other Matter, and the Convention on Biological Diversity. The Wildlife Conservation Ordinance Cap 100, provides for the conservation of wildlife.

Kiribati is particularly vulnerable to climate change as it is comprised of atolls which rise three to four metres above mean sea level and are on average only a few hundred metres wide. The United Nations Framework Convention on Climate Change (UNFCCC) entered into force for Kiribati in May 1995.

9. NATURAL RESOURCES

Mining is governed by the Mineral Development Licensing Ordinance Cap 58. Mining is prohibited without a licence and only I-Kiribati and companies registered in Kiribati may apply. The Seabed Minerals Act 2017 provides for the sustainable management of seabed minerals, and the regulation of prospecting, exploration and mining activities.

Coastal fisheries and forestry are managed by Island Councils under the Local Government Ordinance.[159] Outside the three-nautical-mile limit, the Fisheries Act 2010[160] provides for conservation, management and development of fisheries and control of foreign fishing. In 2017, the Act was amended to bring it into line with obligations under the United Nations Convention on Law of the Sea, art 5 of the United Nations Fish Stocks Agreement and art 5 of the Western Central Pacific Fisheries Convention. The Marine Zone (Declaration) Act 2011 makes provision in respect of the internal waters, the archipelagic waters, the contiguous zone, the territorial sea, the exclusive economic zone, and the continental shelf of Kiribati. The Foreshore and Land Reclamation (Amendment) Act was passed in 2005 to strengthen the recognition of customary rights over the foreshore.

The Phoenix Islands, one of three island groups in Kiribati and consisting of coral atolls and submerged coral reefs, is a UNESCO World Heritage site.

---

159 Cap 51, ss 45 and 116 and Sch.

160 As amended by the Fisheries (Amendment) Acts 2015 and 2017.

It has a combined land area of 28 square kilometres and is one of the largest Protected Areas[161] in the world.

10. CRIMINAL LAW

The criminal law of Kiribati was patriated in 1991 by the Criminal Law and Procedure (Patriation) Act. It replaced United Kingdom legislation relating to criminal law and procedure in force in Kiribati, by amendments to the Penal Code,[162] the Criminal Procedure Code,[163] the Public Order Ordinance,[164] and the Magistrates' Courts Ordinance.[165] The Criminal Law and Procedure (Patriation) Act requires common law meanings to be followed in the interpretation of criminal law, rather than the principles of legal interpretation in England.[166] It also permits the Kiribati courts to determine the meaning of the Penal Code without being bound by decisions from other jurisdictions. The Act abolished a number of common law offences, such as eavesdropping and being a 'common scold'.[167]

10.1. CLASSIFICATION OF OFFENCES

Criminal law is governed mainly by the Penal Code, passed in 1965.[168] Criminal offences are divided into felonies, which are criminal offences punishable by imprisonment for three years or more, and misdemeanours.[169]

The main categories of offences are described in the following sections.

10.1.1. Offences against the State

Treason and sedition,[170] perjury and perverting the course of justice are all offences in Kiribati.[171] The offences of official corruption and abuse of office[172]

161 Phoenix Islands Protected Area Conservation Trust Act 2009.
162 Cap 67.
163 Cap 17.
164 Cap 82.
165 Cap 52.
166 Criminal Law and Procedure (Patriation) Act 1991, s 2.
167 Criminal Law and Procedure (Patriation) Act 1991, s 34.
168 Cap 67.
169 Penal Code Cap 67, s 4.
170 Penal Code Cap 67, ss 47 and 66.
171 Penal Code Cap 67, ss 96 and 102–115.
172 Penal Code Cap 67, ss 85–90.

have been supplemented by provisions relating to secret commissions and corrupt practices.[173]

10.1.2. *Offences against the Person*

As in most common law countries, homicide is divided into murder and manslaughter, based on whether the act was accompanied by 'malice aforethought'.[174]

Sexual offences consist of incest,[175] sexual intercourse without consent[176] and sexual intercourse with a girl under 16.[177] Reasonable belief that the girl is over the age of consent is a defence, provided that the girl was at least 12. Sodomy and indecent practices between males are also prohibited.[178] Other offences include bigamy, fraudulent marriage,[179] and abortion.[180]

10.1.3. *Offences against Reputation*

Defamation is a criminal offence, but only where it is in written form.[181] Justification or truth is not a defence unless the publication was in the public interest.

10.1.4. *Offences Involving Property*

Offences against property include theft, conversion, robbery, extortion, burglary, arson, obtaining property by false pretences, obtaining credit by false pretences, fraudulent statements, and receiving property known to be stolen. Other offences include trespass with intent to commit a crime, malicious damage to property and related interferences with property.[182] The offence of wilfully throwing or projecting an object or fluid into a dwelling house was added in 1980.[183] Forgery of documents, counterfeiting and uttering of forged documents and counterfeit currency are also prohibited.[184]

---

173 Penal Code Cap 67, s 366–370.
174 Penal Code Cap 67, ss 192–193 and 195.
175 Penal Code Cap 67, s 156.
176 Penal Code Cap 67, ss 128 and 129.
177 Penal Code Cap 67, ss 134–135.
178 Penal Code Cap 67, ss 153–155.
179 Penal Code Cap 67, ss 162–164.
180 Penal Code Cap 67, ss 150–152.
181 Penal Code Cap 67, ss 2 and 184–191.
182 Penal Code Cap 67, ss 250–324.
183 Penal Code (Amendment) Act 1980, s 2, adding s 83A to the Penal Code Cap 67.
184 Penal Code Cap 67, ss 325–329.

10.1.5. Public Order Offences

Living off the earnings of prostitution and procuring a woman for prostitution are offences, but loitering or soliciting in a public place for prostitution are not.[185] Practising witchcraft or sorcery is an offence only if designed or believed to harm another person.[186]

10.2. CRIMINAL RESPONSIBILITY AND DEFENCES

The age of criminal responsibility is 10.[187] There is a rebuttable presumption that children over the age of 14 are not criminally responsible.[188] The defence of insanity may be available on proof that at the time of the commission of the offence the accused was affected by a disease of the mind to such extent that they did not know what they were doing or did not know what they were doing was wrong.[189] Mental abnormality not amounting to insanity may diminish responsibility for intentional killing and reduce murder to manslaughter.[190] Intoxication is not a defence, unless the accused does not know what they are doing or that it is wrong, and the intoxication was involuntary, or was such as to cause permanent or temporary insanity.[191] Compulsion is a defence if the accused committed the offence with two or more other offenders, and was compelled to commit the offence by threats of instant death or grievous bodily harm.[192] A married woman is not free from responsibility for an offence which she commits in the presence of her husband unless she proves that he coerced her.[193] Provocation is not a defence, but may reduce murder to manslaughter.[194] Criminal responsibility for the use of force in defence of person or property is determined by the principles of common law.[195]

11. INTERNATIONAL LAW AND TREATIES

Kiribati is a member of the United Nations and of the Commonwealth. It is a dualist state and treaties are required to be ratified by legislation in order to become part

---

185 Penal Code Cap 67, ss 136, 145 and 146.
186 Penal Code Cap 67, s 183.
187 Penal Code Cap 67, s 14.
188 Penal Code Cap 67, s 14(2).
189 Penal Code Cap 67, s 12.
190 Penal Code Cap 67, s 196.
191 Penal Code Cap 67, s 13.
192 Penal Code Cap 67, s 16.
193 Penal Code Cap 67, s 19. The defence does not apply to treason or murder.
194 Penal Code Cap 67, ss 197 and 198.
195 Penal Code Cap 67, s 17.

of domestic law. Many treaties to which Kiribati is a party remain unratified. Exceptions include the Geneva Conventions Act 1993,[196] the Chemical Weapons (Prohibition) Act 2006,[197] the Consular (Conventions) Ordinance,[198] the Diplomatic Privileges and Immunities Act 1983,[199] the Consular Privileges and Immunities Act 1983,[200] and the Maritime Act 2017.[201] One of the conventions domesticated by the Maritime Act is the Maritime Labour Convention 2006. It is notable that the Kiribati Marine Training Centre, established in 1967 in partnership with New Zealand and South Pacific Marine Services, is the only institution in the Pacific to achieve White List status under the Convention.

In the area of human rights, Kiribati has acceded to the following treaties:

- the Convention against Torture and Other Cruel Inhuman or Degrading Treatment or Punishment;[202]
- the Convention on the Elimination of All Forms of Discrimination against Women;[203] and
- the Convention on the Rights of the Child[204] and two Optional Protocols.[205]

Trade agreements to which Kiribati is a party include:

- the Pacific Island Countries Trade Agreement;[206]
- the South Pacific Regional Trade and Economic Cooperation Agreement;[207] and
- the Thailand-Australia Free Trade Agreement.[208]

As discussed above, Kiribati is also party to a number of agreements relating to environmental laws.

---

196 Patriating the Geneva Conventions 1957 (UK), which was extended to the Gilbert and Ellice Islands, with modifications, by the Geneva Conventions Act (Colonial Territories) Order in Council 1959.

197 Domesticating the Convention on the Prohibition of the Development, Production, Stockpiling and Use of Chemical Weapons and on Their Destruction 1997, acceded to by Kiribati on 7 September 2000.

198 Cap 12, conferring powers, immunities and exemptions on consular officers of states that Kiribati has concluded consular conventions with.

199 Domesticating the Vienna Convention on Diplomatic Relations 1961, acceded to by Kiribati on 2 April 1982.

200 Domesticating the Vienna Convention on Consular Relations signed in 1963.

201 Repealing the Shipping Act and domesticating a number of international maritime conventions.

202 Acceded to on 22 July 2019.

203 Acceded to on 17 March 2004.

204 Acceded to on 16 September 2015.

205 Acceded to on 16 September 2015.

206 Ratified on 4 June 2003.

207 Ratified on 10 July 1981.

208 Incorporated by reference in art 403(2) and a related Memorandum of Association.

12. CIVIL SOCIETY ORGANISATIONS

According to the 2015 census, nearly 100 per cent of the population identifies as having a religious affiliation.[209] Most people belong to the Catholic Church or the Kiribati Uniting Church. The umbrella body is the National Council of Churches.

Trade unions are governed by the Trade Unions and Employer Organisation Act 1998, which makes it compulsory for unions to register and introduces accounting requirements.[210]

13. BANABA

The Banaban community live in Rabi, Fiji, but have a right to enter and live on Banaba, which is geographically some way from the main islands of Kiribati. In 1972, the Banabans commenced action against the British government for unpaid taxes and royalties from phosphate mining and for failure to honour an agreement to restore and replant mined lands. The action was only partly successful,[211] but the British government later made an ex gratia payment to the Banabans. On completion of phosphate extraction, the State restored all land on Banaba to the Banaban from whom it was acquired.[212] At the time of the independence, many Banabans wanted to secede. Special provisions were included in the Kiribati Constitution in an attempt to address their concerns. One seat is reserved for a nominated representative of the Banabans,[213] and legislation relating to Banaba must be supported by the nominated member representing Banaba in the Maneaba ni Maungatabu.[214] Banabans' land rights are preserved and it is expressly provided that those rights are not affected by the fact that Banabans live in Fiji.[215] The Constitution establishes the Banaba Island Council.[216] An appeal to the Privy Council from any High Court decision involving the interpretation of the Constitution in applications made on the basis of contravention of the rights of any Banaban or of the Rabi Council has been preserved.[217]

---

209 National Statistics Office *2015 Population and Housing Census* (Kiribati) 56 and 196.
210 Part II.
211 *Tito v Waddell (No 2)* [1977] Ch 106.
212 Banaba Lands (Special Provisions) Act 1988.
213 Constitution of Kiribati 1979, s 117.
214 Constitution of Kiribati 1979, s 124.
215 Constitution of Kiribati 1979, s 119.
216 Constitution of Kiribati 1979, s 121.
217 Constitution of Kiribati 1979, s 123.

BIBLIOGRAPHY

Atanraoi, Pole 'Customary land and development in an Atoll Nation – the case of Kiribati' in Ron Crocombe (ed) *Customary Land Tenure and Sustainable Development: Complementarity or Conflict?* (SPC, 1995).

Corrin, Jennifer and Don Paterson *Introduction to South Pacific Law* (4th ed, Intersentia, 2017).

Lodge, Michael 'Kiribati Legal System' in Guy Powles and Mere Pulea (eds) *Pacific Courts and Legal Systems* (University of the South Pacific, 1988).

Macdonald, Barrie *Cinderellas of the Empire: Towards a History of Kiribati and Tuvalu*, (Institute of Pacific Studies, 2001).

Pacific Islands Legal Information Institute *Kiribati Primary Materials* <http://www.paclii.org/countries/ki.html>.

Secretariat of the Pacific Regional Environment Programme and EDO NSW *Kiribati: Review of Natural Resources and Environment Related Legislation* (SPREP, 2018).

Tsamenyi, Martin 'Kiribati' in Michael A Ntumy (ed) *South Pacific Islands Legal Systems* (University of Hawaii Press, 1993).

Uakeia, Takuia 'Kiribati' in Stephen Levine (ed) *Pacific Ways* (VUW Press, 2016).

NAURU

Gregory DALE

1. CONTEXT

Nauru (*Naoero*) is an island republic, the geography of which barely spans 21 square kilometres and the circumference 20 kilometres. It has 11,550 residents,[1] comprising mainly Nauruans, other Pacific Islanders, asylum seekers resident at the Regional Processing Centre (RPC) and foreign workers either employed at the RPC or employed in fishing. A 20-kilometre coral reef encircles the island[2]

---

[1] Government Information Office 'COVID-19 pacific humanitarian pathway – This is as big as Angam: Appi', *Nauru Bulletin*, Issue 6-2020/210 (21 April 2020) 3–4. This number fluctuates depending upon the number of asylum seekers and business visa holders that are resident on the island.

[2] Carl N McDaniel and John M Gowdy *Paradise for Sale: A Parable of Nauru* (University of California Press, 2000) 13.

and Nauru's territorial sea extends 12 nautical miles from the seaward low-water line of the reef.[3] Its nearest neighbour, Kiribati, is 293 kilometres to the east. Nauruans speak Nauruan (*Dorerin Naoero*). The English language predominates in the legal arena, in spite of the Constitution requiring the government to take 'positive and practical measures to preserve and advance' the Nauruan language.[4] Proceedings in the Supreme and District Courts are conducted in English.[5] Statutes and the *Government Gazette* are published only in English.[6] However, debates in Parliament are conducted in both Nauruan and English.[7] Nauru has a 'narrow economic base',[8] reliant on phosphate mining. Tourism is virtually non-existent and the island is primarily a cash economy.

1.1. LOCAL HISTORY

Before British colonisation, Micronesian people inhabited Nauru for about 3,000 years.[9] It was not until 1798 that Europeans on a British whaling ship, the *Snow Hunter*,[10] chanced upon the island. The ship's captain named the island 'Pleasant Island'. This heralded a period of trading between indigenous Nauruans and Europeans. Whaling ships used the island to replenish their fresh produce, which was bartered in exchange for goods. However, European trade brought violence between locals and European beachcombers.[11] In 1886, Nauru was annexed to Germany under the Anglo-German Convention.[12] It was not until 1900 that non-Nauruans learned that the island was comprised of significant phosphate deposits, a substance highly prized by its Pacific neighbours, Australia and New Zealand, whose agricultural industries were

3 Sea Boundaries Act 1997, ss 2 and 4 (definition of 'baseline of Nauru').

4 Constitution of Nauru, art 2C. See also the Law Revision and Consolidation Act 2019, s 5(3), which requires written laws to be revised and consolidated in English.

5 Supreme Court Act 2018, s 79(1); District Court Act 2018, s 35(1).

6 This is partly due to the lack of a consistent way to write Nauruan: see Xavier Barker 'English Language as Bully in the Republic of Nauru' in Vaughan Rapatahana and Pauline Bunce (eds) *English Language as Hydra* (Multilingual Matters, 2012) 18, and Steven Ratuva 'The gap between global thinking and local living: dilemmas of constitutional reform in Nauru' (2011) 120(3) Journal of the Polynesia Society 241 at 250.

7 Xavier Barker 'English Language as Bully in the Republic of Nauru' in Vaughan Rapatahana and Pauline Bunce (eds) *English Language as Hydra* (Multilingual Matters, 2012) 18 at 23.

8 International Monetary Fund *Republic of Nauru*, IMF Country Report No 20/31 (Washington DC, 2020).

9 Peter Dauvergne *Environmentalism of the Rich* (The MIT Press, 2016) 31.

10 Albert F Ellis *Ocean Island and Nauru: Their Story* (Angus and Robertson, 1935) 29.

11 Nancy Viviani *Nauru: Phosphate and Political Progress* (ANU Press, 1970) ch 1.

12 Declaration between the Governments of Great Britain and the German Empire relating to the Demarcation of the British and German Spheres of Influence in the Western Pacific, 6 April 1886.

struggling with low soil fertility.[13] Suddenly, a substance that had formed over millions of years from either bird guano or the decay of marine life[14] was being mined in earnest. Only seven years after its discovery, the first shipment of phosphate left Nauru, only for the ship to capsize and sink.[15] After World War I, as a former German colony, Nauru became a 'C'-class mandate under the Council of the League of Nations, mandated to the United Kingdom.[16] The UK, Australia and New Zealand entered into an arrangement to divide up phosphate exports, entitling the UK and Australia to 42 per cent each, and New Zealand taking the remaining 16 per cent.[17] At the same time, the influenza pandemic claimed the lives of 18 per cent of the Nauruan population.[18] However, from 1942, the Japanese occupied the island. Two-thirds of Nauruans were exiled to Truk Island, leaving only 600 Nauruans on the island. One-third of those exiled would never return.[19] The Japanese surrendered in 1945,[20] leaving behind an airstrip that has since become the nation's airport. After World War II, Nauru found itself under the administration of Australia as a Trust Territory, this time under the supervision of the Trusteeship Council set up by the United Nations. In 1962, the General Assembly voted in favour of giving Nauru independence, but in the intervening six years Nauru had to settle for a Local Government Council and eventually Legislative and Executive Councils.[21] Australia preferred that Nauru remain an external territory of Australia, albeit one that was self-governed. Australia eventually capitulated to Nauruan demands. On 31 January 1968, Nauru became an independent state.[22]

In 1989, Nauru sought compensation from Australia for paying Nauruans less than the market price for phosphate and for environmental damage sustained from that mining.[23] Proceedings in the International Court of Justice

---

13 S J Gale 'Lies and misdemeanours: Nauru, phosphate and global geopolitics' (2019) 6 The Extractive Industries and Society 737 at 737; Albert F Ellis *Ocean Island and Nauru: Their Story* (Angus & Robertson, 1936) ch 23.

14 Viviani, above n 11, at 33.

15 Gale, above n 13, at 739.

16 Mandate for Nauru 1921 cmd 1202, art 1.

17 The Nauru Agreement of 2 July 1919.

18 James Wightman Davidson 'The Republic of Nauru' (1968) 3(1) The Journal of Pacific History 145 at 145.

19 Carl N McDaniel and John M Gowdy *Paradise for Sale: A Parable of Nauru* (University of California Press, 2000) 19.

20 Albert Ellis *Mid-Pacific Outposts* (Brown and Stewart, 1946) ch 8.

21 Viviani, above n 11, at 150–151. See Nauru Act 1965 (Cth).

22 The Nauru Independence Act 1967 (Cth), s 3 enabled the Nauruan Legislative Council to establish a constitutional convention for the purposes of attaining independence. The Legislative Council adopted the draft constitution on 29 January 1968: Viviani, above n 11, at 176.

23 Christopher Weeramantry, *Nauru: Environmental Damage under International* Trusteeship (Oxford University Press, 1992) ch 16.

were settled in 1993 for AU$107 million.[24] However, as phosphate reserves began to dwindle, wealth was soon squandered through a mixture of misguided investments, corruption, waste and falling prey to foreign con artists.[25] By 2004, the AU$1.8–2 billion Nauru had accrued in profits from phosphate mining since independence had been reduced to around just AU$30 million.[26]

In 2001, faced with domestic political pressures from the perceived influx of asylum seekers, Australia devised the 'Pacific Solution'.[27] Asylum seekers arriving in Australian territorial waters by boat would be removed to 'declared' third countries where their asylum claims would be processed. Given the dire nature of Nauru's finances, it is no surprise that Nauru accommodated Australia's requests to host an immigration detention centre in the interior of the island known as Topside.[28] In the first three years of this arrangement, Nauru is said to have received some AU$130 million in Australian aid.[29] A change in government in Australia saw the dismantling of the detention centre in 2007. However, its closure was short-lived. In 2013, the detention centre reopened and was re-branded as a 'Regional Processing Centre'.[30] Unlike the first iteration of offshore processing, asylum seekers' movements are no longer restricted to the confines of the Centre[31] and Nauruans are now tasked with assessing asylum seekers' claims.[32] Under both guises, the asylum seekers' centres have been mired in controversies and criticisms, mainly relating to human rights.[33]

---

24 Agreement for the settlement of the case in the International Court of Justice concerning certain phosphate lands in Nauru, 1770 UNTS 379; 1993 ATS 26 (signed 10 August 1993; entered into force 20 August 1993).

25 McDaniel and Gowdy, above n 19, at 6; John Connell 'Nauru: The First Failed Pacific State?' (2006) 95 The Round Table 47.

26 Dauvergne, above n 9, at 36.

27 David Scott FitzGerald *Refuge beyond Reach: How Rich Democracies Repel Asylum Seekers* (Oxford University Press, 2019) ch 10.

28 Memorandum of Understanding between the Republic of Nauru and the Commonwealth of Australia for Cooperation in the Administration of Asylum Seekers and Related Issues, signed 11 December 2001.

29 Julia C Morris 'Violence and extractions of a human commodity: From phosphate to refugees in the Republic of Nauru' (2019) 6 The Extractive Industries and Society 1122 at 1126.

30 Memorandum of Understanding between the Republic of Nauru and the Commonwealth of Australia, relating to the transfer to and assessment of persons in Nauru, and related issues, signed 29 August 2012; Memorandum of Understanding between the Republic of Nauru and the Commonwealth of Australia relating to the Transfer to and Assessment of persons in Nauru, and related issues, signed 3 August 2013.

31 FitzGerald, above n 27, at 239.

32 Cait Storr, *International Status in the Shadow of Empire: Nauru and the Histories of International Law* (Cambridge University Press, 2020) 252. Under the Pacific Solution, Nauruans were not employed in any of the roles at the detention centre: Mark Isaacs, *The Undesirables: Inside Nauru* (Hardie Grants Books, 2014) 15. The operation of the RPC is governed by the Asylum Seekers (Regional Processing Centre) Act 2012 and the Nauru Regional Processing Centre Rules 2016.

33 For example, see the Senate Select Committee on the Recent allegations relating to conditions and circumstances at the Regional Processing Centre in Nauru *Taking responsibility: conditions*

1.2. COURT STRUCTURE

Judicial power is vested in the Court of Appeal, the Supreme Court, the District Court and in other courts or tribunals as created by law.[34] The Supreme Court consists of the Chief Justice, and 'such number of other judges that the President in consultation with the Chief Justice deems fit.'[35] It may hear questions referred to it by Cabinet where such question concerns the interpretation or effect of the Constitution.[36] The Chief Justice and Justices of the Supreme Court enjoy tenure until the age of 75 years[37] but may be removed by not less than a two-thirds absolute majority of Parliament on the ground of 'proved incapacity or misconduct'.[38] This protection is also usually stipulated in the judge's contract.[39] In practice, like a number of other Pacific nations, Nauru appoints many of its judges on fixed-term contracts,[40] or on a part-time basis.[41] Judges in the superior courts are expatriates, usually from other nations in the Pacific region.

In 2018, the High Court of Australia was replaced by the Court of Appeal as Nauru's highest court.[42] Appeals from the Supreme Court's original jurisdiction

---

and circumstances at Australia's Regional Processing Centre in Nauru (Report, August 2015); Philip Moss *Review into recent allegations relating to conditions and circumstances at the Regional Processing Centre in Nauru* (Final Report, February 2015).

34 Constitution of Nauru, arts 48 and 57A, amended and inserted by the Constitution (Amendment) Act 2018, ss 4 and 5.

35 Supreme Court Act 2018, s 6(1). Between the abolition of appeals to the High Court of Australia and the creation of the Nauru Court of Appeal, the Full Bench of the Supreme Court (comprised of three judges) sat on a number of occasions: for example, see *Appin v Secretary for Justice* [2014] NRSC 1. The Full Bench can sit, at its discretion, in matters of constitutional importance, national significance, or important points of law: Rules for Empanelment of a Full Bench 2015, r 1.

36 Constitution of Nauru, art 55.

37 Constitution of Nauru, art 50. However, unusually the Supreme Court Act 2018, s 10(1)(d), as amended by the Supreme Court (Amendment) Act 2020, provides that the Chief Justice and other Supreme Court justices hold office until, inter alia, 'attaining the age of 70 years'.

38 Constitution of Nauru, art 51(1).

39 See Submission from the Hon Geoffrey Eames AM QC 'Nauru and the Rule of Law', Select Committee on the Recent Allegations relation to Conditions and Circumstances at the Regional Processing Centre in Nauru, 27 May 2015.

40 These judges are apparently appointed under art 53 of the Constitution of Nauru, which provides for the appointment of acting judges: Peter H MacSporran *Nauru: The Constitution* (Seaview Press, 2007) 117–118. See also the Hon Geoffrey Eames AM QC 'Nauru abandons High Court appeals: Is there a threat to the rule of law?' (Paper delivered to the International Commission of Jurists (Victoria) and the Criminal Bar Association, Essoign Club, Owen Dixon Chambers, Melbourne, 19 April 2018).

41 For example, Dr Ian Freckelton QC has been appointed as a Justice of the Supreme Court on a part-time basis.

42 Article 57. In December 2017, Nauru gave 90 days' notice to terminate the 41-year-old arrangement, as required by art 6 of the Agreement between the Government of Australia and the Government of the Republic of Nauru relating to the High Court of Australia from the Supreme Court of Nauru, 1216 UNTS 151; 1977 ATS 11 (signed 6 September 1975, entered into force 21 March 1977): Michaela Whitbourn 'Nauru scraps appeals for asylum seekers',

to the Court of Appeal lie as of right for convictions on questions of law or mixed law and fact,[43] and for sentences.[44] In other matters, leave of the Court of Appeal is generally required to institute proceedings. For civil matters, appeals to the Court of Appeal lie from any final judgment, decision or order of the Supreme Court.[45] The Court of Appeal is comprised of no fewer than three Justices of Appeal, who are not permitted to serve as a judge after attaining the age of 75 years[46] and can be removed by a two-thirds absolute majority of Parliament on the ground of 'proved incapacity or misconduct'.[47] Under art 57(5) of the Constitution, the Chief Justice of the Supreme Court presides as the President of the Court of Appeal.[48]

The District Court is a court of summary jurisdiction. Its civil jurisdiction is limited to disputes not exceeding AU$3,000,[49] while its criminal jurisdiction is limited to offences punishable by imprisonment of more than five years and a fine not exceeding AU$50,000 in respect of any offence.[50] The Court may be constituted by a Resident Magistrate or a lay magistrate.[51] Lay magistrates are not permitted to hear or determine matters unless a Resident Magistrate is unable to sit on the matter.[52] A Resident Magistrate's appointment terminates upon the appointment of another Resident Magistrate, unless that Resident Magistrate has been appointed in respect of a particular matter.[53] The Resident Magistrate is also the Chairman of the Family Court, which is only properly constituted when he or she sits together with two members[54] appointed by the Nauruan President after consultation with the Chief Justice.[55]

The Age (Melbourne), 3 April 2018, 9. For further information on the now defunct arrangement between Nauru and Australia, see Gregory Dale 'Appealing to whom? Australia's "appellate jurisdiction" over Nauru' (2007) 56(3) International and Comparative Law Quarterly 641.

43 Nauru Court of Appeal Act 2018, s 29(1).

44 Unless the sentence is fixed by a written law: Nauru Court of Appeal Act 2018, s 29(2).

45 Nauru Court of Appeal Act 2018, s 19(2)(a). Appeals from the Supreme Court exercising its appellate jurisdiction from the District Court or other subordinate tribunals or committee lie to the Court of Appeal where a written law provides for such appeals.

46 Article 57(9).

47 Articles 51(1) and 57(10).

48 However, the Chief Justice is not permitted to sit on appeal from any of his or her judgments when sitting on the Supreme Court: art 57(6).

49 District Court Act 2018, s 17.

50 Criminal Procedure Act 1972, s 7. The maximum aggregate sentence of imprisonment that the District Court may impose is 10 years: Criminal Procedure Act 1972, s 9(3)(a). The maximum aggregate fine that the District Court may impose against a person is AU$75,000: Criminal Procedure Act 1972, s 9(3)(b).

51 District Court Act 2018, s 6(1).

52 District Court Act 2018, s 6(2).

53 District Court Act 2018, s 7(2) and (4).

54 Family Court Act 1973, s 4(4).

55 Family Court Act 1973, s 4(1).

Outside of the court hierarchy there are two merits review bodies. The Refugee Status Review Tribunal conducts merits review of refugee status determinations[56] and the Public Service Appeals Board conducts appeals in relation to employee discipline and conditions.[57] The legal profession in Nauru comprises barristers and solicitors, foreign practitioners and pleaders. To be admitted as a pleader, the person must have successfully completed a pleaders' course. Barristers and solicitors must be Nauruan citizens who hold a law degree and already be admitted to practice in a designated country or have practised in Nauru as a pleader for a year.[58] Foreign practitioners may apply for temporary admission.[59]

2. SOURCES OF LAW

The Constitution is the highest source of law in Nauru and a law 'inconsistent' with the Constitution is 'to the extent of the inconsistency, void.'[60] Legislation passed by the Parliament of Nauru is supplemented by English statutes of 'general application' in force in England on 31 January 1968,[61] those referred to in the first schedule of the Custom and Adopted Laws Act 1971. Certain statutes from Australia and Papua New Guinea that were adopted during the colonial era are still in force.[62] The common law and equity in force in England on 31 January 1968 are also in force in Nauru.[63] Authority to make subsidiary legislation is usually given to the relevant minister and, in the absence of specific authority, to Cabinet.[64]

The Custom and Adopted Laws Act 1971 provides that the 'institutions, customs and usages of the Nauruans' existing prior to the commencement of the Act shall 'have full force and effect of law' to regulate interests in land, disposition of property, and inheritance, and 'any matters affecting Nauruans only'.[65] 'Customary law is to be applied by all courts in preference to the common law, but within general limits and only to matters and persons specified by written law',[66] provided that it 'is not repugnant to the Constitution or to any Act'.[67]

---

56 Refugees Convention Act 2012, s 31.
57 Constitution of Nauru, art 70; Public Service Act 2016, Part 8.
58 Legal Practitioners Act 2019, s 7.
59 Legal Practitioners Act 2019, s 13.
60 Constitution of Nauru, art 2.
61 Custom and Adopted Laws Act 1971, s 4.
62 Laws Repeal and Adopting Ordinance 1922, ss 12 and 14.
63 Custom and Adopted Laws Act 1971, s 4.
64 Interpretation Act 2011, s 6.
65 Custom and Adopted Laws Act 1971, s 3.
66 Don E Paterson 'South Pacific Customary Law and Common Law: Their Interrelationship' (1995) 21(2) Commonwealth Law Bulletin 660 at 670.
67 Constitution of Nauru, art 2B(1).

From the perspective of a non-resident, it is difficult to ascertain Nauruan customs because there are few written sources available.[68] Legislation and case law may be accessed through the official website ronlaw.gov.nr or via paclii.org. From time to time, statutes are collated under the Law Revision and Consolidation Act 2019. Some of the more important decisions of the courts may be found in the *Law Reports of the Commonwealth* and in the short-lived serials, the *Nauru Law Reports* and *South Pacific Law Reports*. Copies of unreported cases may be obtained from the registrars of the Court of Appeal and Supreme Court.

3. CONSTITUTIONAL LAW

Parliament elects one of its members to be President.[69] The President is both the head of government and the head of state,[70] although the Constitution is unusually silent as to the President's latter role.[71] The President's dual role is one of three ways in which Westminster conventions differ in application in Nauru. The other differences are that the President is directly elected by Parliament (not the party with the most representatives) and ministers have no individual responsibility.[72] The President appoints a Deputy President[73] and five or six ministers[74] to form the Cabinet. Additionally, the President may appoint Members of Parliament to be deputy ministers who may attend Cabinet meetings but do not participate in its decision-making.[75]

The President enjoys a number of other powers. He or she may advise the Speaker of Parliament to prorogue Parliament. In addition, the President may appoint a person either, upon consultation with Cabinet, to the Supreme Court,[76] or, upon consultation with the Chief Justice, to the Court of Appeal.[77] The President is empowered by statute to declare a state of disaster[78] and by the Constitution to declare a state of emergency.[79]

---

68 Peter H MacSporran 'Nauru Legal Sources' (1993) 1(1) Australian Law Librarian 18 at 20–21.

69 Constitution of Nauru, art 16(1) and (2).

70 Roger Wettenhall and Ian Thynne 'Machinery of Government Innovation in Micro-States: The Cases of Nauru, Niue and Norfolk Island' (1994) 16 Asian Journal of Public Administration 60 at 70.

71 Tony Deklin 'Nauru' in Michael A Ntumy (ed) *South Pacific Islands Legal Systems* (University of Hawaii Press, 1993) 142 at 146–147.

72 Peter H MacSporran *Nauru: The Constitution* (Seaview Press, 2007) 56.

73 Constitution of Nauru, art 21A(1).

74 Constitution of Nauru, art 19.

75 Deputy Ministers Act 2019, s 7.

76 Constitution of Nauru, art 49(2).

77 Nauru Court of Appeal Act 2018, s 9.

78 National Disaster Risk Management Act 2016, ss 26 and 29. This legislation was regularly invoked during the COVID-19 pandemic.

79 Constitution of Nauru, Part IX. Article 78 permits an emergency order or law enacted under Part IX to derogate from certain fundamental rights and freedoms set out in Part II of the Constitution.

The executive is significantly the strongest arm of state. While this is not unusual in countries that have adopted Westminster conventions, the separation of powers commands less respect and understanding among members of the government.[80] There are no formal political parties in Nauru.[81] Instead, politics is dominated by the 'personalities of key individuals'.[82] Subtracting the 12 or so Cabinet ministers and deputy ministers leaves at most six Members of Parliament to constitute an opposition. These Members of Parliament in turn earn less than half the salaries of Cabinet ministers and three-quarters the salaries of deputy ministers.[83]

The executive has on occasion prevailed upon the province of the judiciary. Despite the Constitution protecting judicial tenure and assurances that the courts shall be 'independent',[84] in January 2014, Nauru arrested and deported the Resident Magistrate, Peter Law, in what appears to be retaliation for his decision to give leave to two individuals to have judicial review of their deportations.[85] Chief Justice Eames issued injunctions from Melbourne restraining the government from deporting Magistrate Law. After those orders were ignored, the Chief Justice found his visa to enter Nauru withdrawn. Unable to return to Nauru to exercise his duties as Chief Justice, Eames resigned from that office in March 2014.[86]

Parliament is a unicameral chamber and owes all of its powers to the Nauru Constitution.[87] The Speaker of Parliament presides over Parliament, ensures its business is conducted in accordance with the Constitution,[88] and until he or she

---

80 Ruben Kun, Whitlam Togomae and Roland Kun *National Integrity Systems: Transparency International Country Study Report – Nauru 2004* (Transparency International Australia, 2004) 14–15; Submission from the Hon Geoffrey Eames AM QC 'Nauru and the Rule of Law', Select Committee on the Recent Allegations relation to Conditions and Circumstances at the Regional Processing Centre in Nauru, 27 May 2015.

81 Wettenhall and Thynne, above n 70, at 70. Note that the Nauru Party did exist for a time: Ron Crocombe *The South Pacific: An Introduction* (5th rev ed, University of the South Pacific, 1989) 241.

82 Crocombe, above n 81, at 159.

83 Parliamentary Salaries and Allowances Act 2008, Sch 1.

84 The Constitution of Nauru, art 48(6). Moreover, '[n]either the Republic or any person shall interfere with the functioning of the courts': art 48(7).

85 Mark Isaacs *Nauru burning: An uprising and its aftermath* (Editia, 2016) 56–57. Peter Law and Geoffrey Eames AM QC, like many of Nauru's former judicial officers, hail from Australia. Peter Law is an Australian lawyer and Geoffrey Eames is a former Victorian Supreme Court justice.

86 Jane Lee 'Nauru chief justice quits, citing rule of law breach', *The Age* (Melbourne), 13 March 2014, 9.

87 Constitution of Nauru, art 27. Compare the United Kingdom's Parliament, which enjoys parliamentary sovereignty: Nauru Constitutional Review Commission, *Report* (28 February 2007) 76.

88 Constitution of Nauru, arts 44 and 44A. See also *Parliamentary Services Act 2020*, s 8. Under Part 4 of that Act, the Clerk of Parliament assists the Speaker.

certifies an Act is passed by Parliament, such Act has no operation.[89] Nauru's 14 districts are represented by eight constituencies,[90] each of which are represented by at least two Members of Parliament. Candidates for election must be Nauruan citizens aged over 20 years.[91] Public servants must have resigned three months prior to being nominated for a general election or may find themselves ineligible for reemployment in the event that they are not elected.[92] Members of Parliament are protected by parliamentary privilege.[93]

Only Nauruan citizens aged over 20 are entitled to vote[94] and upon attaining that age they are automatically enrolled.[95] In order to cast a valid ballot, voters must indicate their preference for all candidates on the ballot.[96] Voting is compulsory[97] and failure to vote is an offence, punishable by a penalty not exceeding AU$100.[98] Voting is conducted by secret ballot. Since registering in a district is not based on the application of a single criterion (such as the voter's geographical residence),[99] applications to transfer to another district cannot be made within six months of the last transfer or within 21 days of an election.[100] Such applications are expensive[101] and are determined by an independent Electoral Commissioner. The Commissioner is appointed for terms of four years,[102] and, in addition to determining applications for voters to transfer to other districts, conducts elections and advises members of the executive and legislature on electoral matters.[103] The Supreme Court is the Court of Disputed Returns and its decisions are not subject to appeal.[104]

Other than the articles listed in the Constitution's Fifth Schedule, the Constitution may be amended by a vote of no less than two-thirds of the

89 Constitution of Nauru, art 47.

90 Constitution of Nauru, Second Schedule.

91 Members of Parliament are permitted to hold dual citizenship: *Constitutional Reference No 1 of 2008* [2009] 1 LRC 453 at 463–464.

92 Public Service Act 2016, ss 84(1) and (4). This provision is arguably contrary to art 31 of the Constitution of Nauru: Stewart Firth 'Australia's Detention Centre and the Erosion of Democracy in Nauru' (2016) 51 The Journal of Pacific History 286 at 298.

93 Parliamentary Powers, Privileges and Immunities Act 1976.

94 Constitution of Nauru, art 29; Electoral Act 2016, ss 38 and 40.

95 Electoral Act 2016, s 38.

96 Electoral Act 2016, s 74.

97 Electoral Act 2016, s 54(1).

98 Electoral Act 2016, s 110.

99 A voter may establish his or her entitlement to register in a district if the district is the voter's place of birth, he or she has been living there for more than one month, the voter is connected to the district through Nauru custom, customary links and affiliation, one of the voter's parents were either born or registered in that district, or it is the district of the voter's spouse: see Electoral Act 2016, s 42.

100 Electoral Act 2016, s 47.

101 The fee is currently $1,000: Electoral Act 2016, s 41(3)(b).

102 Electoral Act 2016, s 15.

103 Electoral Act 2016, s 19.

104 Electoral Act 2016, s 10.

Members of Parliament, with at least 90 days elapsing between the introduction and passage of any proposed amendments.[105] Articles listed in the Fifth Schedule require the approval of two-thirds of the votes validly cast at a referendum.[106]

Part II of the Constitution protects fundamental rights and freedoms, including the right not to be deprived of life intentionally, except if sentenced by a court or as the result of an act of self-defence or defence of property;[107] the protection of personal liberties, freedom of expression, freedom of assembly and association, and freedom of conscience; and protection from forced labour, inhuman treatment, unlawful deprivation of property, and unlawful entry to premises or search of the person. Rights and freedoms are enforceable in the Supreme Court.[108]

In 2007, the United Nations Development Programme funded an independent review of the Constitution, which recommended a myriad of constitutional amendments.[109] Most of those changes were effected by the Constitution of Nauru (Parliamentary Amendments) Act 2009. However, at a referendum in 2010, a significant number of other proposed changes failed to garner the required two-thirds majority to effect change. In fact, two-thirds of Nauruans voted against the proposed amendments.[110]

4. LAW OF PERSONS

A person born in Nauru or overseas is a citizen provided that one of his or her parents was, at the time of his or her birth, a Nauruan citizen.[111] A person who is born in Nauru to parents who are non-citizens may apply for citizenship after living continuously in Nauru for 20 years.[112] Citizenship may also be acquired through adoption[113] or marriage,[114] but a person granted citizenship by marriage is deprived of his or her citizenship on the spouse's death or upon marrying a non-Nauruan citizen.[115]

105 Constitution of Nauru, art 84(2).

106 Constitution of Nauru, art 84(3).

107 Article 4.

108 A constitutional proposal to amend art 10 of the Constitution would have inserted a new art 9A providing that '[n]o law shall prevent a citizen bringing civil action against the Republic or its instrumentalities'. However, it failed at referendum.

109 Nauru Constitutional Review Commission, above n 87.

110 Ratuva, above n 6.

111 Naoero Citizenship Act 2017, ss 9 and 12.

112 Naoero Citizenship Act 2017, s 11.

113 Naoero Citizenship Act 2017, s 15.

114 Naoero Citizenship Act 2017, s 13; Constitution of Nauru, art 74. On some occasions, Naoero citizenship has been granted under non-substantive provisions of the Act, such as s 7(6). For example, see GN No 476/2018 (Nauru Government Gazette, No 100, 29 June 2018).

115 Naoero Citizenship Act 2017, s 24(1).

Adoption in Nauru is restricted to prospective adoptive parents of at least 25 years of age[116] and concerns only children under the age of 18 years.[117] Couples jointly seeking to adopt must be married, and a person seeking to adopt solely must generally obtain the consent of their spouse.[118] Power to make adoption orders resides with the Family Court (Resident Magistrate). On the making of an adoption order, the Resident Magistrate must notify the Registrar of Births, Deaths and Marriages.[119]

Births[120] and deaths[121] must be registered. The Resident Magistrate may conduct an inquest into the death of a person.[122] Only funeral officiators can officiate at a funeral.[123] Disposal of human remains is governed by the Funeral Burial and Cremation Act 2017.

Marriage is defined as 'the voluntary union of one man and one woman', each of whom has attained the age of 18 years.[124] At least seven days' notice must be given to the Registrar of an intended marriage.[125]

The laws of divorce are governed by the Matrimonial Causes Act 1973, which provides that the irretrievable breakdown of marriage is the sole ground for divorce.[126] Marriages are voidable if either party 'did not freely consent to the marriage', at the time of the marriage either party was 'unable to understand the nature of the contract and the duties of marriage', as a result of some disease the marriage was not consummated, either party at the time of marriage suffered from 'venereal disease', the female party was pregnant to another male, or either party was 'suffering from mental deficiency or disorder of such a kind or to such an extent as to be unfitted for marriage or the procreation of children.'[127]

The Child Protection and Welfare Act 2016 gives effect to the Convention on the Rights of the Child,[128] which Nauru acceded to in 1994. The Act permits the custody of a child at immediate risk of harm.[129] The core principle for

116 Adoption of Children Act 1965, ss 5 and 6. See generally Unaisi Narawa 'Adoption in Nauru' in Jennifer Corrin and Sue Farran (eds) *The Plural Practice of Adoption in Pacific Island States* (Springer, 2019) 43–66.

117 Adoption of Children Act 1965, s 3.

118 Adoption of Children Act 1965, s 7.

119 Births Deaths and Marriages Registration Act 2017, s 27(1).

120 Births Deaths and Marriages Registration Act 2017, s 12. Stillbirths shall be registered under s 18(1).

121 Births Deaths and Marriages Registration Act 2017, s 36.

122 Inquests Act 1977, s 7(4). In practice, there is not necessarily the capacity to conduct post-mortems in Nauru: Nick Martin 'The Nauru Diaries: Australia is better than this' (2018) 77(1) Meanjin 46 at 62.

123 Births Deaths and Marriages Registration Act 2017, s 87A.

124 Births Deaths and Marriages Registration Act 2017, ss 49 and 50.

125 Births Deaths and Marriages Registration Act 2017, s 54. Notices to marry are published in the *Government Gazette*: s 55.

126 Matrimonial Causes Act 1973, s 8.

127 Matrimonial Causes Act 1973, s 22.

128 1577 UNTS 3 (opened for signature 20 November 1989, entered into force 2 September 1990).

129 Child Protection and Welfare Act 2016, s 17(1).

administering the Act is that 'the safety, wellbeing and best interests of a child are paramount.'[130] Laws concerning children 'must be read and applied subject to the provisions of' the Act and 'in the event of any inconsistency' between the Child Protection and Welfare Act 2016 and any other law, the former will prevail.[131]

5. LAW OF OBLIGATIONS

Contracts and torts are largely governed by case law drawn from the jurisprudence of Nauru and other common law countries. Contracts of employment are governed by the Workers (Contracts of Service) Act 1922 and workers' compensation under the Workers' Compensation Act 1956. The former Act applies to persons or a class of persons gazetted by Cabinet to be workers under the statute.[132] In practice, the Act has limited application because it does not appear that Cabinet has declared anyone to be a worker under the legislation. Since the public service is by far the largest employer,[133] for many Nauruans the terms and conditions of their employment are provided for in the Public Service Act 2016.[134] However, Australians employed at the RPC may be subject to confidentiality requirements set out in Australian legislation[135] and their terms of employment may be dictated by Australian law.

Leave of the Cabinet is required before commencing proceedings against the Republic unless it is an action in contract, administrative law, or to enforce a debt charge on the Treasury Fund.[136] However, any restrictions on the ability of individuals to institute proceedings against the Republic are arguably contrary to art 10(9) of the Constitution.[137] Actions to enforce, rescind, and vary or to claim

---

130 Child Protection and Welfare Act 2016, s 5(1).

131 Child Protection and Welfare Act 2016, s 6(1).

132 Workers (Contracts of Service) Act 1922, s 3. Contracts of service under this Act require ministerial approval: s 4.

133 Jim Arrowsmith and Janet Parker, *Situational Analysis of Employment in Nauru* (International Labour Organization, 2015) 6 <https://www.ilo.org/suva/publications/WCMS_431973/lang--en/index.htm>

134 Arrowsmith and Parker, above n 133, at 22.

135 Australian Border Force Act 2015 (Cth), s 7 and Part 6.

136 Republic Proceedings Act 1972, s 3(3). Proceedings include 'a claim by way of set-off or counterclaim raised in proceedings by the Republic': s 2(2) (definition of 'civil proceedings'). Applications for leave to commence proceedings must be made in writing and accompanied by the proposed statement of claim, counterclaim or third-party notice: Proceedings Against the Republic Regulations 1973, s 3.

137 Nauru Constitutional Review Commission, above n 87, 27–28; Peter H MacSporran *Nauru: The Constitution* (Seaview Press, 2007) 40. See also *Mahdi v Director of Police* [2003] NRSC 3 where Connell CJ dismissed an application by the Secretary of Justice to strike out a habeas corpus application for failing to obtain leave of Cabinet under the Republic Proceedings Act 1972. His Honour found that art 5(4) of the Constitution 'removes by clear implication

damages founded on a simple contract must be commenced within six years of the cause of action accruing.[138] Similarly, actions in negligence, nuisance or breach of duty (arising by virtue of contract or statutorily) must be commenced within six years of the cause of action accruing.[139]

6. PROPERTY LAW

Land is divided into 'phosphate-bearing land', 'non-phosphate-bearing land', and 'worked-out phosphate-bearing land'.[140] *Inter vivos*[141] and testamentary[142] transfers of freehold land to non-Nauruan persons are forbidden and any such attempt to transfer is absolutely void and of no effect. Furthermore, it is an offence to transfer, sell or lease, or grant any estate or interest in land without the written consent of the President of Nauru.[143] The Nauru Lands Committee has power to determine questions as to the ownership of land that arise between Nauruans or Pacific Islanders, between Nauruans and Pacific Islanders,[144] and, under customary law, in relation to the personal estates of deceased Nauruans.[145] The Committee is comprised only of Nauruan citizens.[146] The Nauru Lands Committee publishes its rulings in the *Government Gazette*.[147]

Personal property is governed by common law principles, adjusted pursuant to customary law under s 4(4) of the Custom and Adopted Laws Act 1971. For example, under customary law, objects that would otherwise be considered as fixtures in many other common law countries may be considered personal property. So where a person builds on his or her parents' land, with their approval, the child will continue to hold personal property in the building despite its annexure to the land.[148] In fact, 'Nauruans have never treated or regarded houses

the effect of s 3(1) of the Republic Proceedings Act 1972': [10]. However, the Republic Proceedings Act 1972 has successfully prevented civil actions in the past: see *Heinrich v Nauru Phosphate Corporation* [1987] SPLR 167.

138 Limitation Act 2017, s 6.

139 Limitation Act 2017, s 7.

140 Lands Act 1976. See also Leo D Keke 'Nauru: Issues and Problems' in Ron Crocombe (ed) *Land Issues in the Pacific* (MacMillan Brown Centre for Pacific Studies, 1994) 229–234.

141 Lands Act 1976, s 3. Under subs (6): 'A "Nauruan person" does not include a corporation or an unincorporated body of persons of whom some are not Nauruans'.

142 *Aremwa v Nauru Lands Committee* [1969–82] NLR(B) 17.

143 Lands Act 1976, s 3(3).

144 Nauru Lands Committee Act 1956, s 6(1A).

145 *Agir v Nauru Lands Committee* [2011] NRSC 8.

146 Nauru Lands Committee Act 1956, s 3(2). See also Weeramantry, above n 23, 159–179.

147 Leo Keke 'Land Tenure and Administration in Nauru' in Guy Powles and Mere Pulea (eds) *Pacific Courts and Legal Systems* (University of South Pacific and Monash University, 1988) 144 at 147.

148 *Batsiua v Nauru Lands Committee* [2018] NRSC 47 at [65].

as fixtures.'[149] In a commercial setting, the demarcation between personal and real property is closer to that in other common law jurisdictions.[150]

If RONPHOS (formerly the Republic of Nauru Phosphate Corporation) (discussed below) requires freehold land to be leased for a public purpose, then the consent of the landowner is required.[151] 'Objects of heritage' vest in the Republic[152] and include moveable objects of 'heritage significance', namely 'archaeological, architectural, cultural, scientific or social significance, antiquities, objects, sites or war relics.'[153] Provision is also made for a minister to declare an area surrounding an object of heritage to be a protected site.

Intellectual property is protected through the Copyright Act 2019, the Patents Registration Act 1973, and the Trademarks Act 2019.

7. COMMERCIAL LAW

Since its independence, Australian currency is the legal tender of Nauru.[154] During the 1980s and 1990s Nauru was implicated in a number of money laundering scandals and unwittingly became the conduit for the proceeds of various criminal enterprises.[155] Concerns that the Bank of Nauru was being used to launder money forced its closure in 1998. It was not until 2015 that another financial institution, Bendigo Bank, could be convinced to open a branch on the island. This was achieved by strengthening anti-money laundering and combatting the financing of terrorism legislation.[156] In addition to the Corporations Act 1972 and licensing requirements under the Business Licences Act 2017, Nauru tightened registration requirements for partnerships,[157]

---

149 *Temaki v Bam* [2019] NRSC 22 at [34] (Justice Rapi Vaai). See also Timothy Detudamo (ed) *Legends, Traditions & Tales of Nauru* (IPS Publications, 2008) 55, who states that traditionally the 'property of a Nauruan consisted of coconut land, pandanus land, fruit trees standing on other people's land, a dwelling house, a site for a dwelling house, a fishpond, and a fishing area running from the edge of the reef to about five hundred yards out.'

150 *Detabene v Ronphos* [2011] NRSC 8.

151 Lands Act 1976, s 5.

152 National Heritage Act 2017, s 9(1).

153 National Heritage Act 2017, s 3 (see definitions of 'objects of heritage' and 'heritage significance').

154 Currency Act 1976, s 3. By GN No 295/1976, published in *Gazette* issue 47 on 29 September 1976, the Minister nominated the Commonwealth of Australia for the purposes of this Act.

155 Anthony B van Fossen 'Money Laundering, Global Financial Instability, and Tax Havens in the Pacific Islands' (2003) 15(2) The Contemporary Pacific 237.

156 Anti-Money Laundering Act 2008; Counter Terrorism and Transnational Organised Crime Act 2004.

157 Partnerships Act 2018. Acts done by the partners in a firm bind the partnership and all partners for which partners are jointly and severally liable: s 8(a).

express/charitable trusts,[158] and businesses not trading under their incorporated names.[159] Owners or shareholders of corporations, partnerships, trusts and businesses can be directed to trace and disclose their beneficial owners.[160]

Nauru has made a concerted effort to refute its reputation as a 'true tax haven'.[161] In 2014, an employment tax was introduced, levied at a rate of up to 30 per cent of income.[162] Services rendered by non-residents of Nauru are subject to a services tax of 30 per cent. The Business Tax Act 2016 added a raft of other taxes. Goods and services are not subject to any form of value-added tax. In fact, the price of staples may be limited by ministerial price orders.[163] At the time of writing, diesel, petrol and rice are 'declared goods' for such purposes.[164]

8. ENVIRONMENTAL LAW

The mining of phosphate has left behind limestone pinnacles that now scar the surface of the island's interior.[165] Mining has taken place on approximately 70 per cent of the Nauru's land mass.[166] Australia shirked responsibility for rehabilitating the landscape. The focus of the Nauru Rehabilitation Corporation, a body that was set up in the wake of the settlement of the ICJ case, has perversely turned to secondary phosphate mining.[167]

Nauru acceded to the Kyoto Protocol in 2005,[168] followed by the Paris Agreement in 2016.[169] The Environmental Management and Climate Change Act 2020 and the Ozone Layer Protection Act 2017 give effect to Nauru's international obligations and aim to reduce pollution. The former Act establishes a Climate Change and Environment Protection Fund. These statutes are supplemented by provisions in the Animals Act 1982 and Agricultural Quarantine Act 1999. In addition, the Ports and Navigation Act 2019 provides

---

158 Trusts Act 2018.

159 Business Names Registration Act 2018, s 7.

160 Beneficial Ownership Act 2017.

161 MacSporran, above n 137, at 136.

162 Employment and Services Tax (Amendment to Schedule) Regulation 2020.

163 Prices Regulation Act 2008, s 4.

164 See GN No 344/2008. In the past, wholesale and retail price limitations have also been imposed on Jet A1 fuel.

165 Although some believe the aesthetic qualities of the exposed limestone pinnacles are beautiful and should be exploited as tourism opportunities: S J Gale 'The mined-out phosphate lands of Nauru, equatorial western Pacific' (2016) 63(3) Australian Journal of Earth Sciences 333 at 347.

166 Douglas Fenner 'Nauru' in Charles Sheppard (ed) *World Seas: An Environmental Evaluation* (Academic Press, 2019) vol II, 793 at 793.

167 Storr, above n 32, at 251–252.

168 Kyoto Protocol to the United Nations Framework Convention on Climate Change, 2303 UNTS 162 (opened for signature 11 December 1997, entered into force 16 February 2005).

169 Opened for signature 12 December 2015, entered into force 4 November 2016.

for procedures for the discharge of ballast water, oil and other harmful substances into Nauru's exclusive economic zone.

9. NATURAL RESOURCES

Secondary phosphate mining is managed by RONPHOS, a corporation established under the RONPHOS Act 2005. Nauru's exclusive economic zone extends from the baseline of Nauru to the territorial sea 200 nautical miles seaward from the baseline of Nauru,[170] comprising about 431,000 square kilometres.[171] Nauru is a signatory to the Nauru Agreement, along with seven other Pacific nations.[172] The Agreement controls licensing of vessels in what forms the world's largest tuna purse-seine fishery. As a signatory to the UN Convention on the Law of the Sea,[173] Nauru has sponsored applications by commercial mining companies to the International Seabed Authority to explore the deep seabed for valuable minerals.[174] However, it is unlikely that seabed mining will contribute much to the Nauruan government revenue.[175]

10. CRIMINAL LAW

Up until 2016, Nauru's substantive criminal law was provided by the Queensland Criminal Code as it stood on 1 July 1921.[176] On 12 May 2016, the Criminal Code, as it operated in Nauru, was repealed and replaced by the Crimes Act 2016, which codifies the law.[177] No person under the age of 10 years is criminally responsible for an offence, but between the ages of 10 and 14 years of age the prosecution carries the burden of proving the child knows the child's conduct is wrong.[178] Bodies corporate are able to be prosecuted under the Act. Contempt of court is codified under the Administration of Justice Act 2018. That Act applies

170 Sea Boundaries Act 1997, s 6(1). Within the exclusive economic zone, Nauru has 'sovereign rights for the purposes of exploring and exploiting, conserving and managing the natural resources' of the seabed and jurisdiction over the preservation of the marine environment: Sea Boundaries Act 1997, s 6(4).

171 Fenner above n 166, at 793.

172 Nauru Agreement Concerning Cooperation in the Management of Fisheries of Common Stocks (11 February 1982).

173 1833 UNTS 3 (opened for signature 10 December 1982, entered into force 16 November 1994).

174 See the International Seabed Minerals Act 2015, Part 3.

175 Isabel Feichtner 'Mining for humanity in the deep sea and outer space: The role of small states and international law in the extraterritorial expansion of extraction' (2019) 32 Leiden Journal of International Law 255 at 270.

176 Laws Repeal and Adopting Ordinance 1922.

177 Crimes Act 2016, s 4.

178 Crimes Act 2016, s 41(3).

to corporations and other bodies and provides some defences. The maximum penalty for contempt of court is a fine of AU$20,000 or imprisonment for a term not exceeding two years, or both.[179]

Abortion is unlawful unless is carried out by a medical practitioner up to 20 weeks of pregnancy with the consent of the mother and only where the practitioner considers it is 'appropriate' or 'necessary'.[180] The Cybercrime Act 2015 provides for computer and internet-related offences, including the use of such devices to commit fraud or disseminate child pornography, spam or communications that constitute harassment or threaten 'national defence, public safety, public order, public morality or public health'.[181]

The legal burden of proof is on the prosecution to prove each element of the offence unless a written law expressly provides otherwise.[182] The evidential burden of proof generally rests on the prosecution unless the defendant seeks to rely on an excuse or similar.[183] Trials before the Supreme Court are conducted by judge alone.[184] Proceedings are usually conducted in open court.[185] A public legal defender may provide 'legal aid, advice and assistance' to a person in criminal or civil proceedings.[186] The Court of Appeal's decision in *Batsiua* casts doubt on the ability of a trial judge to direct that the public legal defender represent an accused at trial.[187] The Director of Public Prosecutions represents Nauru in any criminal proceedings before the courts and has the power to enter a *nolle prosequi*. 'Every accused person has the right to be released on bail unless it is not in the interests of justice that bail be granted.'[188] Except for serious offences,[189] a police officer has power to grant bail. Courts have jurisdiction to grant bail in all cases. The presumption in favour of bail[190] is displaced in various circumstances, including where the accused is charged with murder, treason or contempt of court.[191] Judges are permitted to substitute a sentence on appeal only where the court identifies an error of law in the decision-making of the

179 Administration of Justice Act 2018, s 11(1).
180 Crimes Act 2016, ss 63(1) and 68.
181 Cybercrime Act 2015, ss 13, 14, 17, 18, 21 and 22. Police have investigated alleged false posts on social media relating to the presence of the COVID-19 virus under this Act, with President Aingimea describing it as being like calling a false bomb threat at an airport: 'Nauru remains coronavirus-free', *Nauru Bulletin*, Issue 5-2020/209 (8 April 2020) 1–2.
182 Crimes Act 2016, ss 25 and 27.
183 Crimes Act 2016, s 26.
184 Criminal Procedure Act 1972, s 188.
185 Criminal Procedure Act 1972, s 44.
186 Criminal Procedure Act 1972, s 50C.
187 *Republic v Batsiua* (Nauru Court of Appeal, Criminal Appeal No 02/18) at [77].
188 Bail Act 2018, s 4(1).
189 Defined as an offence 'for which the maximum penalty includes imprisonment for 3 years or more': Bail Act 2018, s 3(1).
190 Bail Act 2018, s 4(3).
191 Bail Act 2018, s 4(4).

court below.[192] Penalties and sentences are provided for in Part 15 of the Crimes Act 2016 and alternatives to custodial sentences are provided for in the Criminal Justice Act 1999.

11. ROLE OF INTERNATIONAL LAW AND TREATIES

International law has no effect in Nauru unless it has been incorporated into domestic law by legislation.[193] However, for the purposes of statutory interpretation, s 52 of the Interpretation Act 2011 permits reference to international instruments where Nauru is a party.

Nauru is a member of the Pacific Islands Forum and the Alliance of Small Island States. Nauru is a signatory to the Multilateral Convention for Mutual Administrative Assistance in Tax Matters, sharing tax information with other signatories.

12. CIVIL SOCIETY ORGANISATIONS

A small number of organisations exist on the island, including the Nauru Chamber of Commerce and Industry, the Nauru Law Society and the peak NGO, the Nauru Island Association of NGOs. About two-thirds of Nauruans identify as Protestant and the Nauru Congregational Church is by far the largest church on the island.[194]

News on the island is dominated by government-owned entities including Radio Nauru, Nauru Television and the monthly newspaper, *Mwinen Ko* (let's talk about the issues).[195] In addition, the Government Information Office produces a fortnightly newsletter called the *Nauru Bulletin*.

13. CONCLUSION

Climate change threatens to contract Nauru's already short coastline. President Lionel Rouwen Aingimea MP announced an ambitious 'Higher Ground' initiative to relocate infrastructure to higher interior lands at Topside.[196]

---

192 *Cecil v Director of Public Prosecution (Nauru)* (2017) 91 ALJR 1236 at [10]–[11].

193 *Re BR (Adoption)* [2014] 2 LRC 347, 358 at [47].

194 Gary D Bouma, Rodney Ling and Douglas Pratt *Religious Diversity in Southeast Asia and the Pacific: National Case Studies* (Springer, 2010) 164.

195 Evangelia Papoutsaki and Mario Muliaumaseali'I 'Nauru' in Debra L Merskin (ed) *The SAGE International Encyclopedia of Mass Media and Society* (SAGE Publications, 2020) 1195–1196.

196 *Address by Mr Lionel Rouwen Aingimea, President of the Republic of Nauru*, UN General Assembly, 74th sess, 8th mtg, UN Doc A/74/PV.8 (26 September 2019) 9/62.

A previous proposal to resettle Nauruans to Fraser Island, Queensland failed because both Nauruan sovereignty and identity would have been diminished.[197]

Given its past, Nauruans are understandably wary of foreign influence and anything that threatens to fracture Nauru's harmonious way of life, but this caution has prevented the wider media from undertaking its role as the Fourth Estate.[198] Foreign journalists seeking visas in Nauru must pay a non-refundable fee of AU$8,000.[199] For a brief period, Facebook was banned by the country's sole internet service provider.[200] A recent insertion of sedition offences into the Crimes Act can only have a further chilling effect on the expression of divergent viewpoints.[201]

It is hoped that secondary mining of 'harder-to-reach phosphate' will reach yearly production levels of 200,000 metric tonnes.[202] Whether such yields are achievable remains to be seen. At some point the phosphate will run out and Nauru will need to find other sources of revenue from overseas. A requisite for foreign investment is the maintenance of a stable, open and predictable legal system. Despite the apparent gloom, it would be a mistake to write off Nauru's future.

In 1967, Australian Senator M C Cormack predicted that Nauru was destined to become 'the greatest slum in the oceans of the world',[203] and in 2006, academic John Connell went as far as to declare Nauru a 'failed state'.[204] Both predictions have not come to pass. Time and time again, Nauru has faced adversity and shown its people possess an enduring and resilient spirit. There is much to be learned from Nauru's tumultuous history. It serves as a microcosm for issues such as environmental exploitation, climate change and dominance of the executive arm.

---

197 Gil Marvel Tabucanon and Brian Opeskin 'The Resettlement of Nauruans in Australia: An Early Case of Failed Environmental Migration' (2011) 46(3) Journal of Pacific History 337. See also a 1963 proposal to resettle Nauruans to Curtis Island, Queensland: Jane McAdam *Climate Change, Forced Migration, and International Law* (Oxford University Press, 2012) 149–153.

198 See generally Janey Mac *Janey Mac goes to Nauru* (Ginninderra Press, 2018).

199 'Visa requirements' at <http://www.naurugov.nr/about-nauru/visiting-nauru/visa-requirements.aspx>. See also Nic Maclellan 'Nauru' (2020) 32(1) The Contemporary Pacific 213 at 222.

200 Max Quanchi 'Nauru' in Stephen Levine (ed) *Pacific Ways: Government and Politics in the Pacific Islands* (2nd ed, Victoria University Press, 2016) 148 at 158.

201 The Crimes (Amendment) Act 2020 creates Part 12A, which provides for the offence of sedition, which applies to conduct occurring in and outside of Nauru: s 243D. Sedition is committed if a person utters any 'seditious words or information' through any form of media which has 'sedition intention'. This includes an intention to 'raise discontent or disaffection' amongst residents, to incite residents to 'attempt to procure the alteration of any matter in the Republic as by law established': ss 243A and 243B. A number of lawful exceptions apply including attempting to persuading people 'to procure by lawful means the alteration of any matter established' by law: s 243C.

202 Government Information Office 'Nauru phosphate turns 50', *Nauru Bulletin*, Issue 12-2020/216 (10 July 2020) 5.

203 'Cormack predicts Nauru "a slum"' *The Canberra Times* (Canberra), 4 November 1967, 3.

204 John Connell 'Nauru: The First Failed Pacific State?' (2006) 95 The Round Table 47.

BIBLIOGRAPHY

Davidson, James Wightman 'Nauru' in *International Encyclopedia of Comparative Law* (vol 1, Brill Nijhoff, 1973).

Deklin, Tony 'Nauru' in Michael A Ntumy (ed) *South Pacific Islands Legal Systems* (University of Hawaii Press, 1993).

MacSporran, Peter H 'Land Ownership and Control in Nauru' (1995) 2(2) Murdoch University Electronic Journal of Law.

MacSporran, Peter H *Nauru: The Constitution* (Seaview Press, 2007).

McDaniel, Carl N and John M Gowdy *Paradise for Sale: A Parable of Nature* (University of California Press, 2000).

McDowell, Karen 'The factors behind the constitutional arrangements in Nauru' in Peter G Sack (ed) *Pacific Constitutions: Proceedings of the Canberra Law Workshop VI* (Law Department, Australian National University, 1982).

Mehra, N *Practice and Procedure of the Parliament of Nauru* (1990).

Nauru Constitutional Review Commission, *Report* (28 February 2007).

Pacific Islands Legal Information Institute *Nauru Primary Materials* <http://www.paclii.org/countries/nr.html>.

Quanchi, Max 'Nauru' in Stephen Levine (ed) *Pacific Ways: Government and Politics in the Pacific Islands* (2nd ed, Victoria University Press, 2016).

Ratuva, Steven 'The gap between global thinking and local living: dilemmas of constitutional reform in Nauru' (2011) 120(3) The Journal of the Polynesia Society 241.

Storr, Cait *International Status in the Shadow of Empire: Nauru and the Histories of International Law* (Cambridge University Press, 2020).

Viviani, Nancy *Nauru: Phosphate and Pollical Progress* (ANU Press, 1970).

Weeramantry, Christopher *Nauru: Environmental Damage Under International Trusteeship* (Oxford University Press, 1992).

Williams, Maslyn and Barrie Macdonald *The Phosphateers: A History of the British Phosphate Commissioners and the Christmas Island Phosphate Commission* (Melbourne University Press, 1985).

NEW CALEDONIA – NOUVELLE-CALÉDONIE

Carine DAVID and Victor DAVID

1. CONTEXT

New Caledonia is an archipelagic French overseas territory in the south-west Pacific Ocean, to the north-east of Australia. It consists of a large main island, called Grande Terre (400 kilometres long and 40 kilometres wide), the Loyalty Islands archipelago, low-lying coral atolls and numerous other small islands. The total land area of New Caledonia is 19,100 square kilometres. New Caledonia's exclusive economic zone (EEZ) covers 1,740,000 square kilometres (672,000 square miles), representing 16 per cent of France's EEZ.

New Caledonia was first settled about 4,000 years ago by the ancestors of the Melanesian inhabitants, the Kanak. It was annexed by France in 1853 as part of the 'second French colonial Empire'. The status of New Caledonia as a colony persisted virtually unchanged until after World War II, then New Caledonia became an overseas territory (*territoire d'outre-mer* or TOM) under the French Constitution of 1946. From then on, the Kanak as well as immigrant workers were gradually granted the right to vote. The Kanak then became increasingly involved in local politics.

In 1956, extensive autonomy was granted to New Caledonia, as it was to most French overseas territories. Nevertheless, after 1956, French governments seemed unable to maintain this autonomy and, during the 1960s, the State reneged and reduced the autonomy of New Caledonia, particularly with regard to the management of mineral resources, thereby reducing the potential financial self-sufficiency of the territory.

As a result, from the end of the 1960s, the Kanak started formulating demands for greater autonomy from France. Confronted with France's refusal to return to the autonomy previously granted, the political claim progressively turned into a Kanak independence movement. Under the pressure of this sovereigntist movement, New Caledonia experienced, over a period of about 20 years, a dozen different statutes that granted or withdrew various degrees of autonomy, very well summarised by Professor G Agniel with the figurative expression 'institutional yo-yo'.[1]

The independence struggle led to a near-civil-war situation during the 1980s,[2] which reached a paroxysm in 1988 with a hostage-taking in a cave on the island of Ouvéa, which ended with the deaths of more than 20 people. To get out of the crisis, an agreement was concluded between the French State and the leaders of the loyalist and independence movements, leading to the Matignon Agreements. These paved the way for a return to civil peace, pending a self-determination referendum that was scheduled for 1998. By consensus among local political leaders, a new agreement, the Nouméa Accord, was concluded in May 1998;[3] it extended the self-determination deadline by 20 years.

The current institutional organisation of New Caledonia is the result of this statutory evolution that led to New Caledonia becoming an extremely unique self-governing entity within the French Constitution.[4]

This exceptional legal and political framework is guided by a logic of progressive emancipation, given that New Caledonia appears on the United Nations list of non-self-governing territories. The Nouméa Accord therefore provided for a 20-year cycle, with the organisation of possibly three successive referendums on self-determination.

The first consultation took place on 4 November 2018. The 'concerned populations' of New Caledonia (an electoral body restricted to indigenous

1 Guy Agniel 'L'expérience statutaire de la Nouvelle-Calédonie ou de l'étude du mouvement du yo-yo au service de l'évolution institutionnelle d'un territoire d'outremer' in 'L'avenir statutaire de la Nouvelle-Calédonie. L'évolution des liens de la France avec ses collectivités périphériques', *Les études de la documentation française* (1997) 41.

2 Nic MacLellan 'The Noumea Accord and Decolonisation in New Caledonia', (1999) 34(3) The Journal of Pacific History 245–252, <https://www.jstor.org/stable/25169446>.

3 Accord sur la Nouvelle-Calédonie signé à Nouméa le 5 mai 1998 <https://www.legifrance.gouv.fr/affichTexte.do?cidTexte=JORFTEXT000000555817&categorieLien=id>.

4 The Constitution needed to be amended in order to allow this extensive institutional and normative autonomy <https://www.conseil-constitutionnel.fr/sites/default/files/as/root/bank_mm/anglais/constiution_anglais_oct2009.pdf>.

Kanak people and citizens from other ethnic groups who qualified for permanent residency before December 1994) were asked if they wanted 'New Caledonia to access to full sovereignty and become independent'. 56.67 per cent of voters answered 'No' to this question, and so in line with the Nouméa Accord, a second referendum on the same question was organised on 4 October 2020.[5] The answer was still negative,[6] so a third and final consultation will take place on 12 December 2021, as decided by the French government in June 2021.

The self-determination process as stated by the Nouméa Accord will then be over and the Caledonian people will have made their choice between remaining as a non-sovereign island jurisdiction within the French Republic or becoming an independent state.[7]

2. SOURCES OF LAW

The presentation of the sources of law is an opportunity to highlight the legal pluralism existing in New Caledonia. Due to its societal composition, customs of indigenous populations are a source additional to 'formal law', especially in the field of civil law.[8] The autonomy of New Caledonia within the French Republic is also an explanation for the originality of New Caledonia's sources of law, which allows a mix of national and local regulations even though France is a unitary state.

The New Caledonia Act of 19 March 1999[9] provides the current legal framework for the institutional functioning of the territory.

The basic principle of the current land law of New Caledonia is to be found in s 6 of the New Caledonia Act 1999, which states that there are three different regimes of land ownership in New Caledonia: 'classic' private property, public property, and the customary lands regime (*terres coutumières*).[10]

---

5 Carine David 'The road to sovereignty for New Caledonia? Analysis of the November 2018 consultation on self-determination', (2019) 2(2) Small States and Territories Journal, 141–156, <https://www.um.edu.mt/library/oar/bitstream/123456789/49767/4/SST-2-2-David-FINAL.pdf>.

6 Carine David 'L'hypothèse d'un Etat associé calédonien : sortir du dogmatisme pour trouver une solution pérenne pour la Nouvelle-Calédonie', (2020) 36(2) Revue Juridique, Politique et Economique de la Nouvelle-Calédonie 129–135.

7 Carine David 'L'hypothèse d'un Etat associé calédonien : sortir du dogmatisme pour trouver une solution pérenne pour la Nouvelle-Calédonie', (2020) 36(2) Revue Juridique, Politique et Economique de la Nouvelle-Calédonie 129–135.

8 Oona Le Meur 'Customary Law and Custom in New-Caledonia: Legal Pluralism, Citizenship and the External/Internal Sovereignty Issue' (2015) 2 SOAS Law Journal 230.

9 Loi organique modifiée n° 99-209 relative à la Nouvelle-Calédonie <https://www.legifrance.gouv.fr/loda/id/JORFTEXT000000393606>.

10 See <http://adraf.nc/>.

Most sources of law applicable in New Caledonia are 'formal law', that is to say the law produced by the so-called 'republican' institutions, both at State[11] or local level.[12]

Among these, the Constitution constitutes the primary source of law. Almost all the French 'block of constitutionality' (ie the French Constitution, the Declaration of the Rights of Man and of the Citizen (Déclaration des droits de l'homme et du citoyen) of 26 August 1789, the Preamble to the Constitution of 27 October 1946, the Charter for the Environment of 2004, and all the principles and objectives established by the Constitutional Council) is applicable in New Caledonia. Some derogations were nonetheless granted to New Caledonia, for example the right to vote in local elections (reserved to New Caledonian citizens and excluding 30,000–40,000 French citizens from the electoral body), access to local employment (priority of access is granted to people who have resided in New Caledonia for at least 10 years) and the attribution of legislative power to the local Parliament when the national Parliament normally has the monopoly over legislative power.

International sources of law are also important, but they are significantly different from the national level. On the one hand, since New Caledonia has the status of an Overseas Country and Territory (OCT) of the European Union, European Union law does not apply. On the other hand, most of the international conventions ratified by France are applicable in New Caledonia, unless at the time of negotiation of the convention the State made a reservation of territorial applicability. Finally, some regional conventions are also applicable, for example the Nouméa Convention for the Protection of the Natural Resources and Environment of the South Pacific Region (1986)[13] or the Apia Convention on Conservation of Nature in the South Pacific (1979).[14]

Legislative power is shared between the French Parliament and the Congress of New Caledonia[15] in their respective areas of power as specified in ss 21, 22 and 99 of the New Caledonia Act 1999. Acts and regulations adopted by French national authorities even in matters specified in s 21 are enforceable in New Caledonia only if they expressly say so. Statutes (*lois du pays*) adopted by the local Parliament have the same authority as those passed by the national Parliament.[16]

---

11 National Databank: <www.legifrance.gouv.fr>.

12 New Caledonia Databank: <www.juridoc.gouv.nc>.

13 Convention for the Protection of Natural Resources and Environment of the South Pacific Region (1986), also known as the SPREP Convention or Noumea Convention <https://www.sprep.org/convention-secretariat/noumea-convention>.

14 Convention on Conservation of Nature in the South Pacific (1976), also known as the Apia Convention <https://www.sprep.org/convention-secretariat/apia-convention>.

15 Congrès de la Nouvelle-Calédoni : <www.congres.nc>.

16 Carine Gindre David *Essai sur la loi du pays calédonienne – La dualité de la source législative dans l'Etat unitaire*, (Editions L'Harmattan, 2009).

Currently, and after progressive devolution of powers from the national to the local level over the 20 years of application of the Nouméa Accord (1998–2018), the local legislative field includes matters such as civil law, commercial law, tax law, labour and social security law, and even mining law, public property law and the law relating to Kanak identity.

Case law as a source of law is, on the contrary, exclusively of State origin because justice is a competence still fully exercised by the State at both the national and local level. The judicial system is nevertheless organised in order to take into account local specificities. It is especially interesting to highlight the presence of customary assessors before the civil courts. Indeed, when a dispute involves matters relating to persons and property as well as customary land law, the role of the assessor is to inform the judge about the customary rules and practices in order to allow the judge to apply the traditional rules. Customary assessors are lay judges and they form the customary civil chamber which is presided over by a professional judge.[17] Ordinance n° 82-877 of 15 October 1982 created the customary assessors and gave birth to this judicial institution, unique in the Pacific, which demonstrates an interesting accommodation by the judicial system in its daily operation of non-Western systems of thought.

Finally, the regulation-making power is shared between the State (central and local authorities):[18] New Caledonia (Congress and government of New Caledonia),[19] the provinces (New Caledonia is divided into three provinces), and the municipalities.

Beyond 'formal law' enacted by republican institutions, the situation of persons of customary civil status is governed by their customs regarding matters relating to personal law and customary land law. The application of customary rules and practices is the responsibility of the customary authorities; they govern the daily life of people who have Kanak customary status.

In addition, the Customary Senate – either a consultative authority or co-legislator (in the fields related to custom and Kanak identity) – intervenes in decision-making processes to infuse Caledonian law with Melanesian customary values. This hybridisation of the regulations enacted in New Caledonia remains, however, extremely limited. The exception is the regulations of the province of the Loyalty Islands (whose population is 97 per cent Kanak), in particular in its Environmental Code (in its general principles and in regulations related to protected areas).[20]

17 Cour d'appel de Nouméa: <https://www.cours-appel.justice.fr/noumea>.

18 Haut-commissariat en Nouvelle-Calédonie: <www.nouvelle-caledonie.gouv.fr>.

19 Gouvernement de la Nouvelle-Calédonie: <www.gouv.nc>.

20 <https://www.province-iles.nc/sites/default/files/2019-03/19-033-Code-de-l-environnement-PIL.pdf>.

3. CONSTITUTIONAL LAW

New Caledonia is an autonomous French overseas territory in the process of emancipation, the institutional organisation of which has been the subject of successive developments as a result of independence claims and the shifting balance of power between secessionists and supporters of maintaining the territory as part of the French Republic.

The 1958 French Constitution and all the fundamental guarantees that derive from it are fully applicable in New Caledonia. Any local legislative Act or regulation that does not abide by it can be declared unconstitutional by courts.

Otherwise, except for a restricted number of matters that are usually considered to be the sovereign powers of the State (eg national defence, currency, justice, diplomacy) that are still exercised by the national government, most matters that need normative intervention are within the power of New Caledonia's local authorities.

Since the 1980s, the intensification of the independence movement has led to an increasing territorial division of New Caledonia. The creation of the *pays* by the Lemoine statute in 1984, then of the 'regions' by the Fabius Pisani statute in 1985 mark the awareness of the need for a sharing of political power on a territorial basis to take into account the demographic distribution of the population.

In this context, the provincialisation of the archipelago initiated by the Matignon-Oudinot Agreements in 1988 and confirmed by the Nouméa Accord in 1998 constitutes a key element of the political system put in place to effect a lasting return to civil peace. Indeed, the geographic division of the territory has been used as a tool of territorial federalism, which allows each political group to gain power over the parts of territory where it enjoys majority representation. The provinces have broad powers and significant financial means. The same logic governs the composition of territorial institutions.

First, the local executive is no longer the Haut-Commissaire, the representative of the French State, but the government of New Caledonia, an offshoot of the local assembly. Executive power is vested in the government of New Caledonia, including its President, who represents the territory.

The method of appointment of its members is a specific feature of the government of New Caledonia. Its uniqueness remains in the fact that it is the one extremely rare example of a multi-party government that works. Elected by the Congress of New Caledonia through proportional representation, the local executive thus reflects the different main political trends of the local parliament. As a consequence, parliamentary majorities and minorities coexist within the government. Required by the Nouméa Accord and answering to a consociational logic, the heterogeneous composition of the government reflects the need to build a common destiny for the various elements of Caledonian society. By requiring the majority to discuss with representatives of the opposition, the structure of government is truly original, even though similar approaches can be found in the Good Friday Agreement in Northern Ireland or in the 1997 Fiji Constitution.

After their election by the Congress, members of the government appoint their President and Vice-President and proceed by consensus with the distribution of areas of responsibility for each member.

In this context, the High Commissioner plays a more limited role than previously. This shows the evolution towards autonomy desired by the negotiators of the Nouméa Accord. The High Commissioner is the representative of the French State and, more importantly, ensures that the institutions of New Caledonia are exercising their powers appropriately, including through the review of legality.

The legislative power in New Caledonia is exercised by a partially bicameral Parliament composed of the Congress and the Customary Senate,[21] the latter being involved in the legislative process only in so far as it concerns matters of Kanak identity and custom.

The members of the Congress of New Caledonia are elected for five years. The Congress is an offshoot of the provincial assemblies. The local territorial assembly is composed of 7 of the 14 members of the Loyalty Islands Province assembly, 15 of the 22 councillors of the Northern Province assembly, and 32 of the 40 elected members of the Southern Province assembly. Each province thus forms a constituency for the designation of members of the Congress of New Caledonia.

Elections take place with a party-list proportional representation system. Seats are allocated in the order of presentation of each list. However, there is a threshold and the lists which do not obtain the support of five per cent of registered voters do not participate in the distribution of seats.

Congress has two main roles. The first is to adopt, within its areas of competence, regulations that are binding on Caledonians. These take the form of administrative powers and – a major innovation of the New Caledonia Act 1999 – legislative power. The second of Congress's roles is to elect the government of New Caledonia, and possibly to hold it accountable by way of a no-confidence motion.

In support of specific institutions, the Nouméa Accord recognises the pre-existence of the Kanak people because of their presence in the country before annexation by France in 1853. It was also decided to grant traditional organs the rank of republican institutions in order to offer Kanak people some rehabilitation of their social and cultural identity, to use as a bulwark against Westernisation at the same time as regaining their dignity and their freedom. This explains the creation and role of the Customary Senate in the adoption of the local statutes.

---

21 <https://www.senat-coutumier.nc/>.

In this context, while Congress is in principle the only assembly to approve Bills, the participation of the Customary Senate is expected in the legislative process, for matters relating to custom.

The Customary Senate is composed of 16 members appointed through the traditional practices of each customary area, with two representatives from each customary area of New Caledonia.

4. LAW OF PERSONS

In 1887, indigenous people throughout the French colonial empire became subject to the *Code de l'indigénat*,[22] a statute that imposed restrictions on movement, summary punishments and an authoritarian system of local governance on indigenous populations and immigrant workers. The Indigenous Code distinguished two categories of citizens: French citizens (of metropolitan origin) and French subjects, ie Melanesians as well as immigrant workers. These populations were deprived of their identity. The Indigenous Code was abolished by a law of 7 April 1946.

Since 1946, the law of persons in New Caledonia is characterised by a new form of legal pluralism: the inhabitants of New Caledonia come under either 'ordinary' civil status or customary – Kanak, Wallisian or Futunian – status.

People of ordinary civil status are mainly subject to the French Civil Code,[23] that is to say the rules of French law, with slight differences as the normative power over civil law matters was transferred from France to New Caledonian authorities on 1 July 2013. In this context, most rules applicable to New Caledonian residents belonging to this category remain identical to metropolitan rules, few statutes having been enacted since then. Nevertheless, a differentiation between the two laws will come about gradually as each of the legislators reforms the civil law.[24]

Some aspects of civil law were nonetheless not transferred to New Caledonia. The transfer extends to the matters covered by the first four parts of the Civil Code (law of persons, property law, right of ownership and personal property security law), as well as other matters which, by their nature, are related in civil law, such as co-ownership, residential or professional leases, rural leases, literary and artistic property, or land advertising. The provisions on nationality, as well as art 9 of the Code (the protection of privacy, the principles relating to respect

---

22 Isabelle Merle et Adrien Muckle *L'indigénat. Genèses dans l'Empire français. Pratiques en Nouvelle-Calédonie* (CNRS, 2019).

23 <https://www.legifrance.gouv.fr/affichCode.do?cidTexte=LEGITEXT000006070721&dateTexte=20200209>.

24 <https://juridoc.gouv.nc/JuriDoc/JdCodes.nsf/(mesX-FTP)?SearchView&query=%5bMs_Cat%5d=CL&SearchOrder=4&MaxResults=3000&Start=1&Count=500&Th=CL>.

for the human body) and the provisions of arts 544 and 545 on the fundamental character of property rights, were excluded from the transfer. Also excluded were the provisions which ensure respect for freedom of marriage and the rules on freedom of association. All these fields remain in the hands of the national Parliament. For example, it is not possible for the Congress of New Caledonia to reconsider the same-sex marriage law.

The law of persons also has to comply with the 'block of constitutionality' and the international commitments of France, at the forefront of which is the European Convention on Human Rights.

According to s 7 of the New Caledonia Act 1999, people with customary civil status are governed by their customs for all matters related to civil status, ie filiation, marriage, adoption, divorce, inheritance and matrimonial property regimes. The legal regime applicable to persons in this category therefore differs according to the customary rules existing within their clan, their tribe or their customary area, as New Caledonia is divided into eight customary areas, each one consisting of several districts where tribes, subdivided into clans, live.

According to s 19 of the New Caledonia Act 1999, in the event of litigation relating to the civil status of persons under customary law, where the conflict cannot be settled by the customary authorities, it will be decided by the civil courts, before a panel comprising customary assessors whose job it is to indicate to the judge the customary rules involved. If the dispute involves a common law person and a person with customary civil status, the formal law will apply.

5. TORTS, CONTRACT AND RESTITUTION

Even though New Caledonia has the law-making power for civil law matters, the law of obligations in the territory is still entirely governed by French law. The transfer of this power took place on 1 July 2013, and the provisions applicable in contract law and the law of obligations are still quite close to French law.

In 2016, a major reform of torts and contract law took place in metropolitan France. Because this was after the transfer of power for civil law to Caledonian authorities, it opened up a gap between the two legal systems. However, substantial work to transcribe this reform into Caledonian law is being undertaken; it reveals the difficulties of emancipation for Caledonian law in a newly transferred matter. This deference towards national law can be observed quite often during the years following the transfer of powers from the French State to the New Caledonia authorities.[25]

Inspired by a tradition of Romano-Germanic law, the French law of obligations is based on the rules fixed in the Napoleonic Civil Code of 1804,

[25] For example, the patriation of labour law took nearly a dozen years to become really effective.

nourished by case law that contributes to the modernisation of this law. It has nevertheless remained faithful to classical theory and an obligation remains a personal and subjective right. However, over time, a more economics-orientated approach to obligations has emerged. In this regard, the reform brought about by the Ordinance of 10 February 2016,[26] which might be soon transposed by the Caledonian legislator, confirms this modern approach.

An obligation is today conceived both as a legal link between two people and as a link between two heritages. There is therefore a unique concept of obligation, since all obligations can be defined in the same way as a legal relationship between two people and two heritages, even if this relationship is split depending on whether the subjective aspect of the obligation (link between two people) or the objective one (relationship between two heritages) is taken into account.

Any legal obligation, whatever its source, can be defined as a legal bond uniting the creditor and the debtor, by virtue of which the former (creditor) can obtain from the latter (debtor) the performance of a service, if necessary by coercion and use of public force. Civil obligations are therefore characterised by the possibility of applying to the State courts to obtain judgment against the debtor, and by the use of measures of forced execution thereafter.

There are, however, different kinds of obligations. They have different characteristics and are subject to classifications. According to the drafters of the Civil Code, there were five main sources of obligations (arts 1101 and 1370), which led to the distinction between contractual and non-contractual sources.

Among the contractual sources is contract, which is defined as an agreement of wills, mainly to create obligations. It is defined by the Civil Code as 'an agreement by which one or more persons are bound towards one or more others, to give, to do or not to do something' (art 1101). The contract is therefore a mechanism intended to create obligations, which constitute the promise of services. As such, it is the instrument of economic exchange.

Among the non-contractual sources is quasi-contract, which is a situation similar to contract but which is imposed on the debtor independently of his or her will (eg art 1371, agent of necessity). There is also tort (*délit*) which is an intentional fault (the author has the will to harm and cause damage) and a wrongful act engaging the civil liability of its author (art 1382). Another kind of tort, called *quasi-délit*, is an unintentional wrongful act, recklessness or negligence, which also engages the tort liability of its author (art 1383).

In addition, the law imposes obligations beyond any private will, such as the support obligations between parents and children (the alimentary obligation), obligations towards the guardian, and obligations between spouses.

---

26 Ordonnance n° 2016-131 du 10 février 2016 portant réforme du droit des contrats, du régime général et de la preuve des obligations <https://www.legifrance.gouv.fr/eli/ordonnance/2016/2/10/2016-131/jo/texte>.

The 2016 Ordinance, if transposed into Caledonian law, would establish the modern distinction of legal acts and facts by distinguishing between obligations arising from legal acts, legal facts or the rule of law, or even, as is recognised at the national level, natural obligations, since it is specified in art 1100 para 2 of the Civil Code that the obligations 'may arise from the voluntary performance or from the promise to perform a duty of conscience towards others'.

6. LAWS RELATING TO LAND

Before colonisation, land law was endogenous; customary rules defined how Melanesian families (clans), through migration and matrimonial alliances, occupied – rather than owned – land. Although property lines were not properly mapped out, spatial reference points relating to livelihoods and natural features, covering inhabited or uninhabited areas, did exist and delimited usage rights on land and water. After the French took possession of the archipelago in 1853 and in particular of Grande Terre, they introduced French land law. Based on the prevailing 19th-century European distinctions between civilised and non-civilised nations in colonial contexts, the French authorities exercised their 'right to extinguish primitive titles' to land. They initially restricted the indigenous peoples' land rights to cultivated areas, wrongly assuming that fallow lands and hunting and gathering zones were vacant territories to be annexed to the colony's public domain. In the second half of the 19th century, colonial authorities progressively confiscated most of the land of the Melanesians, forcing them out of their ancestral settlements into reserves, handing out thousands of seized hectares of land to settlers, ranchers and miners. French authorities also replaced the clans' customary land rights with French land property rights but for governance purposes aggregated clans into administrative tribes that were themselves gathered into districts.

Ever since they were forced to live in reserves, sometimes far from their initial homes, the indigenous people constantly fought colonial authorities in order to get their lands back. Since it lost its official colony status in 1946 to become an overseas territory, a large part of New Caledonia's conflictual history between the indigenous peoples, the settlers' descendants and the French State is about the fight for the evolution of applicable land law and the restitution of dispossessed territories – a struggle that has become synonymous with the Kanak people's struggle for independence since the 1970s. The long-awaited evolution started with the Dijoud[27] *réforme foncière* of 1978, which had the official aim of settling 'the land problem with a view to respecting the historic rights of the Melanesian

[27] From the French Minister's name.

communities' and eventually led to the current legal status of land rights in New Caledonia.[28]

The relevant legal rules on private property, which is guaranteed by the French Constitution, are to be found in the Civil Code applicable to New Caledonia. Normative power in civil law was transferred from the French State to the Congress and government of New Caledonia in July 2013. These institutions have full power to modify the French Civil Code as they wish.

Public property rules depend on which level of government is referred to.[29] Public domain pertaining to the French State (courts, national defence infrastructures, etc.) is governed by rules adopted by the French government. They can be found in the French Code Général de la Propriété des Personnes Publiques (CG3P, s L2111.1). New Caledonia's public domain is governed by Acts of the Congress of New Caledonia (*lois du pays*) and local government regulations. The three provinces' public domain rules are also fixed by Acts of Congress.[30] Municipalities' public property rules are fixed by the national government in the Code Général des Collectivités Territoriales (CGCT).

Section 18 of the New Caledonia Act 1999 states that customary lands and all goods situated on them and belonging to persons of customary civil status in New Caledonia are regulated by customary law. Customary lands are inalienable, non-transferable, non-exchangeable and unseizable.

7. COMMERCIAL LAW

As with civil law, commercial law in New Caledonia became a local competence on 1 July 2013 and was therefore little different from French law until recently.

An obvious characteristic of commercial law in New Caledonia is its excessive complexity. It suffers from the same defects as the French law on which it was based. It is thus not surprising that the national Parliament has been recently enacting 'simplification laws' like the Covenant Act of 22 May 2019, or the Company Law Simplification Act of 19 July 2019. Some measures taken by the government of New Caledonia to lighten the burden of administrative formalities for companies reveal the same concern.

New Caledonian commercial law[31] is complex for several reasons. First, it seems obvious that the French national commercial law is not suitable for a

28 The Agence de développement rural et d'aménagement foncier (ADRAF)'s website is a very useful resource on land law in New Caledonia: <http://www.adraf.nc/>.

29 <https://www.collectivites-locales.gouv.fr/biens-relevant-domaine-public-biens-relevant-domaine-prive>.

30 New Caledonia Public Domain : s 44 – Loi n° 99-209 du 19 mars 1999, as well as Maritime Public domain of provinces: ss 45 and 46 – Loi n° 99-209 du 19 mars 1999 and the Loi du pays du 11 janvier 2002 sur le domaine public maritime.

31 Code de Commerce: <https://juridoc.gouv.nc/JuriDoc/JdCodes.nsf/tree2?OpenPage&code=CO>.

small island territory facing different issues and with different needs. Second, the absence (with rare exceptions) of conflict-solving rules in the event of disputes that may fall under both Caledonian and national law aggravates the situation. A third element of complexity is generated by the existence of customary law, which raises difficult questions of delimitation and relationship with formal law. Indeed, the influence of custom in commercial law, and more generally in corporate law, is often underestimated because the application of the New Caledonia Act 1999 encompasses all relations 'under civil law' between people of customary status. But very special issues arise about customary land, which imposes specific conventions on developing entrepreneurial activities and poses difficulties in terms of access to credit and business transfer. Property law, the law of persons, the law of matrimonial property regimes and the law of obligations, which all come under 'civil law', play an essential role in the functioning of businesses. Finally, the originality of corporate law in a customary environment is also marked by the existence of the *groupements de droit particulier local* (GDPLs), innovative legal structures whose primary vocation of managing customary land has today been largely supplanted by their use for entrepreneurial purposes. Legal pluralism leads to complexity in the law applicable in New Caledonia.

To demonstrate the complexity of commercial law, an example may be useful. Today, there are four main categories of independent professions working in the economy: farmers, liberal professions, craftsmen and traders. For each of these professions, the legislation provides different rules. This results in a proliferation of regulations, the knowledge and implementation of which prove to be complex.

Another example is worth mentioning: New Caledonia, by virtue of the continuity of laws inherited from French commercial law, has a very large number of types of entity: civil companies, general partnerships (SNC), limited liability companies (SARL), limited companies (SA), companies by simplified actions (SAS), as well as simple limited partnerships (SCS) or joint stock companies (SCA), non-trading companies (SCM), professional partnership companies (SCP), liberal practice companies (SEL) and limited liberal practice companies (SELARL), cooperative societies, farms with limited liability (EARL), joint farming partnerships (GAEC), agricultural land groupings (GFA), etc.[32] Whether or not such a vast choice can be justified at the national level, it appears to be ridiculous in New Caledonia.

The most recent statistical data reveal that in June 2019 there were 9,904 SARLs (including 711 SELARLs and one EARL), 9,537 civil societies (including 6,950 real estate civil societies, 75 SCMs, 19 SCPs and 522 agricultural civil societies),

---

32 A list of types of commercial companies with a description of them in French can be found at: <https://business.lesechos.fr/outils-et-services/guides/guide-de-la-creation/1417/1423-6-les-differents-types-de-societes-24609.php>.

160 limited companies with boards of directors, 589 SASs and 169 SNCs in New Caledonia. There were no limited partnerships, no public limited companies with management boards, no GFAs and no GAECs.

This excess of complexity has proven to be a major obstacle to economic development in New Caledonia. This is why the Congress of New Caledonia adopted legal provisions in this area in the Support the Growth of the Caledonian Economy Act of 20 January 2020.[33] The Act has four dimensions:

(1) Modernisation and simplification: the statute aims at modernising and simplifying the relations between entrepreneurs and the administration. Two objectives are pursued: to position the administration to be more supportive of economic development and to simplify the lifecycle of businesses. A dozen measures have been enacted, such as the creation of a right to tax error, new tools to improve the administration's payment deadline, and the launch, in mid-2020, of the www.entreprises.nc website to allow the creation of a business in a few clicks.

(2) Economic recovery: the second axis of the law concerns support for the economy and entrepreneurship. Eight measures aim at improving the cash flow of companies and their self-financing capacity in order to allow them to invest, in particular thanks to the early repayment of taxes on stocks or even to the improvement of the remuneration of the accounts of associates. Moreover, the building and automobile sectors, which are important for New Caledonia's economy, benefit from specific provisions.

(3) Boosting purchasing power: purchasing power, consumer protection and competition are the subject of the third part of the law. To fight against high living costs and the continually rising cost of life by encouraging competition, the 'price-quality shield' introduced in 2019 will be continued. Economic recovery through consumption will benefit from a boost to the purchasing power of Caledonians via an exemption from income tax on overtime for employees and the possibility given to employers to pay their employees an exceptional bonus. At the same time, consumer protection is addressed by provisions which seek to improve the efficiency of the New Caledonia Competition Authority; a consumer code will also be drawn up.

(4) Transformation and diversification of the economy: the fourth and last part of this law proposes new tax systems in favour of innovation and rebalancing in order to stimulate the transformation and diversification of the Caledonian economy. Three tools are offered: tax-free zones to encourage companies to set up where economic activity is poorly developed,

33 Loi du pays n° 2020-2 du 20 janvier 2020 de soutien à la croissance de l'économie calédonienne: <https://juridoc.gouv.nc/JuriDoc/JdWebE.nsf/joncentry?OpenPage&ap=2020&page=1491>.

a tax reduction to allow companies to finance research and innovation (30 per cent of spending up to a limit of 5 million francs (about AU$70,000) per year), and a tax credit for crowdfunding of businesses to support investment in the local economy (25 per cent of payments with a ceiling of 500,000 francs (about AU$7,000) per year).

8. ENVIRONMENTAL LAW

The archipelago of New Caledonia, thanks to its geological history, is one of the world's biodiversity hotspots, which means it shelters exceptional species of which more than 75 per cent are endemic. They face many man-made and natural threats, aggravated in recent decades by global environmental change. Strong legal protection is therefore needed to ensure a sustainable future for the terrestrial and marine biodiversity that in turn provides for the livelihoods of New Caledonians.

Despite this well-recognised need for a robust legal framework, environmental law in New Caledonia is anything but simple. To understand why, it is necessary to keep in mind that the power-sharing institutional design has led to a federalist architecture for the territory. Relations between the French State and the Pacific island territory are federal-like. The territory of New Caledonia itself is divided into three provinces on a federal basis.

In the progressive decolonisation process which started with the Matignon Agreements, which were added to the institutional autonomy that had existed since 1957, the current organisation deriving from the 1998 Nouméa Accord and the New Caledonia Act 1999 has led to a devolution of powers on a subject-matter basis between the four different levels of jurisdiction: the French State, New Caledonia, provinces (Loyalty Islands, North and South) and municipalities. All these levels are entitled to make laws regarding the environment.

The State has jurisdiction over constitutional rights related to the environment which are part of the 2005 Constitutional Charter for the Environment.[34] Various fundamental rights and principles are set out in the Charter. France also deals with international matters such as Multilateral Environmental Agreements (MEAs).[35] Unless specifically stated (which is the case for the Aarhus Convention), most of MEAs ratified by France are applicable in New Caledonia; the 1992 Rio Conventions, the Nagoya Protocol and the Paris Agreement on Climate Change are among them.

34 Available in English at <https://www.conseil-constitutionnel.fr/en/charter-for-the-environment>.

35 The Regional Cooperation Service (*Service de la Coopération Régionale et des Relations Extérieures de Nouvelle-Calédonie*) keeps a regularly updated list of MEAs applicable in New Caledonia.

Environmental NGOs are regulated by French national rules whereas New Caledonia is competent to enact rules related to energy production, water, air, mining and all environment-related fiscal rules. Since 2000, New Caledonia has adopted several master management plans (*schémas directeurs*) in fields such as mining,[36] energy production and water.[37] A Mining Code[38] was also enacted to fix the rules for the sustainable exploitation of Grande Terre's mineral resources, which include 25 per cent of the world's reserves of nickel. New Caledonia has also jurisdiction over the exploration, exploitation and management of natural resources (including genetic resources) in its EEZ and decided in 2014 that the entirety of the EEZ (1.4 million square kilometres) would be part of the Coral Sea Natural Park (*Parc Naturel de la Mer de Corail*); it will incorporate marine protected areas, no-take zones and other sustainably managed areas that will allow various kind of activities in line with the 'Blue Economy'.

Municipalities decide on waste collection, drinking water distribution systems, sewerage systems, and electric energy distribution.

According to s 20 of the New Caledonia Act 1999, all matters that are not expressly attributed to the above three levels fall within the competence of the three provinces. Environment is one such matter.

Today each province has its own Environmental Code[39] and they deal in three different ways with the management of natural resources (other than mining and water). The three Environmental Codes have a similar structure but they may differ in content. They include environmental protection principles, such as the right to information and participation in decision-making on environmental matters. The provincial Codes include rules related to environment management administrative structures, environmental impact assessments, protected areas and protected species, invasive species, management of fishing, hunting, forestry, access and benefit-sharing related to genetic resources, quarries, the *installations classées pour la protection de l'environnement* (ICPEs) (any facility – most often but not only industrial or agricultural – that requires specific assessments and preventive measures for identified risks to the natural environment, human and

---

36 Schéma de mise en valeur des richesses minières <https://dimenc.gouv.nc/sites/default/files/download/2009-05_schema_mise_en_valeur_des_richesses_minieres_nc.pdf>.

37 Schéma d'orientation de la Politique de l'Eau Partagée (PEP) <https://davar.gouv.nc/sites/default/files/atoms/files/pep_-_schema_dorientation_pour_une_politique_de_leau_partagee_de_la_nouvelle-caledonie.pdf>.

38 Mining Code: <https://dimenc.gouv.nc/sites/default/files/download/code_minier_de_la_nc_pr_chg_30-04-2019.pdf>.

39 South Province: Code de l'environnement de la province sud (CEPS) <https://www.province-sud.nc/codenv>; North Province: Code de l'environnement de la province nord (CEPN) (2018 edition) <https://www.province-nord.nc/sites/default/files/parutions/code_de_lenvironnement_mis_a_jour_le_16-02-18.pdf>; Loyalty Islands Province: Code de l'environnement de la province des îles loyauté (CEPIL) <https://www.province-iles.nc/sites/default/files/2019-03/19-033-Code-de-l-environnement-PIL.pdf>.

animal health, etc., akin to the SEVESO classification in European law), waste management, and prevention of natural disasters and pollution.

In regard to climate change responses, because there is significant mining and industrial activity in New Caledonia, it chose to focus on sustainable use of fossil energies and the transition renewable energies as much as possible. It has adopted a master plan that covers the 2020s called the *Schéma pour la transition énergétique* (STENC).[40] It has yet to develop a more comprehensive dedicated climate change adaptation plan.

9. CRIMINAL LAW

The exercise of criminal law authority in New Caledonia is quite complex. The first point to note is that criminal procedure is the exclusive domain of the French State. Because criminal law involves guarantees of fundamental rights, the Constitutional Council prohibits all intervention by a local authority in this field.

As far as the substantive criminal law is concerned, there is a division of powers between the French State and the local authorities.

The French Criminal Code is applicable in New Caledonia. This means that criminal law relating to damage to persons and property remains under the jurisdiction of the State. The same rule applies to penal provisions which are attached to powers exercised by the State.

Although s 73 of the Constitution says that criminal law and criminal procedure law are outside the scope of devolution from the State to local governments, local authorities are competent to impose criminal sanctions in the regulations they issue. This is the case, for example, in New Caledonia regarding labour law offences or tax law offences or for the provinces in the area of environmental law offences.

The criminal jurisdiction of local authorities is nevertheless limited by two rules. First, the Congress of New Caledonia and provincial assemblies can impose fines for offences against local regulations where these regulations respect the national classification of offences and do not exceed the maximum penalties provided for offences of the same nature by the laws and regulations of the Republic. They may attach additional penalties to those provided for offences of the same nature by the laws and regulations of the Republic. Second, conditional on the homologation of their local laws by the national Parliament, the Congress of New Caledonia and the provincial assemblies may impose imprisonment. Nevertheless, these measures must respect the classification of crimes in force at

---

40 <https://gouv.nc/sites/default/files/atoms/files/2016.06.23_schema_tranition_energetique_stenc.pdf>.

the national level and should not exceed the maximum provided for offences of the same kind by the laws and regulations of the Republic. Until the entry into force of the homologation law, only the fines and additional penalties that may be provided for by local laws are applicable.

These rules restrict the exercise of local authorities' power by preventing them, for example, from initiating a more repressive policy than the one existing in mainland France. This has been criticised in particular for environmental matters. On the other hand, they do not allow local authorities to innovate in terms of criminalisation because the additional penalties they can provide must be similar to those provided at national level. This means that they can neither use different complementary sanctions nor create new types of complementary penalties if they do not exist at the national level. Here again, the provinces, which have jurisdiction in environmental law, have on several occasions regretted their weak degree of autonomy to issue innovative and educational penalties since such penalties do not exist at the national level.

The Congress of New Caledonia and provincial assemblies may also provide for administrative sanctions in all matters. The fines collected in the application of these provisions are transferred into the budget of New Caledonia. Sworn administrative officers of New Caledonia, the provinces and municipalities may establish breaches of regulations at their respective levels.

There are some demands for an emancipation of local authorities in criminal matters in order to have complete freedom in the areas under their jurisdiction.

10. INTERNATIONAL LAW AND TREATIES

New Caledonia is an overseas autonomous territory within the French Republic, and therefore it is not a subject of international law. International treaties and conventions are signed by France as a party to these international legal agreements and most of them are applicable in New Caledonia. For example, nearly all multilateral agreements on the environment ratified by France like the Convention on International Trade in Endangered Species of Wild Fauna and Flora, the United Nations Framework Convention on Climate Change or the Convention on Biological Diversity are applicable in New Caledonia.

However, in the ongoing decolonisation process that started in 1988 and was confirmed with the 1998 Nouméa Accord, New Caledonia has gained some visibility on the international scene. As part of what is termed 'sovereignty sharing' in the 1998 agreement (between France and New Caledonia) to boost the Pacific territory's autonomy, New Caledonia has a say regarding its own engagement in international treaties signed by France. It can ask to be left out of a treaty (as allowed by international law) or, on the contrary, ask expressly to be part of it, as was the case with the 2015 Paris Agreement on Climate Change.

Two situations should be considered. As mentioned earlier, the French State has transferred its normative jurisdiction in several areas to New Caledonia (s 22, New Caledonia Act 1999) and to the three provinces (s 20, New Caledonia Act 1999), keeping under its own jurisdiction certain matters (s 21, New Caledonia Act 1999) that are usually accepted as attributes of State sovereignty (fundamental rights, justice, diplomacy, currency, national defence, citizenship, criminal law, etc.) or matters that need a high level of skill that is not available locally, like university education or radio and TV broadcasting rights.

First, in the areas that are still within the French State's jurisdiction, s 28 of the New Caledonia Act 1999 says that the national government

> may entrust to the President of the Government [of New Caledonia] the powers to negotiate and sign agreements with one or more States, territories or regional organisations of the Pacific and with regional organisations depending on the specialised agencies of the United Nations.

This provision should be read in conjunction with to s 89, New Caledonia Act 1999, which adds that the Congress of New Caledonia 'is consulted by the High Commissioner on Bills authorising the ratification or approval of treaties or agreements which fall within the competence of the State and are intended to apply in New Caledonia.'

Second, sovereignty sharing in foreign relations takes good account of the decolonisation roadmap. Section 29 introduced, in the areas of New Caledonia's competence, the possibility for the Congress to

> authorise the President of the government to negotiate, in the respect of the international commitments of the Republic, agreements with one or more States, territories or regional organisations of the Pacific and with regional bodies dependent on the specialised agencies of the United Nations.

The French authorities are informed of the authorisation to negotiate and, at their request, are represented in the negotiation as part of the delegation of New Caledonia. This can be considered a big change in the situation.

Section 31 of the New Caledonia Act 1999 states that New Caledonia may, with the agreement of the French authorities, be a member or associate member of international organisations or an observer within them.

New Caledonia is a full member of regional organisations such as the Pacific Community (SPC), the Regional Programme for the Environment (SPREP) and the Pacific Islands Forum (PIF). It is also an associate member of the UN Economic and Social Commission for the Asia-Pacific and a non-voting member of the WHO Western Pacific Region. New Caledonia is a participating territory of the Western and Central Pacific Fisheries Commission, France being a party to the Convention.

Section 32 states that New Caledonia can have representation (in the sense of the Vienna Convention of 18 April 1961) in the states or territories of the Pacific and at the European Community. The authorities of the Republic are informed of the states and territories in which New Caledonia is represented.

The Congress of New Caledonia created in 2017 the legal status of delegations for New Caledonia.[41] Today, there are five delegates in place, one in each for Australia, Fiji, New Zealand, Papua New Guinea and Vanuatu.

Though distinct from international law, New Caledonia's relations with the European Union need special mention as, following Brexit, France is now the only EU member state in the Pacific. New Caledonia is not part of the European Union and EU law is not applicable in New Caledonia. However, it has the status of an Overseas Country and Territory (OCT) attached to France within the European Union. EU–New Caledonia relations are defined in the 2014 Overseas Association Decision.[42]

The Congress of New Caledonia is also consulted by the French Minister for Overseas Territories on the projects and proposals for regulations of the European Union and the European Community relating to the association of the overseas countries and territories with European Union and the European Community.

Section 33 of the New Caledonia Act 1999 introduced decentralised cooperation agreements for New Caledonia and its provinces:

> The president of the government in matters coming under the jurisdiction of New Caledonia, or the president of the provincial assembly in matters coming under the jurisdiction of the province, negotiates and signs, respecting the international commitments of the Republic, decentralised cooperation agreements with French or foreign local authorities, their groups or public establishments.

Although the opening up of New Caledonia to international law is limited to neighbouring Pacific countries and UN agencies, it represents real progress in terms of autonomous regional diplomacy.

---

41 Loi du pays n° 2017-9 du 30 mars 2017 relative aux délégués pour la Nouvelle-Calédonie <https://juridoc.gouv.nc/juridoc/jdtextes.nsf/(web-All)/C83159B06E7BF93D4B25811D0025FDA3/$File/Loi-du-pays_2017-9_du_30-03-2017_ChG.pdf?OpenElement#search=%22d%C3%A9l%C3%A9gu%C3%A9s%22>; Délibération n° 84/CP du 16 mai 2017 portant dispositions relatives aux délégués pour la Nouvelle-Calédonie <https://juridoc.gouv.nc/juridoc/jdtextes.nsf/(web-All)/9F6C768C865979504B2581540073C0D9/$File/D%C3%A9lib%C3%A9ration_N%C2%B0_%2084-CP_du_16-05-2017_ChG.pdf?OpenElement#search=%22d%C3%A9l%C3%A9gu%C3%A9s%22>.

42 Council Decision 2013/755/EU of 25 November 2013 on the association of the overseas countries and territories with the European Union ('Overseas Association Decision') <https://eur-lex.europa.eu/legal-content/EN/TXT/?uri=CELEX%3A32013D0755>.

11. CIVIL SOCIETY ORGANISATIONS

New Caledonia has a rich tradition of trade unionism. Not surprisingly, union ideologies and the system of representativeness[43] bring the Caledonian union landscape closer to the French landscape. The main unions are the USOENC, which defines its action as a demand of social management unionism (close to the French CFDT), and the USTKE, which, on the contrary, would be closer to the approach of the CGT at the national level (with which it has links) and is a protest-oriented union. Other unions represent alternatives to these two extremes.

As in France, there are two large employers' organisations: Medef and CGPME. Medef is the most representative organisation of employers in terms of company size, activity sectors and salaried employment in general. The CGPME represents small and medium-sized enterprises.

Overall, trade unions in New Caledonia are militant and thus industrial relations are highly politicised. This politicisation can be explained in particular by Kanak militancy and its anti-colonial engagement set up within the framework of the policy of 'common destiny' emanating from the Nouméa Accord. More broadly, it can be explained by the persistence of strong inequalities, demands for economic and social rebalancing, and the fight against high prices.

At the religious level, New Caledonia, like mainland France, protects freedom of religion and benefits from laws that ensure the separation of Church and State. Therefore, there is no official religion. New Caledonia is governed, in matters of religion, by the Georges Mandel Decrees of 16 January and 6 December 1939, which slightly modify for some overseas territories the law of separation of Church and State of 1905.[44]

The Kanak people have a cultural background of animist origin, but today they are mostly Christians. Christianity could even be said to be a strong identity component for Kanak society and culture, as well as for the other Oceanian populations present in New Caledonia.

The majority religion in New Caledonia is Christianity. Catholicism is particularly widespread, but there are also a large number of Protestants or Pentecostals, in particular within the Melanesian and Polynesian populations,

---

43 Loi du pays n° 2006-4 du 14 avril 2006 relative à la représentativité des organisations syndicales de salariés: <https://juridoc.gouv.nc/juridoc/jdtextes.nsf/(web-All)/63E2D46B35E168034B2574CE00780419/$File/Loi_du_pays_2006-4_du_14-04-2006.pdf?OpenElement>; also Loi du pays n° 2010-13 du 31 décembre 2010 relative au conseil du dialogue social: <https://juridoc.gouv.nc/juridoc/jdtextes.nsf/(web-All)/4A40AF3C196486294B25780E0005223E/$File/Loi-du-pays_2010-13_du_31-12-2010_ChG.pdf?OpenElement>.

44 Loi du 9 décembre 1905 concernant la séparation des Eglises et de l'Etat <https://www.legifrance.gouv.fr/affichTexte.do?cidTexte=JORFTEXT000000508749>.

due to the presence from the beginning of the 19th century, and even before the takeover by France, of evangelisation missions by the likes of the London Missionary Society.

Minority religions are also present. Islam, in particular, is practised both by members of the community of Indonesian origin and by the descendants of former Algerian deportees who arrived in the second half of the 19th century. The latter mainly live the Bourail region. Judaism is present too, with a community of a few hundred members. There is also a strong Vietnamese community which practises Buddhism, mostly living in Nouméa.

Finally, associations are an important part of life in New Caledonia. This Pacific territory is even, according to a study conducted at the end of 2014, the 'French region' after the Paris region where the most associations are created each year. Open-air centres, sports clubs, cultural and charitable associations, specialised aid providers, environmental associations and consumer protection associations – the goals are varied, and organisations are present even in isolated places. They bring together all ethnic groups. They even carry out certain missions in the general interest, making up for the lack of private suppliers and public services.

The right of association, which was established by a 1901 Act of the French Parliament,[45] has been recognised as a constitutionally guaranteed right since a judgment of the Constitutional Council in 1971.[46]

However, the system of associations has experienced serious difficulties in recent years due to the economic crisis in New Caledonia and the sanitarian crisis, which has led to significant cuts in the public funding which is essential for maintaining the dynamism of associations.

BIBLIOGRAPHY

Agniel, Guy 'L'expérience statutaire de la Nouvelle-Calédonie ou de l'étude du mouvement du yo-yo au service de l'évolution institutionnelle d'un territoire d'outremer' in 'L'avenir statutaire de la Nouvelle-Calédonie. L'évolution des liens de la France avec ses collectivités périphériques', *Les études de la documentation française* (1997).

David, Carine Gindre *Essai sur la loi du pays calédonienne – La dualité de la source législative dans l'Etat unitaire*, (Editions L'Harmattan, 2009).

David, Carine 'The road to sovereignty for New Caledonia? Analysis of the November 2018 consultation on self-determination', (2019) 2(2) Small States and Territories Journal, 141–156, <https://www.um.edu.mt/library/oar/bitstream/123456789/49767/4/SST-2-2-David-FINAL.pdf>.

Faberon, Jean-Yves (ed) *L'outre-mer Français* (La Documentation française, 2004).

---

45 Loi du 1er juillet 1901 relative au contrat d'association <https://www.legifrance.gouv.fr/affichTexte.do?cidTexte=LEGITEXT000006069570>.

46 <https://www.conseil-constitutionnel.fr/decision/1971/7144DC.htm>.

Garde, François *Les institutions de la Nouvelle-Calédonie* (L'Harmattan, 2001).
Lafargue, Régis 'The unity of the republic vs. living together on the same land: New Caledonia from colonization to indigenousness: law at the center of a major culture issue' (2014) 46(2) The Journal of Legal Pluralism and Unofficial Law 172–192, <https://doi.org/10.1080/07329113.2014.902651>.
Le Meur, Oona 'Customary Law and Custom in New-Caledonia: Legal Pluralism, Citizenship and the External/Internal Sovereignty Issue' (2015) 2 SOAS Law Journal 230.
Levine, Stephen (ed) *Pacific Ways: Government and Politics in the Pacific Islands* (2nd ed, Victoria University Press, 2016).
MacLellan, Nic 'The Noumea Accord and Decolonisation in New Caledonia' (1999) 34(3) The Journal of Pacific History. 245–252, <https://www.jstor.org/stable/25169446>.
Mitchell, Kirsty *Custom in New Caledonia: its interaction with French law and prospects for survival* (Monash University, 2001), <https://www.usp.ac.fj/index.php?id=15970>.
New Caledonia databank, <www.juridoc.gouv.nc>.
Ntumy, Michael A 'New Caledonia' in Michael A Ntumy (ed) *South Pacific Islands Legal Systems* (University of Hawaii Press, 1993).
Revue Juridique Politique Economique de la Nouvelle-Calédonie, <www.rjpenc.nc>.

NIUE

Kahealani Sinahemana HEKAU

1. CONTEXT

Niue is a standalone island of 263 square kilometres located at 19.0544° S, 169.8672° W in the middle of the Polynesian triangle of the Cook Islands to the east, Tonga to the south and Samoa to the north. Before the arrival of Christianity in 1844, Niue was governed by customary law. The people lived in settlements and forts and were organised in small family groups led by the head of the family (*magafaoa*). They moved around seeking fertile land for crops, nesting places of fauna for hunting and access to the sea for fishing. Customs were developed around the protection or sharing of resources. Skirmishes between groups were common.

The arrival of missionaries in 1844 brought the influence of the Bible. Natural law and the teachings of Christianity eventually changed the Niuean lifestyle and norms. Settlements gradually coalesced into villages and moved from inland to the coast. Niue has 14 villages joined by a circle island road.

Niue became a British Protectorate in 1900. It was annexed as a territory of New Zealand in 1901 and administered with the Cook Islands. It was separated from the Cook Islands in 1966. By way of the Niue Constitution Act 1974, Niue became a self-governing state in free association with New Zealand.

As at 2019, the Niue resident population was 1,591. Niue has an established government, public health, public schools and a population which retains ownership of the land.

2. SOURCES OF LAW

The Niue Constitution Act 1974 (NZ) established the Constitution of Niue as its supreme law.[1] Niue became a self-governing state in free association with New Zealand. New Zealand, when called upon, assists with external affairs, defence and the provision of necessary economic and administrative assistance.

From Constitution Day (19 October 1974) onward, no Act of the Parliament of New Zealand could extend to Niue as part of its law, unless by request and consent of the Niue Legislative Assembly.[2]

Sources of Niue law[3] include the Constitution, Acts of the Niue Legislative Assembly, regulations approved by Cabinet, Niuean custom,[4] by-laws made by village councils, decisions of the Court of Appeal and of the High Court, and Niue common law.[5]

Key Acts of the Niue Legislative Assembly that have shaped the Niuean legal framework include the Niue Act 1966 for criminal matters and protection of persons;[6] the Public Health Act 1965 for public health and sanitation measures; the Niue Amendment Act (No 2) 1968 and the Land Act 1969 for determining

---

1 Section 4(1).

2 Article 36. This power was rarely used and not at all since 1986.

3 Interpretation Act 2004, s 4.

4 In relation to land only.

5 The decisions of the courts of Niue draw extensively on the judgments of New Zealand courts and courts for persuasive precedent.

6 Now the Criminal Law Code.

land ownership and tenure; the Electricity Power Supply Act 1960 for the power infrastructure; the Education Act 1989 for schools; the Incorporated Societies Act 1908 for non-government organisations; the Water Act 2012 for water resources; the Environment Act 2015 for the natural environment; the Taoga Niue Act 2012 and the Vagahau Niue Act 2012 for culture and heritage.

3. CONSTITUTIONAL LAW

3.1. EXECUTIVE GOVERNMENT

The Constitution establishes the government of Niue. It is designed after the Westminster system and comprises three branches, namely the executive, the legislature and the judiciary. The executive government is led by the head of state[7] who is represented in Niue by the Governor-General.[8] The Governor-General has a limited role in Niue. The exercise of the executive authority is by the Cabinet of Ministers, which consists of the Premier and three members of the Assembly. Members of the Assembly are elected by secret ballot under a system of universal suffrage.[9]

At the first meeting of the Assembly after a general election, the first business is the election of the Speaker, then the election of the Premier. The Premier, within seven days, nominates three members of the Assembly for appointment as ministers. The Speaker appoints as ministers the Premier and members so nominated. Each minister is allocated primary responsibility for a department or function of government.

Members of Cabinet are collectively responsible to the Niue Assembly.

3.2. LEGISLATIVE GOVERNMENT

Members of the Legislative Assembly consist of the Speaker and 20 members elected by secret ballot under a system of universal suffrage.[10] Fourteen members – one from each of the 14 villages – are elected by their respective village constituencies. Six members are elected by persons qualified to be electors of Niue voting on a common roll, which is a roll consisting of the combined village rolls.

Persons qualifying as electors and candidates must be either New Zealand citizens or permanent residents of Niue, have at some point resided continuously

7 Currently Elizabeth II, Queen of the Realm of New Zealand.
8 Letters Patent, 1983 (SR 1983/225) and the Constitution.
9 Constitution; Niue Assembly Act 1966.
10 Constitution, arts 16–19.

in Niue for not less than three years or been ordinarily resident on Niue for the 12 months immediately prior to application for enrolment as an elector or for nomination as a candidate.

Meetings of the Assembly are held at least once every six weeks. Every question before the Assembly is decided by a majority of the votes of the members present. No business can be transacted at any meeting of the Assembly where there are fewer than 10 members present.

All public revenue and expenditure is subject to legislative control. Cabinet is accountable to the Assembly for all expenditure in accordance with the appropriations made by the Assembly.

The Niue Government Account and all public funds and accounts are subject to an annual audit conducted by the Audit Office of New Zealand.[11]

3.3. JUDICIARY

The Court of Appeal[12] is the superior court of record and the highest court in Niue. The Chief Justice is the president of the Court of Appeal. In the absence of the Chief Justice, the judge present who is highest in seniority presides. Judges of the High Court are ex officio members of the Court of Appeal.

Appointment of the Chief Justice is by the Governor-General acting on the advice of Cabinet tendered by the Premier.[13] Any three judges of the Court of Appeal may at any time in Niue or elsewhere exercise the powers of the Court. The Court of Appeal has jurisdiction to hear and determine any appeal from a judgment of the High Court. Judgment of the Court of Appeal shall be in accordance with the opinion of the majority of the judges present.

The Court of Appeal held its first Niue sitting in 2008. Previous sittings were held in New Zealand. Since 2008, the Court of Appeal has held sittings every three years. Any person aggrieved by a decision of the Court of Appeal may petition Her Majesty in Council.[14]

The High Court of Niue has general jurisdiction over civil, criminal and land law matters. Accordingly, the High Court has three divisions – civil, criminal and land.[15] A judge of the High Court may exercise any of the jurisdiction and powers of judges of any division. Judges of the High Court are appointed by the Governor-General, acting on the advice of Cabinet tendered by the Premier. Persons with the requisite qualifications and of not more than 68 years of age may be appointed as judges. All the High Court judges in 2020 are members of

---

11 Constitution, art 60.
12 Constitution, arts 52–55B.
13 Constitution, art 39.
14 Constitution, art 55B.
15 Constitution, art 37.

the New Zealand Maori Land Court. High Court sessions are held at least twice a year, in March and November.

Commissioners of the High Court may be appointed by Cabinet.[16] A Commissioner may exercise such functions and powers of a judge of the High Court as may be prescribed by law. In criminal matters, Commissioners have jurisdiction over minor offences in the Criminal Division of the High Court and non-disputed cases in the Land Division. Serious offences and disputed land matters are dealt with by a judge of the High Court. Cabinet may also appoint justices of the peace; they hold office for such a time as may be prescribed by the warrant of appointment.[17]

There is a handful of legal practitioners, most of whom are public servants. There is one law firm serving the private community and some public contracts. In the absence of a formal law society, legal practitioners maintain a good work reputation through self-discipline. There is a need for more legal practitioners to teach, serve and administer the law for Niue society.

There are also lay persons who act as spokespersons representing parties before court. Notarising of documents is done in accordance with the Notaries Public Act 1998.

The High Court Rules 1916 provide rules for civil proceedings. The Land Court Rules provide for rules for land court proceedings. Criminal procedure is governed by the Criminal Law Code.

A coroner is provided for under the Inquest Act 1964. A judge, a Commissioner or any two justices of the peace act as a coroner.

3.4. NIUE PUBLIC SERVICE

Article 61 of the Constitution sets out that Cabinet is to establish and maintain the institutions and services necessary for public health, education and other services considered necessary to secure a good standard of living and the economic, social and cultural welfare of the people of Niue.[18]

Accordingly, there is a Niue public service consisting of employees whose function is to assist Cabinet to fulfil its executive functions.[19] The service is managed by the Niue Public Service Commission, which is responsible for its general oversight and control. Three persons appointed by Cabinet constitute the Niue Public Service Commission; they serve for a three-year term.[20] The Niue

---

16 Constitution, art 16.
17 Constitution, art 51(1).
18 See also in this regard s 7 of the Niue Constitution Act 1974 and art 69(3)(b) of the Constitution.
19 Constitution, art 62.
20 Constitution, art 64(4).

Public Service Commission reviews the economy and efficiency of departments and offices. The Commission acts independently to appoint and make decisions in relation to employees. It must not receive any direction from Cabinet,[21] but it keeps Cabinet informed on matters affecting the service. An annual report of the state of efficiency and economy of the Niue public service and on the work of the Commission is tabled in the Assembly by 31 March each year. The Commission has other important functions and can also make other reports and recommendations to the Assembly.[22]

The head of the service is the Secretary to Government, who is responsible to Cabinet for the general direction of the work of all departments and offices of the executive government. Each head of department accounts for the work of the department to the Secretary to Government and to the Minister in relation to policy implementation.

The public service departments are organised under ministries. Each ministry is assigned to a Cabinet minister: the Minister for Infrastructure and Finance is responsible for communications, transport, public utilities, finance and planning; the Minister for Natural Resources is responsible for agriculture, forestry and fisheries; the Minister for Social Services is responsible for education, health, justice and Taoga Niue (on the latter, see section 6.2 below); the Premier is responsible for central agencies, namely the executive and legislature, Crown Law, the public service, the police, and commercial and trading bodies. This is an administrative and not a statutory arrangement.

3.5. GOOD GOVERNANCE AND ACCOUNTABILITY

Niue does not have an Ombudsman or official information legislation. In their absence, the Public Service Regulations 2004 set the standard for the performance of public servants in their duties and service to the public.

3.6. PUBLIC HEALTH

The Niue Foou Hospital and the delivery of healthcare services to the Niue public are guided by the Public Health Act 1965. Matters of public health are led by the Director of Health, whose principal functions are to 'prevent, limit, and suppress infectious and other diseases; institute and carry out investigations in respect of public health; and to advise Cabinet on steps necessary to secure the promotion and conservation of human health'.[23] The provision of adequate

---

21 Constitution, art 69(2).
22 Constitution, art 70.
23 Public Health Act 1965, s 5; Niue Act 1966, s 5.

health services is reinforced in the Constitution. Article 61(1) requires Cabinet to 'establish and maintain in Niue such hospitals and other institutions for providing services it considers necessary for public health'. Article 61(3) also provides for the 'establishment and maintenance of institutions and services and for making other provisions as it considers necessary to provide the reasonable standard of living for the people of Niue and to secure their economic, social and cultural welfare'.

The Niue Health Department's regional partner is the Secretariat of the Pacific Community (SPC) and its international partner is the World Health Organization (WHO). Both provide support to Niue to ensure its services are aligned with international standards of healthcare. Niue, along with many Pacific island countries, is most at risk from non-communicable diseases (NCDs). Cardiovascular disease and cancer are the two leading causes of death for Niueans.

The law makes it a priority to prevent and limit infections and other diseases, and to promote and conserve human health. However, budgetary support at Niue Health over the years has been for curative healthcare. Niue is a member of the WHO Framework Convention on Tobacco Control (FCTC), and accordingly enacted the Tobacco Control Act 2018 and adopted tobacco taxation regulations to control tobacco use.[24]

The Niue Health Department provides treatment for basic health problems and to a limited extent undertakes tests for serious health problems. Persons suffering serious accident or disease are referred to Auckland, New Zealand for healthcare. While convenient for the Niue health system, this places a burden on families and encourages them to move away.[25]

3.7. EDUCATION

Article 61(2) of the Constitution provides that 'the Cabinet shall be responsible for establishing and maintaining in Niue such public schools and for making such other provisions as it considers necessary to provide educational opportunities for the people of Niue'.

The Education Act 1989 expands upon art 61(2) and sets provisions for the education of the people of Niue. Cabinet, through the Minister, have control and direction of the Department of Education and its offices. Teachers are public servants appointed by the Public Service Commission.

The Act provides for the establishment of schools, from pre-school, kindergarten, playcentre or similar, through to primary school, intermediate

---

24 Customs Tariff (Cigarettes and Tobacco) Regulations 2006.

25 There are approximately 30,867 Niueans in New Zealand, mainly in Auckland: <https://www.stats.govt.nz/tools/2018-census-ethnic-group-summaries/niuean>.

and secondary school; special education for special needs children; community colleges; training of teachers; and training in technical skills, trades, arts and crafts. Cabinet may allow any other form of education or instruction it deems necessary.

The schools on Niue are government schools and education is free. Any organisation or person may apply to establish a private school. An application can be made to the Director of Education, who may require further information, or upon satisfaction of having received all information may forward the application together with recommendations to the Minister for consideration by Cabinet.

The Niue Certification Authority Act 1978 established a National Certification Authority to provide examinations and grant diplomas or certificates to public servants in a trade or profession.

From the 1960s until 1989 there were at least seven primary schools in Niue. However, with the increase in emigration and a decline in student population, village schools closed down and were merged into one primary school. Primary schooling starts at early childhood education starting at four years old up until ten years old. Intermediate school is merged with high school and provides for students from 11 to 18 years old. The University of the South Pacific has a Learning Centre offering distance learning. Over the years tertiary students have studied abroad, principally in Australia, Fiji, Hawaii, New Zealand and Vanuatu.

4. FAMILY LAW

The family law of Niue as at 31 December 2007 is found in the Family Law Code. The Family Law Code is a consolidation of the law existing at that date made under the Reprint of Statutes Act 1991 and approved by Cabinet in accordance with that Act.[26] There has been no amendment to the Code since that date.

The Family Law Code consolidated the law relating to marriage, divorce, births and deaths, adoption, guardianship, child allowances, maintenance, and wills and succession. The origin of those provisions was found in the Niue Act 1966, the Adoption Act 1955, the Guardianship Act 1968 and the Child Allowance Act 1955. Succession matters were provided for in the Administration Act 1969, the Wills Act 1837 (UK) and the Wills Act Amendment Act 1858 (UK). As the dates of those source Acts indicate, most of the family law of Niue originated in pre-1974 New Zealand legislation. Prior to that, the main principles of the New Zealand legislation would have been derived from English legislation. There is therefore nothing particularly Niuean about any of the key family law principles.

Niuean custom has little impact on the operation of the law, although it is significant socially and at certain points is relevant in land rights matters.

---

[26] CM (07) 498.

5. LAW OF OBLIGATIONS

5.1. CONTRACT

Contracts are in general covered by the principles of the common law of Niue. This in practice means that the English common law will apply. For Niue, the most accessible source of such principles would be in the law of New Zealand. It is however to be noted that much of the law of contract of New Zealand is now in statutory form and therefore represents what is in some cases a significant departure from English common law principles. It is not impossible that the common law of Niue will develop informed by the New Zealand statutory developments. The Minors' Contracts Act 1969 is one Niue statute in this area.

5.2. EMPLOYMENT LAW

There is no general employment law. The main employment is in the public service and that is regulated by the Constitution and the Public Service Regulations 2004.

5.3. TORTS

There is no general torts legislation for Niue. The Interpretation Act 2004 provides sources of law that include Niuean common law. In the absence of specific torts provisions, the fall-back position is the Niue common law. In the absence of Niue common law, judges would refer to the New Zealand common law. New Zealand common law in the 21st century does not extend to personal injury by accident; judges are therefore likely to refer to English common law. The cases where legislation does make provision for torts law are listed below.

(1) The Deaths by Accidents Compensation Act 1952 provides rules for damages for the families of persons killed by accident. A member of the family of a deceased person has a right of action when death is caused by negligence. Section 4(1) provides: 'Where a death of a person is caused by any wrongful act, neglect, or default, and the act, neglect, or default is such as would (if death had not ensued) have entitled the party injured to maintain an action and recover damages in respect of it, the person who would have been liable if death had not ensured shall be liable to an action for damages, notwithstanding the death of the person injured, and although the death was caused under such circumstances as to amount in law to crime.'

Section 5 provides: 'Every such action shall be for the benefit of the wife or husband and the parents and children of the person whose death has so caused.'

(2) The Occupiers Liability Act 1962 provides law relating to the liability of occupiers and others for injury or damage resulting to persons or goods lawfully on any land or other property from dangers due to the state of the property or to things done or omitted to be done there.

(3) The Dogs Act 1966 provides for the registration and control of dogs and liability for injuries and damage caused by dogs. Where a complaint is made to the Chief Officer of the Police or the court that a dog, whether large or not, is dangerous and is not kept under proper control, the court, may, in addition to any fine imposed, order that the dog be destroyed.[27]

The owner of a dog is liable in damages for injury done by the dog. The person seeking damages does not need to show a previous mischievous propensity or that the injury was attributable to neglect on the part of the owner of the dog.[28]

In any action for damages for the act of a dog in attacking a human being or any animal, that the defendant had no knowledge of the dangerous or mischievous character of the dog is not a defence.[29]

(4) The Pig Control Act 1998 provides for the control of pigs. Section 15 provides: 'The owner of a pig that wanders at large is liable in damages for damage done by the pig while wandering at large, and it is not necessary for a person seeking damages to show – (a) A previous propensity in the pig to wander at large; or (b) The owner's knowledge of any such propensity; or (c) That the damage was attributable to neglect on the part of the owner of the pig'.

(5) The Civil Aviation Act 1999 in ss 43 and 44 provides for nuisance, trespass and responsibility for damage. It provides for liability and damages, except no claim can be made in respect of noise or vibration caused by an aircraft or its engines while on, taking off from, or landing at the airport. In respect of loss to property, the fault lies in the act that gives rise to liability in tort. There is no liability in the owner of the aircraft.

6. PROPERTY

6.1. NIUE LAND

The Constitution,[30] the Niue Act 1966, the Niue Amendment Act (No 2) 1968 and the Land Act 1969 provide rules for land tenure. Niuean land is vested in

27 Section 22.
28 Section 24.
29 Section 33.
30 Constitution, art 33.

the Crown but held by Niueans according to the customs and usages of Niue. Therefore, the Land Court determines title to and interests in Niuean land according to the custom and usages of the people of Niue, as far as they can be ascertained.[31]

Ownership of Niuean land is determined by ascertaining and declaring *magafaoa*[32] of that land by reference to the common ancestor and other means that identify the *magafaoa*. A person claiming ownership to Niuean land may apply to the Court[33] and must provide in writing:

(1) the boundaries of the portion of the land which is claimed;
(2) the grounds of the claim;
(3) genealogical tables showing descent from ancestor or ancestors through whom title is claimed, down to and including all persons admitted by the claimant as entitled along with the applicant under the claim;
(4) the names and approximate location of cultivations, villages, burial places – with the names of relatives of the claimant and persons included in the claim who have been buried there – and other places or marks of historical interest;
(5) any other proof or signs of occupation of or connection with the land by the claimant and other persons included in the claim.

Once a common ancestor is determined by the Court, it then proceeds to appoint a *Leveki Magafaoa* to that land. One or several persons can be appointed as *Leveki Magafaoa* to land. In the case of family land belonging to a pool of family land, the *Leveki Magafaoa* will have a trustee-like role. The role is to control the occupation and use of the land under Niuean custom and includes the power to alienate Niuean land. The *Leveki Magafaoa* under Niuean custom must consult with members of the *magafaoa*, whether resident in Niue or elsewhere, and in particular must consult before alienating land by sale or by lease.[34]

The requirement to consult with *magafaoa* resident in Niue levels the playing field for both resident and absentee landowners. Challenges presented by the requirement for consultation can slow down development. However, consultation is a protection against the taking of land without proper procedure.

Any member of the *magafaoa* who has reached the age of 21 is eligible to apply in writing to the Court for an order appointing a *Leveki Magafaoa* of that land. The Court requires the appointment of the *Leveki Magafaoa* to be agreed to in writing and with the signature of the majority of the members of

31 Land Act 1969, s 10. Most land in Niue is held by customary title. There is no privately owned land. There is a small amount of Crown land.
32 *Magafaoa* means family: Land Act 1969, s 12.
33 Land Act 1969, s 11.
34 Land Act 1969, s 15.

the *magafaoa*, whether resident in Niue or elsewhere.[35] Persons domiciled in Niue and who the Court is satisfied are reasonably familiar with the genealogy of *magafaoa* and the history and locations of *magafaoa* land may be appointed *Leveki Magafaoa*. A *Leveki Magafaoa* who is not a member of the *magafaoa* may not acquire beneficial rights in the land.[36]

Title to Niuean land cannot pass on by automatic succession or by will.[37] Provisions for the removal of a *Leveki Magafaoa* apply in the event that a *Leveki Magafaoa* dies. The Court may remove from office any *Leveki Magafaoa* if in its opinion that person cannot by reason of mental or physical disability or for any reason carry out the duties satisfactorily or if the *Leveki Magafaoa* is shown to the satisfaction of the Court to have exercised powers contrary to Niuean custom, equity or good conscience.[38] A *Leveki Magafaoa* may be removed by application for removal on the grounds of death or resignation.[39] Many applications for removal of the *Leveki Magafaoa* fail on the grounds that the applicant did not show failure on the part of the *Leveki Magafaoa* to perform duties in the control and use of the land. The applications for removal instead were based on relationship breakdown or miscommunication.

Sale of Niuean land is limited to the Crown. Sales are not common. The last notable sale of Niuean land to the Crown was for construction of the airport runway extension in 1994. Crown land is concentrated in areas of Alofi South where government infrastructure is located. Questions now arise in relation to Crown land no longer used, or no longer used for the purpose for which it was acquired, and whether owners can reclaim their land.

Most land where churches are built was given to the church by families.[40] Consequently, it is not uncommon to find the exchange of land by way of a gift or exchange among families. That is, families with ample land at the village centre will give land to families who live outside the village in order for them to have a place close to church.[41] The nature of Niuean culture is oral, hence it is often unclear whether gifted land is for the lifetime of the recipient only or whether it extends to descendants.

Leases of Niuean land may be for up to 60 years. Leases for public and church purposes for 60 years can have perpetual rights of renewal. Leases for such purposes may terminate if the land ceases to be used exclusively for

35 See Court of Appeal case – *Tukala M Hekau v Charlie Fuku Togahai, Pt Tapeu*, High Court of Niue, 3 September 2009.

36 Land Act 1969, s 14.

37 Niue Act 1966, s 489.

38 Land Act 1969, s 16(1).

39 Land Act 1969, s 16(2).

40 For example, the land for the church, Alofi Ekalesia; the land on which the New Zealand High Commission buildings stand.

41 *Sapati Laifone v Hana Tauekipaoa and Norma Palana*, High Court of Niue, 10 September 2019.

those purposes.[42] The wharf, the airport, the government administration building, the Niue Assembly (Fale Fono) and the hospital are located on Crown land acquired by purchase. Public roads are land acquired by warrant of Cabinet. Land where the water reservoirs, schools and power generation facilities are located is leased. Most of the Crown lands were acquired by government in the 1950–1970 period during the establishment of the Niue government's basic infrastructure. Many of those leases expired in 2010. Termination or renewal of many of those is pending.

Common mistakes at the Land Court are landowners filing applications out of time, filing for an injunction based on the grounds of lack of consultation, filing for removal of a *Leveki Magafaoa* for reasons other than those set out in the rules, or filing an application for removal on the grounds that the applicant was not aware of an earlier decision of the Court.

Orders of the Court once made are binding on all persons. That is, every order of the Land Court determining or affecting title to Niuean land or to any estate or interest in it binds all persons having any interest in that land, whether or not they are parties to or have notice of the proceedings in which the order is made, and whether or not they are subject to disability.[43]

Common trespasses to Niue land include clearing, planting, building or development on unregistered land.

6.2. TAOGA NIUE, CULTURE AND HERITAGE

At least up until 1986, when the Niue Cultural Council Act[44] was enacted, Niue custom was recognised in only one area of law, that of land. Ownership of Niuean land may be determined in accordance with customs and usages of the people of Niue. Where custom differs from written law, the written law takes precedence.

The Taoga Niue Act 2012 was enacted for the protection and preservation of Taoga Niue culture and heritage. Taoga Niue includes antiquities, objects of national cultural significance, objects of national historical significance, traditional knowledge, expressions of culture, customs, traditions and the history of Niue, Vagahau Niue (language), traditional cultural rights, and traditional knowledge. It recognises both tangible and intangible assets.[45]

The Act recognises traditional knowledge as knowledge created, acquired or inspired for traditional, economic, spiritual, ritual, narrative or recreational purposes, and transmitted from generation to generation. Traditional knowledge

---

42 Land Act 1969, s 29.

43 Niue Amendment Act (No 2) 1968, s 52.

44 Repealed by the Taoga Niue Act 2012.

45 Taoga Niue Act 2012, s 3.

is collectively held by a group known as traditional owners. The publishing or the non-customary use of traditional knowledge requires the prior and informed consent of the traditional owners.[46]

The Act established a standalone Taoga Niue department. It has seven sectors, namely: arts and crafts; cultural bridge; customs and traditions; environment; heritage assets; history; and Vagahau Niue.[47]

The Huanaki Museum, which housed many Niuean artefacts, was destroyed during the category-five cyclone Heta in January 2004. A lot of historical artefacts were lost. A makeshift space was provided to house the artefacts that were salvaged, until a new Taoga Niue building opened in October 2018.

Families practise subsistence farming and hunting on land or fishing and gathering at sea for food and nutrition. This connection with the land and sea lifestyle is crucial for the maintenance of language and culture.

The Vagahau Niue Act 2012 recognises Vagahau Niue as the official language.[48] It established the Niue Language Commission to protect and promote Vagahau Niue. Vagahau Niue is considered an endangered language due to the very few speakers and users of it. This endangerment is due to the bilingual nature of daily life and the increasing exposure to outside influences. School students and youth are most at risk from losing the Vagahau Niue. At primary school level, education is delivered in Niuean for four-year olds only. Five-year-old students to final year high school students are instructed both in Niuean and English. The subjects of arts and crafts and the Vagahau Niue are taught up until intermediate school level only. Tertiary study is undertaken abroad in English. The business language of the public service is English.

7. COMMERCIAL LAW

The principal legislation for commercial matters for Niue is found in the Arbitration Act 1908 and its 1938 amendment, the Bills of Exchange Act 1908, the Business Licence Act 1997, the Chattels Transfer Act 1924, the Cheques Act 1960, the Companies Act 2006, the Development Investment Act 1992, the Incorporated Societies Act 1908, the Mercantile Law 1908, the Merchandise Marks Act 1954, the Niue Bank Act 1994, the Niue Development Bank Act 1993, the Partnership Act 1908, and the Sale of Goods Act 1908. The English provenance of many of these Acts is quite clear from their titles. Niue has inherited those principles through New Zealand Acts of the colonial period. A significant 21st-century development is the Merchants Shipping (Registration of Foreign Vessels) 2012.

46 Taoga Niue Act 2012, s 35.
47 Taoga Niue Act 2012, Sch 1.
48 Environment Act 2015, s 5.

Contemporaneous with the closing of its Offshore Finance Centre, Niue enacted the Niue Companies Act 2006. This Act is a comprehensive modern company law statute of over 200 pages in length. This is the largest statute in the Niue legislation collection. There is specific provision for public, private and overseas companies.

8. ENVIRONMENT

The Environment Act 2015 is for the protection and preservation of the environment and is administered by the Department of Environment – *faahi gahua takatakaimotu*. Such protection involves the requirement of development consent for activities affecting the environment. The 'environment means all natural and physical elements and includes the land, marine areas, freshwater supplies, air, ecosystems and their constituent parts, including people and communities and the natural and physical qualities and characteristics of an area that contribute to a person's appreciation of its aesthetic, cultural and recreational attributes'.[49]

Cabinet may make regulations to set environmental standards for activities that require development consent before their commencement or for activities that do not need consent.[50] This includes activities affecting land use, freshwater supplies, marine areas, animals, plants, air quality or atmosphere, noise control, waste disposal, and asbestos removal.[51]

Activities which require a development consent and which are undertaken without one are punishable by a fine of up to 500 penalty units or a term of imprisonment not exceeding two years in the case of an individual, or in the case of a body corporate a fine of up to 15,000 penalty units.[52]

9. NATURAL RESOURCES

The Territorial Sea and Exclusive Economic Zone Act 1996 provides for the territorial sea and establishes Niue's exclusive economic zone. Niue retains sovereign rights over the exploration, exploitation, conservation and management of the resources of the exclusive economic zone. Section 6 provides: '[t]he baseline from which the breadth of the territorial sea is measured shall be below the low-water mark along the coast of Niue or where there is a coral reef along any part of the coast of Niue, the low-water mark along the outer edge of the coral reef'.

49 Environment Act 2015, s 3.
50 Environment Act 2015, s 13.
51 Environment Act 2015, ss 14–20.
52 Environment Act 2015, s 28. A penalty unit is NZ$100: Interpretation Act 2004, s 5.

Section 10 defines the exclusive economic zone as comprising 'those areas of the sea, seabed and subsoil that are beyond and adjacent to the territorial sea having as their outer limits a line measured seaward from the baseline described in section 6, every point of which line is distant 200 nautical miles from the nearest point of the baseline'.

The protection and preservation of the environment is in close parallel with the Taoga Niue Act 2012. Despite that common interest, the two departments administering these rules work independently of each other.

Fisheries are dealt with by the Domestic Fishing Act 1995, the Territorial Sea and Exclusive Economic Zone Act 1996 and the regulations made under those Acts.

10. CRIMINAL LAW

The main principles of criminal law are now found in the Criminal Law Code of 18 December 2007. The Criminal Law Code is a consolidation of the criminal law legislation approved by Cabinet under the Reprint of Statutes Act 1991.[53]

The Code is in essence a catalogue of offences complemented by rules on penalties and defences, criminal procedure and sentencing. The Code has not been amended since its commencement. The substance of the Code is basically familiar English law principles. The 1879 English Draft Code of Sir James Fitzjames Stephen was the basis for the promulgation of the Criminal Code Act 1893 of New Zealand, which then was used by Sir John Salmond for the Cook Islands Act 1915. In 1966, those provisions were taken over directly for Niue in the Niue Act 1966. There is no death penalty in Niue.

11. INTERNATIONAL LAW

Niue is a party to several international treaties. It is not a member of the United Nations nor does it have a treaty list. Before 1974, treaty obligations affecting Niue were those established during the protectorate and colonial periods. Niue has signed many treaties in its own right, for example the Maritime Boundary Treaty with the United States of 13 May 1997. Under s 6 of the Niue Constitution Act 1974, New Zealand has a duty to assist Niue in respect of international law matters. Since 1988, the pattern of New Zealand treaty-making in this respect was set out in a letter by New Zealand to the United Nations.[54]

---

53 CM (07) 498.

54 Declaration by the Permanent Representative of New Zealand to the United Nations with respect to New Zealand Treaty Actions and its position on Cook Islands and Niue,

Niue is a member of all the key Pacific regional organisations. Treaties have domestic effect only when they have been implemented by legislation.

Niue is bound by five key international human rights conventions: the International Covenant on Civil and Political Rights (ICCPR), the International Covenant on Economic, Social and Cultural Rights (ICESCR), the International Convention on the Elimination of all forms of Racial Discrimination (ICERD), and the Convention on the Elimination of All Forms of Discrimination against Women (CEDAW). Niue became a party to these four key conventions by way of New Zealand's treaty action.

Niue in its own right signed the United Nations Convention on the Rights of the Child. With the exception of the ICERD[55] and the United Nations Declaration on the Rights of Indigenous Peoples,[56] none of the human rights conventions are expressly implemented in Niue law.[57]

BIBLIOGRAPHY

Access to the Niue legislation can be found at <http://www.gov.nu/wb/pages/legislation/niue-laws.php>.

Chapman, Terry *The Decolonisation of Niue* (Victoria University Press, 1976).

Chapman, Terry et al *Niue a History of the Island* (Institute of Pacific Studies, University of the South Pacific, 1982).

Kalauni, Solomona *Land Tenure in Niue* (Institute of Pacific Studies, University of the South Pacific, 1977).

Loeb, Edwin M *History and Traditions of Niue* (Bernice P Bishop Museum, Bulletin 32, 1926).

Pacific Islands Legal Information Institute *Niue Primary Materials* <http://www.paclii.org/countries/nu.html>.

Pointer, Margaret *Niue 1774–1974* (Otago University Press, 2015).

Smith, S P *Niue: The Island and its People* (Institute of Pacific Studies, Niue Extension Centre, University of the South Pacific, 1983).

10 November 1988. As of that time, 'no treaty signed, ratified, accepted or approved or acceded to by New Zealand ... will extend to the Cook Islands or Niue unless the treaty is signed, ratified, accepted, approved or acceded to expressly on behalf of the Cook Islands and Niue'. See also Vienna Convention on Treaties 1969, art 29: 'Unless a different intention appears from the treaty or is otherwise established, a treaty is binding upon each party in respect of its entire territory'.

55 Race Relations Act 1972. Its object is to affirm and promote racial equality in Niue and to implement the International Convention on the Elimination of all Forms of Racial Discrimination.

56 Taoga Niue Act 2012.

57 For instance, there are no domestic laws which state that the ICCPR/ICESCR/CEDAW are law in Niue. There is however the Race Relations Act 1972.

PAPUA NEW GUINEA

Christopher KARAIYE

1. INTRODUCTION

The legal system of Papua New Guinea (PNG) is based on the common law of England. At independence it adopted its own written Constitution as the supreme law.[1] Since independence, PNG has enacted its own laws in an attempt to move away from complete reliance on the principles of common law. Some of the principles of English common law have been replaced by legislation or decisions of the PNG courts, but those principles still play a significant role.

In this chapter, the main elements of PNG's legal system and laws will be discussed, and the principal departures from English common law will be pointed out.

1.1. BRIEF HISTORY OF PAPUA NEW GUINEA AND ITS LEGAL SYSTEM

During the earlier colonial period, PNG was segmented into two regions or protectorates: Papua and New Guinea. The UK government administered Papua and the German government governed New Guinea. The two protectorates were described as British Papua and German New Guinea. Papua was proclaimed by Commodore Eriskines on 6 November 1884 and the annexation[2] was subsequently proclaimed on 4 September 1888 by William MacGregor, the first Administrator.[3] Germany proclaimed New Guinea as a protectorate in 1884 and subsequently annexed it on 17 May 1885.[4]

In 1901 Australia took over the administration of Papua from the UK. Australia also took control of New Guinea as a Trust Territory of the League of Nations after World War I.[5] After World War II, the two territories were jointly governed as the Territory of Papua and New Guinea.[6] That Administration existed until independence on 16 September 1975. On Independence Day, the conjunction 'and' was removed and the new state was named Papua New Guinea.

The legal system of PNG was greatly influenced and shaped by the English legal system through Australia. When Australia colonised Papua and New Guinea, it imposed the common law legal system. Though some of the laws passed by the colonial administration have been repealed, the influence the colonial laws had on the legal system of PNG remains.[7]

---

1 Constitution of the Independent State of Papua New Guinea 1975.

2 Annexation was made in the same year by William McGregor.

3 George Muroa 'The Extent of Constitutional Protection of Land Rights in Papua New Guinea' (1998–99) 26 Melanesian Law Journal 85.

4 George Muroa 'The Extent of Constitutional Protection of Land Rights in Papua New Guinea' (1998–99) 26 Melanesian Law Journal 85.

5 Peter Nagle *Research Guide – Papua New Guinea 1883–1942: Microfilm Collections* (National Archives of Commonwealth of Australia, 2002) 106.

6 Peter Nagle *Research Guide – Papua New Guinea 1883–1942: Microfilm Collections* (National Archives of Commonwealth of Australia, 2002) 108.

7 Christopher Karaiye *Administrative Law and Judicial Review in Papua New Guinea* (Notion Press, 2019).

1.2. DEFINITION OF LAW

In PNG, State law is founded on the concepts of justice and fairness. This notion is rooted in the Constitution, which calls for judges, magistrates and any other persons who dispense justice to be fair and just.[8]

Indigenous societies in PNG were governed by traditional rules before the arrival of the western colonisers. These indigenous rules are called customs[9] or customary law. In some indigenous communities, power is concentrated in one central figure, for instance a traditional chief. Other community members may have little or no power and the customary laws may not be fair or just. Notwithstanding that, customary law was given some recognition during the colonial era, but its application was restricted, to matters including marriage, divorce, ownership of customary land, and barter. As discussed below, at independence, customary laws were given constitutional recognition as part of the underlying law.[10]

2. SOURCES OF LAW

There are number of sources of law. The main source in PNG is the Constitution that was enacted by the House of Assembly in 1975; it took effect on 16 September 1975. The Constitution is stated to take its validity from the will of the people. The Preamble declares: 'We, the people of Papua New Guinea ... hereby establish, adopt and give to ourselves this Constitution'. The Constitution is the supreme law that takes precedence over all other laws in the country.[11] All other laws take their validity from the Constitution. Section 9 of the Constitution provides the hierarchy of laws in PNG. It states:

> 9. The laws.
>
> The laws of Papua New Guinea consist of—
> (a) this Constitution; and
> (b) the Organic Laws; and
> (c) the Acts of the Parliament; and
> (d) Emergency Regulations; and
> (da) the provincial laws; and
> (e) laws made under or adopted by or under this Constitution or any of those laws, including subordinate legislative enactments made under this Constitution or any of those laws; and
> (f) the underlying law, and none other.

---

8 Constitution, s 158(2).

9 Custom is defined as 'the customs and usages of indigenous inhabitants of the country existing in relation to the matter in question at the time when and the place in relation to which the matter arises, regardless of whether or not the custom or usage has existed from time immemorial'. Interpretation Act 1975, Ch 2, s 1.

10 Constitution, Sch 2.1; Underlying Law Act 2000.

11 Constitution, s 11.

The above sources are exclusive and anything that is not prescribed in s 9 cannot be a direct source of law in PNG.[12]

The Organic Laws are the second most important source of law. Both the Constitution and Organic Laws are collectively referred to as constitutional laws. Unlike the Constitution, the Organic Laws and other legislation are enacted by Parliament. Subordinate legislation may be made by other law-making bodies such as the Provincial Assemblies and local level governments (LLGs).

Acts of Parliament are enacted to govern various activities, transactions, conducts, behaviours, operations and management of organisations and individuals alike. They are generally implemented by the servants and agents of the executive arm of the government and in some respects by private persons.

Emergency Regulations are intended to deal with emergency situations, such as disease outbreaks, declaration of war, natural disasters, etc.[13] The head of state, acting on advice of the National Executive Council is empowered to declare state of emergency.[14] Once a state of emergency is declared, Parliament is the sole authority to control the declaration. Parliament must be recalled within 15 days to either continue or dissolve the state of emergency.[15] If Parliament decides to maintain or extend any or the whole of the terms of the declaration, it may set up an emergency committee to take charge of it.[16] Parliament is authorised to extend it for two months, and if it is not further extended, the emergency expires automatically.[17] During the currency of the state of emergency, certain laws may be temporarily suspended.[18] Any state of emergency declaration that fails to comply with the provisions of the Constitution is invalid.[19]

The provincial governments, through their provincial assemblies, are allowed to enact provincial laws to regulate certain activities, for instance liquor, tourism, etc. Similarly, LLGs are allowed to enact laws at the district level for activities such as public marketing, tourism and liquor, amongst others.[20]

At independence, PNG adopted some pre-independence laws, for instance the Admiralty Court Act, the Merchant Shipping Act and the Criminal Code Act.[21] Though many of the adopted laws were either amended or repealed in response to the changing circumstances, some remain intact and unchanged.

---

12 Owen Cox *Papua New Guinea's Law and Legal System* (Pacific Adventist University, 2004) 101.

13 Constitution, Part X (Emergency Powers).

14 Constitution, s 228.

15 Constitution, s 239.

16 Constitution, s 232.

17 Constitution, ss 237 and 238.

18 Constitution, s 233.

19 *Southern Highlands Provincial Government v Somare, Chairman of the National Executive Council* [2007] PGSC 854.

20 See the Organic Law on Provincial Government and Local Level Governments.

21 Edward R Hill and Guy Powles *Magistrates Manual of Papua New Guinea* (Lawbook Co, 2001) 24–27.

The underlying law is comprised of customary law and common law and equity of England that existed immediately before 16 September 1975. Schedule 2.2 of the Constitution and Underlying Law Act adopt the rules of common law and equity as part of the underlying law. The principles of common law and equity cannot be applied if they are inapplicable or inappropriate to the circumstances of the country from time to time, or inconsistent with custom. Pursuant to Sch 2.2 and Underlying Law Act, the principles and rules of common law and equity of England are adopted, and applied and enforced, as part of the underlying law and co-exist with principles of custom as adopted pursuant to Sch 2.1.

Schedules 2.1 and 2.2 provide that 'custom' as defined in Sch 1.2(1) and 'the principles and rules of common law and equity in England' are to be part of the underlying law, subject to various conditions. Some of the obvious conditions are that the particular custom, or the particular principle or rule is not inapplicable or inappropriate to the circumstances of the country or inconsistent with a constitutional law or a statute. The underlying law was applied in line with s 20 and Sch 2.3 of the Constitution until the enactment of the Underlying Law Act 2000, which made the application of Sch 2.3 obsolete.[22]

The common law rules of royal prerogative were abolished both as a source of and application as underlying law.[23] Section 3 of the Underlying Law Act prescribes the sources of underlying law and they are customary law and common law in force immediately before the 16 September 1975. The application of both the customary law and common law are subject to various qualifications set out in s 4. Sections 4 and 5 obligate the courts, especially the National Court and Supreme Court, to develop the rules and principles of the underlying law, with particular emphasis on customary law, as a coherent system in a manner that is appropriate to the circumstances of the country. Apart from the written laws, customary law is superior to common law.[24] In considering different customary laws for a particular proceeding, the courts are required to apply the rule set out in s 17 of the Underlying Law Act 2000.

The decisions of the Supreme Court and National Court are also sources of law. The precedents form the underlying law of PNG.[25] The decisions of the Supreme Court are binding on all other courts but not on itself.[26] The decisions of the National Court are binding on the courts below it, but not on the Supreme Court, although its decisions may be persuasive. Neither the Supreme Court nor the National Court is bound by its own decisions.

---

22 *Re Application by Ila Geno* [2014] SC1313 at [22]. See also Christopher Karaiye *Administrative Law and Judicial Review in Papua New Guinea* (Notion Press, 2019) 30.

23 Underlying Law Act, s 2.

24 Underlying Law Act, ss 6 and 7.

25 Underlying Law Act, ss 4 and 19.

26 See Constitution, Sch 2.5.9(1) and Underlying Law Act 2000, s 19. See also *In re Reference to Constitution section 19(1) by East Sepik Provincial Executive* [2011] SC1154.

3. CONSTITUTIONAL LAW

3.1. NATIONAL LEVEL

PNG is a constitutional monarchy and has a parliamentary democracy based on the Westminster model, with Queen Elizabeth II, the Queen of Papua New Guinea and her heirs, as its head of state.[27] Powers of the head of state are mostly ceremonial and performed by the Queen's representative, a Governor-General, who acts upon the advice of Cabinet or the National Executive Council,[28] Parliament or any instrumentality of State prescribed by law. The Governor-General is elected by Parliament through a secret ballot and the candidate who attains a simple majority of votes is elected the Governor-General.[29]

The formal structure of government is set out in s 99 of the Constitution. The relevant provisions state:

> 99. Structure of Government.
>
> (1) Subject to and in accordance with this Constitution, the power, authority and jurisdiction of the People shall be exercised by the National Government.
> (2) The National Government consists of three principal arms, namely: –
>   (a) the National Parliament, which is an elective legislature with, subject to the Constitutional Laws, unlimited powers of law-making; and
>   (b) the National Executive; and
>   (c) the National Judicial System, consisting of a Supreme Court of Justice and a National Court of Justice, of unlimited jurisdiction, and other courts.
> (3) In principle, the respective powers and functions of the three arms shall be kept separate from each other.
> (4) Subsection (2) is descriptive only and is non-justiciable.

The national Parliament is the supreme law-making body.[30] Together with the judiciary it exercises 'checks and balances' on the executive. PNG has a multiparty system with democratic elections held every five years.[31] A government is formed after every election and it is expected to serve five years in office.[32] Parliament is a single chamber comprising 111 members elected through the limited preferential voting system managed and run by an independent Electoral Commission.[33] Governments remain in office so long as they command a majority in Parliament on matters of confidence (including the annual budget).[34]

---

27 Constitution, Part V.
28 Constitution, Part V.
29 Constitution, s 88.
30 Constitution, ss 99(2)(a) and 100.
31 Constitution, ss 125 and 126.
32 Sean Dorney *Papua New Guinea: People, Politics and History since 1975* (ABC Books, 1990).
33 Constitution, ss 125 and 126.
34 Sean Dorney *Papua New Guinea: People, Politics and History since 1975* (ABC Books, 1990).

The national executive consists of the head of state and National Executive Council.[35] The Council is headed by the Prime Minister as Chairman and his Council of Ministers as members. The Council is responsible to Parliament (and thus the citizens) for the day-to-day administration of policy directives and activities carried out by departments and other public agencies.[36] The Governor-General acting on advice from the Prime Minister appoints ministers and terminates their period in office. Conventionally, the ministers are selected by the Prime Minister from among coalition partners.

The national judicial system is discussed below (section 4).

3.2. SUB-NATIONAL LEVEL

At the sub-national level, there are two levels of government set up by the Constitution and sanctioned by the Organic Law on Provincial Government and Local Level Government (OLPG and LLG). They are the provincial government, which is comprised of the Provincial Assembly[37] and Provincial Executive Council,[38] and the LLG. The administrative function of the province is headed by a Provincial Administrator, who is appointed by the National Executive Council upon recommendation from the Provincial Executive Council.

The LLG is set up in the same fashion as that of the provincial government but at the district level. The LLG is headed by a President as Chairman and ward councillors as members. The administrative functions of the District are headed by the District Administrator, or the Chief Executive Officer as he or she is called after the reform in 2014 pursuant to the District Development Authority Act. The local Open Member of Parliament is the chairman of the District Development Authority and the Presidents of the LLGs within the electorate and three other persons appointed by the Open Member form the Board of the Authority.[39] The District Development Authority's main roles and functions are administrative in nature.

The OLPG and LLG implement Part VIA (Provincial Governments and Local-level Governments) of the Constitution by making provision for and in respect of a system of provincial governments and LLGs for the provinces pursuant to the Second National Goal (Equality and Participation) of the National Goals and

35 Constitution, s 139.

36 Sean Dorney *Papua New Guinea: People, Politics and History since 1975* (ABC Books, 1990).

37 Where the membership is comprised of all open Members of Parliament and the provincial or regional Member of Parliament who is the Governor (unless he or she has taken up a ministerial portfolio in the national government), and all Presidents of LLGs in the province.

38 This is made up of the Governor as chairman and appointed ministers or chairpersons in the province.

39 District Development Authority Act, s 12.

Directive Principles of the Constitution. The purpose of the Organic Law was to bring the government closer to the people and promote greater participation by individual citizens in the development and the decision-making process.

3.3. THE AUTONOMOUS REGION OF BOUGAINVILLE

The Constitution of the Autonomous Region of Bougainville provides for government of the Autonomous Region of Bougainville,[40] which is quite different from that of other provinces. The Bougainville Constitution implements Part XIV of the Constitution[41] and is only applicable to Bougainville.[42] The provincial and local level government system does not apply to Bougainville.[43] The structures of government of Bougainville are set out in the Bougainville Constitution[44] and Organic Law on Peace-Building in Bougainville-Autonomous Bougainville Government and Bougainville Referendum. Sections 288, 289 and 290 of the national Constitution provide the division of powers and functions between the national government and the Bougainville government. Amongst others, the national government retains the powers and functions of defence, foreign relations, international trade, currency, central banking, telecommunications and customs.[45]

The Bougainville Constitution is the supreme law in respect of matters that fall within that jurisdiction. The national laws continue to apply in Bougainville until they are replaced by Bougainville laws.[46] The Bougainville Constitution and other laws passed by the Bougainville Legislature (House of Representatives) form part of the laws of PNG as specified under s 9 of the Constitution.[47] The national judicial system is allowed to carry out its responsibilities in Bougainville.[48] The Bougainville Legislature is permitted to establish its own courts and tribunals,[49] including the appointment of judges[50] to sit on the Bougainville courts. The power to establish courts, tribunals and appointment of judges in Bougainville is unique to the region. Various constitutional institutions are established in Bougainville.[51] Other provinces do not have similar powers or constitutional bodies operating independently there.

40 Formerly the North Solomons Province of Papua New Guinea.
41 Constitution, s 280.
42 Constitution, s 176.
43 Constitution, s 277.
44 Constitution, s 282.
45 See Constitution, s 289.
46 Constitution, s 296.
47 Constitution, s 300.
48 Constitution, s 305. See *Special Reference Pursuant to Constitution, Section 19(1), Reference by the Bougainville Executive* [2020] PGSC 42.
49 Constitution, s 306.
50 Constitution, s 309.
51 See Constitution, ss 310–321.

The above arrangements were done as a result of the Bougainville Peace Agreement of 2001 signed by the national government and the leaders of Bougainville to end a decade-long (1988–2000) civil war over the operation and management of the Panguna Mine in South Bougainville.[52] The Agreement was founded on three pillars: autonomy, independence and weapons disposal.[53] Bougainville was to function as an autonomous region and, amongst other functions, assist in disposing of weapons of the ex-combatants. After 10 to 15 years from the date of the Agreement, the people were to vote in a referendum to decide whether to retain autonomy or for independence.[54] A referendum was conducted on 11 December 2019 and 97.7 per cent of the votes supported independence.[55] The result is non-binding, and consistent with s 342 of the Constitution the national government and the Bougainville government went into consultation over the referendum result.[56] After the consultation, a decision will be made by the national government through the national Parliament and the decision will be presented to the Bougainville government.[57] The law is silent on the kind of things to be considered and discussed during consultation and also the nature of the decision the national government may make.[58]

3.4. CONSTITUTIONAL LAW AND THE PRINCIPLE OF SEPARATION OF POWERS

Constitutional law in PNG is contained in the Constitution and Organic Laws and any law that amends those laws.[59] The Constitution is said to be home-grown or autochthonous,[60] in the sense that it derives its power from the will of the people.[61] Whilst some of the principles which the Constitution

---

[52] Sean Lees and Marilyn Havini et al *Bougainville Peace Agreement: The Burnham I and II Dialogues: Sharing and Exploring Pacific Approaches to Dialogue: A Compendium of Case Studies from Pacific Island Countries* (United Nations Development Programme) 1–3. See also <https://peacemaker.un.org/png-bougainville-agreement2001>.

[53] United Nations Peacemaker, *Bougainville Peace Agreement: Retrieval Document* <https://peacemaker.un.org/png-bougainville-agreement2001>.

[54] Constitution, ss 338–343.

[55] Kylie McKenna '*The Bougainville referendum: Celebrations turn to sadness and hope*' (The Lowy Institute, 2020) <https://www.lowyinstitute.org/the-interpreter/bougainville-referendum-celebrations-turn-sadness-and-hope>.

[56] See also Radio New Zealand, 'Final Bougainville referendum report presented to PNG: Radio New Zealand News' <https://www.rnz.co.nz/international/pacific-news/418349/final-bougainville-referendum-report-presented-to-png>.

[57] Constitution, s 342.

[58] As at the time of publication of this book, the national government and Bougainville government were in consultation and no decision had been made by the national government on the referendum result.

[59] Constitution, Sch 1.2.2.

[60] Moses Aldrin Kimuli *Business Law in Papua New Guinea* (Institute of Business Studies, 1994) 4.

[61] Moses Aldrin Kimuli *Business Law in Papua New Guinea* (Institute of Business Studies, 1994) 6.

promulgates are based on the laws of Australia and England, in many ways it is unique in its outlook. This was highlighted by Amet J in *Wari v Ramoi*,[62] where he said:

> We start from the premise asserted in the Preamble to the Constitution 'that all power belongs to the people'. As Frost CJ said in *The State v Mogo Wonom*:[63]
>
> The Constitution itself is a truly autochthonous Constitution established, as the preamble recites, by the will of the people, to whom 'all power belongs'. Its authority is thus original and in no way derivative from any other source. Unlike the case of Australia where the first settlers brought with them the common law there is, to use the words of Sir Owen Dixon speaking of the American Constitution, 'no anterior law providing the source of juristic authority' for the institutions of government now established.

The aspiration and vision of the people of PNG are contained in the Preamble of the Constitution. It also contains the following five National Goals and Directive Principles, towards which laws and policies developed by the State must be geared:[64]

1. *Integral human development* – promotes the human development of every Papua New Guinean;
2. *Equality and participation* – encourages equality and participation in the development of PNG;
3. *National sovereignty and self-reliance* – strengthens national sovereignty and calls on Papua New Guineans to be self-reliant;
4. *Natural resources and environment* – reminds Papua New Guineans about the importance of their natural resources and their environment; and
5. *Papua New Guinean ways* – calls on Papua New Guineans to promote and utilize Papua New Guinean ways in their dealings with each other, the State and foreigners.

These National Goals and Directive Principles are general guidelines, signposts or broad principles for development, and are non-justiciable.[65]

The Constitution establishes the various institutions of the State.[66] Section 11 provides for the supremacy of the Constitution:

> all acts (whether legislative, executive or judicial) that are inconsistent with [the Constitution or Organic Laws] are to the extent of the inconsistency, invalid and ineffective.

---

62 [1986] PNGLR 12.

63 [1975] PNGLR 311 at 315–306.

64 Eric L Kwa *Constitutional Law of Papua New Guinea* (Lawbook Co, 2001) 14–15.

65 Constitution, s 25(1). See further Vergil Narokobi, *The Implementation of Papua New Guinea's National Goals and Directive Principles and Basic Social Obligations*, PhD Thesis (Victoria University of Wellington, 2016).

66 Eric L Kwa *Constitutional Law of Papua New Guinea* (Lawbook Co, 2001) 1.

The Constitution enshrines the separation of powers,[67] providing that:

(1) the executive power of the people is vested in the executive arm of the Government;[68]
(2) the legislative power of the people is vested in the National Parliament;[69] and
(3) the judicial power of the people is vested in the Judiciary.[70]

Each arm of government holds the others accountable in order to avoid abuse of their respective powers. In practice, the three arms of government do interrelate and depend on each other to function and carry out their designated duties and powers effectively.[71] For instance, the judiciary depends on the executive and legislature to put into effect its orders and also to raise and allocate funds for operation. On the other hand, the executive and legislature depend on the judiciary to guide them on the interpretation and application of the laws.

4. THE JUDICIARY

PNG's judicial system is comprised of the Supreme Court, National Court and other inferior courts.[72] The main function of the judiciary is to interpret and apply laws and maintain the rule of law. The judiciary has maintained independence from Parliament and the executive, in administering the courts and enforcing the laws and rule of law in an impartial manner.

4.1. COURTS

4.1.1. The Supreme Court

The Constitution establishes the Supreme Court[73] as a superior court of record and the highest court of PNG. The Supreme Court has wide powers and jurisdiction guaranteed by the Constitution and specifically it:

(1) is the final court of appeal;[74]
(2) has an inherent power to review all judicial acts of the National Court;[75] and

67 Constitution, s 99(3).
68 Constitution, s 138.
69 Constitution, s 100.
70 Constitution, s 158(1).
71 *Haiveta v Wingti* [1994] PNGLR 160.
72 Constitution, s 155(1).
73 Section 160. The Supreme Court may be constituted by the Full Court (ie the Court constituted by three or more judges in accordance with s 161(2) of the Constitution) or a single judge. The full Supreme Court or simply the Supreme Court has unlimited jurisdiction, whilst a

(3) is the court of first instance for interpretation and application of constitutional laws;[76]
(4) has such other jurisdiction and powers as are conferred on it by the Constitution or any other law.[77]

The Supreme Court's procedure is governed by the Supreme Court Act and the Supreme Court Rules. The necessary forms and procedures are prescribed by these two pieces of legislation. The Supreme Court is constituted by a single judge or three or five judges.

All judges, including the Chief Justice and Deputy Chief Justice, of the National Court may sit on the Supreme Court, except the acting judges.[78] The judges, including the Deputy Chief Justice and acting judges, are appointed by the Judicial and Legal Services Commission.[79] Judges are appointed for 10 years if they are citizens. Non-citizens may only be appointed for a three-year term.[80] All judges are eligible for reappointment until the mandatory retirement age of 70 years. The Chief Justice is appointed for 10 years by the head of state, acting on advice of the National Executive Council.[81]

4.1.2. The National Court

The National Court is a superior court of record,[82] established by s 163 of the Constitution. It is a court of first instance for criminal and civil matters. It has unlimited jurisdiction to deal with any case, unless its jurisdiction is expressly ousted by law.[83] More specifically, the National Court:

(1) has an inherent power to review any exercise of judicial authority and other powers and jurisdiction as are conferred on it by the Constitution or any

single judge exercises limited powers such as dealing with leave applications and certain interlocutory matters, which are not seeking to determine an appeal.

74 Constitution, s 155(2)(a).

75 Constitution, s 155(2)(b).

76 Constitution, ss 18, 19 and 162(1).

77 Constitution, s 155(2)(c).

78 Constitution, s 161(1).

79 Section 170(2) of the Constitution and Organic Law on Judicial and Legal Services Commission. The Judicial and Legal Services Commission is comprised of the Minister for Justice as Chairman, the Chief Justice, the Deputy Chief Justice, the Chief Ombudsman, a Member of Parliament appointed by Parliament, and the Chief Magistrate (only in matters concerning the magisterial services, except the appointment of Chief Magistrate). The Commission is free from control from anyone: s 183, Constitution.

80 Organic Law on the Terms and Conditions of Employment of Judges, s 2.

81 Constitution, s 169(2).

82 Constitution, s 163(2).

83 Constitution, s 166.

law unless jurisdiction or power is conferred upon the Supreme Court or removed by law;[84]

(2) adjudicates on appeals from the District Court[85] and other authorities prescribed by law;[86]
(3) enforces the Constitution;[87] and
(4) enforces the constitutional rights of people.[88]

The National Court is not empowered to deal with the interpretation and application of the constitutional laws. Both the Supreme Court and the National Court have concurrent power to make orders in the nature of prerogative writs and such other orders as are necessary to do justice in the circumstances of a particular case.[89] If the Supreme Court assumes jurisdiction on a particular matter pursuant to s 155(4) of the Constitution, the National Court lacks jurisdiction to deal with the matter.[90]

The procedures of the National Court are set out in the National Court Act and National Court Rules. Most civil claims are brought before this Court. Civil claims are usually instituted in two ways: (a) by writ of summons with a statement of claim endorsed to it, and (b) by originating summons. The nature of the claim dictates the mode of proceedings.

The National Court is usually presided over by a single judge or acting judge,[91] although a number of judges may sit together.[92] Acting judges have the same powers as full-time judges.

4.1.3. *Inferior Courts*

The inferior courts are mandated by s 172 of the Constitution and are established by their respective legislation.

4.1.4. *District Courts*

The District Courts are inferior courts, established by the District Courts Act.[93] They are based in provincial towns and districts.[94] Jurisdiction includes the following:

84 Constitution, s 155(3).
85 District Courts Act, Part XI.
86 See, for instance, the Lawyers Act, which allows appeal from the decision of the Lawyers Statutory Committee: *Ole v Papua New Guinea Lawyers Statutory Committee*[2001] PGNC 7; *Ketan v Lawyers Statutory Committee* [2002] PGNC 57.
87 Constitution, s 22.
88 Constitution, ss 57 and 58.
89 Constitution, s 155(4).
90 See Constitution, s 155(3)(d).
91 Constitution, s 165.
92 Constitution, s 166(3), (4) and (5).

(1) court of appeal from the Village Courts;[95]
(2) civil claims of up to K50,000;[96]
(3) summary offence cases[97] and other minor criminal matters;[98]
(4) applications for search warrants,[99] arrest warrants[100] and bail;[101]
(5) committal proceedings;[102]
(6) family matters especially violence,[103] adultery and enticement,[104] and dissolution of marriage;[105]
(7) juvenile matters;[106] and
(8) customary land disputes.[107]

The magistrates, including the Chief Magistrate, are appointed by the Judicial and Legal Services Commission. Often a single magistrate presides over the court. Generally proceedings are commenced in one of two ways: complaint (for civil claims) and information (for criminal matters). In all proceedings, the rules of evidence under the Evidence Act apply.

4.1.5. Land Courts

There are two land courts established by the Land Disputes Settlement Act: the Local Land Court[108] and the Provincial Land Court.[109] They deal with customary land disputes, to the exclusion of all other courts.[110] Proceedings commence with a complaint or application made orally or in writing to a magistrate of

93 The Act abolished Local Courts and their functions were transferred to the District Courts.
94 Edward R Hill and Guy Powles *Magistrates Manual of Papua New Guinea* (Lawbook Co, 2001).
95 Village Courts Act (as amended).
96 District Courts Act, s 21.
97 Summary Offences Act.
98 For example, firearms offences under the Fire Arms Act 1978; traffic infringements under the Motor Traffic Act.
99 Search Act; District Courts Act.
100 Arrest Act; District Courts Act.
101 Bail Act; District Courts Act.
102 Criminal Code Act and District Courts Act.
103 Family Protection Act 2013.
104 Adultery and Enticement Act.
105 Village Courts Act and District Courts Act.
106 Juvenile Justice Act.
107 Land Disputes Settlement Act.
108 Land Disputes Settlement Act, s 21.
109 Land Disputes Settlement Act, s 45.
110 Land Disputes Settlement Act.

the Local Land Court or to a District Court or a Village Court or on reference from mediation or a land mediator.[111] The application must be accompanied by a general description of the customary land in dispute.[112] The Local Land Court and Provincial Land Court are not bound by any law or rule of law, evidence, practice and procedure in their hearing of the disputes. The Local Land Court is the court of first instance and is composed of a local land magistrate, who is the chairman, and land mediators (not more than four), and the decision is by majority vote.[113] Any decision of that court may be appealed to the Provincial Land Court.[114] The Provincial Land Court may be constituted by a provincial land magistrate, who may elect to appoint land mediators to assist the court. The Provincial Land Court's decision is final and is not subject to further appeal.[115] However, judicial review is available for decisions of the Provincial Land Court[116] and the Local Land Court where there is clear disregard for substantial justice.[117]

4.1.6. *Family Courts*

The Family Court is a court of limited jurisdiction empowered by the Lukautim Pikinini Act under Part XII. The Court was established to deal with child protection issues. The Court's jurisdiction is spelt out in s 88 of the Act and includes:

(1) child protection;
(2) parenting orders (child custody);
(3) maintenance of a child and parent;
(4) access to a child;
(5) guardianship of a child; and
(6) issues involving adopted children.

Family Court proceedings are presided over by District Court magistrates. The strict rules of procedure and evidence do not apply.[118]

111 Land Disputes Settlement Act, s 31.
112 Moses Aldrin Kimuli *Business Law in Papua New Guinea* (Institute of Business Studies, 1994) 32.
113 Land Disputes Settlement Act, s 23.
114 Land Disputes Settlement Act, s 53.
115 Land Disputes Settlement Act, s 60.
116 See *The State v District Land Court at Kimbe, ex parte Casper Nuli* [1981] PNGLR 192; *Nou v Cherake* [2004] PGNC 227; *Afing v Pari* [2006] PGNC 32; *Jimmy v Clan* [2010] PGNC 120.
117 *Application of Nii on behalf of Himself and Other Members of the Toisap Clan* [1991] PNGLR 357.
118 Lukautim Pikinini Act, ss 87 and 89–95.

4.1.7. *Village Courts*

The Village Courts are creatures of the Village Courts Act. They are based in the village communities and they mainly apply custom to resolve customary disputes. They have jurisdiction to deal with civil disputes involving up to K1,000[119] and minor criminal matters.[120] They also deal with customary marriage, and adoption and guardianship of children whose parents are married under custom or unmarried.[121]

The Village Court determines its own procedure.[122] The Act specifically calls for open court in the presence of all parties.[123] The Village Court is not bound to apply technical rules of evidence, but its powers and procedures must be exercised in accordance with the principles of natural justice.[124]

The Court is presided over by one or three village magistrates[125] who are appointed by the minister[126] responsible for Village Courts, usually the Minister for Justice. An appeal lies to the District Court.

4.2. CONSTITUTIONAL RIGHTS

The Constitution expressly guarantees a number of fundamental rights that must be considered and upheld unless they are lawfully restricted. These constitutional rights include the right to freedom (s 32), the right to life (s 35), freedom from inhuman treatment (s 36), protection of the law (s 37), liberty of the person (s 42), freedom from forced labour (s 43), freedom from arbitrary search and entry (s 44), freedom of conscience, thought and religion (s 45), freedom of expression (s 46), freedom of assembly and association (s 47), freedom of employment (s 48), the right to privacy (s 49), the right to vote and stand for public office (s 50), the right to freedom of information (s 51), the right to freedom of movement (s 52), protection from unjust deprivation of property (s 53), equality of citizens (s 55), and other rights and privileges of citizens (s 56).[127]

The rights are enforceable in the National Court[128] and Supreme Court. For example, if a citizen's property is compulsorily acquired, the acquisition must be

---

119 Village Courts Act, s 45.
120 Village Courts Act, ss 77 and 78.
121 Village Courts Act, ss 46 and 47.
122 Moses Aldrin Kimuli *Business Law in Papua New Guinea* (Institute of Business Studies, 1994) 35.
123 Village Courts Act, s 79(1).
124 Village Courts Act, s 59.
125 Village Courts Act, s 7.
126 Village Courts Act, s 17.
127 Christopher Karaiye *Administrative Law and Judicial Review in Papua New Guinea* (Notion Press, 2019) 6.
128 *Kaima v Poga* [2012] PGNC 116; *Gunambo v Upaiga* [2010] PGNC 239; *In the Matter of Enforcement of Human Rights Under S 57 & 58 of the Constitution, Karopo v Provincial Police Commander, New Ireland Province* [2003] PGNC 37.

in accordance with the law, which includes a requirement that the property must be required for a public purpose. A citizen whose property is so acquired must be compensated fairly and justly.[129]

5. LEGAL PROCESS

Every person is guaranteed the right to full protection of the law by s 37(1) of the Constitution.[130] This right is universally applicable to both civil and criminal cases. In all proceedings before the courts, except the Village Courts and quasi-judicial tribunals, the rules of evidence under the Evidence Act apply. In criminal proceedings, the prosecution bears the onus of proving the case beyond reasonable doubt, and in civil cases, the plaintiff bears the onus of proving the case on the balance of probabilities. An appeal or review lies to a higher court from the decision of a court of first instance.[131]

5.1. CRIMINAL LAW

5.1.1. Criminal Offences

Criminal offences are divided into summary and indictable. Summary offences are less serious in nature and are dealt with by the District Court under the Summary Offences Act 1977. Indictable offences are more serious and carry severe penalties. Most indictable offences are set out in the Criminal Code Act, which was originally adopted from the Queensland Criminal Code, but has been substantially altered over time in response to the changing circumstances of PNG.[132]

In most instances, the criminal justice process for both summary and indictable offences is initiated and progressed by the police. The process begins with an arrest of a suspect. Arrest and detention are important aspects of the criminal justice process and they are sanctioned by ss 37 and 42 of the Constitution and regulated by the Arrest Act. Pursuant to s 3 of the Arrest Act, a policeman may arrest a person whom he believes on reasonable grounds (1) is about to commit, or (2) is committing, or (3) has committed an offence. Both arrest and detention involve deprivation of a person's personal liberty

---

129 See Constitution, s 53(1); *The Minister for Lands v Frame* [1980] PNGLR 433.

130 *Yaul v The State* [2005] PGSC 29.

131 *Re Constitution, s 28(5)* [2017] PGSC 48.

132 Donald R C Chalmers, David Weisbrot, Salamo Injia and Warwick John Andrew *Criminal Law and Practice of Papua New Guinea* (UPNG Press (Reprint), 2009). See also *The State v Tulong* [1995] PNGLR 329.

as distinguished from a restriction on his freedom of movement.[133] For this reason, as soon as a person is arrested in relation to an offence, the arresting officer is required by s 42 of the Constitution to strictly observe the principles or safeguards of the right of the accused.

Summary offences are prosecuted in the District Court by a police prosecutor. Indictable offences may be dealt with by a police prosecutor during the committal process in the District Court.[134] Under the committal process, the District Court must be satisfied that there is a prima facie case and sufficient evidence to commit an accused to stand trial at the National Court.[135] If there is insufficient evidence, the District Court is bound to discharge the accused. The police may then elect to compile further evidence and re-arrest the accused or request the Public Prosecutor to exercise ex officio the indictment power under s 526(1) of the Criminal Code Act[136] and commit the accused to the National Court to stand trial. For this process, the Public Prosecutor may assess the evidence and form his or her own opinion whether to commit the accused to stand trial at the National Court.[137]

The National Court is the forum for the trial of indictable offences that are committed to it by the District Court or the Public Prosecutor via ex officio indictment. The decision of the National Court is appealable to the Supreme Court under the Supreme Court Act. Pursuant to s 17 of the Supreme Court Act, an appeal must be filed within 40 days from the date of pronouncement of the decision.[138] An appeal is by way of rehearing[139] and the Supreme Court's decision is final.

The provisions of s 37 of the Constitution are devoted to protecting and safeguarding the rights of a person in custody or charged with an offence. The safeguards are based on common law principles of the fair and impartial administration of justice in open court.[140] The principles include the following:

(1) Except for contempt of court, nobody may be convicted of an offence that is not defined by, and the penalty for which is not prescribed by, a written law (s 37(2)).

---

133 Salamo Injia and Gregory Lay *Constitutional Law in Papua New Guinea* (National Judicial Staff Service, 2018) 159.

134 District Courts Act, Part VI.

135 *R v Wewak Resident Magistrate, ex parte Dyer* [1967–68] PNGLR 511. See s 95 of the District Courts Act.

136 *Paraka v Gauli* [2019] N7975.

137 *Paraka v Gauli* [2019] N7975; *The State v Paraka* [2020] N8229.

138 Supreme Court Act, s 17. An appeal filed outside the 40-day period is incompetent and liable to be dismissed: *Balakau v Ombudsman Commission* [1996] PNGLR 346; *The State v Tuap* [2004] SC765.

139 Supreme Court Act, s 6.

140 Donald R C Chalmers, David Weisbrot, Salamo Injia and Warwick John Andrew *Criminal Law and Practice of Papua New Guinea* (UPNG Press (Reprint), 2009) 2.

(2) A person charged with an offence shall, unless the charge is withdrawn, be afforded a fair hearing within a reasonable time, by an independent and impartial court (s 37(3)).
(3) A person charged with an offence (s 37(4)):
   (a) shall be presumed innocent until proved guilty according to law, but a law may place upon a person charged with an offence the burden of proving particular facts which are, or would be, peculiarly within his knowledge; and
   (b) shall be informed promptly in a language which he understands, and in detail, of the nature of the offence with which he is charged; and
   (c) shall be given adequate time and facilities for the preparation of his defence; and
   (d) shall be permitted to have without payment the assistance of an interpreter if he cannot understand or speak the language used at the trial of the charge; and
   (e) shall be permitted to defend himself before the court in person or, at his own expense, by a legal representative of his own choice, or if he is a person entitled to legal aid, by the Public Solicitor or another legal representative assigned to him in accordance with law; and
   (f) shall be afforded facilities to examine in person or by his legal representative the witnesses called before the court by the prosecution, and to obtain the attendance and carry out the examination of witnesses and to testify before the court on his own behalf, on the same conditions as those applying to witnesses called by the prosecution.
(4) Except with his own consent, the trial shall not take place in his absence unless he so conducts himself as to render the continuance of the proceedings in his presence impracticable and the court orders him to be removed and the trial to proceed in his absence, but provision may be made by law for a charge that a person has committed an offence the maximum penalty for which does not include imprisonment, (except in default of payment of a fine), to be heard summarily in his absence if it is established that he has been duly served with a summons in respect of the alleged offence (s 37(5)).
(5) No person shall be convicted of an offence on account of any act that did not, at the time when it took place, constitute an offence, and no penalty shall be imposed for an offence that is more severe in degree or description than the maximum penalty that might have been imposed for the offence at the time when it was committed (s 37(7)).
(6) No person who shows that he has been tried by a competent court for an offence and has been convicted or acquitted shall again be tried for that offence or for any other offence of which he could have been convicted at the

trial for that offence, except upon the order of a superior court made in the course of appeal or review proceedings relating to the conviction or acquittal (s 37(8)).

(7) No person shall be tried for an offence for which he has been pardoned (s 37(9)).

(8) No person shall be compelled in the trial of an offence to be a witness against himself (s 37(10)).

(9) A determination of the existence or extent of a civil right or obligation shall not be made except by an independent and impartial court or other authority prescribed by law or agreed upon by the parties, and proceedings for such a determination shall be fairly heard within a reasonable time (s 37(11)).

(10) Except with the agreement of the parties, or by order of the court in the interests of national security, proceedings in any jurisdiction of a court and proceedings for the determination of the existence or extent of any civil right or obligation before any other authority, including the announcement of the decision of the court or other authority, shall be held in public (s 37(12)).

(11) In the event that the trial of a person is not commenced within four months of the date on which he was committed for trial, a detailed report concerning the case shall be made by the Chief Justice to the minister responsible for the National Legal Administration (s 37(14)).

(12) Every person convicted of an offence is entitled to have his conviction and sentence reviewed by a higher court or tribunal according to law (s 37(15)).

(13) No person shall be deprived by law of a right of appeal against his conviction or sentence by any court that existed at the time of the conviction or sentence, as the case may be (s 37(16)).

(14) All persons deprived of their liberty shall be treated with humanity and with respect for the inherent dignity of the human person (s 37(17)).

(15) Accused persons shall be segregated from convicted persons and shall be subject to separate treatment appropriate to their status as unconvicted persons (s 37(18)).

(16) Persons under voting age who are in custody in connection with an offence or alleged offence shall be separated from other persons in custody and be accorded treatment appropriate to their age (s 37(19)).

(17) An offender shall not be transferred to an area away from that in which his relatives reside except for reasons of security or other good cause and, if such a transfer is made, the reason for so doing shall be endorsed on the file of the offender (s 37(20)).

5.1.2. Search, Arrest and Detention of an Accused

A search may be conducted by a policeman if he or she reasonably believe that the person has possession of a thing that the person has stolen or otherwise unlawfully obtained or a thing the person intends to use for committing an indictable offence.[141] Search warrants are normally issued by the District Court and the National Court. A search may or may not lead to criminal prosecution.

Some offences require warrants of arrest prior to effecting arrest. For such offences, police, especially commissioned officers, are required to obtain a warrant of arrest at the District Court or National Court before arresting a suspect. If the process is not complied with, the charge and subsequent committal or indictment will be refused by the courts.[142]

Any member of the public may arrest a person whom they believe on reasonable grounds (1) is committing, or (2) has committed an offence.[143] A person arrested by a member of the public must be brought to a nearest police station within a reasonable time.[144]

Section 37 of the Constitution is devoted to protecting and safeguarding the rights of a person in custody or charged with an offence. The safeguards are based on common law principles of the fair and impartial administration of justice in open court.[145] Some of the principles include that a person must be convicted of an offence that is defined by law and that a person charged with an offence is presumed to be innocent until proved guilty according to law.[146]

5.1.3. Bail

Bail is a constitutional right and is readily available to a person who is arrested and charged with an offence, except for the offence of treason and wilful murder pursuant to s 42(6) of the Constitution. The process for bail is regulated by the Bail Act. Section 9 of the Act provides a list of considerations that a bail authority must take into account before granting bail. The factors may vitiate the grant of bail. An applicant for bail must convince the courts that the conditions or factors under s 9(1) will not be violated or they do not apply to him or her or provide a reasonable explanation as why bail should be granted.[147]

---

141 Search Act, s 3.
142 *The State v Tulong* [1995] PNGLR 329.
143 Arrest Act, s 5.
144 Arrest Act, s 16.
145 Donald R C Chalmers, David Weisbrot, Salamo Injia and Warwick John Andrew *Criminal Law and Practice of Papua New Guinea* (UNPNG Press (Reprint), 2009) 2.
146 Constitution, s 37(2) and (4).
147 *Keating v The State* [1983] PNGLR 133.

5.2. CIVIL LAW

The Supreme Court and National Court have unrestricted powers to hear civil cases.[148] However, as a matter of practice, the National Court is the court of first instance where almost all civil disputes are dealt with.[149]

The District Court has jurisdiction over civil claims valuing up to K50,000.[150] The District Court's jurisdiction is limited by the District Courts Act and it cannot exercise powers or jurisdiction that are not expressly authorised by legislation. It is expressly excluded from dealing with dissolution of customary marriages,[151] customary land disputes,[152] and a number of other matters. On this point, in *Emmanuel v Iga*,[153] Kirriwom J had this to say:

> The power of the District Court is limited to what the enabling Act expressly provides. Generally all courts of summary jurisdiction exercise their powers within the limitation imposed upon the court, courts being creatures of Statute.

5.3. LEGAL PROFESSION

The legal profession in PNG is fused. It is governed by the Lawyers Act, which specifies the requirements for admission as a lawyer. The Act requires, among other things, that a person who applies to be a lawyer must have completed a undergraduate law degree from the University of Papua New Guinea or recognised university or institute from a common law jurisdiction, and have received legal training from the PNG Legal Training Institute or a recognised institute, and have a certificate of fit and proper person from the Attorney-General.[154] Application for admission to practice is made to the National Court.[155] The Court, upon satisfaction, admits a lawyer to practise in the National Court and Supreme Court. An admitted lawyer then signs the Lawyers' Roll that is in the custody of the Registrar of the National Court and Supreme Court.[156]

---

148 Constitution, s 155(3).

149 See *Somare v Manek* [2011] SC1118, at [127].

150 District Courts Act, s 21(1)(a). The maximum civil claim in the District Court was raised from K10,000 to K50,000 by the District Court (Amendment) Act 2009.

151 Village Courts deal with the dissolution of customary marriage and the District Courts endorse or certify the dissolution of the customary marriage: Village Courts Act and District Courts Act.

152 The District Court magistrates and land mediators are entitled to preside and decide on customary land disputes: Land Disputes Settlement Act.

153 [2003] PNGLR 20.

154 Lawyers Act, s 25.

155 Lawyers Act, s 26.

156 Lawyers Act, s 31.

An admitted lawyer may not practise law unless a certificate of practice is granted by the Papua New Guinea Law Society.[157]

Admission may be either to restricted or unrestricted practice. Lawyers who are in restricted practice are mostly in employment in the public service, private sector or non-government organisations or working under an unrestricted practice certificate holder. They are not allowed to hold money in trust for their clients and cannot practise on their own accord. Conversely, lawyers in unrestricted practice are allowed to hold trust moneys and they may practise on their own accord.[158] A lawyer's name may be removed from the Roll of Lawyers on grounds including misconduct.[159]

Lawyers are regarded as officers of the court and they are required to assist the courts to resolve disputes and deliver justice to the disputants.[160] Lawyers are also required to deliver legal services to their clients diligently and professionally without fear or favour.

6. ADMINISTRATION AND PERSONNEL OF THE LAW

The following law officers are established by the Constitution and Attorney-General Act:

(1) Attorney-General;[161]
(2) Solicitor-General;[162]
(3) State Solicitor;[163]
(4) Public Prosecutor;[164] and
(5) Public Solicitor.[165]

6.1. ATTORNEY-GENERAL

The office of Attorney-General is established by the Constitution. The appointee must be a qualified lawyer. If the Minister for Justice is a lawyer and admitted

157 Lawyers Act, s 35.
158 Lawyers Act, ss 39, 40 and 41.
159 *Toll v Kara* [1990] PNGLR 71; *Ole v Papua New Guinea Lawyers Statutory Committee* [2006] PGNC 158; *Ole v Papua New Guinea Lawyers Statutory Committee* [2001] PGNC 7; *Kot v Law Society of Papua New Guinea* [2016] PGNC 359; *Papua New Guinea Law Society v Saga* [2006] PGNC 81.
160 *Spirit Haus Ltd v Marshall* [2004] PGNC 166.
161 Constitution, s 156(1).
162 Attorney-General Act, s 11.
163 Attorney-General Act, s 13A.
164 Constitution, s 156(1).
165 Constitution, s 156(1).

to practise law under the Lawyers Act, he will often be appointed Attorney-General.[166] If the Minister for Justice is not legally qualified, the role is assumed by the head of the Department of Justice and Attorney-General, who is an admitted lawyer. The Attorney-General is the principal legal adviser to the national executive.[167] The office also grants certificates of fit and proper person for law graduates for admission to practise law in both the National and Supreme Courts. The Attorney-General also has the power to grant a licence to overseas lawyers to practise in PNG. The Attorney-General instructs the Solicitor-General and State Solicitor on matters that concern the State. The Attorney-General also instructs private lawyers from time to time to act on behalf of the State.[168]

6.2. SOLICITOR-GENERAL

The Office of the Solicitor-General is a branch of the Department of Justice and Attorney-General. It is established by virtue of s 11 of the Attorney-General Act and the incumbent is required to be a lawyer. The Solicitor-General is appointed for a term of three years[169] by the Attorney-General.[170] The Solicitor-General primarily appears as an advocate on behalf of the State in civil matters that go before the courts The Solicitor-General may accept instructions only from the Attorney-General. Other lawyers work under the Solicitor-General and act on behalf of the State in court.

6.3. STATE SOLICITOR

The Office of State Solicitor is established by s 13A of the Attorney-General Act. The State Solicitor must also be a lawyer, and is appointed by the Attorney-General, pursuant to s 13D of the Attorney-General Act, to provide legal advice to the State and its agencies.[171] Like the Solicitor-General, the State Solicitor works within the Department of Justice and Attorney-General. The State Solicitor is not an advocate. Amongst his or her many roles and functions, the

---

166 Attorney-General Act, s 4.

167 See Constitution, s 156(2), and Attorney-General Act, s 7. See also *Independent State of Papua New Guinea v Gelu, Solicitor General* [2003] SC716, where the Supreme Court discussed the application of the constitutional and legislative provisions and functions of the Attorney-General.

168 See ss 7(i) and 8(4) of the Attorney-General Act. See also *The State v Gelu and Manorburn Earthmoving Ltd* [2003] SC716; *Marape v O'Neill* [2016] PGSC 18; *Valu v Ngagan* [2018] PGSC 62.

169 Attorney-General Act, s 12.

170 Attorney-General Act, s 11.

171 Attorney-General Act, s 13B.

State Solicitor provides legal advice and clearance on contracts of employment of departmental heads, on contracts for major works and services of the State, and drafting of legislation.[172]

6.4. PUBLIC PROSECUTOR

The Public Prosecutor[173] is a constitutional office-holder.[174] The duties are spelt out in the Public Prosecutor (Office and Functions) Act and include the conduct of criminal prosecutions in the courts of PNG.[175] In the performance of his or her functions, the Public Prosecutor is not subject to control or direction.

The Public Prosecutor is responsible for the efficient performance of the prosecution function of the State to prosecute persons charged with any criminal offence at their trial before the National Court. The Public Prosecutor is also authorised to advocate on behalf of the State in any criminal appeal before the National Court or Supreme Court.

By law and practice, the Public Prosecutor selects police prosecutors to appear in the District Court on committal matters.

6.5. PUBLIC SOLICITOR

The Office of the Public Solicitor is also a constitutional position.[176] It provides legal aid to members of the general public who are unable to afford to engage a private lawyer.[177]

The Office of the Public Solicitor is funded by the State through the annual budget appropriation.[178] Otherwise, it operates independently from government influence and control. The Public Solicitor is constitutionally obliged to take instruction from any member of the general public and act on their behalf in both criminal and civil proceedings. The Public Solicitor defends and prosecutes cases in courts. The Public Solicitor is allowed to charge nominal legal fees for meeting basic administration expenses but not at the level charged by private law firms.

---

172 See Attorney-General Act.

173 Constitution, s 156.

174 Constitution, s 221.

175 Constitution, s 117.

176 Constitution, s 156(1).

177 See *Constitutional Reference No 1 of 1978* [1978] PNGLR 345, where the Supreme Court discussed the functions of the Public Solicitor.

178 *Constitutional Reference No 1 of 1978* [1978] PNGLR 345.

7. OTHER LAW ADMINISTRATION AND ENFORCEMENT BODIES

7.1. STATE SERVICES

The following State services are established by s 188 of the Constitution:

- the national public service;
- the police force;
- the Papua New Guinea Defence Force; and
- the Parliamentary Service.

7.1.1. National Public Service and Public Service Commission

The national public service constitutes the public service machinery of the State. It is regulated by the Public Services (Management) Act and its General Orders. The appointment of heads of departments and public servants are done under the Act, except the appointment of the heads of statutory bodies, which are facilitated under their respective Acts.

The Public Service Commission is a constitutional body[179] established by s 190 of the Constitution. Section 192 of the Constitution gives independence to the Commission, thus it is not subject to direction or control by anyone in carrying out its functions.[180] Its functions are set out by the Constitution and are further regulated by s 18 of the Public Services (Management) Act. Sections 191(1) and (2) and 193 of the Constitution outline the functions of the Commission, which are:[181]

(1) the review of personnel matters connected with the national public service;
(2) the continuous review of the State services (other than the Defence Force), and the services of other governmental bodies, and advising the National Executive Council and other responsible authorities on organisational matters; and
(3) providing recommendations and views through a process of consultation regarding decisions on appointments, revocation of appointments and suspension from office of some senior public office-holders, including department heads, the Commissioner of Police and the Commander of the Defence Force.

179 See ss 190–194 of the Constitution.
180 *Palaso v Kereme* [2016] PGNC 381.
181 *Re Reference by the Public Solicitor Pursuant to Constitution, Section 19(1)* [2019] SC1871.

The Commission's power to review personnel matters is exclusively governed by the Constitution and Public Services (Management) Act. The Commission's decisions in relation to personnel matters, which mostly concern dismissal or suspension of public servants, become absolute and binding after 30 days from the date of the decision.[182] The Commission does not have power to review personnel matters relating to the statutory authorities, which are not subject to the Public Services (Management) Act.[183]

7.1.2. Police Force

PNG's police force, known as the Royal Papua New Guinea Constabulary, was originally established by the Police Force (Interim Arrangements) Act, and was re-established as one of the State services under Part VII of the Constitution.[184]

The Police Commissioner is the head of the force and has the power of command and control. The Commissioner of Police is responsible for the superintendence, efficient organisation and control of the force in accordance with the Police Act.[185]

The police force is a disciplined force. Its functions are set out in the Constitution.[186] It is entrusted with enforcing the law and maintaining peace and order in the country, as necessary, and enforcing the law in an impartial and objective manner. It is also a function of the police force to lay, prosecute or withdraw charges in respect of offences. The members of the police force are not subject to direction or control by any person outside the force except the National Executive Council through the Minister for Police.[187] The Minister for Police does not have power to control the force, except to advise on policy matters.[188] Operational matters are regulated by the Police Act.

7.1.3. Defence Force

The PNG Defence Force is established by the Constitution. The main functions of the Defence Force, as set out in the Constitution[189] and the Defence Force Act, include the defence of PNG and its territory, assisting in the fulfilment by PNG of its international obligations, providing assistance to civilian authorities

---

182 Public Services (Management) Act, s 18(3)(d)(ii). See *Wakendui v Vagi* [2020] PGNC 31; *Attorney-General v Tetaga, Chairman Public Service Commission* [2005] PGNC 57.

183 *National Agriculture Quarantine & Inspection Authority v Tetaga* [2009] PGNC 220.

184 Section 197.

185 Constitution, s 187.

186 Section 198.

187 Constitution, s 196(1).

188 See *Re Powers, Functions, Duties and Responsibilities of the Commissioner of Police* [2014] PGSC 19.

189 Section 202.

in a civil disaster, and restoring public order and security. It is also under a duty to participate to the maximum in the task of national development and improvement. Its superintendence and control is subject to the National Executive Council through the Minister for Defence. The Commander of the Defence Force is the principal military adviser to the Minister for Defence,[190] and the Secretary for Defence, who is a civilian and has no power of command and control, advises the Minister on administrative matters concerning the Force. The Minister, Commander and Secretary comprise the Defence Council. The Defence Council is subject to the National Executive Council.

The members of the Defence Force are subject to the law, except where the nature of the Force and its functions, duties and responsibilities require otherwise.[191] Members also have a primary duty to obey lawful orders.[192]

7.1.4. Correctional Service

The Correctional Service is an integral part of the State services. It is recognised by the Constitution[193] and governed by the Correctional Service Act 1995. Its function is to detain and reform criminals.

7.1.5. Parliamentary Services

Parliamentary Services exists to serve the administration of Parliament to enable it to function efficiently.[194] The Service is part and parcel of the public service machinery and generally is answerable to the Public Service Commission, particularly in respect of personnel matters.[195] The Clerk of Parliament, who is the head of Parliamentary Services, reports to the Speaker of Parliament.

7.2. THE OMBUDSMAN COMMISSION

The Ombudsman Commission of PNG is an independent institution established by the Constitution.[196] It is comprised of the Chief Ombudsman and two other ombudsmen.[197] The Commission is an integral part of the system of checks and balances embodied in the Constitution to regulate the governance of the country. It is designed to prevent the abuse of power by those in the public sector, ensure

190 See s 201 of the Constitution.
191 Constitution, s 203.
192 Constitution, s 208.
193 Section 188(2).
194 See s 3 of the Parliamentary Service Act.
195 *Kaupa v Aufa* [2015] PGNC 262.
196 Section 217.
197 Constitution, s 217(1).

those exercising public power perform their duties efficiently and fairly, and impose accountability on those who are exercising public power.[198]

The Commission holds leaders in the public domain accountable through the Leadership Code under Part III, Division 2 of the Constitution and Organic Law on the Duties and Responsibilities of Leadership. The Supreme Court, in *Special Reference by the Attorney-General pursuant to Constitution, Section 19*,[199] said, in the context of ss 26 and 27 of Part III.2:

> These provisions are geared towards advancing the purpose of protecting the people of Papua New Guinea from the improper and corrupt conduct of their leaders and to ensure, as far as possible, that such breaches are not committed in the first place.

The Commission's functions are primarily 'investigative'.[200] It looks into allegations of maladministration by government departments, politicians and any leader who holds public office. Leaders expected to abide by the Leadership Code. Leaders include:[201]

(1) all members of Parliament (including the Prime Minister, the Leader and Deputy Leader of the Opposition and all ministers);
(2) all members of Provincial Assemblies and LLGs;
(3) all constitutional office-holders as defined by s 221 which include judges, the Public Prosecutor, the Public Solicitor, the Chief Magistrate, the members of the Electoral Commission, the Clerk of Parliament, the Auditor-General, the members of the Public Service Commission and the members of the Ombudsman Commission;
(4) all heads (Secretaries) of departments of the national public service and Provincial Administrators;
(5) all heads of statutory authorities;
(6) the Commissioner of Police;
(7) the Commander of the Defence Force;
(8) all Ambassadors and High Commissioners and senior diplomatic officials;
(9) the Public Curator;
(10) all personal staff of the Governor-General;
(11) executive officers of registered political parties; and
(12) persons holding such public offices as are declared by law from time to time.

198 See ss 218 (Purpose of the Commission) and 219 (Functions of the Commission) of the Constitution and Organic Law on Ombudsman Commission and Organic Law on the Duties and Responsibilities of Leadership.

199 [2016] SC1534 at [80].

200 Constitution, s 219. See further *Ombudsman Commission v Yama* [2004] SC747.

201 Constitution, s 26.

Complaints may be made by an individual or a group to the Ombudsman in Port Moresby or to representatives in the provinces. Any statement received by the Commission forms part of its investigations. If the Commission forms an opinion that the leader has a case to answer, it refers the matter to the Public Prosecutor for assessment and possible prosecution. The Commission is required to give notice of the right to be heard to the person under investigation before any referral.[202] The decision of the Commission is final and it can only be reviewed by the National Court or Supreme Court on the basis of ultra vires or breach of the principles of natural justice.[203]

The Public Prosecutor's Office is required to form its own opinion based on the evidence and draft statement of charge forwarded by the Commission.[204] If satisfied that the leader has a prima facie case to answer, the matter is referred to the appropriate appointing authorities to deal with. In the case of a Member of Parliament, the matter is referred to the Chief Justice to set up a leadership tribunal to inquire into the allegations.

8. FAMILY LAW

8.1. TWO TYPES OF MARRIAGE: CUSTOMARY AND STATUTORY

There are two types of marriage recognised by law: customary marriage and statutory marriage.[205]

Historically, customary marriage was not officially recognised in the Territory of Papua,[206] as all persons were required to enter into statutory marriages. On the other hand, in New Guinea, marriages entered into in accordance with custom were enforceable by the New Guinea Native Administration Regulations (reg 65); indigenous people were restricted to customary marriages.[207] Since the enactment of the Marriage Act 1963, both statutory and customary marriages are valid. Apart from statutory marriage, which requires documentary proof,[208]

202 *Ombudsman Commission v Yama* [2004] SC747.

203 *Ombudsman Commission of PNG v Donohoe* [1985] PNGLR 348; *Ombudsman Commission v Yama* [2004] PGSC 30.

204 *Special Reference by the Attorney-General pursuant to Constitution, Section 19* [2016] PGSC 52.

205 *Peter v Matthew* [1995] PGNC 31.

206 In accordance with Marriage Ordinance 1912, s 18.

207 In accordance with Marriage Ordinance 1935–36, s 5A, statutory marriage between two natives was not allowed, though statutory marriage was possible between a non-native and a native with written consent from the District Officer. For detailed discussions see Owen Jessep and John Luluaki *Principles of Family Law in Papua New Guinea* (2nd ed, UPNG Press, 1985) 6.

208 Part V of the Marriage Act sets out the formalities of a statutory marriage.

s 3 of the Act recognises customary marriage without any specific statutory requirements.[209] A customary marriage may be formalised in accordance with the custom[210] prevailing at a particular locality at a point in time.[211] It will not be recognised if the woman has been forced into marriage,[212] or if the custom under which the marriage was formed is repugnant to the general principles of humanity.[213] The Village Courts recognise customary marriages under the Village Courts Act 1989.

The customs of some societies in PNG recognise and accept polygamy.[214] However, having one wife is a common practice and in recent times has been strongly supported by the Church.[215] Polygamy has attracted wide criticism over the years, which has resulted in various proposals being advanced to ban the practice; however, none of them has received government approval.[216] It may be argued that polygamy prioritises status and prestige over livelihood and welfare. It is a commonly held view that having multiple wives demonstrates one's prestige (and wealth) and more importantly increases respect and status, as stressed by Kapi DCJ (as he then was) in *Kombea v Peke*:[217] 'It is the custom of people of Ialibu District that a leader may have more than one wife. The status of a leader in custom is determined, amongst other things, by the number of wives he has.' A custom that barred polyandry was declared invalid on the grounds that it was discriminatory on the basis of gender.[218]

Statutory marriage must comply with the formal processes set out in the Marriage Act. In *Kane v Kane*,[219] Kassman J gave an instructive explanation of statutory marriage:

> The marriage is what is commonly called a church marriage being a marriage where the union of a man and woman as husband and wife is solemnized or blessed in a religious ceremony by a minister of religion whether a priest or pastor or other

209 Section 5 of the Customs Recognition Act also recognises customary marriage.
210 The constitutional definition of custom is set out in Sch 1.2 of the Constitution.
211 See Underlying Law Act.
212 Marriage Act, s 5. See also *Application by ICRAF Re Willingal* [1997] PNGLR 119. The District Court (formerly Local Court) has the jurisdiction to deal with such matters.
213 *Application by ICRAF Re Willingal* [1997] PNGLR 119.
214 That is still enforceable under the current marriage legal framework. See Marriage Act, s 3; Customs Recognition Act, s 5; and Constitution, Sch 2.1.
215 Section 3 of the Marriage Act also makes a qualification that a customary marriage is not valid if one of the parties is already married by statute to somebody else. Before that marriage can be recognised, the statutory marriage must be ended. For further details see Owen Jessep and John Luluaki *Principles of Family Law in Papua New Guinea* (2nd ed, UPNG Press, 1985) 22.
216 Jonathan Aleck and Jackson Rannells (eds) *Custom at the Crossroads* (UPNG Press, 1995) 28–29.
217 [1994] PNGLR 572.
218 *Magiten v Beggie (No 2)* [2005] PNGLR 647.
219 [2013] PGNC 203.

authorized celebrant. Further, such ceremonies are performed in accordance with the rites or requirements of the church of both or one or the other partner. This union is at the same time referred to as statutory marriage being a union duly registered in accordance with the requirements of the Marriage Act Chapter 280. Under section 36 of that Act a statutory marriage can also be recorded in a civil marriage ceremony before the Registrar-General or such other person as authorized.

The marriageable age of a male is set at 18 years and female at 16 years.[220] There is no marriageable age specified by customary law for customary marriages. Accordingly, it is arguable that the marriageable ages set out in the Marriage Act apply.

8.2. DISSOLUTION OF MARRIAGE

The present State legal framework is silent on the requirements for the dissolution of a customary marriage in terms of legal requirements,[221] as opposed to recognition of customary marriage. Section 5(f) of the Customs Recognition Act recognises customary divorce, but does not state the process of or requirements for customary divorce.[222]

The Village Courts Act does not empower the Village Courts to grant a divorce, but does allow them to deal with ancillary matters.[223] This dilemma was acknowledged in *Woodham v Undai*[224] by Sawong J, who remarked that there –

> is no express statutory power in a Village Court to dissolve a customary marriage or order compensation payment following such a dissolution under the provisions of the Village Courts Act. However there is general power under S.47, 57 and 58 of the Act, upon which the Village Court derives jurisdiction to dissolve customary marriages and order compensation payments following such a dissolution.

The District Courts are empowered to provide a dissolution certificate upon satisfaction that a customary marriage has been dissolved according to custom.[225]

---

220 Marriage Act, s 7.

221 Owen Jessep and John Luluaki *Principles of Family Law in Papua New Guinea* (2nd ed, UPNG Press, 1985) 56.

222 In addition, as discussed earlier, the Constitution (Sch. 2.1), the Underlying Law Act (ss 4 and 6) and the Marriage Act (s 3) set out the legal requirements for the formation of a customary marriage.

223 Owen Jessep and John Luluaki *Principles of Family Law in Papua New Guinea* (2nd ed, UPNG Press, 1985) 56.

224 [1999] N1868.

225 District Courts Act, s 22A.

Cohabitation does not automatically give rise to customary marriage, and ceasing to cohabit may not be recognised as customary divorce.[226]

Dissolution of statutory marriage is governed by the Matrimonial Causes Act. Statutory marriage may only be dissolved by an order of the National Court.[227] The grounds for dissolution are specified in the Act.[228]

8.3. CUSTODY OF CHILDREN OF MARRIAGE

The guiding principle in awarding custody of children of both customary and statutory marriages is set out in the Matrimonial Causes Act. This principle was reaffirmed by the National Court in *Kane v Kane*:[229]

> This court is reminded of the principal guiding factor and provided in section 74 of the Matrimonial Causes Act which is that 'the court shall regard the interests of the children as the paramount consideration'. In *Bean v Bean* [1980] PNGLR 307 at 320–321, Kapi J (as he then was), said 'the welfare of the child is usually referred to as the comfort, health, moral, intellectual and spiritual welfare of the child. These elements, in turn, are fundamentally dependent on the existence of security, wise discipline and genuine affection in the home'.

The factors the court must take into account when deciding what is in the child's best interest were summarised by Jessep and Luluaki as including:[230]

> diet, health, clothing, accommodation and surroundings, caretaking arrangements, significant persons and relationships affecting the child, daily activities and educational progress, and any relevant wishes of the child ... Details of the parents' behavior and conduct may be important, if it throws light on any aspect of the child's welfare.

In the case of statutory marriages, custody proceedings must be instituted in the National Court under Matrimonial Causes Act. Jurisdiction to deal with custody of children of customary marriages lies with the Village Court, which must apply the rules of custom,[231] taking into account the principles of natural justice and welfare of the children. The jurisdiction to deal with custody of children under the Deserted Wives and Children Act only applies when the father deserted

226 In *Re Maip* [1991] PNGLR 80. See also Edward R Hill and Guy Powles *Magistrates Manual of Papua New Guinea* (Lawbook Co, 2001) 301.

227 Matrimonial Causes Act, s 1.

228 Section 17.

229 [2013] PGNC 203 at [71] and [72].

230 Owen Jessep and John Luluaki *Principles of Family Law in Papua New Guinea* (2nd ed, UPNG Press, 1994) 134.

231 Village Courts Act, s 47.

the child without any means of support or is about to leave the country.[232] In addition, the Family Court has power to deal with child protection under the Lukautim Pikinini Act.[233]

8.4. ADOPTION

Adoption is governed by Part VI of the Adoption of Children Act 1968.[234] The Act regulates both state and customary adoptions. The Act gives the adopting parents the right to adopt a child under custom if that child was being brought up by them as their own.[235] The adoption takes place in accordance with the rules prescribed by custom.[236] After a District Court is satisfied, a certificate of adoption is issued.[237] The Act does not expressly require the welfare of the child to be the paramount consideration, but since this Act is subject to the Custom Recognition Act (s 3),[238] the courts may refuse recognition of those customs that infringe child welfare.

Adoptions under State law are granted by the National Court under the Adoption of Children Act.[239] Section 3 of the Act requires that the child must be in the country and that the applicant was a resident or domiciled in the country. The child's welfare is the paramount consideration[240] and the Court must be satisfied on the factors set out under the Act.[241]

8.5. DISTRIBUTION OF MATRIMONIAL PROPERTY

When a customary marriage ends, there are no written rules governing distribution of matrimonial possessions, such as the house, gardens and livestock. In most instances, it is subject to discussion and intervention by the community leaders. However, it is well established in custom, given the patrilineal society, that whatever is on customary land is retained by the husband, while other possessions are shared between the couple. The inferior

232 *Mura v Gimai* (1997) N1573.
233 Lukautim Pikinini Act, Part XII.
234 *Puri v Puri* [1993] PNGLR 451.
235 Section 53(1).
236 Section 53(2).
237 Section 54. Non-compliance with the requirements of adoption may render certification invalid: *R v Hamboken and Asini* [1973] PNGLR 289.
238 Section 52.
239 Section 9. The Family Court does not have jurisdiction to grant adoption as opposed to the protection and welfare of an adopted child: Lukautim Pikinini Act, s 88.
240 Adoption of Children Act, s 5. See *Adoption of an Infant, R* [1976] PNGLR 81.
241 See s 88 of the Lukautim Pikinini Act.

courts, such as the District Courts,[242] uphold this principle in dealing with the distribution of matrimonial property. The Village Courts may apply custom to resolve these kinds of disputes.[243] They have additional jurisdiction under the Village Courts Act, which Jessep and Luluaki[244] summarise in the following terms:

> Although the Village Court has no specific power to grant customary divorce, it can mediate a settlement between estranged spouses and their respective kin, and its unlimited powers of adjudication in the matters of bride price and custody of children, will in many cases enable the court to produce a situation in which a divorce can occur according to custom.

Under State law, a married woman is entitled to own private property under her own name.[245] Any property acquired during the marriage may be defined as matrimonial property, unless it was acquired prior to the marriage.

Property acquired during a statutory marriage may be distributed between the estranged couple by mutual agreement or by an order of the National Court.[246] In *Robert v Robert*[247] the National Court laid out the following general guiding principles for the distribution of matrimonial property acquired during a marriage:

> I perceive that my task here is firstly, to identify the matrimonial properties then determine the value of each property, if possible, these two issues can be addressed together; secondly, to assess and determine the contributions made by each party towards the properties, taking into account the parties' financial resources, means and time; thirdly, to determine the future needs of each party; fourthly, to consider any other circumstances which are relevant to the issues at hand and fifthly, to make orders for property settlement which are just and equitable in the circumstances of the case.

9. LAW OF OBLIGATIONS

9.1. LAW OF TORT AND CONTRACT

In PNG, tort and contract are governed by the common law, together with a small amount of legislation. With regard to torts, personal injury claims arising

---

242 District Courts Act, s 22A.
243 Village Courts Act, s 57.
244 Owen Jessep and John Luluaki *Principles of Family Law in Papua New Guinea* (2nd ed, UPNG Press, 1985) 81.
245 Married Women's Property Act.
246 Matrimonial Causes Act, ss 73 and 75; *Robert v Robert* [2010] N4003.
247 [2010] PGNC 165 at [52].

from a motor vehicle accident are governed by the Motor Vehicle Insurance Act. Defamation is covered by the Defamation Act.

In contract cases, the Goods Act 1951, the Fairness of Transactions Act 1993 and the Personal Properties Securities Act 2011 may apply. As discussed below, there is also legislation governing employment contracts. Contracts with the public service, using public funds, are governed by the Public Finance (Management) Act; it provides the formalities and requirements and any State contract that fails to comply with the Act is void.

In certain cases, for instance in a claim against the State for tort or breach of contract, a notice to the Solicitor-General or Attorney-General must be given within six months (or within an extended period) from the date when the cause of action arose pursuant to s 5 of the Claims by and Against the State Act. Further, for any tortious action against the State, a claimant must prove that the tort was committed by its servants and agents in the course of performing their duties pursuant to s 1 of the Miscellaneous (Provisions) Act. The State will not be liable for any act committed outside the scope of duties imposed on its servants and agents. Any claim in tort or contract cannot be brought after six years from the date of the tort or breach of contract.[248] Further, an action in tort for a deceased person must be commenced within three years from the date of his or her death.[249]

Formal law to a lesser extent recognises business transactions carried on under customary law, for instance the sale of usufructuary or use rights of customary land, the use of *tabu* (shell money) as a medium of exchange in the Tolai community (in East New Britain Province and others including the Highlands), or the use of food or other items in exchange for food or materials (barter).

9.2. EMPLOYMENT LAW

Employment in PNG is principally regulated by the Employment Act 1978, the Public Employment of Non-Citizens Act 1978, the Employment of Non-Citizens Act 2007, and the Public Services (Management) Act 1995. The Employment Act is of general application and it sets out the parameters for a valid contract of employment, especially in the private sector. Under that Act, both written and oral contracts of employment are valid and a person aged 16 or above may enter into a written contract of employment.[250] Unless provided for in a written contract, the general notice of termination is defined by s 34 of the Act.

248 Frauds and Limitations Act 1988, s 16.
249 Wrongs (Miscellaneous Provisions) Act 1975, s 31.
250 Employment Act, s 18.

However, an employee may be terminated without notice.[251] The common law principles of hire and fire at will apply under this Act.

Employment of non-citizens in the private sector is regulated by both the Employment of Non-Citizens Act and the Employment Act.[252] The Employment of Non-Citizens Act sets out the criteria for non-citizens to find employment in PNG and also provides the procedures for obtaining work permits. Permits are usually granted for specific or specialised senior positions in the employer organisation for a fixed time period, but with the possibility of extension. One of the most important criteria for granting a permit is that the non-citizen and his or her prospective employer must provide a plan for the training, upskilling and transfer of know-how to citizens.

The Public Employment of Non-Citizens Act and the Public Services (Management) Act respectively apply to foreign and local employees in the public service. The Public Employment of Non-Citizens Act applies particularly to non-citizens employed in public authorities, including the public service and other State entities.[253] It sets out the parameters of the employment contract and other terms and conditions of employment. One of the important features under the Act is the localisation requirement, where a non-citizen is required to train and upskill locals.[254] The Act states that any non-citizen employed in the public authorities must be employed on a written contract.[255]

The Public Services (Management) Act and its General Orders apply to all national employees in the public service, except those in the statutory authorities and judicial services, where they have their own legislation governing employment. The Act provides the terms and conditions and also the criteria for employment. Any employment-related grievances under the Public Services (Management) Act must be first addressed through the Public Service Commission. After the Public Service Commission makes its decision, an aggrieved person may pursue an application for judicial review in the National Court.

The common law 'control test', 'integral or organisational test' and 'consistency test' have been held to apply to determine whether a person is an employee or a private contractor.[256]

---

251 The grounds for termination for cause and without notice are provided under ss 34 and 35 of the Employment Act.

252 See s 5 of the Employment of Non-Citizens Act. See also *Air Niugini v Salter* [2001] SC679.

253 Public Employment of Non-Citizens Act, s 4.

254 Public Employment of Non-Citizens Act, s 7.

255 Public Employment of Non-Citizens Act, s 8.

256 *Tingiruan v Rabaul Garage Ltd* [1978] PNGLR 179; Lawrence Kalinoe *Law of Industrial Relations: Texts and Course Material* (Law School, University of Papua New Guinea, 2003) 27. See also *Airfix Footwear Ltd v Cope* [1978] 1 CR 1210; Moses Aldrin Kimuli *Business Law in Papua New Guinea* (Institute of Business Studies, 1994) 281.

10. LAND LAW

The State owns 2.5 per cent of the land in PNG, 0.5 per cent is freehold land and the remaining 97 per cent is customarily owned (customary land)[257] by the indigenous landowners under customary law.[258] Much of the State-owned land was acquired from the customary landowners during the colonial era.

The primary pieces of legislation governing land are the Land Act 1996, which deals with all State land,[259] and the Land Registration Act, which deals with the registration of titles. PNG has adopted the Torrens system for the registration of State leases. It provides conclusive evidence of ownership and indefeasibility of title. In *Mudge and Mudge v Secretary for Lands, The State and Delta Developments Pty Ltd*,[260] the Supreme Court explained that the Torrens system of registered title, which PNG adopted under the Land Registration Act, is not a system of registration of title but a system of title by registration. Once it is registered, the title to a State lease is indefeasible.[261]

In the colonial era, private individuals were barred from acquiring land from the customary landowners.[262] This provision was designed to protect the customary landowners from losing their land to private interests at the expense of their future land requirements, whilst allowing acquisition for development purposes. This prohibition was repeated in successive legislation. The current pieces of legislation continue this policy by preventing customary landowners from disposing of their land other than to citizens in accordance with custom.[263]

However, purchase of customary land by the government is permissible. Under s 53 of the Constitution and s 12 of the Land Act, the government may enter into an agreement with the customary landowners to acquire or lease customary land. Such an agreement must be voluntary. The purchase of customary land for a public purpose will be final if the prerequisites under ss 10 and 11 of the Land Act are fully complied with.[264] Once the land has been purchased, it becomes government land for all purposes. Leased land becomes

---

257 The Land (Tenure Conversion) Act (s 4) defines 'customary land' as land that is owned or possessed by an automatic citizen or community of automatic citizens by virtue of rights of a proprietary or possessory kind that belong to that citizen or community and arise from and are regulated by custom.

258 Harrison A Amankwah, John T Mugambwah and George Muroa *Land Law in Papua New Guinea* (UPNG Press, 2009). The collective native ownership of land was legally recognised by the pre-independence court in *Geita Sebea v The Territory of Papua* (1941) 67 CLR 544.

259 Land Act, s 4.

260 [1985] PNGLR 387.

261 See also *National Council of Young Mens Christian Association of Papua New Guinea (Inc) v Firms Services Ltd* [2017] SC1596 at [3].

262 Land Regulation Ordinance 1888.

263 Section 132.

264 See *Safe Lavao v The State (Re Kerema Town and Airstrip Land)* [1978] PNGLR 15.

government land for the duration of the lease,[265] and reverts to customary status on expiration of the lease.[266]

The Land (Tenure Conversion) Act paves the way for converting customary land to freehold or leasehold under the Land Registration Act.[267] Most of the customary land in PNG is held communally, rather than by individuals. The Land Groups Incorporation Act was enacted to recognise communal ownership through land-holding groups. The Act was intended to encourage greater participation by local people in the national economy, by giving corporate status to certain customary groups and instilling greater certainty of title. The Act also provides a more effective method for the settlement of customary land disputes.[268] The incorporated land groups as corporations have power to acquire, hold, dispose of and manage land, and ancillary powers. The incorporated land group concept was successfully implemented in the palm oil industry, but it remains a challenge in the oil, gas and mining industries.[269]

11. COMMERCIAL LAW

11.1. TAXATION, INVESTMENT, BANKING AND FINANCE

11.1.1. Taxation

The Income Tax Act provides the income tax regime for employees and employers alike.[270] The Income Tax Act and Customs Act provide investment incentives, such as tax holidays, or tax reductions on income taxes or excise taxes, duty-free import of equipment and supplies, and duty-free export of products.[271] These Acts also place conditions or incentives on investments, which include employment opportunities for the local population, requirements to provide training programmes, or requirements to provide local infrastructure such as roads, hospitals or clinics.

---

265 Rudolph William James *Land Law and Policy in Papua New Guinea: Law Reform Commission of Papua New Guinea, Monograph No 5* (Law Reform Commission of Papua New Guinea, 1985) <http://www.paclii.org/pg/lawreform/PGLawRComm/1985/2.pdf>.

266 See *Resena v The State* [1991] PNGLR 475.

267 Part III.

268 Land Groups Incorporation Act, s 1.

269 Tony Power 'Reconciling Customary Ownership and Development: Incorporated Land Groups in Papua New Guinea' <https://www.dfat.gov.au/sites/default/files/MLW_Volume Two_CaseStudy_1.pdf> 12.

270 Sections 209 and 210 of the Constitution authorise Parliament to impose taxes, levies and other income-generating avenues for the government.

271 See Division 1A – Export Incentive and Division 1B – Rural Development Incentives, Income Tax Act.

The Stamp Duty Act provides for the stamp duty levied on the transfer of real property; the Customs Act sets the parameters of custom duty levied on the import and export of goods.

The provincial governments and LLGs are allowed to impose tax in certain areas.[272] When imposing taxes, fees and charges, both the provincial governments and LLGs are required to ensure their respective taxation policies are anti-discriminatory.[273] A tax, fee or charge imposed under a provincial law or a local level law that is discriminatory may be struck down or amended by Parliament. Parliament has powers to repeal or amend the contravening law or to order compensation or restitution to the party aggrieved by the discrimination.

The Constitution of the Autonomous Region of Bougainville gives power to the autonomous Bougainville government to establish its own tax regime for all taxes other than company tax, value-added tax (which was replaced by a goods and services tax) and customs duties.[274] This arrangement is sanctioned by the Constitution, which provides: 'the Bougainville Government [is] to have power to establish its own tax regime for all taxes excluding customs duties, company tax and value added tax.'[275] By agreement with the Internal Revenue Commission, the Bougainville government may collect the three additional taxes.[276]

11.1.2. Banking and Finance

The Central Banking Act establishes the Central Bank, which is known as the Bank of Papua New Guinea. In conjunction with the Central Banking (Regulation) and Banking and Financial Institutions Act, the Central Banking Act provides the platform for the implementation of the State's monetary policy,[277] including the issuance of the national currency (kina and toea) and control the money supply or liquidity in the economy. These laws provide exemptions from exchange control restrictions, ability to repatriate capital and profits, and guarantees against expropriation or nationalisation. The laws provide mechanisms for the regulation and control of banking,[278] super funds (also via the Superannuation (General Provision) Act), finance companies, and savings and loans societies, amongst others. The Central Bank grants licences and provides general oversight in the sector. In 2015 the Anti-Money Laundering

272 Organic Law on Provincial Government and Local Level Government, Part 4, Division 3.
273 Organic Law on Provincial Government and Local Level Government, s 90.
274 Section 154(2).
275 Section 325(c).
276 Constitution of the Autonomous Region of Bougainville, s 154(2)(c).
277 The fiscal policy is implemented by the government budgetary process through the Public Finances (Management) Act, and various other pieces of legislation.
278 Currently there are four commercial banks: Bank South Pacific Limited, Westpac Bank (PNG) Limited, Australia and New Zealand (ANZ) Bank (PNG) Limited, and Kina Bank Limited.

and Counter Terrorist Financing Act was passed to address the global issue of money laundering and financing of terrorism activities. This Act is implemented by the Central Bank.

11.1.3. Corporations

The Companies Act allows incorporation of both local and overseas companies.[279] The Act was based on the New Zealand Companies Act. Once a company is incorporated, it acquires separate legal personality pursuant to s 16 of the Companies Act.[280] It is a separate entity from the shareholders and directors. The Companies Act provides the general framework of powers and functions of the shareholders and directors and issuance of shares.[281] The legislation also allows for amalgamation and compromise,[282] receivership,[283] liquidation[284] and winding up. The Act sets out requirements and procedures for these activities to be conducted in an orderly fashion. Overseas companies may register under the Companies Act to carry on business activities in the country.

Companies or individuals may form partnerships to pursue business ventures pursuant to the Partnership Act. Section 2 of the Act defines a partnership as 'the relationship that subsists between persons carrying on a business in common with a view to profit.' Section 4 sets out the rules for determining the existence of a partnership. Partnerships may be incorporated or unincorporated and, in either case, the provisions of the Act must be complied with.

Associations that are not for profit may be incorporated under the Associations Incorporation Act 1966. Any activity they carry out must be for advancing the interests of the association and its members. Any entity which carries on business in PNG under a name other than its own must register a business name under the Business Names Act.

11.1.4. Intellectual Property

The Copyright and Neighbouring Rights Act provides copyright protection for certain works. In *Aundambui v Post PNG Ltd*,[285] Kandakasi J classified the works protected under the Act as follows:

(a) Literary – covering song lyrics, manuscripts, manuals, computer programs, commercial documents, leaflets, newsletters and articles and so on;

---

279 See Part II – Incorporation and s 383 of the Companies Act.
280 *Pacific Rim Constructors – Singapore PTE Ltd v Huala Hire & Construction Ltd* [2012] N4710.
281 Companies Act, Part VI.
282 Companies Act, Part XIV.
283 Companies Act, Part XVII.
284 Companies Act, Part XVIII.
285 [2014] N5772.

(b) Dramatic - covering plays, dance and the like;
(c) Musical - covering musical recordings and scores;
(d) Artistic - covering photography, painting, sculptures, architecture, technical drawings or diagrams, maps and logos;
(e) Typographical arrangement of published editions - covering magazines, periodicals and so on;
(f) Sound Recording - Covering recordings of sounds not covered in the musicals category; and
(g) Film - covering video footages, films, broadcasts and cable programmes.

Under the Act, copyright comes into existence the moment an individual or a group of individuals or an incorporated entity creates any of these works.[286] The work must be original and exhibit a degree of labour, skill or judgement.[287]

The Trade Marks Act 1978 and Patents and Industrial Design Act 2000 protect trademarks and inventions. Such intellectual properties may be registered with the Intellectual Property Office, an office within the Investment Promotion Authority.

11.1.5. Consumer Protection

The Independent Consumer and Competition Commission Act 2000 was enacted to promote competition and fair trading, regulation of prices for certain goods and services, the protection of consumers' interests, and other related purposes. Section 4 of the Act establishes the Independent Consumer and Competition Commission (ICCC), which is not subject to any form of control by the minister or any other person in the performance of its functions.[288] Unfair trading and anti-competitive behaviour are discouraged by the Act. Prior to any merger, acquisition or amalgamations, approval must be obtained from ICCC on the basis that such activity will not result in unfair trading or lack of competition in the respective sector or industry.

11.2. PUBLIC UTILITIES LAW

Public utilities law governs the protection and promotion of safety, efficiency and effectiveness in the provision of services such as electricity, roads, water, telephone and gas to the public.

---

286 See ss 4(2) and (3) of the Copyrights and Neighbouring Rights Act 2000. See also *Aundambui v Post PNG Ltd* [2014] N5772.

287 *Aundambui v Post PNG Ltd* [2014] N5772.

288 Independent Consumer and Competition Commission Act 2002, s 23.

11.2.1. Electricity

The Electricity Commission Act provided for the establishment of a PNG Electricity Commission to regulate the generation and sale of electricity, and other related purposes. The Commission was replaced by PNG Power Ltd in 2000.

Under the Electricity Industry Act, the regulatory function, including issuing of permits and licences for production and distribution of electricity, are vested in the ICCC.[289] Individuals or organisations may only own, operate and sell electricity with the express approval of the regulator, the ICCC.[290]

11.2.2. Telephone, Television, Internet and Radio Communication

The telephone, internet, voice call, television, etc. radio spectrum systems are regulated by the government through the Telecommunication (Cable Television Service Licence Fees) Regulation, the Telecommunications Act, the Telecommunications Industry Act, the Television (Prohibition and Control) Act, the Telikom PNG Limited Act, and the National Information and Communication Technology Act. Other public utilities such as water and sanitation are also regulated.[291]

11.2.3. Land, Sea and Air Transport

Land, sea and air transport systems are regulated by their respective legislation. The Road Traffic Act regulates all motor vehicles. All vehicles must be roadworthy[292] and be covered by compulsory third party insurance.[293]

The Constitution (s 2(1)) and the Maritime Zones Act define the maritime boundary of PNG. All ships and other maritime vessels including foreign vessels are bound to comply with the Maritime Zones Act and the Merchant Shipping Act. All vessels operating or entering the waters of PNG must satisfy the minimum operational and safety standards prescribed by the Merchant Shipping Act and National Maritime Safety Authority Act. The seaports and their management are covered by the Habours Act.

The Civil Aviation Act applies to civil aviation in the country. It sets out operational and safety standards that are in accordance with the Convention on International Civil Aviation and the International Civil Aviation Organisation. The Act also provides the general rules and guidelines for air accident investigation and the management of airports.

289 See Part IIIA and Part IIIB of the Electricity Industry Act.
290 Electricity Industry Act, s 24D.
291 See National Water Supply and Sanitation Act; Environment Act and Public Health Act.
292 See the Road Traffic Act, s 65(3) and Motor Traffic Regulation, ss 13A and 25B.
293 Motor Vehicle (Third Party Insurance) Act.

12. ENVIRONMENTAL LAW

Environmental laws are intended to promote ecological responsibility and sustainability in the wise use and management of the natural environment, as envisaged by the National Goal and Directive Principle 4 (Natural Resources and Environment). The Environment Act 2000 requires an environmental impact assessment to be prepared whenever any major resource project is proposed. Environment permits are also required.[294] The Act provides for wide consultation and planning,[295] involving various stakeholders, such as the Director of Environment, the Environment Council,[296] the Minister for Environment[297] and various advisory bodies: the Environment Consultative Group,[298] the Provincial Environment Committees[299] and Working Committee.[300] The Act also sets out criteria for formulating and implementing national environmental policies[301] and provincial policies.[302]

The Conservation Areas Act 1978 and the National Parks Act 1982 attempt to conserve the sites and areas related to biological, topographical, geological, historic, scientific or social importance. They also regulate management of those sites and areas. Under the Conservation Areas Act,[303] once land is declared as a conservation area, any development must be within the management plan of the conservation area or be approved by the Minister.

Due to the growing concern about global warming and climate change, the United Nations has established an overarching framework called the United Nations Framework Convention on Climate Change (UNFCCC). This Convention was enacted to curb or mitigate the effects of climate change and adapt to the effects of climate change. The Paris Agreement implements the objectives of the Convention.

PNG signed the Convention on 13 June 1992 and ratified it on 16 March 1993.[304] On 22 April 2016 PNG signed the Paris Agreement and ratified it on 21 September 2016.[305]

Issues relating climate change are regulated by various policies and pieces of legislation. The National Goal and Directive Principle 4 (Natural Resources

---

294 Environment Act, Part 5.
295 Section 15.
296 Environment Act, ss 17–19.
297 Environment Act, s 14.
298 Environment Act, ss 26–28.
299 Environment Act, s 29.
300 Environment Act, s 24.
301 Environment Act, ss 30, 32, 33, 35 and 36.
302 Environment Act, s 39.
303 Sections 17 and 31.
304 United Nations Climate Change, Parties and Observers <http://unfccc.int/tools_xml/country_PG.html>.
305 United Nations Framework Convention on Climate Change <https://unfccc.int/node/61140>.

and Environment) of the Preamble to the Constitution provides for the wise use of natural resources and the protection of the environment. Consistent with this principle, the government in its Vision 2050 and National Climate Change Action Plan aims to attain a 50 per cent reduction in emissions by 2030 and to be carbon neutral by 2050. There are other notable policies on climate which are being developed and implemented in line with the legislative framework.

The Climate Change (Management) Act is the principal piece of legislation governing climate-change-related issues in PNG. Parliament also enacted the United Nations Paris Agreement (Implementation) Act to ratify and implement the Paris Agreement. These Acts are complementary and are implemented concurrently. The Climate Change (Management) Act sets out the regulatory framework for climate change mitigation[306] and adaptation[307] activities. The Act gives recognition and prominence to customary landowners' rights[308] and also accords flexibility to entities in regulated industries to develop their own mitigation and adaptation plans based on their specific circumstances. The Act also provides for free prior informed consent as a mechanism to obtain the consent of customary landowners for the purposes of carrying out climate-change-related projects on their land.[309]

13. NATURAL RESOURCE LAW

Section 115 of the OLPG and LLG provides for the control of natural resources. Subsection (1) provides that where there is a proposal to develop a natural resource in a province or provinces, the appropriate national minister designated by the National Executive Council shall consult with the provincial government in the province or provinces where the natural resource is situated. Subsection (2) provides that governments at all levels must liaise with the customary landowners in relation to the development of natural resources. Section 98 sets out the benefits of natural resources and defines 'natural resources' to include minerals, petroleum, gas, marine products, water, timber (including forest products), fauna, flora and any other product determined by law to be a natural resource.

13.1. MINING AND PETROLEUM LAW

Mining and petroleum resources are governed by the Mining Act and the Oil and Gas Act. The Acts vest ownership over mineral and petroleum resources in

306 Climate Change (Management) Act, Part V.
307 Climate Change (Management) Act, Part VI.
308 Climate Change (Management) Act, Part VIII.
309 Climate Change (Management) Act, s 87.

the State.[310] This is so despite the fact that the bulk of the land where minerals and oil and gas deposits are found is under customary ownership.

The Mining Act deals with exploration, exploitation and extraction of minerals.[311] An exploration licence issued under the Mining Act is required to conduct mineral exploration.[312] Mineral production requires a special mining lease to be obtained under the Act.[313] In addition, the State and the holder of a special mining lease may enter into a mining development contract to govern mineral production within the special mining lease area. The mining development contract is used in respect of large mineral deposits. The Mining Act gives the responsible minister and the Director of Mines[314] wide discretionary powers. Those powers are to be exercised in the circumstances and the manner set out in the mining development contract.[315] State equity participation began in 1967 with the Bougainville Copper Agreement. Since then, equity arrangements have evolved over time. The State may take up to a 30 per cent equity interest.

The Oil and Gas Act governs all dealings in petroleum.[316] A petroleum prospecting licence (PPL) is required in order to conduct exploration within the PPL area.[317] If petroleum resources are discovered in the PPL area, this must be communicated to the Director or Secretary for the Department of Petroleum[318] and the Minister for Petroleum, and they may issue further directions on the discovery. If the discovery and other factors satisfy the Minister, who is also advised by the Petroleum Advisory Board, he or she may issue a petroleum retention licence (PRL) to carry out further tests and assessments on the commercial viability, amongst other things, of the discovery.[319] Social mapping and identification of customary landowners[320] and a project development forum[321] are important aspects of the process of obtaining a petroleum licence. In the project development forum, the State and the affected customary landowners and provincial governments may agree on the terms of the benefit-sharing.[322]

---

310 Mining Act, s 5; Oil and Gas Act, s 6.

311 Section 2 of the Mining Act defines 'minerals' as all valuable non-living substances excluding petroleum obtained or obtainable from land.

312 Mining Act, s 20.

313 Mining Act, s 33.

314 The minister responsible for the administration of the Mining Act and the Director under the Act.

315 Mining Act, ss 17 and 18.

316 Section 3 of the Oil and Gas Act defines 'petroleum' as '(a) any naturally occurring hydrocarbons, whether in a gaseous, liquid, in solid state; or (b) any naturally occurring mixture of hydrocarbons, whether in a gaseous, liquid, or solid state; or (c) any naturally occurring mixture of one or more hydrocarbons, (whether in a gaseous, liquid, or solid state) and any other substance.'

317 Section 21.

318 Oil and Gas Act, s 32.

319 Oil and Gas Act, ss 37–40.

320 Oil and Gas Act, ss 47–49.

321 Oil and Gas Act, s 48.

322 Oil and Gas Act, s 50.

A separate agreement is usually executed between the State and the developer on the development of the resource and also on the terms of equity participation. Once all commercial viability tests and other benefit-sharing issues are sorted out, a petroleum development licence (PPL) may be granted by the Minister[323] for the production of the resource.

Customary landowners of resource areas are critical stakeholders not only on a legal basis but also for policy considerations in respect of the safety and security of the project.

The State may take up to a 22.5 per cent equity in petroleum projects.[324] From this, the State distributes part of the equity to the relevant provincial governments and project area landowners.

13.2. FORESTRY LAW

Forests cover 77.8 per cent of PNG's total land mass of 46,300 square kilometres (representing 1.5 per cent of the world's tropical rainforest).[325] This makes the country one of the most extensively forested nations in the world.[326] There are more than 2,000 species of tree that are of commercial value. However, the forest cover has been extensively reduced since 2000 due to agriculture and logging activities.[327] Most of the tropical rainforests in PNG are held under customary law. The Forestry Act was enacted to protect and regulate forest resources. It sets out the administrative structure, control and regulation mechanisms, including allocation of timber permits throughout the country, and encourages customary landowners to participate actively in the development of forest resources. The Supreme Court, in *Supreme Court Reference No 7 of 1992: Re Forestry Act 1991*,[328] held the legislation to be 'an exhaustive law in the field of national forestry control and development throughout PNG and … a matter of national interest'. In *Madang Timber Ltd v Kambori*,[329] the Supreme Court held that '[t]he provisions of the Forestry Act should be strictly construed as it involves permitting forestry activities which significantly impact on the rights of people in relation to their land'.

---

323 Oil and Gas Act, ss 53–57.

324 Oil and Gas Act, s 165.

325 Eric L Kwa (ed) *Natural Resources Law of Papua New Guinea* (Lawbook Co, 2001) 50. See also Government of Papua New Guinea *Papua New Guinea National REDD+ Strategy 2017–2027* (Climate Change & Development Authority, 2017) 9.

326 Government of Papua New Guinea *Papua New Guinea National REDD+ Strategy 2017–2027* (Climate Change & Development Authority, 2017) 10.

327 Government of Papua New Guinea *Papua New Guinea National REDD+ Strategy 2017–2027* (Climate Change & Development Authority, 2017) 10.

328 [1992] PNGLR 514.

329 [2009] SC1000.

The Act provides for national forests to be declared and for certain trees and species to be protected.[330] The government, through the PNG Forest Authority, may purchase timber rights from the customary landowners under a Forest Management Agreement.[331] The PNG Forest Authority may then grant a timber permit[332] or authority[333] to a business entity to conduct logging activities. Timber reserves can also be declared over Forest Management Agreement areas.[334] Any forest clearing of more than 50 hectares in total for agriculture or other land use development requires prior permission from the PNG Forest Authority.[335] There are various levies imposed on logging companies by the PNG Forest Authority on behalf of the government pursuant to the Act.

13.3. MARITIME LAW

PNG occupies the eastern half of the island of New Guinea and an archipelago of a further 600 islands lying in the western Pacific Ocean.[336] The Constitution (s 2(1)) declares the geographical composition to be 'all the internal waters and the territorial sea and underlying islands'. The Maritime Zones Act 2015 declares 200 nautical miles from the nearest point of the baseline[337] or low-water line to be internal waters. The territorial sea comprises 12 nautical miles from the baseline and archipelagic waters. Hence, 12 nautical miles and the archipelagic waters that constitute the territorial sea are the zones within which customary marine tenure rights are claimed and utilised.[338]

In line with the United Nations Convention on the Law of the Sea, vessels and aircrafts of foreign states have the right of innocent passage through or over the territorial and archipelagic waters of PNG.[339] When foreign vessels and aircrafts are on innocent passage, they are prohibited from carrying out any illegal activity within PNG's territorial and archipelagic waters, including fishing or research, etc., without the express approval or authority of the government of PNG. Any such illegal activity carries severe civil[340] and criminal[341] penalties.

---

330 Sections 3 and 4.
331 Forestry Act, ss 56–58.
332 Forestry Act, ss 73 and 77.
333 Forestry Act, s 87.
334 See Part III of the Forestry Act.
335 Forestry Act, s 90A.
336 Food and Agriculture Organization of the United Nations *Fishery Country Profile: Structure and Characteristics of the Industry* (2002) <http://www.fao.org/fi/fcp/en/PNG/profile.htm>.
337 Maritime Zones Act, ss 27, 28 and 29.
338 Food and Agriculture Organization of the United Nations *Fishery Country Profile: Structure and Characteristics of the Industry* (2002) <http://www.fao.org/fi/fcp/en/PNG/profile.htm>.
339 Maritime Zones Act, ss 14 and 18.
340 Maritime Zones Act, s 16.
341 Maritime Zones Act, s 15.

The exclusive economic zone (EEZ) or exclusive fishing zone is one of the significant products of the Convention on the Law of the Sea. The EEZ accords coastal states the power to conserve, regulate and manage the marine resources within the 200-nautical-mile zone. PNG signed and ratified the Convention and subsequently entered into various regional agreements with other coastal states, particularly Pacific island countries and Australia in relation to the Torres Strait.

The customary rights of the coastal indigenous people to the maritime resources such as fisheries and others are protected by s 8 of the Customs Recognition Act. This implies that the indigenous peoples have ownership rights or use and access rights over areas of sea and reef, or marine flora and fauna. Section 26 of the Fisheries Management Act[342] also recognises customary ownership and use of the marine resources. However, the rights of coastal indigenous people to access marine resources are in some instances limited by national laws to 'waters where they are entitled by custom', and by the Torres Strait Treaty.

The fishery activities of PNG are controlled, managed and regulated by the Fisheries Management Act. The Act also administers and implements the international and regional agreements on fishery resources.

14. TREATIES

Treaty-making is governed by s 117 of the Constitution. Section 177 allows the executive arm of the government to enter into treaties with other countries, but normally with the consent of Parliament.[343]

PNG is a signatory to numerous regional and international treaties and is bound either through ratification or State practice. PNG has entered into over 173 treaties with foreign countries and organisations.[344]

15. CONCLUSION

PNG is a thriving constitutional democracy with the person who is also the monarch of the United Kingdom as its head of state, a model that is centred on the Westminster system of government. The system of government is well

---

342 Formerly this was under s 37(e) of the Fisheries Act (1994) in the terms: 'any traditional rights over or in relation to any area of fisheries waters'. Under the new Fisheries Management Act (1998) (s 26) these rights are stated as 'the rights of the customary owners of fisheries resources and fishing rights shall be freely recognised and respected in all transactions affecting the resources on the area in which the right operates.'

343 The treaty-law making in PNG was criticised by some commentators for being 'weak' and subject to abuse by the executive. See Eric L Kwa 'Treaty Law Making in Papua New Guinea: After Two Decades *Yumi Stap We*?' (1997) 25 MLJ 43.

344 Pacific Legal Information *Pacific Islands Treaty Series* <http://www.paclii.org/pits/en/country/Papua_New_Guinea.shtml>.

entrenched by the Constitution, the country's supreme law. To prevent abuse of public power and resources, there are numerous checks and balances set out by the Constitution. These constitutional arrangements enable the government to continue functioning.

Since independence in 1975, the foreign statutes and principles of common law and equity that PNG adopted from England have undergone considerable reform. These reforms were brought about by legislative action and judicial pronouncements. Hence, many of the laws that are applicable in PNG are of common law origin and home-grown. The Constitution and Underlying Law Act call for the development of local jurisprudence based on custom, amongst other things, but no significant advancement has been made in that area. The Constitution also recognises customary law, which operates alongside State law and sometimes overlaps with it. Customary law remains unwritten and yet over 80 per cent of the population depends on custom to resolve disputes, particularly in the rural settings. This is one of the main challenges that confront the country, especially in the mineral resource sector, where identification of genuine landowners under custom is a rather daunting task and in most instances remains unresolved. Many people in the process are missing out on their rightful benefits, such as royalties and equities from the government and resource developers under the Mining Act and Oil and Gas Act.

Despite the challenges, the three arms of government continue to play their mandated roles and duties to better serve the people. The laws that were enacted and implemented in the country are intended and directed to serve 'public purpose or interest'. To some extent, private interests (tort, contract, etc.) are also protected by the laws of PNG, but often those interests do not override the other well-established legal principles. The courts continue to be vigilant and enforce the rule of law independently from the other two arms of government. By remaining neutral and impartial, the courts have been able to develop principles of law based on the circumstances of PNG and apply them to resolve disputes. It is hoped that the courts will remain a guiding light for the country for years to come.

BIBLIOGRAPHY

Amankwah, Harrison A, John T Mugambwah and George Muroa *Land Law in Papua New Guinea* (UPNG Press, 2009).

Chalmers, Donald R C, David Weisbrot, Salamo Injia and Warwick John Andrew *Criminal Law and Practice of Papua New Guinea* (UPNG Press (Reprint), 2009).

Cox, Owen *Papua New Guinea's Law and Legal System* (Pacific Adventist University, 2004).

Hill, Edward R and Guy Powles *Magistrates Manual of Papua New Guinea* (Lawbook Co, 2001).

Injia, Salamo and Gregory Lay *Constitutional Law in Papua New Guinea* (National Judicial Staff Service, 2018).

Jessep, Owen and John Luluaki *Principles of Family Law in Papua New Guinea* (2nd ed, UPNG Press, 1985).

Kalinoe, Lawrence *Law of Industrial Relations: Texts and Course Material* (Law School, University of Papua New Guinea, 2003).

Kwa, Eric L *Constitutional Law of Papua New Guinea* (Lawbook Co, 2001).

Kwa, Eric L and Nathan Onom 'The Law of Adoption in Papua New Guinea' in Jennifer Corrin and Sue Farran (eds) *The Plural Practice of Adoption in Pacific Island States* (Springer, 2019).

Pacific Legal Information Institute *Pacific Islands Treaty Series: Papua New Guinea* <http://www.paclii.org/pits/en/country/Papua_New_Guinea.shtml>.

Pacific Legal Information Institute *Papua New Guinea Primary Materials* <http://www.paclii.org/countries/pg.html>.

PITCAIRN

Tony ANGELO

1. CONTEXT

Pitcairn is an Overseas Territory in the Pacific Ocean administered by the United Kingdom. It is comprised of one inhabited island (Pitcairn) and three uninhabited islands (Henderson, Oeno and Ducie).[1] Pitcairn island is

[1] Peter Clegg 'Pitcairn' in Stephen Levine (ed) *Pacific Ways: Government and Politics in the Pacific Islands* (2nd ed, Victoria University Press, 2016) 247 at 247; Special Committee

approximately 3 kilometres long and 1.5 kilometres wide with a total land area of 4.35 square kilometres.[2] Access to the island is only by sea.[3] There are two common languages – English and Pitkern (a mixture of 18th-century English and Tahitian).[4] As of 2019, Pitcairn had 43 inhabitants, all of whom lived in the settlement of Adamstown.[5] This population is aging and declining. Unsuccessful attempts to encourage migration to Pitcairn have caused concern for the future viability of the Territory.[6]

Pitcairn was first settled in 1790 by 18 Tahitians and nine mutineers of HMS *Bounty*.[7] Most of the modern-day population can trace their ancestry to these mutineers.[8] A series of attempts by British and Tahitian authorities to relocate the Pitcairn population during the 19th century proved unsuccessful.[9] Although possession of the islands on behalf of the British Crown was taken in 1838, formal oversight from the United Kingdom government remained minimal for much of the 19th century. Pitcairn was brought under the authority of the British High Commissioner for the Western Pacific in 1898.[10] Pitcairn was thus considered a British settlement for the purposes of the British Settlements Acts 1887 and 1945. This gave Britain the authority to legislate for Pitcairn.[11] The British government later enacted the Pitcairn Order 1970 and the Pitcairn Royal Instructions 1970, which established a basic constitutional framework for the islands.[12]

---

on the Situation with regard to the Implementation of the Declaration on the Granting of Independence to Colonial Countries and Peoples *Pitcairn: Working Paper Prepared by the Secretariat* UN Doc A/AC.109/2004/2 (23 March 2004) [Special Committee on Decolonisation (2004)].

2 Special Committee on the Situation with regard to the Implementation of the Declaration on the Granting of Independence to Colonial Countries and Peoples *Pitcairn: Working Paper Prepared by the Secretariat* UN Doc A/AC.109/2019/12 (11 February 2019) [Special Committee on Decolonisation (2019)].

3 Special Committee on Decolonisation (2019), above n 2.

4 Clegg, above n 1, at 247.

5 Special Committee on the Situation with regard to the Implementation of the Declaration on the Granting of Independence to Colonial Countries and Peoples *Pitcairn: Working Paper Prepared by the Secretariat* UN Doc A/AC.109/2020/12 (30 January 2020) [Special Committee on Decolonisation (2020)].

6 Special Committee on Decolonisation (2020), above n 5.

7 Clegg, above n 1, at 248; Special Committee on Decolonisation (2019), above n 2.

8 Special Committee on Decolonisation (2019), above n 2.

9 Clegg, above n 1, at 248. The most notable relocation attempt was to Norfolk Island in 1856. For more on the constitutional arrangements of Norfolk Island and the connection to Pitcairn, see *Bennett v Commonwealth* [2007] HCA 18, (2007) 231 CLR 91.

10 Instructions to the High Commissioner of the Western Pacific from Joseph Chamberlain, Colonial Secretary (1898) *Fiji Royal Gazette* 215; Clegg, above n 1, at 248.

11 British Settlements Act 1887 (UK); British Settlements Act 1945 (UK).

12 Special Committee on Decolonisation (2004), above n 1.

2. SOURCES OF LAW

The sources of law (in descending order of authority) are United Kingdom Acts of Parliament or Orders in Council enacted for Pitcairn, the Pitcairn Constitution 2010, Pitcairn Ordinances made by the Governor, statutes of general application as in force in and for England for the time being, the common law and rules of equity of England, and Island Council Regulations. Most of the laws in force in Pitcairn are accessible to island inhabitants through the Island Secretary's Office and are available on the Pitcairn government website.[13]

2.1. CONSTITUTION OF PITCAIRN 2010

After consultation with Pitcairn Islanders, a Constitution was enacted by the United Kingdom on 4 March 2010 through the Pitcairn Constitution Order.[14] The Constitution replaced the Pitcairn Order 1970 and the Pitcairn Royal Instructions 1970. The Constitution describes the UK's relationship with Pitcairn as a partnership. It provides for the protection of the fundamental rights and freedoms of the individual on the model of the European Convention on Human Rights and the International Covenant on Civil and Political Rights.[15] It also guarantees the existence and independence of a judicial system and provides for the appointment of judges.[16] It codifies the constitutional arrangements and identifies the legal actors of the government of Pitcairn, establishing the offices of Governor and Attorney General and the Island Council.[17]

2.1.1. Governor of Pitcairn

The office of the Governor of Pitcairn is enshrined in the Constitution.[18] The Governor is appointed by the Crown and has executive and legislative authority in Pitcairn.[19] The office of the Governor is usually held by the British High Commissioner in New Zealand.[20] The Governor can enact laws, called 'Ordinances', 'for the peace, order and good government of Pitcairn' after he or she has consulted the Island Council.[21] The Governor is not required

---

13 See the Laws of Pitcairn, Henderson, Ducie and Oeno Islands at <https://www.government.pn/Laws/index.php>.
14 Pitcairn Constitution Order 2010 (UK SI 244/2010).
15 Constitution of Pitcairn 2010, ss 2–26.
16 Sections 43, 44 and 52.
17 Sections 27, 34 and 35.
18 Section 27.
19 Sections 27(1), 33(2) and 36(1).
20 Special Committee on Decolonisation (2019), above n 2.
21 Constitution of Pitcairn 2010, ss 36(1) and 37.

to follow the advice of the Council, but members of the Council have the right to submit their views to a United Kingdom Secretary of State if the Governor acts contrary to the advice of the Council.[22] The Governor retains the ability to legislate without consulting the Council where instructed by a Secretary of State and there are certain matters on which the Governor is not permitted to legislate without instructions from a Secretary of State.[23] Ordinances are subject to disallowance by Her Majesty on the advice of a Secretary of State.[24]

2.1.2. *Attorney General*

Pitcairn has an Attorney General, appointed by the Governor.[25] The Attorney General has authority to initiate criminal proceedings, draft Ordinances, and revise and publish the laws of Pitcairn.[26]

2.1.3. *Commissioner of Pitcairn*

Though a new governance structure, established in April 2009, created four public sector positions in Pitcairn, many administrative and financial functions remain with the Pitcairn Islands Office in Auckland, the Commissioner of which is appointed by the Governor.[27] The Commissioner has responsibility for the financial administration of Pitcairn and liaises between the Island Council and the Governor. Since 2004, Pitcairn has been dependent on budgetary assistance from the United Kingdom for its functioning.[28]

2.1.4. *Island Council*

The day-to-day affairs of Pitcairn are managed by the Island Council, which was established by the Local Government Ordinance of 1964 and is now enshrined in the Constitution.[29] The Island Council has the duty, subject to orders of the Governor, to provide for the enforcement of the laws of Pitcairn.[30] It is empowered to make regulations 'for the good administration of the Islands,

---

22 Section 36(2).
23 Sections 36(3) and 38.
24 Sections 37 and 41.
25 Section 35.
26 Section 35.
27 Special Committee on the Situation with regard to the Implementation of the Declaration on the Granting of Independence to Colonial Countries and Peoples *Pitcairn: Working Paper Prepared by the Secretariat* UN Doc A/AC.109/2011/4 (8 January 2011).
28 Clegg, above n 1, at 250.
29 Constitution of Pitcairn 2010, s 34; Special Committee on Decolonisation (2019), above n 2.
30 Local Government Ordinance 1964 (revised ed, 2019), s 7(1).

the maintenance of peace, order and public safety and the social and economic advancement of the islanders'.[31] The Council consists of seven voting members (the Mayor, the Deputy Mayor and five Councillors) elected by the people of Pitcairn, and three non-voting ex officio members (the Governor, the Deputy Governor and the Administrator) appointed by the Crown.[32]

2.2. UNITED KINGDOM STATUTES

2.2.1. United Kingdom Statutes for Pitcairn

Under the British Settlements Acts 1887 and 1945, the United Kingdom Parliament retains the power to legislate directly for Pitcairn through an Act of Parliament or an Order in Council.[33]

2.2.2. English Statutes of General Application

English statutes of general application can be applied to Pitcairn when the local circumstances of the Territory permit.[34] Statutes of general application are subject to local Ordinances and thus 'fill in the gaps' where there is no Pitcairn Ordinance to govern a circumstance.[35] It is not immediately evident which English statutes are of general application; a court must deem a statute to be such. Such determination by a court in effect amounts to courts retroactively legislating.[36]

2.3. COMMON LAW OF ENGLAND

The common law of England 'for the time being' has been in force in Pitcairn since 1961 and continues to be in force by virtue of the Constitution.[37] The common law is applicable in Pitcairn so far as local circumstances permit and is subject to any Pitcairn Ordinances.[38]

---

31 Section 7(1).

32 Sections 3 and 6.

33 For the Orders in Council that have effect in Pitcairn enacted between 2000 and 2005, see <https://www.government.pn/Laws/UK_Orders_in_Council_2000-2005.html>. For the Orders in Council that have effect in Pitcairn enacted since 2006, see <https://www.government.pn/Laws/UK_Orders_in_Council_since_2006.html>.

34 Constitution of Pitcairn 2010, s 42(1) and (2).

35 Section 42(2).

36 A H Angelo and Andrew Townend 'Pitcairn: A Contemporary Comment' (2003) 1 NZJPIL 229 at 235.

37 Judicature Ordinance 1961; Constitution of Pitcairn 2010, s 42.

38 Section 42.

2.4. LOCAL CUSTOMARY LAW

Customary law, established by the mutineers in the initial settlement of the islands, has influenced certain areas of law in Pitcairn, in particular land law.

3. JUDICIARY

The Pitcairn judicial system has four courts:

- the Judicial Committee of the Privy Council;
- the Pitcairn Court of Appeal;
- the Pitcairn Supreme Court; and
- the Magistrate's Court.

The Island Magistrate is appointed by the Governor from among the residents of the island and has limited jurisdiction to preside over criminal and civil matters in the Magistrate's Court.[39] Where questions of law are concerned, another magistrate, legally qualified in a Commonwealth country, will be appointed to the Magistrate's Court. There is a right to appeal to the Pitcairn Supreme Court, on which the Chief Justice sits.[40] The Supreme Court also has jurisdiction over breaches of the human rights contained in the Constitution and has greater jurisdiction in criminal and civil matters than the Magistrate's Court.[41] There is a right of appeal to the Pitcairn Court of Appeal and to the Judicial Committee of the Privy Council.[42] The courts are able to sit in Pitcairn, New Zealand or the United Kingdom.[43] Several Ordinances regulate judicial procedure and legal representation.[44]

4. SPECIFIC SUBJECT AREAS

A flurry of Ordinances was enacted by the Governor in the early 2000s when international attention was drawn to the Pitcairn legal system due to allegations

39 Judicature (Courts) Ordinance, Part III.

40 Constitution of Pitcairn 2010, s 47.

41 Sections 25 and 47.

42 Section 43; Pitcairn (Appeals to Privy Council) Order 2000 (SI 2000/1816, as amended by SI 2009/224); Judicial Committee (Appellate Jurisdiction) Rules Order 2009 (SI 2009/224).

43 Constitution of Pitcairn 2010, s 43(4); Judicature Amendment Ordinance 2003; Pitcairn Trials Act 2002 (NZ).

44 Many of these were enacted in the early 2000s to prepare for the criminal trials of the alleged sexual abuse of minors. See Evidence (Special Measures Directions) Ordinance 2001 (revised ed, 2002); Judicature Amendment Ordinance 2003 (revised ed, 2005); Judicature (Appeals in Criminal Cases) Ordinance 2000 (revised ed, 2017); Judicature (Courts) Ordinance 2000 (revised ed, 2017); Justice Ordinance 2000 (revised ed, 2019); Legal Aid (Criminal Proceedings) Ordinance 2001 (revised ed, 2009); Legal Practitioners Ordinance 2001; Public Defender in Criminal Proceedings Ordinance 2002.

of sexual abuse of children in Pitcairn and the subsequent trials.[45] The slate of Ordinances in force in Pitcairn is now relatively comprehensive. The common law and English statutes of general application may still apply where there is no applicable local Ordinance. Actions committed prior to the applicable Ordinance would be governed by the English law of the time.

4.1. LAW OF PERSONS

The law of persons is provided in several Ordinances. Adoption is governed by the Adoption of Infants Ordinance.[46] The law of children is in the Children Ordinance.[47] Marriage is provided in the Marriage Ordinance. Homosexual marriage has been permitted in Pitcairn since 2015, with the Ordinance allowing marriage between 'two people, regardless of their sex, sexual orientation or gender identity'.[48] The Marriage (Dissolution of Marriage) Amendment Ordinance was passed in 2012 enabling the dissolution of a marriage.[49] The Probate and Administration Ordinance and the Wills Ordinance govern testamentary matters.[50]

4.2. LAW OF OBLIGATIONS

Some tortious offences like assault, trespass and offences against property are contained in the Summary Offences Ordinance.[51] The Common Law of England, subject to an applicable statute of general application, provides the law of contract and for civil proceedings.

4.3. LAND LAW

Until 1967, land ownership on Pitcairn was determined by a customary system established by the mutineers. Land was held in family groups according to the original division of land by the first inhabitants.[52]

---

45 Angelo and Townend, above n 36, at 231.
46 Adoption of Infants Ordinance 1954 (revised ed, 2014).
47 Children Ordinance 2003 (revised ed, 2014).
48 Marriage Ordinance 1952 (revised ed, 2019), s 1(2).
49 Sections 51–55.
50 Probate and Administration Ordinance 2000 (revised ed, 2014); Wills Ordinance 1967 (revised ed, 2001).
51 Summary Offences Ordinance 2000 (revised ed, 2019).
52 Special Committee on Decolonisation (2004), above n 1.

Ordinances enacted in 1967 reformed the customary tenurial system and the administration of inheritance of land ownership following the death of a landowner.[53] Customary titles were converted and registered as freehold titles. Land not claimed by a Pitcairn Islander within three years from the enactment of the Ordinance was vested in the Island Council for the benefit of the community. Therefore, by 1970, all customary titles were extinguished and replaced with freehold title. However, by the late 1970s, most of Pitcairn was held by Islanders who no longer inhabited the island. Further reform in the 1980s aimed to ensure that every Pitcairn Islander would be allocated a plot of land sufficient for their needs for as long as they lived on Pitcairn.[54] The main categories of land are commercial land, forestry land, garden land, house land, and orchard land.

A further land tenure reform occurred in 2000, which aimed to strengthen the titles of inhabitants of the islands. Ordinances were enacted to establish a system of land tenure based on leasehold relationships between the Island Council as lessor and Pitcairn Islanders as lessees.[55] In 2006, the Governor suspended all existing freehold title to private land.[56] Pitcairn Islanders were then required to apply to the Pitcairn Lands Court to receive a Land Allocation Title.[57] A Land Allocation Title establishes a leasehold estate in the land which is held by the individual lessee from the Island Council as lessor, without payment of rent.[58] Common terms and implied covenants apply to each leasehold interest granted by the Lands Court.[59] A lessee cannot mortgage, sublease or create a charge over their lease.[60] The interest in land cannot be transferred to a person who is not a permanent resident of Pitcairn.[61] After a leasehold interest ends, the interest reverts to the Island Council.[62]

Only permanent residents, former permanent residents and their descendants who intended to reside on the island are entitled to apply for a Land Allocation Title.[63] The Court cannot refuse an application filed by the existing owner of suspended interest in land.[64] However, titles granted in excess of the 'reasonable needs' of the landowner are subject to a land tax.[65] Former residents, or their descendants, can receive a Land Allocation Title if

53 Land and Administration of Estates Ordinance 1967.
54 Special Committee on Decolonisation (2004), above n 1.
55 Lands Court Ordinance 2000; Land Tenure Reform Ordinance 2000 (revised ed, 2006).
56 The Governor's power to do this is in the Land Tenure Reform Ordinance 2000 (revised ed, 2006).
57 Section 4(2).
58 Section 5.
59 Sections 5–6.
60 Section 12.
61 Section 11.
62 Section 5.
63 Section 4(2).
64 Section 4(4).
65 Section 4(5).

the former owner does not apply for the allocation, provided that they return to Pitcairn and reside or work on the land for three years following the grant of their allocation.[66] The Land Tenure Reform Ordinance also provides for what happens to land when a landowner settles overseas indefinitely; the aim is that remaining Pitcairn residents can benefit from the land.[67]

As the Land Tenure Reform Ordinance only suspends private freehold titles, the freehold titles of the Island Council, as public land, remain in force. Communal land is held by the Island Council.

The Constitution introduces a new category of land into Pitcairn, Crown land.[68] However, Crown land is not considered in the Land Tenure Reform Ordinance. There has never been a Crown grant of land to private landowners in Pitcairn, and the lessor of the leasehold estates is the Island Council. Crown land can only refer to land that has been specifically allocated to the Crown or possibly to the land of the uninhabited islands in Pitcairn over which no customary, freehold or leasehold title has been established.

4.4. CRIMINAL LAW

Criminal law in Pitcairn is administered through a combination of Pitcairn Ordinances and regulations, English statutes of general application, and the English common law where it has not been excluded by an Ordinance or a statute of general application.[69] Several Ordinances govern criminal law and criminal procedure matters, including parole,[70] bail,[71] prisons,[72] sentencing,[73] sexual offences,[74] firearms,[75] and protection of victims.[76] Other offences and arrest procedures are covered by the Summary Offences Ordinance.[77]

English statutes of general application and the common law governed criminal law in Pitcairn prior to the enactment of these Ordinances. The Judicial Committee of the Privy Council confirmed in the criminal trials that took place from 2004–2006 that Pitcairn Islanders were subject to English law, including English criminal law, which criminalised their behaviours.[78]

---

66 Section 4(6).
67 Section 8.
68 Constitution of Pitcairn 2010, s 30.
69 Special Committee on Decolonisation (2019), above n 2.
70 Parole Ordinance 2002 (revised ed, 2010).
71 Bail Ordinance 2002 (revised ed, 2017).
72 Prisons Ordinance 2001 (revised ed, 2010).
73 Sentencing Ordinance 2002 (revised ed, 2017).
74 Sexual Offences (Notification and Prevention) Ordinance 2010 (revised ed, 2017).
75 Firearms Offences (Prosecution and Punishment) Ordinance 2003.
76 Victims of Offences (No 2) Ordinance 2002 (revised ed, 2017).
77 Summary Offences Ordinance 2000 (revised ed, 2019).
78 *Christian v R* [2006] UKPC 47 at [10].

A public defender, generally an Auckland barrister, is appointed by the Governor to represent defendants in criminal cases and is paid with legal aid.[79] Several New Zealand lawyers were admitted to the Pitcairn Bar for the purpose of the child abuse trials.[80] Most criminal offences can be tried before the Island Magistrate but certain offences must be heard before the Supreme Court.[81]

4.5. COMMERCIAL LAW

Given the absence of litigation, it is not easy to determine which English statutes of general application would constitute Pitcairn's commercial law. Possible candidates are the Bills of Exchange Act 1882, the Copyright, Designs and Patents Act 1988, the Criminal Injury Compensation Act 1995, the Patents Act 1977, the Sale of Goods Act 1979, and the Trade Marks Act 1994.

4.6. ENVIRONMENTAL LAW

The largest marine protected area in the world was established over Pitcairn's exclusive economic zone in 2016.[82] Fishing, mining, disturbance of the seabed and dumping of waste are prohibited in the marine protected area.[83] Pitcairn residents are permitted to fish.[84] It has been suggested that this protected area could guarantee an economic future for Pitcairn through increased tourism, permit fees and long-term management and maintenance of the reserve.[85] Endangered endemic and indigenous species of animal and plants are also protected and their trade regulated.[86]

4.7. INTERNATIONAL LAW AND HUMAN RIGHTS

As Pitcairn is a United Kingdom Overseas Territory, the United Kingdom government retains responsibility for its international obligations.[87] When the United Kingdom enters into treaties, it can provide for their extension

---

79 Paul Rishworth (Attorney General for Pitcairn Islands) *Country Report for PILON 2012* (2012) available at <www.paclii.org>.

80 Rishworth, above n 79.

81 These offences are treason, piracy, murder, manslaughter, rape or arson. Judicature (Courts) Ordinance 2000 (revised ed, 2017), s 12(1).

82 Pitcairn Islands Marine Protected Area Ordinance 2016 (revised ed, 2017).

83 Sections 8–9.

84 Sections 8–9.

85 Clegg, above n 1, at 254; Special Committee on Decolonisation (2019), above n 2.

86 Endangered Species Protection Ordinance 2004.

87 Rishworth, above n 79.

to Pitcairn.[88] Pitcairn cooperates with the Council of the European Union through the European Union Overseas Countries and Territories Association.[89] Pitcairn is a member of the Secretariat of the Pacific Community.

The question of human rights was addressed specifically in two Pitcairn cases. In *Warren v R* in the Pitcairn Court of Appeal it was said:[90]

> [55] Our first observation is that at least to the extent the matter was argued on appeal, the sentence now criticised was correct. The ECHR is the source of Part 2 of the Pitcairn Constitution and as such is of interpretative value. Section 25(13) directs that in a s 25 proceeding under the Constitution, decisions of stated bodies, which include the European Court of Human Rights, on the interpretation and application of the ECHR are to be taken into account so far as considered relevant. The ECHR was not, however, advanced as a law of Pitcairn directly enforced, and nor could it be. It was not so enacted. While there were international obligations on the part of the United Kingdom and Pitcairn, under s 1(3) of the Constitution no legally enforceable rights or obligations were created.

The Privy Council in *Warren v The State* decided:[91]

> [27] The appellant's reliance on international instruments is similarly misplaced. Here, the appellant relies on articles 1, 73 and 75, UN Charter, on articles 1 and 25, International Covenant on Civil and Political Rights and on article 3, Optional First Protocol to the European Convention on Human Rights ("ECHR"). Neither ECHR nor the First Protocol has been extended to Pitcairn. None of the provisions relied on by the appellant has been implemented into domestic law in Pitcairn.

Any concerns that Pitcairn may have about this absence of direct application of human rights instruments may be able to be addressed by the Special Committee on Decolonisation (C-24),[92] a subsidiary organ of the United Nations General Assembly.

---

88 Rishworth, above n 79. Conventions that have been extended to Pitcairn include the International Covenant on Civil and Political Rights, the International Covenant on Economic, Social and Cultural Rights, the International Convention on the Elimination of All Forms of Racial Discrimination, the Convention against Torture and Other Cruel, Inhuman or Degrading Treatment or Punishment and the Convention on the Rights of the Child.

89 Council Decision 2013/755/EU of 25 November 2013 on the association of the overseas countries and territories of the European Union [2013] OJ L344/1.

90 *Warren v R* (CA 1/2012), <https://www.government.pn/Laws/12-04-2013%20Pitcairn%20COA%20Judgment.pdf/>.

91 *Warren v The State* [2018] UKPC 20, <https://www.jcpc.uk/cases/docs/jcpc-2017-0013-judgment.pdf/>.

92 Full name 'Special Committee on the Situation with regard to the implementation of the Declaration on the Granting of Independence of Colonial Countries and Peoples'.

Since 1946, Pitcairn has been on the United Nations' list of non-self-governing territories. C-24 has monitored decolonisation efforts in Pitcairn since 1961.[93] Each year, the United Nations Secretariat prepares a working paper on Pitcairn which is presented to C-24 at its annual substantive session.[94] An annual regional seminar is also held. These sessions provide an opportunity for representatives of the Territories and the administering powers to be heard; a representative of Pitcairn's Mayor last engaged with the Committee in 2004.[95] C-24 presents an annual report to the United Nations General Assembly, which then adopts a draft resolution on each non-self-governing territory.

The most recent comments from the representative of Pitcairn's Mayor demonstrate that although the Pitcairn Islanders want to choose their own future, they are not fully aware of all decolonisation or self-determination possibilities available to them.[96] It seems as though the Territory does not desire independence. Instead, it desires greater administration and legal autonomy from the United Kingdom, evidenced by the extensive constitutional and legal change that has occurred since 2000.[97]

BIBLIOGRAPHY

Angelo, A H and Kessebohm, R 'The New Constitution of Pitcairn: A Primer' (2009) 7 New Zealand Yearbook of International Law 285.

Angelo, A H and Andrew Townend 'Pitcairn: A Contemporary Comment' (2003) 1 New Zealand Journal of Public and International Law 229.

Clegg, Peter 'Pitcairn' in Stephen Levine (ed) *Pacific Ways: Government and Politics in the Pacific Islands* (2nd ed, Victoria University Press, 2016).

Farren, Sue 'The "Re-Colonising" of Picairn' (2007) 38 Victoria University of Wellington Law Review 435.

Oliver, Dawn (ed) *Justice, Legality, and the Rule of Law: Lessons from the Pitcairn Prosecutions* (Oxford University Press, 2009).

Pacific Islands Legal Information Institute *Pitcairn Islands Primary Materials* <http://www.paclii.org/countries/pn.html>.

Rishworth, Paul (Attorney General for Pitcairn Islands) *Country Report for PILON 2012* (2012) <www.paclii.org>.

93 *The situation with regard to the implementation of the Declaration on the Granting of Independence to Colonial Countries and Peoples* GA Res 1654 XVI, A/Res/1654(XVI) (1961).

94 United Nations 'Pitcairn' (15 May 2019) The United Nations and Decolonization <www.un.org>.

95 *Resolution adopted by the General Assembly on 13 December 2019* GA Res 74/107, A/Res/74/107 (2019).

96 Kevin Young (representative of the Mayor of Pitcairn) *Statement at the Pacific Regional Seminar on Advancing the Decolonization Process in the Pacific Region* PRS/2004/CRP.14 (18–20 May 2004).

97 Clegg, above n 1, at 254. See also Angelo and Townend, above n 36, 244–251.

Srivastava, Dhirendra K 'Pitcairn Island' in Michael A Ntumy (ed) *South Pacific Islands Legal Systems* (University of Hawaii Press, 1993).
Young, Kevin (representative of the Mayor of Pitcairn) *Statement at the Pacific Regional Seminar on Advancing the Decolonization Process in the Pacific Region* PRS/2004/ CRP.14 (18–20 May 2004).

SAMOA

Beatrice Tabangcora

1. CONTEXT

It is believed that the Samoan ancestors first voyaged across the *moana* thousands of years ago from eastern Asia and settled in what is now known as Samoa. Prior to colonisation, Samoan customs and traditional authorities governed the daily lives of Samoans.

The first contact with Europeans occurred in the 18th century. Shortly after the arrival of Europeans, civil unrest grew as prominent Samoan *matai* fought over who should be named the sovereign ruler of Samoa. This unrest was fuelled by the foreigners from Britain, the United States and Germany. They supported different *matai*, but also had an interest in colonising Samoa.[1]

In 1900, the Samoan archipelago was divided between Germany and the United States. The United States claimed Tutuila and the Manu'a islands, while Germany assumed control over Western Samoa. In 1914, after the outbreak of World War I, New Zealand seized Samoa from German control. Upon the formation of the League of Nations in 1919, Western Samoa was declared a mandate, which was to be administered by New Zealand. The New Zealand administration was governed by the Samoa Act 1927.[2] In 1946, the League of Nations mandate was replaced by a United Nations trusteeship.[3] Western Samoa remained under the administration of New Zealand until 1961.

On 1 January 1962, Samoa became the first Pacific island country to gain freedom from colonial administration, following a plebiscite in which a majority

1 See John Waldo Ellison 'The Partition of Samoa: A Study in Imperialism and Diplomacy' (1939) 8 Pac His Rev 259 at 259.

2 Samoa Act 1927 (NZ).

3 Jennifer Corrin and Don Paterson *Introduction to South Pacific Law* (4th ed, Intersentia, 2017) 19; Trustee Agreement for the mandated Territory of Western Samoa, Submitted by the Government of New Zealand to the General Assembly, First Session, Second Part, as Revised by the Assembly, Document A/160/Rev. 2, 12 December 1946.

of the Samoan people voted for independence.[4] It is estimated that there are about 200,000 people currently living in Samoa. A large number of Samoans reside overseas, mainly in New Zealand, Australia and the United States of America.

2. SOURCES OF LAW

2.1. CONSTITUTION

The Constitution of Samoa came into force on 1 January 1962. The Constitution is the supreme law of Samoa and any law that is inconsistent with the Constitution is void.[5] The Constitution of Samoa is published in both the English and Samoan languages. The English version of the Constitution prevails in the event of any inconsistency between the two versions; this was confirmed by the Court of Appeal in *Pita v Attorney-General*.[6]

The Parliament of Samoa may pass legislation to amend any of the provisions of the Constitution. In order for such an Act to be valid, 90 days must have elapsed between the second and third readings, and the bill must, at its third reading, have received at least two-thirds of the votes of the total Members of Parliament.[7] The Constitution provides an additional requirement for the amendment of art 102 of the Constitution, which relates to the alienation of customary land. Proposed amendments to art 102 are subject to a referendum of the electoral constituencies and must receive at least two-thirds of the votes cast.

Since 1962, the Constitution has been amended a number of times. Notable amendments to the Constitution include limitations on the independence of the Controller and Chief Auditor,[8] the change of name from Western Samoa to Samoa in 1997, and the amendment to increase women's participation in Parliament.[9] In December 2020, the Parliament of Samoa passed reforms which significantly altered the structure of the judiciary by making the Land and Titles Court an autonomous court structure with its own appellate division.[10]

4 29,882 out of 37,897 votes were in favour of independence; C G R Mckay 'Western Samoa's Plebiscite on Independence' (1961) J Poly Soc 354 at 356.

5 Constitution of Samoa, art 2(1)(2).

6 Constitution of Samoa, art 112; *In re the Constitution, Pita v Attorney-General* [1995] WSCA 6.

7 Constitution, art 109(1).

8 Constitution Amendment Act (No 1) 1997, s 2.

9 Constitution Amendment Act 2013, s 1(3).

10 Constitution Amendment Act 2020.

2.2. STATUTE LAW

Prior to independence, the laws of Western Samoa consisted of German Ordinances and Decrees, Ordinances of the New Zealand administration, primary and subsidiary legislation passed by the New Zealand and British Parliaments, English common law and equity, and custom. German law was abolished in 1921 in the Samoa Act; the abolishing of German law was confirmed in 1972.[11] After independence in 1962, 26 New Zealand statutes were applicable to Samoa, having been carried over from the period of New Zealand administration. In 1972, all New Zealand and United Kingdom statutes were repealed, except for those provided in the Reprint of Statutes Act 1972.[12] Following further repeals, only three former New Zealand statutes remain applicable to Samoa: the Bankruptcy Act 1908, the Property Law Act 1952, and ss 360 and 362 of the Samoa Act 1921.[13]

Subsidiary legislation is created, amended, passed and repealed by various government officials and bodies, as authorised by Parliament through primary legislation.

2.3. COMMON LAW

At independence, the Constitution also continued in force 'English Common Law and Equity for the time being in so far as they are not excluded by any other law in force in Samoa'.[14] This definition encompasses the law of England as it existed on 14 January 1840 and the rules of English common law and equity as developed in the courts of England and New Zealand, so far as it is consistent with other sources of law in force in Samoa.[15] In addition, the Judicature Act mandates that common law and equity be administered concurrently by the civil and criminal courts.[16] In the event that there is a conflict between common law and equity in the same matter, the rules of equity will prevail.[17]

---

11 Jennifer Corrin 'Colonial legacies? A study of the received and adopted legislation applying in the University of the South Pacific region' (1997) 21 JPacS 32 at 39.

12 The Reprint of Statutes Act 1972 was repealed by the Revision and Publication of Laws Act 2008.

13 Section 11 of the Revision and Publication of Laws Act 2008 notes that the Companies Act 1955 (New Zealand) remains in force in Samoa. However, s 352 of the Companies Act 2001 (Samoa), repealed the Companies Act 1955 (New Zealand).

14 Constitution, art 111(1).

15 Constitution, art 111(1).

16 Judicature Act 2020, s 3.

17 Judicature Act 2020, s 3.

Although the common law is referred to as 'English', the Samoan courts have examined, recognised, applied or given weight to principles of common law as developed by New Zealand, Australian, United States and United Kingdom courts.[18]

2.4. SAMOAN CUSTOM AND USAGE

The Constitution of Samoa also continued in force 'any custom or usage which has acquired the force of law in Samoa or any part thereof under the provisions of any Act or under a judgment of a Court of competent jurisdiction.'[19] The Constitution does not provide a definition of 'custom and usage'. However, the term is defined by the Land and Titles Act 2020 as the custom and usages of Samoa accepted as being in force at the relevant time and includes principles of custom and usage accepted by the people of Samoa in general and accepted as being in force in respect of a particular place or matter.[20]

The Constitution of Samoa makes several references to custom. The Preamble of the Constitution recognises that Samoa is 'an Independent State based on Christian principles and Samoan custom and tradition'.[21] The Constitution recognises that all persons are entitled to the protection of their custom rights.[22] The Constitution also recognises that a proportion of the land in Samoa is held under customary tenure[23] and prohibits the alienation of customary land.[24] *Matai* titles are also to be held in accordance with Samoan custom and usage.[25] Only Samoans are allowed to hold *matai* titles and the powers relating to authority over customary lands.[26]

Should there be any inconsistency between Samoan customary law and the Constitution, the Constitution will prevail.[27] Similarly, legislation will override the customary law. The relationship between Samoan custom and the principles of common law and equity is not specified within the Constitution and thus it is left to the courts to determine which source of law will prevail should there be a conflict.

---

18 Guy Powles 'Samoa' in Michael A Ntumy (ed) *South Pacific Legal Systems* (University of Hawaii Press, 1993) 395 at 398.

19 Constitution, art 111(1).

20 Land and Titles Act 2020, s 2.

21 Preamble to the Constitution.

22 Constitution, art 104(3), as amended by s 7 of the Constitution Amendment Act 2020.

23 Constitution, art 101.

24 Constitution, art 102.

25 Constitution, art 100.

26 Honorary *matai* titles have been bestowed on prominent non-Samoan individuals such as former UN Secretary General *Tupua* Ban Ki Moon, former NZ Prime Ministers *To'osavili* John Key and *Leulua'iali'iotumua* Bill English and several rugby team coaches. These honorary *matai* titles do not have any customary land rights.

27 Constitution, art 2(1).

The Constitution provides that the courts may take customs into consideration in their decisions.[28] Although it is recognised that custom may apply to matters besides land and *matai* titles, Parliament has not given much guidance to the courts as to when custom should be applied.[29] Several decisions of the courts seem to suggest that the application of custom is subject to principles of natural justice and that the customs must be widespread across Samoa.[30]

3. CONSTITUTIONAL LAW

3.1. CONSTITUTION

3.1.1. Executive

3.1.1.1. *O le Ao o le Malo* (Head of State)

The Head of State, known as *O le Ao o le Malo*, is the constitutional head of Samoa. The Head of State is appointed for a term of five years by the Legislative Assembly upon election by the Legislative Assembly.[31] The validity of the election of the Head of State cannot be contested in court.[32] The salary for the Head of State is determined by legislation. The Head of State is prohibited from holding other offices or engaging in work for which they will be remunerated.[33] The Head of State may either resign, or be removed by the Legislative Assembly on the ground of misbehaviour or of infirmity of body or mind.[34]

The position of *O le Ao o le Malo* shows the significance that Samoan custom has in Samoa. The position has only been held by males who hold, or have held, *tama'aiga* titles.[35] To date, four individuals have held the title of Head of State. At independence, this position was jointly held by Tupua Tamasese Meaole and Malietoa Tanumafili II, with a proviso that they would hold the position until their deaths. The Constitution further provided that upon their deaths, a single

---

28 Constitutional Amendment Act 2020, art 71.

29 Jennifer Corrin and Don Paterson *Introduction to South Pacific Law* (4th ed, Intersentia, 2017) 59.

30 Jennifer Corrin and Don Paterson *Introduction to South Pacific Law* (4th ed, Intersentia, 2017) 59.

31 Constitution, arts 18(1) and 19.

32 Constitution, art 18(3).

33 Constitution, art 20.

34 Constitution, art 21(1) and (2).

35 *Tama'aiga*, also known as *tama-a-aiga* (lit. translation: sons of families), titles are prominent *matai* titles within the Samoan chiefly system. The Tupua Tamasese, Malietoa, Mata'afa and Tuimaleali'ifano titles are *tama'aiga* titles. Holders of *tama'aiga* titles have held influential positions in Samoan politics. See Morgan Tuimaleali'ifano 'Titular Disputes and National Leadership in Samoa' (1998) 33 JPH 91 at 92.

Head of State would be elected for a term of five years. Tupua Tamasese Mea'ole died in 1968 and Malietoa Tanumafili II held the position of Head of State until his death in 2007. In 2007, Tui Atua Tupua Tamasese Efi was appointed as the first single Head of State and served for two consecutive terms. In 2017, following a controversial decision by the legislature to not re-appoint Tui Atua Tupua Tamasese Efi, Tuimaleali'ifano Va'aletoa Sualauvi II was appointed as the new Head of State.

3.1.1.2. *Sui o le Fono a Sui Tofia* (Council of Deputies)

The Council of Deputies is established by art 25 of the Constitution. The Council consists of a maximum of three persons elected by the Legislative Assembly.[36] In order to be elected to the Council of Deputies, the candidate must be qualified to be appointed as Head of State.[37] In addition, members of the Council of Deputies are not qualified to be elected as Members of Parliament.[38] In the event that there are no individuals elected to the Council, the Constitution mandates that the Chief Justice is to assume its functions.[39]

3.1.1.3. *Palemia, Sui Palemia ma le Kapeneta* (Prime Minister, Deputy Prime Minister and the Cabinet)

The Constitution provides that the Head of State may appoint the person who commands the confidence of a majority of the Members of Parliament as Prime Minister to preside over Cabinet.[40] The Head of State may also, on the advice of the Prime Minister, appoint eight to 14 Members of Parliament as ministers of Cabinet.[41] From among the appointed ministers, the Head of State, on the advice of the Prime Minister, appoints a Deputy Prime Minister.[42]

The Constitution provides that Cabinet has the general direction and control of the executive government of Samoa and is responsible to Parliament.[43]

3.1.2. Legislature: Palemene *(Parliament)*

The Constitution establishes in Samoa a unicameral Parliament consisting of the Head of State and the Legislative Assembly.[44] The Legislative Assembly

36 Constitution, art 25(1).
37 Constitution, art 25(2).
38 Constitution, art 25(9).
39 Constitution, art 25(1).
40 Constitution, art 32(2)(a).
41 Constitution, art 32(2)(b), as amended by s 3(1) of the Constitution Amendment Act 2020.
42 Constitution, art 32(2)(b.a).
43 Constitution, art 32(1).
44 Constitution, art 42.

consists of 51 members elected from the territorial and urban constituencies.[45] Only holders of *matai* titles are able to contest in an election for a seat in Parliament.

In 2013, the Constitution was amended to increase women's participation in Parliament.[46] It now reserves 10 per cent of the Legislative Assembly seats for women.[47] The Constitution states that there are 'presently five seats' reserved for women; however, the wording of this provision created confusion in the 2021 General Elections in Samoa.[48] In the event that no women are elected to Parliament, the Constitution provides that the prescribed number of women candidates with the most votes will be made additional members of the Legislative Assembly.

Parliament has the power to create laws for Samoa.[49] The law-making process begins with a bill being tabled in Parliament. The bill must undergo three readings before it is presented to the Head of State for assent. The Constitution provides that no bill becomes a law without the assent of the Head of State.[50]

Samoa has been criticised for 'one-party' politics on the basis that the Human Rights Protection Party (HRPP) has been in power since independence.[51] In 2020, several notable members of the HRPP party resigned, including then Deputy Prime Minister Fiame Naomi Mata'afa and former Speaker of the House La'auli Polataivao Leautea.[52]

---

45 Constitution, art 44.

46 Constitution Amendment Act 2013.

47 Constitution, art 44(1A)(a).

48 In the 2021 General Elections, five women were elected outright to Parliament. However, on 20 April 2021, the Head of State issued a Warrant of Election pursuant to art 44(1A) of the Constitution on the grounds that the 10 per cent quota had not been met. As a result, another female candidate, Aliimalemanu Moti Momoemausu Alofa Tuuau, was named as a Member of Parliament. This decision, which has been labelled as an unconstitutional political maneuver, has been contested in the courts.

49 Constitution, art 43.

50 Constitution, art 60.

51 Afamasaga Toleafoa 'One Party State: The Samoan Experience' in David Hegarty and Darrell Tryon (eds) *Politics, Development and Security in Oceania* (ANU Press, 2013) 69 at 70.

52 The author acknowledges the claim that the correct title for La'auli is La'aulialemalietoa. The author has used the title used by the Honourable La'auli when he took his parliamentary oath in 2020. La'auli Polataivao Leautea, upon leaving the HRPP, established a new political party, 'Fa'atuatua i le Atua Samoa Ua Tasi' (FAST). Fiame Naomi Mata'afa was elected as the leader of the FAST Party in March 2021. In the 2021 General Elections, the FAST Party won 25 of the 51 Parliament seats. The sole independent candidate elected in 2021 later joined the FAST Party, bringing their total number of seats to 26. The HRPP, led by Prime Minister Tuilaepa Sailele Malielegaoi, also won 25 seats. However, after the creation of an additional seat for a female candidate under art 44(1a) of the Constitution, the HRPP had 26 seats. As at 1 June 2021 there is a political stalemate in Samoa.

3.1.3. *Judiciary*

3.1.3.1. Civil and Criminal Courts

The civil and criminal courts deal with matters that fall outside of the jurisdiction of the Land and Titles Court. The Chief Justice, who is the head of the Bench, is appointed by the Head of State on the advice of the Prime Minister.[53] The Supreme Court judges and Senior Supreme Court Judge are appointed by the Head of State on the advice of the Judicial Service Commission.[54] The Judicial Service Commission advises the Head of State on the appointment, promotion, transfer and dismissal of the judges of the civil and criminal courts. The Judicial Service Commission consists of the Chief Justice (who is the Chairperson), the Attorney-General, a person nominated by the Minister of Justice, the Chairman of the Public Service Commission, a retired Supreme Court judge appointed by the Head of State on the advice of Cabinet, and the Supreme Court Registrar as the Commission Secretary.[55]

In order to be appointed as a judge of the Supreme Court, the candidate must meet the qualifications prescribed by the Head of State on the advice of the Judicial Service Commission and have practised as a barrister in Samoa, or an approved country, for at least 15 years.[56]

Article 74 provides that the judges of the Court of Appeal may be the Chief Justice and Supreme Court judges, retired judges of the Supreme Court and individuals possessing the qualifications of a Supreme Court judge appointed by the Head of State on the advice of the Judicial Service Commission.[57] Non-citizen judges, who are usually from New Zealand and Australia, are often appointed to preside over Court of Appeal matters.[58]

Upon appointment, the Chief Justice, the Senior Supreme Court Judge, Supreme Court judges and any persons appointed as judges of the Court of Appeal must take and subscribe an oath before the Head of State.[59] The Chief Justice and Supreme Court judges hold office until they reach the age of 68 years, resign, or are suspended or removed from office.[60] The Chief Justice may only be removed from office on the grounds of 'stated misbehaviour' or 'infirmity of the mind'.[61] The Head of State may remove the Chief Justice by addressing

---

53 Constitution, arts 65 and 66(1).
54 Constitution, art 80(1)(3).
55 Constitution, art 79(1).
56 Constitution, art 66(2).
57 Constitution, art 74(1); Court of Appeal judges appointed under art 74(2)(c) may be appointed for a period of time or for a particular matter.
58 Constitution, art 81(2).
59 Constitution, art 80(1)(2).
60 Constitution, art 67(1) and (4)–(6).
61 Constitution, art 67(6).

two-thirds of the Legislative Assembly and praying for the removal of the Chief Justice.[62] If the Legislative Assembly is not meeting, the Head of State on the advice of the Prime Minister, may suspend the Chief Justice.[63] The Senior Judge and judges of the Supreme Court may be removed by the Head of State on the advice of the Judicial Service Commission.[64]

Fa'amasinoga Sili o Samoa (Supreme Court)

Article 65 of the Constitution establishes the Supreme Court of Samoa as a superior court of record, consisting of the Chief Justice and Supreme Court judges. The Supreme Court has original, appellate and revisional jurisdiction and possesses the power and authority to administer the laws of Samoa.[65] The Supreme Court also has the jurisdiction to address and determine questions involving the interpretation of the Constitution.[66] In addition, the Head of State, on the advice of the Prime Minister, may also seek the opinion of the Supreme Court on any questions relating to the interpretation of the Constitution.[67]

Fa'amasinoga o Talosaga (Court of Appeal)

The Court of Appeal is established by art 74 of the Constitution. The Court of Appeal is a superior court of record in Samoa and has the general jurisdiction to hear appeals from the Supreme Court.[68] The Court of Appeal has the jurisdiction to hear appeals on matters which involve a substantial question of law regarding the interpretation of the Constitution, and may do so if it receives certification from the Supreme Court or if the Court of Appeal grants special leave.[69] The Court of Appeal has the power to affirm, reverse or vary the judgment appealed from, order a new trial, dismiss the appeal or make any orders and award costs as it thinks fit.[70] The decisions of the Court of Appeal are final.[71]

The Chief Justice is the President of the Court of Appeal.[72] The Chief Justice, Supreme Court judges, retired Supreme Court judges and non-citizen judges appointed by the Head of State may sit on the Court of Appeal.[73] Any three

---

62 Constitution, art 67(6).

63 Constitution, art 67(5).

64 Constitution, art 79(4); formerly, Supreme Court judges could not be removed unless approved by two-thirds of the Legislative Assembly.

65 Constitution, art 71(1).

66 Constitution, art 71(2); excluding matters in Part IX of the Constitution.

67 Constitution, art 71(3).

68 Constitution, art 75(1).

69 Constitution, art 75(2).

70 Constitution, art 77.

71 Constitution, art 75(4).

72 Constitution, art 75(3); the senior judge of the Court present at the appeal or a judge designated by the Chief Justice may preside in the absence of the Chief Justice.

73 Constitution, art 73(2); apart from the Chief Justice and Supreme Court judges, the Samoan Court of Appeal is presided over by former judges of the New Zealand Court of Appeal, High Court and Supreme Court.

judges of the Court of Appeal may exercise all of the powers of the Court.[74] The Constitution further provides that the majority of the Court of Appeal presiding over a matter must be retired or current Supreme Court judges; however, one of the three judges may be a non-Samoan judge appointed in the interest of justice.[75] Judges are not permitted to hear appeals on their own decisions.[76] The final decision of the Court of Appeal is the opinion of the majority of the judges presiding over the matter and can be delivered by any of the members.[77]

Fa'amasinoga Fa'aitūmalō (District Court)

Article 78 of the Constitution makes provision for subordinate courts. The District Court (formerly known as the Magistrates Court) is the subordinate court in the Samoan court system. The District Court has a limited jurisdiction with civil and criminal matters. It also has several divisions, namely the Family Court, the Family Violence Court and the Youth Court.[78]

A District Court hearing can be presided over by a District Court judge or a *fa'amasino fesoasoani*. Under the District Courts Act 2016, in order for a person to be appointed as a District Court judge they must have been admitted and have practised as a barrister in Samoa, or any other approved country, for a minimum of eight years.[79] Appointments are made by the Head of State acting on the advice of the Judicial Service Commission, provided that the above requirement is met.[80] Similarly, *fa'amasino fesoasoani* (assistant magistrates) are appointed by the Head of State on the advice of the Judicial Service Commission.

In relation to civil matters, the District Court when presided over by a judge may hear and determine:

(1) contract or torts actions where:
  (a) the debt, demand or damage, or value of the chattels claimed does not exceed $20,000 tala;
  (b) the debt or demand claimed does not exceed $20,000 tala after deduction of any set-off admitted by the plaintiff;[81]

---

74 Constitution, art 74(1).
75 Constitution, art 75(1)(a) and (b).
76 Constitution, art 75(3).
77 Constitution, art 75(2) and (1)(c).
78 In 2016, a Drugs and Alcohol Court was established as a division of the District Court. However, there is no mention of this in the laws of Samoa as of the last consolidation in 2019.
79 District Courts Act 2016, s 6(3). The Head of State, acting on the advice of the Judicial Commission, may designate by Order any country as an approved country, if the Commission is satisfied that the country has a legal system similar to that of Samoa.
80 District Courts Act 2016, s 6(2).
81 District Courts Act 2016, s 19(1).

(2) actions for the recovery of any penalty, expenses, contribution or other similar demand which is recoverable by law where:
    (a) there is no express provision stating that the demand can be only be recovered in another court, and
    (b) the amount claimed does not exceed $20,000 tala.[82]

Fa'amasino fesoasoani have more limited jurisdiction. They may hear and determine:

(1) contract or tort actions where the debt, demand or damage does not exceed $2,000 tala;[83]
(2) actions for the recovery of money where:
    (a) the law expressly provides that the District Court may hear the matter; and
    (b) the amount claimed does not exceed $2,000 tala.[84]

In relation to criminal matters, District Court judges have jurisdiction to hear and determine or pronounce a sentence for offences punishable by fine, forfeiture or a term of imprisonment not exceeding seven years.[85] However, the Act provides that a District Court judge presiding over a Youth Court proceeding may impose a sentence that exceeds seven years if the maximum penalty of the committed offence exceeds seven years.[86] *Fa'amasino fesoasoani* have a more limited jurisdiction, as they are only able to deal with matters where:

(1) the maximum penalty for the offence is an imprisonment term of less than one year;[87] or
(2) the value of the stolen property does not exceed $500 tala (when dealing with the offence of theft).[88]

3.1.3.2. *Fa'amasinoga o Fanua ma Suafa* (Land and Titles Courts)

Article 104 of the Constitution makes provision for the Land and Titles Courts, which have supreme authority over the subject of Samoan customs and

82 District Courts Act 2016, s 19(2).
83 District Courts Act 2016, s 19(3)(a).
84 District Courts Act 2016, s 19(3)(b).
85 District Courts Act 2016, s 30(1).
86 District Courts Act 2016, s 30(1)(b).
87 District Courts Act 2016, s 30(1).
88 District Courts Act 2016, s 30(3).

usages and the exclusive jurisdiction to hear and determine matters involving Samoan customary land and *matai* titles.[89] Notably, the Constitution expressly provides that the Land and Titles Courts govern a legal system that is 'different and separate from that of the Civil and Criminal Courts', acknowledging the plural legal system of Samoa.[90] Decisions of the Supreme Court and Court of Appeal are not binding on the Land and Titles Courts.[91]

The President is the head of the Land and Titles Court.[92] The Head of State appoints the President of the Land and Titles Court on the advice of the Prime Minister.[93] The President of the Land and Titles Court must be a Samoan legal practitioner with at least 10 years of practice experience and a *matai* who has rendered at least seven years of service to their village.[94] Once appointed, the President of the Land and Titles Court holds office until the age of 68 years.[95] The Head of State may remove the President of the Land and Titles Court, only on the grounds of 'unbecoming conduct' or 'physical and mental disability', after gaining the approval of two-thirds of the Members of Parliament.[96]

The *Komisi o le Faamasinoga o Fanua ma Suafa* advises the Head of State on the appointment, removal and suspension of the Deputy President, Vice President and judges of the Land and Titles First Court.[97] The *Komisi o le Faamasinoga o Fanua ma Suafa* consists of the President of the Land and Titles Court, as Chairperson; a Supreme Court judge nominated by the Chief Justice; the Chairperson of the Public Service Commission; and the Registrar of the Land and Titles Court as Secretary of the Commission.[98]

Once appointed, the President, Deputy President, Vice President and judges of the Land and Titles Courts must take and subscribe an oath before performing the functions of their office.[99]

Land and Titles First Court

The Land and Titles First Court is established by art 104A of the Constitution. The Land and Titles First Court is presided over by the Assistant

---

89 Constitution, art 104.
90 Constitution, art 104(2).
91 Land and Titles Act 2020, s 57(1).
92 Constitution, art 104B(2).
93 Constitution, art 104D(1).
94 Constitution, art 104D(1)(a) and (b).
95 Constitution, art 104D(1)(d).
96 Constitution, art 104D(3).
97 Constitution, art 104E(4); *Komisi o le Faamasinoga o Fanua ma Suafa* is translated as the 'Commission of the Land and Titles Court'.
98 Constitution, art 104E(1).
99 Constitution, art 104F; depending on the position, the oath must be sworn before the Head of State or the President of the Land and Titles Court.

President and at least two Land and Titles Court judges.[100] The Land and Titles First Court has original and appellate jurisdiction and the power and authority to administer the laws provided under Part IX of the Constitution. It has the jurisdiction:

- to determine matters relating to Samoan names and titles;
- to make orders or declarations in respect of Samoan names and titles, as necessary to preserve or define the same, or to determine the rights and obligations attached to the names and titles in accordance with Samoan customs;
- to determine claims and disputes relating to customary lands and the right of succession to property held in accordance to customs;
- to exercise powers inherent in a court of record; and
- as may be conferred by Act.[101]

In addition, the Land and Titles First Court has the power to determine disputes involving right of way or access on customary land.[102] The Constitution mandates that the Land and Titles First Court must apply the custom and usages of the Samoan people, the law relating to custom and usage, as well as the Constitution and other legislation that apply to the Court when determining a matter.[103] The Land and Titles First Court must also determine matters according to what it considers to be 'fair and just' between the parties.[104]

The Land and Titles Court has the power to make decisions and orders on all petitions before it.[105] The decision of the majority of judges hearing the matter will constitute the decision of the Court.[106] Decisions of the Land and Titles First Court may be reviewed by way of appeal to the Land and Titles High Court.[107]

Land and Titles High Court

Article 104B establishes the Land and Titles High Court as a superior court of record, consisting of the President of the Land and Titles Court, as the presiding judge and head of the Bench, and two Land and Titles Court Vice Presidents, who are appointed by the President.[108] The Land and Titles High

---

100 Constitution, art 104A(2); the Constitution makes no further reference to an 'Assistant President' but to a 'Deputy President' and 'Vice President'.
101 Constitution, art 104A(5).
102 Land and Titles Act 2020, s 38.
103 Constitution, art 104A(6).
104 Constitution, art 104A(7).
105 Constitution, art 104A(8).
106 Constitution, art 104A(9).
107 Constitution, art 104A(10).
108 Constitution, art 104B(2)(a) and (b); the Constitution provides that judges of the Land and Titles First Court may be appointed if the Vice President(s) of the Court is not present.

Court has original, appellate and revisional jurisdiction and possess all the power and authority to administer the laws under Part IX of the Constitution. It has the jurisdiction to hear appeals from the Lands and Titles First Court and may:

- uphold the appeal;
- set aside, vary or reverse a decision of the Land and Titles Court;
- order the Land and Titles Court to rehear the matter; or
- make orders relating to the appeal; and
- award costs as it thinks.

Land and Titles Court of Appeal and Review

Article 104C of the Constitution establishes the Land and Titles Court of Appeal and Review as a superior court of record. The Land and Titles Court of Appeal and Review has original, appellate and revisional jurisdiction and possesses all the power and authority necessary to administer the laws pertaining to the Land and Titles Court.[109] In particular, the Land and Titles Court of Appeal and Review has the jurisdiction to hear and determine appeals and applications for judicial review of the decisions of the Land and Titles High Court.[110]

The Land and Titles Court of Appeal and Review is composed of a retired Samoan Supreme Court judge or a retired President of the Land and Titles Court as the Chairperson, a Samoan Supreme Court judge, the President or a retired Deputy President or retired Vice President of the Land and Titles Court, and a Samoan lawyer who is a *matai* and who is qualified to be a Supreme Court judge.[111] Any three members of the Land and Titles Court of Appeal and Review may exercise the powers of the Land and Titles Court of Appeal and Review.[112] In relation to appeals, the Land and Titles Court of Appeal and Review has the power to uphold an appeal, set aside, vary or reverse the decision of the Land and Titles High Court or order the Land and Titles High Court to rehear the matter.[113] In relation to reviews, the Land and Titles Court of Appeal and Review may grant the remedies or prerogative writs sought by the parties, revoke the petition or make any order relevant to the review.[114]

---

109 Constitution, art 104C(5).

110 Constitution, art 104C(6).

111 Constitution, art 104C(2); Members of the Court of Appeal are appointed by the Head of State on the advice of Cabinet, the Chief Justice or the President of the Land and Titles Court.

112 Constitution, art 104C(3).

113 Constitution, art 104C(7)(a); there is a discrepancy in the terminology used to refer to the Land and Titles Court of Appeal and Review. In this section, the term used is 'Court of Final Appeal and Review'.

114 Constitution, art 104C(7)(b).

Previously, the Supreme Court had the jurisdiction to review questions relating to fundamental rights that arose in Land and Titles Court proceedings.[115] However, the Constitution Amendment Act 2020 removed this right of review.[116] The Constitution now mandates that the decisions of the Land and Titles Court of Appeal and Review are final and cannot be questioned by any other court by way of appeal, review or investigation.[117] The Land and Titles Court of Appeal and Review may also determine, dispose of or remit to another court questions that arise in relation to the interpretation or effect of any provision under Part IX of the Constitution.[118] Furthermore, the Head of State, on the advice of the Prime Minister, may also refer any questions regarding the interpretation or effect of any provision under Part IX of the Constitution to the Land and Titles Court of Appeal and Review for its opinion.[119]

Fono a le Nu'u (Village Councils)

Although village *fono* are not part of the formal State court system, their decisions can be appealed to the Land and Titles Court.[120] Out of the 275 villages in Samoa, 192 of these villages are considered traditional villages, or *nu'u*, which are governed by the village *fono* or council.[121] Village *fono* govern the day-to-day life in the Samoan villages. Village *fono* are recognised and protected by the Village Fono Act 1990, and empowered to create by-laws for a wide range of reasons, ranging from hygiene and sanitation, to development of land for economic purposes, to improvement of living standards, to promoting natural justice and fairness, harmony and social cohesion, to protecting Samoan customs and traditions and natural resources.[122] Village *fono* also have the power to impose customary punishment on anyone who fails to abide by the by-laws set by the village.[123] Village *fono* have the power to impose a fine of food, fine mats, animals or money, order that the offender and their family be banished or ostracised, or order the offender to work on the village land.[124]

---

115 Constitution, arts 4 and 73(2).

116 Section 2 of the Constitution Amendment Act 2020 amended art 4 of the Constitution to expressly exclude persons from seeking judicial reviews on matters arising from Land and Title Courts proceedings.

117 Constitution, art 104C(8).

118 Constitution, art 104C(9).

119 Constitution, art 104C(10).

120 Village Fono Act 1990, s 11.

121 This figure contradicts the statistics on the official Government of Samoa website. It states that there are 265 villages in Samoa and 45 in the vicinity of Apia; Leasiolagi Malama Meleisea, Measina Meredith, Muagututi'a Ioana Chan Mow, Penelope Schoffel, Semau Ausage Lauano, Hobert Sasa, Ramona Boodoosingh, Mohammed Sahib *Political Representation and Women's Empowerment in Samoa: Volume 1 Findings and Recommendations* (NUS Centre for Samoan Studies, 2015) 21.

122 Village Fono Act 1990, s 5(2).

123 Village Fono Act 1990, s 6(1).

124 Village Fono Act 1990, s 6(1)(a), (aa) and (b).

The Act provides a minimum standard of procedure which village *fono* must follow before making an order of banishment; this acts as a safeguard to ensure that the powers granted to the village are not abused. Village *fono* must inform the alleged offender of the allegations and evidence supporting the allegations, allow the offender an opportunity to respond within a reasonable time, allow for the offender to have the option of having a support person or representative when responding to the allegations, and give the offender the opportunity to make a submission on what they think is the appropriate penalty for the misconduct.[125] In order to impose the customary punishment of banishment on an offender, the village *fono* is required to file a petition with the Land and Titles Court, which in turn decides whether to uphold the decision. Banishment orders made by the village *fono* are subject to appeal to the Land and Titles Court.[126]

There are two significant banishment cases decided by the Court of Appeal. *Pitomoa Mauga* involved the village *fono* of Lotofaga and its attempt to justify the banishment of the appellant under s 3 of the Village Fono Act 1990. The Court of Appeal, in upholding the decision of Vaai J, clarified that the Act did not grant village *fono* the power to banish individuals who offended village protocol and stated that there was a 'need to marry modern democratic ideals and human rights with indigenous customs and traditions'.[127] The Court of Appeal also held in *Ta'amale v Attorney-General* that while the customary practice of banishment infringed on the right to freedom of movement protected by the Constitution, it was a reasonable restriction to maintain public order. However, the Court of Appeal emphasised that banishment orders were only to be used as an 'extreme measure of social control' and only for the purposes of preserving the stability of village life.[128]

3.2. CONSTITUTIONAL OFFICES AND ENTITIES

3.2.1. Komesina o Sulufaiga *(Office of the Ombudsman)*

The Office of the Ombudsman is established by art 82A of the Constitution. It is an independent office of the Government.[129] The Ombudsman Act 2013 outlines the functions and powers of the Office. The Ombudsman is appointed

---

125 Village Fono Act 1990, s 6(2).

126 Village Fono Act 1990, s 6(7).

127 *Pitomoa Mauga et al v Fuga Leituala* (unreported, CA March 2005, Lord Cooke of Thorndon P, Casey and Bisson JJ) at [10]; Leulua'ialii Tasi Malifa 'Village Fono Act Reforms' (Paper presented at the Samoa Law Society Biennial Law Symposium, Samoa, December 2015).

128 *Taamale v Attorney-General* [1995] WSCA 12.

129 Ombudsman (Komesina o Sulufaiga) Act 2013, s 6.

by the Head of State on the recommendation of the Legislative Assembly for a term of six years. Members of Parliament, ministers, public servants, or a director or employee of a public body are not eligible for appointment to this position.[130] Appointment, removal and the remuneration of the Ombudsman are determined by the Act.

The Ombudsman Act 2013 sets out a number of functions for the Office: administrative review, human rights protection and special investigations. The Ombudsman's Office can initiate an investigation, either on its own initiative or by a complaint, concerning any administrative decisions that affect a person made by a government ministry or organisation or an officer when carrying out a power or function under law.[131] The Ombudsman's Office may also investigate and report on matters referred to it by the Prime Minister or parliamentary committees.[132]

The Ombudsman functions as the national human rights institution in Samoa. Under the Act, the Office is responsible for:

- promoting public awareness of human rights and efforts to combat all forms of discrimination or corruption;
- inquiring into and reporting on alleged human rights violations;
- monitoring and promoting compliance with international and domestic human rights laws;
- participating in judicial proceedings involving human rights issues with the approval of the court;
- consulting, engaging and cooperating with relevant civil society organisations and national regional and international human rights bodies;
- advising on any matter referred to the Ombudsman by the Government; and
- producing and publicising reports on the Office's human rights functions.[133]

The Act gives the Ombudsman the power to establish a special investigation unit for the purposes of receiving and determining complaints about a police or prison officer, or an officer of prescribed disciplined forces, and of carrying out any other functions, duties or powers prescribed by law.[134] The Act provides that the Office may not investigate a matter if it is already being investigated by the police, prisons or other disciplined force. However, the Act provides

130 Ombudsman (Komesina o Sulufaiga) Act 2013, Sch 3, s 1(2).

131 Ombudsman (Komesina o Sulufaiga) Act 2013, s 18(1).

132 Ombudsman (Komesina o Sulufaiga) Act 2013, s 19(3); in May 2019, the Office of the Ombudsman completed an Investigation Report under this section entitled 'Power Struggle at the National University of Samoa', available at <https://ombudsman.gov.ws/special-investigations-unit-documents/>.

133 Ombudsman (Komesina o Sulufaiga) Act 2013, s 33.

134 Ombudsman (Komesina o Sulufaiga) Act 2013, s 41.

that if the Ombudsman has reason to believe that there is an abuse of process, unreasonable delay or an inappropriate investigation of the matter, the Ombudsman may investigate.[135] The Special Investigations Unit was established in 2016. No special investigations have been undertaken under this section.

3.2.2. Ofisa o le Loia Sili *(Office of the Attorney-General)*

In addition to art 83(g) of the Constitution, the Office of the Attorney-General is established by s 3 of the Attorney-General's Office Act 2013. The Attorney-General is appointed by the Head of State on the advice of the Prime Minister.[136] In order to be appointed to this position, the candidate must be qualified to be a judge of the Supreme Court.[137] The Attorney-General is responsible for providing advice on legal matters referred to him or her by the Head of State, Cabinet, the Prime Minster or a minister and have the power to institute, conduct or discontinue proceedings for any alleged offences.[138] The Attorney-General, when carrying out a constitutional, statutory or common law function, can only be directed by the Head of State, Prime Minister, Cabinet, a minister, a court or if required by Act.[139]

The Office of the Attorney-General is divided into a Civil Division, a Prosecution Division, a Legislative Drafting Division and a Corporate and Finance Division, each with its own statutory functions.[140]

3.2.3. Ofisa o le Pule ma Suetusi Sili *(Samoa Audit Office)*

The Samoa Audit Office is established by the Constitution and governed by the Audit Act 2013.[141] The Controller and Auditor-General is appointed for a term of 12 years by the Head of State on the advice of the Prime Minister, who is also required to consult with the parliamentary committee responsible for the officers of Parliament.[142] The Controller and Auditor-General is an independent officer of Parliament and is required to report annually to Parliament.[143] The Act sets out the functions of the Controller and Auditor-General and grants the officer general and ancillary powers to seize, and enter premises to seize, any information needed to perform their functions.[144] The powers to seize

135 Ombudsman (Komesina o Sulufaiga) Act 2013, s 41(2).
136 Constitution, art 41(1).
137 Constitution, art 41(1).
138 Constitution, art 41(2).
139 Attorney-General's Office Act 2013, s 7.
140 Attorney-General's Office Act 2013, s 5.
141 Constitution, arts 93 and 97–99.
142 Constitution, art 97(1) and (2).
143 Constitution, arts 9(5) and 98(1).
144 Audit Act 2013, ss 12–13 and 20.

required information overrides any rights to secrecy or confidentiality, meaning that legal professional privilege cannot be claimed.[145] There are limited grounds for dismissing the Controller and Auditor-General. Article 99F(2) of the Constitution states that the Controller and Auditor-General may only be removed by the Head of State on the advice of the Prime Minister if he or she is convicted of an offence punishable by a minimum of 12 months' imprisonment or involving tax evasion, becomes bankrupt, becomes incapable of or fails to perform his or her constitutional or statutory function, or engages in conduct that conflicts with the office of the Controller and Auditor-General.[146]

3.2.4. Komisi o Galuega a le Malō *(Public Service Commission)*

The Public Service Commission is the entity that is responsible for the planning, management, policy formulation, monitoring and evaluation of human resources for the Public Service. Encompassed in this function is the responsibility to appoint, promote, discipline or remove public servants. There are certain offices which are excluded from the definition of the Public Service, namely that of the executive, legislative and judicial branches of Government, as well as the Attorney-General, Controller and Auditor-General, police, prisons and other defence force officers, village representatives (*sui o le nu'u*), and the employees of the Legislative Assembly.[147]

3.3. LEGAL PROFESSION

Lawyers in Samoa may be admitted as a barrister or solicitor or both. The Lawyers and Legal Practice Act does not set out clear parameters between the work of barristers and solicitors. However, it provides that the preparation of a conveyance, will or tenancy agreement is work to be exclusively done by solicitors.[148] Practitioners in Samoa are usually barristers and solicitors; however, there are lawyers who are registered as barristers sole.[149] There are three types of practising certificates issued by the Samoa Law Society: unrestricted, restricted or barrister sole. Unrestricted practising certificates are

145 Audit Act 2013, ss 22–23.

146 Constitution, art 99F(2).

147 Constitution, art 83.

148 Lawyers and Legal Practice Act 2014, s 34(2); Guy Powles 'Samoa' in Michael A Ntumy (ed) *South Pacific Legal Systems* (University of Hawaii Press, 1993) 395 at 428.

149 The Samoa Law Society reported that as of March 2020, 162 lawyers were registered as having practising certificates. A majority (94) of the registered lawyers were employed by the Government, while 62 lawyers were employed by private law firms or as in-house counsel. The remaining five lawyers were registered as barristers sole.

issued to lawyers who are permitted to practise on their own account as a sole practitioner.[150] Restricted practising certificates are issued to lawyers who may only practise law as an employee of a lawyer with an unrestricted practising certificate or as a Government employee.[151] Barrister sole practising certificates are issued to lawyers who may only act as counsel and cannot take money directly from any clients.[152]

Practitioners working in the public sector either work in the Attorney-General's Office, the Samoa Law Reform Commission or as in-house counsel for various ministries and departments. Samoa does not have a Public Solicitor's Office. In 2015, the Parliament of Samoa passed the Community Legal Centre Act to 'provide free legal services to the people of Samoa'. An amendment was made to the Act restricting the provision of legal aid to criminal proceedings. Although plans were set for the building of the Centre, development has been postponed for a few more years. Samoa has a thriving private legal sector with 39 private law firms.

3.3.1. Admission

In order to be admitted to the bar as a barrister or solicitor of the Supreme Court, a person must:[153]

- be at least 21 years of age;
- have good character; and
- hold the prescribed qualifications; specifically, the Council of the Law Society must be satisfied that the applicant holds an academic or professional qualification in law.[154] The Council may accept academic or professional law qualifications from any country if it is satisfied that the legal system is sufficiently similar to that of Samoa.[155]

Individuals who satisfy these requirements may be admitted and enrolled on the permanent or temporary roll. Admission and enrolment on the permanent roll requires Samoan citizenship.[156] The temporary roll is for non-citizens. The length of time for which a person may be enrolled on the temporary roll is determined by the Supreme Court on the recommendation of the Council.

150 Lawyers and Legal Practice Act 2014, s 32(1).
151 Lawyers and Legal Practice Act 2014, s 32(4).
152 Lawyers and Legal Practice Act 2014, s 34(2).
153 Lawyers and Legal Practice Act 2014, s 23(1).
154 Lawyers and Legal Practice Act 2014, s 23(3).
155 Lawyers and Legal Practice Act 2014, s 23(3)(c).
156 Lawyers and Legal Practice Act 2014, s 24.

The Lawyers and Legal Practice Act provides a maximum period of five years for temporary roll enrolment, which can be extended by application.[157]

3.3.2. Council of the Law Society

The Lawyers and Legal Practice Act sets out the organisational structure and outlines the various functions of the Council of the Law Society. These functions range from reviewing applications for admission[158] and promoting and encouraging proper conduct amongst lawyers,[159] to the maintenance of the rule of law, the development of laws,[160] and protecting and representing the interests of the legal profession.[161] The Act empowers the Council of the Law Society to:[162]

- issue practising certificates;
- inquire into the character and qualifications of individuals applying for admission;
- conduct investigations into complaints made against lawyers or into ethical and professional misconduct of lawyers or law firms;
- prosecute lawyers in breach of the Act or laws that relate to practising law;
- require lawyers to undergo further legal training and development; and
- exercise other powers to enable the Society to carry out its functions.

The Act also empowers the Law Society to create rules for the regulation of the Society and the legal profession. Should the Council of the Law Society find that a lawyer is guilty of professional misconduct or of breaking the rules, the Secretary of the Council will issue a certificate to strike the name of the lawyer from the roll. Reinstatement of a lawyer's name to the roll can be done by Supreme Court order.

3.3.3. Legal Education

A substantial number of the law graduates in Samoa gained their qualifications from the University of the South Pacific School of Law after it was established in 1994.[163] Several lawyers in Samoa also hold undergraduate and postgraduate

---

157 Lawyers and Legal Practice Act 2014, s 25(1)–(3).
158 Lawyers and Legal Practice Act 2014, s 5(c).
159 Lawyers and Legal Practice Act 2014, s 5(a).
160 Lawyers and Legal Practice Act 2014, s 5(f) and (h).
161 Lawyers and Legal Practice Act 2014, s 5(i) and (j).
162 Lawyers and Legal Practice Act 2014, s 6(1) and (2).
163 In January 2021, the University of the South Pacific underwent an internal restructure. The School of Law is now the 'Discipline of Law' and falls under the School of Law and Social Science.

qualifications from universities in New Zealand, Australia, the United Kingdom and the United States.

3.4. COURT PROCEDURE

Proceedings in the State legal system are adversarial, with the exception of the Land and Titles Court, which seems to adopt an inquisitorial approach.[164] The standard of proof for civil proceedings is 'on the balance of probabilities', while in criminal proceedings the standard is 'beyond reasonable doubt'. In civil proceedings, the burden to prove the elements of the claim rests on the plaintiff. In criminal proceedings, the burden rests on the State to prove that the accused committed the offence. Civil proceedings are tried by a judge alone. Both the English and Samoan language may be used in civil and criminal proceedings, either in the documents submitted to the court or in the examination of witnesses.[165]

3.4.1. *Civil Proceedings*

The Supreme Court Rules 1980 set out the procedures for civil proceedings in the Supreme Court, while the District Court Act 2016 establishes procedures for civil proceedings in the District Court.

Civil actions are initiated by filing a statement of claim with the Registrar.[166] The statement of claim must include the names and descriptions of the plaintiff and defendant, the nature of the cause of action and the relief sought.[167] It must also include relevant facts needed by the court and the defendant to understand the basis of the claim.[168] The Supreme Court Rules allow for parties to be joined to the claim, either as plaintiffs or defendants, at any stage of the proceedings by order of the court.[169] Amendments to the statement of claim can be made at any time by the plaintiff, with the leave of the court.[170] Parties are able to apply for interlocutory orders in the Supreme Court.[171]

---

164 Supreme Court (Civil Procedure) Rules 1980, r 115; Jennifer Corrin and David Bamford *Civil Procedure and Courts in the South Pacific* (2nd ed, Intersentia, 2016) at 265.

165 Supreme Court (Civil Procedure) Rules 1980, r 201; Criminal Procedure Act 2016, s 40: in criminal proceedings, documents must be written in English if the Registrar is satisfied that the defendant understands English but may be written or translated into Samoan in the event that the defendant does not.

166 Supreme Court (Civil Procedure) Rules 1980, r 13.

167 Supreme Court (Civil Procedure) Rules 1980, r 10.

168 Supreme Court (Civil Procedure) Rules 1980, r 15(1).

169 Supreme Court (Civil Procedure) Rules 1980, rr 31–34.

170 Supreme Court (Civil Procedure) Rules 1980, r 17.

171 Supreme Court (Civil Procedure) Rules 1980, Part VIII.

Under the Supreme Court Rules, defendants must file a response in the court office, within 10 days of being served with summons.[172] If a defendant fails to file a response, the plaintiff may make an application to the court for a default judgment against the defendant.[173]

Plaintiffs may apply for a discontinuance of action at any time before the trial.[174] This does not affect the plaintiff's ability to bring a subsequent action.[175]

3.4.2. *Criminal Proceedings*

The Criminal Procedure Act 2016 is applicable to all criminal proceedings. Although the State is the prosecutor in most cases, private prosecutions may also be brought. Private prosecutions have been brought against individuals who had allegedly committed statutory offences[176] who failed to comply with court orders;[177] however, most private prosecutions have been in relation to offences contained in the Electoral Act 1963.[178]

All criminal proceedings in the Supreme Court are tried by a judge alone.[179] In cases involving a charge with an offence punishable by life imprisonment, the defendant must be tried by a judge of the Supreme Court sitting with five assessors.[180] Assessors are Samoan citizens between the ages of 25 and 68 years, whom the Judicial Services Committee is satisfied possess good character, education, ability and reputation.[181] A person charged with an offence punishable by life imprisonment may elect trial before a judge alone.[182] Requests to be tried by a judge sitting alone are prevalent in high-profile cases, such as the trial of Kolani Lam, who was convicted of murdering his wife, Sa'u Justina Sa'u, the former CEO of the Unit Trust of Samoa, and the trial of Herman Westerlund and Suapaina Petelo Savaiinaea, who were acquitted of the assault and murder of Jeremiah Malaki Tauiliili.[183]

Criminal proceedings are commenced by the laying of information in either the Supreme Court or District Court, depending on the jurisdiction of each

172 Supreme Court (Civil Procedure) Rules 1980, r 96.
173 Supreme Court (Civil Procedure) Rules 1980, r 97.
174 Supreme Court (Civil Procedure) Rules 1980, r 109.
175 Supreme Court (Civil Procedure) Rules 1980, r 110.
176 *Toailoa Law Office v Duffy* [2005] WSSC; *Churchward v Curtiss* [1930–49] WSLR 23.
177 *Meredith Ainu'u Lawyers v Muagututagata Peter Ah Him* [2006] WSSC 55.
178 See *Sia v Peteru* [1998] WSSC 37; *Teo v Attorney-General* [2001] WSSC 25; *Vui v Ah Chong* [2006] WSSC 452; *Samoa Party v Attorney-General* [2009] WSSC 23; *Sione v Ponifasio* [2017] WSDC 30.
179 Criminal Procedure Act 2016, s 6(1).
180 Criminal Procedure Act 2016, s 6(2).
181 Criminal Procedure Act 2016, s 127.
182 Criminal Procedure Act 2016, s 125.
183 See *Police v Lam* [2020] WSSC 21; *Police v Westerlund* [2020] WSSC 47.

court.[184] Any information must be sworn or affirmed, refer to the statutory provision of the offence that the defendant has allegedly committed, and contain sufficient facts to ensure that the defendant and the court are fairly informed of the substance of the alleged offence.[185] The laying of information must generally be done within a year of the time that the offence had allegedly been committed.[186] A charging document must also be filed within 21 working days of the laying of information in the court, in order for a hearing to commence. Charging documents must set out the charges that the Attorney-General will proceed with against the defendant.[187]

The Act provides that defendants may be tried together by order of the court, in situations where the allegations are sufficiently linked by time, place, circumstances or other significantly related factors, or where the court is satisfied that, in the interests of justice, a joint trial is desirable or expedient.[188]

With the exception of judge-alone trials, in order for a defendant to be convicted there must be concurrence of four out of five of the assessors as well as the presiding judge.[189] In the event that a guilty verdict is found against the defendant, depending on the penalties prescribed by the Act for a particular offence, the court may make an order for imprisonment, the payment of a fine or community service. The Sentencing Act 2016 provides guidelines that the court must follow when imposing a sentence on an offender. Interestingly, the court must also take into account any penalties that were imposed by village *fono* on the offender as a mitigating factor in sentencing.[190]

The Criminal Procedure Act provides that a person must not be arrested without warrant unless expressly provided for by statute.[191] A person must be informed by the arresting officer of the grounds of the arrest and any charges against them, as well as their right to silence and counsel.[192] Judges may issue warrants to search and seize and for forensic samples.[193] Police are provided with the power to arrest without warrant and the power to enter premises without warrant to arrest an offender under the Act.[194] Other powers of the police may be found in the Police Powers Act 2007.

The Criminal Procedure Act also provides the procedure for the taking of evidence. Other procedures and rules relating to evidentiary matters – such

---

184 See *District Court* in section 3.1.3.1 above.
185 Criminal Procedure Act 2016, ss 18 and 24.
186 Criminal Procedure Act 2016, s 16.
187 Criminal Procedure Act 2016, s 19(1).
188 Criminal Procedure Act 2016, s 23(1) and (2).
189 Criminal Procedure Act 2016, s 136.
190 Village Fono Act 1990, s 8.
191 Criminal Procedure Act 2016, s 29(1).
192 Criminal Procedure Act 2016, s 32.
193 Criminal Procedure Act 2016, ss 33 and 34.
194 Criminal Procedure Act 2016, ss 29 and 30.

as the admissibility of evidence, the examination and cross-examination of witnesses, improperly obtained evidence, identification evidence, and privilege and confidentiality – are found in the Evidence Act 2015.

Children under the age of 10 cannot be charged with a criminal offence.[195] The Young Offenders Act 2007 established the Youth Court division of the District Court and provides the special procedure to be followed by the Court when determining matters concerning offenders who are between the ages of 10 and 17.[196]

3.4.3. *Appellate Procedure*

The relevant procedure for appeals is outlined in the Judicature Ordinance 1961, the Supreme Court Rules and the Court of Appeal Rules. Appeals from District Court decisions are made to the Supreme Court, while appeals from Supreme Court decisions are made to the Court of Appeal. Appeals may be from both civil and criminal proceedings and may be brought by either party to the proceedings. The decisions of the Court of Appeal, and of the Supreme Court on appeal from the District Court, are final.[197] However, the Court of Appeal may, with leave, hear an appeal from a Supreme Court decision on an appeal from a District Court decision on a civil matter.[198]

An appeal lies as of right in civil cases involving an amount in excess of $3,000 tala, and with leave where the Court of Appeal or the Supreme Court is of the opinion that the question involved in the appeal is one of general or public importance.[199]

In criminal proceedings, both the Attorney-General and accused parties may appeal a decision of the District Court to the Supreme Court or of the Supreme Court to the Court of Appeal. Appeals can be made against conviction, acquittal, sentence or orders.[200] In appeals against conviction, the court may confirm the conviction, set aside the conviction and order a re-trial, or amend the conviction as it sees fit.[201] In appeals against acquittals, the court may dismiss the appeal, uphold the appeal and direct a re-trial, uphold the appeal and convict the respondent, or convict the respondent on a related charge.[202] In appeals against sentences, the court may confirm the sentence or amend the sentence,

195 Young Offenders Act 2007, s 3.
196 Young Offenders Act 2007, Part 2.
197 Judicature Ordinance 2020, s 21.
198 Judicature Act 2020, s 11(a) and (b).
199 Judicature Ordinance 1961, s 51(a) and (b).
200 Criminal Procedure Act 2016, s 154.
201 Criminal Procedure Act 2016, s 154(2)(a).
202 Criminal Procedure Act 2016, s 154(2)(c).

and in appeals against orders, the court may confirm, set aside or amend the order as it sees fit.[203]

3.4.4. *Land and Titles Courts*

3.4.4.1. Land and Titles First Court

Before any case commences in the Land and Titles Courts, the parties to a matter must make a genuine effort to resolve the dispute by participating in mediation or Samoan conciliation.[204] Samoan conciliations are conducted by the Registrar of the Court.[205]

Proceedings in the Land and Titles First Court commence on the filing of the petition with the Registrar of the Court.[206] Upon receiving the filed petition, the Registrar must publish the petition in three consecutive monthly issues of the Government-owned newspaper, the *Savali*.[207] Once the petition has met the publishing requirements, the Registrar will set the matter for a judicial settlement conference with a judge of the Land and Titles Court as the mediator and facilitator.[208] If the matter is settled, the decision will be called and confirmed in open court as an order.[209]

If the parties are unable to settle, the Registrar will set the matter for hearing.[210] In exceptional cases, the Land and Titles First Court may grant special leave to hear unpublished petitions.[211]

The full judgment of the Land and Titles First Court must be delivered in open court by the presiding Vice President or a member of the panel appointed by the Vice President within three months of the last day of the proceedings.[212] As a general requirement, the Land and Titles Courts must give reasons for every decision on a petition, appeal or application for review.[213]

Decisions of the Land and Titles First Court may be appealed to the Land and Titles High Court. In addition, the Land and Titles First Court may, in any proceedings before it, reserve a case stated for consideration by the Land and Titles High Court.[214]

203 Criminal Procedure Act 2016, s 154(2)(d).
204 Land and Titles Act 2020, s 31.
205 Land and Titles Act 2020, s 32(1).
206 Land and Titles Act 2020, s 35(1).
207 Land and Titles Act 2020, s 35(2); the *Savali* is published online at <https://www.samoagovt.ws/category/savali-newspaper/>.
208 Land and Titles Act 2020, s 33(1)–(3).
209 Land and Titles Act 2020, s 33(4).
210 Land and Titles Act 2020, s 35(3).
211 Land and Titles Act 2020, s 35(4).
212 Land and Titles Act 2020, s 54(1)(a).
213 Land and Titles Act 2020, s 55(1).
214 Land and Titles Act 2020, s 45(1).

3.4.4.2. Land and Titles High Court

The President or Deputy President of the Land and Titles High Court must give leave for an appeal to be heard.[215] The aggrieved party must file an application for leave to appeal within 40 days of the Land and Titles First Court delivering its decision.[216] Applications for leave must be supported by documentation containing the grounds of appeal.[217] Once the respondent is served with the leave application, they have 30 days to file a response.[218]

When determining whether to grant leave, the President or Deputy President of the Land and Titles High Court may hear submissions from both parties and make orders on the application as he or she sees fit.[219]

Leave to appeal decisions of the Land and Titles First Court to the Land and Titles High Court may be granted on the grounds that:

- new and material evidence has been found since the hearing of the petition which the applicant had no knowledge of, or could not have been reasonably adduced at the hearing of the petition;
- the successful party or a witness is guilty of misconduct that affected the result of the case;
- a mistake was identified and proven to affect the result of the case;
- the Court acted outside of its jurisdiction;
- the decision was wrong in law or not in accordance with custom and usage;
- the decision or order was manifestly against the weight of the evidence adduced at the petition hearing; or
- a substantial wrong or miscarriage of justice has occurred.[220]

Judges are prohibited from hearing and determining appeals on matters that they presided over in the first instance in the Land and Titles First Court.[221] The Land and Titles High Court has the discretion to re-hear the matter in whole or in part.[222] Decisions of the Land and Titles High Court may be appealed to the Land and Titles Court of Appeal and Review.[223] In addition, the Land and Titles High Court may, in any proceedings before it, reserve a case stated for consideration by the Land and Titles Court of Appeal and Review.[224]

---

215 Land and Titles Act 2020, s 40(1).
216 Land and Titles Act 2020, s 40(2).
217 Land and Titles Act 2020, s 40(2).
218 Land and Titles Act 2020, s 40(3).
219 Land and Titles Act 2020, s 41(1)–(3).
220 Land and Titles Act 2020, s 39.
221 Constitution, art 104B(3).
222 Land and Titles Act, s 42(1).
223 Constitution, art 104B(8).
224 Land and Titles Act 2020, s 45(2).

The full judgment of the Land and Titles High Court must be delivered in open Court by the President, the presiding Deputy President or a member of the panel appointed by the President within three months of the last day of the proceedings.[225]

3.4.4.3. Land and Titles Court of Appeal and Review

The Land and Titles Court of Appeal may hear appeals and applications for judicial review of decisions of the Land and Titles High Court.

The Chairperson of the Land and Titles Court of Appeal and Review must grant leave for an appeal to be heard by the Court.[226] When determining whether to grant leave to appeal, the Chairperson may hear submissions from both parties and must deliver a decision within 10 days of the date of the hearing.[227] Appellants are required to file their application for leave to appeal and notice of appeal with the Registrar of the Court within 40 days of the Land and Titles High Court delivering its decision.[228] Upon being served with the appeal application, respondents have 30 days to file their response.[229]

The Land and Titles Court of Appeal and Review may only grant leave to appeal if it is satisfied that it is 'necessary in the interests of justice' for the appeal to be heard and determined.[230] The Land and Titles Act provides that it is 'necessary in the interests of justice' to hear and determine where:

- the appeal involves a matter of general or public importance;
- a substantial miscarriage of justice may have occurred or may occur if the appeal is not heard; or
- the appeal involves a matter of general customary or cultural significance.[231]

The Land and Titles Court of Appeal and Review may hear appeals on decisions of the former Land and Titles Court and its appellate division by way of special leave.[232] Special appeals may be heard by the Land and Titles Court of Appeal and Review if the case involves substantial questions of law in the interpretation or effect of art 104A(5) and (6) or questions of general, customary or public importance that ought to be considered by the Court.[233] Applications for special

225 Land and Titles Act 2020, s 54(1)(b).
226 Land and Titles Act 2020, s 47(1).
227 Land and Titles Act 2020, s 48(2) and (3).
228 Land and Titles Act 2020, s 47(2).
229 Land and Titles Act 2020, s 47(3).
230 Land and Titles Act 2020, s 46(1).
231 Land and Titles Act 2020, s 46(2).
232 Land and Titles Act 2020, s 43(1); this special leave to appeal only applies to decisions that were made before the Land and Titles Act 2020 commenced.
233 Land and Titles Act 2020, ss 43 and 44.

leave must be made within 12 months from the date that the Land and Titles Act 2020 commenced and include a copy of the notice of appeal, certified copies of all relevant documents, records and evidence, and the required fee.[234] Once the application has been received by the Registrar, the respondents must be served in person and the notice of appeal must be published in three consecutive monthly issues of the *Savali*.[235] The Act provides that the respondent has 40 days to file their response with the Registrar.[236] When leave is granted, the Registrar will set a date for the hearing and notify the parties.[237]

The full judgment of the Land and Titles Court of Appeal and Review must be delivered in open court by the Chairperson or a member of the panel appointed by the Chairperson within three months of the last day of the hearing.[238]

3.5. DISPUTE RESOLUTION

There are several avenues for dispute resolution in Samoa: the State court system, alternative dispute resolution and customary dispute resolution.

3.5.1. Alternative Dispute Resolution

Alternative dispute resolution is defined in the Alternative Dispute Resolution Act 2007 as 'any process used to resolve disputes between parties in civil and criminal proceedings which is outside the usual court-based litigation model'.[239] The Act provides the procedures for mediation, arbitration, settlement, reconciliation and conciliation.[240]

In 2013, the Act was amended to include mediation as a form of dispute resolution. The former Chief Justice Patu Tiava'asu'e Falefatu Sapolu likened mediation to traditional methods of reconciliation; His Honour did, however, clarify that, unlike Samoan custom, mediation was purely facilitative and not determinative.[241] The Act establishes the Mediation Council, which consists of the Chief Justice, a District Court judge, the President of the Samoa Law Society, the Attorney-General, the Ombudsman, the CEO of the Ministry of Justice and the Presidents of the Accredited Mediators of Samoa Association

234 Land and Titles Act 2020, s 44(1).
235 Land and Titles Act 2020, s 44(2).
236 Land and Titles Act 2020, s 44(3).
237 Land and Titles Act 2020, s 44(6).
238 Land and Titles Act 2020, s 54(1)(c).
239 Alternative Dispute Resolution Act 2007, s 2.
240 Alternative Dispute Resolution Act 2007, s 5.
241 Sapeer Mayron 'Conference speaker delves into mediation' *Samoa Observer* (online ed, 8 September 2018).

and the Chamber of Commerce.[242] The Council is responsible for regulating and controlling mediation and mediators, ensuring good and acceptable standards of practice and ensuring that mediators receive proper training as required.[243]

The Act provides that reconciliation or conciliation should be encouraged in disputes of a substantially personal or private nature and not aggravated in degree.[244]

Several Acts of Parliament also provide for special tribunals. The decisions of such tribunals may be subject to appeal to the courts. For example, under the Planning and Urban Management Act 2004, decisions of the Planning and Urban Management Agency may be appealed to the Planning Tribunal.[245] The Tribunal, which consists of a judge appointed by the Chief Justice and two persons appointed by the Head of State on the advice of Cabinet, may hear the appeal and decide on the proceedings and may confirm, amend or cancel the decision that is subject to the appeal.[246] The decision of the Tribunal may be appealed to the Supreme Court on a matter of law.[247]

3.5.2. Customary Dispute Resolution

Although there has been an increase in the use of the formal State court system to solve disputes, the *matai* chiefly system continues to play a role in resolving disputes, particularly in rural areas. Village *fono*, which consists of *alii ma faipule* or *matai*, use Samoan custom to resolve disputes within the village.[248]

Under Samoan custom, disputes were resolved using *fa'aleleiga* and *ifoga*.[249] An *ifoga* is a ceremonial request for forgiveness made by the offender and his *aiga* (family) to those injured.[250] *Ifoga* are performed primarily to show remorse for the wrongdoing but also to prevent further violence from occurring and maintain peace within a community.[251] *Ifoga* are public acts of self-humiliation, involving the wrongdoers and/or members of their *aiga* sitting under an *ie toga* (fine mat) on the ground in front of the victim's home and at the mercy of the victim's family, until the victim's family accepts or rejects the apology.[252]

---

242 Alternative Dispute Resolution Act 2007, s 6A.
243 Alternative Dispute Resolution Act 2007, s 6C.
244 Alternative Dispute Resolution Act 2007, s 15.
245 Planning and Urban Management Act 2004, s 54.
246 Planning and Urban Management Act 2004, s 74.
247 Planning and Urban Management Act 2004, s 77.
248 Teleiai Lalotoa Mulitalo Seumanutafa and Jennifer Corrin 'Plural Procedures for Adoption and "Vae Tama" in Samoa' in Jennifer Corrin and Sue Farran (eds) *The Plural Practice of Adoption in Pacific Island States* (Springer, 2019) 87 at 99.
249 *Fa'aleleiga* means 'reconciliation' while *ifoga* is 'the act of bowing'.
250 *Attorney-General v Matalavea* [2007] WSCA 8 at [26].
251 Leilani Tuala-Warren 'A Study into the Ifoga: Samoa's Answer to Dispute Healing' (Te Matahauariki Institute, 2002) 20.
252 Leilani Tuala-Warren 'A Study into the Ifoga: Samoa's Answer to Dispute Healing' (Te Matahauariki Institute, 2002) 19.

Generally, *ifoga* are accepted quickly and forgiveness is symbolised by the removal of the fine mat.[253] When the *ifoga* is accepted, gifts of money, *ie toga*, food items and livestock are given by the wrongdoer's family to the victim's family. The acceptance of the *ifoga* traditionally meant complete forgiveness and an understanding that neither party would bring the matter up again.[254]

The practice of *ifoga* remains prevalent in modern Samoan society and has been recognised and incorporated into the formal legal system. The performance and acceptance of an *ifoga* does not diminish the criminal responsibility of the accused. However, an *ifoga* is considered as a mitigating factor in criminal sentencing, with the weight given to *ifoga* varying depending on the circumstances in each case.

On the other hand, the concept of *fa'aleleiga* has also been incorporated into statute, such as the Young Offenders Act 2007.[255]

4. LAW OF PERSONS

4.1. BIRTH, MARRIAGE AND DEATH

All births, marriages and deaths must be registered with the Registrar under the Births, Deaths and Marriages Registration Act 2002.

The Marriage Ordinance 1961 places several restrictions on marriage. Individuals are not allowed to marry their close relatives, that is, their grandparents, parents, parent's siblings, or their own siblings or children.[256] There are no provisions for same-sex marriage in the Act. The minimum age of marriage is 18 years for the husband and 16 years for the wife.[257] In relation to the marriage of minors (under the age of 21 years for the husband and 19 years for the wife), the parents or guardians of the minors must give consent.[258] A District Court judge may grant an exception to this requirement if they think fit to do so.[259]

253 It is suggested that the family of the victim will accept *ifoga* quickly to avoid being perceived in a negative manner (eg unforgiving, un-Christian-like). The decision to accept the *ifoga* is made by the *matai* of the family – it is not clear whether the victim plays a role in this process; Leilani Tuala-Warren 'A Study into the Ifoga: Samoa's Answer to Dispute Healing' (Te Matahauariki Institute, 2002) 19.

254 Leilani Tuala-Warren 'A Study into the Ifoga: Samoa's Answer to Dispute Healing' (Te Matahauariki Institute, 2002) 19.

255 Young Offenders Act 2007, s 2.

256 Marriage Ordinance 1961, Sch 1.

257 Marriage Ordinance 1961, s 9.

258 Marriage Ordinance 1961, s 10(1).

259 Marriage Ordinance 1961, s 10(2).

4.2. SEPARATION, DIVORCE AND NULLITY

Termination of marriage is governed by the Divorce and Matrimonial Causes Ordinance 1961. The Ordinance gives the Supreme Court jurisdiction to deal with matters concerning divorce and other matrimonial matters.[260]

4.2.1. *Judicial Separation*

Under s 4 of the Ordinance, spouses are able to present a petition for judicial separation on the grounds that the marriage has broken down irretrievably.[261] If the Court is satisfied that the allegations contained in the petition are true, it may make a decree for judicial separation.[262] When a decree is made, the petitioner is no longer obliged to live with their spouse.[263] The Court also has the power to reverse the decree.[264]

4.2.2. *Divorce*

In order for the Court to grant a decree of divorce, it must be satisfied that:

(1) the marriage has broken down irretrievably;
(2) the parties have been separated and living separately for a continuous period of at least 12 months prior to submitting the application; and
(3) there is no reasonable likelihood of cohabitation being resumed by the parties.[265]

The Ordinance provides an exception to the separation requirement for instances when the Court is satisfied that a party to the marriage is the subject of domestic violence.[266] Furthermore, the law requires that the Court and legal practitioner representing the party must consider whether reconciliation is a possibility for the parties.[267] If the Court is satisfied that a reconciliation is possible, it is required that the parties undergo marriage counselling.[268]

---

[260] Divorce and Matrimonial Causes Ordinance 1961, s 3(1).
[261] Divorce and Matrimonial Causes Ordinance 1961, s 4.
[262] Divorce and Matrimonial Causes Ordinance 1961, s 5.
[263] Divorce and Matrimonial Causes Ordinance 1961, s 5.
[264] Divorce and Matrimonial Causes Ordinance 1961, s 6.
[265] Divorce and Matrimonial Causes Ordinance 1961, s 7.
[266] Divorce and Matrimonial Causes Ordinance 1961, s 7(3).
[267] Divorce and Matrimonial Causes Ordinance 1961, s 7E(1).
[268] Divorce and Matrimonial Causes Ordinance 1961, s 7E(2).

If there are children of the marriage, the Court must also be satisfied that:

(1) all of the children of the marriage are 18 years of age and over; or
(2) proper arrangements have been made for the care, welfare and development of children who have not reached 18 years of age. In the event that the Court is not satisfied that the proper arrangements have been made, a divorce order may still take effect, if the circumstances require it.

A divorce order can be rescinded, before it takes effect, if the parties reconcile.[269]

4.2.3. Nullity

Marriages are void, even if no decree for nullity has been granted, in the following circumstances:

(1) one of the parties to the marriage was already married;
(2) there was an absence of consent by one of the parties, whether by duress, mistake, insanity or otherwise;
(3) the marriage is within the prohibited degrees of relationship, and therefore void under s 7 of the Marriage Ordinance 1961; or
(4) the marriage was not solemnised.

Applications for the annulment of marriages can be presented to the Court if one of the parties to the marriage is domiciled in Samoa at the time of the filing of the petition or the marriage was celebrated in Samoa.[270] Marriages are considered voidable in the following circumstances:

(1) the marriage was not consummated due to incapacity or wilful refusal of the respondent;
(2) either party of the marriage, at the time of the marriage, was deemed a mentally defective person within the Mental Health Act 2007 but was capable of consenting to the marriage;
(3) the respondent, at the time of the marriage, suffered from a communicable venereal disease; or
(4) the respondent was, at the time of the marriage, pregnant with someone else's child.[271]

---

269 Divorce and Matrimonial Causes Ordinance 1961, s 7F.
270 Divorce and Matrimonial Causes Ordinance 1961, s 9.
271 Divorce and Matrimonial Causes Ordinance 1961, s 9(c).

4.2.4. *Maintenance and Alimony*

Following any proceedings for the decree of divorce or nullity, the Court may also make orders appropriate for the provision of alimony or maintenance.[272] It appears under the Ordinance that only males are required to pay alimony. The legislation specifies that orders are to be made to the husband or his personal representatives to pay the wife an amount deemed reasonable by the Court until her death.[273]

4.2.5. *Custody*

When determining matters relating to the custody or upbringing of a child, the Court must consider the welfare of the child to be of first and paramount importance.[274] Either parent of the child can make an application for the custody and upbringing of the child, as well as the right of access.[275] However, if the Court considers the parents of the child to be unfit, they will appoint another person as a guardian.[276]

4.3. ADOPTION

Adoptions in Samoa are governed by the Infants Ordinance 1961. This statute was based on the Adoption Act 1955 of New Zealand. There is no mention of local culture or the practice of customary adoptions, even though customary adoptions are more prevalent than State adoptions in Samoa.[277]

The law allows individuals and married couples to make applications for the adoption of infants. The law does not require the applicants or the infant to be domiciled in Samoa.[278] The Ordinance defines an infant as a person who is under the age of 21.[279] It is unlawful for a person to give, receive or promise any payments or rewards for the arrangement or proposal of an adoption, without the consent of the court.[280]

---

272 Divorce and Matrimonial Causes Ordinance 1961, s 22(1).

273 Divorce and Matrimonial Causes Ordinance 1961, s 22(2).

274 Infants Ordinance 1961, s 3.

275 Infants Ordinance 1961, s 4(1).

276 Infants Ordinance 1961, s 4(2).

277 Teleiai Lalotoa Mulitalo Seumanutafa and Jennifer Corrin 'Plural Procedures for Adoption and "Vae Tama" in Samoa' in Jennifer Corrin and Sue Farran (eds) *The Plural Practice of Adoption in Pacific Island States* (Springer, 2019) 87 at 99.

278 Infants Ordinance 1961, s 7.

279 Infants Ordinance 1961, s 2.

280 Infants Ordinance 1961, s 9.

There are several conditions of which the court must be satisfied before an adoption order is made:

- the infant must be under the age of 21;
- no payment was made or reward offered in relation to the adoption;
- the applicant must be of good repute, a fit and proper person to have care and custody of a child, and have sufficient ability to bring up, maintain and educate the infant;[281]
- the welfare and interests of the infant will be promoted by the adoption;[282]
- the infant, if over the age of 12 years, must consent to the adoption;[283] and
- the living parents of the infant (or their legal guardian, if both parents have died) must consent to the adoption.[284]

The Ordinance provides that the court has a discretion to forgo the consent of a person who is permanently absent from Samoa, incapable of giving consent, is unfit to have the custody or control of the infant, or who has deserted the infant.[285]

The law was amended to introduce additional safeguards for overseas adoptions, which are defined as applications for the adoption of an infant by non-citizens. The law specifies that if one of the applicants is a Samoan citizen, it is not considered to be an overseas adoption.[286] The Ordinance mandates that an overseas adoption order will not be made unless the court receives certification from the Attorney-General that:

> The infant does not have any suitable person or family in Samoa who is or are willing to provide for the care, support or welfare of the infant; and
>
> There are no other suitable arrangements available in Samoa for the care, support and welfare of the infant.[287]

When granted, the adoption order has a number of effects, namely that:

(1) the name of the adopting parent will be conferred on the infant with such proper or Christian name as the court may fix;[288]
(2) the infant is deemed to have been born in lawful wedlock of the adopting parents;[289]

---

281 Infants Ordinance 1961, s 8(a).
282 Infants Ordinance 1961, s 8(b).
283 Infants Ordinance 1961, s 8(c).
284 Infants Ordinance 1961, s 8(d).
285 Infants Ordinance 1961, s 8(d).
286 Infants Ordinance 1961, s 7A(5).
287 Infants Ordinance 1961, s 7A(2).
288 Infants Ordinance 1961, s 10(1).
289 Infants Ordinance 1961, s 10(1) and (2)(a)(ii).

(3) the infant is, for all purposes civil and criminal or otherwise, taken in law to be the child of the adopting parent;[290]
(4) all rights and legal responsibilities between the infant and his or her natural parents are terminated. The infant is entitled to take property as an heir or next-of-kin of his or her natural parents either directly or by representation.[291]

The adopted infant will not, by virtue of the adoption, be entitled to:

> Acquire any right, title or interest in any property on any issue of the adopting parent by virtue of any deed, will or instrument prior to the date of the adoption order unless it is expressly stated in the instrument;
>
> Take any property that is expressly limited to the heirs of the adopting parent nor property from the lineal or collateral kindred of such parent by right of representation; or
>
> Acquire any property vested in any issue of lawful wedlock of the adopting parent in the case of intestacy.[292]

The Ordinance provides that the court may vary or discharge an adoption order subject to terms and conditions as it thinks fit.[293] In the event that an adoption order is discharged, the infant and their natural parents are taken to be restored to the position inter se that existed immediately before the order of adoption was made.[294] However, the discharge of the adoption order does not affect anything lawfully done or the consequences of anything unlawfully done while the order of adoption was in force.[295]

4.4. CHILDREN

4.4.1. Ill-Treatment and Neglect

Under the Infants Ordinance 1961, it is an offence to wilfully ill-treat or neglect a child. A person who is found guilty of this is liable to a fine of up to five penalty units or a term of imprisonment of a maximum of one year.[296]

---

290 Infants Ordinance 1961, s 10(1) and (2)(a)(i).
291 Infants Ordinance 1961, s 2(b).
292 Infants Ordinance 1961, s 10.
293 Infants Ordinance 1961, s 11(1).
294 Infants Ordinance 1961, s 11(2).
295 Infants Ordinance 1961, s 11(2).
296 Under the Infants Ordinance 1961, s 12 and the Fines (Review and Amendment Act) 1998, s 4, a person may be fined $500 WST if they are found guilty of ill-treating or neglecting a child.

4.4.2. *Reasonable Punishment*

Parents, teachers and other persons having lawful control or charge of children are given the right to administer 'reasonable punishment' to children in their care.[297] Although Samoa abolished corporal punishment in schools, it reintroduced the use of reasonable force by teachers on students in 2019,[298] despite objections by both the Ombudsman's Office and Supreme Court Justice Vui Clarence Nelson.[299] The provision only allows the teacher to use reasonable force to prevent the child from harming themselves or others, engaging in criminal conduct or engaging in threatening, offensive or disruptive behaviour.[300] The Act is also clear that the use of any object by the teacher to impose force is not 'reasonable force'. Should an object be used, the teacher is liable to be charged for assault under the Crimes Act 2013.[301]

4.4.3. *International Obligations*

Samoa is a party to the United Nations Convention on the Rights of the Child, the Convention on the Elimination of all Forms of Discrimination against Women and the Convention on the Rights of Person with Disabilities, but not to the Hague Convention. Supreme Court Justice Vui Clarence Nelson became a member of the Committee on the Rights of the Child in 2015, with a term that will run until 2023. In March 2020, Samoa hosted the Extraordinary Convention on the Rights of the Child Committee Session, the first United Nations treaty body meeting to be held outside of Geneva.[302]

5. LAW OF OBLIGATIONS

5.1. TORTS

Courts in Samoa generally apply the principles of English common law and equity to determine claims in tort. Claims may be based on intentional or negligent conduct which results in loss or damage. The courts in Samoa have

---

297 Infants Ordinance 1961, s 14.

298 Education Amendment Act 2019.

299 Dateline Pacific 'Opposition to reinstating corporal punishment in Samoa' *Radio NZ* (online ed, 7 September 2018).

300 Education Amendment Act 2019, s 23(3)(a)–(c).

301 Education Amendment Act 2019, ss 3A and 3B.

302 Sapeer Mayron 'Convention summit a chance to improve children's rights' *Samoa Observer* (online ed, 1 March 2020).

considered and applied wide-ranging common law tort principles which relate to: trespass to person, land and chattels; negligence; defamation; vicarious liability; nuisance; deceit; misfeasance in public office; and intimidation. The remedies of damages and injunction may be ordered by the court if the tort action is successful.

There are a few statutory provisions which relate to tortious liability in Samoa. The Contributory Negligence Act 1964 allows the apportionment of liability where it is held that the partial defence of contributory negligence applies.[303] The Defamation Act 1993 outlines the parameters of the tort of defamation, the procedure to be followed in these cases and the defences to defamation claims.[304] Under the Fatal Accidents Act 1974, actions are available to the surviving dependents of a person whose death was caused by a wrongful or negligent act.[305] The Law Reform Act 1964 provides for proportionate liability, which allows tortfeasors to be held jointly liable for a matter and also claim damages from one another.[306] The Law Reform Act also abolished the defence of common employment.[307] Furthermore, the Accident Compensation Act 1989 provides that a person who is injured as a result of another's negligence may also pursue a civil claim against the tortfeasor, although the court will take into account any compensation received under the Accident Compensation Scheme.[308]

5.2. CONTRACTS

Contracts are governed by the principles of English common law. In some cases, there is also statutory regulation. For example, contracts relating to the sale of goods are subject to the provisions of the Sale of Goods Act 1975. The Frustrated Contracts Act 1975 provides remedies that are available when a contract becomes impossible to perform.[309]

5.3. RESTITUTION

The law of restitution is applicable to situations where a defendant has been unjustly enriched to the detriment of the plaintiff. Restitution is governed by

303 Contributory Negligence Act 1964, s 3.
304 Defamation Act 1993.
305 Fatal Accidents Act 1974, ss 3 and 4.
306 Law Reform Act 1964, s 8.
307 Law Reform Act 1964, s 9.
308 Accident Compensation Act 1989, s 65.
309 Frustration of Contracts Act 1975, s 3.

the principles of equity. The court may make an order for a claim of damages to indemnify the plaintiff: 'so far as money can do it, the injured person should be put in the same position as he or she would have been if he or she had not sustained the wrong'.[310]

6. PROPERTY

6.1. LAND

There are three types of land tenure in Samoa: customary, freehold and public. Freehold land is defined as land held 'for an estate in fee simple'[311] and accounts for about four per cent of the land in Samoa.[312] Freehold land is freely transferable.

Public land, which is defined as 'land that is free from customary title and from any estate in fee simple', accounts for about 12 per cent of the total land in Samoa.[313] The Constitution also provides that all land lying below the high-water mark is public land.[314] Public land may be leased to any foreign State or organisation by the Minister of Natural Resources under the Land for Foreign Purposes Act 1993.[315]

Customary land is defined in the Constitution as land that is held 'in accordance with Samoan custom and usage and with the law relating to Samoan custom and usage' and is a fundamental aspect of Samoan culture and identity.[316] The value of customary land cannot be equated with money. Customary land in Samoa accounts for 83 per cent of the total land in Samoa.[317] Authority over customary land is vested in *matai* titles associated with the land and held for the *aiga* rather than any individual.[318] The Constitution provides that customary land cannot be alienated in any way, unless permitted under an Act of Parliament.[319]

---

310 *Burke v Toluono* [2013] WSSC 9.

311 Constitution, art 101(3).

312 Jennifer Corrin 'Resolving Land Disputes in Samoa' in *Making Land Work* (Australian Agency for International Development, 2008) Vol 2, 199 at 203.

313 Constitution, art 101(4).

314 Constitution, art 103(1), as amended by s 5 of the Constitution Amendment Act 2020.

315 Land for Foreign Purposes Act 1993.

316 Constitution, art 101(3); Jennifer Corrin 'Resolving Land Disputes in Samoa' in *Making Land Work* (Australian Agency for International Development, 2008) Vol 2, 199 at 204.

317 Constitution, art 101(2).

318 Jennifer Corrin 'Resolving Land Disputes in Samoa' in *Making Land Work* (Australian Agency for International Development, 2008) Vol 2, 199 at 204.

319 Constitution, art 102.

The first exception to the prohibition of alienation of customary lands is found in the Taking of Lands Act 1964, which empowers the Government to compulsorily acquire customary land for public purposes. The definition of 'public purpose' in the Act covers a wide range of areas: public health, education, public recreation, burial of the dead, forestry, electricity, communication services, the control of coasts and rivers, protection of natural resources, and the provision of government infrastructures.[320] The Act further provides that where the Government has compulsorily acquired land, all persons with an interest in the land are entitled to full and just compensation by the Government. If the parties are unable to come to an agreement on compensation, a claim may be filed with the Supreme Court. This claim may be subject to an appeal. *Siva Afi Investment Limited and Siva Afi Designs Limited v Attorney-General* involved the compulsory acquisition of a piece of land which had been leased by the appellants for the conduct of their business. There, the Court of Appeal discussed the underlying principles to 'full and just compensation' and adopted the approach of the English Court of Appeal, which established three conditions that must be satisfied before an award for compensation is made:[321]

(1) there is a causal connection between the acquisition and the loss in question;
(2) the loss is not too remote; and
(3) the claimant must have taken reasonable steps to eliminate or reduce the loss suffered.

The Government is permitted by the Taking of Lands Act to sell or lease land that has been compulsorily acquired, but is deemed in excess.[322] Should customary land that had been acquired by the Government be sold, the title is then converted to freehold title. The Government has been criticised for failing to follow the proper procedure set out in the Taking of Lands Act 1964.[323]

320 Taking of Land Act 1964, s 2.

321 *Siva Afi Investment Limited and Siva Afi Designs Limited v The Attorney-General* [2012] WSCA 17.

322 Taking of Land Act 1964, ss 22, 23 and 23A.

323 Chris Grant 'Accessing land for public purposes in Samoa' in *Making Land Work* (Australian Agency for International Development, 2008) Vol 2, 265 at 266; Ruiping Ye *Torrens and Customary Land Tenure: A Case Study of the Land Titles Registration Act 2008 of Samoa* (2009) NZACL Yearbook 15 at 99.

The second exception to the prohibition of the alienation of customary lands is through lease or licence of customary land. Customary land can be registered and then leased, with the Government acting as trustee for the customary owners.[324]

In an effort to increase economic growth in Samoa, Parliament passed the controversial Land Titles Registration Act 2008, which establishes a register for the registration of customary land leases. The legality and constitutionality of the Land Titles Registration Act 2008 has been challenged by the Samoa Solidarity International Group, who has brought a $5 million tala lawsuit against the Government; the Group alleges that the Government was also in breach of the Constitution by failing to hold a referendum, as required by art 109 of the Constitution.[325]

In 2013, Parliament passed the Customary Land Advisory Commission Act. The purpose of the Commission is to 'encourage, facilitate and promote greater use of customary land for the purpose of enhancing the social, cultural, economic and commercial development of Samoa'. The Commission may make suggestions to Cabinet on measures to perform its functions, conduct public consultations on the law affecting customary land, and undertake a review of customary land laws and any other functions provided by the Act.[326]

The Supreme Court may determine whether land is customary, public or freehold land, in the event that title to the land is disputed.[327] This is illustrated in *Board of Trustees of the Congregational Church of Samoa v Pouvi*, which involved a dispute as to whether a particular piece of land was freehold or customary. The Court held that part of the land was freehold and the remainder customary.[328]

6.2. TANGIBLE PROPERTY AND INTANGIBLE PROPERTY

Personal property is generally governed by the principles of English common law.[329]

---

324 Alienation of Customary Land Act 1965, s 4.

325 The matter has yet to be decided. Lanuola Tusani Tupufia 'A-G moves to strike out $5 million lawsuit' *Samoa Observer* (online ed, 13 August 2019); Joyetter Feagaimaali'i-Luamanu 'P.M in $5 million lawsuit over land Act' *Samoa Observer* (online ed, 22 August 2018).

326 Customary Land Advisory Commission Act 2013, s 6.

327 Judicature Ordinance 1961, s 31; Land and Titles Court Bench Book (2003) at 26.

328 Land and Titles Court Bench Book (2003) at 15; *Board of Trustees of the Congregational Church of Samoa v Pouvi* [2003] WSSC 4.

329 Guy Powles 'Samoa' in Michael A Ntumy (ed) *South Pacific Legal Systems* (University of Hawaii Press, 1993) 395 at 424.

6.3. INTELLECTUAL PROPERTY

6.3.1. Protection of Intellectual Property Rights

Intellectual property is the term used to describe creations of the mind and the protection afforded to those ideas by law. All matters pertaining to intellectual property in Samoa are governed by the Intellectual Property Act 2011, with the exception of copyright matters, which are governed by the Copyright Act 1998. Types of intellectual property rights that are afforded by law are copyright, patents, trade marks, designs, plant breeders' rights, rights to geographical location, and layouts. The Registrar, who is the Chief Executive Officer of the Ministry of Commerce, Industry and Labour, is responsible for maintaining the Intellectual Property Registry.[330] The Act permits individuals to pursue a claim of relief should their intellectual property rights be infringed.[331]

6.3.2. International Law on Intellectual Property Rights

There are also international laws which apply to intellectual property of which Samoa is a signatory. As a member of the World Trade Organization, Samoa is a party to the Agreement on Trade-Related Aspects of Intellectual Property Rights (TRIPS) and to the Paris Convention, the Madrid Agreement and the Madrid Protocol. These international instruments are considered to be a minimum standard for the protection of intellectual property.

6.3.3. Protection of Traditional Knowledge

The intellectual property regime, both domestic and international, has been criticised for failing to adequately protect cultural and traditional knowledge. The systems implemented by the regime are considered to be Western and individualistic and to fail to account for the nature of traditional knowledge, which is generally owned by a community. The UN Declaration on the Rights of Indigenous Peoples recognises that 'indigenous peoples have the right to maintain, control, protect and develop their intellectual property over [their] … cultural heritage, traditional knowledge, and traditional cultural expressions'.[332] Samoa abstained from voting on this Declaration.

In 2015, the Samoa Law Reform Commission published a report on the protection of traditional knowledge, recommending that new legislation be

330 Intellectual Property Law Act 2011, ss 2 and 118.
331 Intellectual Property Law Act 2011, s 125.
332 United Nations Declaration on the Rights of Indigenous Peoples, art 31(1).

passed to protect traditional knowledge from misuse and misappropriation and that a substantive reform to existing laws be undertaken.[333] However, as at June 2021, no legislation regarding the protection of traditional knowledge has been passed.

7. COMMERCIAL LAW

7.1. COMPANY LAW

The Companies Act 2001 governs private and public companies in Samoa. The incorporation of private and public companies in Samoa occurs after an application is made and accepted by the Registrar. Applications for the incorporation of a company must include the company's name, type, rules, and residential and postal address, as well as the full names and addresses of the directors and/or shareholders.[334] Once the application for incorporation is approved, the company name is entered into the Companies Registry and the company must be issued a certificate of incorporation.[335] Further included in Part 2 of the Act is the procedure for the changing of company names, rules and registered addresses.

The Act also outlines procedures relating to shares and the rights of shareholders with regard to the ownership of shares and the payment of dividends. The Act classifies shares as personal property, which can be disposed of by way of sale or transfer.

The Act further provides for the powers, duties and liabilities of the director or directors of a company, who are responsible for the management, direction and supervision of a company.[336] Directors are obligated to act in good faith and in the best interest of the company and in compliance with the Companies Act and the rules of the company.[337] Directors are also expected to act with reasonable care, diligence and skill when performing their directorial duties.[338]

The Act also makes provision for the procedure to be followed when dealing with insolvent companies, the removal of companies from the Register and the re-instatement of companies to the Register.

333 Samoa Law Reform Commission *Protection of Samoa's Traditional Knowledge: Final Report* (2015).
334 Companies Act 2001, s 6.
335 Companies Act 2001, s 7.
336 Companies Act 2001, s 64.
337 Companies Act 2001, s 65.
338 Companies Act 2001, s 70.

7.2. PARTNERSHIPS

Partnerships are governed by the Partnership Act 1975. The Act defines a 'partnership' as a relationship between 'persons carrying on a business in common with a view to profit'.[339] The Act essentially provides rules for the relationship between partners, their relationship with people who deal with them and the dissolution of partnerships and the consequences thereof.

7.3. SECURITIES

The Securities Act 2006 governs all transactions involving securities. The Act defines 'securities' as 'an interest or right to participate in any capital, assets, earnings, royalties, or other property of a person'.[340] A security can be an equity security, a debt security, an interest in a superannuation scheme, a life insurance policy, an interest that is declared by regulations to be a security, and a renewal or variation of the terms or conditions of an interest of right.[341] The Act places restrictions on offering securities to the public as it prohibits misleading or deceptive conduct in relation to information memorandums, advertisements or an offer of securities.[342] In the event of non-compliance with the prohibition of misleading or deceptive conduct, the court may make an order: declaring the contract void, varying the contract, or requiring the person guilty of misconduct to provide a refund or return property or to pay damages for the losses suffered as a result of their misconduct.[343] The Act also empowers the Head of State to create regulations pertaining to securities. To date, there have been no such regulations.

In addition to the Securities Act 2006, there is the Personal Property Securities Act 2013, which commenced on 27 February 2017. The Personal Property Securities Act 2013 created a security interest in movable property, prioritised competing interest in movable property, created a Registry for the filing of personal property securities, provided the procedure for the simplified and expedited enforcement against collateral in the event of a debtor's default, and repealed the Chattel Transfer Act 1975.[344]

---

339 Partnership Act 1975, s 4.
340 Securities Act 2006, s 5(a).
341 Securities Act 2006, s 5(b).
342 Securities Act 2006, ss 14–16.
343 Securities Act 2006, s 18(2).
344 Personal Property Securities Act 2013.

7.4. INSOLVENCY

The law relating to insolvency is the Bankruptcy Act 1908. The Supreme Court has jurisdiction to hear bankruptcy matters and is empowered by the Act to decide all questions of law and fact relating to bankruptcy matters, make orders or decrees in relation to the property of the debtor, punish those in contravention of the Act, and exercise other powers given to it by the Act.[345]

The Act outlines acts of bankruptcy, provides for the procedure for adjudicating bankruptcy matters, establishes the duties of the bankrupt person, and outlines the effect of bankruptcy and the administration of the bankrupt's property.

7.5. CARRIAGE BY AIR AND SEA

The Carriage by Air Act 1964 governs carriage by air. The Act gives effect to the Warsaw Convention as amended in 1955. The Convention is therefore enforceable by law. The Convention provides a number of documentation requirements and duties in relation to carriage of persons, baggage and cargo. The liability of the carrier and available avenues of redress are also provided by the Act. In relation to liability, the Act specifies that the relevant provisions of the Fatal Accidents Act 1974 and the Contributory Negligence Act 1964 apply.

In 1975, the Parliament of Samoa passed the Carriers Act 1975, which amended the law relating to the liability of carriers. Carriers are defined in the Act as 'any common carrier of passengers or goods by land, sea or water'.[346] The Act provides for the liability of carriers in relation to negligence causing death, personal injury and loss or damage to goods. However, the Act limits the liability of carriers for goods, unless the value of the goods was declared and a charge paid.[347]

7.6. BANKING

The Central Bank of Samoa is the primary advisor to the Government in relation to the supply and stability of money and the supervision of financial institutions in Samoa.[348] The Central Bank of Samoa is established and

345 Bankruptcy Act 1908, ss 3 and 9.
346 Carriers Act 1975, s 2.
347 Carriers Act 1975, s 6.
348 Guy Powles 'Samoa' in Michael A Ntumy (ed) *South Pacific Legal Systems* (University of Hawaii Press, 1993) 395 at 412.

governed by the Central Bank of Samoa Act 2015. The Act sets out the structure, objectives, functions and administration of the Bank and empowers the Bank to deal with currency, foreign exchange and financial stability matters.

8. ENVIRONMENTAL LAW INCLUDING RESPONSES TO CLIMATE CHANGE

Both the Ministry of Natural Resources and Environment and the Ministry of Agriculture and Fisheries are responsible for the protection and conservation of the environment. Samoa has an extensive legislative framework of environmental law, consisting of several pieces of legislation.

The Land Surveys and Environment Act 1989 is the legislation which provides the national guidelines for conservation and the environment. The Act empowers the Ministry to also create subsidiary legislation such as the Ozone Layer Protection Regulations 2006 and the Plastic Bag Prohibition Importation Regulations 2006.[349]

8.1. NATURAL RESOURCE MANAGEMENT

In comparison to other South Pacific island countries, Samoa does not have a large amount of natural resources to exploit. There are few minerals to exploit, either on land or in the sea. Samoa's exclusive economic zone is also one of the smallest in the Pacific, which in turn limits the fisheries resources.[350] There are several pieces of legislation which relate to natural resource management: the Agriculture and Fisheries Ordinance 1959, the Forestry Management Act 2011, the National Parks and Reserves Act 1974, the Water Resources Management Act 2014, and the Fisheries Management Act 2016.

8.2. PLANNING AND URBAN MANAGEMENT

The Planning and Urban Management Act 2004 governs planning and urban development. The Act establishes and empowers the Planning and Urban Management Agency to ensure that the use, development and management of land is done sustainably and that an appropriate urban structure is developed.[351]

---

349 SPREP and EDO NSW 'Review of Natural Resource and Environment Related Legislation – Samoa' (January 2018) 8.

350 As defined in the Maritime Zones Act 1999.

351 Planning and Urban Management Act 2004, s 8.

Proposals for any development on land are subject to approval by the Planning and Urban Management Agency.[352] In making its decision, the Planning and Urban Agency may take into consideration a variety of factors, ranging from potential environmental, social and economic effects, to the likely effects on culture, to the sustainability of the development, to the adequacy of arrangements for access, waste and sanitation, to safety measures and the public interest in the development.[353] Decisions of the Planning and Urban Management Agency are subject to an appeal to the Planning Tribunal. Such appeal must be made within 28 days of the Agency's decision.[354]

The Act also provides that a person may seek financial redress from the Government if they suffer a loss as a consequence of the decisions of the Agency.[355]

8.3. WASTE MANAGEMENT AND POLLUTION

The Waste Management Act 2010 governs all matters relating to the collection, disposal and management of solid waste in Samoa, both on land and on the sea. The Act empowers the Ministry of Natural Resources and Environment to formulate policy, make arrangements, manage and regulate the disposal of waste. The Chief Executive Officer of the Ministry can serve notice on a person who fails to meet the waste requirements established in the Act. The Act makes it an offence to fail to comply with a served notice.[356]

The Marine Pollution Prevention Act 2008 provides measures for the prevention of and responses to marine pollution caused by vessels. The Act also deals with matters relating to international marine pollution conventions.

8.4. CLIMATE CHANGE

Samoa does not have any domestic legislation that specifically relates to climate change. However, Samoa is a strong advocate for climate action on the international stage and has implemented sustainable policies within Government. Research conducted shows a need to better involve the communities in the resilience development process.[357] Samoa became a party to the United Nations

352 Planning and Urban Management Act 2004, s 37.
353 Planning and Urban Management Act 2004, s 46.
354 Planning and Urban Management Act 2004, s 54.
355 Planning and Urban Management Act 2004, s 64(1).
356 Waste Management Act 2010, s 17.
357 Science Daily 'Samoa climate change resilience challenges Western perceptions' (online ed, 22 November 2019).

Framework Convention on Climate Change on 29 November 1994, the Kyoto Protocol to the United Nations Framework Convention on Climate Change on 27 November 2000, and the Paris Agreement on 22 April 2016. In October 2017, the Government of Samoa and the United Nations Development Programme (UNDP) announced the Improving the Performance and Reliability of Renewable Energy Power System in Samoa (IMPRESS) project, in an effort to make the entire country reliant on renewable energy for electricity generation by 2025.[358] The IMPRESS project recognised the prioritisation of sustainable and renewable energy by the Government of Samoa and was funded by the Government and the Global Environment Facility (GEF).

9. INTERNATIONAL LAW AND TREATIES

9.1. ENFORCEABILITY OF INTERNATIONAL LAW

Samoa is a dualist State, which means that any international instruments that Samoa has signed are not enforceable domestically until enacted in domestic legislation. There is no mention of international law in the Constitution of Samoa.

9.2. HUMAN RIGHTS

Samoa has acceded to and ratified a number of international human rights treaties, such as the Universal Declaration of Human Rights (UNDHR),[359] the Convention on the Elimination of all Forms of Discrimination against Women (CEDAW),[360] the Convention on the Rights of a Child and its Optional Protocols relating to the involvement of children in armed conflict and child prostitution and pornography (CRC),[361] the International Convention on Civil and Political Rights (ICCPR),[362] the Convention for the Protection of All Persons from

---

358 UNDP 'Samoa is ready to IMPRESS with launch of large-scale renewable energy project' (online ed, 31 October 2017).

359 United Nations Universal Declaration on Human Rights (10 December 1948) UN Doc GA/Res/217A (III).

360 United Nations Convention on the Elimination of all Forms of Discrimination against Women (18 December 1979) 1249 UNTS 13 (opened for signature 18 December 1979, entered into force 25 September 1992).

361 United Nations Convention on the Rights of the Child 1577 UNTS 3 (signed on 30 September 1990, entered into force 29 November 1994).

362 United Nations International Covenant on Civil and Political Rights 999 UNTS 171 (opened for signature 16 December 1966, entered into force on 15 February 2008).

Enforced Disappearance (CED),[363] the Convention on the Rights of Persons with Disabilities (CRPD),[364] and the Convention against Torture and Other Cruel or Degrading Treatment or Punishment (CAT).[365]

Samoa also has a national human rights institution (NHRI), which is the Office of the Ombudsman. The NHRI has produced State of Human Rights Reports, which cover women's rights, domestic violence, disability, climate change and other pressing human rights issues.[366] In 2016, the NHRI was awarded an 'A' status by the Global Alliance of National Human Rights Institutions (GANHRI), making Samoa the first NHRI in the Pacific to achieve that status.[367]

The Samoan courts have also used conventions that Samoa was not a party to as guidance when deciding on matters not provided for in domestic laws. *Wagner v Radke* was a case regarding an international kidnapping involving German nationals and their child.[368] After failing to be granted custody of his eight-year-old child, the father kidnapped the child and took him to Samoa, along with his new wife. When the mother of the child found out about this, she made an application to the Supreme Court of Samoa requesting that the child be returned to her. In this case, the Court held that the principles of the Hague Convention were applicable as international customary law, because it contained widely accepted principles regarding child abduction. It was inconsequential that Samoa was not a party to the Convention.

9.3. TRADE

Samoa is a member of the World Trade Organization and is party to a number of regional trade agreements. Samoa is a party to the Pacific Island Countries Trade Agreement (PICTA) and a signatory to the South Pacific Regional Trade and Economic Cooperation Agreement (SPARTECA), the Pacific Agreement on Closer Economic Relations (PACER) and the PACER Plus Agreement. In 2018, Samoa acceded to the multilateral ACP-EU Partnership Agreement between African, Caribbean and Pacific countries and the European Union.[369]

---

363 United Nations Convention for the Protection of All Persons from Enforced Disappearance 2716 UNTS 3 (signed on 6 February 2007, entered into force 27 November 2012).

364 United Nations Convention on the Rights of Persons with Disabilities A/RES/61/106 (signed on 24 September 2014, entered into force 2 December 2016).

365 United Nations Convention against Torture and Other Cruel or Degrading Treatment or Punishment 1465 UNTS 85 (opened for signature 10 December 1984, entered into force 28 March 2019).

366 All Samoa NHRI Reports are available on the official website of the Office of the Ombudsman, <https://ombudsman.gov.ws/state-of-human-rights-reports/>.

367 Government of Samoa 'Samoa's Second Voluntary National Review of the implementation of the Sustainable Development Goals Report' (2020) 71.

368 *Wagner v Radke* [1997] WSSC 6.

369 ACP-EU Partnership Agreement.

Exports from Samoa, like most Pacific island countries, consist mainly of agricultural and fisheries products. Samoa's export destinations are New Zealand, Australia, American Samoa, the Cook Islands, Japan, Tokelau, Malaysia, Singapore, Philippines, the United Kingdom and the United States. A major criticism of the Pacific trade agreements, particularly PACER Plus, is the fact that the Pacific island nations are not benefiting as much from the agreements as their developed nation partners Australia and New Zealand.[370] This criticism led to other countries, such as Fiji, Papua New Guinea and Tonga, refusing to sign the agreement.

10. CRIMINAL LAW

The Crimes Act 2013 repealed the Crimes Ordinance 1961. The Act sets out the acts or omissions which constitute criminal offences in Samoa. The Act specifies the elements of each offence and the punishment for which an offender is liable, and other matters relating to criminal liability in Samoa. In Samoa, the Prosecutions Division of the Attorney-General's Office is generally responsible for prosecuting individuals accused of committing an offence, although private prosecutions are also permitted. In criminal proceedings, the prosecution bears the burden of proving beyond reasonable doubt that the elements of the offence as established by the Act have been satisfied. Failure to do so will result in a 'not guilty' verdict.

The Crimes Act outlines a number of defences to criminal charges, namely infancy, insanity, compulsion, self-defence and defence of property.[371] However, the Crimes Act also stipulates that ignorance of the law and consent to death by the victim are not valid excuses.[372] The Act stipulates that persons who are permitted to use force will attract criminal liability if the force used is deemed to have been excessive.[373] The Crimes Act also outlines a number of legal justifications and excuses in relation to arrest.[374]

370 Jane Kelsey *A People's Guide to PACER: The Implications for the Pacific Islands of the Pacific Agreement on Closer Economic Relations (PACER) Final Report* (Pacific Network on Globalisation, 2004); Matthew Dornan 'PACER Plus is not much to celebrate' *East Asia Forum* (online ed, 2 June 2017); Radio New Zealand 'Pacific trade deal signatories to take heavy losses' (online ed, 24 October 2018); Grant Wyeth 'PACER Plus, Minus Tonga' *The Diplomat* (online ed, 30 March 2018).

371 Crimes Act 2013, ss 12–14 and 17–20.

372 Crimes Act 2013, ss 15 and 16.

373 Crimes Act 2013, s 21.

374 Crimes Act 2013, Part 4.

11. CIVIL SOCIETY ORGANISATIONS

There is currently no legal framework in place in Samoa for civil society engagement. Non-government organisations (NGOs) and civil society organisations (CSOs) fall under the Samoa Umbrella for Non-Governmental Organisations (SUNGO), which was established in 1997 with a vision of a Samoa that 'has a competent and confident civil society sector that promotes sustainable development and quality of life for the people of Samoa'.[375] NGOs and CSOs may apply to be a part of SUNGO. In addition, the Civil Society Support Program (CSSP) was set up in March 2010, funded by the Australian and Samoan governments. The CSSP provides grants for NGO or CSO projects that align with the CSSP's objectives and the national development strategies of Samoa.[376]

Religion is an important aspect of Samoan society. In 1966, the National Council of Churches of Samoa was established. Although Samoa is a predominantly Christian nation, there is a small number of individuals who practise the Baha'i and Muslim faiths. The Samoa Bureau of Statistics reported in 2011 that about 97 per cent of the population identified as Christian: 31 per cent belonged to the Congregational Christian Church, 19.4 per cent to the Roman Catholic Church, 15.1 per cent to the Latter Day Saints, 13.7 per cent to the Methodist Church; eight per cent to the Assemblies of God, and 3.9 per cent to the Seventh Day Adventists.[377]

12. COMMENTARY

Like many Pacific island countries, there is room for improvement to the legal system of Samoa. Samoa has been criticised in the past for its 'one-party politics' due to the lack of opposition.[378] Further criticisms of the Samoan legal system include passing laws rapidly, failing to hold public consultations when introducing or reforming laws and failing to uphold the doctrine of the separation of powers.[379] These criticisms cast an unfavourable light on Samoa's reputation as a free and democratic nation.

---

375 SUNGO 'Vision and Mission' (n.d.) <www.samoa.sungo.ws>.

376 Government of Samoa's Strategy for Development 2016–2020 and the Ministry of Women, Community and Social Development Community Development Plan 2016–2021.

377 Samoa Bureau of Statistics 'Population and Housing Census: Vol 2' (2011).

378 Afamasaga Toleafoa 'One Party State: The Samoan Experience' in David Hegarty and Darrell Tryon (eds) *Politics, Development and Security in Oceania* (ANU Press, 2013) 69 at 70.

379 See Beatrice Tabangcora 'Ua se vaa tu matagi: the revival of criminal libel in Samoa' (2018) 24 CLJP 39.

Nevertheless, as the first Pacific island country to achieve independence from colonial rule, Samoa has made tremendous progress in cultivating its unique legal system. Samoa has been commended for its robust judiciary, constitutional stability and its sensitive and cautious approach to the harmonisation of its customs and its legal system.[380] It is one of the few Pacific island countries to have replaced almost all introduced law with local laws and has a judiciary that is primarily composed of persons of Samoan descent. Samoa shares the same issues of legal pluralism as other Pacific island nations and has made efforts to ensure that Samoan custom and traditions continue to play a meaningful role in its post-colonial society.

BIBLIOGRAPHY

Corrin, Jennifer 'Resolving Land Disputes in Samoa' in *Making Land Work* (Vol 2, Australian Agency for International Development, 2008).

Grant, Chris 'Accessing land for public purposes in Samoa' in *Making Land Work* (Vol 2, Australian Agency for International Development, 2008).

Pacific Islands Legal Information Institute *Samoa Primary Materials* <http://www.paclii.org/countries/ws.html>.

Powles, Guy 'Samoa' in Michael A Ntumy (ed) *South Pacific Legal Systems* (University of Hawaii Press, 1993).

Trustee Agreement for the mandated Territory of Western Samoa, Submitted by the Government of New Zealand to the General Assembly, First Session, Second Part, as Revised by the Assembly, Document A/160/Rev. 2, 12 December 1946.

380 Jennifer Corrin 'Resolving Land Disputes in Samoa' in *Making Land Work* (Australian Agency for International Development, 2008) Vol 2, 199 at 217; Tony Angelo 'Steady as she goes: The Constitution and the Court of Appeal of Samoa' *New Zealand Association of Comparative Law Yearbook 18*, 427.

SOLOMON ISLANDS

Jamie MOLEA and Joel FANGALASUU

1. CONTEXT

Solomon Islands is an independent state and a member of the Commonwealth. It comprises six large islands and over 900 smaller ones, covering a land area of 28,370 square kilometres. The exclusive economic zone is 1,589,477 square kilometres. The country's capital is Honiara, located on the island of Guadalcanal. Solomon Islands had an estimated population of 670,000 as at 2019.[1] It has a significantly homogenous population, with more than 95 per cent Melanesian, three per cent Polynesian and one per cent Micronesian, with additional Chinese- and European-descent minorities.[2] English is the official language of the country, with 69 per cent of the population aged five and over having basic proficiency. Solomon Islands Pidgin is the most common language and is widely used as the lingua franca. There is no vernacular common to the whole country; about 87 different languages are in use.

The dominant religion of Solomon Islands is Christianity, and the church is a central part of most villages. The Church of Melanesia is the largest denomination, with 32 per cent of the population as members, followed by the Roman Catholic Church, with 20 per cent of the population. Persons with no religion comprise less than one per cent of the population (2009 census).

Solomon Islands' primary earnings come from the export of copra, timber, fish products, palm products, cocoa and gold; its major trade partners are Australia, New Zealand, China and the European Union. The collapse of Asia's timber market in 1998 adversely affected Solomon Islands, with a 10 per cent decrease in the country's GDP that year.[3] Economic activity was further disrupted the following year by civil conflict on Guadalcanal. In 2017, Solomon Islands' GDP per capita was US$2,200.

Solomon Islands was established as a British Protectorate in 1893.[4] The first resident administrator was sent by Britain in 1896 and was based in Tulagi. He was answerable to the Colonial Office through the Western Pacific High

1 World Population Prospects 2019: Data booklet <https://population.un.org/wpp/Publications/Files/WPP2019_DataBooklet.pdf> 20.

2 Solomon Islands Population & Housing Census 2009, National Report, Vol 2 at 83 <https://www.statistics.gov.sb/statistics/demographic-statistics/census>.

3 1999 Annual Report – Central Bank of Solomon Islands <http://www.cbsi.com.sb/wp-content/uploads/2016/09/AR-1999.pdf> 12.

4 Pacific Order in Council 1893 SO&I 1893/78, art 6.

Commission, which was based in Fiji. The High Commissioner had extensive powers to make orders for the Western Pacific.[5] British administration of the British Solomon Islands Protectorate was continued after World War II, but headquarters were moved to Honiara, using infrastructure installed by the Americans during the war.

After World War II, all administrative and law-making powers remained with the High Commissioner. Provisions were made for the first Legislative Council in 1964.[6] The Legislative Council consisted of the High Commissioner (who was President), three ex officio members, eight official members, eight elected members and two nominated members.[7] These provisions provided for elected members from each of the five main districts of the Solomons, including the capital Honiara. Notwithstanding the existence of the Legislative Council, extensive powers remained with the High Commissioner. The 1964 Order provided that the High Commissioner could execute all powers under the Order at his or her discretion and that no action could be enquired into by any court.[8]

Discussions on self-governance with a view to independence began in 1967.[9] In 1970, an Order was put in place which established a Governing Council. The 1970 Order increased the number of elected members from eight to 17 members.[10] The Protectorate was divided into 17 constituencies under the Order, with each of the Governing Council's elected members representing a constituency.[11] Solomon Islands was granted self-governance in 1976 and achieved independence on 7 July 1978.[12]

2. SOURCES OF LAW

The Solomon Islands Independence Order 1978[13] provided for the adoption of the Solomon Islands Constitution, which is a Schedule to the Solomon Islands Independence Order 1978 (UK).

Section 75 of the Constitution authorises the Solomon Islands Parliament to make provision for the application of laws, including customary laws.

---

5 Article 7(4).

6 British Solomon Islands Order 1964 SO&I 1964/1572.

7 British Solomon Islands Order 1964 SO&I 1964/1572, s 19.

8 British Solomon Islands Order 1964 SO&I 1964/1572, s 4.

9 John Nonggorr 'Solomon Islands' in Michael A Ntumy (ed) *South Pacific Islands Legal Systems* (University of Hawaii Press, 1993) 269 at 269.

10 British Solomon Islands Order 1970 SO&I 1970/482, s 7.

11 Section 10.

12 Solomon Islands Independence Order 1978, SO&I 1978/783. Note also Solomon Islands Act 1978 (UK).

13 Solomon Islands Independence Order 1978, SO&I 1978/783. Note also Solomon Islands Act 1978 (UK).

In doing so, the customs and values of Solomon Islanders have to be given particular regard.[14] Schedule 3 of the Constitution makes interim[15] provision for the application of laws, subject to the Constitution and any Acts of Parliament. It continues in force Acts of Parliament of the United Kingdom of general application in force on 1 January 1961.[16] It also provides for and recognises the application of customary law, and the principles and the rules of common law and equity. In theory, customary law is superior to common law and equity.

3. CONSTITUTIONAL LAW

The Constitution's supremacy is provided for in s 2. This declares that the Constitution 'is the supreme law of Solomon Islands and if any other law is inconsistent with this Constitution, that other law shall, to the extent of inconsistency, be void'.

The Constitution can be amended only through a special majority in Parliament.[17] Generally, an amendment to constitutional provisions requires a two-thirds' majority. However, there are specific provisions which require a three-quarters' majority for amendment, for example the provisions on fundamental rights and freedoms, the legislature, the legal system, the office of the Ombudsman, the office of the Auditor-General, and an amendment to the provisions that require three-quarters' majority.

3.1. LEGISLATURE

The national legislature is provided for in the Constitution under Chapter VI. It consists of a single chamber and is known as the National Parliament of Solomon Islands. Parliament is made up of representatives of 50 constituencies, each constituency being represented by a single member.[18] To be eligible for election to Parliament, a person must be a citizen of Solomon Islands and be at least 21 years of age. There are certain factors that disqualify a person: allegiance to a foreign state, holding a public office, having been declared bankrupt, being of unsound mind, having a criminal conviction, being disqualified

14 Constitution of Solomon Islands 1978, s 75(2).

15 Customs Recognition Act 2000 was enacted to deal with some of these matters but has not been brought into force.

16 Constitution of Solomon Islands 1978, Sch 3, para 1.

17 Constitution of Solomon Islands 1978, s 61(3).

18 Constitution of Solomon Islands 1978, s 46.

from membership of Parliament or from registration as an elector or voting at elections, or holding any office function which involves responsibilities connected with the elections to Parliament.[19]

Members may lose their seats in numerous ways. These include dissolution of Parliament, resignation, being elected Speaker or appointed Governor-General, absence from two consecutive meetings without obtaining consent, or where a condition for disqualification exists.[20]

Parliament has the power to 'make laws for the peace, order and good government of the Solomon Islands'.[21] Theoretically, any Bill or amendments to a Bill can be brought forward by a Member. A Bill which provides for imposing or increasing tax or increases to the Consolidated Fund or other funds cannot be introduced except with the approval of Cabinet.[22] A Bill becomes law when it has been passed by Parliament and assented to by the Governor-General.[23] A Bill does not come into operation until it has been published in the *Gazette*, although Parliament has the power to postpone the coming into operation of some laws.[24] Courts have however held that Parliament cannot undermine or alter the separation of powers of the three branches of government.[25] This means for example that Parliament cannot enact legislation which would undermine the judiciary.

Parliamentary proceedings are overseen by a Speaker and Deputy Speaker, who are elected by Members of Parliament. The rules of procedure in Parliament are found in its Standing Orders.[26] Where matters arise which are not provided for in the Standing Orders, the usage and practice of the Commons House of Parliament of Britain are followed.[27] Courts have held that the Speaker has jurisdiction to determine issues which raise points of order that may also have bearing on certain constitutional provisions, and that such a declaration does infringe the courts' power to interpret constitutional law.[28] It has also been held

---

19 Constitution of Solomon Islands 1978, ss 48–49.

20 Constitution of Solomon Islands 1978, s 50.

21 Constitution of Solomon Islands 1978, s 59.

22 Constitution of Solomon Islands 1978, s 60.

23 Constitution of Solomon Islands 1978, s 59(2).

24 Constitution of Solomon Islands 1978, s 59(3).

25 *Kenilorea v Attorney-General* [1984] SILR 179. In this case, Parliament had retrospectively sought to validate provisions of an Act that had not been brought into force. The provisions sought to be validated were the subject of a claim before the courts. The Court of Appeal stated the Constitution makes a clear separation of powers between legislature, the executive and the judiciary, and judicial power cannot be usurped by the legislature or executive.

26 Standing Orders of the National Parliament of Solomon Islands <http://www.paclii.org/sb/other/parliamentstandingorders.pdf>.

27 Standing Orders of the National Parliament of Solomon Islands, r 82.

28 *Speaker v Philip* [1991] SBCA 1.

that the constitutional powers of the Speaker during parliamentary proceedings are not subject to judicial review.[29]

3.2. JUDICIARY

3.2.1. Court of Appeal and High Court

The High Court and Court of Appeal are established by the Constitution. The High Court has unlimited original jurisdiction to hear and determine any civil or criminal proceeding.[30] This jurisdiction also extends to appeals from subordinate courts.[31] The High Court also has original jurisdiction to hear issues of constitutional interpretation and make declarations accordingly.[32] If matters of constitutional interpretation are brought up in subordinate courts, they are referred to the High Court.[33]

The Chief Justice and puisne judges of the High Court are appointed by the Governor-General on advice from the Judicial and Legal Service Commission.[34] If the office of the Chief Justice is vacant, then the Governor-General may appoint a puisne judge to the office. Generally, judges of the High Court may hold office until they are 60 years of age, with the exception of foreign judges, whose tenure depends on their contract.[35]

The Court of Appeal has jurisdiction to hear and determine civil and criminal appeals as of right from decisions of the High Court sitting at first instance and on questions of law arising from the High Court's exercise of appellate jurisdiction. In other cases, leave is required. In some cases, an appeal is not allowed, including decisions of the High Court that are provided by statute to be final.[36] The judges that make up the Court of Appeal include the President of the Court Appeal and the Justices of Appeal, the Chief Justice and puisne judges of the High Court are judges of the Court of Appeal ex officio.[37]

The President of the Court of Appeal and the Justices of the Court of Appeal are appointed by the Governor-General according to the advice of the Judicial

---

29 *Wale v Governor-General* [2019] SBHC 43; Jamie Molea '*Wale v Governor-General*: The Bounds of Judicial Review in Solomon Islands' (2019) Comparative Law Journal of the Pacific, Hors Serie Vol XXIV: Small Countries: A Collection of Essays, 127.
30 Constitution of Solomon Islands 1978, s 77.
31 Section 84.
32 Section 82.
33 Section 84(2).
34 Section 78.
35 Section 80(2).
36 See further, Jennifer Corrin *Courts and Civil Procedure in the South Pacific* (2nd ed, Intersentia, 2016) 27–28 and 43.
37 Constitution of Solomon Islands 1978, s 85.

and Legal Service Commission.[38] If the office of the President of the Court of Appeal is vacant, then the Governor-General may appoint another qualified judge to act as President of the Court of Appeal.[39]

Judges cease to preside when their term expires or through resignation. They may also be removed for inability to discharge the functions of their office. The Governor-General may remove a judge on advice from a tribunal appointed to investigate the ability of a judge to perform his or her functions or for misbehaviour.[40]

3.2.2. Subordinate Courts

There are three different subordinate courts: the Magistrates' Courts, the Customary Land Appeal Courts and the Local Courts.

The Magistrates' Courts have jurisdiction in civil and criminal matters within the area in which they are established. Magistrates' Courts are known respectively as Principal Magistrates' Courts and Magistrates' Courts of the First Class or of the Second Class. A Principal Magistrates' Court exercises jurisdiction throughout the country. Every other Magistrates' Court exercises jurisdiction within the limits of the district it is situated in.[41]

The Chief Justice establishes Magistrates' Courts and decides on the jurisdiction to be exercised by a magistrate. The Chief Justice may also assign individual magistrates extraterritorial jurisdiction to a particular district or districts and may transfer magistrates from one district to another.[42]

The Magistrates' Courts' civil jurisdiction includes all personal claims where the value of the claim does not exceed SI$20,000, or if in the Principal Magistrates' Court, SI$50,000. If it is a claim for rent between landlord and tenant or for land or other property, the value must not exceed SI$5,000, or SI$20,000 in the Principal Magistrates' Court.[43] A magistrate can commit to imprisonment of up to six weeks persons who default in payment of judgment debts if they have the means to pay the debt.[44]

The criminal jurisdiction for a Principal Magistrates' Court covers offences where the maximum punishment for the offence does not exceed 14 years' imprisonment or a fine or both. But the maximum punishment a Principal Magistrate's Court may impose is a prison term not exceeding five years or fine of SI$1,000.[45] The jurisdiction for Magistrates' Courts of the First or Second Class

38 Section 86(1).
39 Section 86(5).
40 Section 87(3)–(6).
41 Magistrates' Courts Act (Cap 20), ss 3 and 4.
42 Section 8.
43 Magistrates' Court (Amendment) Act 2007.
44 Magistrates' Courts Act, s 19.
45 Magistrates' Courts Act, s 27.

covers offences which have a maximum penalty of one year's imprisonment or fine of SI$200.

The Local Courts are established by the Chief Justice and are governed by the law or customs of people in the area in which the court has jurisdiction. The Local Courts Act empowers the Chief Justice to confer jurisdiction upon any local court to determine any criminal or civil matter.[46] The courts also have jurisdiction to hear customary issues, including land disputes.[47] However, local courts must be satisfied that the matter has already been referred to local chiefs and all traditional forms of dispute resolution have been exhausted before they can accept jurisdiction.[48] In 2020, the Solomon Islands Parliament began assessing a Bill which establishes a 'tribal lands panel' aimed at resolving disputes relating to tribal land.[49] This panel should assess tribal land disputes before they are referred to Local Courts.

There are also the Customary Land Appeal Courts. These courts have exclusive jurisdiction to hear appeals from the Local Courts on customary land issues.[50] A subsequent appeal to the High Court lies only on points of law and not on issues of fact or customary law.[51]

3.2.3. *Legal Profession*

The Legal Practitioners Act and the Legal Practitioners (Admission) Rules 1996 regulate the legal profession and practitioners. A person who desires to be admitted as a legal practitioner in Solomon Islands must apply to the Registrar of the High Court.[52] The Registrar issues a practising certificate if the applicant meets the necessary criteria. Persons who are entitled to practise as a barrister, solicitor or legal practitioner in any Commonwealth country and have practised for at least five years preceding the application can be admitted as legal practitioners.[53] Persons who hold a law degree or legal qualification are qualified to apply for provisional admission.[54] Provisional admission holders cannot gain full admission until they have had practical experience for a period of 12 months, during which they cannot appear as an advocate in the courts or hold money in trust for a client.[55] After the required practical experience

---

46 Local Courts Act (Cap 19), s 9.
47 Land and Titles Act (Cap 133), s 254.
48 Land and Titles Act (Cap 133), s 12.
49 Tribal Land Panels Bill 2019.
50 *Manubili & Or v Fenda* [1984] SILR 1.
51 Land and Titles Act (Cap 133), s 231B; see also *Campbell v Mafuara* [1984] SILR 4.
52 Legal Practitioners Act (Cap 16), s 3.
53 Legal Practitioners (Admission) Rules 1996, r 3.
54 Rule 6.
55 Rule 9.

is completed, provisionally admitted practitioners are entitled to apply for full admission.[56]

The Legal Practitioners Act requires the Registrar to keep a roll of legal practitioners. The Act outlines a set of offences that apply to legal practitioners. In particular, the Act provides that it is an offence for an unqualified person to act as a legal practitioner.[57] A disciplinary panel, which includes the Attorney-General, was introduced by the Legal Practitioners (Amendment) Act 2003 to investigate complaints on legal practitioners.[58] The Chief Justice appoints the members of the disciplinary committee and may refer complaints about the conduct of any legal practitioner to the committee to investigate.[59]

3.3. CONSTITUTIONAL OFFICES

The offices of the Director of Public Prosecutions and the Public Solicitor are established in the Constitution. Both the Director of Public Prosecutions and the Public Solicitor are appointed by the Governor-General.[60] The Director of Public Prosecutions generally has the power to undertake criminal proceedings against any person.[61] During a period where the office of the Director of Public Prosecutions is vacant, those functions shall be performed by the Attorney-General.[62] The Public Solicitor's functions are to provide legal aid, advice and assistance to persons who have been charged with a criminal offence or when directed to do so by the High Court.[63]

The Constitution also establishes the office of the Ombudsman. The functions of the Ombudsman are to enquire into the conduct of officials and authorities, assist in the improvement of practices and procedures of public bodies and ensure elimination of arbitrary and unfair decisions.[64] The Ombudsman may receive complaints from any person who is aggrieved by the conduct of an official in the exercise of powers or performance of their functions.[65] Officials subject to review by the Ombudsman include public agencies, police, government officials and bodies corporate as prescribed by Parliament. The Ombudsman cannot review decisions of judges, magistrates or registrars in the exercise of their judicial functions.[66]

56 Rule 10.
57 Legal Practitioners Act 1987, s 14.
58 Legal Practitioners (Amendment) Act 2003, s 2.
59 Legal Practitioners Act 1987, ss 8 and 8A.
60 Constitution of Solomon Islands 1978, ss 91(2) and 92(2).
61 Section 91(4).
62 Section 91(9).
63 Section 92(4).
64 Section 97.
65 Ombudsman Act 2017.
66 Section 97(4).

The Ombudsman is not subject to the direction of any authority and no proceedings can be brought against the Ombudsman in any court of law for actions taken in the discharge of functions.[67] The Ombudsman is appointed by the Governor-General on the advice of a committee made up of the Speaker of Parliament, the Chairman of the Public Service Commission and the Chairman of the Judicial and Legal Service Commission.[68]

The office of Auditor-General is established by the Constitution.[69] The public accounts of all ministries, offices, courts and authorities of government, as well as of provincial governments, are audited and reported on annually by the Auditor-General. The Auditor-General has access to all books, records, returns and other documents relating to accounts.[70] The Auditor-General submits his or her reports to the Minister of Finance and Speaker who lays them before Parliament. The Auditor-General is not subject to the direction or control of any person or authority.[71]

4. LAW OF PERSONS

4.1. MARRIAGE

The Islanders Marriage Act regulates marriage of Solomon Islanders in Solomon Islands. The Act provides that a marriage is valid if it is in accordance: (1) with the custom of Solomon Islands; (2) with the provisions of the Pacific Islands Civil Marriages Order in Council 1907; or (3) is celebrated before a minister of religion or a district registrar.[72] Marriages celebrated before a registered minister of religion must be celebrated in a church;[73] a marriage before a district registrar must take place in his or her office.[74] The Act provides for the voluntary registration of customary marriages.[75]

The Act also imposes limitations on who can be married. The age of capacity to marry is 15.[76] Further, no person may be married under the age of 18 without the consent of his or her parents, guardians, or in their absence, of a judge or magistrate.[77]

---

67 Section 98.
68 Section 96.
69 Constitution of Solomon Islands 1978, s 108.
70 Constitution of Solomon Islands 1978, s 108.
71 Section 108(4)–(5).
72 Islanders' Marriage Act (Cap 171), s 4.
73 Section 8.
74 Section 9.
75 Section 18.
76 Section 10.
77 Section 10.

Expatriates may be married by a minister of religion under the Pacific Order 1893 (UK) or contract a civil marriage under the Pacific Islands Civil Marriages Order 1907 (UK). These regimes generally cover marriages in Solomon Islands and try to encapsulate legal plurality considerations. Given the colonial nature of some of the legislation, reform is much needed.[78]

4.2. TERMINATION OF MARRIAGE

The Islanders' Divorce Act (Cap 170) covers three main areas: divorce, judicial separation and nullity of marriage. Regarding divorce, the Islanders' Divorce Act specifically applies to only two types of marriages: a marriage made under the Islanders' Marriage Act and a registered customary marriage. The Islanders' Divorce Act does not regulate divorce for a customary marriage that is not registered under the Act; this is regulated by custom. However, courts have dealt with divorce of parties who are not Solomon Islanders but who are domiciled in Solomon Islands.[79]

4.2.1. Divorce and Judicial Separation

A person seeking divorce may file a petition in the High Court.[80] Under this fault-based system,[81] a petition for divorce can be based on several grounds: adultery, desertion of a partner for over three years without cause, cruel treatment of a partner,[82] living apart for at least five years, and the unsound mind and continuous care of the respondent of at least five years.[83] Additional grounds are available if the petitioner is the wife. These are if the husband has committed rape, sodomy or bestiality.[84]

A person seeking judicial separation may petition the High Court on the same grounds as for divorce. If the Court grants a decree for judicial separation, the petitioner is no longer obliged to live together with the respondent.[85]

---

78 See Jennifer Corrin Care and Kenneth Brown 'Marit Long Kastom: Marriage in the Solomon Islands' (2004) 18 IJLPF 52.

79 *Emmett v Emmett* [2009] SBHC 29.

80 Islanders' Divorce Act (Cap 170), s 5(1).

81 Kenneth Brown and Jennifer Corrin Care 'Putting Asunder: Divorce and Financial Relief in Solomon Islands' (2005) OUCLJ 85 at 93.

82 Section 5(1).

83 Islanders Divorce (Amendment) Act 1998, s 5(1).

84 Islanders' Divorce Act (Cap 170), s 5(1)(d).

85 Section 16; similar to the laws around marriages, colonial legislation around divorce and nullity of marriages exists trying to capture western ideologies as well as customary law. This has proven challenging. Reform is needed to fully integrate the dual legal regimes while reflecting the modern social climate of Solomon Islands; see Kenneth Brown and Jennifer Corrin Care 'Putting Asunder: Divorce and Financial Relief in Solomon Islands' (2005) OUCLJ 85 at 85.

4.2.2. *Nullity of Marriage*

A marriage can be declared a nullity on the grounds that:[86]

(1) the respondent refuses or is unable to consummate the marriage; or
(2) at the time of the marriage:
 (a) a party to the marriage was of unsound mind;
 (b) the respondent was suffering from a venereal disease in a communicable form; or
 (c) the wife was impregnated by a person other than the husband.

In order for the petitioner to succeed on grounds (b) or (c), three other conditions must be met. These are that the petitioner:

(1) was ignorant of the facts alleged at the time of the marriage;
(2) brought the petition within a year of the date of the marriage; and
(3) since discovering the grounds, has not consented to sexual intercourse.

4.3. ADOPTION

The Adoption Act 2004 regulates adoption in Solomon Islands. Since coming into force in 2007, it has had several amendments.

As a starting point, the Adoption Act gives courts the power to grant an adoption order once several conditions are met.[87] These conditions, as established in the case of *Re Boboria*,[88] are summarised in *The Plural Practice of Adoption in South Pacific States*[89] as follows:

1 the applicant and child must be ordinary residents of Solomon Islands;
2 the applicant must give at least 3 months' notice of the proposed adoption to the relevant local authority within whose area the applicant was living at the time of the application;
3 the parents of child consent to the adoption;
4 the parents understand that they are consenting to being permanently deprived of their parental rights;
5 the order must be for the welfare of the child;

---

86 Islanders' Divorce Act (Cap 170), s 13; see also Kenneth Brown and Jennifer Corrin Care 'Putting Asunder: Divorce and Financial Relief in Solomon Islands' (2005) OUCLJ 85 at 95.

87 Adoption Act 2004, s 3(1).

88 *In re Adoption Act 2004, Application by Boboria and Sua* [2014] SBHC 109.

89 Philip Kanairara and Jennifer Corrin 'Adoption in Solomon Islands' in Jennifer Corrin and Sue Farran (eds) *The Plural Practice of Adoption in Pacific Island States* (Springer, 2019) 115.

6 the parents must not have been promised or received, any payment or other reward in consideration of the adoption;
7 the applicants must be in good health;
8 the order must accord with the wishes of the child, having regard to his or her age and understanding;
9 the child must have been in the continuous care and possession of the applicant for at least 3 months immediately preceding the date of the order.

Two 2019 cases have shown interesting developments in the conditions required for adoption in Solomon Islands. In the case of *Adoption of Rapuinoni*,[90] Keniapisia J highlighted the welfare and best interest of the child as being the 'one important requirement' for consideration in adoption cases. The same judge in *Re Adoption of Ezinta Rozma*[91] expanded on the scope of the 'ordinary resident' to cover those who have natural 'family connections' to Solomon Islands, as opposed to those who come from 'an overseas country, just to adopt a child, without any attachment to this country'.

Customary adoption is regulated by customary law. In *R v Takabea*, the customary adoption must be done according to customary practices of Solomon Islands and not of a foreign country or else it will not be recognised.[92] The 2019 case of *Re Ne'e*[93] provides an additional view. The applicants in that case applied for formal recognition of a customary adoption which occurred 15 years earlier. Keniapisia J granted recognition of the customary adoption. In his reasoning, Keniapisia J stated that customary adoption, under customary law, was recognised under the law of Solomon Islands, provided it did not contradict the Constitution or statutes. The judge further said that under s 28 of the Adoption Act, customary adoption is endorsed and recognised.

4.4. CHILDREN

In 2017, Solomon Islands passed the Child and Family Welfare Act 2017. This Act establishes a robust legal framework for the welfare and protection of children as it revolves around the best interest of the child. The Act also recognises the importance of children remaining within existing societal structures such as families and communities. As such it works towards promoting and encouraging the proper care and protection of children within these structures. It takes a further step to establish avenues for the care and protection of children when these structures are unable to do so.

90 [2019] SBHC 48.
91 [2019] SBHC 63.
92 *R v Takabea* [1993] SBHC 81.
93 *Adoption of Ne'e* [2019] SBHC 47.

The Act operates both in a reactive and proactive sense. The Director, established under the Act, is responsible for its administration. Section 5 casts a wide net in defining a child in need of care and protection.[94] It covers the living environment of children and the different types of abuse and exploitation that children might experience. The Act provides three ways in which the Director can assist or intervene for the best interest of the child: the parents themselves can seek assistance from a social welfare officer,[95] a person can report that a child needs care and protection,[96] or the court can refer a child who is deemed to be in need of care and protection to the Director.[97] In receiving a request, report or referral from the relevant officers, the Director can take appropriate actions which ensure the wellbeing and protection of the child.[98] Unless contrary to the best interests of the child,[99] an action made by the Director must involve the participation of the child and family members of the child.[100] The Act further establishes proactive measures such as protection programmes.[101] The responsibility to implement these programmes rests with the Director.

Under the Act, the following are considered general offences: (1) the contravention of a care and protection order without a reasonable excuse;[102] (2) making public the identity of a child who is the subject of a proceeding under the Act;[103] (3) obstructing, threatening or intimidating the Director or any other social worker in the execution of his or her duties under the Act;[104] and (4) obstructing, threatening or intimidating a registered service provider in the course of providing services to a child.[105]

5. LAW OF OBLIGATIONS

Generally, Solomon Islands has adopted the principles of common law and equity for contract and tort law.[106] The Constitution's general referral to 'the principles of Common Law and Equity' has seen varied interpretations by courts as to the extent which common law principles can be applied. Courts have

94 Child and Family Welfare Act 2017, s 5.
95 Section 17.
96 Section 18.
97 Section 22(1).
98 Section 25.
99 Section 25(2)(a).
100 Section 26(1).
101 Section 16.
102 Section 55.
103 Section 56.
104 Section 57.
105 Section 58.
106 Jennifer Corrin and Don Paterson *Introduction to South Pacific Law* (4th ed, Intersentia, 2017) 37.

stated that the principles which apply are not limited to those of England.[107] In a later ruling, this view was rejected; it was stated that the common law and equity principles which the Constitution referred to were only the common law and equity principles of England.[108] This means that courts must apply the law as determined by courts in England even though English courts have no jurisdiction over Solomon Islands courts.[109]

The Constitution states that Solomon Islands courts are not bound by decisions of foreign courts after independence.[110] Although not expressly stated, it has been interpreted by courts as providing a cut-off date for the application of common law and equity principles.[111] This has made it slightly complicated for courts when applying principles that have been overruled in England after the cut-off date.

5.1. TORTS

Some statutes of general application that were adopted at independence govern certain aspects of tortious liability.[112] Otherwise common law principles have been relied on in courts as the basis of numerous torts and negligence claims.[113]

5.2. CONTRACT

The general principles of contract law – which include offer, acceptance, intention to create legal obligations, consideration, illegality, frustration, privity, misrepresentation and mistake – are all based on English common law.

Other than the application of common law and equity to contract law, there are a few pieces of legislation that regulate contract law, the notable ones being the Bills of Sale Act,[114] the Sale of Goods Act 1893 (UK) and the Consumer Protection Act.[115]

---

107 *Official Administrator for Unrepresented Deceased Estates v Allardyce Lumber Co Ltd* [1980–81] SILR 66.

108 *Cheung v Tanda* [1984] SILR 108; Corrin and Paterson, above n 106, at 38.

109 Corrin and Paterson, above n 106, at 38.

110 Constitution of Solomon Islands, Sch 3, s 4(1).

111 *Cheung v Tanda* [1984] SILR 108.

112 Eg Occupiers Liability Act 1957 (UK) and Workmen's Compensation Act (Cap 78).

113 *Lenga v Solomon Taiyo Ltd* [1991] SBHC 9; *Ngelea v Bulu* [1998] SBHC 120; *Kirite'e v Ome* [2018] SBHC 25; all these cases were based on negligence claims in which the court judgment referred to the House of Lords case of *Donoghue v Stevenson* [1932] AC 562.

114 Bills of Sale Act (Cap 174).

115 Consumer Protection Act (Cap 63).

However, there have been some deviations from common law principles by courts. In *Success v Premier of Guadalcanal Province, Rima, Attorney-General,*[116] the Court of Appeal held that the concept of privity did not apply to a customary land agreement.

6. LAND LAW

During the British Protectorate era of the 1890s, regulations were put in place that enabled land to be granted as freehold estates in fee simple to the Crown for the purpose of trading stations.[117] Some of the acquisitions during these early periods were very contentious. The Regulations provided that the High Commissioner oversee land transactions to ensure compliance. Non-Solomon Islanders were further enabled to acquire land through a 'waste lands' scheme; waste land was land said to be not owned, cultivated or occupied by natives.[118]

By the late 1950s, further regulations converted all existing freehold estates into 'perpetual estates' and leasehold estates into 'fixed-term estates'.[119] Post-independence legislation established a 'Torrens'-type system of registration which recognised these regimes and allowed perpetual estates to be owned only by Solomon Islanders or Solomon Islands institutions.[120] Fixed-term estates held by Solomon Islanders were not to exceed 99 years, while for non-Solomon Islanders or institutions they were not to exceed a period of 75 years.[121] As a result, the English common law regime of freehold estates no longer exists in Solomon Islands. Land may also be held as leasehold. All leases of two years or more must be registered.[122]

The Constitution provides for the compulsory acquisition of land by the government. This provision states that the government may not acquire any land unless the taking is necessary in the public interest, where there is reasonable justification for any hardship that may result to any person having an interest in a property, and where provision has been made to pay for prompt compensation.[123] This same provision gives the High Court power to review

116 *Success v Premier of Guadalcanal Province, Rima, Attorney-General* [2011] SBCA 19 – the plaintiffs were parties to an agreement with trustees for a timber licence under a statutory scheme. Upon application of renewal of their licence, a third party had also reached agreement with the trustees for a licence which covered the same area. The plaintiffs sought an injunction. It was held by the court that the concept of privity did not apply to customary land agreements.
117 Solomon (Land) Regulation 1896, regs 4–6.
118 Solomon (Waste Lands) Regulation 1900, reg 2.
119 Land and Titles Regulation 1959, Sch 2, s 13.
120 Land and Titles Act (Cap 133), s 112(3).
121 Land and Titles Act (Cap 133), s 100.
122 Section 146.
123 Constitution of Solomon Islands 1978, s 8.

compulsory acquisition. Section 112 of the Constitution further provides that if compulsory acquisition is to be made of customary land, the government must negotiate with the owners of the land, the owners must have independent legal advice, and if practicable the interest acquired is to be only for a fixed term.

Customary land is a matter of major importance. The majority of land in Solomon Islands is customarily owned. The vast differences in customs and norms within the Solomons poses difficulty when defining customary land rights. Generally, under custom, land is a communal asset which has religious, social and political significance. Customary land is therefore owned by communities. Individuals in the communities have rights to use the land.

All land registration is regulated by the Land and Titles Act Cap 133. This has made it challenging when dealing with customary land, given that there is no requirement for customary land to be registered. Although the Land and Titles Act recognises the need to define customary land boundaries, during colonial times this was undertaken only for land required for national development.[124] Suggestions have been made to improve legislation for recording customary land boundaries with the intent of protecting rights of traditional landowners. The Customary Land Records Act 1992 was passed to address this problem.[125]

Given that the majority of land in Solomon Islands is customary, access to land by the government and private enterprise has been difficult. Land governance is unstable and international investors have generally been unwilling to engage in business.[126]

7. COMMERCIAL LAW

Commercial law in Solomon Islands is complex from a legislative perspective. On the one hand, a number of laws have been passed locally. On the other hand, statutes of general application still apply in areas not covered by legislation enacted locally.

7.1. COMPANY LAW

The Companies Act 2009 primarily focuses on the formation and governance of private, public and community companies in Solomon Islands. Under the Act, any person, either individually or with another person, can apply for

124 John Cook and Genesis Eddie Kofana 'Reconciling Customary Ownership and Development; Recording land rights and boundaries in Auluta Basin, Solomon Islands' (Australian Agency for International Development, 2008) 50.

125 Cook and Kofana, above n 124, at 50.

126 Cook and Kofana, above n 124, at 52.

registration of a company.[127] All applications for registration must be made to the Registrar of Companies.[128] The Registrar, in receiving an application, will check whether the application complies with the requirements outlined in the Act. If all requirements are met, the Registrar will enter the company on the Solomon Islands register[129] and issue a certificate of incorporation.[130] The Registrar has the authority to remove a company from the register if there are grounds for its removal under the Act.[131]

Organisations may also register under the Co-operative Societies Act if their objective is the promotion of economic interests of their members.[132] Organisations that register under the Co-operative Societies Act must register with the Registrar of Co-operative Societies.

7.2. PARTNERSHIP

Solomon Islands has not passed an Act with regard to partnerships. The Partnership Act 1890 of the United Kingdom[133] still applies in Solomon Islands as a statute of general application. Any business which subsists between persons carrying on a business in common with a view of profit is broadly viewed as a partnership and is governed by the Act.[134] In contrast to that, the Act excludes companies or associations falling within the scope of s 1(2) of the Act from that definition.[135] A number of cases have gone on to clearly outline what constitutes a partnership. A partnership arrangement with a view to profit, according to *Aujare v Sasasgo*,[136] only begins to constitute a partnership when the two parties actually carry out the business.

7.3. INSOLVENCY

In 2009, Solomon Islands passed the Companies (Insolvency and Receivership) Act 2009. This Act, which came into effect in July 2010, provides for the management and administration of insolvent companies and receivers in

127 Companies Act 2009, s 6(1).
128 Section 6(2).
129 Section 8(1)(a).
130 Section 8(1)(b).
131 Companies Act 2009, s 140.
132 Co-operative Societies Act (Cap 164), s 4.
133 Partnership Act 1890 (UK).
134 Partnership as defined by s 1 of the Partnership Act 1890 (UK).
135 Partnership Act 1890 (UK), s 1(2)(a), (b) and (c).
136 *Aujare v Sasasgo* [2004] SBHC 7.

Solomon Islands. According to the Act, liquidation of a company begins at the time a liquidator is appointed.[137] Sections 15–19 of the Act establish the guidelines as to who can be a liquidator, and the process of appointing a liquidator. Once a liquidator is appointed, a liquidator is obliged under the Act, amongst other things, to administer and manage the assets of the company to serve the creditors of the company in the manner outlined within the Act.[138] Once all obligations are fulfilled, the liquidator should deliver the relevant documents to the Registrar of Companies.[139] The liquidation ends once either of these two requirements are complied with.

It is important to note that a compromise can also be proposed to creditors when there is reason to believe that a company is or will be unable to settle its debts in the normal course of business.[140] This proposal, however, can be made only by a director of the company, the company's receiver, or its liquidator. The process of a compromise is established under ss 7–12 of the Act.

7.4. INTELLECTUAL PROPERTY

Trade marks, design and patents are provided for in specific legislation: the Registration of United Kingdom Trade Marks Act (Cap 180); the United Kingdom Designs (Protection) Act (Cap 181); and the Patents Act 1949 (UK).

The Copyright Act 1987 provides a framework for protection of every original literary, dramatic, musical or artistic work that is unpublished by a 'qualified person', which is defined as a Solomon Islands individual or body corporate.[141] It further covers sound recordings, cinematograph film and other broadcasting.[142] Copyright protection is conferred if the work was first published in Solomon Islands by a qualified person.

For original literary, dramatic, musical or artistic work, a copyright exists for the work for 50 years at the time it is published. If the work is not published before the death of the author, the 50-year period begins when the author dies.[143] For sound recordings, cinematograph film and other broadcasting, copyright protection exists for a period of 50 years from the time of publication.[144] There have been no Copyright Act claims in Solomon Islands courts since the inception of the Act.

---

137 Companies (Insolvency and Receivership) Act 2009, s 14(1).
138 Companies (Insolvency and Receivership) Act 2009, s 13(1)(a).
139 Companies (Insolvency and Receivership) Act 2009, s 53.
140 Companies (Insolvency and Receivership) Act 2009, s 6.
141 Copyright Act 1987, s 3.
142 Section 11.
143 Section 3.
144 Section 11(3).

7.5. CARRIAGE BY AIR AND SEA

The Carriage of Goods by Sea Act regulates the carrying of goods by sea in ships from and to ports in Solomon Islands, or to ports outside Solomon Islands.[145] The Act, in cases of damages and loss, outlines the circumstances in which liability may or may not rest with the carrier.

Registration of vessels is outlined in the Shipping (Registration) Regulations 2010. These regulations provide for application requirements, the registration process and safety requirements. Solomon Islands is also a party to international maritime conventions, including the Standards of Training, Certification and Watchkeeping for Seafarers (STCW).[146]

7.6. BANKS

The operation of banks and other financial institutions in Solomon Islands is regulated by the Banking Act 1995. A body corporate wishing to conduct banking business can apply through the Central Bank of Solomon Islands for a licence.[147] The power to approve or refuse the granting of a licence rests with the Minister.[148] The Act also establishes other ministerial powers, including the power to revoke licences and the power to appoint an examiner to check the books and affairs of banks for any contraventions or non-compliance with the Act.[149] Furthermore, it grants the Court the power to order a moratorium against any licensed banking business to prohibit its operation for a certain period of time.[150] A banking business licence is suspended during the time the moratorium is in effect.[151]

8. ENVIRONMENTAL LAW

The Environment Act 1998 establishes a regime which is intended to manage environmental impacts generally. The object of the Act is to provide for development control, monitor pollution, reduce risks to human health

145 Carriage of Goods by Sea Act (Cap 158), s 2; this Act incorporates the Hague Rules.
146 Shipping (STCW Convention) Regulations 2010 – this Convention sets minimum qualification standards for masters, officers and watch personnel on seagoing merchant ships and large yachts.
147 Banking Act 1995, s 5(2).
148 Section 6.
149 Section 20.
150 Section 21(1)(a)(b).
151 Section 21(2).

and degradation of the environment, promote recycling, and comply with regional and international conventions relating to the environment.[152] When considering any existing or proposed developments, there is a general duty on the environmental regulatory authority to consider the effects that the developments have on the environment.[153] An advisory committee is established under the Act. Its primary function is to report to the Environment Division and Minister all matters concerning the Act.[154]

Solomon Islands is a signatory of the 2015 Paris Agreement.[155] Solomon Islands is yet to enact legislation that is specifically aimed at implementing the Paris Agreement or its principles.[156]

9. NATURAL RESOURCES

9.1. MINERALS

The Mines and Minerals Act[157] regulates mining operations in Solomon Islands. The Act vests the right over minerals in all lands in the people and the government of Solomon Islands.[158] No person can carry out any reconnaissance, prospecting or mining unless done in accordance with the procedures established under the Act.

The administrative body that acts to regulate and control mining operations is the Minerals Board.[159] Applications for permits, licences and leases are sent to the Director, who brings the application before the Board for consideration.[160] Based on the advice of the Board, the Minister may then grant a permit, licence or lease with regard to the particular mining operation. Mining operations in Solomon Islands have included gold and bauxite mining.

In cases where the proposed site for prospecting or mining is within customary land, surface access rights must also be obtained from the

152 Environment Act 1998, s 3.
153 Section 15.
154 Section 14.
155 Paris Agreement, United Nations Treaty Collection, No. A-54113, <https://treaties.un.org/doc/Publication/UNTS/No%20Volume/54113/A-54113-Solomon%20Islands-080000028047fea3.pdf>.
156 For example, the UK enacted the Climate Change Act 2008 and New Zealand enacted the Climate Change Response (Zero Carbon) Amendment Act 2019.
157 Mines and Minerals Act (Cap 42).
158 All lands include customary, freehold, water and land covered by water.
159 Mines and Minerals Act (Cap 42), s 10.
160 Under s 5(2) the Director is appointed by the Minister. The Director also takes the role of Chief Geologist under s 5(3). Schedule 3(1) then goes on to state that the Chief Geologist is also the Chairman of the Board.

landowners. This involves the establishment of trustees for the payments of fees and damages for the landowners. The Board is involved in facilitating this consultation.

9.2. FORESTRY

The Forest Resources and Timber Utilisation Act[161] regulates logging and milling operations in Solomon Islands. All logging and milling operations must operate under a licence. The power to grant a licence rests with the Commissioner of Forest Resources. The Commissioner may grant a licence if he or she is satisfied that all the required legal conditions are met.[162]

An additional step exists if the logging or milling operations are to occur on customary land – the applicant must obtain timber rights from the customary landowners. The applicant must apply to the Commissioner for consent to negotiate with the appropriate local government. If this is granted, the provincial government is responsible for facilitating and ensuring that a meeting takes place between the applicant and the landowners.[163] If an agreement is reached between the customary landowners and the applicant, the provincial government will send a certificate to the Commissioner of Forestry.[164] The Commissioner, once satisfied that all requirements are met, will recommend to the provincial government to grant approval for the agreement.[165] The Act also gives the Minister of Forestry the power to impose levies and to impose restrictions on certain areas by declaring them to be state forests[166] or reserves.[167]

9.3. FISHERIES

Marine resources contribute significantly to the national economy and local livelihoods in Solomon Islands. This is reflected in the Fisheries Management Act 2015. The Act[168] aims to ensure the proper, sustainable use and management of Solomon Islands' marine resources.[169] This Act establishes several legal frameworks and mechanisms designed to achieve the principles of the Act under s 5.

---

161 Forest Resources and Timber Utilisation Act (Cap 40).
162 Section 5(2).
163 Forest Resources and Timber Utilisation (Amendment) Act 2000, s 8(1).
164 Section 9(2)(c).
165 Forest Resources and Timber Utilisation Act, s 11.
166 Section 20.
167 Section 24.
168 It repealed the Fisheries Act 1998.
169 Fisheries Management Act 2015, s 4.

The Act establishes the Fisheries Management Plan. This is a plan which implements the proper use and management of marine resources at three levels: the national, provincial and community level.[170] Additionally, the Act uses a licensing system which prohibits a person from engaging in several fishing-related activities without a valid licence or authorisation.[171] The power to grant, renew or deny a licence lies with the Director.[172] This is made based on the recommendations given by the Fisheries Licensing Committee.[173] The applicant can appeal to the Fisheries Appeals Committee if the applicant is not satisfied with the Director's decision.[174]

The Act uses the prohibition of certain areas and activities to achieve its objective. The Minister may declare a particular area to be a national marine protected area or a managed area.[175] Once a particular area is declared to be protected, no person is allowed to engage in any activity that is prohibited under that declaration, or engage in any activity that would negatively impact the fishery resource in that area. This is similar to provisions under the Protected Areas Act 2010, which is aimed at conserving biological diversity.

10. INTERNATIONAL LAW AND TREATIES

Parliament considers foreign relations through its Standing Select Committee, the Foreign Relations Committee, which oversees and makes recommendations on, inter alia, international treaties and conventions and diplomatic obligations.[176] There is no legislation which provides for the processes that a government must go through in acceding to an international treaty. Common practice is to rely on the provisions of each specific treaty when dealing with the formalities of ratification. Solomon Islands is a party to the Vienna Convention on the Law of Treaties and relies on the provisions of the Convention in acceding to or ratifying treaties. A treaty becomes part of law only after incorporation into domestic legislation.

The country's foreign policy for international relationships and diplomatic ties is guided by the following broad objectives:[177]

1 Promotion of democracy and respect for human rights, and contribute to effective global governance and international security;

---

170 Section 17(1).
171 Section 43.
172 Fisheries Management Act 2015, s 45(1).
173 Section 10(1).
174 Section 11(1)(a).
175 Section 19.
176 Standing Orders of the National Parliament of Solomon Islands, Order 71B.
177 'Foreign Policy' Solomon Islands Ministry of Foreign Affairs and External Trade <http://www.mfaet.gov.sb/about-us/foreign-policy.html>.

2 Effective collaboration with the UN and development partners in attaining the existing Millennium Development Goals (MDGs) and the post 2015 Sustainable Development Goals (SDGs) for Solomon Islands;
3 Enhancement of engagements and strengthening of partnerships with international organisations and donor partners;
4 Enhancement and strengthening of partnership with European Union;
5 Exploring of greater opportunities through South-South relations – building on existing regional frameworks;
6 Establishing bilateral Technical Cooperation partnerships.

The country's foreign trade is based on the Trade Policy Framework, which sets out the main principles that guide trade policy. The framework concentrates on economic performance, recognition of trade commodities, foreign investment and services, trade policy and the business environment, and trade agreements and market access.[178]

Solomon Islands is a member of a number of regional and international organisations, including the African, Caribbean and Pacific Group of States, the Secretariat of the Pacific Community, the Pacific Islands Forum, the Melanesian Spearhead Group, the World Trade Organisation and the United Nations.

11. CIVIL SOCIETY ORGANISATIONS

There is no central government registry of civil society organisations.[179] However, NGOs and their partners are coordinated and facilitated by the Development Services Exchange, which is the national umbrella body for NGOs in Solomon Islands. Most civil society organisations are registered under the Charitable Trusts Act 1964, which provides for registration of 'any association for religious, educational, literary, social or charitable purpose'.[180] 'Charitable purposes' in the Act is broadly defined and includes organisations with the following purposes: supply the physical wants of the sick; education for children of the poor; reformation and employment of criminals; provision of religious instruction; support of libraries; and the promotion of athletic sports.[181] Organisations that register under the Charitable Trusts Act do so with the Registrar of Companies.[182] Civil society organisations may also be registered under the Co-operative Societies Act 1953.

---

178 'Solomon Islands Trade Policy Framework' Solomon Islands Ministry of Foreign Affairs and External Trade <http://www.mfaet.gov.sb/about-us/trade-policy.html>.
179 'Civil Society Briefs – Solomon Islands' Asian Development Bank (2017) <https://www.adb.org/sites/default/files/publication/228836/csb-sol.pdf>.
180 Charitable Trusts Act 1964 (Solomon Islands), s 3.
181 Section 2.
182 Sections 3–5.

For some organisations, there is specific legislation that regulates their activities. These include religious groups such as the Church of Melanesia[183] and the Solomon Islands Red Cross.[184]

Civil society organisations are generally exempt from tax. Tax exemptions vary with the nature of the tax. Income tax legislation provides exemptions that may be provided if the Minister is of the opinion that it would assist any business operations of a Solomon Islander.[185] Goods tax legislation enables tax exemptions for goods, provided the organisation is non-profit. These include goods for organisations such as educational institutions, institutions or organisations established for promotion of a university or school, organisations which promote sport, and organisations which promote religious, charitable or benevolent institutions.[186] These exemptions generally benefit civil society organisations.

BIBLIOGRAPHY

Brown, Kenneth and Jennifer Corrin Care 'Putting Asunder: Divorce and Financial Relief in Solomon Islands' (2005) Oxford Commonwealth Law Journal 85.

Cook, John and Genesis Eddie Kofana 'Reconciling Customary Ownership and Development; Recording land rights and boundaries in Auluta Basin, Solomon Islands' (Australian Agency for International Development, 2008).

Corrin, Jennifer and Don Paterson *Introduction to South Pacific Law* (4th ed, Intersentia, 2017).

Corrin Care, Jennifer and Kenneth Brown 'Marit Long Kastom: Marriage in the Solomon Islands' (2004) 18 International Journal of Law Policy and Family 52.

Kanairara, Philip and Jennifer Corrin 'Adoption in Solomon Islands' in Jennifer Corrin and Sue Farran (eds) *The Plural Practice of Adoption in Pacific Island States* (Springer, 2019).

Nonggorr, John 'Solomon Islands' in Michael A Ntumy (ed) *South Pacific Islands Legal Systems* (University of Hawaii Press, 1993).

Pacific Islands Legal Information Institute, *Solomon Islands Primary Materials*, <http://www.paclii.org/countries/sb.html>.

'Solomon Islands' in Norman Douglas and Ngaire Douglas (eds) *Pacific Islands Year Book* (17th ed, Fiji Times, 1994).

---

183 Church of Melanesia Trust Board (Incorporated) Act Cap 156, and the Church of the Province of Melanesia (Solomon Islands) Property Act Cap 157.

184 Solomon Islands Red Cross Society Act Cap 167.

185 Income Tax Act (Solomon Islands) Cap 123, s 9.

186 Goods Tax Act (Solomon Islands) Cap 122, First Schedule.

TOKELAU

Lise Hope-Suveinakama

1. BACKGROUND

Tokelau is a non-self-governing territory of New Zealand comprising the islands of Fakaofo, Nukunonu and Atafu. Tokelau is administered by the government of New Zealand under the Tokelau Act 1948.[1]

Tokelau has experienced periods of great sadness: the 1860s Peruvian slavers took most of the able-bodied men from all the villages;[2] a flu epidemic further depopulated the islands; and its fourth island, Olohega (or Swains Island), was lost to American Samoa in 1925.[3]

Tokelau surmounted those tragic events through the strength of its customs and traditional practices. During colonialism and to this day, the villages thrive under the leadership of the Taupulega (Village Council of Elders). The vibrant customs and traditional practices of Tokelau helped sustain it, as did the strong historical and cultural links between Olohega and the three atolls of present-day Tokelau.

The local history of Tokelau has been shaped by the various administrations that it has had tracing back through periods of colonisation. This constitutional history proceeded from being a British protectorate (1889–1915), to a United Kingdom colony (1916–1926), to a United Kingdom dependency (1926–1948), to a New Zealand territory administered by New Zealand government departments (1949–1993), to a New Zealand territory with increasing self-governing powers (1994 onwards).[4]

The focus here is on some key constitutional developments that emerged for Tokelau whilst it was administered by New Zealand as a British dependency, through to its current legal system. The UK and New Zealand agreed that Tokelau would become part of New Zealand in 1948. Tokelau was then incorporated

---

1 Tokelau Act 1948, Preamble and s 3.

2 H E Maude, *Slavers in Paradise* (ANU Press, 1981).

3 Guano Act 1856 (48 USC ch 8 paras 1411–1419); *Matagi Tokelau* (University of the South Pacific, 1991). The territory now known as Tokelau was in British colonial times known as the Union Islands. The name was changed in 1946 by the Tokelau Nomenclature Ordinance 1946 (made by the Administrator of Western Samoa).

4 Administration Rules 1993 and delegations made under them had a significant role to play. The delegations of 2004 were to the Taupulega. The Taupulega then subdelegated to the General Fono. The three delegations were basically of 'all the powers exercisable by me [the Administrator] in respect of Tokelau under any enactment.' As at November 2020 there are very few such powers; two significant ones are under the Tokelau (Exclusive Economic Zone) Fishing Regulations 2012 (SR 2012/278) and under the Commissions of Inquiry Rules 1991.

as a territory of New Zealand. The Queen is the head of state of the Realm of New Zealand, which includes Tokelau.[5] The Queen is represented in the Realm by the Governor-General of New Zealand. The people of Tokelau are New Zealand citizens.[6] Tokelau has been administered by the Ministry of Foreign Affairs and Trade since 1974, and by an Administrator who is the head of the Special Relations Unit in that Ministry.[7]

Later Acts and amendments to the Tokelau Act 1948 reflect the changes of approach by New Zealand as Tokelau continued to strengthen its national government. The legal recognition of the Fono Fakamua (Parliament) as the executive government of Tokelau for the whole of Tokelau was a significant development for Tokelau. In 1994 the Administrator of Tokelau delegated his executive power to the General Fono and to the Council of Faipule[8] when the General Fono was not in session. This delegation was revoked in 2004 and a new delegation was made to the three Taupulega who then partially (on national matters) sub-delegated to the General Fono.

The Constitution of Tokelau established the rules for the government of Tokelau and the composition of the General Fono and of the Council for the Ongoing Government. This followed the grant of power to the General Fono to make rules for Tokelau subject to the principal Act.[9] The relationship with New Zealand was further developed with the 2003 Joint Principles of Partnership Agreement, which outlines the relationship between sources of law in New Zealand and Tokelau.

The incorporation of Tokelau as part of New Zealand by virtue of s 3 of the Tokelau Act 1948 makes this Act the primary source of constitutional law that governs the relationship of Tokelau with New Zealand. This Act authorises the Governor-General to legislate for Tokelau and the General Fono to make rules for Tokelau. The Act confirms that existing laws and the Common Law of England continue in force.[10]

2. SOURCES OF LAW

The sources of law, in order of importance, are: the Tokelau Act 1948; Acts of the New Zealand Parliament which have been extended to Tokelau;[11] Regulations

---

5 Letters Patent cls 1 and 6 (SR 1983/225).

6 Citizenship Act 1977 (NZ).

7 Administration Rules 1993.

8 Now the Council for the Ongoing Government of Tokelau (Te Fono a te Malo Fakaauau).

9 Tokelau Amendment Act 1996; Constitution of Tokelau, rr 3 and 6.

10 Tokelau Act 1948, s 4B.

11 There are very few such Acts. The main statute is the Tokelau Act 1948. Also of major significance is the Tokelau (Territorial Sea and Exclusive Economic Zone) Act 1977. The other Acts primarily involve constitutional matters, such as the Royal Titles Act 1974 and the

made by the Governor-General; General Fono Rules; Village Rules; custom; pre-1949 legislation (existing law); and the common law of England.

Custom is, in practice, the primary source of law for Tokelau. It existed in the villages and was inherited from past ancestors prior to colonialism and during colonialism. Custom is usually oral and unwritten. It is based on Tokelau's traditional practices and way of life. Traditional authority in Tokelau is in its villages, and the needs of Tokelau at a local level are generally met through the administration of custom by the elders.

The traditional set-up of the villages of Tokelau was little influenced during colonialism. The British authorities and the New Zealand authorities which followed them rarely created or imposed structures that had any significant impact on the management of village affairs. Generally the colonial powers advanced their governance purposes by building on existing structures.

The Customs Rules 2004 stipulate that the custom of Tokelau is a source of law and, if it is referred to in any proceedings of the High Court of Tokelau, set out the procedure that must be followed in sourcing an expert opinion on the custom of Tokelau.

3. THE EXECUTIVE

3.1. GENERAL FONO

The General Fono is the government of Tokelau charged with the executive power to manage national matters in the interest of the nation of Tokelau. It is the duty of the General Fono to manage the following matters:[12]

- national budget appropriation;
- national resources;
- national public service;
- international relations;
- telecommunications;
- the relationship of Tokelau with New Zealand;
- national integrity;
- national transport;
- postal services;
- policy and structures for national health and education;
- Tokelau currency for coin collectors; and
- any matter referred by the Taupelga of each village to the General Fono.

Citizenship Act 1977, or matters of international interest, such as the Diplomatic Privileges and Immunities Act 1968 and the United Nations Act 1946.

12 Constitution, r 5.

The General Fono is required to meet at least twice a year. The Standing Orders of the General Fono give the General Fono the power to appoint officers to support its work. These officers include the Chairperson, who is responsible for the good conduct of the General Fono meetings and General Fono Committees. The Secretariat of the General Fono is designated by the General Fono. The General Fono conducts its business in accordance with the law of Tokelau and its Standing Orders. Proceedings of the General Fono may not be questioned by any court of law nor may the validity of any certificate given by the Chairperson of the General Fono in the exercise of his or her functions.

The General Fono consists of the Faipule and the Pulenuku of each village and one delegate from each village for every 100 inhabitants of the village based on the latest available census figures rounded to the nearest 50 inhabitants. Based on the population count for the three villages in December 2019, the General Fono consists of 22 delegates (seven from Atafu, seven from Nukunonu and eight from Fakaofo). The General Fono has the power to suspend any of its members on grounds set out in the law[13] and must inform the village concerned if it does so.

The Kauhauatea are senior elders of Tokelau. They have a place of right in the General Fono. There are six elders of 60 years of age or more, two designated by each Taupulega for the Kauhauatea in the General Fono. The members of the Kauhauatea have a right to speak and assist the General Fono as they see fit and also when the General Fono asks for their advice. The Kauhauatea do not vote on matters before the General Fono.

3.2. THE COUNCIL FOR THE ONGOING GOVERNMENT OF TOKELAU

The Council for the Ongoing Government comprises the three Faipule and one General Fono delegate from each village, designated by the Taupulega. The Council has the power under the Constitution to suspend any of its members. The members of the Council for the Ongoing Government hold ministerial portfolios as decided by them.

The Council for the Ongoing Government choose the Ulu o Tokelau from among their members to become the Chair of the Council. The Ulu o Tokelau represents the Council, the General Fono and the nation as determined by the Council.

The Council is responsible for conducting the government of Tokelau in accordance with General Fono decisions.[14] This includes implementing the decisions of the General Fono, unless there is a necessity to do otherwise and

[13] Constitution, r 3(4).
[14] Constitution, 5.

then only after consultation with the members of the General Fono. The Council is also responsible for responding to national emergencies.

3.3. VILLAGE GOVERNANCE

The Village Incorporation Rules 1986 gave legal personality to the Taupulega as the *pule*, or authority, in their respective villages. The Taupulega determines its composition based on village custom. The responsibility of the Taupulega is to manage the village in accordance with the objectives set out in r 4 of the Village Incorporation Rules 1986.

3.4. THE PUBLIC SERVICE

The Constitution and the Tokelau Public Service Rules 2004 authorise the General Fono to establish public service positions for the national public service of Tokelau and the village public service. The General Fono appoints a Tokelau Employment Commissioner.[15]All other national public service positions are under the control of the Council for the Ongoing Government.

3.5. DEVOLUTION OF POWERS

On 3 September 1993 there was a significant shift in the New Zealand government's approach towards Tokelau pertaining to the control of the Tokelau public service. The delegation of the State Services Commissioner's power to Tokelau Public Service Commissioners vested self-government in respect of the Tokelau public service in Tokelau. This led to the abolition of the post of Official Secretary and the established Tokelau Public Service Commission in 2001. The Tokelau Public Service Commission of three Tokelau Commissioners was abolished in 2004 and the Public Service Rules 2004 established the Council for the Ongoing Government as the employer of Tokelau's national public servants and the Taupulega as the employer in each village for the village public servants.

In 2016 the General Fono made the Tokelau Employment Commissioner Rules 2016. These Rules provide for the establishment of the position of the Tokelau Employment Commissioner, with specific responsibilities relating to the national public service; the Commissioner reports to the General Fono. The Tokelau Public Service Manual provides a resource for both the national and village public service in relation to employment-related issues. The Public Service

15 Tokelau Employment Commissioner Rules 2016, r 3.

Rules 2004 provide equal opportunities for both men and women and employees are appointed on merit. The village public service is under the Taupulega.

4. THE LEGISLATURE

The New Zealand Parliament is the highest legislature for Tokelau and Acts are the supreme laws of Tokelau. The Tokelau Act 1948 is the principal Act.

The Governor-General of New Zealand legislates for Tokelau via Regulations.[16] Any Regulations made by the Governor-General can override General Fono Rules or Village Rules.

4.1. GENERAL FONO RULES

The Tokelau Amendment Act 1996 granted the General Fono power to make rules internal to Tokelau. The Preamble of the 1996 Amendment Act captured the views of the Taupulega: 'The elders of Tokelau have for many years wished to have a greater and more direct involvement in the government of Tokelau at a national level.' The General Fono rules are the supreme rules made in Tokelau.

The Tokelau Act 1948 gives the General Fono the power to make such rules as it thinks necessary for the peace, order, and good government of Tokelau.[17] Such General Fono Rules have no effect outside Tokelau and must be consistent with any Act of the Parliament of New Zealand that is in force in Tokelau, any regulation made specifically for Tokelau and any international obligation that applies in respect of Tokelau.

The laws that are within the control of the General Fono fall into two main categories: Rules made by the General Fono itself in the exercise of its rule-making power under s 3A of the Tokelau Act 1948, and Regulations made before 1 August 1996 by the Governor-General in Council under s 4 of the Tokelau Act 1948. The General Fono has the power under s 3A(2) of the Tokelau Act 1948 to declare that Regulations made under s 4 are not in force in Tokelau, and in certain cases has used that power to amend them.[18]

The Constitution of Tokelau stipulates that sources of law made in Tokelau are, in descending order of priority, the Constitution of Tokelau, General Fono Rules, Village Rules and the custom of Tokelau.

At the self-government level, the General Fono is the national legislature. General Fono Rules may be disallowed by the Administrator of Tokelau within

16 Tokelau Act 1948, s 4.

17 Tokelau Act 1948, s 3A(2).

18 For example, the Administration Rules 1993 were originally promulgated as regulations – SR 1993/257; that legislation has been amended three times by the General Fono.

30 days of receipt of a copy of the Rules. General Fono rules apply within the territorial limits of the villages of Tokelau and on any ship or aircraft that operates in the service of Tokelau.

The Constitution of Tokelau is a General Fono law; it is not entrenched but there is special provision for amendment. The Constitution consolidated the rules and procedures that explain the internal government of Tokelau, its functions and how it is managed. The Constitution has a Preamble which speaks to the foundation of Tokelau as a nation that is based on God and the three villages – 'Tokelau is founded upon God' – and spells out the values of the people of Tokelau that are protected in the Constitution. The Constitution establishes the General Fono to deal with national issues for Tokelau. The General Fono usually sits three times a year. The Council for the Ongoing Government continues the business of the government when the General Fono is not in session. The Council for the Ongoing Government reports to the General Fono on how the business of the government is conducted between sessions.

The Constitution of Tokelau under r 7 stipulates the law-making procedure that the General Fono must follow. The General Fono must submit draft rules to the Taupulega for consideration. Rule 7 of the Constitution authorises the General Fono to make emergency rules for Tokelau prior to consideration by the Taupulega.

4.2. VILLAGE RULES

The Village Incorporation Rules 1986 provide legal recognition of the Taupulega as the *pule* (power) for each village and grants it law-making powers for its village. Village rules made by a village must not contradict Acts of Parliament that are in force in Tokelau, or any regulation that is in force in Tokelau, or any international obligation of Tokelau applying in respect of Tokelau, or any General Fono Rule.

The Village Rules are specific and unique to each village based on longstanding customs and traditional practices for the purpose of sustaining peace and order in the villages. All villages have written village rules which are accessible to members of the community.

5. THE JUDICIARY

5.1. COURTS OF TOKELAU

The first courts of Tokelau were established in 1912 by the British government with the appointment of a Faamasino (magistrate) to settle grievances and deal with crimes. Improvements in the Tokelau judiciary came with the establishment in 1970 of a Commissioner's Court in each village of Tokelau.

The courts of Tokelau as established under the Tokelau Amendment Act 1986 are the Commissioner's Court in each village, the High Court and the Court of Appeal of New Zealand as courts of Tokelau. A Village Appeal Committee in each village was established under the Crimes, Procedure and Evidence Rules 2003.

5.2. LAW COMMISSIONERS

The Law Commissioners are lay judges appointed by the Governor-General of New Zealand on the recommendation of the Minister of Foreign Affairs and Trade after consultation with the Taupulega of the relevant village. If the Law Commissioner is incapable by reason of sickness or otherwise of performing the office of the Law Commissioner, or where there is a vacancy in the office of the Law Commissioner, the person performing the functions of the Faipule becomes the default Law Commissioner in the village.

A Law Commissioner has jurisdiction only in respect of the island to which that Law Commissioner is appointed and for the territorial sea of Tokelau that surrounds that island. The civil and criminal authority of Commissioners is to hear civil claims of up to NZ$1,000 and to deal with criminal offences punishable by a fine or up to one year's imprisonment. The sentencing power of the Commissioners is limited to imposing a fine of up to NZ$150 and imprisonment of three months.

Appeals to the Village Appeal Committee may be made within 15 days from the day the judgment was delivered by the Commissioner. The decision of the Appeal Committee is final.[19]

The Governor-General, on the recommendation of the Minister of Foreign Affairs made after consultation by that Minister with the elders of the village concerned, may appoint any Tokelauan to be the Commissioner for the village. Every Commissioner shall hold office for a term of three years and shall be eligible for reappointment.

The Governor-General may, if he or she thinks fit, remove a Commissioner for inability or misbehaviour. A Commissioner may resign the office of Commissioner by notice in writing addressed to the Administrator of Tokelau.

The work of the Law Commissioners mostly concerns minor criminal offences.[20] The Law Commissioners have no jurisdiction in relation to land matters or family matters, and in practice hear very few civil claims.

---

19 Crimes, Procedure and Evidence Rules 2003, r 140.

20 For statistics, *Tokelau Judicial Annual Report 2016–2017*; *2017–2018*.

5.3. APPEAL COMMITTEES

An appeal committee[21] is appointed ad hoc by the Taupulega to hear an appeal against the decision of the Commissioner. The appeal committee consists of no fewer than three persons.

5.4. COURT CLERKS

The role of the Court Clerk was formally established under the Crimes, Procedure and Evidence Rules 2003.[22] The Court Clerk is to keep a record book in which are registered all cases commenced in the Commissioner's Court and every order made by the Commissioner.

5.5. LAW PROFESSION

Entitlement to practise in the courts of Tokelau is addressed in r 95 of the Crimes, Procedure and Evidence Rules. The basic requirement is that an applicant has been admitted to practise law in a Commonwealth jurisdiction and possesses sufficient knowledge of the law of Tokelau. Approval to practise is granted by the Council for the Ongoing Government. Few lawyers have been admitted to appear in the courts of Tokelau – some only on a case-specific basis. There are no lawyers in private practice in Tokelau.

5.6. COURT PROCEDURE

All cases in the Court of a Commissioner take place before the Commissioner and such members of the Taupulega as choose to be present. The procedure is oral and inquisitorial. The Commissioner may discuss the case with the members of the Taupulega who are present before giving judgment. The Appeal Committee will follow the same rules of procedure as the Commissioners.

The procedures for the High Court for Tokelau are stated in the Tokelau Amendment Act 1996[23] to be subject to General Fono Rules but otherwise cases proceed 'in the same manner in all respects as if Tokelau was for all purposes part of New Zealand'.

At present, the law lacks detail on court procedure in the High Court for Tokelau. The High Court may sit in Tokelau or New Zealand, or elsewhere[24] at

21 Crimes, Procedure and Evidence Rules 2003, r 140.

22 Initially, the role was performed by the Village Secretary (the Failautuhi).

23 Section 3.

24 Tokelau Act 1986, s 3(3).

the discretion of the Chief Justice. The current law presents difficulties for the people of Tokelau to effectively access the High Court.

5.7. THE HIGH COURT

The High Court of New Zealand has jurisdiction to administer the law of Tokelau as a separate court of justice in and for Tokelau. The jurisdiction of the High Court includes hearing criminal appeals from judgments of the Commissioner, criminal cases transferred by Commissioners, criminal trials on serious matters, such as murder, manslaughter and treason, and civil cases involving more than $1,000. Only two cases have been brought to the High Court; both involved public service employment matters.[25]

5.8. DISPUTE RESOLUTION

Dispute resolution for Tokelau is embedded in its customs and traditional practices. Traditional village systems used by the Taupulega and village civil groups, like the Aumaga (Able-bodied Men's Group) or the Fatupaepae (Women's Committee), are used almost without exception for resolving disputes. Land and custom disputes have always been the prerogative of the Taupulega if families or individuals are not able to resolve them.

The Crimes, Procedure and Evidence Rules recognise alternative dispute resolution and that it may be preferable to resolve disputes outside of court. In criminal cases, the court may promote reconciliation and encourage and facilitate the settlement of some proceedings before or during trial. The court may facilitate reconciliation only in relation to offences of a personal or private nature.[26] In such cases, the accused may agree to pay compensation or make amends in some other way. The court must approve the terms of the agreement.[27]

Where settlement of a criminal matter is approved by the court, the court must order that the proceedings be stayed. The accused is neither discharged nor convicted. If the accused breaches the agreement, he or she may be in contempt of court, and the criminal proceedings may resume.

---

25 *Sam v Council for the Ongoing Government of Tokelau* [2012] NZHC 2775; *Suveinakama v Council for the Ongoing Government of Tokelau* [2019] NZHC 1787 – see Jennifer Corrin 'Tokelau's day in court' (2019) Comparative Law Journal of the Pacific, Hors Serie Vol XXIV: Small Countries: A Collection of Essays, 141. The presumption is that civil cases and criminal appeals in the High Court will 'be decided on the papers', Crimes Procedure and Evidence Rules, r 87. Rule 147 states that in civil matters a court should promote reconciliation and amicable settlements.

26 Crimes, Procedure and Evidence Rules, r 130(1).

27 Crimes, Procedure and Evidence Rules, r 130(1).

In civil cases, the court must, so far as it is possible, promote reconciliation among the parties and encourage them to settle their dispute amicably.[28] The Civil Arbitration Rules 2004 provide another mechanism to resolve civil disputes between parties. The Commissioner has the power under these Rules to appoint an arbitrator to settle disputes between parties.[29]

The alternative dispute resolution mechanisms provided under the Crimes, Procedure and Evidence Rules have yet to be utilised by the Commissioners. This provides an opportunity to look again at creating an independent mechanism outside the court for alternative dispute resolution easily accessed by members of the communities. This can be looked at in the context of reviewing the law to allow a new structure under the law and also for personnel. On the other hand, having custom as the mechanism to resolve land disputes has worked for years, but this can be strengthened in order to address the increasing number of land disputes handled by the Taupulega. Some land disputes have remained unresolved for years.

The establishment of an Appeal Committee system for each village in 2003 further strengthened the judiciary of Tokelau.[30]

5.9. FINAL APPEALS

The Court of Appeal of New Zealand hears appeals on any judgments of the High Court acting as a Tokelau court. The decision of the Court of Appeal is final. There is also a prerogative right of appeal to the head of state.

6. FAMILY LAW

6.1. GENERAL

Civil matters relating to adoption and divorce applications are dealt with by the Council for the Ongoing Government of Tokelau.[31] Decisions of the Council on these matters are final.

Births, deaths and marriage registration was an early preoccupation of the Western Pacific High Commissioner. Provision was first made in respect of foreigners by regulation in 1896.[32] This provision was gradually strengthened

---

28 Crimes, Procedure and Evidence Rules, r 146.
29 There has not been any arbitration carried out in Tokelau.
30 Crimes, Procedure and Evidence Rules, r 140.
31 Divorce Rules 1987, r 10; Adoption Rules 1966, r 8.
32 Queen's Regulation 1 of 1896, Fiji Royal Gazette 1896 no 85.

until 1917, when the registration of births, deaths and marriages was made a formal requirement for Tokelauans and non-Tokelauans alike.

The New Zealand government made new regulations for births and deaths in 1969 and for marriages in 1986. The General Fono amended the birth and death rules in 2014.[33] The equal status of children was formally established by the Tokelau Islands Amendment Act 1969.

The legislation on adoption dates from 1966. The Adoption Rules provide only for adoptions of Tokelauan children. The adoptions are administered by the Council for the Ongoing Government of Tokelau. Foreign adoptions are governed by r 162 of the Crimes Procedure and Evidence Rules.

6.2. DIVORCE

Tokelau divorce laws adapted to the local circumstances were promulgated in 1987 following extensive discussion in Tokelau. The dissolution of marriages under the Divorce Rules is decided by the Council for the Ongoing Government following the recommendation provided by the Taupulega concerned.[34]

The Divorce Rules 1987 give the Taupulega a significant role to bring about reconciliation between the parties to the marriage and to make every effort to resolve their differences. The Taupulega can refer the couple to the Church for counselling, include other family members in the discussion and also reconcile the parties. At the end, the Taupulega provides its recommendation on the divorce application to the Council for the Ongoing Government.

Divorce is rare. The question that is often asked is why applications are required to go through the Taupulega. The Taupulega's role in divorce procedures captures its role in maintaining peace and order in the village and also in families. The involvement of the Taupulega and the Church is significant and it represents the role of custom, traditions and the values of families.

6.3. SUCCESSION

Matters of succession are dealt with by the Succession Rules 2004. The Succession Rules 2004 provide for the succession to moveable property. Succession to land (immovable property) is determined by the Taupulega in accordance with custom.[35]

In the event of intestacy, the family of the deceased will distribute the property of the deceased in accordance with custom. If there is dispute among

33 Births and Deaths Registration Rules 1969.

34 Divorce Rules 1987, r 10.

35 Constitution, r 15.

the family in relation to the distribution of the property, the Taupulega will decide the matter. The village is the ultimate successor of a person who dies leaving no *kaiga* (family) successors.[36]

Wills may be formal and signed and witnessed, or holographic. Testate succession to moveable property is governed by the terms of the will.

7. LAW OF OBLIGATIONS

During the British period there were laws for the control of trade, particularly with relation to arms and alcohol, but subsequently also with relation to the registration of companies, merchant shipping, business licences, and labour contracts. Many of these colonial laws were specifically addressed to non-Tokelauans, but the effect of prescribing for one party to a contract effectively controlled the behaviour of the Tokelauan party to the contract. Intellectual property laws and taxation came at an early date.

The Contract Rules 2004 provide for the administration of all contracts for Tokelau except land and sales by way of judgment execution authorised by law. The rules establish procedures on the formation of contract, the parties to the contract, interpretation of obligations of the parties, and dealing with any fundamental breaches under the contract and remedies for breaches. These Rules are based on and are to be read together with the principles of the UN Convention on Contracts for the International Sale of Goods (CISG).[37]

To date, Tokelauans have not made a clear distinction between what the common law identifies as criminal and tortious actions. Tokelau has an established system of compensation for those who suffer injury. Rule 143 of the Crimes Procedure and Evidence Rules provides that 'there is no right to claim damages for other than property loss in any action at Tokelau law.'

8. LAND LAW

Land in Tokelau is governed by the custom of the village. Matters relating to customary land are not within the jurisdiction of the courts of Tokelau.[38]

The arrival of Europeans in the Western Pacific brought with it demands for land. An early reaction from the High Commissioner of the Western Pacific was to promulgate in 1896 a regulation prohibiting the sale of land to non-native persons and seriously restricting the right to take leases of land.

---

36 Succession Rules 2004.

37 Contract Rules 2002, r 2.

38 Constitution, r 15(1). Jurisdiction over the one piece of privately owned land (about 40 acres) is dealt with in r 15(4).

In the early period of contact with Europeans, some land in Fakaofo was sold to a European trader. In 1963, a portion of that land was acquired from the descendants of the trader by the New Zealand government and vested in the village of Fakaofo.[39] The remaining portion is the only piece of non-customary land in Tokelau.

In 1967 the New Zealand government repealed all existing legislation relating to land in Tokelau and vested all land in the Crown, subject to the rights of ownership in the land as determined in accordance with the customs and usages of the inhabitants of Tokelau. Consistent with the previous legislation, transactions by Tokelauans disposing of land among themselves were not restricted.

The Tokelau Amendment Act 1967 was repealed by the Tokelau Amendment Act 2007 following the enactment by the General Fono of its own land rules. Those rules are now found in r 15 of the Constitution. They vest full control once again in the villages of Tokelau and retain the restriction on alienation of any kind to non-Tokelauans.[40]

9. COMMERCIAL LAW

Tokelau has an array of law relating to commercial matters, arbitration,[41] banking,[42] money lending and insurance,[43] carriage of goods,[44] contract,[45] legal tender,[46] income tax,[47] incorporated bodies,[48] maritime transport,[49] salvage,[50] and telecommunications.[51] The Civil Aviation Act 1990 provides the basis for aviation in Tokelau should the need arise. The English common law and equity remain as the default system, but all references to New Zealand statutes have been repealed or replaced by laws made by the General Fono. In particular, the Application of New Zealand Law Rules 2004 provide for the law of New Zealand on bills of exchange, marine insurance, partnership and intellectual property for the time being in force in New Zealand to be the law of Tokelau on those matters.

---

39 Tokelau Amendment Act 1963.
40 Constitution, r 15(5).
41 Civil Arbitration Rules 2004.
42 The Banking Rules 2004 establish a Tokelau Savings Bank and a Tokelau Development Bank.
43 Business Restrictions Rules 1989.
44 The Carriage of Goods by Sea Rules 2004 incorporated the Hague Rules.
45 Contract Rules 2004.
46 Interpretation Rules 2003, r 12.
47 Income Tax Rules 1997.
48 The Incorporation Rules 2003 provide a set of general rules for the incorporation of bodies for a wide variety of purposes.
49 Inter-Atoll/Shipping Rules 2015; Transport Tokelau Corporation Rules 1997.
50 Shipping (Salvage) Rules 1992.
51 Telecommunication Rules 1996.

10. ENVIRONMENTAL LAW INCLUDING RESPONSES TO CLIMATE CHANGE

The environment of Tokelau is fragile and legislation is essential for its sustainability, given human activities, exotic pests and other organisms, and natural hazards such as climate change phenomena.

The Biosecurity Rules 2003 protect and sustain the fragile environment of Tokelau from being destroyed by the introduction and spread of exotic pests and diseases and other organisms, and provide facilities for biosecurity services for the import and export of animals and plants, of animal products and plant products, and of other goods safely into and out of Tokelau. The rules provide procedures for containment and eradication of new incursions and support international cooperation in the prevention of the movement of pests and diseases.[52]

Under the Emergency Rules 2003, the Ulu of Tokelau must advise the outside world if Tokelau is affected by an emergency. The pronouncement of such an emergency happens after discussions between the Ulu of Tokelau and the Faipule of a particular village about the condition of the village concerned and the nature of the emergency.

The emergency can take different forms: it can be a serious threat to the environment of that village or of Tokelau as a whole or it can endanger life or property on one of the villages of Tokelau. The emergency could be a fire, a storm or a disease outbreak.[53]

Tokelau has yet to develop substantive environmental rules that will address the specifics of the approach (government and village) for the protection and preservation of its pristine environment from the impacts of climate change and natural disasters.

As Tokelau is a non-self-governing territory of New Zealand, it is the overall responsibility of New Zealand to assist Tokelau. The Joint Statement of the Principles of Partnership between Tokelau and New Zealand 2003 provides for the defence and security of Tokelau. New Zealand discharges this responsibility as the need arises, in close consultation and collaboration with Tokelau. The Tokelau National Disaster Plan plays a vital role.

Tokelau has a Memorandum of Understanding (MOU) of 2003 and a Waste Management MOU of 2007 with Samoa. Both MOUs provide extra support for Tokelau in terms of reducing waste and further impact on the environment, and support for the implementation of Tokelau law.

The Village Rules of Fakaofo, Atafu and Nukunonu provide procedures for the management of waste and instructions for waste disposal in specified locations.

---

52 Biosecurity Rules 2003. See also the Rhinoceros Beetle Rules 1957.

53 Tokelau Emergency Rules 2003, r 2.

The customary concept of *lafu* is used by the Taupulega as a means to control access to land resources.

11. NATURAL RESOURCES

Tokelau has support through New Zealand especially pertaining to the management of its exclusive economic zone.[54] Fisheries are Tokelau's major resource.[55]

The Taupulega have, under the Village Incorporation Rules 1986, established Village Rules to effectively manage fisheries and protect the marine resources from pollution and the environment from being exploited. These Village Rules are very detailed in terms of the measures and restrictions for conservation and preservation, and declare protected areas covering marine and terrestrial ecosystems. The Rules relate to the lagoon, reef areas and territorial sea.

While there is law to manage and protect Tokelau's natural resources, it is critical that the law be updated to address specific procedures for the management of the limited natural resources and their sustainability for the survival of the people and to cover any areas of Tokelau's natural resources that are not currently addressed.

12. CRIMINAL LAW

The first criminal legislation for Tokelau was the Native Laws of the Union Group of 1912 published by the Western Pacific High Commission. These rules, inspired by British notions of criminal law and punishment, were basic in form and reflected not only some traditional offences but also some of the realities of Tokelau life, such as the provision for the payment of fines by coconuts. These rules were confirmed and elaborated on in the Native Laws Ordinance 1917. The Tokelauan language was not used in either the 1912 or 1917 laws, but the Samoan versions would have been accessible to the people and to the local magistrate as a consequence of the missionary influence and the use of the Samoan Bible.

The 1917 system remained in force until 1975. It had not been followed extensively; the preference was to deal with socially unacceptable behaviour in accordance with tradition. In 1975 the New Zealand government imposed a new

---

54 Tokelau (Exclusive Economic Zone) Fishing Regulations 2012 made pursuant to ss 8 and 11 of the Tokelau (Territorial Sea and Exclusive Economic Zone) Act 1997 and s 4 of the Tokelau Act 1948.

55 The revenue from fisheries was US$14 million in 2019 (reported to the General Fono of March 2020 by the Administrator of Tokelau via video link on 11 March 2020 due to COVID-19 travel restrictions).

criminal law system which was modelled on the criminal law of New Zealand but taken directly from the law of Niue. This body of law never became part of the social ordering system of Tokelau.

The 1975 system was replaced by the Crimes, Procedure and Evidence Rules 2003, which were promulgated by the General Fono after an extensive review of offences and criminal procedures. These Rules include the most common and most serious of customary offences. Criminal offences also exist under other legislation, such as the Electricity, Gas, and Dangerous Goods Rules 2003.

It is time now to review of the Crimes, Procedure and Evidence Rules 2003 and other rules with criminal offences to match the current state of development of Tokelau. There are new offences which must be incorporated into the Rules. Likewise, the penalties and the jurisdiction of the Commissioners must be reviewed.

13. INTERNATIONAL LAW

Tokelau and New Zealand acknowledge that, subject to United Nations General Assembly Resolution 2625 (XXV), Tokelau does not have an international legal personality separate from that of New Zealand. New Zealand accordingly continues to enter into binding treaty obligations on Tokelau's behalf.[56]

Tokelau is administered by New Zealand in accordance with art 73 of the Charter of the United Nations. New Zealand is therefore under an international obligation and 'sacred trust' to develop self-government in Tokelau. The ultimate goal of the development of self-government is the exercise by Tokelau of its right to self-determination. Further, the Joint Principles of Partnership 2003 provide that New Zealand will encourage Tokelau to engage in foreign relations with its support.

New Zealand supports Tokelau's aspirations to enter into arrangements with other countries or to join regional or international organisations in its own right, where such participation is consistent with Tokelau's status as a non-self-governing territory. Tokelau consults New Zealand about any such developments. This has led Tokelau to enter into regional organisations and full membership of the Forum Fisheries Agency, the South Pacific Regional Organization and the Secretariat of the Pacific Community, as well as becoming an observer in the FAO and an associate member of the Pacific Islands Forum. It also has MOUs with other countries, for example Samoa and Tuvalu.

In conducting foreign affairs on Tokelau's behalf, New Zealand advises Tokelau as to which international instruments to extend to Tokelau through New Zealand's treaty action. This process is to ensure adequate consultation with

---

[56] Eg maritime boundary treaties.

Tokelau with regard to treaty actions that New Zealand is intending to take, and to refrain from extending any treaty action to Tokelau unless Tokelau expressly requests to be included. New Zealand assists Tokelau, through the provision of advice and administrative assistance, to implement treaty obligations as required.

The Tokelau (Territorial Sea and Exclusive Economic Zone) Act 1977 established an exclusive economic zone for Tokelau in accordance with the United Nations Convention on the Law of the Sea. Consistent with international practice on the delimitation of maritime boundaries, there are boundary treaties with the United States (in respect of American Samoa), France (in respect of Wallis and Futuna) and the Cook Islands.

The individual human rights and freedoms for all the people of Tokelau are those described in the Universal Declaration on Human Rights and reflected in the International Covenant on Civil and Political Rights.[57] The rights of individuals in Tokelau must be exercised having proper regard to the rights of other individuals and to the community to which the individual belongs.

Complaints concerning any breach or alleged breach of a human right are dealt with by the Council for the Ongoing Government. The Council for the Ongoing Government has original and final authority to determine all matters of human rights. Should the Council of Ongoing Government agree with the complaint, it may make any order it thinks appropriate for the protection of the right. An order made by the Council of Ongoing Government may be enforced in the same manner as a judgment of the High Court. The Council is the mechanism to protect and promote the rights and freedoms of the people of Tokelau.[58]

Tokelau is subject to the provisions of the First Optional Protocol to the International Convention on Civil and Political Rights.

The extension of the human rights conventions to Tokelau was through New Zealand's ratification. New Zealand therefore reports on how the rights of the people of Tokelau are protected and promoted.

In addition, Tokelau is bound by and reports regularly, as required on: the International Covenant on Economic, Social and Cultural Rights; the International Convention on the Elimination of All Forms of Racial Discrimination; the Convention on the Elimination of All Forms of Discrimination against Women; the Convention against Torture and Other Cruel, Inhuman or Degrading Treatment; and on several ILO Conventions.

Tokelau is affiliated to the International Labour Organization through New Zealand's treaty ratification. This requires Tokelau to report annually, through New Zealand, on the employment conditions of women and men in Tokelau and ensure the laws provide for equal opportunities for their employment, mechanisms to voice employment grievances and safe working conditions.

---

57 Constitution, r 16.

58 No human rights case has been referred to the Council.

The role of international law and treaties for Tokelau is significant to the advancement and development of Tokelau towards becoming more self-reliant. The longstanding relationship shared by Tokelau and New Zealand has enabled Tokelau to engage with regional organisations and enter international regional agreements that provide long-term benefits for Tokelau. This manner of engagement can however be frustrating, because Tokelau as a colony is not free to fully exploit international law and treaties that would assist Tokelau's development as a nation.

14. CIVIL SOCIETY ORGANISATIONS

The historical evidence available at the time of first European contact with the islands of Tokelau indicates a system of village organisation, with the communities organised as a feudal domain dominated by the ruler of Fakaofo.[59]

The Constitution of Tokelau in the Preamble clearly states that the community groups will have clear aims and constitutions and will have a role in the development of Tokelau.

In the context of Tokelau, one of the community groups is the Able-bodied Men's Group, usually known in Tokelau as the Aumaga or Taulelea. This group comprises all the men of the village aged between 16 and 65. The other traditional group is the Women's Committee, or Fatupaepae. This group includes all the women and girls of the village.

The youth and sports groups[60] are organised differently in each village of Tokelau: some are split into two groups; some have one group for both youth and sports.

These community groups operate under the umbrella of the Taupulega. In Tokelau they are the backbone of the village. They carry out the wishes of the Taupulega to keep the village thriving and in order.

The Church is firmly established in the three villages of Tokelau and the established Churches are the Catholic Church in both Fakaofo and Nukunonu and the Ekalehia Fakapotopotoga Kelihiano Tokelau (EFKT) in Atafu and Fakaofo.[61] The Preamble of the Constitution of Tokelau makes it clear that Tokelau is founded upon God. Tokelau is a Christian nation. The Church has a crucial role in the development of Tokelau. In all the villages of Tokelau the Church is the backbone for providing peace and stability in the lives of the communities of Tokelau.

---

59 A Hooper 'Ghosts of Hierarchy I' (Paper presented at conference on Hierarchy, Ancestry and Alliance at the Australian National University, 1990).

60 'Youth' in Tokelau as defined under the Tokelau Youth Policy 2013–2015 and in the context of Tokelau are those between the ages of 15 and 39. The main common sports are netball, rugby league and rugby sevens, cricket, volleyball, rowing and relays.

61 Successor to the London Missionary Society.

There are no trade unions in Tokelau. However, the Public Service Manual provides procedures to address grievances of public servants. The procedures and processes stipulated are for national and village employees. A human resource adviser at the national or village level acts as a contact person to hold discussions and negotiations between the employers and the employees in relation to any grievance pertaining to work conditions. The government and the villages are the main employers.

15. CONCLUDING REMARKS

The history of Tokelau is relevant to its current legal system. The system has gained more and more strength since the beginning of colonialism. The significant political and constitutional changes that occurred for Tokelau under the administration of New Zealand were timely, with the development of its national governance, the General Fono and the Council for the Ongoing Government and external engagements. As for the villages, their structures and systems remained unaltered, but were strengthened by the legal recognition of the Taupulega as the *pule*, or authority, and as having the power to legislate for the village.

The focus at present is for Tokelau to become more self-reliant. The Joint Principles of Partnership Agreement 2003 is a key document that outlines the responsibilities of the partners. Its relevance and whether it is effectively serving Tokelau, to advance developments that would increase its capacity to exercise its right to self-determination, need to be examined.

The Tokelau Public Service Manual provides a mechanism for public servants of Tokelau to lodge grievances relating to employment issues. The decisions of the employer are final. There is no appeal from the decision of the employer. The employers at both national and village level are political institutions and this may inhibit public servants from taking their grievances to the court level by way of judicial review or otherwise.

A review of the Public Service Manual and the implementation of the Tokelau Employment Commissioner Rules will ensure there are adequate mechanisms for dispute resolution that will enable public servants at the national and village levels to voice their grievances in a fair and transparent process and provide an appeal process should matters not be resolved satisfactorily.

On a broad view, the inclusion of the Kauhauatea in the General Fono of Tokelau is unique to Tokelau. The place of elders is rightfully in the village in the Taupulega. The inclusion of Kauhauatea in the General Fono as the highest national political institution of Tokelau is a great accomplishment and an acknowledgement of the importance of the elders in the culture of Tokelau, and of their wisdom and knowledge.

The judicial system can be traced back to colonialism and Tokelau is free of prisons and serious crime. The system has had a positive impact for many years but times are changing and judicial needs are growing. The members of the community are increasingly becoming aware of their rights under the law and therefore demanding timely and responsive justice.

The place of traditions and customs in the development of Tokelau as a nation is very special. The civil society organisations in Tokelau are the best examples of this. These civil society organisations exist to serve the purposes of the village and the will of the Taupulega, rather than their own needs. It is best to keep these traditions alive rather than make them formal civil society organisations under rules and procedures enacted by the General Fono.

The mechanism provided under the Public Service Manual to address any grievances of national and village public servants is rather challenging, especially for the village employees, who have to take their grievances to the Taupulega. This mechanism is rarely used.

During the period of colonialism, the islands of Tokelau operated as individual islands until the elders saw the need for a national body and started meeting, despite the challenges presented by transportation and communication. The Tokelau Amendment Act 1982 marked the formal recognition of the General Fono, with 45 members equally representing all the islands. This represents the wisdom and the hearts of the elders that led Tokelau to the current era. In contrast to the 45 General Fono members of 1982, there are now 22 in the General Fono based on the formula in the Constitution. The number in the General Fono will continue to change as the population count for each village is updated before the national elections every three years.

BIBLIOGRAPHY

Huntsman, Judith and Anthony Hooper *Tokelau* (Auckland University Press, 1996).

Macgregor, Gordon *Ethnology of Tokelau Islands* (Bernice P Bishop Museum, Bulletin 146, 1937, reprinted 1971).

Matagi Tokelau (Office for Tokelau Affairs, 1991).

Pacific Islands Legal Information Institute *Tokelau Primary Materials* <http://www.paclii.org/countries/tk.html>.

Tokelau – A History of Government (Office of the Council of the Ongoing Government, 2008).

Tulafono a Tokelau (Council for the Ongoing Government, Tokelau, 2016) [a collection of the legislation as at 2016].

TONGA

Reimen Hii

1. INTRODUCTION

The Kingdom of Tonga is an independent sovereign state comprising some 170 islands spread over 700,000 square metres in the Polynesia subregion of the South Pacific. Its islands are divided into three main groups – Tongatapu, Ha'apai, Vava'u – along with the Niuas, isolated islands to the far north.

Colloquially known as the 'Friendly Islands' because of the congenial reception accorded to Captain James Cook on his first visit in 1773, contemporary Tonga is homogeneous in language and culture, with a population of over 100,651 people,[1] most of whom reside on the main island of Tongatapu.

Tonga's geographical and historical context has had a significant impact on the shape of its culture and the development of its legal institutions and jurisprudence. Tonga has a traditionally hierarchical organisation and extensive kinship groups that were conducive to the formation of a centralised chiefly system, which had evolved by the 12th century into a hierarchal system of monarchy similar to that of European dynasties.

Settled over 3,000 years ago, Tonga sits at the historical heart of growth and spread of Polynesian civilisation. The period between 1200 AD and 1500 AD was one of great expansion and dominance, where the kings of the Tu'i Tonga Empire conquered a territory stretching as far as Wallis and Futuna, Tokelau, Tuvalu, Nauru, parts of Fiji, the Marquesas, Solomon Islands, Kiribati, Niue, the Cook Islands and parts of Samoa.

1 Overall total population – 'World Population Prospects: The 2019 Revision' (xslx). <population.un.org> (custom data acquired via website). United Nations Department of Economic and Social Affairs, Population Division. Retrieved 9 November 2019.

The 15th to 17th centuries marked the arrival of Europeans to the Tongan islands. By 1845, Taufa'ahau, the inheritor of a powerful regional chiefdom as *Tu'i Kanokupolu*, had unified Tonga under his leadership as King George Tupou I after converting to Christianity.

Upon his ascension as the undisputed leader of Tonga in 1852, Tupou I saw the institution of far-reaching reforms to the Tongan political and legal system, including abolishing serfdom in the Vava'u island groups in 1835, publishing the Vava'u Code – Tonga's first written laws (and forerunner to the first Tongan Constitution) – and, with the help of English missionary Shirley Baker, declaring Tonga a constitutional monarchy in 1875.

Though exposed to colonial forces, Tonga is unique in the Pacific in that it has never lost indigenous governance. From 1900, Tonga concluded a Treaty of Friendship with the United Kingdom, making it a British Protectorate – the Kingdom remained self-governing, with the British responsible for foreign and defence affairs.[2] Tonga ceased its status as a British Protectorate on 4 June 1970, following the exchange of letters between King Tupou IV and Queen Elizabeth II requesting the termination of the treaty under arrangements established by the third monarch Queen Salote.

In 2010 Tonga experienced a series of democratic reforms whereby the sovereign, Tupou V, voluntarily relinquished much of his power and surrendered his day-to-day role in government to the Prime Minister and Cabinet. This resulted in the balance of power shifting from a traditional hereditary or absolute monarchy towards a constitutional monarchy. The reforms also resulted in significant changes to the composition of the executive government (termed the Cabinet in the Constitution), the legislature, and appointments to the judiciary, by adopting aspects similar to those in the modern UK constitutional framework and neighbouring countries. The reforms signify a form of law-making and dispute resolution unique in the South Pacific.

2. SOURCES OF LAW

The sources of law of Tonga's legal system are the Constitution, statutes and subsidiary legislative instruments, and English common law.[3] There has also been a significant increase in the development of a Tongan common law since the early 1990s.

Over the past 150 years, Tonga has been engaged in the formation and preservation of key institutions. Initially, the successful ordering of a Tongan

---

2 Treaty of Friendship Between the United Kingdom and the Kingdom of Tonga, signed 18 May 1900.

3 Brill Nijhoff, *International Encyclopaedia of Comparative Law Online*, Volume 1: National Reports 1974, 'Tonga: II/IX Sources of Law and Present Law'.

nation required the adoption of compatible concepts from two distinct legal cultures by combining the authoritarian elements of Tongan chiefly law with the command theory of English jurisprudence. These forces, together with the Christian notions of individual responsibility and morality, eroded other characteristics of Tongan legal culture, such as reciprocity of obligation and the kinship group, to the point where such characteristics are now scarcely reflected in the legal framework of the State.

Tonga's first Constitution tied together the threads of Tongan and English law and initiated an active process of law-making which acknowledged the Constitution as the source of its legitimacy. As a result, little in Tongan law can be discerned as based solely on Tongan norms or customs. The structure of central government and the law of land tenure and local government reflect an amalgam of traditional and introduced thinking. Nevertheless, these longstanding statutory provisions are now regarded as legitimately Tongan.[4]

2.1. CONSTITUTION

The Constitution of Tonga (Cap 1.01) is the supreme law of Tonga;[5] any law inconsistent with the Constitution is void to the extent of the inconsistency.[6]

The Constitution may be amended (and has been amended at least 39 times) by the Legislative Assembly passing an amending Act that is unanimously accepted by the Privy Council and approved by the sovereign.[7]

The Constitution begins with a Declaration of Rights that sets out fundamental legal principles applicable in the Kingdom and guarantees a number of rights applicable to all persons within the realm, including a declaration of freedom and abolishment of slavery,[8] freedom of worship and of the press,[9] and a guarantee that the same law applies to all persons regardless of their social status or nationality, thus reinforcing the rule of law.[10]

The Constitution also establishes the institutions of government – Cabinet,[11] legislature,[12] and judiciary[13] – and their form, as well as protecting

4 Guy Powles 'Tonga' in Michael A Ntumy (ed) *South Pacific Islands Legal Systems* (University of Hawaii Press, 1993) 317.
5 Constitution, cl 82.
6 Constitution, cl 82, as amended by Constitution Amended Act 1990.
7 Constitution, cl 79.
8 Constitution, cls 1 and 2.
9 Constitution, cls 5 and 7.
10 Constitution, cl 4.
11 Constitution, cls 31–35.
12 Constitution, cls 56–83.
13 Constitution, cls 83A–103A.

the order of succession to the throne,[14] and titles and hereditary estates of the nobles.[15] Similar to many other Pacific island nations, land is given preeminent treatment and specifically enshrined in the Constitution. Land vests in the sovereign and is granted to the nobles and titular chiefs to become their hereditary estates.[16]

2.2. STATUTES AND SUBSIDIARY LEGISLATION

From 1966 until 2003, the Civil Law Act (Cap 5.01) provided that the courts of Tonga 'shall apply the common law of England and the rules of equity, together with statutes of general application in force in England'. To be of general application, statutes were required to be 'of general relevance to the conditions of other countries, and in particular, not based upon politics or circumstances particular to England'.[17] In 2003 the Civil Law (Amendment) Act 2003 deleted references to 'statutes of general application', resulting in a lacuna in the law if there was no local Act on point.

Since 2003, the Tongan legislature has embarked on a legislative reform programme which has bridged many of the gaps, such as the Guardianship Act 2003 (Cap 6.04), the Admiralty Act 2008 (Cap 3.10), the Copyright Act 2008 (Cap 17.05), and legislation against unfair business practices, such as the Protection Against Unfair Competition Act (Cap 17.11). However, as of 2020, Tonga lacks a Bankruptcy Act[18] and an Act to deal with ancillary relief to replace the defunct Matrimonial Causes Act 1973 (UK). New legislation is commonly based on foreign models, due to Tonga's foreign aid obligations to enact legislative reform; this creates a level of consistency and homogeneity across South Pacific legal systems. To the extent that there is a lacuna, the courts have applied English common law and rules of equity or resorted to other Tongan statutes of similar application to fill those gaps.[19] Tongan statutes (including the 2020 Current Revised Edition) are accessible on the Tongan Attorney General's Office's website[20] and on the PacLII website.[21]

---

14 Constitution, cl 32.

15 Constitution, cls 111–112.

16 Constitution, cls 104–114.

17 *Teta v Ulrich* [1981–88] Tonga LR 127; *Tu'itavake v Propert* [1989] Tonga LR 14.

18 A Bankruptcy Act has been foreshadowed as references to such Act have been made in the Receivership Act 2015 (Cap 17.14).

19 See for example *Fresha Exports Ltd v Tonga Co-operative Federation Ltd* [2010] Tonga LR 200 at [9]; *Edwards v Tapueluelu* [2018] TOSC 21 at [51]; *Fonokalafi v Tonga Communications Corporation Ltd* [2010] TOSC 3.

20 <www.ago.gov.to>.

21 <www.paclii.org>. References in this chapter to the Tongan Constitution, and subsidiary legislation are up to date through to 1 December 2020 and have been published in the Revised Edition of the Laws of Tonga consolidated to the end of 2020 pursuant to the Laws Consolidation Act 1988.

2.3. COMMON LAW AND EQUITY

Prior to 1966, English common law had been applied by the Supreme Court of Tonga without question where Tongan law was silent. This included assuming inherent jurisdiction to issue prerogative writs, giving guidance on the hearing of appeals, and applying the principles of natural justice and substantive common law in areas such as tort and contract law.

In 1966 the application of common law and equity was given statutory force by the Civil Law Act, which provided that the Tongan courts were to 'apply the common law of England and the rules of equity'. These laws apply only so far as no other Act or legislative provision has been made in the Kingdom, and 'as the circumstances of the Kingdom and of its inhabitants permit and subject to such qualifications as local circumstances render necessary'.[22]

English common law is binding on the Tongan courts, but judicial decisions from other common law jurisdictions (particularly New Zealand, Australia and Fiji) are often cited in the decisions of the Tongan courts as persuasive and relevant. This is a by-product of Tonga sourcing its superior court judges from its Commonwealth neighbours. Since 1990, there has been significant development of a Tongan common law, with a critical mass of published decisions from the superior courts of Tonga in all areas of public and private law, primarily criminal and constitutional law. Where there is a relevant Tongan decision, the courts have generally preferred those cases over English decisions for their precedent value, which conforms with s 4 of the Civil Law Act.

Tongan cases are reported in the Tonga Law Reports, an authorised series of reports which publishes selected decisions from the Court of Appeal, Supreme Court and Land Court commencing from 1908. The [2016] Tonga LR is the latest edition of the reports and available at the Tongan Attorney General's Office's website.[23] The 2016 decisions are also available on the PacLII website.[24]

2.4. CUSTOM AND TRADITIONAL LAW

Until recently, Tonga did not recognise customary law as a distinct source of law, unlike other neighbouring South Pacific legal systems. In *Faletau v 'Akau'ola*[25] Lewis J of the Supreme Court held in relation to an application to strike out a claim based on a customary law cause of action:

> The phenomenon which has brought about inroads into custom in Tonga has been the passage of laws in accord with the principles set out in the Constitution Act of 1875

22 Civil Law Act Cap 14.03, s 4.
23 <www.ago.gov.to>.
24 <www.paclii.org>.
25 [1997] Tonga LR 185.

> and other legislation by the Tongans themselves. That is, the law in Tonga has evolved by statutes made by the Tongans in a Tongan Parliament embracing and discarding custom as the Tongan Parliament representing all Tongans, deemed appropriate.

On 15 October 2020, the Legislative Assembly unanimously passed a Bill to amend the Constitution by inserting a clause 89A requiring every court or tribunal in the Kingdom to take Tonga's 'customs, traditions, practices, values and usages' into consideration, where relevant, in deciding any matter before it. Clause 89A defines:

> Customs in Tonga comprises all reasonable and sufficiently certain customs, traditions, practices, values and usages of Tongans: and every Court or Tribunal in the Kingdom, where relevant, shall have regard thereto when deciding any matter before them for decision. Custom requires to be established in evidence but in so doing a Court or Tribunal shall not apply technical rules of evidence but shall admit and consider such information as is available. Tongan Customs shall not be lost by reason of lack of recent usage.

The amendments were passed without consultation and have been met with criticism by the Tonga Law Society as 'disturbing', 'rushed', and 'made without prior notice'.[26] As of 1 June 2021, they have not been assented to by the sovereign and promulgated as law.

The proposed constitutional requirement to take into account unwritten custom will raise practical difficulties in terms of the method and standard of proof of custom, and its unwritten and evolving nature. During legislative debates, concerns were expressed 'over the unknown perimeters of traditional culture and the possibility for Clause 89A to become a hiding place for crimes'[27] such as corruption.

Regardless of whether the sovereign assents to the insertion of clause 89A of the Constitution, custom has and will continue to play a role in Tongan jurisprudence in so far as it has been transformed into statute, and informs the content of substantive law in areas such as kinship relations, mitigation of sentences and land law. Tongan custom, practice and conventions about government processes also form an important part of the constitutional framework, and help give it practical effect.[28] Tongan custom in relation to the authority of chiefs and property law has long been transformed into a codified amalgam of local statutes: see below under sections 3, 6 and 9.

---

26 See 'Tonga Law Society Statement on the Constitutional Amendment passed by parliament on 15 October 2020' (online 21 November 2020) <https://matangitonga.to/2020/10/22/tonga-law-society>.

27 See 'Parliament amends Tongan Constitution to include unwritten "customs"' *Matangi Tonga Online* (online 17 October 2020) <https://matangitonga.to/2020/10/17/parliament-amends-tongan-constitution-include-unwritten-customs>.

28 *Cabinet Manual of His Majesty's Cabinet* (Cap 01.01.02) at [41].

3. CONSTITUTIONAL LAW

Traditional Tongan rulers created a hierarchal system of monarchy similar to that of European dynasties. Tonga's traditional complex social structure is essentially broken into three tiers: the sovereign (typically, a male king with the royal title passed from father to eldest son), the nobles, and the commoners. Between the nobles and commoners are *Matapule*, sometimes called 'talking chiefs', who are associated with the monarch or a noble and who may or may not hold estates. The enactment of the Constitution transformed the pre-1875 concepts of traditional leadership and control of land into a constitutional model of intermediary nobles and hereditary land estates, whilst retaining the sovereign's authority over tribal chiefs or local leaders. Today's Tongan monarchy remains an influential and powerful entity in the Kingdom, though under King George Tupou V the Crown made concessions to accommodate a more democratic state.

Despite the constitutional overlay, status and rank play a powerful role in personal relationships, even within families. Traditional custom obligations still impose reciprocal responsibilities on commoners and nobles; the nobility are able to extract favours from people living on their estates, and likewise must extend favours to their people.

3.1. THE SOVEREIGN

The sovereign is accorded preeminent status in law, tradition, and by his or her constitutional function. The Constitution provides that the form of government for the Kingdom is a constitutional monarchy under the sovereign and his or her successors.[29] The sovereign has two roles, as the head of state of the Kingdom of Tonga,[30] and as the *Hau 'o e Fonua*, the supreme head of the traditional kingship system of the Kingdom.[31] The sovereign is also the head of the executive[32] and commander-in-chief of the armed forces of Tonga.[33]

The Tongan monarchy has perpetual succession through the male line and, if there is no male heir, through the female line. The royal line is protected by the requirement that the sovereign's consent be given to the marriage of any member of the royal family, which includes all persons related by descent either lineally

29 Constitution, cl 31.
30 Constitution, cl 31.
31 Constitution, cl 41.
32 Constitution, cls 31, 41 and 50.
33 Constitution, cl 36.

or collaterally to the sovereign up to 20 times removed.[34] The sovereign may cancel the right of such persons and his or her heirs to succeed to the Crown of Tonga, and such persons whose rights are cancelled shall be regarded as dead. The Constitution also forbids a person who is insane or imbecile, or found guilty of an offence punishable by imprisonment for more than two years, from succeeding.[35]

In the absence of a lawful heir, the sovereign may appoint a successor, subject to the approval of nobles of the Legislative Assembly, who may, as a last resort, choose the successor to the throne as 'the first of a new dynasty': cl 32 Constitution. The present sovereign, King Tupou VI, succeeded to the throne on 18 March 2012 upon the death of his elder brother King George Tupou V.

The sovereign's prerogative powers are routinely exercised by Cabinet, ministers and officials on behalf of the government as a whole. However, unlike other neighbouring constitutional monarchies in the Commonwealth, the Tongan sovereign may and commonly does exercise some powers personally. These include calling or dissolving the Legislative Assembly and initiating elections to that body;[36] assenting, vetoing or refusing to sign legislation passed by the Legislative Assembly;[37] making treaties with foreign states;[38] proclaiming martial law in the event of war;[39] and appointing judges with the advice of the Judicial Appointments and Discipline Panel (JADP).[40]

In an emergency, the sovereign in council may make regulations 'for securing the public safety, the defence of the Kingdom, the maintenance of public order and for the maintaining of supplies and services essential to the life of the community'. Such regulations may provide for arrest and trial, detention, or the taking of property – notwithstanding any enactment to the contrary and without affecting the prerogative of the sovereign.[41] In recent times, states of emergency have been declared in the wake of the 2008 pro-democracy riots, and in 2020 to deal with the extraordinary challenges posed by the coronavirus (COVID-19) pandemic.

The Constitution does not contain any provision which allows for the impeachment or removal of the sovereign, his or her descendants by royal succession, or royal estates and lands. The Constitution also provides that there can be no amendment to the Constitution without the sovereign's consent (cls 41, 56, 68 and 70).

34 Constitution, cl 32.
35 Constitution, cl 35.
36 Constitution, cl 38.
37 Constitution, cls 41 and 79.
38 Constitution, cl 39.
39 Constitution, cl 46.
40 Constitution, cls 85, 86, 86A and 88.
41 Emergency Powers Act (Cap 20.06).

3.2. THE EXECUTIVE

3.2.1. *Privy Council*

The Privy Council presided over by the sovereign constitutes the highest executive authority in Tonga's constitutional arrangements. Its members consist of 'such people whom the King shall see fit to call his Council'.[42] Its function is to provide the sovereign with general advice or in particular in the discharge of the sovereign's functions as head of the executive. The Prime Minister and elected government ministers are not automatically granted membership to the Privy Council.

The Privy Council also acts as the final appellate court in relation to disputes from the Land Court about hereditary estates and titles. The Privy Council is rarely called to sit in its judicial capacity, and has delivered only one judgment in the last 10 years.[43]

The Privy Council's legislative powers under the Constitution were repealed by the 2010 amendments.

3.2.2. *Cabinet*

The Cabinet exercises the executive authority of the Kingdom and has collective responsibility to the Legislative Assembly.[44] 'Executive authority' is defined under the Constitution to exclude all powers vested in the sovereign or sovereign in council.

Headed by the Prime Minister, ministers meet collectively in Cabinet to consider the business of government in the tradition of a Westminster-style system. Ministers are responsible for specified government ministries, departments and portfolios pursuant to statute and (less commonly) Privy Council decisions. This operating principle is reflected in cl 51(1) of the Constitution and in s 17(3) of the Government Act, which requires the Prime Minister not to decide 'any grave or important matter' without the consent of Cabinet. By convention, this requirement for the consent of Cabinet applies to policy and government decisions, and not for the advice the Prime Minister might give the sovereign on appointments and dismissals of ministers.[45]

The Constitution also gives a number of significant powers of decision either to Cabinet directly or to the sovereign with the consent of Cabinet,

---

42 Constitution, cl 50.

43 *Fielakepa v Aleamotu'a* (unreported, Privy Council of Tonga, PC Appeal 1/16, 12 August 2016, His Majesty King Tupou VI, Lord Tupou KC, Lord Dalgety QC, Lord Madraiwiwi, Paulsen LCJ, Cato J).

44 Constitution, cl 51.

45 *Cabinet Manual of His Majesty's Cabinet* (Cap 01.01.02) at [20].

including decisions on the currency of Tonga;[46] the determination of the terms of leases of land up to 99 years in length, and the approval of leases of land to religious bodies and on beach frontages;[47] and approval of government expenditure during emergencies (with a requirement to report to the Legislative Assembly on such decisions).[48] Additionally, many other Acts provide powers and functions for Cabinet, including powers to make regulations and other delegated legislation.

The Prime Minister is appointed and dismissed by the sovereign on the recommendation of the Legislative Assembly. The Prime Minister presides over Cabinet and leads the government in the Legislative Assembly and is the government's principal spokesperson. The Prime Minister also has residual responsibility for the administration of any department or government property not otherwise specifically provided for.[49] By convention, the Prime Minister chairs Cabinet meetings and is responsible for Cabinet procedure. The Constitution requires the Prime Minister to report to the sovereign regularly on matters that have arisen with the government and upon the state of the country.[50]

The Deputy Prime Minister is formally appointed by the sovereign on the Prime Minister's recommendation and exercises all powers and performs all duties of the Prime Minister if the Prime Minister is absent, unwell or otherwise unable to perform the duties of office.[51]

Members of Cabinet consist of the Prime Minister and other such ministers nominated by the Prime Minister and appointed by the sovereign from amongst the members of the Legislative Assembly. The Constitution also allows the Prime Minister to appoint up to four non-elected representatives as Cabinet Ministers.[52] Appointed Cabinet members are entitled to sit and exercise all the rights, duties and responsibilities of an elected representative, except for participating in any vote of no confidence in the Prime Minister.

The Constitution requires ministers to prepare a report each year on the affairs of each Ministry for the sovereign to forward to the Legislative Assembly.[53] The Legislative Assembly may question a minister on the report and the activities of the department. Ministers can also be 'impeached' by the Assembly on specified grounds. For practical purposes, the impeachment process for ministers has been overtaken by other methods of accountability,

---

46 Constitution, cl 45.
47 Constitution, cls 105, 108, 109 and 114.
48 Constitution, cl 19(ii).
49 Government Act (Cap 8.06), s 17(1).
50 Constitution, cl 50A(3).
51 Government Act, s 18.
52 Constitution, cl 51(2)(a).
53 Constitution, cl 51(5).

including the powers of the Assembly to ask questions and to express lack of confidence, and the general operation of civil and criminal law. As discussed below, the impeachment process is more relevant for the impeachment of elected representatives under cl 75 of the Constitution. The more likely consequence for a minister guilty of a serious failure in office is dismissal from Cabinet by the sovereign on the advice of the Prime Minister, who would consult other ministers.

The total number of Cabinet members including the Prime Minister must not exceed half the number of elected members of the Legislative Assembly less the Speaker. Currently, the Cabinet of Prime Minister Reverend Dr Pohiva Tu'ioneta consists of 12 members, including two women[54] and three nobles.

The Tonga police force is under the command and direction of the Minister of Police. Under the Tonga Police Act (Cap 7.07), the sovereign in Privy Council, after receiving advice from the JADP, appoints a Police Commissioner, who is responsible for the administration of the Tonga Police Act, and the management and command and control of the Tonga police. While the Commissioner is required to comply with written directions of the Minister of Police, he or she exercises his or her duties independently in relation to the maintenance of order, the enforcement of the law, investigation of crime, and decisions about Tonga police members.[55]

3.3. LEGISLATIVE ASSEMBLY

Since the 2010 constitutional reforms, the Legislative Assembly (*Fale Alea*) has been composed of 17 elected representatives of the people and nine elected representatives of the nobles.[56] The electoral boundaries are determined by the Electoral Boundaries Commission, an independent statutory body.[57]

The Speaker presides over all Legislative Assembly meetings and is responsible for its business and affairs. The responsibilities extend to ruling on questions of interpretation and application of the Rules of Procedure of the Legislative Assembly.[58] The Speaker is appointed from one of the elected nobles' representatives by the sovereign on the Legislative Assembly's recommendation, no later than five days after the Prime Minister's appointment.[59]

---

54 To date, Tonga has only had a total of seven women enter Parliament. The first female Member of Parliament was HRH Princess Mele Siu'ilikutapu elected in 1975 to 1977. The first woman to be appointed a Cabinet minister was 'Alisi Taumoepeau (Minister of Justice) who was elected in 2006.

55 Tonga Police Act, s 20.

56 Constitution, cl 56.

57 Constitution, cl 60 and Electoral Boundaries Commission Act (Cap 2.04), s 16

58 Constitution, cls 61 and 62; Legislative Assembly Act (Cap 2.06), s 15; Rules of Procedure of the Legislative Assembly of Tonga (Cap 4.16.3).

59 Constitution, cl 62.

Members are immune from arrest (except for indictable offences) and judgment whilst the Assembly is sitting, and parliamentary privilege, as established under English common law, applies to the procedures of Tonga's Legislative Assembly. Decisions[60] have confirmed that in the absence of a breach of the Constitution, the courts have no jurisdiction to inquire into or judicially review the Assembly's internal proceedings. The Assembly may punish, by fine or imprisonment, anyone who speaks or acts disrespectfully in the Assembly or publishes any material defamatory of the Assembly.[61]

The Legislative Assembly's plenary power is to make laws for the Kingdom.[62] Clause 51 of the Constitution expressly vests the sovereign and the Legislative Assembly with power to enact laws, following a process whereby a Bill is read in the Legislative Assembly and, if voted for by a majority three times, is presented to the sovereign for assent. Bills relating to the sovereign, royal family or the titles and inheritances of nobles may only be voted on by representatives of the nobles of the Legislative Assembly.[63] After receiving the sovereign's assent and signature, the Bill becomes law upon publication in the *Government Gazette*. While the sovereign seldom withholds approval,[64] there is no convention that approval must be given to a law which has been presented by the Assembly. If approval is withheld, it is unlawful for the Bill to be discussed further until the following session of the Legislative Assembly.[65]

The principal power of the Legislative Assembly in relation to the executive (primarily Cabinet) is to delay or decline to pass appropriation Bills or approve expenditure under cl 78 of the Constitution and to debate and scrutinise government Bills.

Elections are held simultaneously for the representatives of the nobles and people every four years, subject to the sovereign's prerogative power to convene or dismiss the Legislative Assembly at any time.[66] All 34 nobles are competent to vote in an election for representatives of the nobles, and to sit in the Assembly if chosen, unless they are declared insane or an imbecile, or are disqualified by reason of having been convicted of a criminal offence with a sentence of two

---

60 *Sanft v Fotofili* [1987] TOPC 1; [1988] LRC (Const) 110 (3 August 1987); *Fotofili v Siale* [1987] TOPC 2; [1988] LRC (Const) 102 (3 August 1987) decisions of the Privy Council sitting as Tonga's Court of Appeal as the then Court of Appeal Act 1988 provided that appeals were heard to the King in Council: see ss 9 and 31 of Court of Appeal Act 1988.

61 Constitution, cl 70.

62 Constitution, cl 67.

63 Constitution, cl 67.

64 For example, in 2012 King Tupou V refused to assent to the Arms and Ammunitions (Amendment) Bill which had been passed by the Assembly (10 to eight) and would have reduced the possible criminal sentences for illicit possession of firearms to less than two years' imprisonment. At the time, two members of the Assembly had been recently charged with illicit possession of firearms.

65 Constitution, cl 68.

66 Constitution, cl 77.

years' imprisonment.[67] Life peers appointed by the sovereign may also vote in elections for the nobles' representatives but may not be elected as a noble's representative.[68] In relation to elections of representatives of the people, every Tongan subject aged 21 years or older is entitled to vote, and is qualified to run for office upon registration, unless disqualified by the Constitution.[69] Candidates who are civil servants must resign upon registration for election.[70] Candidates are prohibited from spending more than T$100,000 on an election campaign, and the judiciary has adjudicated on numerous cases involving allegations of bribery or election offences and defined these offences.

Voting is not compulsory, and is conducted by secret ballot. Election disputes may be initiated on petition by candidates or electors, and are heard by the Supreme Court sitting in its jurisdiction as a court of disputed returns.

Any member may be impeached for breach of the laws or the resolutions of the Legislative Assembly, maladministration, incompetency, destruction or embezzlement of government property, or the performance of acts which may lead to difficulties between Tonga and another country.[71] The Assembly is required to conduct a trial of the offences, presided over by the Chief Justice – if found guilty by the Assembly, the impeached person may be dismissed from office.[72] Prior to the 2010 constitutional reforms, judges were also liable to be impeached under cl 75, though the investigation and dismissal of judges has now been taken over by the JADP of the Privy Council.[73]

3.4. LOCAL GOVERNMENT

The Governors of each of the island groups of Vava'u and Ha'apai are appointed by the sovereign on the advice of the Prime Minister, and are responsible for representing the government, and administering and enforcing laws in their respective districts. They hold office at the sovereign's pleasure. The Governors are responsible for enforcement of the law, supervision of government officers, and annual reports to the Prime Minister.[74] They have no legislative powers.[75]

While there is no express provision for local government in the Constitution, under the District and Town Officers Act (Cap 8.03) the Kingdom is divided into 22 districts, each with a district officer and specified towns under the

67 Constitution, cl 63.
68 Electoral (Elections of Representatives of the Nobles) Regulations (Cap 2.03.02), r 2(1).
69 Constitution cl 23; Electoral Act (Cap 2.03), s 25.
70 Public Service Act (Cap 2.11), s 21.
71 Constitution, cl 75.
72 Constitution, cl 75.
73 Constitution, cl 83C.
74 Constitution, cls 54 and 55; Government Act, s 24.
75 Constitution, cl 55.

jurisdiction of town officers to carry out defined duties on behalf of the government. These include conducting regular public health and agricultural inspections, and keeping record of Tongans resident in their district or town. The officers are elected every three years. The duties of the district officers include inspections for public health, agriculture and licence compliance and reporting back regularly to the Prime Minister (or the Governor, for Ha'apai and Vava'u divisions), and informing the police should any breach of the law be identified.

The town officer supports the district officer in public health, agriculture and licence compliance inspections, as well as by announcing any *fonos* (public meetings). Along with their oversight duties, both district and town officers have other duties, such as the recording of births and deaths. As chairmen or members of most village committees, they are also able to assist in the improvement of the local water supply, garbage disposal and agricultural roads, and to implement measures to increase cultivation.

Town officers also bear responsibility for informing the Registrar General of every death that occurs within their jurisdiction where the head of the family is absent, the closest adult relative is absent from the same island as the deceased, and there is no other occupier of the deceased's premises.[76] There are presently 23 district officers and 156 town officers.

Traditionally, government communicated with the people by *fono*, summoned by the district officer, the noble, Governor or Prime Minister, depending on the size and importance of the occasion. There are penalties for non-attendance at such *fonos* where proper notice has been given.[77] With the widespread adoption and use of modern telecommunication devices, such as the internet, radio and television, *fonos* have become increasingly rare in modern Tonga.

3.5. JUDICIARY

The judicial power of the Kingdom is vested in the Court of Appeal, Supreme Court, Magistrates' Court and Land Court, with limited appeal to the Tongan Privy Council.[78]

Following the 2010 constitutional reforms, the Constitution was amended to establish the JADP and create the position of the Lord Chancellor. The JADP is a Committee of the Privy Council whose fixed membership comprises the Lord Chancellor, the Lord Chief Justice, the Attorney General, and Law Lords appointed by the sovereign from time to time. The JADP advises on

76 Births, Deaths, and Marriages Registration Act, s 3.

77 Fonos Act (Cap 8.05).

78 See Constitution, cls 84–104, Court of Appeal Act (Cap 3.04), Supreme Court Act (Cap 3.16), Land Act (Cap 20.01), and Magistrate's Court Act (Cap 3.12).

the sovereign's judicial-related functions, including the appointment and dismissal of judges.[79] The Lord Chancellor is appointed by the sovereign in Privy Council on advice from the JADP. Candidates must be qualified for appointment as a judge of the Supreme Court. The Lord Chancellor's primary responsibilities are for: (1) the administration of the courts; (2) all matters relating to the judiciary and its independence; and (3) the maintenance of the rule of law, and other such matters specified by the Constitution of any other Act.[80] The Lord Chancellor has, unless otherwise provided for by law, complete discretion to exercise his functions without interference, and sits as the Chairman of the JADP. The present Lord Chancellor is a New Zealand-born Tongan who replaced the former interim Lord Chancellor, a New Zealander, in February 2020.

The creation of the JADP under the 2010 constitutional reforms had previously been criticised by the former Minister of Justice as 'splitting' the Ministry, such that the Lord Chancellor administered the courts, and the Minister administered the Ministry and its budget, and as being unworkable and incompatible with the principles of modern constitutional monarchies. In August 2014, the Legislative Assembly passed a Bill to abolish the JADP (replacing it with the former Judicial and Legal Services Commission) and the Lord Chancellor's post. The Bill never received royal assent and lapsed upon the dissolution of the Legislative Assembly in November 2014. In March 2019, Bills were introduced in the Legislative Assembly to abolish the JADP, and introduce the Judicial and Legal Services Commission. The Bills lapsed when the Legislative Assembly was prorogued in November 2019 with the elections following the death of Prime Minister 'Akilisi Pohiva.

The Lord Chief Justice is the head of the Tongan judiciary, which comprises the Lord President of the Court of Appeal, judges of the Court of Appeal, judges of the Supreme Court, the Lord President of the Land Court, judges of the Land Court, the Chief Magistrate, and magistrates.[81]

The Chief Justice holds the office of President of the Court of Appeal pursuant to s 4 of the Court of Appeal Act and by convention. In the Chief Justice's absence, the senior member of the Court of Appeal at the hearing presides as Vice-President.

The Chief Justice also holds the office of President of the Land Court ex officio, by convention. Judges of the Supreme Court also sit ex officio as judges of the Land Court. The Lord Chancellor, Chief Justice and other judges hold office 'during good behaviour', subject to any contractual arrangements.[82]

---

79 Constitution, cl 83C.

80 Constitution, cl 83B.

81 Constitution, cl 81(2).

82 Constitution, cls 83B(4) and 87.

The bulk of judicial work is carried out by the Chief Magistrate and magistrates (currently eight in total, including the Chief Magistrate), all Tongans, two of whom are formally legally trained, who sit at the times and places determined by the Chief Magistrate.[83] The Chief Magistrate is appointed by the sovereign, after receiving advice from the JADP, and is the administrative head of the Magistrates' Court. Magistrates are also appointed by the sovereign, upon advice from the JADP, on such terms as the sovereign may establish, though in principle they are equivalent to senior civil servants.[84] Magistrates must retire at the age of 72 years, unless they have been appointed as required by the exigencies of judicial service to continue as a magistrate.[85] Tonga's first female magistrate was appointed in 1999 and held office until 2000. The second female magistrate was appointed Senior Magistrate on 4 April 2018 and continues to hold office.

Each magistrate has jurisdiction to issue warrants, try persons charged with offences, issue subpoenas, take or administer oaths, determine civil matters, make orders of maintenance, admit to bail, conduct criminal committal inquiries, or make a temporary order needed either in the interests of justice or to preserve peace and order in an area.[86] Magistrates also may hold an inquest into suspicious deaths under the Inquests Act (Cap 3.09).

Proceedings in the Magistrates' Court are conducted summarily and usually exclusively in the Tongan language. A magistrate's criminal jurisdiction extends to offences punishable by up to three years' imprisonment or a fine of T$10,000. They may also determine more serious offences by consent or upon remittal from the Supreme Court.[87] The Chief Justice may also invest a named magistrate with enhanced criminal jurisdiction to deal with matters by consent punishable by up to seven years imprisonment or $T50,000.[88] The Magistrates' Court's civil jurisdiction extends to actions in which the amount claimed does not exceed T$10,000, and cases there are tried without a jury.[89] Civil procedure is governed by Part V of the Magistrate's Court Act (Cap 3.12) and the Magistrate's Court (Civil) Rules (Cap 3.12.03). Criminal procedure is governed by the provisions in Part II of the Magistrate's Court Act.

The Magistrate's Court Act was amended in 2012 to insert s 94A, which allowed the sovereign, upon the recommendation of the Chief Justice, to appoint by royal warrant up to 20 persons as justices of the peace for terms of one year which may be renewed. The amendments were introduced in an effort to improve access to justice, and legal services for Tongans particularly those residing outside the capital Nuku'alofa. Justices of the peace are invested with powers to witness

---

83 Magistrate's Court Act, s 6.
84 Magistrate's Court Act, s 2.
85 Magistrate's Court Act, s 3.
86 Magistrate's Court Act, s 8.
87 Magistrate's Court Act, ss 11, 35 and 36.
88 Magistrate's Court Act, s 11(4).
89 Magistrate's Court Act, s 59.

documents, take oaths and other such powers of commissioners of oaths, grant bail, and issue search warrants and subpoenas, along with any powers assigned to them under any Act or regulation.

The Magistrates' Court (Justice of the Peace) Regulations (Cap 3.12.04) provides that a person may be appointed as a justice of the peace if he or she is at least 35 years of age, a Tongan citizen, of good character, normally resides in his or her nominated area for at least two consecutive years, and has a good knowledge of local customs, cultures and traditions, and a reasonable command of the English language. The inaugural justices of the peace were sworn in at Nuku'alofa on 18 June 2014.

The Land Court is established under cl 86A of the Constitution and ss 144 and 149 of the Land Act, with exclusive jurisdiction to hear all disputes and questions of title affecting land or any interest in land.[90] The Land Court consists of the President and other judges assisted by assessors (lay Tongans) appointed by the sovereign with the consent of the Privy Council after receiving advice from the JADP.

Land Court trials are conducted by a judge sitting with an assessor selected from a panel of assessors, though chamber proceedings may be conducted by a judge alone. The assessor's function is to assist the judge with explanation and advice about Tongan usages and customs. The Land Court's procedures are governed by the Supreme Court Rules (Cap 3.16.05), to the extent that they do not conflict with the provisions of the Land Court Rules (Cap 20.01.07). The limitation period in the Land Act is 10 years from the date when the action accrued.[91] The question of the limitation period is a matter solely for the Land Court, with no prospect of judicial review in the Supreme Court;[92] the Crown, however, is not bound by the limitation period.[93]

The Supreme Court has unlimited jurisdiction, except in land cases. The Court's powers include all the powers for the time being vested in or capable of being exercised by the High Court of Justice in England and Wales.[94] It also hears matters on appeal from the Magistrates Court pursuant to s 74 of the Magistrate's Court Act.

The Constitution guarantees that persons accused of indictable offences are entitled to a trial by jury in the Supreme Court. There also exists a right to a jury trial in civil cases.[95] In practice, this right is rarely exercised. Civil procedure is governed by the Supreme Court Rules and other such rules made by the Court for the practice and procedure of the courts.[96]

---

90 Constitution, cl 90.
91 Land Act, s 170.
92 *Isoloi v Nuku*, Unreported, Privy Council of Tonga, 1988.
93 *Minister of Lands v Leger* [1987] SPLR 352.
94 Supreme Court Act, s 5(1).
95 Constitution, cl 99.
96 Supreme Court Act, s 6.

Since 1910, the Supreme Court judges have been exclusively expatriates appointed from Commonwealth countries, particularly the UK, Australia, New Zealand and Fiji. This process overcomes the limitations of a small pool of local judicial talent and avoids perceptions of bias. The practice continued until 2018, when the sovereign appointed the first Tongan Supreme Court judge, signalling a move towards a greater sense of national identity and ownership of Tonga's judicial system.

The Court of Appeal is the final appellate court in all criminal, civil and land matters (save for disputes relating to hereditary estates and titles, which are determined by the sovereign in Privy Council).[97] In civil cases, appeal is as of right, except from decisions on interlocutory matters or costs, and where the sum awarded is less than T$1,000. In criminal cases, appeal lies as of right on question of law alone. Leave is required for appeals against the sentence, and for grounds of appeal based on a question of fact alone and on questions of mixed law and fact. Leave to appeal in criminal matters may also be given by the judge who tried the appellant.

Judges of the Court of Appeal are appointed on a contractual basis by the sovereign in Privy Council on the advice of the JADP; they are typically senior or retired superior court judges from Commonwealth countries. In 2015, the first Tongan Court of Appeal judge was appointed. The Court of Appeal sits on an ad hoc basis at times determined by the President, but at least twice a year. Hearings of the Court of Appeal require at least three members, save for interlocutory matters, where two judges may sit.

There are also a number of statutory tribunals with specific jurisdiction to determine matters established by their enabling Acts, such as the Tax Tribunal,[98] the Public Service Tribunal,[99] the Police Board,[100] and the Disciplinary Committee of the Tonga Law Society.[101]

3.6. ATTORNEY GENERAL AND LEGAL PRACTITIONERS

The 2010 reforms enshrined the position of the Attorney General in the Constitution as the principal legal advisor to Cabinet and the government, and placed him or her in charge of all criminal proceedings on behalf of the Crown, as well as of performing any other functions and duties required by law.[102] The constitutional enshrinement of the First Law Officer of the Kingdom was intended to create a role that is to be non-partisan, independent and

97 Constitution, cl 92 and Court of Appeal Act, ss 10 and 16.
98 Revenue Services Administration Act (Cap 11.07), s 58.
99 Public Service Act, s 21A.
100 Tonga Police Act, s 35.
101 Law Practitioners Act (Cap 3.11), s 19.
102 Constitution, cl 31A.

free of interference from the Minister of Justice and government of the day. The Attorney General has, unless otherwise provided by law, complete discretion to exercise his or her functions without interference.

Qualifications for appointment as the Attorney General are the same as appointment for a judge to the Supreme Court. The Attorney General is appointed by the sovereign in Privy Council on advice of the JADP. Subject to any contractual arrangements, office is held during good behaviour. The Supreme Court has recently held that the Attorney General's responsibility for all criminal proceedings under s 41A of the Constitution extends to allow intervention in, and termination of, private prosecutions.[103]

The Solicitor-General is the Attorney General's deputy and head of the Department of Crown Law. He or she is responsible for implementing all the directions of the Attorney General and the daily administration and operations, as well as being responsible for all civil and constitutional matters, including legislative drafting at the direction of the Attorney General. There also exists a Director of Public Prosecutions, who is responsible for the conduct of all criminal prosecutions for the Crown. The Director of Public Prosecutions is not a constitutional office, though in 2019 the Act of Constitution of Tonga (Amendment) (No 2) Bill was introduced to the Legislative Assembly to constitutionally enshrine the position of Director of Public Prosecutions with the responsibility for all criminal proceedings in the Kingdom. This Bill has now lapsed.

The practice of law in Tonga is regulated by the Law Practitioners Act, which makes it unlawful for a person to practise as a law practitioner if they are not on the Roll of Law Practitioners and do not hold a valid practice certificate. The Law Practitioners Act also permits the Chief Justice to appoint law practitioners as commissioners for oaths with the power to take affidavits and declarations. Appointments as commissioners for oaths are only valid whilst the law practitioner has in force a valid practice certificate. While many practitioners were licensed to act as advocates for fees approved by the Supreme Court, now the majority of practitioners are degree-qualified and university-educated Tongans (many from the University of the South Pacific or New Zealand universities). There are a handful of overseas-based counsel, including non-Tongans, who practise in the Tongan superior courts.

3.7. OMBUDSMAN

A recent development is the creation of the statutory Ombudsman's Office under the Ombudsman Act (Cap 2.02), with responsibility for investigating decisions and for making recommendations relating to the administration of

[103] *Attorney General v Lavulavu* [2019] TOSC 35.

government departments (including decisions by ministers or Governors) and to investigations received on complaint or carried out on his or her own motion.

4. LAW OF PERSONS

4.1. NATIONALITY AND CITIZENSHIP

The Nationality Act (Cap 10.02) deems a person to be a Tongan subject if he or she is: (1) born in Tonga to a Tongan parent; (2) born abroad to a Tongan father or Tongan mother; (3) a non-Tongan who marries a Tongan upon providing a written declaration to the Minister of Foreign Affairs that she or he wishes to assume Tongan nationality, and takes the oath prescribed by the Act; or (4) naturalised under the Act. The sovereign has a discretion to grant naturalisation provided an applicant meets the standards of residence (at least five years), good character and knowledge of the Tongan language, demonstrates an intention to continue residing in the Kingdom, and takes an oath of allegiance.[104]

The Nationality Act confers all the rights of a natural-born subject, except in relation to the grant of hereditary land allotment.[105] Amendments to the Act in 1991 and 1996 also permitted the Privy Council and sovereign to naturalise persons identified in the Third Tonga *Government Gazette* dated 15 February 1991 whom they wish to declare naturalised persons and holders of a Tongan Protected Person Passport. These provisions were the culmination of Tonga's passport sale scandal from the early 1980s, which resulted in widespread protest, condemnation, and subsequent litigation and prosecutions, including the prosecution of former government ministers.[106]

In 2007, the Nationality Act was further amended to insert a new s 17, which revoked the ban on dual citizenship for Tongans. The amendments allowed any person who had ceased to be a Tongan subject prior to the enactment of the amendments to apply to the Minister for Foreign Affairs for a certificate of re-admission to Tongan nationality. Applicants for re-admission are not required to meet the residence requirements under the Act. Persons who regain their Tongan nationality are entitled to all the rights of natural-born subjects. While the amendments have allowed Tongan women who marry non-Tongans to retain their citizenship, they have also revived the ability of Tongan males to make a claim for, reclaim or revive their constitutionally guaranteed right

104 Constitution, cl 29; Nationality Act, s 9.

105 Nationality Act, s 9.

106 See further Anthony Van Fossen 'Citizenship for Sale: Passports of Convenience from Pacific Island Tax Havens' (2007) 45(2) Commonwealth & Comparative Politics 138; and also the prosecution of former Prime Minister Lord Tu'ivakano (then Minister of Foreign Affairs) *R v Tu'ivakano* [2020] TOSC 15 and in *Tu'ivakano v R* [2020] TOCA 8.

to land in Tonga under cl 113 of the Constitution. This has created challenges for Tonga's courts.[107]

4.2. STATUS

The status of being a Tongan is required for a number of purposes, including holding land allotments and voting in elections. The status of holding a noble title confers rights and privileges. While the Constitution protects such statuses, it also declares that there is but one law for chiefs and commoners, for non-Tongans and Tongans.[108]

4.3. MARRIAGE

The minimum age for marriage is 15 years, though parental or guardian consent is required for marriage under 18 years.[109] In 2016, the Deputy Prime Minister reported that 183 child marriages had been recorded in the country in the preceding three years, and there has been a push by civil society to review the law regarding the age of marriage.[110]

Births, deaths and marriages are registered with the Registrar General of Births, Deaths and Marriages. The Registrar General is appointed by the Prime Minister with the consent of Cabinet. The Registrar General is supported by sub-registrars; their office is part of the Ministry of Justice.

Marriage in Tonga must be between a man and woman, and requires solemnisation by a registered minister of religion in the presence of two witnesses, after the issue of a marriage licence, for which 16 months' residence is required. If the residence requirement is not met, the Registrar General has discretion to grant a special licence to marry where at least one of the applicants has an established link to the Kingdom. There is no recognition of any other form of celebration of marriage in Tonga. The Births, Deaths, and Marriages Act also prohibits marriage within specified degrees of consanguinity.

---

107 See for example *Sunia v Kava* [2020] TOLC 2; LA 4 of 2018; and *The Crown v Schaumkel* [2012] TOCA 10.

108 Constitution, cl 4.

109 Births, Deaths and Marriages Registration Act (Cap 6.01), s 6.

110 See for example Helen Griffiths 'Time for Tonga to End Child Marriage' *Human Rights Watch Dispatches* (online 8 June 2017) <https://www.hrw.org/news/2017/06/08/time-tonga-end-child-marriage>; Bruce Hill 'Teen Marriage in Tonga often caused by Parental Pressure' *ABC News: Pacific Beat* (online 25 August 2016) <https://www.abc.net.au/radio-australia/programs/pacificbeat/teen-marriage-in-tonga-often-caused-by-parental/7787504>.

4.4. DIVORCE

Tonga's divorce system is based on fault. The principal grounds for divorce are adultery, a sentence of five years' imprisonment, bigamy, wilful and continuous desertion for two years, affliction with an incurable contagious disease, unsound mind for five years, incapacity (on limited grounds) to consummate the marriage, continuous separation for two years without intention to resume normal marital relations, and behaviour by a respondent such that the petitioner cannot expect to live with the respondent.[111]

There is no jurisdiction for a court to make a declaration of nullity or order of separation. Annulment may be obtained by Act of the Legislative Assembly, as has occurred in cases of marriage of a royal family member without the sovereign's consent.[112]

The Supreme Court may make orders for maintenance in conjunction with divorce proceedings or at any time, in favour of the parties or children.[113] The courts also have power to make orders in favour of deserted wives under the Maintenance of Deserted Wives Act (Cap 6.06).

4.5. CHILDREN

Illegitimacy affects a child's status and entitlements, particularly in relation to inheritance. Every married parent and the mother of an illegitimate child has an obligation to register the birth within three weeks of delivery or be liable to a fine of T$100.[114]

4.6. ADOPTION, CUSTODY AND GUARDIANSHIP

A court order known as Letters of Adoption is required for a valid adoption. Only illegitimate children may be adopted.[115] The best interest of the child is the paramount consideration in adoption and custody proceedings.[116] This is in line with Tonga's international treaty obligations under the Convention on the Rights of the Child.[117]

---

[111] Divorce Act (Cap 6.09).

[112] Mele Siulikutapu New Zealand Marriage Annulment Act 1970, and Fatafehi Tuku'aho Marriage Annulment Act 1980.

[113] Divorce Act, ss 17 and 18.

[114] Births, Deaths, and Marriages Registration Act, s 3(2).

[115] Maintenance of Illegitimate Children Act (Cap 6.07).

[116] *Saavedra v Solicitor General* [2013] TOCA 7.

[117] Convention on the Rights of the Child 1577 UNTS 3 (opened for signature 20 November 1989, entered into force 2 September 1990).

Generally, the mother's consent to the adoption is required, though it may be dispensed with in limited circumstances, such as when the mother cannot be found or unreasonably withholds her consent.[118] The court may refuse the adoption if it considers the petitioner not to be fit or proper. The court will, as part of its duty to consider whether the adoption is in the child's best interest, inquire if the petitioner has demonstrated that he or she is sufficiently acquainted with the children he or she wishes to adopt – this has been colloquially known as the 'six-month rule', though the Court of Appeal and Supreme Court has held this is not an inflexible requirement, particularly in the case of very young children who might never have come to know their natural mothers.[119]

While non-Tongans are not prohibited from adopting Tongan children, the courts are not prepared to allow such petitions unless all other means of caring for the child in Tonga have been exhausted, having regard to Tonga's obligations under art 21 of the Convention on the Rights of the Child.[120] There is precedent for the mother of an illegitimate child to petition the Supreme Court jointly with a man she marries who is not the father of the child to be successfully granted Letters of Adoption.[121]

Once adopted, the child will bear the name and be deemed to be of the same nationality as the person to whom Letters of Adoption have been granted. Any adopted person of Tongan nationality by birth who has attained the age of 21 years and has by reason of the adoption become of another nationality may apply to the Supreme Court for Letters of Admission to be again admitted as a Tongan subject.

There is no provision for children who are born within wedlock to be adopted, though the court may make orders in relation to custody and guardianship (both interim and permanent) under the Guardianship Act (Cap 6.04). The Supreme Court may also make custody orders in divorce proceedings pursuant to the provisions of the Divorce Act. The Solicitor-General is appointed guardian ad litem in all custody and adoption proceedings. The office conducts investigations and prepares a report for the court with recommendations about the application.

5. LAW OF OBLIGATIONS

5.1. TORTS

The courts apply the English common law of tortious liability for intentional or negligent harm so far as the circumstances of Tonga and its inhabitants

118 Maintenance of Illegitimate Children Act, s 15(2).

119 *Hatch v Solicitor General* [2010] To LR 177; and *Saavedra v Solicitor General* [2013] TOCA 7.

120 *Saavedra v Solicitor General* [2013] TOCA 7.

121 *In the Matter of Maintenance of Illegitimate Children Act and Application for adoption by J* [2012] TOSC 58.

permit.[122] The Defamation Act (Cap 5.02) makes statutory provision for civil and criminal defamation; the Act contains rules relating to truth as a defence and certain defamatory matter that do not require proof of actual loss, while leaving other matters, such as the method in which a defamatory statement is conveyed (ie innuendo, by natural and ordinary meaning, etc.), to the common law.

5.2. CONTRACT

The English common law of contract applies, subject to statutory protections which impose standards for certain types of contractual arrangements, such as in the Consumer Protection Act (Cap 17.04). Generally, insurance is governed by the law of contract. The only statutory provision for insurance is that which deals with marine risks. The Marine Insurance Act (Cap 48.10) applies the insurance principles adopted internationally.

6. PROPERTY LAW

6.1. LAND AND NATURAL RESOURCES

All land in Tonga is vested in the Crown. There is no provision for freehold in fee simple. In formal terms, all other interests in land are life interests in favour of individual persons. Land cannot be sold or devised by will.[123] However, limited leasing or mortgaging of life interests in land are permitted.[124]

There are three types of life interests: royal estates, *tofi'a*, and *api*.

Royal estates are set aside from Crown lands for the use of the sovereign for the time being and royal families, from which the sovereign may grant life interests from time to time.

Holders of the 33 noble titles and six hereditary chiefships have life interests in the *tofi'a* – inherited estates associated with their titles. Succession to titles and estates was originally granted and guaranteed by the Constitution and passes, according to the Constitution and Land Act, to a legitimate descendant, with a preference for the eldest male descendent. In the absence of male children, the eldest female will inherit and pass the interests to her sons. Failing direct heirs, the rights pass to brothers, and then to sisters. In the absence of an heir, the rights revert to the Crown and the sovereign may determine to whom they

122 Civil Law Act (Cap 14.03), s 4.
123 Constitution, cl 104.
124 Constitution, cl 104.

should be granted.[125] There are certain titles and estates associated with the royal family that are treated as *tofi'a* under the Royal Estates Act and Land Act.

Every Tongan male over the age of 16 is in principle entitled to two *api* (allotments), an agricultural allotment of up to five hectares, and a small town allotment for use as a residence.[126] Due to the scarcity of land, a person is not entitled to hold two allotments of the same kind, and any such grant is null and void.[127] The grants are made from *tofi'a* or Crown lands, depending on where the grantee resides. When the *api* holder dies, his widow holds a life interest, unless she remarries or is found by the Land Court to have committed fornication or adultery.[128]

Unlike succession to *tofi'a* and the royal line, succession of *api* cannot descend through females. Subject to the widow's interests, succession of *api* passes to the holder's eldest son or his male heir. If there is none, then it passes to the next eldest son of the original holder and so on. If there is no heir through sons, a daughter may acquire a life interest, which she cannot pass on. If there are no daughters, succession passes to the original holder's brothers and sisters. Where succession through the male line fails, the *api* reverts to the *tofi'a* holder or the Crown as the case may be.[129]

The law relating to land tenure and its administration is found in the Land Act, which, subject to the Constitution, is treated by the Land Court and Privy Council as an exhaustive code.[130] However, the Land Court will apply common law and equitable principles such as estoppel and constructive trusts in the adjudication of disputes.[131] Section 44 of the Land Act provides that a person who has been granted an allotment and has abandoned it for more than two years will forfeit the allotment to the Crown or *tofi'a* as the case may be.

The Land Act provides for resident Tongan males to apply for *api* allotments and grants of *api* by the Minister. No person may hold more than one agricultural allotment. Once procedures have been completed, including the approval of the *tofi'a* holder in the case of land on *tofi'a*, the applicant is entitled to register the life interest, which is inheritable in accordance with the Act. Registration provides statutory protection, and the *api* holder cannot lose his interest other than through court action. A small annual rental is payable to the *tofi'a* holder or Crown.

While the Constitution guarantees every adult male his own allotment, the reality is that this is far from achieved because of population pressures

---

125 Constitution, cl 111.

126 Constitution, cl 113 and Land Act, ss 45 and 46.

127 Land Act, s 48.

128 Land Act, s 80.

129 Land Act, s 82.

130 *Baron Tuita v Vete, Lolohea and Ors* LC 1987 Nos 12 and 13 (4 March 1988).

131 See for example *Makoni v Koloamatangi* [1990] Tonga LR 50; *Fie'eiki v 'Ilavalu (No 2)* [1995] Tonga LR 192; and *OG Sanft and Sons v Tonga Tourist and Development Co Ltd* [1981–88] Tonga LR 26.

and land scarcity. Other factors include *tofi'a* holders' reluctance to approve registration and preference by some families for informal arrangements.

Subject to Cabinet approval, an allotment holder may lease the *api* to a Tongan or foreigner for up to 20 years. *Tofi'a* and *api* may be mortgaged in favour of the government or Westpac Bank of Tonga by creating a mortgage lease for a period not exceeding 30 years. On default by a mortgagor, the mortgagee may not sell the land but may take possession for the balance of the period and may sublease the land and sell buildings. The Land Act does not permit any other power of sale.

The government may compulsorily resume any land for public purposes, subject to the obligation to pay a 'fair value' guaranteed by cl 18 of the Constitution. The process is entirely administrative, and involves the Minister of Lands giving 30-day notice of intention to resume possession. The rates of compensation payable in respect of crops, buildings and land are determined by Privy Council regulation.

All minerals are reserved as the property of the Crown and all mining activity is regulated by the Minerals Act (Cap 20.02) and the Petroleum Mining Act (Cap 20.05). Tonga has recognised the importance and value of its offshore resources located in deep seabeds and enacted the Seabed Minerals Act 2014 (Cap 20.07) to regulate mining activity within its jurisdiction.

6.2. ROYAL TITLES

As a customary concept, the noble title, like the royal title, exists independently of its holder. The title is a dignity, a status from which rights and obligations flow. The titles are akin to incorporeal hereditary English titles – intangible, inalienable (except for treason), permanently associated with *tofi'a* and inheritable in accordance with terms imposed by the sovereign in conformity with the Constitution and Land Act.

While the sovereign has retained authority in relation to the appointment to noble titles, trusteeship of estates during a noble heir's minority, the revision of interests in the absence of an heir and succession to titles are strictly governed by the Constitution.[132]

6.3. TANGIBLE AND INTANGIBLE PROPERTY

Ownership of chattels is governed by contractual rules, common law bailment rules, and torts such as conversion, trespass, detinue and trover. Under general

132 Constitution, cls 44, 104 and 112; Land Act.

common law principles, possession gives title of property as against a stranger. An idiosyncrasy of Tonga law is that a house is considered personal property and does not form part of the land; buildings are treated as chattels detachable from the land upon which they stand.[133] Chattels may be disposed of by will under the Probate Act (Cap 6.08) by persons aged at least 16 who are of sound mind.

Trusts are governed by English common law and equity, so far as Tongan circumstances permit. In 2010, the Legislative Assembly enacted the Personal Property Securities Act (Cap 17.09), which creates a system of attachment, priority, publication and enforcement of security interests in personal property, which may be searched in a publicly accessible register.

Tonga has an Industrial Property Act (Cap 17.07), a Copyright Act (Cap 17.05), and a Protection of Layout-Designs (Topographies) of Integrated Circuits Act (Cap 17.13), which are administered by the Business Registry and Intellectual Property Office within the Ministry of Commerce, Consumer, Trade, Innovation and Labour. Under the Industrial Property Act, applicants may apply for protection for patentable inventions, utility model certificates, industrial designs, and trade marks and other link marks.

Tonga is a signatory to the Berne Convention for the Protection of Literary and Artistic Works,[134] and protection of moral and economic rights is afforded automatically under the Copyright Act during the lifetime of the author of the work plus 50 years after his or her death. The Legislative Assembly has also enacted the Protection of Geographical Indications Act 2002 (Cap 17.12) to grant protection over goods identified as originating from the territory of a country, region or locality where the quality, reputation or other characteristic of the product is essentially attributable to its geographical origin. The common law tort of passing-off is also available to protect intangible property rights.

6.4. CULTURAL PROTECTION

Under the Preservation of Objects of Archaeological Interests Act (Cap 13.05), the sovereign appoints a Tongan Traditions Committee with oversight over

---

133 *Cowley v Tourist Services Ha'apai Ltd and Fund Management Limited* [2001] Tonga LR 183 (CA); *Mangisi v Koloamatangi* [1999] TOCA 9. Unsuccessful litigants who are ordered to give up possession of land may remove the buildings from the land. Otherwise, they are entitled to compensation from the landowner for making improvements to the land, see for example: *Schaumkel v 'Aholelei* [2012] TOLC 2 at [55]; and *Finau v Minister of Lands* [2012] TOLC 1 at [30].

134 Berne Convention for the Protection of Literary and Artistic Works 1160 UNTS 231 (opened for signature 9 September 1886, revised 2 June 1928, 26 June 1948, and 14 July 1967, entered into force 24 July 1971).

archaeological explorations. The committee current consists of six persons, including the chairman and secretary. They serve at the sovereign's pleasure. The removal of objects or articles of Tongan culture listed in the customs regulation is prohibited without consent. The sovereign is a party to the Polynesian Heritage Trust deed pursuant to the Polynesian Heritage Trust Act (Cap 13.04), under which representatives from Fiji, New Zealand, Samoa and Tonga form a trust board and undertake projects to foster Polynesian values, heritage and culture.

7. COMMERCIAL LAW

7.1. BUSINESS ENTITIES

Tongan law recognises juridical personality. Companies are incorporated under the Companies Act (Cap 17.03), non-profit organisations under the Incorporated Societies Act (Cap 17.06), charitable trusts and societies under the Charitable Trusts Act (Cap 16.04), co-operatives under the Co-operative Societies Act (Cap 17.02) and credit unions under the Credit Unions Act (Cap 16.05). Registered entities are capable of owning properties, suing and being sued. In each case, there are appointed registrars that supervise the incorporated bodies. Partnerships are governed by the common law.

7.2. COMMERCE

All persons and entities carrying on business in the Kingdom must hold an annual licence issued by the Ministry responsible for Commerce, under the Business Licences Act (Cap 17.01). Certain activities have been prohibited under the Business Licences Act on the grounds of morality, safety or national security.[135]

There are various statutory bodies, agencies and officials which perform regulatory functions. Under the Price and Wage Control Act (Cap 17.10), an appointed competent authority may control the prices of goods and services, and wage rates in order to secure availability at fair prices. There are provisions for investigations and appeal, subject to the final determination of Cabinet. There is also further statutory protection for consumers in the Consumer Protection Act; businesses may rely on the provisions of the Protection Against Unfair Competition Act and common law passing-off claims to protect against unfair competition and damage to their goodwill or reputation.

135 Examples of prohibited activities include gambling, sex work and businesses with undisclosed foreign ownership: see *Prasad v Minister of Revenue and Customs* [2018] TOSC 28 at [9].

7.3. INSOLVENCY

Insolvent incorporated bodies are dissolved and their assets are distributed to creditors and members under provisions in their incorporating statutes. Insolvent companies are dissolved under the supervision of the Supreme Court and its Winding up Practice Directions. Since the Civil Law Act was amended to prevent recourse to the Bankruptcy Act 1914 (UK),[136] there has been no statutory provision for the bankruptcy of individuals.

7.4. CARRIAGE BY AIR AND SEA

Carriage of goods and persons is regulated under the Carriage of Goods by Sea Act (Cap 22.01), the Carriage of Passengers and Luggage by Sea Act (Cap 22.02), the Carriage by Air Act (Cap 23.01), and the Civil Aviation Act (Cap 23.02), which are modelled on New Zealand's civil aviation rules.

7.5. BANKING AND TAXATION

Tonga has a small number of financial institutions. There are four registered commercial banks: the Westpac Bank of Tonga, the Australia New Zealand Banking Group (ANZ), MBF Bank, and Bank of the South Pacific Tonga. There is a government-owned developmental financial institution, the Tonga Development Bank, incorporated under the Tonga Development Bank Act, which lends money to key sectors of the business community, such as agriculture and tourism, and provides savings accounts.

Regulation of finance and financial institutions is governed by a host of statutes, including the National Reserve Bank of Tonga Act (Cap 16.12), which creates the National Reserve Bank of Tonga, which is responsible for the Kingdom's currency, monetary policy and supervising financial institutions.[137]

Tonga's economy, like many of its South Pacific neighbours, is heavily reliant on remittances sent by Tongans living abroad. Orders for payment of money, such as bills of exchange, cheques and promissory notes, are governed by rules in the Bills of Exchange Act (Cap 16.02). The government levies a range of direct and indirect taxes, such as a consumption tax on most goods and services at a rate of 15 per cent, pursuant to the Consumption Tax Act (Cap 11.01), and excise

---

136 Civil Law (Amendment) Act 2003, s 3.

137 Other Acts include the Financial Institutions Act (Cap 16.06), the Foreign Investment Act (Cap 16.09), the Foreign Exchange Control Act (Cap 16.07), the Foreign Exchange Levy Act 2015 (Cap 16.08), and the Moneylenders Act 2018 (Cap 16.10).

tax on imported goods, under the Excise Tax Act (Cap 11.04), to finance the Kingdom's various operations.

7.6. LABOUR LAW

The Ministry of Commerce, Consumer, Trade, Innovation and Labour is responsible for employment and industrial relations in the Kingdom. There are no general statutory provisions for conditions of employment or the handling of industrial disputes, save for a handful of specified occupations such as the Tonga police, the public service and law practitioners under their respective regulatory Acts. The Trade Unions Act (Cap 8.15) allows for the formation of unions that may act in restraint of trade and enjoy immunity from actions in tort law.

Tonga has also implemented a mandatory retirement savings scheme requiring every employer to make contributions from an employee's wages to a fund established under the National Retirement Benefits Fund Act (Cap 8.08) to access in cases of retirement, permanent and total disability before retirement age, death before retirement or early release. A similar savings scheme exists for public servants under the Retirement Fund Act (Cap 2.12).

8. ENVIRONMENTAL AND PLANNING LAW

The Environment Management Act (Cap 21.03) specifically creates a ministerial portfolio charged with co-ordinating the role of government in relation to all environmental management, including climate change issues, and decision-making processes. The Act's purpose is ensuring the Kingdom's observance of its international obligations relating to the protection of the environment, facilitating the assessment of environment impacts and likely impacts of proposed activities, promoting meaningful public involvement in relation to issues of environmental management, including climate change, and implementing measures to increase the resilience of the Kingdom and its environment to climate change.

The Minister of Lands, Survey, Natural Resources and Environment and Climate Change is responsible for administering the Environmental Impact Assessment Act (Cap 21.04), which requires environmental impact assessments to be carried out as part of development projects within the Kingdom. Development projects which do not have environmental approval or are assessed as having an inappropriate environmental impact may not be undertaken.

Under the Forests Act (Cap 19.04), Cabinet may declare any unalienated land to be a forest reserve or reserve area, and a Parks and Reserves Authority established under the Parks and Reserves Act (Cap 13.03) may, with the consent of Cabinet, declare any area of land or sea to be a park or reserve for the benefit and enjoyment of all people of Tonga. Such declared areas enjoy protection and efforts to preserve their natural heritage.

Tonga has enacted legislation prohibiting the import, manufacture, export and use of certain hazardous chemicals and toxins under the Ozone Layer Protection Act (Cap 21.07) and Hazardous Wastes and Chemicals Act (Cap 21.05), and providing for their control and safe management if found.

Species of birds and marine life are protected under the Birds Preservation Act (Cap 21.02) and Fisheries Management Act (Cap 18.02), and penalties may be imposed for taking protected species, polluting or damaging protected areas, or (in the case of fishing) breaches of prohibitions on illegally importing fish, exceeding maximum permitted fishing quotas, or engaging in fishing with prohibited gear or methods such as explosives.

The Biosafety Act (Cap 21.01) establishes a National Biosafety Advisory Committee charged with responsibility for monitoring the development, use, handling and transboundary movement of living modified organisms, and overseeing the Kingdom's implementation of all aspects of the Cartagena Protocol on Biodiversity[138] to protect the Kingdom's fragile environmental ecosystems.

Like its South Pacific neighbours, food and water security remain live issues in Tonga. The Water Resources Act (Cap 20.08) vests all water resources in the Crown. The Act also empowers the Minister responsible for water to manage water resources through implementing a National Water Management Plan, issuing licences for drilling for or taking water, and environmental impact assessments.

As a Small Island Developing State, Tonga is extremely vulnerable to the adverse impacts of climate change and disaster risk. Since 2005, it has developed and implemented a National Climate Change Policy.[139] The nation has established the Tonga Climate Change Trust Fund, the Pacific region's first, and currently only, existing national fund with a specific focus on climate change. The Fund provides supplementary financial support to pipeline and current adaption and mitigation efforts through solar electrification projects and implementing coastal protection measures.

9. CRIMINAL LAW

The Constitution guarantees no punishment without conviction, certain minimum rights for the accused in relation to indictments and searches of premises, the right not to be a witness in one's own trial, and protection from retrospective offences and being tried twice for the same offence.[140]

---

138 Cartagena Protocol on Biodiversity to the Convention on Biological Diversity 2226 UNTS 208 (opened for signature 29 January 2000, entered into force 11 September 2003).

139 National Strategic Development Framework 2015–2035; see also Tonga Climate Change Policy: A Resilient Tonga by 2035.

140 Constitution, cls 10–16 and 20.

The framework of Tonga's criminal laws is found in a large number of statutes creating offences. The major and most commonly prosecuted criminal laws are contained in the Criminal Offences Act (Cap 4.04), the Order in Public Places Act (Cap 7.06), the Town Regulations Act (Cap 8.14), and the Traffic Act (Cap 24.03).

In Tonga, the minimum age of criminal responsibility is set at seven years of age; children aged between seven and 12 years may not be convicted unless they were aware of the nature and consequence of their conduct.[141] A person who is found insane is not criminally culpable, though may be ordered by the Supreme Court to be detained in safe custody.[142] Intoxication does not relieve a person from criminal responsibility, except where the intoxication was caused without the person's consent by the malicious or negligent act of another, or the person was rendered temporarily insane by the intoxication.[143]

The criminal law includes provision for inchoate offences (such as attempt or conspiracy to commit an offence), abetting of crime, and the harbouring of offenders.[144] Offences against the State include treason (which carries a mandatory death penalty or life imprisonment), sedition, and attempts to injure or alarm the sovereign.[145] Offences against 'justice, public peace and public morals' include perjury and interference with the course of justice, forming or assisting an unlawful society, unlawful assembly, riot, bigamy, and prostitution.[146] Offences against the person include homicide, manslaughter, bodily harm, assault, infanticide, and suicide.[147] The Criminal Offences Act also contains numerous offences against property, including wilful damage to property and animals.[148]

Contemporary concerns, such as financial and technological offences, are captured by the Money Laundering and Proceedings of Crime Act (Cap 4.07), the Computer Crimes Act (Cap 4.02), and the Genocide Act (Cap 4.05).

In 2014, Tonga enacted the Family Protection Act (Cap 6.02), which provides a framework for the protection of survivors of domestic violence and offences for breaches of protection orders.

In addition to regulating the procedure for civil actions in defamation, the Defamation Act creates the offences of defaming the character of the sovereign and other persons. The defence of truth in criminal proceedings for defamation must be established on the balance of probabilities, and that the publication of the defaming materials was for the public benefit.

---

141 Criminal Offences Act, s 16.
142 Criminal Offences Act, ss 17–20.
143 Criminal Offences Act, s 21.
144 Criminal Offences Act, Part I.
145 Criminal Offences Act, ss 44–62.
146 Criminal Offences Act, ss 63–84.
147 Criminal Offences Act, ss 85–142.
148 Criminal Offences Act, ss 143–191.

There are also special offences relating to the exercise by the government of its emergency and public order powers, as noted above. Tonga is seeing an increase in drug-related offending. Under the Illicit Drugs Control Act (Cap 4.06), the import, export, possession, manufacture, cultivate, use, or supply of certain prescribed drugs attracts heavy penalties of imprisonment and/or fines. Tonga also has a number of specific 'moral' offences contained in the Pornography Control Act (Cap 4.09) and Adultery and Fornication Act (Cap 4.01).

Local government is assisted by regulatory Acts in addition to the Criminal Offences Act and the Order in Public Places Act. It is an offence to fail to support near relatives, to plant sufficient food to keep oneself and dependents, and to neglect dwellings, frontages and cemeteries. Whilst customary offences are not directly recognised by the court, they are reflected in some legislative provisions. For example, a traveller 'to a distant place upon a government road, if he be thirsty may peel and drink coconuts growing by the roadside ... but only to relieve thirst'. Similarly, it is unlawful to pass any of the nobles on horseback or in a vehicle 'without stopping until the noble is passed and saluting by raising the hand'.[149] Prosecutions of such offences are relatively rare – prosecutions under the Order in Public Places Act are more commonly conducted for drunken or disorderly behaviour.[150]

Punishments provided for in the Criminal Offences Act include payments of compensation, fines (with mandatory imprisonment for failure to pay), whipping, community service, imprisonment, and death. Tongan criminal law recognises the role of custom in sentences – traditional Tongan reconciliation and apologies are taken into account as mitigating factors.[151]

Whilst Tongan criminal law recognises corporal and capital punishment as forms of sentences imposed for serious crimes, Tonga has been a de facto abolitionist state, with the last known execution having taken place in 1982. Sentences of death may only be carried out with the assent of the sovereign and Privy Council. Males between the ages of seven and 16 may be ordered to be whipped by a police officer with a light cane instead of other punishment, and males of 16 years and over may be sentenced to whipping on conviction for prescribed offences. The last known sentences of whipping being carried out were in the early 1980s. In 2010, the Court of Appeal overturned a decision when a sentence of whipping was handed down as part of a sentence for offences of escaping from lawful custody, housebreaking and theft. The Court accepted that the component of the sentence ordering whipping was punishment that was cruel and unusual and, arguably, unconstitutional.[152]

---

149 Town Regulations Act, ss 13 and 14.

150 See for example *Hekeheke v Police* [2010] Tonga LR 34 (public intoxication); *Schaper v Kaho* [2013] TOSC 45 at [8] (failing to observe the Sabbath).

151 *Kaufusi v Lasa* [1990] Tonga LR 139.

152 *Fangupo v R; Fa'aoa v R* [2010] Tonga LR 124.

The Legislative Assembly has also enacted the Rehabilitation of Offenders Act (Cap 3.15), which allows eligible offenders to obtain a certificate that their conviction has expired and to clear their police record of any conviction. The scheme only applies with respect to convictions that receive a non-custodial sentence of no more than two years' imprisonment, and after the applicant has served a rehabilitation period of four or seven years without any more convictions.

10. INTERNATIONAL LAW AND TREATIES

Tonga is a party to a number of international and regional treaties and conventions. It joined the Commonwealth of Nations in 1970 and the United Nations in 1999. It is also a member of the Pacific Islands Forum and the Secretariat of the Pacific Community. The Minister and Ministry of Foreign Affairs are responsible for the conduct of Tonga's foreign affairs.

Clause 39 of the Constitution retains the sovereign's right (or those to whom the sovereign may delegate the right) to make treaties with foreign states. In practice, proposed treaties are considered in Cabinet, and are often signed by the Minister for Foreign Affairs. Treaties do not become domestic law until ratified and implemented by statute. However, the sovereign may cancel the government's ratification of treaties, as in 2015 when King Tupou IV cancelled the ratification of the UN Convention on the Elimination of Discrimination against Women following a popular petition from opponents in the community, including church representatives.[153]

Tonga has implemented portions of the Vienna Convention on Diplomatic and Consular Relations[154] and the New York Convention on Special Missions[155] by enacting domestic legislation to confer the usual privileges and immunities on personnel from overseas representing foreign governments, including immunity from suit and process, and exemption from taxation.[156]

---

153 See 'Tongans seek royal intervention to stop CEDAW' *Radio NZ* (online 22 May 2015) <https://www.rnz.co.nz/international/pacific-news/274357/tongans-seek-royal-intervention-to-stop-cedaw>; 'Tonga's King and Privy Council say "no" to CEDAW' *Radio NZ* (online 1 July 2015) <https://www.rnz.co.nz/international/pacific-news/277663/tonga's-king-and-privy-council-say-no-to-cedaw>; and Melenaite Taumoefolau 'Why Tongan has no word for human rights' *The Ideas Room* (online 8 April 2019) <https://www.newsroom.co.nz/@ideasroom/2019/04/08/521574/when-are-human-rights-a-right-for-tonga>.

154 Vienna Convention on Diplomatic and Consular Relations 500 UNTS 95 (opened for signature 18 April 1961, entered into force 24 April 1964).

155 Convention on Special Missions 1400 UNTS 231 (opened for signature 8 December 1969, entered into force 21 June 1985).

156 See for example Diplomatic Relations Act (Cap 25.04), the Diplomatic Privileges Act (Cap 25.03), the Consular Relations Act (Cap 25.02), the Consular Conventions Act (Cap 25.01) the Special Missions' Privileges and Immunities Act (Cap 25.06), and the International Organisations Act (Immunities and Privileges of Certain Officers) Act (Cap 25.05).

The following countries maintain physical missions in Tonga: Australia, New Zealand, the People's Republic of China, Japan and the United Kingdom. Further, the governments of the Netherlands and Finland have appointed indigenous Tongans as Honorary Consuls to perform specific diplomatic duties.

According to 2019 World Bank data, Tonga's foreign trade represents 87.6 per cent of the country's GDP.[157] Tonga is a member of the Pacific Island Countries Trade Agreement (PICTA), the South Pacific Regional Trade and Economic Cooperation Agreement (SPARTECA), and the World Trade Organization (WTO). Agricultural and food products, including fish, make up more than two-thirds of total exports. The main imports are petroleum oils, meat and diodes. Its major export partners are the United States, South Korea, Australia, New Zealand and Japan. Its main suppliers are Fiji, New Zealand, China, and Japan.

The archipelago suffers from a chronic trade deficit, due to imports exceeding exports – a situation which is likely to continue for some years despite substantial international aid. The WTO estimates that in 2019 Tonga exported US$20 million and imported US$238 million in goods, while commercial services exports and imports stood at US$84 million and $93 million respectively.

11. CIVIL SOCIETY ORGANISATIONS

Community and faith-based groups and churches have long been a distinctive feature of civil society organisations in the South Pacific, including Tonga. Tonga's civil society organisations are made up of a range of non-governmental organisations across a spectrum of the community to advocate and advance their respective partisan interests. Churches of various Christian denominations play a major and influential role in the Kingdom's political and social development; this reflects the historical influence of Protestant missionaries when modern Tonga was born in 1845. Tongans are ardent churchgoers, the overwhelming majority considering themselves Christian. The Free Wesleyan Church is the largest denomination and Tonga's State Church (in 2016, 35 per cent of the population was affiliated with the Free Wesleyan Church),[158] followed by the Church of Latter-Day Saints (19 per cent in 2016),[159] the Catholic Church (14 per cent in 2016),[160] and the Free Church of Tonga (12 per cent in 2016).[161] Other religious faiths, such

157 See for World Bank country economic data (online 4 May 2021) at <https://data.worldbank.org/indicator/NE.TRD.GNFS.ZS?locations=TO>

158 Tonga Statistics Department *Tonga 2016 Census of Population and Housing: Volume 1* (2016) 13.

159 Tonga Statistics Department *Tonga 2016 Census of Population and Housing: Volume 1* (2016) 13.

160 Tonga Statistics Department *Tonga 2016 Census of Population and Housing: Volume 1* (2016) 13.

161 Tonga Statistics Department *Tonga 2016 Census of Population and Housing: Volume 1* (2016) 13.

as Buddhism, Islam and Baha'i, are present in Tonga, though with relatively few adherents.

The Constitution establishes freedom of religion, which is respected in practice by the government and general society, though there are laws which restrict commerce and broadcast media in accordance with Christian religious norms, including a mandatory day of rest on the Sabbath.

Prior to independence, overseas chapters of international civil society organisations were set up in Tonga and other Pacific states, for example the Tonga Red Cross, established pursuant to the Tonga Red Cross Society Act (Cap 12.18) as an independent and voluntary society that carries on work for the improvement of health, prevention of disease, and mitigation of suffering during peace and war throughout the world. The Tonga Red Cross enjoyed the patronage of the late Queen Salote Tupou III.

The transition towards greater democratic engagement has seen an increase in government ministries working with civil society organisations to shape the Kingdom's development. The Civil Society Forum Tonga is the key umbrella organisation for capacity building and coordinating civil society in Tonga. Its members include the Tonga National Youth Congress, the National Council for Women, *Ma'a Fafine mo e Famili*, the *'Ofa, Tui, 'Amanaki* Centre, the Women and Children Crisis Centre Tonga, the Tonga Family Health Association, the Tonga Leitis' Association, the Mango Tree Respite Centre Tonga, the On the Spot arts initiative, and the Tonga National Disability Congress.

The development of civil society capacity in Tonga has been a significant focus of government, the sector and aid donors. Tonga has participated in a number of civil society strengthening initiatives, including the Tonga Governance Strengthening Program, funded by the United Nations Development Programme and the Australian government, an electoral civics education programme in the lead-up to Tonga's 2010 elections, and a participatory governance project led by CIVICUS: the Participatory Governance Project – Leadership Development and Civil Society Strengthening in the Pacific in 2012.

From the 1990s, Tongan civil society developed its collective voice to advocate for social change in addition to providing humanitarian assistance in accordance with the organisations' respective purposes. Civil society has also become increasingly vocal in its criticism of the government, and in recent years has provided robust assessments of its performance. The government allows national and international civil society organisations to operate in a free and open environment without restrictions, but these organisations do face capacity restraints over uncertain funding and the retention of staff and expertise.[162]

162 Asian Development Bank 'Civil Society Briefs: Tonga' (2015) 4.

12. CONCLUSION

Tonga's legal and political development has been shaped by its unique system of constitutional monarchism and its status as the only South Pacific state not to have been colonised by a foreign power.

The historical amalgam of pervasive systems of traditional authority and introduced law from the United Kingdom has had a tendency to foster attitudes of respect, deference and compliance towards those exercising lawful power. It has also contributed to Tonga's confidence and faith in its system of constitutional monarchy. These attitudes are most marked where the sovereign is concerned, and to a significant extent have contributed to the absence of questioning and debate surrounding the implications of the sharing of executive powers under a reformed Constitution.

The 2010 constitutional reforms have created a form of law-making and dispute resolution unique in the South Pacific. They also signal a shift towards greater indigenous ownership and agency by the people over the Kingdom's political and legal systems. As Tonga's democratic aspirations continue to mature, it will need to continue the delicate balancing of its traditional and cultural values against its people's changing values and priorities in an ever-shrinking globalised society threatened by the potentially devastating effects of climate change.

BIBLIOGRAPHY

Attorney General's Office, Tonga <www.ago.gov.to>.

Corrin, Jennifer and Don Paterson *Introduction to South Pacific Law* (4th ed, Intersentia, 2017).

Pacific Islands Legal Information Institute *Tonga Primary Materials* <http://www.paclii.org/countries/to.html>.

Powles, Guy 'Political and Constitutional Reform Opens the Door: The Kingdom of Tonga's Path to Democracy' (2012) Comparative Law Journal of the Pacific, Hors Serie Vol XV.

TUVALU

Jennifer CORRIN*

1. BACKGROUND

Tuvalu, formerly known as the Ellice Islands, is located in the west-central Pacific Ocean about halfway between Hawaii and Australia. There are nine small coral islands,[1] with a total land area of 26 square kilometres, dispersed in a chain over a distance of around 676 kilometres.[2] From the 2017 census, Tuvalu has

* This chapter is an Editorial Team effort.

1 Composed of three reef islands and six atolls. The atolls – Nanumea, Nui, Nukufetau, Funafuti and Nukulaelae – all have islets encircling a shallow lagoon. The reef islands – Nanumanga, Niutao, Vaitupu and Niulakita – are compact with a fringing reef.

2 The average height of the islands is less than two metres above sea level, which makes them particularly susceptible to rising sea level and storms/tidal surges. The islands are predicted to be uninhabitable in 50–100 years. Some research suggests the islands will change shape but not necessarily disappear. There has been some expansion due to sediment, corals and other debris being washed ashore by storms and waves. Rising sea levels may also help hard

a population of 10,507. Funafuti[3] is an atoll as well as the capital of the island nation, and is the centre of government and commerce. Around one-third of the country's population lives there, while the rest of the population inhabits the outer islands in extended family groups clustered in villages.

The island of Funafuti was named Ellice's Island in 1819,[4] with Great Britain claiming control in the late 19th century. Captain Gibson of HMS *Curacoa* announced each of the Ellice Islands as a British Protectorate between 9 and 16 October 1892. A Resident Commissioner administered the Ellice Islands from 1892 to 1916 as part of the British Western Pacific Territories. Together with what is now Kiribati (originally the Gilbert Islands), Tuvalu formed the British Gilbert and Ellice Islands Colony in 1916.

From the 1960s, there was tension and competition over employment between the Gilbertese and Ellice Islanders. The demands from Ellice Islanders for secession resulted in a referendum in 1974. The referendum determined that the Gilbert Islands and Ellice Islands should each have their own administration. This led to the transition to separation of the groups between October 1975 and January 1976. Finally, in 1976, the Gilbert and Ellice Islands Colony and the old administration were officially separated, forming the separate British colonies of Kiribati and Tuvalu. On 5 September 2000, Tuvalu became the 189th member of the United Nations.

The main priorities of Tuvalu after separation were to establish the foundation for a separate, if small, nation and to look for foreign assistance in order to match political independence with economic viability.

The Tuvalu Parliament has 16 elected members[5] and each island has its own local government. There are no political parties. The head of state is Queen Elizabeth II, represented by the locally selected Governor-General.

Tuvaluans are Polynesian and speak Tuvaluan, a language closely related to Tokelauan. English is taught in schools and is widely used in Tuvalu. Most of the population belong to the Church of Tuvalu (formerly the Ellice Islands Protestant Church).

The rain catchment and wells provide the only fresh water in the country. Tuvalu's porous soil limits agriculture. Coconut palms, breadfruit trees, pandanus, taro and bananas grow, pigs and chickens are raised, and seabirds, fish and

---

coral reefs just below the water surface to grow, building up the living shelf that protects shorelines; however, increased carbon dioxide in the water and high temperatures may actually produce the opposite effect. Erosion has been caused by quarrying for rocks, gravel, and sand. Construction materials for big building projects are now imported.

3 Funafuti has a population of 6,320 (2017 census). Tuvalu Population & Housing Mini-Census 2017, Preliminary Report. 3, Tuvalu Central Statistics Division <https://tuvalu.prism.spc.int/>.

4 The name applied to all of the nine islands after the work of English hydrographer Alexander George Findlay.

5 Electoral Provisions (Parliament) Amendment Act 2019.

shellfish are caught for food. However, the islands increasingly depend on foreign aid and on food imported from overseas.

2. SOURCES OF LAW

The sources of law for Tuvalu are, in order of priority, the Constitution, Acts, customary law, the common law of Tuvalu[6] and the applied law. These matters are dealt with in the Laws of Tuvalu Act (Cap 1.06).[7] Customary law is defined in s 5 as 'the customs and usages, existing from time to time, of the natives of Tuvalu'. Customary law is superior to the common law and is a matter of law not of fact.[8] Schedule 1 of the Act provides a process for identifying customary law. This process is controlled by the judiciary.

Sections 6–12 deal with the applied law, which consists of imperial enactments in force on 1 January 1961.[9] These statutes have effect if they are of general application and not inappropriate to the circumstances of Tuvalu. The sections provide a system for patriating the applied laws; sale of goods and arbitration are examples of such patriated laws.[10]

Precedent is dealt with in s 13. Decisions of the Judicial Committee of the Privy Council in London on appeal from a Tuvalu case bind all courts of Tuvalu. In other instances, decisions of the Privy Council are of persuasive effect only. A court of Tuvalu is bound by the decisions of any court superior to it in the judicial hierarchy. It is unclear whether decisions of the courts of England and Wales continue to have any binding effect, although they are clearly persuasive.[11]

3. CONSTITUTION

In 1986, the government of Tuvalu established an autochthonous constitution by the Constitution of Tuvalu Ordinance 1986. The Constitution appeared as a Schedule to the Ordinance in the same way as did the Independence Constitution of 1978.[12]

---

6 This is comprised of 'the relevant rules', which are defined to mean 'the rules generally known as the English common law and the doctrines of equity': Laws of Tuvalu Act Cap 1.06, s 6(5).

7 Key definitions are also dealt with in the Constitution, Sch 1, and in the Interpretation and General Provisions Act Cap 1.04.

8 Laws of Tuvalu Act Cap 1.06, s 6(3)(b) and Sch 1.

9 Laws of Tuvalu Act Cap 1.06, s 7(1), read with Western Pacific (Courts) Order 1961 (UK), s 15.

10 Sale of Goods Act Cap 40.60; Arbitration Act Cap 7.04.

11 See further, Jennifer Corrin and Don Paterson *Introduction to South Pacific Law* (4th ed, Intersentia, 2017) 40.

12 The Constitution is the subject of ongoing reform discussion. A report on the latest endeavours can be found in 'Tuvalu Constitutional Review Project Report' <https://www.pacific.undp.org/content/dam/fiji/docs/TuvaluCRProjectUpdateReport.pdf>. The Constitution is numbered Cap 1.02 in the 2008 consolidation.

The Preamble to the Constitution in paras 4 and 6 sets out guiding principles for the State. Paragraph 4 states, 'Amongst the values that the people of Tuvalu seek to maintain are their traditional forms of communities, the strength and support of the family and family discipline', and para 6 states, 'The life and the laws of Tuvalu should therefore be based on respect for human dignity, and on the acceptance of Tuvaluan values and culture, and on respect for them'. Schedule 1 of the Constitution[13] affirms that the Preamble forms part of the Constitution. The matter is put beyond doubt by s 1 of the Constitution: 'Tuvalu is a sovereign democratic State, governed in accordance with this Constitution and in particular in accordance with the Principles set out in the Preamble'. Section 4(2) continues, 'In all cases this Constitution shall be interpreted and applied consistently with the principles set out in the Preamble'. The matter is reaffirmed in ss 10 and 13. Section 13 is particularly direct: 'The Principles set out in the Preamble are adopted as part of the basic law of Tuvalu, from which human rights and freedoms derive and on which they are based'. Section 29 is in similar vein.

The role of the Preamble in relation to human rights and freedoms – in the particular instance, the freedom of religion – was the subject of extended discussion in the case of *Teonea v Pule o Kaupule of Nanumaga and Nanumaga Falekaupule*. In its judgment[14] the Court by a majority held in favour of the petitioner and against the action of the traditional authority. In practical terms, the judgment was untenable, and by the Constitution (Recognition of Traditional Standards, Values and Practices) Amendment Act 2010, the declaration of the Court of Appeal was effectively reversed to 'protect the island communities of Tuvalu from the spread of religious beliefs which threaten the cohesiveness of island communities'.[15]

The Constitution is the supreme law of Tuvalu[16] and is entrenched; by s 7, a two-thirds majority of the total membership of the Parliament is required in most cases for a change to the Constitution.

There is a Bill of Rights in Part II,[17] which follows a recognisable British Colonial Office pattern and reflects the influence of the European Convention on Human Rights and Freedoms.

The head of state is 'the sovereign of Tuvalu'. Her Majesty Queen Elizabeth II of the United Kingdom agreed to the request of Tuvalu that she be their head

13 Section 3(1).

14 Given in 2009. Tuvalu CoA, Civil Appeal 1 of 2005. See further Tony Angelo '"Steady as She Goes" – The Constitution and the Court of Appeal in Samoa' (2012) 18 New Zealand Association of Comparative Law Yearbook 145.

15 Section 4.

16 Section 3.

17 Sections 9–42.

of state and that consequently Tuvalu be added to the realms of which she is sovereign.[18] The sovereign is the 'symbol of unity and identity of Tuvalu'; the sovereign acts on advice of Cabinet or the Prime Minister in most cases. The sovereign's representative is a Governor-General, who must be a citizen of Tuvalu aged between 50 and 65.

The Parliament of Tuvalu is unicameral. There are 16 members and the head of government is the Prime Minister. The Prime Minister is elected by Members of Parliament in a meeting chaired by the Governor-General. Cabinet is collectively responsible. The term of Parliament is four years.

Other constitutional offices include the Secretary to Government, who is the key public officer providing liaison between the ministers and the public servants. The Secretary's role is similar to that of the Secretary to Government in Niue. The Secretary attends Cabinet meetings but is not a member of Cabinet.

The Attorney-General is a constitutional officer appointed by the head of state on advice of the Public Service Commission. The Attorney-General is the principal legal advisor to the government.

4. LEGISLATURE

Legislation follows the Westminster pattern. The Parliament passes Bills, which, when signed by the sovereign, become law as Acts. The sovereign has no discretion in the matter and by s 86 of the Constitution must 'promptly assent' to a Bill presented to him or her when it has passed through the parliamentary procedures. The Speaker of the Parliament is elected by the Parliament from among its members.

Other constitutional offices are the Public Service Commission, which is an independent employer of all public servants, and the Auditor-General, who is an independent officer responsible for inspecting and reporting on the public accounts of Tuvalu.

5. LOCAL GOVERNMENT

The Falekaupule Act (Cap 4.08) is the principal law dealing with local government. It repealed the Local Government Act and established a new relationship between the traditional governance bodies and the national government at island level. The former Island Councils and the Funafuti Town Council were replaced by the Falekaupule and the Kaupule. The Falekaupule is the traditional assembly of each island and is governed in accordance with the custom of the island.

18 Section 48.

The Kaupule is the executive arm of the Falekaupule and is responsible for the island budget, the promulgation of local subordinate legislation, and liaison with the central government in Funafuti. Each Kaupule has six members, who are elected by registered voters unless the Falekaupule resolves to elect and terminate its Kaupule members directly.[19]

6. THE COURTS

The hierarchy of the courts in Tuvalu consists of Magistrates' Courts,[20] the High Court and the Court of Appeal.[21] A further appeal lies to the Judicial Committee of the Privy Council in England.[22] There are also special courts established to deal with land: the Lands Court and the Lands Courts Appeals Panel.[23] The Island Courts Act[24] makes provision for inferior courts to deal with local disputes.

The Privy Council has jurisdiction to hear appeals from the decisions of the Court of Appeal, with leave from the Court of Appeal, on certain constitutional matters. It may also hear appeals involving questions of great general or public importance, and from decisions in certain other civil cases.[25] The Constitution makes no reference to a specific criminal jurisdiction of the Privy Council. To date, it appears that no appeal has been taken to the Privy Council.

The Court of Appeal consists of the judges of the High Court and at least three judges of appeal.[26] Judges of appeal are appointed by the Governor-General acting in accordance with the advice of Cabinet.[27] The Court of Appeal has jurisdiction to hear appeals as of right from the High Court exercising any type of civil jurisdiction, except where an order was made by consent or is as to costs only or where an order or judgment is interlocutory, except where prescribed by rules of court, leave is required.[28] No appeal is allowed from decisions allowing an extension of time in which to appeal; orders giving unconditional leave to defend an action; or decisions provided by statute to be final.[29] In criminal

19 Falekaupule (Amendment) (No 1) Act 2019, s 3.
20 Magistrates' Courts Act Cap 7.36.
21 Constitution of Tuvalu Cap 1.02, ss 119(a), 134 and 136.
22 Tuvalu (Appeals to Privy Council) Order 1975 (SI 1975 No 1507).
23 Native Lands Act Cap 46.20.
24 Cap 7.32.
25 Superior Courts Act Cap 7.68, s 13(1)(b).
26 Superior Courts Act Cap 7.68, s 7(2).
27 Superior Courts Act Cap 7.68, s 8(2).
28 Superior Courts Act Cap 7.68, s 9(2)(d).
29 Superior Courts Act Cap 7.68, s 9(2).

cases, appeals lie as of right from decisions of the High Court, both original and appellate, to the Court of Appeal.[30]

The High Court is constituted by the Chief Justice, who is appointed by the sovereign acting in accordance with the advice of Cabinet.[31] The current appointee is based in Australia and visits approximately once every three years. Additional judges may be appointed by the head of state, acting in accordance with the advice of Cabinet after consultation with the Chief Justice.[32] When sitting to hear appeals on customary land matters, the Chief Justice may appoint two or more assessors to assist him.[33] The High Court has original jurisdiction to determine questions as to the interpretation or application of the Constitution,[34] and to determine applications for breach of human rights.[35] The High Court has unlimited original jurisdiction in civil cases.[36] It hears appeals as of right from all decisions of the Senior Magistrate's Court,[37] other than orders made ex parte, by consent, or as to costs only, where special leave is required.[38] The High Court's jurisdiction to hear appeals from the Senior Magistrate's Court exercising appellate jurisdiction includes decisions on appeal from the Lands Courts Appeals Panel.[39] The High Court may also decide a question of law referred to it by way of case stated from the Senior Magistrate's Court.[40] The High Court also has a supervisory jurisdiction over inferior courts[41] and unlimited original jurisdiction in criminal matters.[42] The High Court hears appeals from decisions of the Senior Magistrate's Court.[43] In practice, both civil and criminal appeals go directly to the High Court from the ordinary Magistrates' Courts, as the Senior Magistrate's Court is not sitting. Appeals lie as of right and may be made in relation to questions of fact and/or law, including the matter of sentence, which is deemed to be a question of law. In addition, there is provision for appeals to be made by way of case stated.

The Magistrates' Courts Act establishes the Magistrates' Courts. This court is theoretically divided into two levels, namely the Senior Magistrate's Court and the Magistrates' Court. When sitting to hear appeals on customary land

---

30 Superior Courts Act Cap 7.68, s 9(1)(a).
31 Constitution of Tuvalu Cap 1.02, s 122.
32 Constitution of Tuvalu Cap 1.02, s 123. No such appointment has yet been made.
33 Native Lands Act Cap 46.20, s 27.
34 Constitution of Tuvalu Cap 1.02, s 131(1). See also s 130(1).
35 Constitution of Tuvalu Cap 1.02, ss 38(1) and 130(1)(a).
36 Superior Courts Act Cap 7.68, s 3(2)(a).
37 Magistrates' Courts Act Cap 7.36, s 39.
38 Magistrates' Courts Act Cap 7.36, s 39(2).
39 Native Lands Act Cap 46.20, s 26(2).
40 Magistrates' Courts Act Cap 7.36, s 41.
41 Superior Courts Act Cap 7.68, s 3(2)(d).
42 Superior Courts Act Cap 7.68, s 3(2)(a).
43 Superior Courts Act Cap 7.68, s 3(2)(e); Pt IX of the Criminal Procedure Code Cap 7.

matters, the Senior Magistrate is empowered to appoint two or more assessors to assist.[44] A Magistrates' Court has original jurisdiction to hear civil cases involving actions for up to $500. The Senior Magistrate's Court has jurisdiction to hear civil cases involving actions for up to $10,000.[45] The Senior Magistrate may also make adoption orders. The Senior Magistrate's Court has jurisdiction to hear appeals from any other Magistrates' Court as of right in all matters[46] other than orders made ex parte, by consent, or as to costs only, where special leave is required.[47] The only Magistrates' Court operating is the Resident Magistrates' Court. In criminal matters Magistrates' Courts have summary jurisdiction only. The Senior Magistrate's Court may deal with offences where the maximum punishment does not exceed 14 years' imprisonment and/or a fine, or where jurisdiction has been expressly conferred on the court.[48] The maximum punishment that may be imposed by the Senior Magistrate's Court is imprisonment for five years or a fine of $1,000 or both.[49] Other Magistrates' Courts may only deal with offences cases where the maximum punishment is imprisonment for one year or less or a fine of up to $200 or both, or where jurisdiction has been expressly conferred on the court.[50] The Magistrates' Courts hear appeals from decisions of the Island Courts within their district,[51] and may review any Island Court decision.[52] The Senior Magistrate's Court also has jurisdiction to hear appeals from other Magistrates' Courts,[53] and from the Lands Courts Appeals Panel.[54] The Senior Magistrate's Court may decide a question of law referred to it by way of case stated by a magistrate.[55] In practice, all these matters go directly to the High Court, as the Senior Magistrate's Court is not currently operating.

Island Courts are established by the Island Courts Act[56] on each island that the Governor-General designates.[57] They are subordinate to Magistrates' Courts and are presided over by three Island Magistrates, being the President, the Vice President and an ordinary member.[58] Appointments are by the

44 Native Lands Act Cap 46.20, s 27(1).
45 LN 2/88 made under Magistrates' Courts Act Cap 7.36, s 22(3). The dominant currency is Australian.
46 Magistrates' Courts Act Cap 7.36, s 39.
47 Magistrates' Courts Act Cap 7.36, s 39(2).
48 Magistrates' Courts Act Cap 7.36, s 25(1)(a) and (b).
49 Magistrates' Courts Act Cap 7.36, s 25(1)(b).
50 Magistrates' Courts Act Cap 7.36, s 25(2)(a) and (b).
51 Magistrates' Courts Act Cap 7.36, Part VI; Island Courts Act Cap 7.32, s 28.
52 Islands Courts Act Cap 7.32, s 37.
53 Magistrates' Courts Act Cap 7.36, s 43(1).
54 Native Lands Act Cap 46.20, s 26(1).
55 Magistrates' Courts Act Cap 7.36, s 41.
56 Cap 7.32.
57 Island Courts Act Cap 7.32, s 3(1)–(2). There are currently eight Island Courts.
58 Island Courts Act Cap 7.32, s 9(1).

Governor-General acting in accordance with the advice of the Public Service Commission and subject to the approval of the Chief Justice.[59] A clerk of court is appointed by the Senior Magistrate to each Island Court.[60] Island Courts have jurisdiction within the boundaries of the island on which they were established and over inland and adjacent waters.[61] They may deal with divorce and associated proceedings provided both parties are domiciled in Tuvalu, claims in contract and tort where the amount involved does not exceed $60, and applications for maintenance,[62] and for custody.[63]

Island Courts do not have jurisdiction over customary land disputes.[64] Island Courts may deal with criminal offences set out in Sch 2 of the Island Courts Act or where the maximum punishment is imprisonment of six months or less or a fine of $100 or both.[65]

The Lands Court is constituted by at least six members, appointed by the local government council with the approval of the Land's Officer.[66] The Lands Courts Appeals Panel is constituted by the President, a Vice President and at least three other members, all of whom are appointed by the Minister.[67] The Lands Court has jurisdiction to determine all customary land disputes.[68] It also deals with native wills,[69] adoption and related conveyances of land,[70] customary fishing rights,[71] disputes concerning customary leases,[72] and paternity disputes.[73] Appeals lie from the Lands Court to the Lands Courts Appeals Panel.[74]

7. LEGAL PROFESSION

There are few lawyers in Tuvalu and most are in government service. There is a People's Lawyer, an Office established by the People's Lawyer Act 1988, who provides legal advice and legal representation for members of the public. The legal profession is regulated by the Legal Profession Act 2015. The Act establishes

59 Island Courts Act Cap 7.32, s 9(2).
60 Island Courts Act Cap 7.32, s 12(1).
61 Island Courts Act Cap 7.32, s 4.
62 Maintenance (Miscellaneous Provisions) Act Cap 17.20.
63 Island Courts Act Cap 7.32, Sch 1; Custody of Children Act Cap 17.15.
64 Native Lands Act Cap 46.20, ss 12, 14, 15, 16 and 17.
65 Island Courts Act Cap 7.32, Sch 2. See also s 6 of the Act.
66 Native Lands Act Cap 46.20.
67 Native Lands Act Cap 46.20, s 9.
68 Native Lands Act Cap 46.20, s 12.
69 Native Lands Act Cap 46.20, s 15.
70 Native Lands Act Cap 46.20, s 16.
71 Native Lands Act Cap 46.20, s 17.
72 Native Lands Act Cap 46.20, s 18.
73 Native Lands Act Cap 46.20, s 20.
74 Native Lands Act Cap 46.20, s 10.

the Legal Practitioners Committee, consisting of the Attorney-General, the Chief Ombudsman, the People's Lawyer, and the Commissioner of Police. The Committee deals with admission to practice and discipline of legal practitioners. It is an offence to practise law without a certificate of admission.[75] Lawyers admitted to practice in England who have at least five years' practical experience are automatically entitled to practise in Tuvalu.[76]

8. EVIDENCE AND PROCEDURE

As Tuvalu does not have its own Evidence Act, the rules are provided by the English evidence legislation in force on 1 January 1961.[77] Unfortunately, the English legislation at that time was spread across a large number of statutes dating back to the beginning of the 19th century. A further complicating factor was that these Acts were superimposed on the common law of evidence. The relevant statutes include the Evidence Act 1845, the Evidence Act 1851, the Bankers' Books Evidence Acts 1879 and 1859, the Documentary Evidence Act 1882, the Criminal Evidence Act 1898, and the Evidence Act 1938.

Procedure is governed by pre-independence provisions. In the case of civil procedure this is the Western Pacific (High Court) Rules 1964. Criminal procedure is governed by the Criminal Procedure Code (Cap 10.05), originally enacted in 1963.

9. CRIMINAL LAW

The principal and general legislation for criminal law is the Penal Code (Cap 10.20). It is in a standard form and reminiscent of the Queensland Criminal Code 1899.

10. LAND LAW

The Native Lands Act (Cap 46.20) includes the Tuvalu Lands Code. Most land in Tuvalu is held in accordance with custom. It is divided into plots which are owned by dissent groups; most groups own more than one plot. Land may not be sold to a non-Tuvaluan. Leases are however not uncommon and families earn income from land by the rentals, for example to the government for essential

---

75 Legal Profession Act 2015, s 14.
76 Legal Profession Act 2015, s 7(3).
77 Laws of Tuvalu Act Cap 1.06, s 7(1).

community services. If there is a dispute, the Land Court decides. The maximum period for a lease is 75 years. Land is scarce and therefore rents are relatively high, especially in Funafuti.

In the absence of agreement, the government may take land under the Crown Acquisition of Lands Act (Cap 46.05). Typically, the acquisition is of a leasehold interest.

Land use custom allows passage through land but does not permit the taking of produce from another's land without permission. The taking of produce from another's land without permission is trespass, but not the physical presence. The foreshore is owned by the government. Land is registered.

The Native Lands Act provides for the survey of land and for registration of title to native lands. A title which has been registered is indefeasible. The Act deals extensively with leases, and in the Part dealing with alienation has provision for native wills, native adoptions, customary fishing right and native leases. Section 20 of the Act permits the court to conduct an inquiry into the paternity of an illegitimate child and to make an order in relation to his or her land rights and in relation to maintenance.

11. FAMILY LAW

Marriage is dealt with in the Marriage Act (Cap 17.25). The minimum age for marriage is 18. A Family Protection and Domestic Violence Act was enacted in 2014. Adoption is dealt with specifically in the Adoption of Children Act (Cap 17.05) and has special significance because of its relationship to land rights.

Succession matters are dealt with by the English Wills Act 1837 and its amendment of 1852. Intestacy is covered by the Administration Act 1925 (UK) and family protection by the Inheritance (Family Provision) Act 1938 (UK).

In addition to the specific provisions relating to the rights of children in the Native Lands Act, children's rights are addressed in the Custody of Children Act (Cap 17.15). In custody matters, 'the welfare of the child [is] the first and paramount consideration'.

The Matrimonial Proceedings Act (Cap 17.30) provides for marriage breakdown in a very succinct manner. The approach is secular and social as indicated in s 2 of the Act:

> To minimize the ill-effects of a breakdown, attempts at reconciliation and the lessening (if possible) of the common bitterness resulting from a marriage failure must be given prominence, and if the divorce does go ahead it must be remembered that if there are children what is being broken up is not just a family but a family unit, and the children, as members of that unit, must be given every care and protection.

There are peremptory grounds for divorce in cases of failure to consummate or fraud, duress or mistake. The single alternative ground is 'that the marriage has completely broken down'. Jurisdiction is with the Island Courts. By s 12, 'the welfare of the children is of paramount importance'. The court may make any order it thinks necessary or desirable to adjust the property rights of any person affected by matrimonial proceedings (s 13). To the extent possible, the court is required to reduce 'the continuing bad effects of the breakdown of a marriage', and shall endeavour to settle all property matters before granting a divorce; it shall do this by consent wherever possible.

12. LAW OF OBLIGATIONS

The fields of contract, torts and restitution are predominantly covered by the rules of English common law and equity. There are few statutory variations. Prominent examples are the Sale of Goods Act (Cap 40.60) and the Workmen's Compensation Act (Cap 40.72).

13. COMMERCIAL LAW

The principal legislation in this field is the Bills of Sales Act (Cap 40.04), the Companies Act (Cap 40.08), the Companies and Business Registration Act (Cap 40.12), the Cooperatives Act (Cap 40.20), the Copyright Act (Cap 40.24), the Income Tax Act (Cap 26.16), the International Companies Act 2009, the Law of Property Act 1925 (UK), the Partnership Act (Cap 40.36), the Registration of United Kingdom Patents Act (Cap 40.48), the Registration of United Kingdom Trade Marks Act (Cap 40.52), and the Sale of Goods Act (Cap 40.60). Tuvalu uses Australian currency but also has its own coinage.

Bills of sale allows movable property to serve as security for a loan. The transfer is required to be in writing and to be registered.

A group of at least five people may obtain registration as a cooperative society and upon registration the cooperative society becomes a corporation with its own separate legal identity.

Corporations can be established by royal charter because the British Crown is still recognised as head of state, but this is rare. Usually the creation of a corporation is authorised under legislation.

The Hire-Purchase Act 1938 (UK), as amended in 1954, and the Bills of Exchange Act 1882 are in force in Tuvalu as part of the applied law.

The Statute of Frauds, s 4, and the Law of Property Act 1925 (UK), as amended by the Law Reform (Enforcement of Contracts) Act 1954, apply in Tuvalu as part of the applied law. This legislation provides that contracts of guarantee and contracts for dispositions of land must be in writing. Section 53 of the Law of Property Act 1925 provides that a disposition of any equitable interest must be in writing and signed by the person disposing of that interest. Section 136 provides that any legal chose or thing in action can be assigned in writing, provided that notice is given to the debtor or other person from whom the assignor would have been able to claim the thing in action.

14. THE ENVIRONMENT AND INTERNATIONAL LAW

Tuvalu is party to a number of treaties.[78] In order to be enforceable as a matter of domestic law, treaties must be implemented by an Act.

Tuvalu has been very active on matters relating to global warming and has been outspoken on these matters since the Rio Conference of 1992. It is a consistent leader among the Pacific nations in climate change negotiations. In 2019, it enacted the Climate Change Resilience Act to build an effective climate change response, ensure long-term climate resilience and transition to a lower carbon economy.

Fisheries are extremely important for Tuvalu. Legislation which deals with marine pollution is the Marine Pollution Act (Cap 48.16), while the Marine Resources Act (Cap 48.2) deals with marine resources. There is also an Ozone Layer Protection Act (Cap 30.30).

15. COMMENT

Tuvalu began its life as an independent state with an inter-island vessel as its main asset other than the land and sea itself. A marine training institute was established to provide merchant seamen for the future. This is recognised in the Tuvalu Maritime Training Institute Act 2000. Remittances from Tuvaluan seamen on foreign vessels have provided an important source of income over the years. However, employment opportunities are decreasing. Remittances from overseas workers (mostly seafarers) more than halved in the period from 2008 to 2012.

Tuvalu was assigned the domain suffix .tv by the Internet Corporation for Assigned Names and Numbers in 1995. In 2000 .tv was leased for $50 million over 12 years. Under the current agreement, which was signed in 2011 (and expires in 2021), Tuvalu earns about $2.2 million a year in royalties.

A particular feature of the current Tuvalu legal and financial situation is its intergenerational trust funds. The model pioneered by Tuvalu immediately after independence is the International Trust Fund of 1987.[79] Tuvalu entered

---

[78] Eg Tuvalu is a signatory of the United Nations Framework Convention on Climate Change and ratified it in 1993.

[79] NZTS 1987, no 29, art 1.

its independent existence essentially resourceless. It appealed for help in the early 1980s but was unsuccessful. Other approaches for one-off assistance were rejected. It then developed the concept of a reserve fund, to which contributions were invited from Australia, New Zealand and the United Kingdom. The result was the establishment of an international trust fund by treaty with a sum of AU$27.1 million contributed in equal shares by Australia, New Zealand and the United Kingdom, AU$1.6 million contributed by Tuvalu, and smaller amounts contributed by Japan and South Korea. The Fund now stands at AU$172.3 million.[80] The money of the Fund is not Tuvalu government money. The Tuvalu government receives the income from the Fund and that money goes into the Consolidated Account. Initial investments were on a 30:70 (growth/defensive) basis and in the Australian share market. The first call on earnings of the Fund is to maintain the real value of the Fund. In a bad year, therefore, there might be no distribution to the government. To counter this difficulty and to make national budgeting easier, a second account was established within the Fund to which earnings in good years were contributed so that in bad years drawings could be made from that second account to maintain regular budget support for the government.

The Tuvalu Trust Fund is a national fund established to provide the government with a reliable source of revenue. Following its success, it was decided to establish an intergenerational trust fund for the islands. That was done by the Falekaupule Trust Fund Deed in 1999, complemented by the Tupe Fakanaa a Falekaupule Act. The Falekaupule Trust Fund works on principles similar to those of the Tuvalu Trust Fund and has the advantage of pooling assets with the Tuvalu Trust Fund for investment purposes.

Cyclones and similar disasters not infrequently cause massive damage in Tuvalu. Aid is typically available to meet the post-disaster needs, but it became apparent from experience that much needs to be done at the time of the disaster and immediately after it and before international aid arrives. To meet this need, the Climate Change and Disaster Survival Fund Act 2015 was established and again the pattern of the Tuvalu Trust Fund was used: this time establishment was not by a treaty, nor a deed, but by an Act of Parliament.

BIBLIOGRAPHY

Angelo, Tony '"Steady as She Goes" – The Constitution and the Court of Appeal in Samoa' (2012) 18 New Zealand Association of Comparative Law Yearbook 145.

80 As at 2017. In the Trust Fund's report of 30 September 2016, the value of the fund was AU$6.7 million greater than the inflation-adjusted value. AU$6.7 million was distributed; AU$5 million was reinvested in the Fund.

Angelo, Tony, Brian Bell and Bayley Roylance 'Intergenerational Funds in the Pacific' (2017) 23 Comparative Law Journal of the Pacific 135.

Crocombe, Ron (ed) *Land Tenure in the Atolls* (Institute of Pacific Studies, University of the South Pacific, 1987).

Isala, Tito 'Land Tenure and Development Dollars in Tuvalu' in Ron Crocombe (ed) *Land Issues in the Pacific* (Institute of Pacific Studies, University of the South Pacific, 1994).

Pacific Islands Legal Information Institute *Tuvalu Primary Materials* <http://www.paclii.org/countries/tv.html>.

Tsamenyi, Martin 'Tuvalu' in Michael A Ntumy (ed) *South Pacific Islands Legal Systems* (University of Hawaii Press, 1993).

VANUATU

Morsen MOSSES

1. CONTEXT

The New Hebrides, an island group in the South Pacific, was first discovered by Europeans in 1606.[1] In 1906, Britain and France agreed to a Convention establishing a sphere of joint influence in the country, under which they had parallel jurisdiction each over their own subjects.[2] In 1914, the two colonial

1 The Islands of New Hebrides were discovered by the Spanish explorer Pedro Fernández de Queirós, who landed in 1606 on Espiritu Santo (now known simply as Santo). The archipelago was later mapped and named New Hebrides by the English explorer Captain James Cook in 1774. See Sue Farran 'Pacific Punch: Tropical Flavors of Mixedness in the Island Republic of Vanuatu' in Anna Koppel, Vernon Valentine Palmer and Mohammed Y Mattar (eds) *Mixed Legal Systems, East and West* (Ashgate, 2015) 124.

2 The Convention was signed in London on 20 October 1906, and is known as the London Convention.

powers agreed to a new Protocol establishing the Anglo-French Condominium over the New Hebrides. The Protocol provided for greater mixed juridical functions, including the administration of a joint court, the making of joint regulations for the order and good governance of the islands, and certain services to be undertaken in common.[3] Due to World War I, the Protocol of 1914 was not ratified or implemented until 1922.

Calls for independence began in the mid-1960s. This was sparked by disputes over the system of land ownership under the Condominium, which allowed for appropriation of customary lands by Europeans.[4] While a number of French-speaking parties opposed the idea of immediate independence, the English-speaking pro-independence movement that became the Vanua'aku Pati repeatedly called on the two colonial powers to grant the New Hebrides independence.

In 1978, with the consent of the British and French administrations, a temporary government was established. In 1979, the latter appointed a constitutional planning committee with a specific role to draft the written Constitution. An Exchange of Notes between the UK and France approved the final draft of the document on 23 October 1979. On 30 July 1980, the New Hebrides acceded to its independence and became the Republic of Vanuatu.

2. SOURCES OF LAW

Vanuatu was jointly administered by the UK and France from 1906 until 1980. As a result of this, the country has several sources of law. The Constitution, statutory law, British and French laws, colonial Joint Regulations, common law and indigenous customary law apply.

2.1. CONSTITUTION

The Constitution of Vanuatu is the supreme law of the land.[5] It lays out, among other things, the basic structure of the government, the requirements of citizenship, the basic tenets of land ownership and provides for fundamental rights and freedoms of individuals.

---

3 The protocol respecting the New Hebrides signed at London on 6 August 1914, by representatives of the British and French governments. Farran, above n 1, at 125.

4 Howard Van Trease 'The Colonial Origins of Vanuatu Politics' in Howard Van Trease (ed) *Melanesian Politics: Stael Blong Vanuatu* (Macmillan Brown Centre for Pacific Studies, University of Canterbury and Institute of Pacific Studies, University of South Pacific, 1995) 13; Miranda Forsyth *A Bird that Flies with Two Wings: Kastom and State Justice Systems in Vanuatu* (ANU Press, 2009) 2.

5 Article 2 of the Constitution.

The procedures for amending the Constitution are different from those covering Acts of Parliament. Article 85 of the Constitution provides that Parliament may amend the Constitution by a vote of no less than two-thirds of all members at a special sitting attended by at least three-quarters of members. Alternatively, if there is no such quorum, Parliament may meet a week later and make a decision by the same majority even if only two-thirds of the members are present. Article 86 of the Constitution requires that any amendment regarding the status of the three official languages (English, French, Bislama), the electoral system or the parliamentary system shall not come into effect unless approved by a national referendum.

2.2. STATUTORY LAW

Parliament is authorised by the Constitution to 'make laws for the peace, order and good government of Vanuatu'.[6] Any Bill passed by Parliament becomes law after it is assented to by the President of the Republic and gazetted by the State Law Office. The laws made are to be consistent with the Constitution.

The Constitution provides that the pre-independence laws and regulations, which were still in force in the country after 30 July 1980, continue to form part of the laws of the Republic of Vanuatu. The Acts of Parliament adopted since independence and the pre-independence regulations that are still in force are compiled in the *Laws of Vanuatu*, and were published in two revised editions in 1988 and 2006. In these revised editions, the laws are designated by chapter numbers (Cap).

2.3. COLONIAL LAWS

In accordance with art 95(2) of the Constitution, the British and French laws in force or applied in Vanuatu immediately before 30 July 1980 continue to apply after independence to the extent that they are not expressly revoked or incompatible with the independent status of Vanuatu. The same article also provides that the application of these colonial laws should, wherever possible, take into account custom or customary law.

During the time that Vanuatu (then New Hebrides) was under the administration of the UK and France, the Anglo-French Protocol of 1914, which regulated the government of New Hebrides, provided that the laws of Britain and France were to apply to their respective nationals and to nationals of other countries, including indigenous New Hebrideans who chose to be subject to

6 Article 16(1) of the Constitution.

such laws. Indigenous New Hebrideans who did not choose to be subject to those laws were subject to customary law.

The French legislation and subsidiary legislation that applied to French nationals and optants was provided by the French Codes, together with legislation specifically stated (by these same laws) to apply to New Caledonia or New Hebrides, or applied to New Hebrides by the French Commissioners in Nouméa.

Similarly, English laws were applied to UK citizens and optants living in the territory of New Hebrides in accordance with art 20 of the Pacific Order in Council 1893 (UK), which provided for the application of 'the substance of the law for the time being in force in England'. In 1961, the statutes of general application in force in England on 1 January 1961were applied in New Hebrides in accordance with art 15 of the Western Pacific (Courts) Order 1961 (UK). The High Court of New Hebrides Regulation 1976 later extended the date of the application of English statutes of general application to 1 January 1976. Accordingly, prior to independence, British nationals and optants were, inter alia, subject to statutes of general application in force in England on 1 January 1976. They were also subject to legislation and subsidiary legislation expressly stated to apply to the New Hebrides.

2.4. COMMON LAW AND EQUITY

Before independence, French nationals and optants were not subject to the common law and equity of England.[7] As far as the UK citizens and optants were concerned, the High Court of New Hebrides Regulation 1976 provided for the reception of the common law and equity, so far as the local circumstances of the New Hebrides permitted.[8]

The Constitution of Vanuatu does not expressly provide for the reception of the common law and equity. However, in accordance with art 95(2) of the Constitution, the British and French laws in force or applied in Vanuatu immediately before 30 July 1980 continue to apply after independence, unless they are expressly revoked or are incompatible with the independent status of Vanuatu. The Constitution of Vanuatu, in effect, continues in force the above Regulation of 1976, which permits the application of common law and equity in the country.

---

7 Principles of common law and equity are principles evolved by the UK courts on the basis of the common practices of the Kingdom in early times, with some additions from other sources; and principles developed by the Court of Chancery in the interests of equity and fairness. See Jennifer Corrin and Don Paterson *Introduction to South Pacific Law* (4th ed, Intersentia, 2017) 30–31.

8 The High Court of New Hebrides Regulation 1976 (UK).

2.5. JOINT REGULATIONS

Prior to independence, the Resident Commissioners of the UK and France were specifically authorised by the Anglo-French Protocol of 1914 to issue jointly local regulations binding on all inhabitants of New Hebrides.[9] Accordingly, a large number of Joint Regulations were issued, some of which authorised the making of rules or orders by local public authorities.[10]

The Constitution provides in art 95(1) that these Joint Regulations and subsidiary legislation made thereunder in force immediately before 30 July 1980 continue to apply after independence and will be construed with adaptations necessary to bring them into conformity with the Constitution.

The Joint Regulations that are still in force are included in the compilation *Laws of Vanuatu*, published in two revised editions in 1988 and 2006. They are now called Acts of Parliament.

2.6. CUSTOMARY LAW

The Constitution recognises custom as a source of law in Vanuatu. Article 95(3) of the Constitution provides that '[c]ustomary law shall continue to have effect as part of the law of the Republic of Vanuatu'. Article 47(1) of the Constitution provides that custom is a source of law in dispute resolution.[11] Article 95(2) states that the application of colonial laws should, wherever possible, take into account custom.

With regard to land transactions, art 74 of the Constitution provides that rules of custom form the basis of ownership and use of land in Vanuatu.[12] Article 51 of the Constitution states that Parliament may provide for the manner of the ascertainment of relevant rules of custom, which influences the courts in applying custom. Parliament, however, has yet to exercise its powers under this provision.

The Island Courts Act 1983, which provides for the establishment of Island Courts, specifically requires the Island Courts to 'administer' the customary law prevailing within the territorial jurisdiction of the court, so far as the same is

---

9 Article 7 of the Anglo-French Protocol Respecting the New Hebrides.

10 See Don Paterson 'Vanuatu' in Michael A Ntumy (ed) *South Pacific Islands Legal Systems* (University of Hawaii Press, 1993) 368.

11 Article 47(1) provides: 'the administration of justice is vested in the judiciary, who are subject only to the Constitution and the law. The function of the judiciary is to resolve proceedings according to law. If there is no rule of law applicable to a matter before it, a court shall determine the matter according to substantial justice and whenever possible in conformity with custom'.

12 Article 74 of the Constitution states: 'The rules of custom shall form the basis of ownership and use of land in the Republic of Vanuatu'.

not in conflict with any written law and is not contrary to justice, morality and good order.[13]

3. CONSTITUTIONAL LAW

The expression 'constitutional law' generally refers to written and unwritten laws, established conventions and practices that provide for the establishment and functioning of the national government.[14] In Vanuatu's context, the Constitution is the principal written law regulating, among other things, the operation of the government. In addition to the Constitution, unwritten principles of common law and customary law, as well as established conventions and practices, operate to regulate the functioning of the national government. This section will focus on the written Constitution and then on those aspects of the Constitution that are provided in other legislation, the common law and constitutional conventions.

3.1. THE WRITTEN CONSTITUTION

During the constitutional transition towards independence, with the agreement of Britain and France, the written constitution was drafted by a Committee comprised of representatives of different political parties and groupings and with the assistance of two constitutional experts, one appointed by the UK and one by France.

The draft constitution was then approved and enacted by the UK and France in an Exchange of Notes in 1979.

3.1.1. Structure and Format of the Written Constitution

The Constitution of Vanuatu commences with a preamble which emphasises the unity of the country and its struggle for nationhood, and proclaims the establishment of the Republic of Vanuatu based on Melanesian values and Christian principles.[15]

The Constitution then continues with the substantive parts in chapter 1. This consists of some general provisions about the nature of the state, the status of the Constitution, the national and official languages, and the national sovereignty,

---

13 Section 10 of Island Courts Act 1983 Cap 167.

14 Corrin and Paterson, above n 7, at 77.

15 See Preamble of the Constitution; Constitutional Committee, *Republic Blong Vanuatu* (1979) 157.

electoral franchise and political parties.[16] Article 1 of the Constitution provides that '[t]he Republic of Vanuatu is a sovereign democratic state' and art 2 stipulates that '[t]he Constitution is the supreme law of the Republic of Vanuatu'.

Chapter 2 provides for fundamental rights, freedoms and duties of individuals. Chapter 3 sets out the rights to citizenship. In chapter 3, the original art 13 dealt with the avoidance of dual nationality; it was amended in 2013 to allow for dual citizenship.[17] Chapter 4 contains provisions establishing the legislative branch of the government. Chapter 5 establishes the Malvatumauri Council of Chiefs, and prescribes its function and organisation. Chapter 6 contains provisions establishing the head of state (President). Chapters 7 and 8 provide respectively for the executive and judicial branches of the government. Chapter 9 contains provisions creating the public service and the Ombudsman. Chapter 10 provides the Leadership Code. Chapter 11 deals with emergency powers.

Chapter 12 contains provisions about land. It is to be noted that due to significant problems related, among other things, to the failure by the government to protect the interests of customary landowners, art 78, which comes under this chapter, was amended in 2013 to allow the creation of customary land management, which is a customary institution intended to resolve land ownership and disputes over custom land.

Chapter 13 deals with decentralisation. Chapter 14 regulates the amendment of the Constitution and chapter 15 contains transitional provisions allowing for the continued existence of laws, certain public offices and institutions.

3.1.2. *Interpretation of the Written Constitution*

The courts in Vanuatu have held that constitutional provisions must be interpreted broadly unless the terms of the provisions are precise and unambiguous; consideration must be given to the purpose of the Constitution, which is to advance the constitutional objectives, taking due account of the country's circumstances and resources.[18] However, it has been held that the courts should not use an ordinary statute, such as the Interpretation Act, to interpret the Constitution. This is because such an approach would undermine the Constitution, which is the supreme law of the land.[19] When interpreting ambiguous words and expressions of the Constitution, the courts are to rely not

---

16 Corrin and Paterson, above n 7, at 86.

17 Constitution (Sixth) (Amendment) Act No 27 of 2013.

18 *Timakata v Government of Vanuatu* [1989–94] 2 Van LR 691; *Virelala v Ombudsman* [1997] VUSC 35; *President of the Republic of Vanuatu v Speaker of Parliament* [2008] VUSC 77.

19 *Silas v Public Service Commission* [2014] VUCA 9; *Union Electrique du Vanuatu Ltd v Republic of Vanuatu* [2017] VUSC 96.

only on the substantive terms of the Constitution, but also on the Preamble of the Constitution.[20] It has also been noted that the Preamble of the Constitution is not a substantive provision such as arts 1–95. Rather, the Preamble is an introductory statement expressing some underlying principles, philosophies and aspirations, which form the basis of the new nation.[21]

3.2. THE LEGISLATURE

The legislature consists of a single chamber known as Parliament. It has the power, among other things, to make laws for the peace, order and good government of Vanuatu. Members of Parliament are elected by universal suffrage through an electoral system that includes an element of proportional representation, so as to ensure fair representation of different political groups and opinions.[22] Subject to certain qualifications and restrictions imposed by the Representation of People Act 1982[23] and the amendments of art 13 of the Constitution in 2013,[24] every citizen of Vanuatu who is at least 25 years of age is eligible to stand for election and every citizen of at least 18 years of age is eligible to vote.

Parliament is required under the Constitution to meet twice a year in ordinary session. In addition, it may meet in extraordinary session at the request of the majority of its members, the Speaker or the Prime Minister. Parliament makes its decisions by a public vote of a simple majority of the members voting. The quorum for Parliament is two-thirds of its members, or if there is no such quorum, Parliament is to meet three days later and a simple majority of members will suffice.

Parliament has power to control the executive. It may pass, by an absolute majority of members, a motion of no confidence in the Prime Minister, causing the Prime Minister and other ministers to cease to hold office, although they may continue to exercise their functions until a new Prime Minister is elected.[25]

The life of a Parliament is four years from the date of its election, unless it is dissolved by the vote of an absolute majority of the members at a special meeting when at least three-quarters of the members are present.[26] Parliament may be dissolved by the President on the advice of the Council of Ministers. However, no dissolution of Parliament is allowed within the first 12 months after a general election.

---

20 *President of the Republic of Vanuatu v Speaker of Parliament* [2008] VUSC 77.

21 *President of the Republic of Vanuatu v Speaker of Parliament* [2008] VUSC 77. The Court cited a Solomon Islands case to support this view: *Minister of Provincial Government v Guadalcanal Provincial Assembly* [1997] SBCA 1.

22 Article 17(1) of the Constitution.

23 Representation of People Act 1982 Cap 146.

24 Constitution (Sixth) (Amendment) Act No 27 of 2013.

25 Article 43 of the Constitution.

26 Article 28 of the Constitution.

Article 18 of the Constitution establishes an Electoral Commission, which has general responsibility for the registration of electors and the conduct of elections for Parliament, for the Malvatumauri Council of Chiefs, and for local government and municipal elections. The Electoral Commission consists of a Chairman and two members appointed by the President, with the advice of the Judicial Service Commission.

3.3. THE JUDICIARY

Chapter 8 of the Constitution contains provisions providing for the judiciary. The main function of the judiciary is to resolve proceedings according to law. Article 49 of the Constitution establishes the Supreme Court with unlimited jurisdiction in civil and criminal matters. The Supreme Court also has jurisdiction to hear and determine all cases relating to claims that constitutional rights have been infringed.[27] Moreover, when a question concerning the interpretation of the Constitution arises before a subordinate court, and the court believes that the question concerns a fundamental point of law, the court must submit the question to the Supreme Court for determination.[28] The Supreme Court also has jurisdiction to hear and determine the validity of any Bill or regulation referred to the Court by the President.[29] Article 54 provides that the Supreme Court may hear and determine any question regarding whether a person has been validly elected, vacated or has become disqualified to sit in Parliament, or in the Malvatumauri Council of Chiefs or a local government council. As an appellate court, the Supreme Court has jurisdiction to hear appeals from Magistrates' Courts, review convictions, receive referrals from the Magistrates' Courts on questions of law and hear land appeals from Island Courts on questions relating to procedure.

The Chief Justice of the Republic of Vanuatu is appointed by the President after consultation with the Prime Minister and the leader of the opposition. All judges of the Supreme Court are appointed by the President on the advice of the Judicial Service Commission.[30]

The Constitution also provides for a Court of Appeal to be composed of two or more judges of the Supreme Court sitting together. It has the jurisdiction to hear all criminal and civil appeals from the Supreme Court exercising its original and appellate jurisdiction.[31]

27 Article 53(1) and (2) of the Constitution.
28 Article 53(3) of the Constitution.
29 Article 16(4) of the Constitution.
30 Articles 49(3) and 47(2) of the Constitution.
31 Article 50 of the Constitution.

Magistrates' Courts are not referred to in the Constitution, but are established under the Judicial Services and Courts Act.[32] Magistrates' Courts are courts of summary jurisdiction and are subordinate to the Supreme Court. They have jurisdiction to hear and determine, in a summary way, proceedings for an offence for which the maximum punishment does not exceed imprisonment for two years.[33] Magistrates' Courts also have jurisdiction to hear and determine, in a summary way, civil proceedings:

(1) in which the amount claimed or the value of the subject matter does not exceed 1,000,000 VT (not including claims relating permanent physical damage to a person);
(2) relating to disputes between landlords and their tenants where the value of the claim does not exceed 2,000,000 VT;
(3) relating to undefended suits for divorce or judicial separation, subject to the directions of the Chief Justice; and
(4) relating to claims made under the Maintenance of Family Act,[34] the Maintenance of Children Act,[35] or any other law providing for the maintenance of children, mothers of children or wives where the annual sum claimed does not exceed 1,200,000 VT.[36]

Magistrates' Courts may hear appeals from decisions of Island Courts, except those which concern the ownership of land. Magistrates are appointed by the President of the Republic on the advice of the Judicial Service Commission.

The Constitution provides that all members of the judiciary hold office until they reach the age of retirement.[37] Removal of a judge from office may only occur if he or she is convicted and sentenced on a criminal charge, or he or she is found guilty by the Judicial Service Commission of gross misconduct or professional incompetence.[38] It has also been held that the principles of natural justice must be observed when removing a judge from office. Thus, a judge against whom allegations are made must be given an adequate opportunity to respond to those allegations.[39]

Article 52 of the Constitution requires Parliament to establish village and island courts with jurisdiction over customary and other matters and to provide

---

32 Judicial Services and Courts Act No 54 of 2000 Cap 270.

33 Section 14(2) of the Judicial Services and Courts Act 2000 Cap 270.

34 Maintenance of Family Act 1966 Cap 42.

35 Maintenance of Children Act 1966 Cap 46.

36 Magistrates' Court (Civil Jurisdiction) Act No 4 of 1981 Cap 130, s 1, as amended by s 1 of Magistrates' Court (Civil Jurisdiction) (Amendment) Act No 8 of 1984.

37 The retirement age in Vanuatu is 55 (s 54 of Employment Act 1983 Cap 160).

38 Article 47(3) of the Constitution.

39 *D'Imecourt v President of Vanuatu* [1988] VUSC 59; see also Corrin and Paterson, above n 7, at 109.

for the role of chiefs in such courts. A system of Island Courts was established in 1983 by the Island Courts Act. The Island Courts have jurisdiction to hear and determine minor civil claims and criminal matters and to administer the customary law that prevails in their territorial jurisdictions.[40] In relation to its criminal jurisdiction, an Island Court cannot impose a fine exceeding 24,000 VT or a sentence of imprisonment exceeding six months.[41] In the exercise of its civil jurisdiction, an Island Court may award compensation or damages not exceeding 50,000 VT.[42] Section 10 of the Island Courts Act provides that an Island Court is to apply, among other things, customary law prevailing within its territorial jurisdiction, unless it is in conflict with any written law and is contrary to justice, morality and good order.

3.4. CONSTITUTIONAL OFFICES AND ENTITIES

3.4.1. Executive Government

The executive power is vested in the Prime Minister and Council of Ministers, and is to be exercised as provided by the Constitution or a law.[43] The Prime Minister is elected by an absolute majority of the Members of Parliament voting by secret ballot. The Prime Minister appoints the other ministers from among the Members of Parliament and may designate one of them as Deputy Prime Minister.[44] The Prime Minister assigns responsibilities for the conduct of government to the ministers and may remove them from office. Ministers remain Members of Parliament. The Council of Ministers (Prime Minister and all other ministers) are collectively responsible to Parliament. A motion of no confidence against the Prime Minister, if supported by an absolute majority of the Members of Parliament, will cause the Prime Minister and other ministers to cease to hold office. The Council of Ministers may also be terminated whenever the Prime Minister resigns or dies, but the ministers continue to exercise their functions until a new Prime Minister is elected.

3.4.2. Head of State

Chapter 6 of the Constitution provides for the head of state, known as the President. The President must be an indigenous Ni-Vanuatu citizen qualified

---

40 Sections 7, 8 and 10 of the Island Courts Act. See also Anita Jowitt 'Island Courts in Vanuatu' (1999) 3 Journal of South Pacific Law <http://www.paclii.org/journals/fJSPL/>.

41 Section 11 of the Island Courts Act.

42 Section 12 of the Island Courts Act.

43 Article 39(1) of the Constitution.

44 Article 42 of the Constitution.

to be elected to Parliament.[45] The head of state is elected by an electoral college consisting of the Members of Parliament and the chairmen of the local government councils. The President is elected by a vote of three-quarters of the members of the Electoral College present at the first meeting.[46] If there is no such quorum, the Electoral College is to reconvene 48 hours later and elect the President with a vote of at least two-thirds of the members present.

The head of state symbolises the unity of the nation; the role is essentially honorific. The Constitution however does give the head of state some powers. Some of these powers are not required to be exercised on advice: the head of state has the power to refer a Bill or a regulation to the Supreme Court for its opinion, if the head of state considers that it is inconsistent with the Constitution.[47] Article 44 of the Constitution provides that in the case of the death of the Prime Minister and that there is no Deputy Prime Minister, the President may appoint a caretaker Prime Minister. The head of state is also authorised to appoint the five members of the Public Service Commission after consultation with the Prime Minister.[48] The head of state appoints the Ombudsman after consultation with the Prime Minster, Speaker of Parliament, leaders of political parties, the President of the Malvatumauri Council of Chiefs, the chairs of provincial councils and the chairs of the Public Service Commission and of the Judicial Service Commission.[49]

Article 38 of the Constitution provides that the President may, on the advice of a parliamentary committee, pardon, commute or reduce a sentence imposed on a convicted person. The President may also dissolve Parliament on the advice of the Council of Ministers; this power is to be exercised at the discretion of the President.[50]

The term of office of the President is five years. The President may be removed from office by the Electoral College for gross misconduct or incapacity.[51] The Constitution does not expressly provide for the suspension or resignation of the President. However, this has occurred in practice: a President resigned in 1984.

3.4.3. Malvatumauri Council of Chiefs

Chapter 5 of the Constitution provides for the Malvatumauri Council of Chiefs, composed of custom chiefs elected by their peers sitting in District

45 Article 35 of the Constitution.
46 Article 34 (Sch 1) of the Constitution.
47 Articles 16(4) and 39(3) of the Constitution.
48 Article 59 of the Constitution.
49 Article 61 of the Constitution.
50 *President of Vanuatu v Korman* [1998] VUCA 3; *Vohor v Abiut* [2004] VUCA 1.
51 Article 36 of the Constitution.

Councils of Chiefs.[52] The Council elects its own President. The Council is to meet at least once a year. The Council itself, Parliament or the government may call additional meetings.

Prior to the 2013 constitutional reforms, art 30 of the Constitution provided that the Council had general competence to discuss matters relating to land, custom and tradition, and that it could be consulted on questions relating to land, custom and tradition.[53] This article was amended in 2013 and the government must now consult with the Council of Chiefs in areas related to land, custom and tradition. However, there is still no requirement that the government follow the advice of the Council. The amendment also provided that the Malvatumauri Council may make recommendations for the preservation and promotion of Ni-Vanuatu culture and languages.[54]

3.4.4. Public Administration

3.4.4.1. The Public Service

Public servants are appointed by the Public Service Commission. Only citizens of Vanuatu are appointed to public office. For as long as their posts exist, they are not to be removed, except in accordance with the Constitution.[55] This security of tenure does not apply to personal political advisors to the Prime Minister and ministers, and senior public servants may be transferred by the Prime Minister to other posts of equivalent rank. Public servants leave the public service upon reaching retirement age or upon being dismissed by the Public Service Commission.[56]

The Public Service Commission is established under art 59 of the Constitution and is composed of five members appointed for three years by the President after consultation with the Prime Minister. Every year the President may appoint one of the members to be the Chair of the Commission.

In accordance with art 60 of the Constitution, the Public Service Commission is responsible for the appointment and promotion of public servants, and the selection of those to undergo training courses. The Public Service Commission is also responsible for the discipline of public servants. It has, however, no authority over the members of the judiciary, the armed forces, the police or the teaching services. The Public Service Commission is an independent body; in exercising its functions, the Commission is not subject to the direction or control of any other person or body.[57]

---

52 Article 29(1) of the Constitution.
53 Article 30 of the Constitution.
54 Constitution (Sixth) (Amendment) Act No 27 of 2013; art 30(1) of the Constitution.
55 Article 57(5) of the Constitution.
56 Article 57(7) of the Constitution.
57 Article 60(4) of the Constitution.

3.4.4.2. The Ombudsman

The Ombudsman is appointed for five years by the President after consultation with the Prime Minister, the leaders of political parties, the President of Malvatumauri Council of Chiefs and the chairpersons of the Public Service and the Judicial Service Commission.[58] The Ombudsman is an independent body whose main function is to investigate and report upon administrative action taken by officials of the central, provincial and local government, by statutory bodies and other public officials.[59] Moreover, the Ombudsman is authorised to investigate complaints that an individual has not obtained, in the official language he or she uses, the services which the individual may rightfully expect from the administration.[60] The Ombudsman Act 1998 also authorises the Ombudsman to investigate breaches of the Leadership Code.[61]

3.4.5. *Provincial and Local Government*

Chapter 13 of the Constitution provides for decentralisation in order to enable the people of Vanuatu to fully participate in the affairs of their local government. The same chapter also authorises Parliament to enact legislation to realise that ideal. Accordingly, the Decentralisation Act 1980 established local government regions and local government councils.[62] The same legislation provides for the election of local government councils every four years. Each Council consists of representatives of customary chiefs.

A local government council is responsible for the good government of its local government region and the welfare of its people.[63] It has, for instance, the power to deal with the choice of location, construction and maintenance of schools, clinics, dispensaries, health centres, bridges, roads (other than those under the responsibility of the national government), water supplies, wharves, markets, libraries, museums and cultural centres.[64] Each Council is also authorised by the same Act to regulate and control markets, supervise and control area and village councils, and provide staff for village courts and information services.[65]

The Council is authorised to license cinemas, business premises and premises for sale of liquor or for trading. Each Council also has indirect power to levy and collect various kinds of taxes (ie head tax, liquor licensing tax, trading tax), control vehicular traffic, and register births, deaths and marriages.[66]

---

58 Article 61 of the Constitution.

59 Articles 61–65 of the Constitution; see also Corrin and Paterson, above n 7, at 111–112.

60 Article 64 of the Constitution.

61 Section 12 of the Ombudsman Act No 7 of 1998.

62 Sections 2 and 3 of the Decentralization Act 1980 Cap 230.

63 Section 23(1) of the Decentralization Act 1980 Cap 230.

64 Part I(A) of the Schedule, Decentralization Act 1980; see also Paterson, above n 10, at 373.

65 Part I(A) of the Schedule, Decentralization Act 1980.

66 Part I(B) of the Schedule, Decentralization Act 1980.

In accordance with s 26(1) of the Decentralization Act, local government councils may make laws for the good government of the region and the welfare of its people. These regional laws are to be consistent with the Constitution and any written law.

3.4.6. *Custom Land Management Office*

Land rights and interests of customary landowners are protected under the Constitution.[67] However, due to significant problems, related, among other things, to the failure by the government to protect the interests of customary landowners, the Constitution was amended in 2013 to allow for the creation of a customary institution. This customary institution was created to resolve land ownership and disputes over customary land.[68] The amended version of art 78 of the Constitution also provides that the final decisions reached by customary institutions, after being recorded in writing, are binding and are not subject to appeal or review by any court of law.

After the constitutional amendment of 2013, a new piece of legislation, the Custom Land Management Act, was enacted in 2013. This Act was passed to give effect to the new art 78 of the Constitution. In fact, the new law formalises the recognition of customary institutions, specifically nakamals and custom area land tribunals. Such customary institutions determine the rules of custom relating to the ownership and use of land.[69] The new law also specifies that final decisions reached by these customary institutions, when appropriately recorded, are binding and are not subject to appeal or judicial review by any court of law.[70] These decisions may be reviewed by the Supreme Court, but only on the grounds of incorrect composition, improper process or fraud (matters of process). Reviews on merit are not permitted.

3.5. THE LEGAL PROFESSION

The legal profession in Vanuatu is not referred to in the Constitution. It is governed by the Legal Practitioners Act 1980. This piece of legislation establishes a Law Council consisting of the Chief Justice, who is the chairperson, the Attorney-General and one legal practitioner appointed by the Minister of Justice.

In accordance with s 5 of the Legal Practitioners Act, the Law Council has general responsibility for the control and supervision of legal practitioners. The Law Council is authorised by the same section to prescribe the qualifications

---

67 Article 73 of the Constitution.

68 Constitution (Sixth) (Amendment) Act No 27 of 2013.

69 Section 1(1) of the Custom Land Management Act 2013.

70 Section 1(2) of the Custom Land Management Act 2013.

for legal practitioners, keep a Register of Legal Practitioners, control the registration of notaries public, and be responsible for the discipline, legal education and conduct of legal practitioners.

The Law Council is also authorised, under s 7 of the Act, to establish a Disciplinary Committee, which is to receive and hear complaints against legal practitioners and their employees. The Disciplinary Committee is composed of a judicial officer nominated by the Chief Justice, a legal practitioner nominated by the Attorney-General, and three other persons who are not registered as legal practitioners under the law, but are considered suitable by the Law Council.

It has been noted that after lawyers are qualified to practise, there is little supervision and continuing education to help them acquire suitable legal experience.[71] To address, among other things, this issue, the Law Society Act was passed in 2010 to provide for mandatory continuing legal education for legal practitioners.[72]

3.6. COURT PROCEDURE

3.6.1. Civil Proceedings

The procedures for civil proceedings before the Supreme Court and the Magistrates' Court are regulated by the Civil Procedure Rules of 2002.[73] Proceedings in the Supreme Court are started by filing a claim in an office of the Supreme Court anywhere in Vanuatu.[74] Proceedings in the Magistrates' Court are started by filing a claim in the office of the Magistrates' Court in the district where the claimant or defendant lives, where the actions that led to the proceedings happened, or where the property that is the subject of the claim is located.[75] Before both the Supreme Court and Magistrates' Court, a person may apply during proceedings for an interlocutory order.[76]

In accordance with r 4.3 of the Civil Procedure Rules, a claim must contain a statement of the case, set out the claimant's address, be in a specific form, and have with it a response form. In addition, a claim filed in the Magistrates' Court must show the facts that give the Court jurisdiction to examine the claim. In both the Supreme Court and the Magistrates' Court, the defendant must file and

71 See Caroline Penfold 'Contextualising Program Outcomes for Pacific Island Law Graduates' (2012) 22 Legal Education Review 51 at 67 and 69; also Jennifer Corrin 'Dispute Resolution Options in Vanuatu: An Extensive Menu for a Small State' (2019) Comparative Law Journal of the Pacific, Hors Serie Vol XXIII: Small States: A Collection of Essays, 154–155.

72 Section 4 of the Law Society Act 2010.

73 Civil Procedure Rules of 2002 No 49 of 2002.

74 Rule 2.3 of the Civil Procedure Rules of 2002.

75 Rule 2.4 of the Civil Procedure Rules of 2002.

76 Rule 2.7 of the Civil Procedure Rules of 2002.

serve a response within 14 days of the date of service of the claim.[77] The failure to do so risks a default judgment.

The procedure for civil proceedings in Island Courts is regulated by the Island Courts (Civil Procedure) Rules 2005. These require that every civil claim is started by the claimant filing a written statement of claim. The claim is to be signed by the claimant at an office of an Island Court. The claim is to be within the jurisdiction of the Island Court (as authorised by the warrant establishing the Island Court). In addition, a statement of claim must be filed at the office of the Island Court where the defendant ordinarily resides or carries on business, or where the course of action arose, or if the claim is about ownership of customary land, where the land in question is situated.[78] The statement of claim must specify the name, occupation and address of both the claimant and defendant, and also the grounds of the claim.[79] If the claim relates to the ownership or boundary of customary land, the claim should contain a description of the boundaries and a map of the land. The defendant must file and serve a response at the office of the Island Court where the statement of claim was filed, at least seven days before the date of hearing of the claim.[80]

3.6.2. *Criminal Proceedings*

Criminal proceedings in the Supreme Court and Magistrates' Court are regulated by the Criminal Procedure Code Act 1981. The Act, which has been amended a number of times, allows any person who has reasonable and probable cause to believe that an offence has been committed by any person to make a complaint to a judicial officer.[81] The Criminal Procedure (Amendment) Act 1984 further requires that complaints be made under oath, whether submitted orally or in writing, and be signed by both the private prosecutor and judicial officer. Proceedings may be instituted by a private prosecutor or a public officer, namely a public prosecutor.[82] The judicial officer is then required to draw up and sign a formal charge. However, if he or she is of opinion that a complaint does not disclose any offence, he or she may refuse to admit the complaint and provide the reasons for doing so.[83]

77 Rules 4.4 and 4.13 of the Civil Procedure Rules of 2002.

78 Rule 1(2) of the Island Courts (Civil Procedure) Rules 2005.

79 Rule 1(3) of the Island Courts (Civil Procedure) Rules 2005.

80 Rule 2 of the Island Courts (Civil Procedure) Rules 2005.

81 Section 35(1) Criminal Procedure Code Act 1981, as amended by the Criminal Procedure (Amendment) Act No 13 of 1984.

82 Section 33 of Criminal Procedure Act 1981; section 35 of the Criminal Procedure (Amendment) Act 1984.

83 Section 35(2) and (3) of the Criminal Procedure Code Act 1981, as amended by the Criminal Procedure (Amendment) Act of 1984.

The Criminal Procedure Code Act also authorises a police officer to institute criminal proceedings by bringing before the court a person arrested without a warrant.[84] In such circumstances, the judicial officer must draw up and sign a charge containing a statement of the offence the accused is charged with.[85]

The procedure for criminal proceedings in the Island Courts is regulated by the Island Courts (Criminal Procedure) Rules 2005. A police officer is to initiate criminal proceedings. After receiving a complaint or becoming aware that a person may have committed a criminal offence, the police officer must make a full investigation, and if it appears that a criminal offence has been committed, he or she must file a charge at an office of the Island Court.[86] The charge sheet must contain the name and address of the accused, the offence with which he or she is charged, and the date and place of the alleged offence. The Court may permit the complainant to withdraw the charge. If the accused is not in custody, a police officer must send him or her a summons in which the details of the charge and the date of the hearing are indicated.[87]

3.6.3. *Appellate Proceedings*

In civil proceedings, appeals from the Magistrates' Court to the Supreme Court, or from the Supreme Court to the Court of Appeal, may be brought by any party to the proceedings. The appeal may concern questions of law or fact or mixed law and fact.[88] Appeals must be filed within 28 days of the date of the decision.[89] The Civil Procedure Rules also state that filing an appeal against a civil judgment does not affect the enforcement of the judgment, unless the appellant applies for a suspension and the court grants such suspension.[90]

Civil appeals from the Island Court to the Magistrates' Court may be brought within 30 days from the date of the decision of the Island Court.[91] The Island Courts Act provides that notwithstanding the 30-day requirement, an application may be granted by a judge if the application is made within 60 days from the date of the decision.[92] Customary land decisions from the Island Courts may be brought directly to the Supreme Court if the questions raised relate to procedure; questions based on merit cannot be brought directly to the Supreme Court.

---

84 Section 12 of the Criminal Procedure Code Act 1981.

85 Section 379(1) of the Criminal Procedure Code Act 1981.

86 Rule 1 of the Island Courts (Criminal Procedure) Rules 2005.

87 Rule 1(5) of the Island Courts (Criminal Procedure) Rules 2005.

88 Rule 16.27(1) and (2) of the Civil Procedure Rules 2002.

89 Rule 16.28(1) of the Civil Procedure Rules 2002.

90 Rule 13.4 of the Civil Procedure Rules 2002.

91 Section 22(1) of the Criminal Procedure Code Act 1981, as amended by s 7 Schedule Island Courts (Amendment) Act No 15 of 2001.

92 Section 22(5) of the Island Courts Act 1982.

In criminal proceedings, appeals from the Magistrates' Court to the Supreme Court or from the Supreme Court to the Court of Appeal are brought by either the criminal defence lawyer or the representative of the offender giving notice of appeal to the Registrar of the Court within 14 days after the sentence has been rendered.[93] It has been held that if an appeal is brought by a prosecutor, the accused must be personally served with the notice of appeal.[94] Criminal appeals from the Island Court to the Magistrates' Court follow the same rules as civil appeals from Island Courts to the Magistrates' Court.

3.7. DISPUTE RESOLUTION

Diverse options for dispute resolution exist in Vanuatu.[95] While some options are provided by the State, others emanate from the chiefly traditional systems, which resolve disputes in accordance with customary law.

As seen earlier, the State provides for ordinary State courts (in other words, a three-tier hierarchy of common law courts), which are the central means for dispute resolution. This includes the Magistrates' Courts, the Supreme Court and the Court of Appeal. They are established to adjudicate disputes between parties and administer justice in accordance with the rule of law in civil, criminal and administrative matters. Island Courts are hybrid courts; they hear and determine not only minor civil and criminal matters, but also administer the application of customary law.

The State also provides for the establishment of customary institutions to resolve customary land disputes. These are nakamals and area land tribunals, established by the Custom Land Management Act 2013.[96] Nakamals are authorised to determine the ownership of customary land within their custom area.

The Public Service Act 1998 also provides for the establishment of an administrative tribunal, called the Disciplinary Board of the Public Service Commission, to hear and determine disciplinary offences relating to public servants.[97]

Moreover, traditional forums for the resolution of disputes exist throughout the islands of Vanuatu. The vast majority of Ni-Vanuatu people live in accordance with their custom. Customary ways of resolving disputes are very much present. Chiefs are responsible for conducting resolution of disputes between individuals in local communities. Conflict between individuals in

93 Section 201 of the Criminal Procedure Code Act 1981.
94 *Public Prosecutor v Toa* [2003] VUCA 13.
95 See for example Corrin, above n 71.
96 Sections 1 and 2 of the Custom Land Management Act 2013.
97 Section 37 of the Public Service Act No 11 of 1998.

local communities is often resolved through customary reconciliation. It is to be noted that Island Courts, which were established to, among other things, administer custom, are encouraged to promote reconciliation and facilitate settlement in an amicable way.[98]

Finally, it should be noted that the Rules of Civil Procedure of 2002 provide that the courts may, by order, refer a matter for mediation if they consider that mediation may help to resolve issues in dispute and if no party to the dispute raises a substantial objection.[99] Suitable mediators may be trained mediators, chiefs, church leaders or elders in the communities.

4. LAW OF PERSONS

4.1. MARRIAGE

The Civil Status (Registration) Act 1970 requires that all marriages, including dissolutions and nullifications of marriage, must be recorded by district registrars.[100] Moreover, the Marriage Act 1970 requires that marriages are to be celebrated before a district registrar or a minister approved for celebrating marriages, or be made in accordance with custom.[101] By doing so, the law recognises civil, religious and customary marriages in Vanuatu.

All marriages, including the ones made in accordance with custom, must fulfil the requirements of age, specifically that males must be over 18 years and females over 16. There must also be parental consent for any party to the marriage who is under 21 years of age.[102] There are additional, miscellaneous requirements concerning prior notice, procedure, witnesses and formalities after the ceremony, namely registration.[103] All marriages, whether civil, religious or customary must be registered.

4.2. ANNULMENT AND DIVORCE

4.2.1. Void and Voidable Marriages

A marriage may be annulled by a decree of nullity on the grounds that it is void or voidable.

---

98 Section 20 of the Island Courts Act.

99 Rule 10.3 of the Civil Procedure Rules of 2002.

100 Sections 23 and 24 of the Civil Status (Registration) Act 1970 Cap 61.

101 Section 1 of the Marriage Act 1970 Cap 60.

102 Sections 2 and 3 of the Control of Marriage Act 1966 Cap 45.

103 Parts 2–4 of the Marriage Act 1970 Cap 60; see also Paterson, above n 10, at 386.

A marriage that is void is never a marriage. Section 1 of the Matrimonial Causes Act 1986[104] provides that a marriage will be held by the courts to be void if:

- marriage was induced by duress or mistake;
- at the time of the marriage one of the parties was, because of mental illness, incapable of understanding the nature of the marriage ceremony;
- the parties were too closely related to each other; or
- the marriage did not follow proper legal procedure.

A voidable marriage is a full and proper marriage until it is set aside by the courts. Section 2 of the Act provides that a marriage may be held to be void on the following grounds:

(1) lack of consummation by the respondent;
(2) unsoundness of mind or recurrent fits of insanity or epilepsy at the time of the marriage;
(3) venereal disease of the respondent at the time of marriage; or
(4) pregnancy of the wife by a man other than the husband.[105]

Section 2 states that in the last three cases, the petitioner must, in addition, show that he or she was unaware of the facts alleged, that he or she has commenced the proceedings within a year of the date of marriage, and that he or she has had no sexual intercourse with the respondent since becoming aware of the facts alleged. A decree of nullity of voidable marriage operates only to annul the marriage from the date of the pronouncement of the decree. Therefore, any children born as a result of the marriage are legitimate.

4.2.2. Divorce

The Matrimonial Causes Act 1986 also provides for the dissolution of marriage. Section 4 states that a customary marriage may be dissolved only in accordance with the rules of custom. Section 5 states that a civil or religious marriage may be dissolved if the respondent has committed adultery, has deserted the petitioner without just cause for a period of at least three years, has treated the petitioner with persistent cruelty, has an incurable unsoundness of mind for a period of at least five years, or has been absent for at least seven years without any

[104] Section 1 of the Matrimonial Causes Act 1986 Cap 192. For more on the explanation of these grounds, see Sue Farran *A Digest of Family Law in Vanuatu* (University of the South Pacific, 2003) 44–45.

[105] Section 2 of the Matrimonial Causes Act 1986 Cap 192. See also Paterson, above n 10, at 386–387.

communication. The wife may also petition for divorce on the ground that her husband has, after the marriage, been convicted of rape or an unnatural offence.

There are a number of restrictions on divorce. Section 6 states that a petition for divorce may not be presented within the first two years of the marriage, unless exceptional hardship has been suffered by the petitioner or exceptional depravity has been practised by the respondent. Section 9 provides that the courts may not proceed with the hearing of a petition for divorce unless they are satisfied that reconciliation between the parties is impossible. Moreover, a court must dismiss the petition for divorce if it is satisfied that the petitioner has aided, connived at, or condoned the adultery complained of, has condoned the cruelty complained of, or has acted in collusion with the respondent. Finally, s 16 of the Matrimonial Causes Act provides that the courts must dismiss a petition for divorce if they are not satisfied that proper arrangements have been made for the care and upbringing of any child of the marriage who is under 16 years of age.

4.3. ADOPTION

4.3.1. Legal Adoption

There was no Joint Regulation providing for adoption in Vanuatu. Since independence, Vanuatu has not yet enacted its own Act of Parliament in this respect. An Adoption Bill was drafted in 2019. During the final stage of the writing of this chapter, the Bill is still under consultation. The Explanatory Note of the Bill provides that this Bill not only sets out the process and requirements for formal adoption in Vanuatu, but it also regulates formal adoption and does not apply to custom adoption.[106]

The current written laws relating to adoption are an English colonial law, the Adoption Act 1958 (UK),[107] and the French Civil Code applicable in Vanuatu on 30 July 1980. As noted earlier, in accordance with art 95(2) of the Constitution, existing colonial laws continue to apply after 30 July 1980 to the extent that they are not expressly revoked or incompatible with the independent status of Vanuatu, and whenever possible taking due account of custom. The French laws applicable in Vanuatu after 30 July 1980 are rarely used due to the fact that most of the legal practitioners in Vanuatu are trained in common law jurisdictions and are not familiar with French law.[108]

---

106 Bill for the Adoption Act 2020.

107 Adoption Act 1958 (UK).

108 See Sue Farran 'Family Law and French Law in Vanuatu: An Opportunity Missed?' (2004) 35 Victoria University of Wellington Law Review 382.

Under the UK Adoption Act 1958 and other adoption-related laws, including the Adoption Act 1926 (UK),[109] adoptive parents must be over 25 years of age and at least 21 years older than the person in respect of whom the adoption application is being made. An exception to this rule exists where the adopter is closely related to the adoptive child. In such circumstances of close relation, the 21-year gap requirement may be waived. Adoption of a female child by a single male is prohibited, unless there are exceptional circumstances.

The Supreme Court of Vanuatu has held that the adoption of a female child by a gay couple is prohibited in Vanuatu.[110] This is on the basis that it is contrary to Vanuatu customs and traditions, and contrary to s 2(2) of the Adoption Act 1926 (UK) left in place by the Adoption Act 1958 (UK).[111]

In accordance with the English legislation applicable in Vanuatu, where spouses are adopting, the consent of both spouses is required.[112] In addition, the consent of any natural parent of the child, or guardian or person who has actual custody of the child must be obtained, unless the child is abandoned or the required consent cannot be obtained because the relevant person cannot be found, or is incapable of giving consent or has persistently rejected the child.[113] Any payment or reward for giving a child up for adoption renders the adoption illegal, unless the court has approved the payment.[114]

4.3.2. *Custom Adoption*

In Vanuatu, a child may also be adopted in accordance with custom. Customary rules relating to adoption vary from one area to another. Custom adoption has been recognised as legal adoption in Vanuatu.[115]

4.4. MAINTENANCE AND CUSTODY OF CHILDREN

4.4.1. *Maintenance*

Children under 18 years of age have a right to be supported by their parents. In accordance with s 1 of the Maintenance of Family Act 1966, it is an offence for a man to fail to maintain, for a period exceeding one month, his wife or his

---

109 Section 2 of Adoption Act 1926 (UK); see also the explanation of Farran, above n 104, at 32–33.

110 *In Re MM Adoption Application by SAT* [2014] VUSC 78.

111 Section 2(2) of the Adoption Act 1926 (UK); Adoption Act 1958 (UK).

112 Section 2(3) of the Adoption Act 1926 (UK).

113 Section 2(3) and (4) of the Adoption Act 1926 (UK); see also the explanation by Farran, above n 104, at 33.

114 Section 9 of the Adoption Act 1926 (UK).

115 *M v P, Re the Child G* [1998] VUSC 2.

legitimate children under 18 years of age. The same section also makes it an offence for a mother to desert, for a period exceeding one month, her children under 18 years of age. In these two cases, if found guilty, the punishment is one or both of a fine not exceeding 20,000 VT and imprisonment for a term not exceeding three months. Such conduct can be excused if the offender is financially incapable of providing the maintenance. This financial incapacity must be by reason of illness or injury, imprisonment, or any other circumstances beyond the person's control.

4.4.2. Custody

In the case of divorce, parents are free to make their own arrangements regarding the custody of any children of the marriage. Generally, courts will not interfere if both parties accept the arrangements regarding the custody of the children. The courts will intervene only when parents cannot agree on custody arrangements. Section 15(1) of the Matrimonial Causes Act 1986 provides that a court, when making a decree of divorce or nullity of marriage, may make an order for, among other things, the custody of the children of the marriage. It has been held that the guiding principle is the interests of the child, which is a principle recognised and affirmed in the Convention on the Rights of Child ratified by Vanuatu in 1995.[116]

5. LAW OF OBLIGATIONS

5.1. TORTS

There was no Joint Regulation relating to tort liability in Vanuatu. Since independence, Vanuatu has not passed an Act of Parliament in this respect. However, as noted earlier, art 95(2) of the Constitution, in effect, continues in force the UK Regulation of 1976, which permits the application of common law and equity and the French Code Civil in Vanuatu.

The current law of torts in Vanuatu is made up of principles of common law and equity. Generally, these principles were used by the English courts as the basis for determining what kind of conduct should give rise to liability to pay compensation or damages to persons suffering injury or damages from such conduct. The main kinds of conduct giving rise to liability are trespass (to land, person or things), nuisance, negligence, failure to keep animals known to be dangerous under proper control, and deceitful or defamatory statements.[117]

---

116 *Molu v Molu* [1998] VUSC 15; Convention on the Rights of Child Ratification (Ratification) Act No 26 of 1992.

117 For more details on the law of torts, see Corrin and Paterson, above n 7, at 287–316.

5.2. CONTRACT

There is no Joint Regulation relating to the law of contract. In conformity with art 95(2) of the Constitution, the basic principles of contract law in Vanuatu are provided by the rules of common law and equity, although post-independence legislation has intervened to some extent.[118]

The principles of common law and equity have determined when promises made by a person are binding and enforceable by the courts. Generally, in accordance with the rules of common law and equity, there are two kinds of undertakings that are binding. The first is that made in a written document called a deed. The second is that made in exchange for something of value given or promised to be given, unless illegal, contrary to public policy, or based upon certain fundamental mistakes of fact.[119]

It is important to note that custom is also recognised as a relevant source of law applicable to contract law, at least at the village level. Generally, contractual disputes arising in the local villages are governed by the rules of custom.

5.3. RESTITUTION

The rules of common law and equity also regulate the law of restitution in Vanuatu. There was no Joint Regulation or post-independence legislation in this respect. Generally, when it is proven that a party breaches a contract, the available remedies are damages, injunctions, specific performance and restitution. Independently of contract, under the law of restitution a defendant may be ordered to restore money or the benefit of work done, goods supplied, or services rendered to the plaintiff if it is shown that he or she would otherwise be unjustly enriched.[120]

6. PROPERTY LAW

6.1. LAND LAWS

The Constitution provides that all land in Vanuatu belongs to the indigenous custom owners and their descendants,[121] that the rules of custom form the basis of ownership and land use in Vanuatu,[122] and that only indigenous citizens of Vanuatu who acquired land in accordance with a recognised system of land

---

118 See for example the Law Reform (Contract) Act No 23 of 2009 requiring, among other things, contractual documents to be described as a deed or an agreement under seal (s 3(1)(c)).

119 For more details on the law of contract, see Corrin and Paterson, above n 7, at 237–285.

120 Corrin and Paterson, above n 7, at 283.

121 Article 73 of the Constitution.

122 Article 74 of the Constitution.

tenure will have perpetual ownership of their land.[123] The Constitution provides, however, that the government may acquire and own land for the public interest.[124] The government may also buy land from custom owners for the purpose of transferring the ownership to indigenous citizens or indigenous communities.[125]

Any land transaction between an indigenous citizen and a non-indigenous citizen or a non-citizen must be approved by the government.[126] No approval should be given if the transaction is prejudicial to the interests of the landowners, the indigenous citizens (who are not custom owners), the community in which the land is situated or the Republic.

There are also a number of Acts relating to land in Vanuatu. The Land Reform Act and Land Leases Act were enacted to provide, among other things, for the lease of land. Accordingly, land may be leased by custom owners to other persons for a maximum period of 75 years[127] and may be mortgaged.[128]

The Land Reform Act also provides that all land owned by the British government, the French government, the Condominium or the municipality was, on 30 July 1980, automatically transferred to the government of Vanuatu, and is considered public land held for the benefit of the Republic.[129]

New laws passed in 2013 related to, among other things, the government's failure to adequately protect the interests of landowners, including custom owners. The new laws consisted of amendments to the Constitution, amendments to the Land Reform Act and Land Leases Act, and a new Custom Land Management Act. The purpose of this series of reforms was, essentially, to reduce the power which had been given to the Minister of Lands to approve land leases. The reforms require that the Minister sign leases only after they are approved by the Land Management Planning Committee.[130] In addition, leases for development on customary land will not be concluded until free, prior and informed consent of the custom owner group is obtained.[131]

6.2. LAWS RELATING TO TANGIBLE AND INTANGIBLE PROPERTY, AND TO CULTURAL PROTECTION

In Vanuatu, property law is influenced by ideas and structures introduced through the common law of England, customary law, indigenous ideas relating to property, and international law.[132]

123 Article 75 of the Constitution.
124 Article 80 of the Constitution.
125 Article 81 of the Constitution.
126 Article 79 of the Constitution.
127 Section 32(1) of the Land Leases Act 1984.
128 Section 52(1) of the Land Leases Act 1984.
129 Section 9 of the Land Reform Act 1980.
130 Section 8(B)(b) of the Land Reform (Amendment) Act 2013.
131 Section 6(E)(a)(ii) of the Land Reform (Amendment) Act 2013.
132 Sue Farran and Don Paterson *South Pacific Property Law* (Cavendish Publications, 2004) 1.

In Vanuatu, rights to corporeal things, including land and personal property or chattels, are protected under a number of land laws and the common law. Rights in incorporeal things, however, are not well protected by the law, though Vanuatu has started to enact pieces of legislation in this respect. These rights affected include the right to medicinal knowledge, magic, skills in making traditional artefacts and clothing, song and oral history, methods of cultivation and food preparation, and other forms of indigenous knowledge.[133]

There are a number of Acts which relate to the protection of intellectual property rights. These include the Trademarks Act 2003, the Patents Act 2003, the Designs Act 2003, the Copyright Act 2000, the Trade Secrets Act 2000, the Geographical Indication (Wine) Act 2000 and the Circuit Layout Act 2000. The Protection of Traditional Knowledge and Expressions of Culture Act 2019 aims to protect, regulate and manage traditional knowledge and expressions of culture in Vanuatu.

7. COMMERCIAL LAW

Vanuatu has enacted a number of pieces of legislation in the area of commercial law. The Companies Act 2012 provides for the formation, registration and governance of companies in Vanuatu. It should be mentioned that this particular Act repealed and replaced the old Companies Act, which was adopted in 1986. The Companies Act provides that any person may, either alone or together with another person, apply to have his, her or their company registered under the Act. This is subject to requirements relating to incorporation, as prescribed by s 6, being fulfilled.[134] A company may be registered as a private company, public company or community company. The Companies Act also provides for the director or directors of the company who will have the powers necessary for managing, directing and supervising the management, business and affairs of the company.[135] In exercising the powers and duties, the director or directors must act in a good faith and in the interests of the company.[136]

The Companies Act prohibits, among other things, certain misleading and deceptive conduct. All advertisements relating to offers of securities to the public are prohibited.[137] Accordingly, a person must not engage in any conduct relating to advertisement for debt and equity securities that is misleading or deceptive or that is likely to mislead or deceive. A person found guilty of this offence is liable

133 Farran and Paterson, above n 132, at 6.
134 Section 6 of the Companies Act 2012.
135 Section 63 of the Companies Act 2012.
136 Section 64 of the Companies Act 2012.
137 Section 138 of the Companies Act 2012.

to a fine not exceeding 500,000 VT or to an imprisonment term not exceeding five years, or to both a fine and imprisonment.

The Financial Dealers Licensing Act 1971, as subsequently amended by the Dealers in Securities (Licensing) Amendment Act 2017 and the Financial Dealers Licensing (Amendment) Act 2018, makes provision for regulating the business of dealing in securities, the protection of the public by creating penalties for fraudulently inducing persons to invest money, and other related matters. Any person carrying on or purporting to carry on the business of dealing in securities (among others, debenture stocks, loan stocks, bonds, certificates of deposit, proceeds of foreign exchange) is required to hold a licence under this Act.[138] The failure to do so is an offence punishable on conviction by a fine of 25 million VT or imprisonment for a term not exceeding 15 years, or both (if the person is a natural person), or a fine not exceeding 125 million VT (if the person is a body corporate).

The Partnership Act 1975 declares the law of partnership and provides for the formation of limited partnerships. Accordingly, a partnership is the relationship that subsists between persons carrying on a business (which expression includes every trade, occupation or profession) in common with a view of profit.[139] This definition of partnership excludes the relationship between members of any company or association that is registered as a company or formed or incorporated under the Company Act or any related legislation.

A limited partnership consists of not more than 20 persons and must consist of one or more general partners liable for all debts and obligations of the firm and one or more persons (limited partners) whose contribution consists of a certain amount of capital or property specified at the time of the creation of the partnership.[140] The limited partners are not liable for debts and obligations of the firm beyond the amount so contributed.

In 2013, Parliament passed the Companies (Insolvency and Receivership) Act, which provides for the management and administration of insolvent companies and for related purposes. In relation to insolvent companies specifically, the Act provides for the possibility of compromises with creditors[141] and for the liquidation of such companies.[142] A liquidator of an insolvent company takes possession of, protects, realises and distributes the assets, or the proceeds of the realisation of the assets, of the company to its creditors, and if there are surplus assets, distributes them or the proceeds of the realisation of the surplus assets in accordance with the Act.

---

138 Section 2 of the Financial Dealers Licensing Act 1971, as amended by the Dealers in Securities (Licensing) Amendment Act No 11 of 2017 and the Financial Dealers Licensing (Amendment) Act No 31 of 2018.

139 Section 1 of the Partnership Act 1975 Cap 92.

140 Section 47 of the Partnership Act 1975 Cap 92.

141 Division 1, Part 2 of the Companies (Insolvency and Receivership) Act No 3 of 2013.

142 Division 2, Part 2 of the Companies (Insolvency and Receivership) Act No 3 of 2013.

The relevant law relating to international carriage by air in Vanuatu is the Convention for the Unification of Certain Rules for International Carriage by Air, adopted in 1929, as amended and replaced by the Hague Protocol to the Warsaw Convention of 1955 and the Montreal Convention of 1999. Vanuatu ratified the Convention for the Unification of Certain Rules for International Carriage by Air in 2005 and therefore is obliged to comply with its provisions. This Convention provides for the documentation and duties of the parties relating to the carriage of passengers, baggage and cargo.[143] It also provides for the liability of the carrier and the extent of compensation for related damages.[144]

The Maritime Act 1981 regulates the carriage of goods by sea by providing for the responsibilities and liabilities of the vessels and carriers travelling within the islands and waters of Vanuatu.[145]

With regard to the carriage of passengers by sea, Vanuatu has ratified a number of international conventions, including the Athens Convention relating to the Carriage of Passengers and their Luggage by Sea of 1974, and its Protocol.[146] That Convention provides, among other things, for liability of the carrier for the damage suffered as a result of the death of or personal injury to a passenger and the loss of or damage to luggage if the incident which caused these damages occurred in the course of the carriage and was due to the fault or neglect of the carrier or of his servants or agents acting within the scope of their employment.[147]

Finally, banking in Vanuatu is regulated under the International Banking Act 2002, which repealed the Banking Act 1970. The Act provides that any person carrying on banking business in Vanuatu must hold a licence to do so. Such licence is issued by the Reserve Bank of Vanuatu.[148] The Act also provides for supervision and enforcement to be exercised by the Reserve Bank of Vanuatu.[149]

8. ENVIRONMENTAL LAW

Since independence, Vanuatu has enacted a number of environmental laws. The current overarching environmental law is the Environment and Conservation Act;[150] it provides essentially for the conservation, sustainable development

143 Chapter II of the Convention for Unification of Certain Rules for International Carriage by Air (Ratification) Act 2005.

144 Chapter III of the Convention for Unification of Certain Rules for International Carriage by Air (Ratification) Act 2005.

145 Section 70 of the Maritime Act 1981 Cap 131.

146 Protocol to the Athens Convention Relating to the Carriage of Passengers and their Luggage by Sea, 1974. See also Ratification of Certain Conventions and Protocols Act No 38 of 2017.

147 Article 3 of the Athens Convention relating to the Carriage of Passengers and their Luggage by Sea, 1974.

148 Sections 6 and 7 of the International Banking Act No 4 of 2002.

149 Part 3 of the International Banking Act No 4 of 2002.

150 Environment and Conservation Act 2003, Cap 283 (title of Act amended by Act No 28 of 2010).

and management of the environment. The Act formally establishes the Department of Environmental Protection and Conservation (DEPC), including providing for its functions and responsibilities.[151] It also provides a process of identification and management of the environmental impacts of proposed development projects.[152] Moreover, the Act provides for the recognition of community conservation areas and gives direction to communities in relation to registration of their conservation areas at the national level and to bioprospecting (research).[153]

It should be noted that the above Act started as the Environmental Management and Conservation Act in 2002. In 2011, it underwent a name change, after it had combined three different Acts: the Environmental Management and Conservation Act; the Environment Management and Conservation (Amendment) in Statute Law (Miscellaneous Provisions) Act; and the Environmental Management and Conservation (Amendment) Act.

The Pollution (Control) Act 2013 creates a framework for the DEPC to develop and introduce pollution standards and permit systems and allows the department to take compliance action when pollution is occurring. DEPC officers can, for instance, issue notices under this Act ordering any person to take measures or extra measures to prevent, control or reduce pollution.

Further, the Waste Management Act 2014 provides for the protection of the environment by establishing specific responsibilities to be undertaken by the DEPC, the municipal and provincial councils, the Ministry of Health and the Department of Biosecurity in relation to the identification, collection and disposal of waste, planning and reporting on waste management, and management of hazardous waste. In accordance with this legislation, three orders were signed in 2018 by the Minister of Lands and Natural Resources to implement the decision of the Council of Ministers to ban certain non-biodegradable plastics.[154]

In 1991, Vanuatu passed the International Trade (Flora and Fauna) Act to implement Vanuatu's obligations as a party to the Convention on International Trade in Endangered Species of Wild Fauna and Flora. The Act provides for the control and regulation of the export and import of certain species of fauna and flora, and for related purposes.

In 1995, Parliament passed the National Parks Act, making provision for the declaration of national parks and nature reserves, for the protection and preservation of such areas, and for related matters.

---

[151] Part 2 of the Environment and Conservation Act 2003.

[152] Part 3 of the Environment and Conservation Act 2003.

[153] Part 4 of the Environment and Conservation Act 2003.

[154] Waste Management Regulation Order No 15 of 2018; Private Waste Operator's License Fees Order No 16 of 2018; and Waste Management (Penalty Notice) Regulation Order No 17 of 2018.

In relation to its response to climate change, Vanuatu has ratified the United Nations Framework Convention on Climate Change (UNFCCC), the Kyoto Protocol to the United Nations Framework Convention on Climate Change (Kyoto Protocol) and the Paris Agreement. In 2016, Vanuatu submitted its first Nationally Determined Contribution (NDC) under the Paris Agreement.[155]

Being one of the countries most vulnerable to climate change, Vanuatu has adopted a number of important policies dedicated to climate change adaptation and disaster risk reduction.[156] Vanuatu is also one of a few countries having a dedicated Climate Change Ministry; it was established in 2014. This Ministry oversees the National Disaster Management Office, which is responsible for the coordination of preparation for and responses to emergencies and disasters in Vanuatu.

9. NATURAL RESOURCES

9.1. MINERALS

Since independence, Vanuatu has passed a number of laws regulating natural resources. The Mines and Minerals Act[157] was passed in 1986 to regulate and control the search for and exploitation of minerals. Section 2 of the Act provides that the property in minerals, in their natural condition in land, is vested in the Republic of Vanuatu. It is stated in the same section, however, that this should not prejudice the grant or the exercise of rights under or pursuant to the Act. The Mines and Minerals Act also specifies that all rights exercisable in relation to minerals, by the government of Vanuatu with respect to the continental shelf or the exclusive economic zone, are vested in the Republic.[158]

The Petroleum (Exploration and Production) Act 1993 makes provision for the search for and production of petroleum. The Minister responsible has the power to grant a petroleum prospecting licence to an individual or a body corporate under conditions prescribed.[159] A licensee whose petroleum prospecting licence is in force, or any person, may apply for the grant of a petroleum production licence under the conditions prescribed by the Act.[160]

---

155 Republic of Vanuatu 'Intended Nationally Determined Contribution (INDC)' Submission to the United Nations Framework Convention on Climate Change (2015).

156 See for instance, National Advisory Committee on Climate Change 'Republic of Vanuatu: National Adaptation Programme for Action (NAPA)' (Policy, Government of Vanuatu, December 2007); Government of the Republic of Vanuatu 'Vanuatu Climate Change and Disaster Risk Reduction Policy 2016–2030' (Project Report, Government of Vanuatu, 2015).

157 Mines and Minerals Act 1986 Cap 190.

158 Section 3 of the Mines and Minerals Act 1986.

159 Sections 11 and 14 of the Petroleum (Exploration and Production) Act 1993.

160 Sections 28 and 29 of the Petroleum (Prospection and Production) Act 1993.

The Quarry Act was enacted in 2013 to provide for the regulation of quarries. This Act establishes a Commissioner who is authorised to issue quarry permits to extract building materials.[161]

The Geothermal Energy Act 1987 was passed by Parliament to regulate and control the exploitation of geothermal energy and to provide for incidental related matters. The Act authorises the Minister responsible to grant prospecting and production licences for geothermal energy.[162]

9.2. FORESTRY

In 2001, Parliament passed the Forestry Act, which makes provision for the protection, development and sustainable management of forests and for the regulation of the forestry industry. The Act provides, among other things, that in performing their functions, forest authorities must have regard to the following principles: (1) the forests of Vanuatu must be sustainably managed, developed and protected so as to achieve greater social, environmental and economic benefits for current and future generations; (2) the diversity of the forests and forest ecosystems of Vanuatu must be protected; (3) the rights of custom owners and other Ni-Vanuatu with customary interests in forests must be recognised; and (4) any relevant international obligations undertaken by Vanuatu must be respected.[163]

The Act also provides for commercial forestry operations. These operations may be conducted only in accordance with a licence granted by relevant authorities under the Act.[164] Accordingly, among others, the following licences may be granted: timber licence, mobile sawmill licence and sandalwood licence.[165]

9.3. FISHERIES

In 2014, the Fisheries Act was passed. It repealed the old Fisheries Act of 2005.[166] The Act makes provision for the management, development and regulation of fisheries within Vanuatu waters, and for the control of the fishing vessels entitled to fly the flag of Vanuatu outside of Vanuatu waters in a manner consistent with Vanuatu's international obligations. The Act provides that the Department of

---

161 Sections 2 and 19 of the Quarry Act 2013.

162 Parts V and VII of the Geothermal Energy Act 1987.

163 Section 4 of the Forestry Act 2001.

164 Part 5 of the Forestry Act 2001.

165 Part 5 of the Forestry Act 2001.

166 The Fisheries Act No 55 of 2005 Cap 315 repealed the Fisheries Act 1982.

Fisheries has the principal function of, and authority for, the conservation, management and development of the fisheries resources in Vanuatu.[167] The Act also provides that a person must not use a Vanuatu vessel for commercial fishing or related activities in Vanuatu waters unless he or she has a fishing licence.[168] The Director of the Department of Fisheries is authorised by the Act to issue fishing licences.[169]

10. CRIMINAL LAW

The Penal Code of Vanuatu[170] is the main statute that provides for the acts or omissions which will be regarded as criminal offences and for the rules related to the criminal law in the country.

One of the important principles in criminal law is that the accused is innocent until proved guilty. Unless and until the prosecution proves that the accused is guilty of an offence, he or she is innocent in the eyes of the law.[171] Another important principle is that the prosecution has the burden of proving its case. The prosecution has to prove beyond reasonable doubt that the offence has been committed by the person charged.[172] The courts must decide, after the parties have presented their submissions and produced evidence, whether the prosecution has proved its case beyond reasonable doubt. Where the prosecution fails to produce evidence for all of the elements of the offence, there is no case to answer.

It is to be noted that the Penal Code of Vanuatu lists a number of exemptions from criminal responsibility. Section 12 of the Code provides that a mistake of fact can be a defence to a criminal charge.[173] The mistake must, however, be a reasonable and genuine belief in a fact which, had it existed, would have rendered the conduct innocent. Moreover, an accused is not criminally responsible if, by reason of a disease of the mind at the time of the act, he or she was unable to understand the nature of the act or to know that the act was wrong.[174] It is important to note, however, that for a successful insanity defence, the accused has to prove that he or she was insane at the time of the offence.[175] In Vanuatu, children below the age of 10 are not criminally responsible.[176] Section 21 of the

---

167 Section 3(2) of the Fisheries Act 2014.

168 Section 35(a) and (b) of the Fisheries Act 2014.

169 Section 36 of the Fisheries Act 2014.

170 Penal Code of Vanuatu, 1981 Cap 135.

171 Among other cases, see *Public Prosecutor v Arnhabat* [2003] VUSC 50; see also Pacific Judicial Education Programme, *Vanuatu Magistrates Bench Book* (2004) 69.

172 *Public Prosecutor v Taleo* [2001] VUSC 8.

173 Section 12 of the Penal Code.

174 Section 20 of the Penal Code.

175 Section 20(1) of the Penal Code.

176 Section 17 of the Penal Code.

Code provides that voluntary intoxication will not constitute a defence, unless the offence charged is one in which the degree of intoxication was such as to deprive the accused of the capacity to form the criminal intention.[177] Involuntary intoxication is deemed to be a mental disease.[178] In accordance with s 11 of the Code, ignorance of the law is not a defence to any criminal charge.

11. ROLE OF INTERNATIONAL LAW AND TREATIES

Vanuatu adopts a dualist approach to international law; treaties are not part of domestic law and do not create domestic rights and obligations unless and until the national Parliament enacts legislation to that effect.[179] This approach is provided for in art 26 of the Constitution, which states:

> Treaties negotiated by the Government shall be presented to Parliament for ratification when they – (a) concern international organizations, peace or trade; (b) commit the expenditure of public funds; (c) affect the status of people; (d) require amendment of the laws of the Republic of Vanuatu; (e) provide for the transfer, exchange or annexing of territory.

It is in the field of human rights treaties that the effect of this dualist approach is particularly noticeable. In practice, however, this approach has not been consistently adopted by the courts. While in *Noel v Toto*[180] the Supreme Court of Vanuatu applied the Convention on the Elimination of all Forms of Discrimination against Women to grant equal land rights to women, in *Joli v Joli*[181] the Court of Appeal refused to apply the same Convention, even though Vanuatu was a party to it. In the latter case, the Court held that it was the role of Parliament to decide how gender equality in matrimonial property must operate in the country.

Vanuatu has ratified the following human rights conventions: the International Covenant on Civil and Political Rights in 2008,[182] the Convention on the Elimination of all Forms of Discrimination against Women in 1995,[183] the Convention against Torture in 2010,[184] the Convention on the Rights of

---

177 Section 21 of the Penal Code.

178 Section 20(4) of the Penal Code.

179 See Dejo Olowu *International Law: A Textbook for the South Pacific* (CDPublishing.Org, 2013) 113.

180 *Noel v Toto* [1995] VUSC 3.

181 *Joli v Joli* [2003] VUCA 27.

182 Covenant on Civil and Political Rights (Ratification) Act 2008.

183 Convention on the Elimination of all Forms of Discrimination against Women (Ratification) Act 1995.

184 Convention against Torture and Other Cruel, Inhuman and Degrading Treatment or Punishment (Ratification) Act 2010.

Child in 1992,[185] and the Convention on the Rights of Persons with Disabilities in 2008.[186]

Upon ratification, Vanuatu is under an obligation to amend and develop domestic legislation to comply with these treaties. Thus, after ratifying the Convention on the Elimination of all Forms of Discrimination against Women, Vanuatu passed the Family Protection Act 2008; it aims to improve family relations by providing for an offence of domestic violence and family protection orders in the case of domestic violence. Vanuatu also amended a number of pieces of legislation, including the Municipalities Act,[187] to create reserved seats for women in municipal councils.

Treaties in the field of trade also need to be specifically incorporated by an Act of Parliament. Vanuatu has ratified a number of trade agreements, including the Trade Agreement Among the Melanesian Spearhead Group Countries in 1994,[188] the ACP-EU Partnership Agreement in 2001,[189] the Pacific Island Countries Trade Agreement (PICTA) in 2003,[190] and the Protocol Amending the Marrakesh Agreement Establishing the World Trade Organization in 2019.[191] Upon ratification, these trade treaties became part of Vanuatu's domestic law.

12. CIVIL SOCIETY ORGANISATIONS

In addition to the chiefly systems, churches are regarded as important civil society organisations because they play a significant role in the maintenance of peace and stability in the communities. In Vanuatu, most NGOs are registered under the Charitable Associations Act, but churches are not required to be registered. Individuals are free to form a Christian association, as freedom of association is provided for in the Constitution.[192]

Trade unions are regulated under the Trade Unions Act 1983, which provides for the registration of trade unions, the conditions for registration and the powers of the registrar of trade unions. A trade union operating in the country must be registered in accordance with the Act.

---

185 Convention on the Rights of the Child (Ratification) Act 1992.

186 Convention on the Rights of Persons with Disabilities (Ratification) Act 2008.

187 Municipalities (Amendment) Act 2013.

188 Trade Agreement Among the Melanesian Spearhead Group Countries (Ratification) Act 1994.

189 ACP-EU Partnership Agreement Act 2001 Cap 273.

190 Pacific Island Countries Trade Agreement (PICTA) Act 2003 Cap 292.

191 Protocol Amending the Marrakesh Agreement Establishing the World Trade Organization No 27 of 2019.

192 Article 5 of the Constitution.

In ending this chapter, it is interesting to note that Vanuatu is not only one of the most culturally diverse countries in the world, with many different languages, cultures and traditions, but it also has a very complex legal system as a result of its colonial past. Economically, however, Vanuatu is one of the least developed countries, relying heavily on overseas aid, agriculture and tourism. Mineral exploitation is almost non-existent.

BIBLIOGRAPHY

Corrin, Jennifer 'Dispute Resolution Options in Vanuatu: An Extensive Menu for a Small State' (2019) Comparative Law Journal of the Pacific, Hors Serie Vol XXIII: Small States: A Collection of Essays, 139–162.

Corrin, Jennifer *Contract Law in the South Pacific* (2nd ed, Intersentia, 2020).

Corrin, Jennifer and Sue Farran 'The Law on Adoption in Vanuatu' in Jennifer Corrin and Sue Farran (eds) *The Plural Practice of Adoption on Pacific Island States* (Springer, 2019).

Corrin, Jennifer and Don Paterson *Introduction to South Pacific Law* (4th ed, Intersentia, 2017).

Farran, Sue 'Family Law and French Law in Vanuatu: An Opportunity Missed?' (2004) 35 Victoria University of Wellington Law Review 367.

Farran, Sue 'Pacific Punch: Tropical Flavors of Mixedness in the Island Republic of Vanuatu' in Anna Koppel, Vernon Valentine Palmer and Mohammed Y Mattar (eds) *Mixed Legal Systems, East and West* (Ashgate, 2015).

Farran, Sue and Don Paterson *South Pacific Property Law* (Cavendish Publications, 2004).

Forsyth, Miranda *A Bird that Flies with Two Wings: Kastom and State Justice Systems in Vanuatu* (ANU Press, 2009).

Judiciary of the Republic of Vanuatu <https://courts.gov.vu/>.

Pacific Islands Legal Information Institute *Vanuatu Primary Materials* <http://www.paclii.org/countries/vu.html>.

Paterson, Don 'Vanuatu' in Michael A Ntumy (ed) *South Pacific Islands Legal Systems* (University of Hawaii Press, 1993).

WALLIS AND FUTUNA – WALLIS ET FUTUNA

Yves-Louis SAGE

1. BACKGROUND

The three islands of Wallis,[1] Futuna[2] and Alofi[3] are located in the Western Pacific. They cover a surface area of 124.2 square kilometres, are of volcanic origin and are in the sub-equatorial zone with a hot and humid climate. The islands are 16,000 kilometres from France and thus are the most distant from France of all the French Territories.[4] The main town of Wallis and Futuna is Mata Utu. According to the latest census, there were 11,600 people living in Wallis and Futuna in 2018. That figure was 5.2 per cent lower than the 2013 figure.[5]

The currency used in Wallis and Futuna is the Pacific franc (XPF or F CFP), France's second official currency also used in New Caledonia and

1 77.9 km^2.
2 46.28 km^2.
3 17.78 km^2. This island is virtually uninhabited.
4 Wallis and Futuna is 8,000 km from Los Angeles, 4,000 km from Sydney, 480 km from Fiji, 1,871 km from New Caledonia and 2,891 km from Tahiti.
5 Insee Wallis-et-Futuna: the population continues to decrease, but more gradually – Insee Première No 1775 (26 September 2019) <https://www.insee.fr/fr/statistiques/4219031>.

French Polynesia. The Pacific franc is pegged to the euro at a fixed exchange rate.[6]

Generally presented as a tax haven, Wallis and Futuna has a specific tax regime which is based on indirect taxation. There is no income tax, corporate tax, capital gains tax, wealth tax or value-added tax. The Territorial Assembly has sole responsibility for establishing taxes, the tax base and taxation rates.[7] These advantages have attracted a number of foreign and maritime companies to register in Wallis and Futuna.[8]

According to the the Chamber of Commerce, Industry, Trades & Agriculture of Wallis & Futuna:[9]

> Freight cost aid of up to 50% is granted to Wallis & Futuna businesses to offset extra costs linked to the air or sea transport of raw materials and intermediate products imported from the European Union for processing purposes. Transport of such incoming products between the islands of Wallis and Futuna is also offset, as is the transport of goods produced in the islands for shipment to France.

The island of Wallis (which in the Wallisian language is Uvea) takes its name from Captain Samuel Wallis, who was the first Western navigator to land there, in 1767.

Wallis is surrounded by a lagoon and a coral reef which has four passes, of which the main one (Honikulu in the south) allows access to the wharf at Mata Utu. This is the only place where boats can be moored in relative safety.

Around 230 kilometres southwest of Wallis are Futuna and its neighbouring islet of Alofi, which is uninhabited. These are also called the Horn Islands after

---

6 The Institut d'Emission d'Outre-Mer (IEOM – the central bank for French overseas territories) has sole authority to issue the currency. 1,000 XPF is equal to 8.38 euros; 1 euro is equal to around 119.33 XPF.

7 In accordance with art 74 of the Constitution, Statute No 61-814 of 29 July 1961 and Decree No 57-811 of 22 July 1957.

8 Jean-Francois Boudet 'Les Codes Fiscaux Outre-Mer' (2015) Comparative Law Journal of the Pacific, Hors-Série Vol XVIII: Regards Sur La Fiscalité Dans Le Pacifique Sud: Australie, Nouvelle-Calédonie, Nouvelle Zélande, Polynésie Française, Vanuatu, Wallis-et-Futuna/Issues on Taxation in the South Pacific: Australia, New Caledonia, New Zealand, French Polynesia, Vanuatu, Wallis and Futuna <https://www.wgtn.ac.nz/law/research/publications/about-nzacl/publications/special-issues/hors-serie-volume-xviii,-2015/Boudet.pdf> 60; Jean-Francois Boudet 'La Polynésie Française est-elle un Paradis Fiscal?' (2013) 19 Comparative Law Journal of the Pacific 35 at 42–43 <https://www.wgtn.ac.nz/law/research/publications/about-nzacl/publications/cljpjdcp-journals/volume-19,-2013/Boudet.pdf>; William Gilles 'La fiscalité à Wallis-et-Futuna: entre faiblesse, paradoxe et apparence' (2015) Comparative Law Journal of the Pacific Hors-Série Vol XVIII: Regards Sur La Fiscalité Dans Le Pacifique Sud: Australie, Nouvelle-Calédonie, Nouvelle Zélande, Polynésie Française, Vanuatu, Wallis-et-Futuna/Issues on Taxation in the South Pacific: Australia, New Caledonia, New Zealand, French Polynesia, Vanuatu, Wallis and Futuna.

9 Investing in Wallis & Futuna <https://www.wallis-et-futuna.wf/en/investing>.

the port of departure of two Dutch sailors, Willem Schouten and Jacob Le Mair, who landed there in 1616. Both the islands are mountainous and difficult to access from the sea.

Writers agree that the first Austronesian inhabitants of Wallis and Futuna arrived respectively in 1200 BC and 800 BC.[10] Wallis and Futuna were both subject to Samoan[11] and Tongan influence as a result of regular mixed marriages based on the main chieftainships of the area.[12]

Structurally, Wallisian society is similar to the more autocratic and monarchic Tongan model; Futuna was influenced by the Samoan system and is more participatory and oligarchic.[13]

First contact with Europeans began in 1616 and 1767, but was sporadic. It was only from 1837, with the arrival of four missionaries from the Society of Mary,[14] that Western influence became significant through the process of evangelisation. By 1843 the two archipelagos were entirely Christianised, and until 1877 the representatives of the Catholic Church were advisors to the local chiefs and exercised a major political influence.

The creation of the three customary monarchies of Uvea, Alo and Sigave, which gave them thus the appearance of Western-style royalty, can be attributed to the missionaries.[15] The missionaries had from 1842 proposed and organised requests for protectorate status with France.[16]

After the failure of the first protectorate request in 1842, there was a gap until 1886, when the joint requests of the Queen of Wallis and the King of Futuna were successful. The decree of 5 April 1887 placed the island of Wallis under French protection, and that was extended to Futuna on 16 February 1888. As Angleviel notes:[17]

> These two symbolic protectorates ... protected the interests of the missionaries and of the high chiefs while at the same time avoiding the Ministry for Colonies having disproportionate expenses relative to the insignificance of archipelagos at the end of the world.

---

10 Frédéric Angleviel 'Wallis et Futuna (1801–1888): Contacts, Évangélisations, Inculturations' (Dissertation, Montpellier, 1989).

11 Although the island of Wallis was invaded in the 15th century by a wave of people from Tonga, Futuna did not come under the influence of Samoa until the 17th century.

12 Even today the royal lines established from contact with Tongan civilisation occupy a predominant place within Wallis and Futuna society.

13 Frédéric Angleviel, 'Wallis-et-Futuna (1942–1961) ou comment le fait migratoire transforma le protectorat en TOM' (2006) 122–123 Journal de la Société des Océanistes 61.

14 Caroline Duriez-Toutain *Présence et perceptions maristes à Tonga, 1840–1900* (Presses Universitaires de Bordeaux, 1996).

15 From 1851 there were collections of customary rules in the form of 'Futuna legislation' and (in 1870) the 'constitutions of the kingdom of Wallis'.

16 Ratified by France on 5 April 1887.

17 Angleviel, above n 13.

In the early days of the protectorate, the role and powers of the French Resident were limited to simple matters of representation and to that of advisor to the customary chiefs.

From 1905, France started sending military doctors as residents. From 1909, the rules of the protectorate were amended to require the customary chiefs to consult the French Resident on all general matters concerning the kingdoms.[18] In the course of time, the presence and influence of France grew significantly at both the administrative and financial levels.[19] In 1940 Wallis had three public officers (the Resident, a secretary-treasurer and a telephonist). This arrangement was complemented in 1945 by an administrative delegate to Futuna. French influence took a more concrete form on 29 July 1961 when Wallis and Futuna was granted the status of an overseas territory (TOM) of France. That grant had been preceded by a vote of the population on 27 December 1959, which was 99 per cent in favour of the status.

Wallis and Futuna is on several scores a territory that is exceptional within the Republic.[20] Its integration, from the time of the constitutional revision of 28 March 2003,[21] into the category of overseas collectivities[22] which have a special status under art 74 of the Constitution, did not result in repeal of the law of 29 July 1961. From 2003 any amendment to the status of Wallis and Futuna had to be made by an organic law approved after the advice of the local assembly.[23]

In a general way, the laws of 1961 and of 2003 show the desire of France to preserve institutional and social stability in the collectivity,[24] taking account of its cultural and social specificities.

The status of Wallis and Futuna 'rests on a balance which has no other example in the French collectivities between the republican legality of the common law

18 Dr Brochard, who was the doctor with the French troops who arrived in August 1909, suggested that the priests be sent away. On the affair, see Jean-Claude Roux 'Espaces coloniaux et société polynésienne de Wallis-Futuna' (Dissertation, Université de Paris I: Panthéon-Sorbonne, 1991) <http://www.documentation.ird.fr/hor/fdi:36043>.

19 This allowed the creation of a true road infrastructure, the building of dispensaries; the teaching of the French language was encouraged by way of subsidies granted to Catholic schools.

20 Sophie Joissains and Jean-Pierre Sueur 'Les îles Wallis et Futuna: assurer le développement dans le respect des spécificités locales. Rapport d'information fait au nom de la commission des lois. No 103 (2014–2015)' (Senate report, 19 November 2014) <https://www.senat.fr/notice-rapport/2014/r14-103-notice.html>.

21 Concerning the reform of the decentralised organisation of the Republic.

22 A form of 'contract of free association' which links Wallisians and the people of Futuna to France.

23 This was notably the case in respect of Organic Law No 2007-224 of 21 February 2007, which defined the status of Wallis and Futuna, and also for Organic Law No 2010-704 of 28 June 2010, art 21(V).

24 Joissains and Sueur, above n 20.

and recognition of customary power'.[25] The principles were confirmed in art 3 of the Law of 29 July 1961:

> [T]he Republic guarantees to the peoples of the territory of Wallis and Futuna … respect for their beliefs and their customs so long as they are not contrary to the general principles of law and the provisions of this statute.

The success of the statute of 1961 results from the fact that it is not defined by the co-existence of customary power alongside republican power but by the integration of the customary authorities into the heart of the institutions put in place by the Republic.[26]

The statute of 2003 confirms the existence of the three customary kingdoms as the constituencies for which administrative authority is conferred on agents from France.

The three kingdoms also correspond to administrative areas and each is ruled by a sovereign assisted by a Prime Minister and ministers:

- Uvea, on the island of Wallis which is further subdivided into three districts;
- Sigave, on the western part of the island of Futuna;
- Alo, on the eastern part of the island of Futuna and on the island of Alofi.

The French State gives each sovereign an annual grant to cover his or her costs and also provides an allowance to the ministers and customary chiefs.

Since 2003, the institutional arrangement of Wallis and Futuna is characterised by three specific traits:

- an executive for the collectivity guaranteed by the representative of the State;
- the involvement of the customary authority in the management of territorial matters;
- a Territorial Assembly which has limited functions and is the deliberative organ of the collectivity.[27]

The 20 members of the Territorial Assembly are elected by universal suffrage in a proportional, multi-candidate vote of one round. This occurs every five years in each of the five constituencies.[28] The Territorial Assembly debates principally financial matters and gives advice on matters relating to the powers of the

[25] 'Wallis et Futuna: L'évolution dans La Continuité?' (Senate report, 9 September 2003) <https://www.senat.fr/rap/r03-216/r03-2168.html>.

[26] Joissains and Sueur, above n 20.

[27] Joissains and Sueur, above n 20.

[28] Wallis is represented by 13 elected members (six for the district of Mu'a, four for the Hahake district, and three for the Hihifo district), and Futuna by seven elected members (four for the Alo district and three for Sigave).

Assembly and its wishes on matters relating to the power of the French State. The Assembly appoints from among its members a permanent commission of four members: two representing Wallis and one each for the constituencies of Sigave and Alo.

Statutory provisions set out the powers of the Territorial Assembly. These powers govern: the general status of the territorial agents, the civil status of custom, the public domain of the territory, land rights, external trade and handicrafts, agriculture, forests, water other than the sea, the environment, animal husbandry, fishing, internal transport, hygiene and public health, the protection of children and the mentally ill, tourism, hunting, urbanisation and natural habitat, social welfare and the protection of monuments and significant sites.

Administratively speaking, the Territory of Wallis and Futuna is divided into three areas, each administered by a Territorial Council made up of customary authorities and presided over by the local kings. Since 1980, each of the three areas has enjoyed legal personality and has its own budget. Since 1987, the central government has been represented by a Senior Administrator, who is head of the Territory (a member of the French prefectural service). The Administrator is in turn represented in Futuna by a delegate designated by decree.

The Senior Administrator represents the Territory in litigation and in all acts of civil life, and approves the decisions of the Territorial Assembly.

As Joissains and Sueur note:

> The powers of the territorial governments extend to matters of civil status, the management of the roads in the villages, the delivery of identity documents, the maintenance of the electoral lists and the organisation of elections, the maintenance of public structures, oversight of buildings to which the public has access, the collection of rubbish and is responsible for good relations with the chieftainship and the maintenance of the Royal Palace.[29]

As the head of the local public services, the Administrator manages the Territory's budget, which comes only[30] from the French government.[31] The customary authority has the powers that flow from the ancestral traditions of Wallis and Futuna which have been preserved to this day. The customary institutions retain considerable power in the territory's social life and organisation, and customary law is enforced by the customary chiefs.

---

29 Joissains and Sueur, above n 20.

30 The territorial governments have no local, fiscal resource of their own. There is no income tax, no company tax, no tax on interest, no wealth tax and no value-added tax.

31 The head of the Territory oversees expenditure and implements the decisions of the territorial council.

The chiefdom remains the basis of the whole traditional organisation of society. There is, however, a marked shift in the attitudes of the younger generations because of the conservative views of the chiefs.[32]

Each king governs and also fulfils the role of arbiter, is elected by the noble families, and nominates the chiefs of the district.[33]

The customary authorities are also represented in the Territorial Council. The Council has only a consultative function in relation to local business and has the role of assisting the Administrator.

The Territorial Council is presided over by the Administrator. It comprises the three kings, who are Vice-Presidents by right, or their substitutes who are appointed by the Administrator on the advice of the title holders, as well as three members designated by the Administrator after agreement with the Territorial Assembly.

The kings participate in the Territorial Council; their role is to set the main political and economic directions of the Territory. They appoint a representative to the permanent commission of the Territorial Assembly. Before each session of the Territorial Assembly, the Territorial Council provides comment on all the matters on the agenda of the forthcoming session.

Village matters are directly dealt with by meetings of the inhabitants, who can appoint and also dismiss customary chiefs.

At the level of the collectivity, each king presides over a *fono*, which takes place every month in the *fale fono*. The *fono* deals with the current problems of the community in accordance with their secular traditions. The *fono* is the final recourse in all customary matters.

2. SOURCES OF LAW: DUALITY OF THE APPLICABLE LAW

In 1959, the inhabitants of the archipelago adopted the status of French Overseas Territory, which was legally endorsed by Law n° 61-814 of 29 July 1961.[34]

Under the 1961 statute the Territory is governed by: (1) statutes of the Republic and decrees applicable by reason of their object and reference to the whole of the national territory; and (2) from the time of the promulgation in the Territory by the statutes, decrees and ministerial orders which are declared

---

32 Culture et patrimoine / Politiques publiques / Accueil – Les services de l'État à Wallis et Futuna <https://www.wallis-et-futuna.gouv.fr/Politiques-publiques/Culture-et-patrimoine>.

33 The situation of Lavelua is secure. The royal authority in Futuna is less secure because the village chiefs can easily depose the monarch.

34 Loi n° 61-814 du 29 juillet 1961 conférant aux îles Wallis et Futuna le statut de territoire d'outre-mer, Titre I, art 4, modifié par Loi n° 78-1018 du 18 octobre 1978, art 1, JORF 20 octobre 1978.

to be expressly for the overseas territories or to the Territory of Wallis and Futuna (in accordance with the principle of legislative speciality).[35]

Regulations are made by the administration of the Territory, through the High Commissioner of the Republic in the Pacific Ocean, or by its deputy, the Administrator Superior of the Territory of Wallis and Futuna, each according to their jurisdiction as set out in the statute or by decrees which have been issued in relation to the 1961 statute's application.[36]

Customary law has been described by Sophie Chave-Dartoen in the following way:[37]

> Wallisians are French citizens but they are governed by a special law a kind which allows almost all disputes which involve villagers to be settled according to custom whose content varies over time and which meet the need principally of preserving order and stability. Thus, the result of disputes is often compensatory in nature and takes the form of pigs or woven mats.

This special law status is applicable only for civil disputes which go through the customary councils and between persons who have customary status.

As Antonia Trouilhet-Tamole and Emeli Simete note:

> The law of 29 July 1961 allowed all traditional organisations to continue side by side with the authorities of the Republic, and these two authorities coexist perfectly. It is a peaceful coexistence which, despite certain small clashes from time to time, has lasted for 33 years.[38]

Customary councils manage the current affairs of the Territory, such as land problems which, in the absence of a cadastral survey and by reason of the legal impossibility of the alienation of land to non-locals, are dealt within the clan 'Kutuga'. Disputes may then eventually be dealt with at the level of villages, before being settled, if necessary, by the chieftainship. The decisions made by

---

35 The Code of Commerce has been implemented by Ordonnance No 2019-848 of 21 August 2019.

36 Statutes, decrees, orders and regulations that existed before the date of the local promulgation of the statute of 1961 are still applicable in Wallis and Futuna without any special promulgation where they are not contrary to the provisions of the statute of 1961.

37 Sophie Chave-Datoen 'Le paradoxe Wallisien: une royauté dans la Republique' (2002) 32 Ethnologie française 637. See also Allison Lotti 'Droit coutumier à Wallis et Futuna, entre tradition et modernité' (Working with Legal Pluralism, Australian National University, 25 September 2014). On the application of customary land rules, see TA Wallis et Futuna, 15 mai 2017, n° 1560023–1560024; Éric Landot 'La coutume peut être une source du droit … enfin … à Wallis et Futuna' (blog, 18 September 2017) <https://blog.landot-avocats.net/2017/09/18/la-coutume-peut-etre-une-source-du-droit-enfin-a-wallis-et-futuna/>.

38 Antonia Trouilhet-Tamole and Emeli Simete in Paul de Deckker and Jean-Yves Faberon (eds) *Custom and the Law* (Asia Pacific Press, Australian National University, 2001), 118.

the chief are *tapu*.[39] It is not uncommon for inhabitants of Wallis and Futuna to be involved in criminal litigation and the common law courts are then seized in matters of appeal from the decisions of those councils.[40]

It should be noted that the inhabitants of Wallis and Futuna also use the common law courts when the customary punishments seem unsuitable for offenders; this is particularly the case in matters of family violence.

3. JUDICIARY: JUSTICE WITH LOCAL CHARACTERISTICS[41]

3.1. STATE COURTS

By a decree of 19 February 1962,[42] the Court of Common Law was established in the form of a detached section of the Court of First Instance of Noumea in New Caledonia. This court has full jurisdiction in criminal matters and also in civil and commercial matters, but subject to the powers reserved for the court of local law. All the decisions of this court may be appealed to the Court of Appeal in Nouméa.

The court established in 1962 was converted into a Court of First Instance of Mata Utu by a decree of 26 December 1983, and by a decree of 27 December 1983, a juvenile court was created.

The Labour Court was created by an order of the High Commissioner of 2 December 1968.

The Court of First Instance has one judge who makes decisions sitting as a single judge and is responsible for the functioning of the court. The judge acts as an investigatory judge, a sentencing judge, a judge in family matters, a judge for the execution of judgments and also as a public officer who acts as a prosecutor for the Republic.

39 Joissains and Sueur, above n 20.

40 Chave-Dartoen, above n 37. On land, see Olivier Aimot and Antonia Tamole 'Traitement Coutumier Des Problèmes Fonciers A Wallis' (2011) Comparative Law Journal of the Pacific, Hors-Série Vol XII: Droit Foncier et Gouvernance Judiciaire dans le Pacifique Sud: Essais Comparatistes/Land Law and Judicial Governance in the South Pacific: Comparative Studies <https://www.wgtn.ac.nz/law/research/publications/about-nzacl/publications/special-issues/hors-serie-volume-xii,-2011>.

41 Joissains and Sueur, above n 20. See also Régis Lafargue 'La justice outre-mer: justice du lointain, justice de proximité' (2002) 101(1) Revue française d'administration publique at 36 for Wallis and Futuna.

42 Décret n°62-189 du 19 février 1962 Relatif à l'organisation de la juridiction de droit commun instituée sur le territoire des iles Wallis & Futuna, JORF 21 February 1962. See also Article L533-1 et s Code de l'Organisation judiciaire; see also art 21(V) Loi n° 2007-224 du 21 février 2007, – art 21 (V) JORF 22 février 2007.

The court's personnel is made up of a registrar, an interpreter and a secretary; there are no court officers such as barristers, sheriffs or notaries. Those functions are often fulfilled by the police or by a public defender.

3.2. ADMINISTRATIVE TRIBUNAL AT MATA UTU

Pursuant to art 68 of Statute No 2002-1138 of 9 September 2002 relating to the organisation and scheduling of matters of justice, the French government created, by an ordinance of 26 September 2003, an administrative tribunal for Wallis and Futuna. It replaced the previous administrative dispute council.[43]

3.3. FINANCE COURT

In matters of financial law, Wallis and Futuna remains under the direct control of the Court of Accounts in France.

3.4. LOCAL LAW JURISDICTION

The local law jurisdiction[44] provided for by art 5 of the Law of 29 July 1961 has not been altered over the years. It settles disputes relating to customary civil status and to customary land rights. Customary law applies in this court.

Appeal is possible from that jurisdiction to the Review Chamber of the Court of Appeal in Nouméa. This deals with lack of jurisdiction, excess of jurisdiction, and actions contrary to legislation. French law governs procedural matters and breaches of public order.

On the basis of a joint application by the parties, these cases can be brought before a common law court, and custom will be applied there to those cases.

However, this jurisdiction has not been exercised because of lack of local agreement, so the court operates under the 'same conditions as under the French protectorate'.[45] Preference is given to methods of dispute resolution of a conciliatory nature, and notably this is the case when the dispute concerns members of the same family or a land matter.

In practice, cases are decided first before the village chief and his council. The district chief and his council, which comprises the village heads and the chief of the customary police, can then establish an appeal jurisdiction to hear appeals

[43] Article 1 of the Ordinance sets up an administrative tribunal in Wallis and Futuna and art 2 repeals the council for administrative disputes of Wallis and Futuna.

[44] Organised by the Decree of the Administrator of 20 September 1978.

[45] Joissains and Sueur, above n 20.

from the decision of the village chief and his council. Finally, if the matter is still not resolved, the Council of Ministers (the six ministers and the three chiefs of the district) will decide the matter in a collegial manner; if no decision can be agreed on, the matter is taken to the king.

4. CONCLUSION

According to Article 75 of the French Constitution, citizens of Wallis and Futuna who do not have ordinary civil status shall retain their personal status so long as they have not renounced it. Therefore, as Régis Lafarge notes, 'there thus coexist two systems of civil law each providing for a community governed by its own law'.[46]

The recognition for Wallis and Futuna of a status that is different from that of metropolitan France is clearly established by the Decree of 20 September 1978,[47] which created customary courts. For land matters, the role of custom is a logical consequence of the recognition of the Territory's special status.[48]

As to the criminal law, the Court of Cassation in France reaffirmed, on 10 October 2000, that it is the same for everyone.[49]

BIBLIOGRAPHY

Angleviel, Frédéric (ed) *Les Outre-Mers Français Actualités et Etudes* (coll. 'Portes océanes', Vo. 1, L'Harmattan, 2012).

Angleviel, Frédéric, Bernadette Papilio-Halagahu, Adriano Favole and Daniel Frimigacci (eds) *Wallis et Futuna, 3500 ans d'histoire [Ko le afe tolu kaulelau lima fetu'u o fakamatala o le isitolia o Futuna mo Uvea – Faka-matala kite histolia o Uvea mo Futuna talu mai ta'u e toluafenimageau (3500)]* (Groupe de Recherche en Histoire Océanienne Contemporaine, comité du cinquantième, 2014).

Bright, Phil and Jean-Paul Mailagi *Atlas de la population de Wallis et Futuna* (Secrétariat général de la Communauté du Pacifique, 2007).

Chave-Dartoen, Sophie *Royauté, chefferie et monde socio-cosmique à Wallis ('Uvea): Dynamiques sociales et pérennité des institutions* (Pacific-credo Publications, 2017).

---

46 Lafargue, above n 41.

47 Arrêté du 20 septembre 1978, n° 2063, du Haut-commissaire de la République dans l'Océan Pacifique, portant organisation d'une juridiction de droit local dans le territoire de Wallis-et-Futuna (Journal Officiel de Wallis).

48 On the application of customary land rules, see TA Wallis et Futuna, 15 mai 2017, n° 1560023–1560024; Landot, above n 37. Régis Lafargue 'La distinction du droit à la différence en droit civil et en droit pénal' in Jean-Yves Faberon and Paul De Deckker (eds) *L'État pluriculturel* (Bruylant, 2003).

49 Cass crim, 10 October 2000, n° 5871, *Siwel Waehnya et autres (affaire des coutumiers de Chepenehe).*

Favole, Adriano 'La royauté oscillante. Ethnographie et histoire de la cérémonie d'investiture du Tu'i Agaifo d'Alo (Futuna)' (2000) 111 Journal de la Société des Océanistes 195.

Grant Burrows, Edwin *Ethnology of Uvea (Wallis Island)* (Bernice P Bishop Museum, 1937).

Huffer, Elise, Mikaele Tui et al (eds) *Uvea, Suva, Fidji / Mata'Utu, Wallis* (trans Neil Carruthers, Institute of Pacific Studies/Services des affaires culturelles de Wallis, 2004).

Leleivai, Hapakuku 'Wallis and Futuna' in Stephen Levine (ed) *Pacific Ways: Government and Politics in the Pacific Islands* (2nd ed, Victoria University Press, 2016).

Loi n° 61-814 du 29 juillet 1961 conférant aux îles Wallis et Futuna le statut de territoire d'outre-mer (1) Version consolidée au 14 février 2018 <http://www.wallis-et-futuna.gouv.fr/layout/set/print/Publications/Legislation-et-reglementations-relatives-aux-institutions-du-territoire/Loi-statutaire-de-1961/2.-Statut-1961>.

Lotti, Allison *Le Statut De 1961 À Wallis Et Futuna: Genèse de trois monarchies républicaines (1961–1991)* (L'Harmattan, 2011).

Moyse-Faurie, Claire 'L'identité futunienne' in Darrell Tryon and Paul de Deckker (eds) *Identités en mutation dans le Pacifique à l'aube du troisième millénaire. Hommage à Joël Bonnemaison* (Presses Universitaires de Bordeaux, 1998).

Moyse-Faurie, Claire and Frédéric Angleviel 'Futuna ou "l'enfant perdu"... un timide biculturalisme' (2002) 32–33 Hermès 377.

Ntumy, Michael A 'Wallis and Futuna' in *South Pacific Islands legal Systems* (University of Hawaii Press, 1993) 622.

O'Reilly, Patrick 'Bibliographie méthodique analytique et critique des Iles Wallis et Futuna' (1963) Volume XIX, Journal de la Société des Océanistes 231.

Pechberty, Dominique and Epifania Toa, *Vivre la coutume à 'Uvea (Wallis)* (L'Harmattan, 2004).

Rensch, Karl H, *Le wallisien en poche* (Archipelago Press, 2002).

Rensch, Karl H *Parler Wallisien* (Archipelago Press, 2002).

Roux, Jean-Claude *Espaces coloniaux et société polynésienne de Wallis-Futuna (Pacifique central)* (Dissertation, Université de Paris I: Panthéon-Sorbonne, 1991).

Van der Grijp, Paul 'Development Polynesian style: Contemporary Futunan social economy and its cultural features' (2005) 114(4) Journal of the Polynesian Society 311.

INDEX

ABOUT THE EDITORS

Jennifer Corrin is Professor Emerita at The University of Queensland. She is an academic, researching on law reform and development in plural legal regimes and legal issues affecting small states, and is a former legal practitioner. Before joining The University of Queensland, she spent five years at the University of the South Pacific, having joined the Faculty after nine years in her own legal firm in Solomon Islands. She is author of *Contract Law in the South Pacific* (now in its second edition) and co-author of *Introduction to South Pacific Law* (now in its fourth edition) and *Courts and Civil Procedure in the South Pacific*.

Tony Angelo is Professor Emeritus at Victoria University of Wellington. He has a long-standing interest in the law of small states and has published extensively on the laws of Mauritius, Seychelles and the small countries of the Pacific. His major current research involves private international law monographs for the South Pacific and articles on aspects of constitutional development and decolonisation in the South Pacific.

www.ingramcontent.com/pod-product-compliance
Ingram Content Group UK Ltd.
Pitfield, Milton Keynes, MK11 3LW, UK
UKHW051918100926
8556IPUK00021B/1243

9 781839 701535